ANNOTATED INSTRUCTOR'S MANUAL
FOR

BEEBE, BEEBE, & REDMOND

INTERPERSONAL COMMUNICATION
RELATING TO OTHERS

SECOND EDITION

Prepared by

Mark Butland

AUSTIN COMMUNITY COLLEGE

With Contributions from
Nan Peck, Northern Virginia Community College

and

Stephanie K. Ludwig, Southwest Texas State University

Allyn and Bacon

BOSTON LONDON TORONTO
SYDNEY TOKYO SINGAPORE

CONTENTS

INTRODUCTION

USING THE INSTRUCTOR'S RESOURCE MANUAL

This Annotated Instructor's Manual is designed to make the use of *Interpersonal Communication: Relating to Others,* Second Edition, simple, enjoyable, and effective. In this introduction, an overview of what it is to teach a course in Interpersonal Communication is given. Descriptions of suggested criteria for semester assignments are provided, along with a sample syllabus for organizing the semester.

Ample materials for planning and organizing units of instruction are provided in Part I, the Instructor's Guide. Preparation for the teaching of each chapter is made simple.

- Instructional objectives for each chapter provide an overview of the quantity and nature of the concepts to be covered;

- Cross-references to text learning tools direct the instructor to: key-term recaps, application activities, discussion and review suggestions, journal entry guidelines, and group activities.

- Chapter overviews contain capsules of the major chapter concepts.

- Detailed complete-sentence outlines for each chapter serve as expeditious lecture notes. Thus, much of the instructor's work is already done.

- Activities follow each outline.

Part II, the Annotated Text, contains the complete student text, annotated with a wealth of helpful teaching suggestions:

Teaching Strategy annotations offer suggestions for introducing concepts to the class.

Instructional Goals and Tips provide ideas for helping students meet the basic communication goals of the text.

Discussion and Writing present high-interest questions you can use for in-class discussions and writing exercises.

Media and Outside Resources offer numerous suggestions for using popular media, guest speakers and other outside resources.

Skill Development annotations suggest a variety of exercises and activities, such as role playing, that students can perform collaboratively to enhance specific skills discussed in the text. They also offer suggestions for using the Building Your Skills feature in class.

Research and Literature suggest journals, articles, conference proceedings and other resources you can use as additional background information or as enrichment for your more advanced students.

Activity annotations are cross references to materials located in the Instructor's Guide Section.

Web Activities offer hands-on suggestions for using the World Wide Web in your teaching of Interpersonal Communication.

Internet Resources offer URLs for relevant Internet resources.

Focus on Comprehension provides a brief summary of important chapter concepts.

TEACHING INTERPERSONAL COMMUNICATION

Interpersonal communication might be thought of as the primary building block for other communication contexts. It begins where all human, social phenomena begin, with the self. It continues as an ongoing process of sharing meanings with others. It pervades group communication and organizational communication. Its precepts cross over to public communication and mass communication.

For example, when students make inquiry into interpersonal communication, they learn that practicing other orientation, or empathy, is critical to interpersonal relationship development and maintenance. They will learn the same skills are necessary for relationships with multiple others in groups and in organizations. When they consider public speaking and mass communication, they must concern themselves with audience analysis and adaptation—other orientation.

Students often remark that it is the most immediately useful course for other reasons. Interpersonal communication is a process in which we all constantly participate. We need only go about the business of our daily lives to encounter countless opportunities to apply the concepts of the course. When students look "out there" for what is discussed in the classroom, they find it everywhere.

They also will seek to find it in you, the instructor. You—as a human instrument—can serve as the primary tool for the students' journey to understanding, appreciating, and using interpersonal communication skills. The saying goes, "We believe some of what you say and all of what you do." Modeling perception checking, active listening, response skills, and the like will illustrate course concepts better than any other aid.

Demonstrating interpersonal communication skills will also open and enhance a climate such that students are more than willing to actively, verbally participate in the sharing of meaning in the classroom. If you do, yourself, what you ask them to do, everyone involved will part with richer understanding.

ASSIGNMENTS AND SCHEDULES

The study of interpersonal communication is an ongoing process of examining self in relation to others. The instructor's personal vision will, of course, determine the methods by which students' integration of the course concepts will be gauged. A variety of assignment types readily apply to the subject matter.

ASSIGNMENTS

1. Participation
   Interpersonal communication is ubiquitous, and students invariably offer a wealth of illustrations for chapter concepts—if they are asked. Including participation as part of the course grade rewards these contributions.

2. Journals
   Student journals are highly appropriate for the exploration of interpersonal communication. Clearly-established criteria for and regular instructor feedback on journals are necessary to ensure their effectiveness.

   For journals to perform their potential integrative function, students must transcend the tendency to write: (a) diary entries having no clear relation to course concepts (e.g., "My dog ran away this morning. I'm going to make hamburgers for dinner.") or (b) summaries of chapter material (e.g., "Chapter one is about communication models and principles. Feedback is a message sent in response to another message." Content criteria for journals may be established as:

   1. a detailed description of an interpersonal communication (between at least two people) episode;
   2. a definition of at least one course concept (or at least two or three) evidenced in the episode; and

3. a (transcending) explanation of the link between the concept and the description or piece of the description.

Journals encourage students to make immediate, ongoing applications of course material. They are most helpful when collected and commented upon regularly by the instructor. This provides students ongoing evaluation of their progress and provides the instructor opportunity to communicate with every student. The instructor's schedule is a factor to consider regarding the inclusion of journals, as they are quite time-consuming.

3. Short writing assignments.
   Interpersonal Communication: Relating to Others is unique in its thoughtful inclusion of text annotations for the instructor. "Discussion and Writing" suggestions for each chapter may be assigned as out-of-class writing assignments. Many of the text's "Building Your Skills" and "Learning with Others" supplements include thoughtful questions for brief writing assignments.

4. Book or Movie Review Term Paper
   Almost every popular movie or book at least includes illustrations of interpersonal communication. The text "Media and Outside Resources" annotations often include examples of these. In addition, the AIM cites popular movies to accompany each chapter concept. Student-selected movies or books serve as exciting data for analysis in term papers. Suggested content criteria for the assignment of movie or book review paper include:

   1. a brief overview of the story contained in the book or movie;
   2. a definition, suitable for the naive reader, of each of at least three applicable text concepts;
   3. "thick description" (C. Geertz, 1973, *The Interpretation of Cultures*, New York: Basic Books) of several instances in which each of the chosen text concepts was evidenced (Descriptions should include as much dialogue as possible and figuratively transfer the reader to the scene.);
   4. clear explanations of how the text concepts were illustrated in all supporting instances.

5. Self-improvement project report
   Students may be asked to submit brief, written descriptions of areas of interpersonal communication behavior that they would like to improve. The instructor may then quickly provide written feedback on related text chapters and outside research areas. Students should also be instructed to (a) consciously monitor their communication for occurrences of the selected behavior, (b) identify themes in occurrences of the behavior, i.e., "I seem to do this

more when I'm talking to a teacher." (c) identify variables related to the behavior (i.e., status), (d) collect written research on the behavior and its related variable(s), and prepare a written report of findings. Content criteria for a self-improvement project term paper may include:

1. an explanation of the chosen interpersonal communication behavior;
2. an explanation of the theme(s) in occurrence of the behavior, including specific examples of occurrences;
3. an analysis of the relationship(s) between the behavior and the communication context;
4. a summary of the findings of related research;
5. a discussion of implications of the research for the student's case; and
6. a logical plan for altering the behavior.

6. Presentations

Students may be asked to deliver individual or group presentations. These are lively and interesting learning aids provided they are assigned as: extemporaneous presentations, of a uniform skeleton format, within set time limits.

Individual presentations of book or movie review findings serve as strong concluding arguments for the universal value of the study of interpersonal communication. Student presentations in general contribute greatly to community building in the classroom. The instructor may assign or contract volunteers of individuals or groups for brief presen-

tations of text concepts as well. Suggested oral content criteria include:

1. an overview of the topic;
2. a preview of sub-topics to be discussed;
3. transitions between treatment of sub-topic areas;
4. explanation of each sub-topic;
5. supporting examples that illustrate each sub-topic;
6. a review of chosen sub-topic; and
7. a concluding statement regarding the information's usefulness, importance, and the like.

7. Examinations

Students often appreciate the use of several examinations of relatively low numerical weights. The Test Bank for *Interpersonal Communication: Relating to Others,* Second Edition, includes ample questions of varying types for three exams.

SCHEDULE

This sample schedule is based on a 15-week semester and may be adapted to a quarter system of 10 weeks (4 class meetings per week) by:

1. having only two exams—a midterm covering Chapters 1–5 and a final covering Chapters 6–11;
2. covering chapter 3 in 3 days.
3. covering chapter 5 in 3 days.
4. covering chapter 7 in 3 days.

Sample Schedule

Day	Discussion Topic	Assignment
1	Introduction to the course	Student Introductions
2	Defining Interpersonal Communication The Importance of Interpersonal Communication to Our Lives An Evolving Model for Human and Interpersonal Communication Mediated Interpersonal Communication: A New Frontier	Chapter 1 AIM Activity 1.1
3	Principles of Interpersonal Communication	Chapter 1 AIM Activity 1.2
4	How to Improve Your Own Interpersonal Communication	Chapter 1 Building Your Skills, p. 29

continued

Day	Discussion Topic	Assignment
5	Self-Concept: Who Are You?	Chapter 2 Building Your Skills, p. 42 AIM Activity 2.1
6	Self-Esteem: Your Self-Worth How Self-Concept and Self-Esteem Affect Interpersonal Communication and Relationships	Chapter 2 Building Your Skills, p. 55
7	Improving Your Self-Esteem	Chapter 2 Building Your Skills, p. 63
8	Understanding the Interpersonal Perception Process	Chapter 3 Building Your Skills, p. 72 AIM Activity 3.1
9	Perception and Interpersonal Communication How We Organize and Interpret Interpersonal Perceptions	Chapter 3 AIM Activity 3.2
10	Barriers to Accurate Perceptions	Chapter 3 Building Your Skills, p. 87
11	Improving Your Perceptual Skills	Chapter 3 Building Your Skills, p. 93 AIM Activity 3.3
12	The Nature of Culture	Chapter 4 Building Your Skills, p. 103
13	Barriers to Effective Intercultural Communication	Chapter 4
14	Improving Intercultural Competence	Chapter 4 Building Your Skills, pp. 118, 120, 121, 123 AIM Activity 4.1 AIM Activity 4.2
15	Exam One	Unit One
16	Listening Defined Why You Listen	Chapter 5 Building Your Skills, p. 147
17	Listening Barriers	Chapter 5 Building Your Skills, p. 148, 152
18	Improving Your Listening Skills	Chapter 5 Building Your Skills, p. 163 AIM Activity 5.1 AIM Activity 5.2
19	Responding with Empathy Improving Your Responding Skills	Chapter 5 AIM Activity 5.3

continued

Day	Discussion Topic	Assignment
35	Self-Disclosure: A Foundation for Relational Escalation	Chapter 9 Building Your Skills, p. 313, 315 AIM Activity 9.1
36	Two Models for Self-Disclosure	Chapter 9 Building Your Skills, p. 323
37	Stages of Interpersonal Relationships	Chapter 10 AIM Activity 10.1
38	Skills for Starting Relationships	Chapter 10 Building Your Skills, p. 335
39	Interpersonal Communication Skills for Escalating and Maintaining Relationships	Chapter 10 AIM Activity 10.2
40	Identifying and Acting on Trouble Signs in Relationships	Chapter 10 AIM Activity 10.3
41	De-Escalating and Ending Relationships	Chapter 10 Building Your Skills, p. 354
42	Relating to Family	Chapter 11 AIM Activity 11.1, 11.2, 11.3
43	Relating to Friends and Lovers	Chapter 11 AIM Activity 11.4, 11.5, 11.6
44	Relating to Colleagues	Chapter 11 Building Your Skills, p. 396 AIM Activity 11.7
45	Exam Three	Unit Three

PART I
Instructor's Guide

CHAPTER 1 Introduction to Interpersonal Communication

INSTRUCTIONAL OBJECTIVES

After studying this chapter, students should be able to:

1. Compare and contrast definitions of communication, human communication, and interpersonal communication.
2. Explain why it is useful to study interpersonal communication.
3. Compare and contrast communication as action, interaction, and transaction.
4. Describe the key components of the communication process.
5. Discuss five principles of interpersonal relationships.
6. Identify strategies that can improve communication effectiveness.

LEARNING TOOLS

TOOLS	TEXT PAGES
Building your skills activities	29
Chapter glossary	33
Discussion and review questions	31
Electronic connections	13, 18, 19
Journal entry guidelines	32
Key term recaps	11, 16, 17, 30
Learning with others activities	30
Understanding diversity	20

CHAPTER OVERVIEW

CHAPTER ONE: INTRODUCTION TO INTERPERSONAL COMMUNICATION

A. Defining Interpersonal Communication: Communication, human communication, and interpersonal communication are defined and contrasted. Interpersonal communication is discussed as a special form of communication, involving simultaneous interaction between individuals with mutual influence in order to manage our relationships. The concepts of mass, public, and small-group communication are contrasted with interpersonal communication.

B. The Importance of Interpersonal Communication: Interpersonal communication permeates our lives. Being skilled in interpersonal communication can improve your relationships with family, friends, and work and school colleagues, as well as improve your physical and emotional health.

C. Models for Human and Interpersonal Communication: Three models for understanding communication are outlined within an historical perspective. Message Transfer models focus on the actions involved in communication. Message Exchange models introduce the concepts of feedback and context to emphasize a less static and more interactive perspective. Message Creation models introduce the notion of "simultaneous" interaction involving mutual and concurrent sharing of ideas and feelings.

D. Mediated Interpersonal Communication: Today, technology has allowed various types of media to be used to transmit interpersonal messages. Mediated messages are often less effective because information is often filtered out inadvertently. Electronic communication is increasingly a part of our lives and continually evolving and changing. One way to view mediated communication is according to the "richness of the channel" being used.

E. Principles of Interpersonal Relationships: Relationships are governed by five principles: they are systems with processes; they are concerned with both message content and personal feelings; they are defined by the roles assumed by interactants; they are governed by social rules; and they may be complementary, symmetrical, or parallel.

F. Improving Your Interpersonal Communication Effectiveness: A five-part strategy is offered, including: knowing how communication works; developing communication skills; increasing motivation to be effective; increasing communication options and communication flexibility; and decreasing self-focus through other-orientation and empathy.

DETAILED CHAPTER OUTLINE

I. Defining Interpersonal Communication: Interpersonal communication is inescapable and at the core of the human experience.
   A. Between 80 and 90 percent of our waking hours are spent communicating with others.

B. We develop interpersonal relationships through these interactions.

II. Defining Interpersonal Communication: To define interpersonal communication, two broader categories must first be defined.

A. Communication is the process of acting on information.
   1. Experts disagree on one single definition.
      a. Decades of controversy.
      b. One research team counted over 126 published definitions for communication.
   2. Communication is not unique to humans.
      a. Communication across species (for example, man and dog).
      b. Communication within species (for example, a colony of ants).

B. Human communication is the process of making sense of the world and sharing that sense with others.
   1. We make sense of the world by listening, observing, tasting, touching, and smelling.
   2. We share conclusions about the world with others in face-to-face interactions and via many media (such as speeches, songs, radio, television, e-mail, letters, books, articles, poems, advertisements, and others).

C. Interpersonal communication is a special form of human communication that occurs when we interact with another person and mutually influence each other, usually for the purpose of managing relationships.
   1. Interpersonal communication is a special form of human communication.
      a. The quantity of interactants must be two.
      b. The quality of interaction must be personal rather than impersonal.
         1) Personal interaction is more intimate in nature and implies treating one another as unique human beings.
         2) Impersonal interaction is less intimate in nature and implies treating one another as means to our own personal ends and goals.
   2. Interpersonal communication involves simultaneous interaction between individuals. Both participants interact at the same time.
      a. May be verbal (such as talking) or nonverbal (such as listening).
      b. May be brief or enduring.
   3. Interpersonal communication involves mutual influence between individuals. Both participants affect and respond to each other.
      a. Degree of influence varies.
      b. Impact of influence varies.

4. Interpersonal communication is the fundamental means we use to manage our relationships.
   a. Interpersonal relationships are defined as the ongoing connections we make with others through interpersonal communication.
   b. Relationships move through identifiable and predictable stages.
   c. Most of our relational management through interpersonal communication occurs indirectly.

III. The Importance of Interpersonal Communication to Our Lives:

A. Being skilled at interpersonal communication can improve relationships with family.
   1. Virginia Satir calls family communication "the largest single factor determining the kinds of relationships [we make] with others.
   2. Family communication affects self-concept formation.
   3. Self-concept influences how we interact with others.

B. Being skilled in interpersonal communication can improve relationships with friends.
   1. Unmarried people have reported that developing friendships and falling in love are the top-rated sources of satisfaction and happiness.
   2. Losing a relationship is among the most stressful.
   3. Individuals between the ages of 19 and 24 years report to have already had five to six romantic relationships and to have been in love once or twice.
   4. Studying interpersonal communication can offer insight into our behaviors in friendship, romance, and love.

C. Being skilled in interpersonal communication can enhance relationships with your colleagues.
   1. Can help avoid stress and effectively deal with conflict.
   2. Can increase our sense of satisfaction.
   3. Success and promotions often hinge upon how well we relate with supervisors and peers.

D. Being skilled in interpersonal communication can improve your physical and emotional health.
   1. Loneliness can kill.
      a. Widowed or divorced patients experience more medical problems than do married people.
      b. Grief-stricken spouses are more likely than others to die prematurely, especially around the time of the departed spouse's birthday or their anniversary.

c. Childless middle-aged wives were almost two and one-half times more likely to die in any given year than those who had at least one child.

d. Terminally ill patients with limited social support die sooner than those with stronger ties to friendships.

2. Connectedness heals. Support from people who care about us helps us become better adjusted to adversity in life.

IV. An Evolving Model for Human and Interpersonal Communication: Models are useful in helping us understand complex processes. Three models are discussed in order of oldest to newest.

A. Message Transfer models emphasize human communication as action.

1. In 1942, Harold Lasswell summarized the process as: "Who (sender) says what (message) in what channel (channel) to whom (receiver) with what effect."

2. The linear input/output process is defined by key components, including information source, encoding, decoding, receiver, message, channel, noise (external or psychological).

3. This model is simple and straightforward, but overlooks the complexities of real-life human communication.

B. Message Exchange models emphasize human communication as interaction.

1. In the 1940s and early 1950s two new components were added to the earlier model: feedback and context.

a. Feedback emphasized a response to a message sent.

1) Could be verbal or nonverbal.

2) Could be intended or unintended.

b. Context emphasized the importance of the particular environment within which the communication takes place.

1) All communication takes place within a context.

2) Context encompasses the physical environment, the number of people present, the relationship between communicators, the communication goal, and the impact of culture.

2. This model is more realistic because of the addition of feedback and context.

3. The model is limited because it characterizes communication as a linear, step-by-step sequence.

C. Message Creation models emphasize human communication as transaction.

1. Most scholars view this as the most realistic model for interpersonal communication.

2. Employs the same components as the other models.

3. Adds the notion of simultaneous interaction of components. As we talk (sender), we also listen (receiver).

4. Adds the notion of message creation.

a. Participants monitor the degree to which each understands messages being sent.

b. Participants mutually define the symbols used in the episodes of interaction because each participant's message influences the other participant's next message and symbol selections.

c. Meaning is created based upon a mutual, concurrent sharing of ideas and feelings.

5. While no model is completely realistic, this model most accurately describes interpersonal communication.

V. Mediated Interpersonal Communication, A New Frontier: New technologies have expanded the definition of interpersonal communication to include mediated interpersonal messages.

A. New technologies expand the traditional "face-to-face" interaction aspect of the definition of interpersonal communication.

1. An assortment of new devices allows us to communicate interpersonally as well as impersonally, including telephone, fax, e-mail, and electronic chat rooms on the Internet.

2. These new media are often less satisfying and less comfortable due to the nature of interacting through a medium such as a computer.

a. We are accustomed to communicating our feelings in a face-to-face environment where there are no media filters to interfere with the clarity of the message.

b. People do develop meaningful, lasting relationships through the new media, however.

3. Nonverbal signals that tend to be filtered out by the new media have begun to be replaced by symbolic cues.

a. Screaming at someone with e-mail messages is accomplished by using ALL CAPITAL LETTERS.

b. In other situations, we might describe our emotions for the other person (for example, "I am frowning right now").

c. Emoticons are symbols developed by e-mail users to carry the emotional content of a message being sent (see examples in text).

4. Some of the new media employs "richer" channels than others.

a. The richness of a communication channel is based upon four criteria:

1) Amount of feedback that can be received.
2) Number of cues that the channel can convey and that can be interpreted by a receiver.
3) Variety of language communicators use.
4) Potential to express emotions and feelings.
    b. For example, face-to-face is richer than voice mail, which is still richer than a memo.
VI. Principles of Interpersonal Relationships:
    A. Interpersonal relationships are both systems and processes.
        1. A system is a set of interconnected elements; a change in one element affects all the other elements.
        2. A process implies constant change rather than stasis.
        3. The system/process perspective of interpersonal relationships makes possible several conclusions:
            a. Any change in one interactant has the potential to affect the other.
            b. Prior interactions affect future interactions.
            c. Our communication with others is irreversible.
            d. Because all relationships are continually changing, greater energy is required to renegotiate our relationships in light of the new circumstances.
            e. Due to the symbolic nature of communication as well as the process nature of relationships, misunderstandings are inevitable. Several pessimistic maxims, offered by Osmo Wiio, suggest the difficulty of understanding each other:
                1) If communication can fail, it will.
                2) If a message can be understood in different ways, it will be understood in just that way that does the most harm.
                3) There is always somebody who knows better than you what you meant by your message.
                4) The more communication there is, the more difficult it is for communication to succeed.
    B. Interpersonal relationships emphasize both message content and personal feelings.
        1. Content refers to the information aspect of a message.
        2. Personal feelings always accompany content and give emotional information about the content of the message.

3. Metacommunication means communication about communication, and refers to the cues present in interpersonal exchanges.
    a. Feelings about the issue at hand.
    b. Clues about how intimate a relationship is.
    c. Clues about the power structure of the relationship.
C. Interpersonal relationships are defined by the roles that we assume.
    1. A role is a set of expected behaviors that we associate with a particular situation.
    2. The roles we assume reflect our expectations of behaviors appropriate to the particular environment.
    3. The roles we assume reflect our perceptions of self and other. At least six different perceptions can come to bear on the roles we select:
        a. Who you think you are.
        b. Who you think the other person is.
        c. Who you think the other person thinks you are.
        d. Who the other person thinks he or she is.
        e. Who the other person thinks you are.
        f. Who the other person thinks you think he or she is.
    4. The varied number of roles we assume increases the potential for different perceptions with our partners.
        a. Successful relationships tend to spend more time aligning their perspectives.
        b. Successful relationships tend to share more common perceptions of their relationship.
D. Interpersonal relationships are governed by social roles.
    1. Rules are "a followable prescription that indicates what behavior is obligated, preferred, or prohibited in certain contexts.
        a. Rules may be explicit or implicit.
        b. Rules help us to define appropriate and inappropriate communication in a given situation.
        c. Rules are developed by those involved in the interaction and by the culture.
        d. Rules are mutually defined and agreed upon.
    2. Interpersonal rules of greatest importance, according to research by Michael Argyle, et al., include:
        a. Partners should respect the other's privacy.
        b. Partners should not reveal each other's secrets.
        c. Partners should look the other person in the eye during conversation.
        d. Partners should not criticize the other person publicly.

3. Interpersonal rules are learned from experiences with family members and friends.

VII. How to Improve Your Own Interpersonal Communication: A Five-Part Strategy.

A. Be knowledgeable: You must know how interpersonal communication works by learning theories, principles, concepts, and rules.

B. Be skilled: You must translate that knowledge into social skills.
1. Learning skills requires four steps: Hear it, see it, do it, and correct it.
2. Skills require practice.

C. Be motivated: You must want to improve.

D. Be flexible: You must examine your interpersonal options in light of the situation.

E. Be other-oriented: You must not focus exclusively on yourself.
1. We tend to be self-concerned.
2. Other-oriented communication suggests that you:
   a. Consider the needs, goals, desires, and motives of your partner.
   b. Consider the timing and location of your messages with regard to the other.
3. Other-orientation is a collection of essential communication skills.
   a. Accurately understanding yourself.
   b. Accurately perceiving yourself and others.
   c. Adapting to those different from yourself (age, culture, gender, and so on).
   d. Developing positive, healthy attitudes about others. Carl Rogers suggests:
      1) Genuine, positive regard for the other.
      2) An open and supportive communication climate.
      3) Listening carefully.
   e. Being sensitive to both verbal and nonverbal messages.

ACTIVITY 1.1

COMMUNICATION MODELS FOR LUNCH

Objective

To visually demonstrate the complexity of communication and why the models have evolved over the years.

Directions

1. Bring two slices of bread, one jar of peanut butter, one jar of jelly, one knife, one spoon, and two napkins to class. You will also need one desk or table, at the front of the room.

2. Ask for two volunteers to come to the front of the room.

3. In front of the class, explain to the volunteers that one of them will give directions on how to make a peanut butter and jelly sandwich to the other, who will make the sandwich.

4. Show both of the volunteers (and the class) the materials with which they will work.

5. Explain that there are several important rules for this procedure:

• The source (direction giver) must face away from the sandwich maker (receiver).

• The receiver must face away from the source and toward the class.

• The receiver may not speak or make any sounds.

• The receiver must do everything that the source instructs and nothing that the source does not instruct.

6. If necessary, stop the receiver from performing steps the source did not include. Typically, the source forgets to include steps (for example, "Take the lid off of the peanut butter jar" before "Put the knife in the peanut butter.")

Discussion Questions

The class will find the resulting efforts very amusing. Depending on the efficiency of your source volunteer, some or all of the following questions should illustrate the limitations of the communication as action model and support the need for the more complex transactional model.

1. Does communication really work in a linear way?
2. What effect does the absence of feedback have on the communication process?
3. Did the number of people present in the context have an effect on the source's and receiver's communication?
4. Did the audience bring physical noise to the communication process?
5. Were either of the volunteers experiencing psychological noise while participating in this demonstration?
6. Were there any necessary elements missing in the encoding of the message?
7. Were there any difficulties in the decoding of the message?

ACTIVITY 1.2 X

CONTENT AND RELATIONSHIP DIMENSIONS ROLE-PLAYS*

Objective

Demonstrate how the content of messages is affected by relational cues.

Directions

Students should be grouped in pairs, given a copy of the dialogue and situations, assigned a situation—per pair—and given a minute to decide who will perform which role. Pairs of students should then perform the dialogue, using nonverbal cues to illustrate their relationship to each other. The rest of the class should attempt to guess the natures of the illustrated relationships.

The Dialogue

Person A: Hi . . .

Person B: Hey.

Person A: What's going on?

Person B: Pretty cool storm we're having, huh?

---

*From Russell Wittrup, Southwest Texas State University.

Person A: Yeah, that lightning is intense. Hey, did you see (current movie) yet?

Person B: No, but I've heard it's good.

Person A: Wanna go?

The Situations

1. Two people who work together but don't know one another well
2. Two roommates who know each other quite well
3. Two people who are madly in love after knowing each other for five months
4. Two people, in an established relationship, when one is quite angry with the other
5. An employee and his or her supervisor
6. A parent and his or her son or daughter
7. A very outgoing person who senses that the other is shy
8. Two actors trying out for a play
9. Two people who are making up, after just having had a fight
10. One person is jealous of the other person
11. One person has a hidden agenda with the other person
12. One person feels intimidated by the other person

CHAPTER 2 Communication and Self

INSTRUCTIONAL OBJECTIVES

After studying this chapter, students should be able to:

1. Define, compare, and contrast the meanings of self-concept and self-esteem.
2. Identify factors that shape the development of self-concept.
3. Describe how an individual's self-concept affects his or her relationships with others.
4. Identify the effects of an individual's communication styles on relationships with others.
5. Present strategies for improving self-esteem.

LEARNING TOOLS

TOOLS	TEXT PAGES
Building your skills activities	38, 42, 55, 63
Chapter glossary	67
Communication experience	51
Considering others	60
Discussion and review questions	65
Journal entry guidelines	66
Key term recaps	39, 41, 56, 64
Learning with others activities	66
Understanding diversity	43

CHAPTER OVERVIEW

CHAPTER TWO: COMMUNICATION AND SELF

A. Coming to terms with who we are requires understanding the term *self-concept*. Who you are is reflected in your attitudes, beliefs, and values, and can change over time and circumstances. Aspects of who you are include your "spiritual," "social," and "material" selves.

B. Our self-concept develops from at least three sources: interaction with others, association with groups, and the roles we assume.

C. Closely related to self-concept is self-esteem; whereas self-concept is who you are, self-esteem is your evaluation of who you are.

D. Awareness of self-concept and self-esteem benefits interpersonal relationships by increasing "other-orientation." Each of us also has varying levels of interpersonal needs for affection, inclusion, and control. Self-concept, self-esteem, and interpersonal needs allow for self-fulfilling prophecies, subjective interpretations of messages, selective exposure, and unique message formation. People tend to have a predominant communication style and a backup style that are based on their sense of self and others.

E. Self-esteem can be improved by positive intrapersonal communication, visualization, avoiding comparisons to others, reframing past events, developing honest relationships, processing and letting go of the past, and seeking professional assistance.

DETAILED CHAPTER OUTLINE

I. The question "Who are you?" is the starting point for understanding self-concept.
   A. We can view self-concept as the labels we consistently use to describe ourselves to others.
   B. Who you are is reflected in your attitudes, beliefs, and values.
      1. An attitude is a learned predisposition to respond to a person, object, or idea in a favorable or unfavorable way.
      2. Beliefs are conceptions of what is true and what is false.
      3. Values are enduring concepts of good and bad, right from wrong.
   C. Our concept of self can and does change, depending upon circumstances and influences.
      1. Your material self is a total of all the tangible things you own: your possessions, your home, your body.
      2. Your social self is the part of you that interacts with others.
      3. Your spiritual self consists of all your internal thoughts and introspection about your values and moral standards.
II. How does self-concept develop?
   A. We form our self-concept by seeing ourselves in a figurative looking glass when we interact with others.
   B. We form our self-concept based on attitudes, beliefs, and values of groups with whom we associate.

C. We form our self-concept based on roles we assume.

III. What is self-esteem?

    A. Self-esteem is closely related to your self-concept.

        1. Through your self-concept you describe who you are.

        2. Through your self-esteem you evaluate who you are.

    B. Berne (1964) identified four life positions to describe our overall sense of our own worth and that of others.

        1. I'm OK, you're OK.

        2. I'm OK, you're not OK.

        3. I'm not OK, you're OK.

        4. I'm not OK, you're not OK.

IV. Self-concept and self-esteem affect interpersonal communication and relationships.

    A. Knowing yourself and understanding how others see you is prerequisite to becoming other-oriented.

        1. George Herbert Mead suggests that we develop an "I" which is based upon our own perspective of ourselves, and a "Me" which is an image of ourselves based upon the collective responses we receive and interpret from others.

        2. When we begin the decentering process, we often interpret false assumptions about others, using our own selves as a frame of reference.

            a. When you use a specific-other perspective, you rely on information that you have observed or that you can imagine about a particular person.

            b. When you use a generalized-other perspective, you apply knowledge about people in general or about specific subgroups to the person with whom you are interacting.

    B. We refer to the tendency for what we believe about ourselves often coming true because we expect it to come true as self-fulfilling prophecy.

    C. Self-concept and self-esteem color how we interpret messages.

        1. Perhaps you know someone whose low self-esteem colors how he or she interprets messages and interacts with others.

        2. The principle of selective exposure suggests that we tend to place ourselves in situations consistent with who we think we are.

    D. How we communicate with others reflects the interaction of our self-concept and our need to interact with others. Social psychologist Will Schutz suggests that three primary social needs affect our need to interact with others:

        1. Inclusion—the need to be included in the activities of others, and have others involved in our activities.

        2. Control—the need to have some degree of influence over the relationships we establish with others. Also, the need to allow others to have some influence over their relationships with us, which may lead to increased stability and comfort.

        3. Affection—the need to give and receive love, support, warmth, and intimacy.

        4. The levels of inclusion, control, and affection vary enormously from person to person.

        5. The greater a person's interpersonal needs for inclusion, control, and affection, the more actively interpersonal relationships will be pursued.

        6. Our self-concept, self-esteem, and interpersonal needs not only influence how we communicate with others, they also impact how we communicate intrapersonally (messages said to one's self).

    E. Self-concept and self-esteem also influence our communication styles: the way we deliver messages and treat other people.

        1. Norton (1983) identified nine styles and the behaviors that illustrate each style.

        2. The Wilson Learning Corporation classifies our communication styles by the degree to which we display assertive and responsive behaviors.

            a. Assertiveness, according to the Wilson Learning model, refers to our efforts to control others.

            b. Responsiveness refers to our efforts to place the feelings of others above our own.

            c. Drivers are highly assertive.

            d. Analyticals are high on assertiveness and low on responsiveness.

            e. Expressives are high in both assertiveness and responsiveness.

            f. Amiables are the most responsive and least assertive types.

        3. According to the Wilson Learning model, each of us has a predominant communication style and we tend to interact most effectively with others who have a similar style.

        4. But we also have a backup communication style that we may use under stress if our primary style does not achieve the desired results.

        5. Recognizing styles that you and others use will help you adapt your messages to others, develop flexibility and sensitivity to

feedback, and use it to enhance your self-concept.

V. There are at least seven proven techniques for improving your self-esteem.

   A. Practicing positive intrapersonal communication—communication within yourself—can improve self-esteem.

      1. Realistic, positive self-talk can have a reassuring effect upon your level of self-worth.

      2. Conversely, repeating negative messages about yourself can keep you from trying and achieving.

   B. Visualization takes the notion of self-talk one step further.

      1. You can actually try to "see" yourself emphasizing some desirable behavior.

      2. Visualizing yourself performing well can yield positive results in changing long-standing feelings of inadequacy.

   C. Avoiding comparisons to others can improve self-esteem.

      1. Rather than finding others who seemingly are better off, focus on unique attributes that make you who you are.

      2. A healthy, positive self-concept is fueled not by judgment by others, but by a genuine sense of worth that we recognize in ourselves.

   D. Reframing is the process of redefining events and experiences from a different point of view.

      1. Reframing events that cause us to devalue our self-worth can change our perspective.

      2. Looking at the big picture places negative experiences that we all have in a realistic context.

   E. Developing honest relationships can be beneficial in fostering a healthy self-image.

      1. Having at least one person who can help you objectively and honestly reflect on your virtues and vices can be helpful.

      2. The more credible the person, the more likely we are to believe the information they offer us.

   F. Letting go of the past may be necessary.

      1. Individuals with low self-esteem may be locking on to events and experiences that happened years ago and refusing to let go of them.

      2. Becoming aware of the changes that have occurred and can occur in your life can assist you in developing a more realistic assessment of your value.

   G. Seeking support may be necessary if your self-image problems are deeply ingrained.

      1. Counselors, clergy members, and therapists can help you sort through problems.

      2. If you are not sure to whom to turn for a referral, you can start with your school counseling services.

ACTIVITY 2.1

THE "IF I WERE A . . ." GAME

Outline how self-concept develops from chapter two. Ask for several volunteers from the class to stand up in front of the group. Instruct them to wear a "poker face" during the first part of the exercise. In part one of the exercise, ask the class to brainstorm out loud the answers to the following questions for each volunteer: "If I were a vehicle, what kind would I be? If I were music, what type would I be? If I were food, what kind would I be? If I were an animal, what would I be? Help the class reach consensus for each of these questions for each volunteer and record the class answers on the board. Part two requires that each volunteer answer the same questions about him/herself. As answers are revealed, circle correct class answers and cross out incorrect answers on the board. Which volunteers were more accurately identified? Why would they be easier? What label was totally wrong? How did that information make the volunteer feel? What communicative behaviors create this image? What will the volunteer do about the disparity between self-image and public image? Could repeated messages from others that are incongruous with self-image alter someone's entire communication with others, creating a self-fulfilling prophecy? Are there any safeguards against such unhealthy influences? Review for the class the looking glass self, social comparisons, and self-concept and interpretation of messages as they may relate to the above exercise.

CHAPTER 3 Interpersonal Communication and Perception

INSTRUCTIONAL OBJECTIVES

After studying this chapter, students should be able to:

1. Define perception and interpersonal perception.
2. Identify and explain the three stages of interpersonal perception.
3. Describe the relationship between interpersonal perception and interpersonal communication.
4. Explain the interpersonal perception processes of impression formation, implicit personality theory, attribution theory, and constructs.
5. Identify ten factors that distort the accuracy of interpersonal perceptions.
6. Identify seven suggestions for improving interpersonal perceptions.

● LEARNING TOOLS

TOOLS	TEXT PAGES
Building your skills activities	72, 78, 87, 93
Chapter glossary	96
Discussion and review questions	95
Journal entry guidelines	95
Key term recaps	78, 85, 90
Learning with others activities	96
Understanding diversity	92

CHAPTER OVERVIEW

CHAPTER THREE: INTERPERSONAL COMMUNICATION AND PERCEPTION

A. The perception process involves selecting, organizing, and interpreting stimuli in our environment.
B. We form perceptions in interpersonal relationships according to how we organize information. Four theories explain how we organize interpersonal perceptions: impression formation, implicit personality, constructs, and attribution.
C. At least ten barriers impede our accurate perceptions: ignoring details, overgeneralizing, holding on to preconceptions and stereotypes, imposing consistency, presuming causes and effects, preferring simple explanations, ignoring circumstances, crediting irrelevant information, focusing on the negative, and seeing only the good or bad.
D. We can improve our perceptual skills in seven ways: by increasing our understanding of the perception process, increasing our observational accuracy, recognizing how we attribute meaning, checking our perceptions, increasing our awareness of perceptual inaccuracies and compensating for them, seeking honest feedback, and developing social decentering, empathy, and other-orientation.

DETAILED CHAPTER OUTLINE

I. What is the process of interpersonal perception?
   A. Perception is simply the arousal of any of our senses.
   B. Interpersonal perception is the three-stage process by which we decide what people are like and give meaning to their actions.
   C. Interpersonal perception begins with selecting stimuli to attend to.
      1. The number of sensations we can attend to at any given time is limited.
      2. This selectivity can also cause us to fail to perceive information that is important.
      3. During the selection stage, we attempt to simplify the stimuli that flood in through our senses.
      4. Directing our attention to specific stimuli and consequently ignoring others is called *selective perception*.
      5. We also simplify stimuli by categorizing information and inventing stereotypes.
         a. When we stereotype people, we place them into inflexible, all-encompassing categories.
         b. The *halo effect* occurs when we attribute a variety of positive qualities to people simply because we like them.
         c. Attributing a variety of negative qualities to people simply because we do not like them is called the *horn effect*.
   D. The second stage of interpersonal perception is organizing and imposing structure on what we observe.

1. After we select stimuli to attend to, we start to organize them into convenient, understandable, and efficient patterns that allow us to make sense of what we have observed.
2. The way we organize information depends partly upon the way we punctuate, or separate, it.
3. When it comes to punctuating relational events and behaviors, we each develop our own separate set of standards.
4. The way we organize information depends partly upon the way we superimpose, or fill in, missing information to create closure.

E. The final stage of perception is interpreting: attributing meaning to what we observe.

II. How does interpersonal perception affect interpersonal communication?

A. How much we notice about another person's communication behavior relates to our level of interest and need.

B. Perception can be either a passive or an active process.
1. Passive perception occurs simply because our senses are in operation.
2. Active perception occurs when we are motivated to select particular information.

III. Interpersonal perception involves three processes: forming impressions of others; applying implicit personality theories, which we use to organize information about people; and finally developing attribution theories, which help us explain why people behave the way they do.

A. What characterizes impression formation?
1. Impressions are collections of perceptions about others that we maintain and use to interpret their behaviors.
2. We select, organize, and interpret all of these perceptions to create a general impression.
3. We tend to form these impressions readily and part with them reluctantly.
4. When the first impressions we form about someone affect our interpretation of subsequent perceptions of them, the primacy effect has occurred.
5. When we attend more to the last thing we observed of a person, the recency effect has occurred.

B. What is an implicit personality theory?
1. In addition to developing impressions about specific people, we also organize our perceptions by developing our own implicit theories to explain how people in general behave.
2. Your implicit personality theory is your own set of beliefs and hypotheses about what people are like.

3. The "halo effect" involves attributing a variety of positive attributes to someone we like without confirming the existence of these qualities.

C. Personal constructs represent qualities that allow us to categorize people into one of two groups of polar opposites: friendly or unfriendly, intelligent or unintelligent, and the like.
1. Cognitive complexity refers to the ability to develop long lists of constructs to describe others. People's cognitive complexity varies according to differentiation, elaboration, and integration.
2. Cognitive complexity is shaped and shapes our perceptions.

D. Attribution theory relates to our tendency to attribute specific motives and causes to the behaviors we observe.
1. Developing the most credible explanation for the behavior of others is the goal of the attribution process.
2. According to one attribution theory, correspondent inference theory, we try to determine the intentionality of the person in causing the effect—determining how intentional the act was.
3. Causal attribution theory identifies three potential causes for any person's action: circumstance, a stimulus, or the person herself or himself.
4. A number of factors affect the accuracy of our attributions: our ability to make effective and complete observations; the degree to which we are able to directly observe the cause and effect; the completeness of our information; and our ability to rule out other causes.

IV. There are at least ten barriers to accurate perception.

A. Ignoring details involves giving too much weight to information that is obvious and superficial.

B. Overgeneralizing is treating small amounts of information as if they were highly representative.

C. Holding on to preconceptions involves distorting or ignoring information that violates our expectations or preconceptions.

D. Imposing consistency involves overestimating the consistency and constancy of others' behaviors, ignoring fluctuations.

E. Causation preconnecting causes and effects involves relying on pre-existing ideas about underlying causes and what we observe.

F. Simplifying involves choosing simple explanations over complex ones.

G. Ignoring circumstances involves diminishing the effect of external circumstances on another's behavior.
 1. We tend to explain our own negative actions in terms of circumstances, while attributing others' actions to their personality.
 2. We also fail to compare one person's behavior with that of others under the same circumstances.
H. Crediting irrelevant information is treating irrelevant information as if it were relevant.
I. Focusing on the negative is giving more weight to negative information than to positive information.
J. Seeing good or bad involves distorting our attributions to match our like or dislike for someone.

V. There are at least seven strategies for improving your interpersonal perceptual skills.
 A. Increase your understanding of the perceptual process.
  1. Studying this chapter is a start.
  2. Continue by questioning your perceptions and analyzing the process through which you arrive at perceptual conclusions.
 B. Increase your observational acuity.
  1. You can increase the amount of information that you process from your senses by consciously attending to the input.
  2. When you interact with others, try to identify new details to observe, while keeping the entire picture in view.
 C. Recognize the elements to which you attribute meaning.
  1. Try to become aware of the stimuli to which you attribute meaning.
  2. Decide whether you are giving proper weight to the elements you are perceiving.
 D. Check your perceptions.
  1. Indirect perception checking involves seeking additional information through passive perception to either confirm or refute your interpretations.
  2. Direct perception checking involves asking straight out if your interpretations of a perception are correct.
 E. Increase your awareness of perceptual inaccuracies and compensate for them.
 F. Increase your awareness of others' perceptions of you and seek honest and constructive feedback.
 G. Develop decentering, empathy, and other-orientation.

  1. Gather as much knowledge about the circumstances that are affecting the other person as possible.
  2. Gather as much knowledge about the other person as possible.

ACTIVITY 3.1

DYADIC PERCEPTION: JUST THE SIX OF US

Objective

To illustrate the impact perception has on our relationships with others.

Directions

Have students partner up and discuss the "six people" involved in their exchange. Each couple should come up with a statement from each of the six perspectives that might influence the outcome of a first meeting of the two.

Discussion Questions

 1. Does perception have an interpersonal impact?
 2. Which of your own three people has the loudest voice? At what times?
 3. How can these perceptions create positive or negative spirals of interaction? What can you do to stop a negative spiral's effects?

ACTIVITY 3.2

IMPRESSION FORMATION IN THE CLASSROOM

Objective

To illustrate the pervasiveness of impressions based upon general physical qualities, behaviors, and disclosed information.

Directions

 1. Divide the class into pairs.
 2. Instruct students to spend a few minutes getting to know their partners.
 3. Provide copies of the following variables for all students.
 4. Ask students to record their impressions of each other, according to these variables.
 5. Ask them to also record the stimuli that gave rise to their impressions.
 6. Carefully instruct students to refrain from speaking while recording their impressions.
 7. When everyone has finished recording, have the pairs share their impressions and their bases with each other.
 8. As a class, discuss the accuracy of the impressions formed. Question the speed and confidence with which we form them.

Variables

Variable	Impression	Stimuli for This Impression
Age	_____	_____
	_____	_____
Marital status	_____	_____
	_____	_____
Occupation	_____	_____
	_____	_____
Income level	_____	_____
	_____	_____
Socioeconomic background	_____	_____
	_____	_____
Religious preferences	_____	_____
	_____	_____
Political affiliations or beliefs	_____	_____
	_____	_____
Hobbies or interests	_____	_____
	_____	_____
Personality characteristics	_____	_____
	_____	_____

ACTIVITY 3.3

DIRECT PERCEPTION-CHECKING ROLE-PLAYS

Objective

To provide experience in the process of asking others to confirm perceptions.

Directions

1. Ask for several pairs of volunteers or divide the entire class into pairs.
2. Give each pair of students one of the following pairs of perception-checking scenarios.
3. Ask students to create several lines of dialogue to enact their scenarios.
4. Have the pairs perform their scenarios for the class; have the class provide comments and suggestions on the handling of each type of scenario.

Scenarios

1. This morning, your boss told you that he or she wants to speak with you this afternoon and that you need to arrive at his or her office on time. You have been wondering what your boss meant by this and now you see an opportunity to ask your boss, before the afternoon meeting.

2. You found a bouquet of flowers at your doorstep this morning. The flowers came with no note. You have been crazed with curiosity about the flowers. Now you run into a colleague who, you believe, has a crush on you.

3. Your significant other said that he or she would telephone you last night, but you received no calls. Now you have an opportunity to speak with him or her, face to face.

4. Yesterday was your birthday and you heard nothing from one of your closest friends. Now you encounter this friend.

5. Your instructor insisted that you promptly turn in an assignment and had been unwilling to allow you one extra work day you had requested. It has been two weeks since you turned in the assignment and you have not received it back. You see your instructor in the hall.

6. You just heard the end of a group conversation in which one of the participants concluded loudly, "That sounds like some people I know," and then looked quickly at you. Now that person is walking away from the group, toward you.

7. This morning, one of your acquaintances looked straight at you, but did not respond when you said "Hello." Now you see this person again.

8. Lately, you have noticed a change in the appearance of one of your friends. He or she looks thinner, is constantly perspiring, and trembles most of the time. What do you say to your friend?

9. A classmate of yours is looking at you every time you look in his or her direction. The classmate does not look away, even if you stare at him or her for a long time. Now you encounter each other outside of class.

10. You have just gone to a family member to seek advice on a problem you are having. This person is usually very helpful to you, but today, he or she is quickly flipping through the pages of a magazine the entire time you are talking. What do you say to him or her?

CHAPTER 4 Communication and Diversity: Adapting to Others

INSTRUCTIONAL OBJECTIVES

After studying this chapter, students should be able to:

1. Define culture.
2. Identify cultural elements, values, and contexts.
3. Discuss differences and similarities in verbal and nonverbal communication in different cultures.
4. Discuss barriers to effective intercultural communication.
5. Identify strategies for developing knowledge, motivation, and skills that can improve intercultural competence.

LEARNING TOOLS

TOOLS	TEXT PAGES
Building your skills activities	103, 118, 120, 121, 123
Chapter glossary	135
Considering others	114
Discussion and review questions	131
Journal entry guidelines	132
Key term recaps	108, 109, 119, 122, 129
Learning with others activities	133
Understanding diversity	104, 128

CHAPTER OVERVIEW

CHAPTER FOUR: INTERPERSONAL COMMUNICATION AND CULTURAL DIVERSITY: ADAPTING TO OTHERS

A. Culture is learned and shared by a group of people. Cultural elements may include things and ideas, institutions, beliefs, aesthetics, and language. Cultural change occurs through enculturation and acculturation. Cultural values provide insights into behavior. Cultural context provides insights into verbal and nonverbal message formation and interpretation.

B. Intercultural communication often suffers from barriers, including ethnocentrism, ambiguity, stereotypes, prejudice, and erroneous assumptions.

C. Bridging cultural differences requires seeking information about the culture, increasing other-orientation, asking for more information, becoming mindful, flexible, and tolerant, and avoiding making negative judgments about other cultures. Through development of knowledge, motivation, and specific skills, one can acquire and hone intercultural competence.

DETAILED CHAPTER OUTLINE

I. Diversity is guaranteed because we all have different experiences, backgrounds, and perceptions. Diversity can interfere with developing relationships. An increase in diversity awareness is based upon several factors: the United States is becoming increasingly culturally diverse, the world marketplace requires successful competitors to be sensitive to cultural differences, and improvements in transportation systems increases the likelihood that you will yourself be traveling abroad.

II. Culture is a learned system of knowledge, behavior, attitudes, beliefs, values, and norms that is shared by a group of people.

A. Categories of things and ideas that identify the most profound aspects of cultural influence are known as *cultural elements* and include:
1. Material culture: things and ideas.
2. Social institutions: schools, governments, religious organizations.
3. Individuals and the universe: system of beliefs.
4. Aesthetics: music, theater, art, dance.
5. Language: verbal and nonverbal communication systems.
6. As we grow, we learn to value these cultural elements through enculturation: the process of communicating a group's culture from generation to generation.
7. Cultures change as new information and influences penetrate their stores of knowledge.
8. Other changes take place through acculturation: acquiring approaches, beliefs, and values by coming into contact with other cultures.

B. Cultural values constitute the second component of culture.

1. Identifying what a given group of people values or appreciates can provide insight into the behavior of an individual raised within that group.
2. According to Hofstede (1980), there are four variables for measuring values that are significant in almost every culture.
    a. Some cultures emphasize traditional male values, while others place greater value on female perspectives.
        1) Masculine cultures value achievement, assertiveness, heroism, and material wealth.
        2) Feminine cultures value relationships, caring for the less fortunate, and overall quality of life.
    b. Some cultures tolerate more ambiguity and uncertainty than others.
        1) Those in which people need certainty to feel secure are more likely to have and enforce rigid rules for behavior and develop elaborate codes of conduct.
        2) People from cultures with a greater tolerance for uncertainty have more relaxed, informal expectations for others.
    c. Some cultures value an equal or decentralized distribution of power, whereas others accept a concentration of hierarchical power in a centralized government and other organizations.
    d. Some cultures value individual achievement, while others value collective, group achievement.
  C. Cultural contexts are the third component of culture.
    1. In high-context cultures, nonverbal cues are extremely important in interpreting messages.
    2. Low-context cultures rely more explicitly on language, and use fewer contextual cues to send or interpret information.
III. The first step in building bridges between cultures is to find out what barriers keep us from connecting with people from other cultures.
  A. Ethnocentrism stems from a conviction that your own cultural traditions and assumptions are superior to those of others.
  B. Different codes for verbal and nonverbal communication may also impede your ability to connect with someone of another culture.
  C. Stereotyping and prejudice are barriers to effective intercultural communication as well.
    1. To stereotype someone is to push him or her into an inflexible, all-encompassing category, failing to consider the uniqueness of individuals, groups, or events.
    2. Two anthropologists say that every person is, in some respects:
        a. like all other people,
        b. like some other people, and
        c. like no other people.
    3. Our challenge when meeting others is to sort out how they are alike and how they are unique.
    4. Prejudice—prejudging someone before you know all the facts—inhibits effective communication.
  D. Just as it is inaccurate to assume that all people who belong to another group are worlds apart from you, it is usually erroneous to assume that others act and think as you do.
IV. Improving cultural diversity requires appropriate knowledge, motivation, and skills.
  A. Intercultural communication—communication between people with different cultural backgrounds—can be challenging.
    1. Misunderstandings and miscommunication occur between people from different cultures because of different coding rules and cultural norms, which play a major role in shaping our patterns of interaction.
    2. When you encounter a culture that has little in common with your own, you may experience culture shock, or a sense of confusion, anxiety, stress, and loss.
  B. Developing knowledge helps us understand those who are different from us. We develop knowledge by seeking information, asking questions, and developing a "third culture."
  C. Developing the proper motivation requires learning strategies of accepting others who are different from yourself.
    1. Tolerate ambiguity: Remind yourself that communicating with someone from another culture produces uncertainty.
    2. Develop mindfulness.
        a. To be mindful is to be consciously aware of cultural differences, to acknowledge that there is a connection between thoughts and deeds when you interact with a person from a background different from your own.
        b. Also try to consider the other individual's frame of reference or world view and use his or her cultural priorities and assumptions when you are communicating.
        c. You can become more mindful through self-talk.
    3. Avoid negative judgments about another culture.

a. The ethnocentrism that underlies many such judgments is a communication barrier.

b. It is also an underlying cause of suspicion and mistrust and, in extreme cases, a spark that ignites violence.

c. Try to simply acknowledge cultural differences and to view them as an interesting challenge rather than as an obstacle to be eradicated.

D. Developing skills or strategies to adapt to others who are different from you involves flexibility and other-orientedness.

1. Develop flexibility.

a. When you interact with someone from another background, your responding skills are crucial.

b. Pay close attention to the other person's nonverbal cues and adjust your communication style and language if necessary to put the person at ease.

c. Avoid asking questions or making statements based on generalizations.

2. Become other-oriented.

a. Being other-oriented does not mean that you should try to communicate in ways for which you are not equipped.

b. Trying to use slang or jargon from another culture to impress someone may result in embarrassing errors and do more harm than good.

c. Try to respond to the other person's interests, needs, and rules.

E. In actually visiting or living in another culture, or in simply trying to communicate with someone from a very different background from your own, the following suggestions may be helpful.

1. Seek information about the culture.

a. Prejudice stems from ignorance, and knowledge is power.

b. Learning about another person's values, beliefs, and behaviors can help you understand his or her messages and their meaning.

c. Every person has a world view based upon cultural beliefs about the universe and key issues such as death, God, and the meaning of life.

d. These beliefs shape our thoughts, language, and behavior.

e. Only through intercultural communication can we hope to understand how each individual views the world.

f. You can also prepare yourself by studying about the culture.

g. Given the inextricable link between language and culture, the more you learn about another language, the more you

will understand the traditions and customs of the culture.

2. Be other-oriented.

a. Being other-oriented does not mean that you should try to communicate in ways for which you are not equipped.

b. Trying to use slang or jargon from another culture to impress someone may result in embarrassing errors and do more harm than good.

c. But you can try to respond to the other person's interests, needs, and rules.

3. Develop a "third culture" by combining aspects of two different cultures into a unique, shared hybrid culture. The goal of a "third culture" is to reduce the tendency of viewing cultural differences with an "us versus them" mentality.

a. A third culture can create unique values and norms.

b. Attempts to understand another culture that are necessary in creating a third culture can increase relational empathy.

c. Cultural rules and behaviors become more explicit as the third culture must acknowledge and manage differences.

4. Ask questions.

a. When you encounter someone from another background, asking questions is a simple technique for gathering information and also for confirming the accuracy of your expectations and assumptions.

b. Be prepared to share information about yourself.

c. Communication helps to reduce the uncertainty that is present in any relationship.

5. Develop mindfulness.

a. To be mindful is to be consciously aware of cultural differences, to acknowledge that there is a connection between thoughts and deeds when you interact with a person from a background different from your own.

b. Also try to consider the other individual's frame of reference or world view and to use his or her cultural priorities and assumptions when you are communicating.

c. You can become more mindful through self-talk.

6. Develop flexibility.

a. When you interact with someone from another background, your responding skills are crucial.

b. Pay close attention to the other person's nonverbal cues and adjust your communication style and language if necessary to put the person at ease.

   c. Avoid asking questions or making statements based on generalizations.
7. Tolerate ambiguity: Remind yourself that communicating with someone from another culture produces uncertainty.
8. Avoid negative judgments about another culture.
   a. The ethnocentrism that underlies many such judgments is a communication barrier.
   b. It is also an underlying cause of suspicion and mistrust and, in extreme cases, a spark that ignites violence.
   c. Try to simply acknowledge cultural differences and to view them as an interesting challenge rather than as an obstacle to be eradicated.

ACTIVITY 4.1

INTERCULTURAL ENCOUNTERS

Identify the intercultural encounters you have had during the past week. Use the space below to organize your experiences.

1. Friends or family members who are from a culture other than my own:

   _____   _____
   _____   _____
   _____   _____
   _____   _____

2. People I have met from a culture other than my own:

   _____   _____
   _____   _____
   _____   _____
   _____   _____

3. Ethnic foods I have eaten (not counting pizza):

   _____   _____
   _____   _____
   _____   _____
   _____   _____

4. Situations in which I have heard someone speaking a language other than my own:

   _____
   _____
   _____
   _____

ACTIVITY 4.2

CULTURAL EFFECTS ON COMMUNICATION

Objective

To illustrate the impact that differing world views have on communication.

Directions

1. Make enough copies of the "world views" and case study to distribute to students. (One sheet accommodates three people.)
2. Explain that students will be placed into groups, to make a decision about a case study. Also explain that each student will be given a world view to enact (for example, they will have to communicate as if they held their assigned view).
3. Place students into groups.
4. Give group members varying "world views."
5. Give students the case study they are to discuss with their fellow group members.
6. Watch group interaction carefully, noting any conflicts that arise. If students need prompting, tell them to ask the question, "What might a person who believes this say?"
7. When interaction slows, ask groups to present their decisions and their means of arriving at them.
8. Read all of the world views to the class. Ask them about difficulties they encountered or would encounter, in similar situations outside the classroom.

World Views

View 1

You believe that there is no higher power above humans. There is no spiritual realm. Truth is scientifically documentable. Though science has validated some evidence for spiritual beliefs, it has not proven a higher power. We live one life. When we die, we cease to exist. There is no supreme justice.

View 2

You believe in a higher power and in a spiritual existence. Only the highest power can know all of the truth. We live one life on earth and a different, spiritual life after death. We pay for our life mistakes, after death.

View 3

You believe in a higher power and in a spiritual existence. Humans also contain this power and live many lives. Different humans have different amounts of the power. People with the largest amounts of the divine power are those with the oldest souls. We pay for the mistakes of any given life in the life that follows it.

Case Study

A young woman is suffering a strange phenomenon. For the last two days, she has been trapped in her own home. The doors and windows of the home seemingly close themselves, barring her from exiting. Objects inside the home have been moving—seemingly of their own will—through the air. Visitors are able to enter the home, but no one has been able to help the young woman or remove her from the home. Those who have visited her—her parents, a nun, and a family doctor—have observed that the young woman experiences periods of which she has no recollection during which she speaks in unrecognizable voices and languages.

What needs to be done?

CHAPTER 5 Listening and Responding

INSTRUCTIONAL OBJECTIVES

After studying this chapter, students should be able to:

1. Describe four elements of the listening process.
2. Understand why we listen and list barriers to effective listening.
3. Identify four ways to improve other-orientation and listening skills.
4. Identify responding skills and understand strategies for improving them.

LEARNING TOOLS

TOOLS	TEXT PAGES
Building your skills activities	147, 148, 152, 163
Chapter glossary	171
Considering others	157, 159
Discussion and review questions	167
Journal entry guidelines	168
Key term recaps	145, 154, 158, 164, 166
Learning with others activities	169
Understanding diversity	150

CHAPTER OVERVIEW

CHAPTER FIVE: LISTENING AND RESPONDING

A. Listening is defined as a process of selecting, attending, understanding, and remembering.
B. We listen for a number of reasons, including enjoyment, evaluation, information, and empathy.
C. Six barriers interfere with our listening ability: personal agendas, emotional noise, criticizing the speaker, speech rate versus thought rate, information overload, and external noise.
D. Effective listening is a skill that can be improved. You can become a stronger listener by stopping distractions, looking at the speaker, listening to the entire message, determining your listening goal, transforming barriers into strengths, and improving your memory.
E. Responding with empathy requires you to understand your partner's feelings, ask questions, paraphrase content, and paraphrase feelings.
F. You can improve your ability to respond to others more appropriately by providing well-timed responses, providing usable information, avoiding unnecessary details, and being descriptive rather than evaluative.

DETAILED CHAPTER OUTLINE

I. What is listening?
   A. Listening is different from hearing in that hearing is the physiological process of decoding sounds.
   B. Listening is a complex process we use to make sense out of what we hear.
   C. The first step of listening is selecting: focusing on one sound as you sort through the various sounds competing for your attention.
   D. The second step of listening is attending: focusing on the sound you select.
   E. The third step of listening is understanding: assigning meaning to the sounds you select and to which you attend.
      1. People understand best if they can relate what they are hearing to something they already know.
      2. The greater the similarity between individuals, the greater the likelihood for more accurate understanding.
      3. You understand best that which you also experience.
   F. The fourth step of listening is remembering: recalling information.
      1. Short-term memory is where you store almost all of the information you hear.
      2. The information we store in long-term memory includes events, conversations, and other data that are significant for us.
   G. We confirm that listening occurs by responding.
      1. You respond to people to let them know you understand their messages.
      2. Responses can be nonverbal or verbal.
II. Why do you listen?
   A. You listen to enjoy.
   B. You listen to learn.

C. You listen to evaluate.

D. You listen to empathize.

1. To empathize with someone is to try to feel what he or she is feeling.

2. Do you listen empathically without giving advice?

III. There are at least six barriers to effective listening.

A. Most interpersonal listening problems can be traced to a single source: focusing on a personal agenda.

1. We often wait our turns in conversations, formulating what we are going to say next.

2. How can you remedy this problem?

a. Diagnose it: Note consciously when you find yourself drifting off.

b. Mentally remind yourself to listen with greater energy and focus.

B. Emotional noise occurs when our emotional arousal interferes with communication effectiveness.

1. Certain words may be distracting to you.

2. Sometimes concepts, rather than specific words, cause an emotional eruption.

3. The emotional state of the speaker may also affect your ability to understand and evaluate what you hear.

4. Your challenge is to avoid emotional sidetracks.

C. Being critical of the speaker may distract us from focusing on the message.

1. Chapter three showed us that most people form impressions of others based solely on nonverbal information.

2. Good listeners say to themselves, "While it may be distracting, I am simply not going to let the appearance of this speaker keep my attention."

D. Your ability to think faster than people speak is another listening pitfall.

1. The average person speaks at a rate of 125 words a minute, while you as a listener are able to process up to 600 or 800 words a minute.

2. You can turn your listening speed into an advantage if you use the extra time to summarize what a speaker is saying.

E. Information overload is another barrier to listening.

1. We are all constantly bombarded with sight and sound images.

2. Don't assume that because you are ready to talk, the other person is ready to listen.

F. External noise is another barrier to listening.

1. Sounds in the environment compete with your attention while you are listening to others.

2. You can attempt to listen through the competing distractions or you can modify the environment to reduce them.

IV. There are three steps to improving your listening skills.

A. Stop.

1. You must tap into your own internal dialogue and stop your own running commentary about issues or ideas that are self-focused.

2. Maslow suggests that we operate at one of four skill levels.

a. The first level is unconscious incompetence—Before reading this chapter, you simply may not have been aware that you are distracted by internal dialogue.

b. The second level is conscious incompetence—You may now be aware that you are an easily distracted listener, but you do not know how to solve the problem.

c. Level three is conscious competence—We are aware that we know something, but it has not yet become an integrated habit.

d. The final level is unconscious competence—At this level, your skills have become second nature to you.

B. Look.

1. Nonverbal messages are powerful and are the primary ways we communicate feelings, emotions, and attitudes.

2. Another reason to look at another person is to establish eye contact, which signals that you are focusing your interest and attention on him or her.

C. Listen.

1. Mentally summarize the details of the message.

2. Mentally weave these summaries into a focused major point or series of major ideas.

D. Transform listening barriers into listening goals.

E. Practice listening to challenging material.

F. Determine your listening goal: to learn, to enjoy, to evaluate, or to provide support.

V. Above all, good listening is an other-oriented ability.

A. To listen passively is to avoid displaying any behavior that lets the speaker know we are listening.

B. Active listeners respond mentally, verbally, and nonverbally to a speaker's message.

1. This can be a measure of how accurately you understood the message.

2. Your responses indicate whether you agree or disagree with the comments others make.

C. Understand your partner's feelings.
D. Ask questions.
E. Reflect content by paraphrasing.
F. Reflect feelings by paraphrasing.
VI. How can you improve your responding skills?
   A. Provide well-timed responses.
      1. Feedback is usually most effective when you offer it at the earliest opportunity.
      2. Sometimes, however, if a person is already sensitive and upset about something, delaying feedback can be wise.
   B. Provide usable information.
   C. Avoid unnecessary details.
   D. Be descriptive rather than evaluative.

ACTIVITY 5.1

SHARPENING LISTENING SKILLS

The following listening activities can help you sharpen your listening skills.

1. Make a list of "red flag" words that have derailed your listening ability in the past. Ask another student to make up a paragraph about an important issue, using these words, and read it aloud to you. Monitor your reactions to the words and see whether you can steer your internal conversation back to the issue. Also notice how you begin to feel about the speaker and what you do about those feelings.

2. In a group, assign one student to speak very slowly on a difficult subject. Write down short summaries during pauses in the speech, then compare the summaries with those of others in the group.

3. List the things in your home—TVs, stereos, computers, newspapers, and so on—that might distract from conversation. Bring a radio into class and try conversing with a partner with music and news broadcasts in the background. Then have a conversation without the extra noise. Compare the results.

ACTIVITY 5.2

LISTENING TEST

Read the following situation. If you are alone, read it only once and then write the details in the message as well as the key idea. Or, as a real test of listening, have a roommate, friend, or family member read the situation out loud. Check your answers by rereading the situation.

Imagine that you are working in a fast-food restaurant. Your boss approaches you with a concerned look on his face and says: "We have a problem. I have had three customers in the past hour call and complain that they have been given the wrong order when they left the drive-thru window. We have to correct this problem immediately. The first incident happened at ten this morning. We had another problem at ten-thirty. I just had another call a few minutes ago. I think Jan is working the drive-thru now. I'd like you to investigate and let me know what you find out."

1. What are the details in the message? _____

_____

_____

_____

2. What is the main point? _____

_____

_____

ACTIVITY 5.3

RESPONDING WITH EMPATHY

Objective

To provide students the opportunity to practice responding with empathy.

Directions

1. Write the strategies for responding with empathy and using reflecting skills on the chalkboard.
2. Divide the class into pairs.
3. Give one of the following situations to each pair.
4. Explain that one member of each pair will describe his or her situation to the other member.
5. Explain that the listener in each pair will respond using all four strategies.
6. Have the pairs demonstrate their efforts to the class.
7. Ask the class to comment on the difficulties experienced.

Situations

1. You have just learned that a family member has died.
2. You are failing two classes and have decided to quit school.
3. You and your spouse have just decided to get a divorce.
4. You just found a wallet containing several hundred dollars.
5. You have just decided that giving your child up for adoption is the best thing you could do for him or her.
6. You have just been disowned by your family.
7. You have just learned that a friend of yours is having an affair with your significant other.
8. You have just been informed that you have a terminal illness.
9. You just met the mate of your dreams.

10. You have just been expelled from school for a breach of ethics.
11. You just received lavish praise from your instructor about a paper one of your fellow classmates wrote.
12. You just realized that you won a four-million-dollar lottery.
13. You just forgot to turn in a final project and slept through a final exam.
14. You have just decided to become a priest.
15. You were just fired from your job.

STRATEGIES FOR RESPONDING WITH EMPATHY

1. Understand your partner's feelings.
2. Ask questions.
3. Reflect content by paraphrasing.
4. Reflect feelings by paraphrasing.

GUIDELINES FOR USING REFLECTING SKILLS

1. Use your own words.
2. Don't go beyond the information communicated by the speaker.
3. Be concise.
4. Be specific.
5. Be accurate.

CHAPTER 6 Communicating Verbally

INSTRUCTIONAL OBJECTIVES

After studying this chapter, students should be able to:

1. Describe the relationship between words and meaning.
2. Understand how words influence us and our culture.
3. Identify word barriers and means of managing them.
4. Discuss how the words we use affect our relationships with others.
5. Understand supportive approaches to relating to others.
6. Understand how to confirm other people's sense of themselves.

LEARNING TOOLS

TOOLS	TEXT PAGES
Building your skills activities	194, 196, 201
Chapter glossary	210
Considering others	203
Discussion and review questions	206
Electronic connections	176, 198, 201
Journal entry guidelines	207
Key term recaps	178, 192, 197, 202, 203
Learning with others activities	207
Understanding diversity	177

CHAPTER OVERVIEW

CHAPTER SIX: COMMUNICATING VERBALLY

A. Humans are symbolic by nature and use words. Words are symbolic, arbitrary, and context-bound. Words have both denotative and connotative meanings and can communicate about the concrete or abstract.
B. The words we use can be powerful. Words have the power to create something new or unfamiliar. Words have the power to affect our thoughts and actions. Words have the power to affect and reflect their host culture. Words should be used carefully and thoughtfully.
C. Verbal communication can be challenging at times. At least eight barriers can interfere with our effec-

tive use of words: bypassing, bafflegab, lack of precision, allness, static evaluation, polarization, fact-inference confusion, and biased language.
D. A number of verbal strategies can enhance interpersonal relationships by establishing a positive and supportive climate and communicating a sense of value for others. We use words to establish a supportive relationship when we describe rather than evaluate, solve problems rather than control others, are genuine rather than manipulative, empathize rather than remain detached, are flexible rather than rigid toward others, and present ourself as an equal rather than a superior. Words can communicate a value for others when we use confirming responses. Words communicate a lack of value for others when we use disconfirming responses.

DETAILED CHAPTER OUTLINE

I. To understand the relationship between words and meaning, we must look at what words are and how they function.
   A. Words are symbols that represent something else.
      1. We use words as symbols in relationship to referents and thoughts.
      2. Referents are the things the symbols (words) represent.
      3. Thought is the mental process of creating a category, idea, or image triggered by the referent or the symbol.
   B. Words are arbitrary.
      1. In English, words arbitrarily represent something else.
      2. There is not necessarily a logical connection between the referent and the symbol.
      3. Further, English is a living language that will continue to evolve as we develop the need to name and describe new phenomena.
   C. Words are context-bound: They derive their meaning from the situation in which they are used.
   D. Words are culturally-bound.
      1. Culture consists of the rules, norms, values, and mores of a group of people that have

been learned and shaped from one generation to the next.

2. The meaning of a symbol such as a word can change from culture to culture.

3. The study of words and meaning is called *semantics*.

4. One important body of semantic theory, known as *symbolic interaction,* suggests that as a society we are bound together because of our common use of symbols.

5. The theory of symbolic interaction also illuminates how we use our common understanding of symbols to form interpersonal relationships.

E. Words have denotative and connotative meaning.

1. Language is the vehicle through which we share our sense of the world with others.

2. Messages convey both content and feelings.

3. Our language conveys meaning on two levels.

   a. The denotative level conveys content.

   b. The connotative level of language conveys feelings.

F. Words communicate concrete or abstract meaning.

1. Words can be placed along a continuum from abstract to concrete.

   a. We call a word concrete if we can experience its referent with one of our senses.

   b. If we cannot experience the referent with our senses, then the word is abstract.

2. In general, the more concrete the language, the easier it is for others to understand.

II. Words have power.

A. Words have the power to create.

1. Words give us tools to create our world by naming and labeling what we experience.

2. Words give us the symbolic vehicle to communicate our creations and discoveries to others.

3. One theorist believes that you also create your moods and emotional state with the words you use to label your feelings.

4. Research demonstrates that your words and corresponding outlook have the power to affect your health.

B. Words have the power to affect thoughts and actions.

1. Advertisers have long known that the way a product is labeled affects our propensity to purchase it.

2. Words also have the power to affect policy and procedures.

C. Words have the power to affect and reflect culture.

1. A theory called *linguistic determinism* explains this by means of a hypothesis of re-

ciprocity: Language shapes your culture and culture shapes your language.

   a. To understand your culture, you should study the words you use.

   b. There is evidence that words not only reflect your culture but they also mold it.

2. The words we use and listen to affect our world view—how we interpret what we experience.

III. There exist many communication barriers: things that interfere with the sharing of meaning.

A. Bypassing occurs when the same words mean different things to different people.

1. Meaning is fragile and the English language is imprecise in many areas.

2. One researcher estimated that the 500 words we use most often in our daily conversations with others have over 14,000 different dictionary definitions.

B. Bafflegab is the use of highly abstract language.

C. Why do some people use bafflegab?

1. They may be trying to dazzle their listener with evidence of their education or they may simply not be other-oriented.

2. They may be focused on impressing the receiver rather than on conveying meaning.

3. Another reason people use big words, overly formal language, or evasive phrases is to hide their ignorance.

D. Lack of clarity may be created through improper or imprecise use of words.

1. A malapropism is a confusion of one word or phrase for another that sounds similar to it.

2. Other imprecisions include using words out of context, using inappropriate grammar, or putting words in the wrong order.

3. It is vital to remember that meanings are in people, not in words.

4. For most communication, the object is to be as specific and concrete as possible.

5. Yet you are being too precise if you use a restricted code: words that have a particular meaning to a subgroup or culture.

6. Groups that rely upon restricted codes may have greater cohesiveness because of this shared "secret" language or jargon.

7. When people have known one another for a long time, they may also use restricted codes for their exchanges.

D. Using language to make unqualified, often untrue generalizations is called *allness.*

1. Allness statements deny individual differences or variations.

2. Reality rarely, if ever, provides evidence to support sweeping generalizations.

3. Incorporating the words "to me" in your pronouncements can help communicate to others (and remind yourself) that your view of something is uniquely yours.

4. Indexing your comments and remarks by noting the particular persons to which they apply is another way to help you avoid generalizing.

E. A static evaluation is a statement that fails to recognize change.

1. Labels in particular have a tendency to freeze-frame our awareness.

2. In addition, some of us suffer from having a world view so rigid that we can never change or expand our perspective.

3. It is important to acknowledge that perception is a process, and to avoid trying to nail things down permanently into all-inclusive categories.

4. To avoid static evaluation yourself, try dating your observations and indicate to others the time period from which you are drawing your conclusions.

5. Most importantly, try to observe and acknowledge changes in others.

F. Describing and evaluating what we observe in terms of extremes is known as *polarization*.

1. The world in which we live comes not in black and white but in a variety of colors.

2. If you describe things in extremes, leaving out the middle ground, then your language does not accurately reflect reality.

3. Family counselors who listen to family feuds find that the tendency to see things from an either/or point of view is a classic symptom of a troubled relationship.

4. Few relational difficulties are exclusively one-sided.

G. Fact-inference confusion occurs when we pronounce something as a fact without directly observing it or verifying it through the authority of an expert's research or observation.

1. A fact is something that has been proven to be true.

2. An inference is a conclusion based upon speculation.

3. The semantic problem occurs when we respond to something as if it were a fact, when in reality it is an inference.

H. Using words that reflect your biases toward other cultures or ethnic groups, or someone's gender, can create a word barrier for your listeners.

1. Although many debate the merits of political correctness, it is clear that sexist or racially stereotypical language can offend others.

2. In addition, such language ignores the fact that the world is constantly changing.

3. Sexist language can reflect stereotypical attitudes or describe roles in exclusively male or female terms.

4. Consciously remembering to use nonsexist language will result in several benefits.

a. First, monitoring your speech for sexist remarks can help you monitor your attitudes about sexist assumptions you may hold.

b. Second, using nonsexist language will help you become more other-oriented.

c. Third, nonsexist language will make your speech more contemporary and unambiguous.

d. Finally, your nonsexist language will empower others.

5. In addition to monitoring your language for sexual stereotypes, avoid racial and ethnic stereotypes.

a. Monitor your speech so that you are not, even unconsciously, using phrases that depict a racial group or ethnic group in a negative, stereotypical fashion.

b. The underlying principle in avoiding biased language is to imagine how the listener might react to your words.

IV. Words may be used to establish supportive relationships with others.

A. For more than three decades, Jack Gibb's observational research has been used as a framework for both describing and prescribing verbal behaviors that contribute to feelings of either supportiveness or defensiveness.

B. Words and actions are tools we use to let someone know whether we support them or not.

C. You can use words to create a supportive climate rather than an antagonistic one.

D. Describe your own feelings rather than evaluate others.

1. Most of us don't like to be judged or evaluated.

2. One way to avoid evaluating others is to eliminate the accusatory "you" from your language.

3. Instead, use the word "I" to describe your own feelings and thoughts about a situation or event.

4. In doing this you are, in essence, taking ownership of your thoughts and feelings.

5. This approach leads to greater openness and trust because your listener does not feel rejected or as if you are trying to control him or her.

E. Solve problems rather than control others.

1. When people treat you like a child, it often means they are trying to control your behavior.

2. In truth, we have little or no control over someone else's behavior.

3. Most of us don't like to be controlled against our will.

4. Using open-ended questions creates a more supportive climate than critical comments or commands.

F. Be genuine rather than manipulative.

1. To be genuine means that you honestly seek to be yourself rather than someone you are not.

2. It also means taking an honest interest in others and considering the uniqueness of each individual and situation, avoiding generalizations or strategies that focus only on your own needs and desires.

3. A manipulative person has hidden agendas.

4. A genuine person uses words to discuss issues and problems openly and honestly.

G. Empathize rather than remain detached from others.

1. Empathy is one of the hallmarks of supportive relationships.

2. The opposite of empathy is neutrality.

3. To be neutral is to be indifferent or apathetic toward another.

4. Even when you express anger or irritation toward another, you are investing some energy in the relationship.

H. Be flexible rather than rigid toward others.

1. Most people don't like someone who always seems certain that he or she is right.

2. Instead of making pronouncements, you can verbally acknowledge that your way of viewing is one way of viewing.

3. This manner of speaking gives your opinions a softer edge that allows room for others to express a point of view.

I. Present yourself as equal rather than superior.

1. You can antagonize others by letting them know that you view yourself as better or brighter than they are.

2. Although some people have the responsibility and authority to manage others, "pulling rank" does not usually produce a cooperative climate.

3. Also avoid using bafflegab to impress others.

4. When you communicate with someone from another culture, you may need to use an elaborated code to get your message across.

5. This means that your messages will have to be more explicit, but they should not be condescending.

V. One of the key skills in maintaining a long-term relationship is to know how to demonstrate that you value the other person.

A. A confirming response is a statement that causes others to value themselves more.

B. A disconfirming response is one that causes others to value themselves less.

C. There are several kinds of confirming responses.

1. Direct acknowledgment: When you respond directly to something another person says to you, you are acknowledging not only the statement, but also that the person is important.

2. Agreement about judgments: When you confirm someone's evaluation of something, you are also affirming that person's sense of taste and judgment.

3. Supportive response: When you express reassurance and understanding, you are confirming a person's right to his or her feelings.

4. Clarifying response: When you seek greater understanding of another person's message, you are confirming that he or she is worth your time and trouble.

5. Expression of positive feeling: We feel confirmed or valued when someone else agrees with our expression of joy or excitement.

6. Compliment: When you tell people you like what they have done or said, what they are wearing, or how they look, you are confirming their sense of worth.

D. There are also several categories of disconfirming responses to avoid using and to recognize in others' attempts to chip away at your self-image and self-esteem.

1. Impervious response: When a person fails to acknowledge your statement or attempt to communicate, even though you know he or she heard you, you may feel a sense of awkwardness or embarrassment.

2. Interrupting response: When people interrupt you, they may be implying that what they have to say is more important than what you have to say, or that they are more important than you are.

3. Irrelevant response: An irrelevant response is one that has nothing at all to do with what you were saying and suggests that your partner is not listening to you at all.

4. Tangential response: A tangential response is one that acknowledges you, but that is only minimally related to what you are talking about.

5. Impersonal response: A response that intellectualizes and uses the third person distances the other person from you and has the effect of trivializing what you say.

6. Incoherent response: When a speaker mumbles, rambles, or makes some unintelligible effort to respond, it may leave you wondering if what you said was of any value or use to the listener.

7. Incongruous response: An incongruous response is one in which the verbal message is inconsistent with nonverbal behavior.

ACTIVITY 6.1

ORIGINS OF WORDS

Objective

To help students understand how language is dynamic and always changing. To emphasize the cultural and regional impact on certain names and words.

Directions

Have students work in small groups comparing the names they each use for the following popular foods:

1. Carbonated drinks
2. Sandwiches made on long rolls
3. Drinks made with ice cream
4. Cut and fried potatoes
5. Tubular links of processed meat, often seen on barbecue grills

Discussion Questions

1. How does our language change?
2. What influences impact our language?
3. What are some examples of "new" slang terms?
4. Why do some groups create their own language adaptations?

ACTIVITY 6.2

FIDO OR FLUFFY: CONNOTATIVE MEANINGS

Objective

To clarify the distinction between denotative and connotative meaning.

Directions

Ask each person in turn to describe the first thing that pops into his or her head for each of the following nouns: dog, house, flag, God.

Discussion Questions

1. For each of the nouns, can we agree on a common definition (the denotative meaning)?
2. Where do our personal (connotative) meanings for these nouns come from?
3. Which nouns created in you a more positive association and why?
4. Which has greater impact on you, denotative or connotative meanings? When?

5. What kind of connotative meanings seem to be connected to very strong emotions? Why would that be? Do these emotionally charged nouns seem more or less abstract than others? Why would that make a difference?

6. Do people (poets, protesters, or others) ever use the connotative power of words as a weapon? Does it work? What defense is there against that?

ACTIVITY 6.3

DENOTATIVE/CONNOTATIVE MEANINGS

1. Provide both denotative (literal) and connotative (personal) definitions for the following terms. Compare your answers with those of your classmates.

	Denotative Definition	Connotative Definition
Winter	_____	_____
Prom	_____	_____
Piano	_____	_____
Car	_____	_____
Spring Break	_____	_____

2. Practice describing something, starting with an abstract description, and then becoming more concrete. Make this a game you play with one or more of your classmates. Think of something concrete, such as the name of your communication teacher or your state governor. Make your first clue an abstract hint such as "person" or "human," and then provide increasingly more concrete clues.

ACTIVITY 6.4

WHAT'S IN A NAME?

For most people, the most attention-catching word is their name. Given the power that words have to create and affect thoughts and actions, consider the implications of names.

1. Rank the following names according to status (1 = most status), then share and discuss the results with your classmates.

Mr. Smith	_____
Miss Smith	_____
Ms. Smith	_____
Mrs. Smith	_____
Fr. Smith	_____
Dr. Smith	_____
Prof. Smith	_____
Officer Smith	_____
Smith	_____

2. If you marry, should you change your name? Imagine that John Smith marries Mary Jones. Discuss the communication implications of the following names with your classmates. Which name would you prefer? Explain your choice.

John Smith-Jones/Mary Smith-Jones

John Jones-Smith/Mary Jones-Smith

John Smith and Mary Smith

Mr. John Smith/Mrs. Mary Jones

Mr. and Mrs. Smith-Jones

Mr. John Smith/Ms. Mary Jones

John Jones/Mary Jones

Mr. and Mrs. John Smith

ACTIVITY 6.5

RECOGNIZING BARRIERS IN COMMUNICATION

Objective

To help students analyze speech for communication barriers that may be present.

Directions

Read the following statements aloud to the class. Ask students to identify the barrier to effective communication present in each statement.

Statements

1. "You can't love me, but not want to marry me; 'love' means 'marriage.' " (Bypassing)
2. "I would attempt to rectify your aborted attempt at symbolic convergence were your very premise not misinformed by an outmoded bourgeois paradigm." (Bafflegab)
3. "Once a liar, always a liar." (Static evaluation)
4. "The French are outstanding cooks." (Allness)
5. "Either you're with me or you're against me." (Polarization)
6. "You left dirty dishes in the sink. The fact is you are self-centered." (Fact-inference confusion)
7. Either I get the job I want when I graduate, or college was a total waste of time." (Polarization)
8. "So, are you studying to become a black doctor?" (Biased language)
9. "College students spend most of their time partying." (Allness)
10. "Perhaps you should consider becoming an authoress." (Biased language)
11. "His speech was memorable because of his gestation." (Lack of clarity; malapropism—"gestation" is the period of carrying developing offspring in the uterus after conception; "gesticulation" is the act of using gestures.)

12. "You have never in your life considered a single person, other than yourself." (Allness)
13. "An hour is not 'running a little late'; ten minutes is 'running a little late.' " (Bypassing)
14. "You can't teach an old dog new tricks." (Static evaluation)
15. " 'I feel a lot more like I do now, than I did when I got here.' " (Lack of clarity)

ACTIVITY 6.6

RECOGNIZING DEFENSIVE-CLIMATE COMMUNICATION

Objective

To help students recognize communication that contributes to a defensive climate.

Directions

1. Explain that students will work in groups to change defensive climate strategies into supportive ones.
2. Divide the class into small groups.
3. Distribute several of the following statements to each group for revision.
4. Have the groups report their revisions to the class.

Statements

1. "I'm perfectly willing to admit when I'm wrong—I am just never wrong."
2. "Do it my way or hit the highway."
3. "You are obviously not understanding the program here."
4. "Well, when you reach my level of education, you might be able to make such intellectual leaps."
5. "Maybe some big, strong, manly man would be so kind as to move this stack of books for little, dainty me."
6. "Okay, let me try to explain this to you in itsy-bitsy, teeny-tiny baby steps."
7. "I know what you're thinking; you're thinking you can get away with this, but you can't."
8. "Look, here's how you should feel about this . . ."
9. "Certain persons should know that speaking to someone like myself in that manner will not benefit certain persons."
10. "You obviously do not care about my feelings."
11. "Did I ever tell you how ravishingly beautiful you are when you're angry?"
12. "I'm not mad; why should I care what you do?"
13. "I'm not interested in your opinions; I already told you what the right answer is."
14. "I am the boss here and I can terminate your employment at any time."
15. "No, we don't need to discuss our feelings; they're your feelings—not mine."

CHAPTER 7 Communicating Nonverbally

INSTRUCTIONAL OBJECTIVES

After studying this chapter, students should be able to:

1. Explain why nonverbal communication is an important and challenging area of study.
2. Describe the functions of nonverbal communication in interpersonal relationships.
3. Summarize research findings that describe codes of nonverbal communication behavior.
4. Describe three bases for interpreting nonverbal behavior.
5. Formulate a strategy for improving ability to interpret nonverbal messages accurately.

LEARNING TOOLS

TOOLS	TEXT PAGES
Building your skills activities	222, 227, 240
Chapter glossary	245
Discussion and review questions	242
Electronic connections	227
Journal entry guidelines	243
Key term recaps	217, 224, 226, 231, 234, 237, 239
Learning with others activities	243
Understanding diversity	219, 235

CHAPTER OVERVIEW

CHAPTER SEVEN: COMMUNICATING NONVERBALLY

A. Studying nonverbal communication is important and often undervalued. Nonverbal messages communicate our feelings and attitudes. Nonverbal messages are more believable and taken to be more honest than verbal messages. Nonverbal communication plays a major role in all interpersonal relationships.
B. Interpreting nonverbal messages can be challenging. When compared to verbal messages, nonverbal messages are often more ambiguous. Nonverbal messages are continuous rather than having a clear and distinct beginning and ending. Nonverbal cues, unlike words, tend to employ multiple channels. Nonverbal messages cannot be accurately understood without an understanding of the larger culture.
C. Codifying nonverbal communication is challenging. Researchers have focused on many elements of nonverbal signals, but eight codes are most common: body movement, eye contact, facial expression, vocal cues, personal space, territory, touch, and appearance.
D. When interpreting nonverbal communication, meaning can be derived from messages clustered around three concepts: immediacy, arousal, and dominance. Immediacy messages communicate a sense of attraction. Arousal messages communicate the level of excitement being felt. Dominance cues give insight into how powerful a person feels at that time.
E. Interpreting nonverbal messages is skill-based and can be improved. Nonverbal interpretations are more likely to be accurate when we consider the cues in context. Interpreters should attribute meaning to clusters of cues rather than just one isolated cue. Consider past experiences when interpreting the present. Become adept at checking your perceptions of nonverbal cues with others.

DETAILED CHAPTER OUTLINE

I. Why should we study nonverbal communication?
   A. Nonverbal messages communicate our feelings and attitudes.
      1. Mehrabian (1972) concluded that 93 percent of the emotional meaning of our messages is communicated nonverbally.
      2. When we interact with others, we base our feelings and emotional responses not upon what our partner says, but rather upon what he or she does.
   B. Nonverbal messages are more believable: nonverbal messages are more difficult to fake.
   C. Nonverbal communication plays a major role in interpersonal relationships.
      1. One researcher suggests that as much as 65 percent of the social meaning in our messages is based upon nonverbal communication.

2. We begin making judgments about strangers just a fraction of a second after meeting them, based upon nonverbal information.

3. Nonverbal cues are important not only when we initiate relationships, but also as we maintain and develop mature relationships with others.

4. Although we rely heavily on nonverbal messages, they do not operate independently of spoken messages in our relationships.

   a. First, nonverbal cues substitute for, repeat, contradict, or regulate verbal messages.

   b. Second, nonverbal messages accent and complement emotional messages.

II. There are difficulties inherent in attempting to classify nonverbal behaviors.

  A. Nonverbal messages are often ambiguous

    1. The meaning of nonverbal messages may be known only to the person displaying them.

    2. That person may not intend for the behavior to have any meaning at all.

    3. Some people have difficulty expressing their emotions nonverbally.

  B. Nonverbal messages are continuous.

    1. Words are discrete entities.

    2. Nonverbal cues occur in a continuous stream, so they are difficult to categorize and interpret.

  C. Nonverbal cues are multichanneled.

    1. Nonverbal messages come from a variety of sources simultaneously.

    2. Although you can move among them very rapidly, you can only actually attend to only one nonverbal cue at a time.

  D. Nonverbal interpretation is culture-based.

    1. Research suggests that there is some underlying cross-cultural basis for expressing emotion.

    2. Yet each culture may develop unique rules for displaying and interpreting these nonverbal messages.

III. There are at least six categories of nonverbal information that researchers have studied.

  A. Kinesics is the study of body movement, posture, and gestures.

    1. One paradigm identifies four stages of "quasi-courtship behavior."

     a. In stage one, courtship readiness, we may suck in our stomach, tense our muscles, and stand up straight.

     b. The second stage includes preening behaviors: we manipulate our appearance by combing our hair, applying makeup, straightening our tie, pulling up our socks, and double-checking our appearance in the mirror.

     c. In stage three, we demonstrate positional cues, using our posture and body orientation to be seen and noticed by others.

     d. In the fourth stage, appeals to invitation, we use close proximity, exposed skin, open body positions, and eye contact to signal our availability and interest.

    2. Another team of researchers focused on nonverbal behaviors that make us label a person warm and friendly or cold and distant.

     a. "Warm" people face their communication partners directly, smile more, make more direct eye contact, fidget less, and generally make fewer unnecessary hand movements.

     b. "Cold" people make less eye contact, smile less, fidget more, and turn away from their partners.

    3. Posture and body orientation reveal important information.

     a. Open body posture (uncrossed arms and legs) communicates that we are receptive and responsive listeners.

     b. When we are trying to decrease our contact with someone, we are likely to turn away from him or her.

    4. Mehrabian (1972) found that nonverbal cues of open body and arm position, a forward lean, and a more relaxed posture communicate liking.

    5. Another team of researchers tried to classify movement and gestures according to their function.

     a. Emblems are nonverbal cues that have a specific, generally understood meaning in a given culture and may substitute for a word or phrase.

     b. We frequently accompany a verbal message with illustrators that either contradict, accent, or complement the message.

     c. Nonverbal movements and postures used to communicate emotion are called *affect displays*.

     d. We use regulators to control the interaction or flow of communication between ourselves and another person.

     e. Adaptors are nonverbal behaviors that help us to satisfy a personal need and adapt to the immediate situation.

     f. These five categories of nonverbal behavior give you a new and more precise way to think about your own behavior.

  B. Eye contact serves at least four functions in interpersonal interactions.

    1. First it serves a cognitive function because it gives you information about another person's thought processes.

2. Second, we use eye contact to monitor the behavior of others.
3. Third, eye contact is one of the most powerful regulatory cues.
4. Finally, the area around our eyes serves an expressive function.

C. The face is the exhibit gallery for our emotional displays.
1. Although we often try to manipulate our facial cues to project a premeditated feeling, our faces may still betray our true emotions to others.
2. To interpret our partner's facial expressions accurately, we need to put our other-orientation skills to work, focusing on what the other person may be thinking or feeling.
3. According to one research team, your face is capable of producing over 250,000 different emotions.
4. Yet all of our expressions can be grouped under six primary emotional categories: surprise, fear, disgust, anger, happiness, and sadness.
5. Interpretation is still difficult because, even though our faces provide a great deal of information about emotions, we have learned how to control our facial expressions.
6. In addition, our facial expressions seem to be contagious.

D. The pitch, rate, and volume at which we speak, and our use of silence all provide important clues to our feelings in the form of vocal cues.
1. Your voice is a primary tool for communicating information about the nature of relationships between yourself and others.
2. Some vocal expressions of emotion are easier to identify than others.
   a. Expressions of joy and anger are obvious ones.
   b. Shame and love are the most difficult to identify based on vocal cues alone.
   c. We are also likely to confuse fear with nervousness, love with sadness, and pride with satisfaction.
3. Our voices also provide information about our self-confidence and our knowledge of the subject matter in our messages.
4. In addition to providing information about emotions, self-confidence, and knowledge, vocal cues serve a regulatory function, signaling when we want to talk and when we don't.
5. Sometimes it is not what we say, or even how we say it, that communicates our feelings: Silence may communicate volumes and serves many functions.
   a. We may be silent because we may simply not know what to say.
   b. There is evidence that when someone tells a lie, he or she may need a few moments to think of a credible ruse.
   c. We may use silence to distance ourselves from those around us.
   d. We may use silence to think about what we want to contribute to the conversation.
   e. Silence, too, may be a sign of respect.
   f. Sometimes you are silent with someone because words would diminish the experience you are sharing.
   g. Baker's theory of silence suggests that the more at ease we are when we share a silence with a close friend, the more comfortable we are with just being together and enjoying each other's companionship.

E. Proxemics is the study of personal space.
1. Hall (1966) identified four spacial zones that we unconsciously define for ourselves.
   a. When we are between zero and one and one-half feet from someone, we are occupying *intimate space*.
      1) This is the zone in which the most intimate interpersonal communication occurs.
      2) It is open only to those with whom we are well-acquainted.
   b. The zone that ranges from one and one-half to four feet is called *personal space*.
      1) Most of our conversations with family and friends occur in this zone.
      2) If someone we don't know well invades this space on purpose, we may feel uncomfortable.
   c. Zone three, *social space*, ranges from four feet to twelve feet.
      1) Most group interaction and many of our professional relationships take place in this zone.
      2) The interaction tends to be more formal than in the first two zones.
   d. *Public space*, the fourth zone, begins at twelve feet.
      1) Interpersonal communication does not usually occur in this zone.
      2) Many public speakers and teachers position themselves even more than twelve feet from their audience.
2. The specific space that you and others choose depends upon several variables.
   a. The more you like someone, the closer you will stand.
   b. We allow high-status individuals to surround themselves with more space than we do lower-status people.

c. Large people also usually have more space around them than smaller ones.

d. Women stand closer to others than men do.

e. All of us tend to stand closer to others in a large room than we do in a small room.

f. In groups, more dominant group members tend to select seats at the head of a table, while more shy individuals often select a corner seat at a rectangular table.

F. The next category of nonverbal codes is territory.

1. Territoriality is the study of how animals use space and objects to communicate occupancy or ownership of space.

2. We announce our ownership of space with territorial markers: things that signify that the area has been claimed.

3. We also use markers to indicate where our space stops and someone else's starts.

G. Touch is another category of nonverbal codes.

1. Normally, we touch to express intimacy.

2. Countless studies have shown that intimate touching is vital to our personal development and well-being.

3. The amount of touch we need, tolerate, receive, and initiate depends upon many factors.

a. The amount and kind of touching you receive in your family is one big influence.

b. Studies show that most of us are more likely to touch people when we are feeling friendly, happy, or under other specific circumstances:

1) When we ask someone to do something for us.

2) When we share rather than ask for information.

3) When we try to persuade someone to do something.

4) When we are talking about intimate topics.

5) When we are in social settings that we choose rather than in professional settings that are part of our job.

6) When we are thrilled and excited to share good news.

7) When we listen to a troubled or worried friend.

H. In all of our interactions appearance counts.

1. American culture places a high value upon how much we weigh, the style of our hair, and the clothes we wear.

2. These things are especially important in the early stages of relationship development.

3. Attractive females have an easier time persuading others than do those who are perceived as less attractive.

4. In general, we think attractive people are more credible, happier, more popular, more sociable, and even more prosperous than less attractive people.

5. The shape and size of your body also affect how others perceive you.

a. Heavier and rounder individuals are often perceived to be older, more old-fashioned, less good-looking, more talkative, and more good-natured than thin people.

b. Thin people are perceived to be more ambitious, more suspicious of others, more uptight and tense, more negative, and less talkative.

c. Muscular and athletically, fit folks are seen as better looking, taller, and more adventurous.

6. Our clothes also affect how others perceive us.

IV. Mehrabian (1972) has found that we synthesize and interpret nonverbal cues along three primary dimensions: immediacy, arousal, and dominance.

A. Immediacy cues are behaviors that communicate liking and engender feelings of pleasure.

1. The principle of immediacy is simple: We move toward persons and things we like and avoid or move away from those we dislike.

2. In brief, to communicate that we like someone, we use these cues:

a. Close proximity and forward lean.

b. Direct and possibly side-by-side body orientation.

c. Eye contact and mutual eye contact.

d. Smiling

e. Head nods and movement.

f. Open posture with arms oriented toward others.

g. Cultural- and context-appropriate touch.

h. Higher and upward pitch in our voice.

B. Arousal cues indicate responsiveness and interest.

1. The face, voice, and movement are primary indicators of arousal.

2. Forward lean, a flash of the eyebrows, and a nod of the head are other cues that implicitly communicate arousal.

C. Dominance cues communicate status, position, and importance.

1. A person of high status tends to have a relaxed body posture when interacting with a person of lower status.

2. High-status individuals usually have more space around them, have bigger offices, and have more "barriers" protecting them.

3. Other power cues that communicate feelings of dominance include our use of furniture, clothing, and locations.

4. Argyle (1988) summarizes the nonverbal cues that communicate dominance according to:
   a. Use of space (height, facing a group, more space).
   b. Eye contact (less with lower status, more when talking, more when initially establishing dominance, more when starting to establish power).
   c. Face (no smile, frown, mature adult features).
   d. Touch (initiating touch).
   e. Voice (loud, low pitch, greater pitch range, slow, more interruptions, more talk, slight hesitation before speaking).
   f. Gesture (pointing at the other or at his or her property).
   g. Posture (standing, hands on hips, expanded chest, more relaxed).

V. There are no universal dictionaries to which we can turn for help in interpreting nonverbal behaviors, but there are some principles and key skills.
A. Consider nonverbal cues in context.
   1. Context can change the meaning of nonverbal cues.
   2. Trying to draw conclusions from an isolated behavior or a single cue can lead to misinterpretations.
B. Look for clusters of nonverbal cues.
   1. Instead of focusing on a specific cue, look for corroborating cues that can lead us to a more accurate conclusion about the meaning of a behavior.
   2. Always consider nonverbal behaviors in conjunction with other nonverbal cues, the environment, and the person's verbal message.
C. Consider past experiences when interpreting nonverbal cues.
   1. Familiarity with another person increases our ability to interpret his or her nonverbal behavior.
   2. After knowing someone over a period of time, you begin to increase your sensitivity to certain glances, silences, and vocal cues that might be overlooked or misunderstood by others.
D. Check your perceptions with others.
   1. You judge others by their behavior, not by their intent.
   2. The only way to know what people intend is to ask them whether you have interpreted their behavior correctly.
   3. The key skill in doing this is called *perception checking*.
      a. First, observe the person's nonverbal cues, making a point to note such variables as amount of eye contact, posture, use of gestures, facial expression, and tone of voice.
      b. Second, try to interpret what the individual is expressing through his or her nonverbal behavior.
      c. Finally, check your perception by asking him or her if it is accurate.
   4. Overusing this skill would be irritating to most people, but it may be called for when you are uncertain of how someone feels and it is important for you to know.
   5. Addressing your question to a specific nonverbal cue will help you interpret your partner's behavior in future interactions as well.

ACTIVITY 7.1

REVERSE CHARADES

Objective

To visually and kinesthetically review categories of nonverbal communication, nonverbal communication codes, and dimensions of interpretation of nonverbal cues.

Directions

1. Provide each student with a six-inch piece of masking tape. (Small pieces of paper with scotch tape or self-adhesive memo notes work as well.)
2. Ask students to write the name of a popularly known person or a label for a "type" of person (for example, "teacher," "Mel Gibson," or "garbage collector") on the tape.
3. Explain that students will need to:
   a. Place their piece of tape on the back of another student.
   b. Walk around the room, viewing the characters listed on classmates backs.
   c. Respond—nonverbally—to each classmate, as they would respond if they actually met the person listed on the classmate's back.
4. Stress that verbal communication may not be used.
5. Ask students to begin.
6. When nonverbal interaction has slowed, tell students they may look at the tape on their own back. (Others may need to help them remove it.)
7. Have students return to their seats to report the responses they received, based on their assigned character. Ask them to place the examples they give in the appropriate category of nonverbal communication, nonverbal communication code, and dimension for interpretation of nonverbal cues.

Categories

Emblems
Illustrators (not possible for this activity)
Affect displays
Regulators
Adaptors

Codes

Kinesics (body movement, gestures, posture, eye contact, and facial expression)
Vocal cues
Personal space and territory
Touch
Appearance (not applicable for this activity)

Dimensions

Immediacy (degree of liking)
Arousal (degree of interest and responsiveness)
Dominance (degree of power and status)

ACTIVITY 7.2

NONVERBAL COURTSHIP BEHAVIORS

Visit a public place where social interaction takes place, such as a restaurant, bar, or sports event. Make notes about the quasi-courtship behaviors you observe. Compare your observations with those of your classmates.

ACTIVITY 7.3

NONVERBAL SKILL ASSESSMENT

Rate your current level of skill attainment (10 = High; 1 = Low) on the following factors:

	Rating Today	Desired Rating
1. I know the functions of nonverbal messages when I communicate with others.	_____	_____
2. I know how to interpret other people's postures and movements to determine whether people like me or feel more powerful than I am.	_____	_____
3. I know how to interpret the use of space around me and others to assess whether people like me or feel more powerful than I am.	_____	_____
4. I know the role voice plays in communicating my emotions and others' emotions.	_____	_____
5. I know the role facial expressions play in communicating and interpreting emotions.	_____	_____
6. I know how to interpret the eye contact of other people to assess dynamics of power, control, leadership, and credibility.	_____	_____
7. I know the nonverbal cues that communicate that people like me and that I like them.	_____	_____
8. I know the nonverbal cues that communicate power and status relationships.	_____	_____
9. I know the nonverbal cues that communicate that people are interested and responsive to me and my message.	_____	_____

Overall Nonverbal Assessment

| 10. I do an excellent job of interpreting nonverbal messages. | _____ | _____ |

CHAPTER 8 Conflict Management Skills

INSTRUCTIONAL OBJECTIVES

After studying this chapter, students should be able to:

1. Define conflict.
2. Compare and contrast three types of interpersonal conflict.
3. Identify commonly held myths about interpersonal conflict.
4. Describe differences between destructive and constructive approaches to managing conflict.
5. List and describe five stages of conflict.
6. Discuss five types of power.
7. Describe three types of conflict management styles.
8. Identify and use conflict management skills to help manage emotions, information, goals, and problems when attempting to resolve interpersonal differences.

LEARNING TOOLS

TOOLS	TEXT PAGES
Building your skills activities	259, 277, 281
Chapter glossary	288
Communication experience	262
Considering others	267, 269
Discussion and review questions	284
Journal entry guidelines	285
Key term recaps	253, 255, 260, 266, 279, 283
Learning with others activities	286
Understanding diversity	250

CHAPTER OVERVIEW

CHAPTER EIGHT: CONFLICT MANAGEMENT SKILLS

A. Interpersonal conflict, a struggle between two people who cannot agree upon a way to meet their needs, can vary in intensity and goal, and is tied to our unique experiences. Our inherent differences coupled with our unique experiences provide fuel for conflict.

B. Most conflict can be categorized in one of three types: pseudo, simple, and ego conflict. Pseudo conflict can occur when conflict is sparked because we miss someone's intended meaning. Simple conflict stems from differences in ideas, definitions, perceptions, or goals. Ego conflict involves personal attacks and defensiveness.

C. We tend to view conflict negatively because we often subscribe myths about the nature of conflict. Four myths that can create negative feelings toward conflict are: conflict can always be resolved, conflict is always because of misunderstandings, conflict is a sign of poor interpersonal relationship, and conflict is always bad.

D. Conflict in our relationships can be constructive, allowing for growth and new insights, or destructive, dismantling relationships without restoring them. Conflict can be understood as a process with a prior condition stage, a beginning, a middle, an end, and an aftermath stage.

E. Conflict styles, or how each of us patterns our behavior in conflict, can be categorized into three patterns: nonconfrontational, confrontational, and cooperative. A nonconfrontational style involves avoiding or giving in. A confrontational style involves attempts to control or coerce others to compliance. A cooperative style views conflict as a series of problems to be solved to the satisfaction of both participants.

F. Managing conflict is not always easy. Several suggestions can help you generate options, promote understanding, and provide cooperation. Managing emotions, the flow of information, and goals can improve effectiveness in conflict. Managing conflict should also involve both parties adequately defining the problem, analyzing the problem, determining goals for the conflict, generating possible solutions, and selecting a solution that is mutually satisfactory.

G. At times in conflict, others may aggressively violate your rights. These are times that call for assertive behavior on your part. Being assertive involves describing the situation as you see it, disclosing how you feel about the situation, identify the potential effects of the other's aggressive behavior, be silent and wait for a response, reflect back the content and feelings offered in response. Assertiveness is a skill that can be improved.

DETAILED CHAPTER OUTLINE

I. What is conflict?
   A. Simply stated, interpersonal conflict is a struggle that occurs when two people cannot agree upon a way to meet their needs.
   B. The intensity level of a conflict usually relates to the intensity of the unmet needs.
   C. At the bedrock of all conflict are differences—different goals, experiences, genders, cultures, and other factors.
   D. Since most of what we do is based upon achieving a desirable goal, it is not surprising that most conflict is goal-driven.
   E. Our inherent differences, coupled with our experiences, provide fuel for conflict.

II. One research duo found that most conflicts fit into three different categories.
   A. Pseudo conflict is triggered by a lack of understanding.
      1. "Pseudo" means false or fake.
      2. Pseudo conflict occurs when we simply miss the meaning in a message.
      3. But unless we clear up the misunderstanding by asking for more information, a real conflict might ensue.
      4. Listening well and testing your understanding of a message with questions and feedback can help you keep these kinds of conflicts from escalating.
   B. Simple conflict is the second category of conflict types.
      1. Simple conflict stems from differences in ideas, definitions, perceptions, or goals.
      2. A key to unraveling a simple conflict is to keep the conversation focused on the issues at hand so that the expression of differences does not deteriorate into a battle focusing on personalities.
   C. Ego conflict is based upon personal differences.
      1. A personal attack puts your partner on the defensive.
      2. As each person in the conflict becomes more defensive about his or her position, the issues become more entangled.
      3. If you find yourself in ego conflict, try to refrain from hurling personal attacks and emotional epithets back and forth.
      4. Instead, take turns expressing your feelings without interrupting each other; then take time to cool off.

III. According to one researcher, many of us were raised with five myths that contribute to our negative feelings about conflict.
   A. Myth 1: Conflict can always be avoided.
      1. Most of us learned that conflict is unnatural and that we should eliminate it from our conversations and relationships.

   2. Yet evidence suggests that conflict arises in virtually every relationship.
   B. Myth 2: Conflict always occurs because of misunderstandings.
      1. Conflicts do sometimes flare up because of a lack of understanding or empathy, but there are times when individuals simply have different needs or goals.
      2. These differences, not lack of understanding, are the source of the conflict.
   C. Myth 3: Conflict is always a sign of a poor interpersonal relationship.
      1. It is an oversimplification to assume that all conflict is rooted in underlying relational problems.
      2. Overly polite, stilted conversation is more likely to signal a problem than are periodic disagreements.
      3. In fact, the free expression of honest disagreement is a hallmark of a healthy relationship.
   D. Myth 4: Conflict can always be resolved.
      1. Not all disagreements can be resolved by listening harder or paraphrasing your partner's message.
      2. Some disagreements are so intense and the perceptions so fixed that individuals may have to agree to disagree and live with it.
   E. Myth 5: Conflict is always bad.
      1. In fact, if a relationship is conflict-free, the individuals are probably not being honest with each other.
      2. Although it can be destructive, conflict can also help us identify issues that need further discussion and lead to negotiations that give us fresh insights into the relationship.

IV. What is the difference between constructive and destructive conflict?
   A. Constructive conflict helps build new insights and establish new patterns in a relationship.
      1. The airing of differences can lead to a more satisfying relationship in the long run.
      2. A well-managed disagreement that includes sharing personal needs or revising goals can lead couples or friends to first examine and then repledge their commitment to one another.
      3. It can revitalize the relationship, enabling both people to view its elements from different perspectives, even if the information shared seems negative at first.
   B. Destructive conflict dismantles relationships without restoring them.
      1. If both individuals are dissatisfied with the outcome of the conflict, then it has been more destructive than constructive.
      2. The hallmark of destructive conflict is a lack of flexibility in responding to others.

3. Conflict can become destructive when people view their differences from a win-lose perspective, rather than looking for solutions that allow each individual to gain.

4. A rapidly spiraling conflict can be as destructive as a tornado churning through a trailer park.

5. One way to minimize destructive conflict cycles is to understand the sequence of conflict-triggering causes so you can stop them at an early stage.

V. Conflict is a process with a beginning, a middle, an end, and an aftermath.

A. The source or prior conditions constitute the first phase in the process as the one that sets the stage for disagreement.

1. It begins when you become aware that there are differences between you and another person.

2. The differences may stem from role expectations, perceptions, goals, or resources.

3. In interpersonal relationships, many potential sources of conflict may smolder below the surface and take some time to flare up into overt conflict.

4. Moreover, they may be compounded with other concerns, making them difficult to sort out.

B. Stage two is the beginning: *frustration awareness*.

1. At this stage at least one of you becomes aware that the differences in the relationship are increasingly problematic.

2. When the differences interfere with something you want to accomplish, then your frustration level rises.

C. The middle is termed *active conflict*.

1. When you bring your frustration to the attention of others, a conflict becomes an active, expressed struggle.

2. Active conflict does not necessarily mean that the differences are expressed with shouting or emotional intensity.

3. To keep this from happening, many experts advocate that you do not wait until your frustration level escalates to peak intensity before you approach someone with your conflict.

D. The end stage is termed *resolution*.

1. When you begin to try to manage the conflict, it has progressed to the resolution stage.

2. Of course, not all conflicts are ultimately resolved.

E. The final stage is the *aftermath*, or follow-up.

1. This stage involves dealing with hurt feelings or managing simmering grudges, and checking with the other person to confirm

that the conflict has not retreated into the frustration awareness stage.

2. Conflict does progress in stages, but your resolutions can backslide unless you confirm your understanding of the issues with your partner.

VI. How is power related to conflict?

A. Power refers to the resources an individual has to influence another person.

B. Even if the person does not use it, sometimes just having power determines a person's role in the relationship.

C. The person with the most resources to control the conflict management process will have more influence in shaping the outcome of disagreement.

D. Knowing what the sources of power are and how those sources can be tapped in a conflict can help you both to predict how you and others will behave in conflicts and to resolve conflicts more effectively.

E. Power does not reside in individuals; it is a product of our interpersonal interactions.

F. One pair of researchers developed a classic framework for defining bases, or sources, of power that we use to influence others.

1. Legitimate power is power based upon an appointed, elected, or designated position.

2. Referent power is based on interpersonal attraction.

a. If people like us and value our company, friendship, and advice, then we have power and influence that we can use to manage conflicts.

b. People rarely acknowledge the role of interpersonal attraction in managing conflicts, but this referent power may be enough to tip the balance in that person's favor.

3. Expert power is based upon the influence derived from a person's knowledge and experience.

a. If you are an expert in some specialized field, you have the potential for greater influence in how decisions are made about matters relating to this field.

b. Of course, when two individuals in conflict assume expert status, clashes can result in heated controversy.

4. Reward power is based upon the ability to give gifts, money, status, power, or other things we might desire.

a. People who have this kind of power have the ability to manage a conflict with their resources.

b. Of course, those who exercise this kind of power must know what rewards will be meaningful to the person they are trying to influence, or the power will be useless.

5. Coercive power involves the use of sanctions and punishments to influence outcomes.
    a. Often individuals who can reward you also dish out punishment.
    b. Sometimes, in interpersonal relationships, individuals who have no legitimate power and negligible referent, expert, and reward power will try to use coercion.
6. The conscious use of any type of power should be based on careful consideration of the short-term effect it will have upon your partner and the long-term effect it is likely to have upon your relationship.

VII. Most of us do not have a single way of dealing with differences, but we do have a tendency to manage conflict following patterns that we have used before.
    A. The pattern we choose depends on several factors: our personality, the individuals with whom we are in conflict, the time and place of the confrontation, and other situational factors.
    B. A widely accepted approach to identifying patterns of conflict organizes conflict styles into three types.
        1. A nonconfrontational style is characterized by backing off, either avoiding the conflict or giving in to the other person.
            a. A placating response is an attempt to please.
                1) Generally placaters adopt this approach because they fear rejection if they rock the boat.
                2) They appear to be other-oriented, but in fact they are simply seeking self-protection.
            b. Another nonconfrontational style is distracting: attempting to change the subject and avoid conflict or stress, rather than face issues directly.
            c. A third nonconfrontational style is computing.
                1) Computers remove themselves from conflict by remaining aloof and cool.
                2) The computing style is characterized by low empathy and minimal involvement with the issues at hand.
            d. Withdrawing from conflict, either physically or psychologically, is another nonconfrontational approach.
            e. Some people simply give in when faced with conflict.
        2. People who take a controlling approach to managing conflict have a win-lose philosophy—they want to win at the expense of the other person.
            a. Controllers often resort to blaming, or seeking a scapegoat, rather than assuming responsibility for a conflict.
            b. If this strategy does not work, controllers may resort to coercive power, using hostile name-calling, personal attacks, or threats and warnings.
                1) Threats refer to actions they can actually carry out and are powerful to the extent that the other person would genuinely find the threatened actions punishing.
                2) Warnings are negative prophecies they cannot actually control.
                3) Those who take a cooperative approach to conflict management view conflicts as a set of problems to be solved, rather than games in which one person wins and another loses; they use other-oriented strategies and foster a win-win climate using the following techniques:
                    a. Separate the people from the problem: Leave personal grievances out of the discussion, describing problems without making judgmental or evaluative statements about personalities.
                    b. Focus on shared interests: Ask questions such as "What do we both want?" and "Where are we already agreeing?"
                    c. Generate many options to solve the problem: Use brainstorming and other techniques to generate alternative solutions. (You will learn more about these techniques later in this chapter.)
                    d. Base decisions on objective criteria: Try to establish standards—involving cost, timing, and other factors—for an acceptable solution to a problem.

VIII. Managing conflict is not easy, but the following skills can help you generate options that promote understanding and provide a framework for cooperation.
    A. Manage your emotions.
        1. Often the first sign that we are in a conflict situation is a feeling of anger, frustration, fear, or even sadness that sweeps over us.
        2. Try to avoid taking action when you are in such a state.
        3. If we feel powerless to control our own fate, then we will have difficulty taking a logical

or rational approach to managing the conflict.

4. When we are emotionally charged we experience physical changes, such as increased adrenaline flow.

   a. Such changes fuel our fight-flight responses.

   b. If we choose to stay, verbal or physical violence may erupt.

5. You can draw upon some specific strategies when an intense emotional response to conflict clouds your judgment and decision-making skills.

   a. Select a mutually acceptable time and place to discuss a conflict.

      1) If you are upset, or even tired, you are at risk for an emotionally charged shouting match.

      2) If you ambush someone with an angry attack, don't expect him or her to be in a productive frame of mind.

      3) Of course, sometimes issues need to be discussed on the spot and you may not have the luxury to wait.

      4) But whenever it is practical, make sure the other person is ready to receive you and your message.

   b. Plan your message.

      1) Take time to organize your message, including identifying your goal and your desired outcome.

      2) You might also consider talking with a trusted friend or colleague or writing down your key ideas first.

   c. Monitor nonverbal messages.

      1) Monitoring your nonverbal messages can help to de-escalate an emotion-charged situation.

      2) Speaking calmly, using direct eye contact, and maintaining a natural facial expression will signal that you wish to collaborate rather than control.

      3) Also be sure that your nonverbal messages are not contradicting your verbal message.

   d. Avoid personal attacks, name-calling, and emotional overstatement.

      1) Using threats and derogatory names can turn a simple conflict into an ego conflict.

      2) Try to avoid exaggerating your emotions and you can take the sting out of your description.

   e. Use self-talk.

      1) Rather than immediately responding—outwardly—to an upsetting message, take a slow breath and question your-

self about the likely outcomes of your potential responses.

      2) Self-talk has a powerful effect on how we feel and respond to others.

B. Manage information.

1. Skills that promote mutual understanding are important for cooperative conflict management.

2. The following specific suggestions can help you reduce uncertainty and enhance the quality of communication during conflict.

   a. Clearly describe the conflict-producing events.

      1) Attempt to deliver your complaints in a brief, well-organized speech.

      2) Describing events in chronological order works well when describing a conflict.

   b. "Own" your statements by using descriptive "I" language.

   c. Use effective listening skills.

      1) Give the speaker your full attention and make a conscious point of tuning out your internal messages.

      2) Focus not only on the facts or details, but also analyze so you can understand the major point the speaker is making.

      3) Remember to "seek to understand rather than to be understood."

   d. Use effective response skills.

      1) Respond clearly and appropriately.

      2) Check perceptions, especially when emotions run high.

      3) Ask questions if you are genuinely unsure about facts, issues, or major ideas addressed.

      4) Summarize your understanding through paraphrasing.

C. Manage goals.

1. Both individuals involved in an interpersonal conflict want something.

2. To manage conflict, it is important to seek an accurate understanding of these goals and to identify where they overlap.

   a. Identify your goal and your partner's goal.

      1) Ask yourself what you would like to have happen.

      2) Next, you need to identify what the other person wants in order to manage the conflict.

   b. Identify where your goals and your partner's goals overlap.

      1) Armed with an understanding of what you want and what your partner wants, you can then determine whether the goals overlap.

2) If you focus on shared interests (common goals) and develop objective, rather than subjective, criteria for the solution, there is hope for finding a resolution that will satisfy both parties.

D. Manage the problem: You can apply all of the preceding skills in a proven method for problem solving.

1. First, define the problem. (Most problems boil down to something you want more or less of.)

2. Second, analyze the problem.
   a. To analyze is to break something down into its components.
   b. With your partner, consider the following problem components:
      1) Conflict-producing events in chronological order.
      2) The type of conflict present.
      3) The symptoms, effects, and obstacles.
      4) Whether the conflict stems from several subproblems.

3. Third, determine the goals of you and your partner.
   a. Also, generate objective criteria for a solution.
   b. The more measurable, verifiable, and objective the criteria, the greater the likelihood that you and your partner will be able to agree when the criteria have been met.

4. Fourth, generate multiple solutions.
   a. The more solutions you can generate, the greater the probability of finding a mutually acceptable one.
   b. One way to generate options is through brainstorming.
      1) Make sure the problem and the goals are clear to both of you.
      2) Try to temporarily suspend judgment and evaluations.
      3) Specify a certain time period for brainstorming.
      4) Consider having each partner brainstorm ideas separately before a meeting, or write ideas down before verbalizing solutions.
      5) Try to develop at least one unique or far out idea.
      6) Piggyback off the ideas of your partner and encourage him or her to use or modify any of your ideas.
      7) Write down all of the ideas suggested.
      8) Review each idea, noting ways to combine, eliminate, or extend them.

5. Finally, select the best solution.

6. Sometimes it may take several attempts at defining, analyzing, goal-setting, and generating before a mutually agreeable solution emerges.

7. Though these steps are presented as prescriptive suggestions, remember that conflict rarely follows a linear, step-by-step sequence of events.

8. These skills are designed to serve as a general framework for collaboratively managing differences.

IX. In using all of the preceding skills, you will need to assert yourself, especially if someone has aggressively violated your rights.

A. To assert yourself is to let your communication partner know that his or her behavior or message is infringing on your rights.

1. We each have rights.

2. In interpersonal communication, you have the right to:
   a. Refuse a request someone makes of you.
   b. Express your feelings as long as you don't trample on the feelings of others.
   c. Have your personal needs met if they don't infringe upon the rights of others.

B. Aggressiveness means pursuing your interests by denying the rights of others.

C. You can develop your skills in asserting yourself by practicing five key suggestions.

1. Describe how you view the situation.

2. Disclose your feelings.

3. Identify effects of the other person's behavior upon you or others.

4. Wait for a response while carefully monitoring your own for contradictions to your verbal message.

5. Reflect the content and feelings the other person presents to you in his or her response.

6. If the other person is evasive, unresponsive, or aggressive, you'll need to cycle through the steps again.

7. If you tend to withdraw from conflict, you can work on your assertiveness using several methods.
   a. Visualize past situations in which you wished you had been more assertive and replay them, imagining what you might have said.
   b. Practice verbalizing assertive statements.
   c. When you are appropriately assertive, consciously congratulate yourself for sticking up for your rights.

ACTIVITY 8.1

CREATE A CONFLICT ROLE-PLAY

Objective

To give students the opportunity to participate in and analyze different conflict types and styles.

Directions

1. Explain that students will work in pairs to create brief conflict scenario dialogues, using different conflict sales.
2. Divide the class into pairs.
3. Give a scenario with corresponding roles to each pair.
4. Allow students a few minutes to discuss their task with their partner.
5. Have each pair perform their scenario, asking the class to identify which type of conflict was created and which conflict styles were evidenced.

Scenarios

1. Roommates disagreeing over whose television program should be watched.

   Role A: nonconfrontational, using placating responses
   Role B: controlling, using threats

2. A student and a teacher disagreeing about the student's grade on a paper.

   Role A: cooperative, attempting to generate many solutions to solve the problem
   Role B: nonconfrontational, using distracting

3. A parent and daughter or son disagreeing about whether the parent will come to visit the daughter or son this weekend.

   Role A: nonconfrontational, using computing
   Role B: cooperative, focusing on shared interests

4. A cashier and a customer disagreeing about whether the customer gave the cashier a twenty-dollar bill or a ten-dollar bill

   Role A: controlling, using blaming
   Role B: controlling, using threats

5. Two motorists who have just had a minor collision, disagreeing about who is at fault for the accident.

   Role A: cooperative, basing decisions on objective criteria
   Role B: nonconfrontational, using withdrawing

6. A parent and his or her adult child disagreeing about whether the parent will come to live with the adult child.

   Role A: controlling, using warnings
   Role B: nonconfrontational, computing

7. Two fans at a ball game disagreeing about who should get the last beverage a vendor has to sell.

   Role A: cooperative, separating the people from the problem
   Role B: controlling, using blaming

8. A taxicab driver and a customer disagreeing over the amount of the cab fare.

   Role A: nonconfrontational, using distracting and then using giving in
   Role B: cooperative, basing decisions on objective criteria

9. An intimate couple, disagreeing about which one of two parties to attend.

   Role A: cooperative, generating many options to solve the problem
   Role B: controlling, using warnings

10. Two friends disagreeing over both wanting to date the same person.

    Role A: nonconfrontational, using withdrawing
    Role B: cooperative, focusing on shared interests

CHAPTER 9 Understanding Interpersonal Relationships

INSTRUCTIONAL OBJECTIVES

After studying this chapter, students should be able to:

1. Explain relationships of circumstance and relationships of choice.
2. Describe three dimensions of interpersonal relationships.
3. Explain what interpersonal attraction is.
4. Describe the elements that contribute to interpersonal attraction.
5. Explain the relationship between attraction and interpersonal communication.
6. Describe the principles of self-disclosure.
7. Construct two models of self-disclosure.

LEARNING TOOLS

TOOLS	TEXT PAGES
Building your skills activities	296, 301, 308, 313, 315, 323
Chapter glossary	326
Considering others	296
Discussion and review questions	324
Electronic connections	312
Journal entry guidelines	325
Key term recaps	301
Learning with others activities	325
Understanding diversity	302, 310

CHAPTER OVERVIEW

CHAPTER NINE: UNDERSTANDING INTERPERSONAL RELATIONSHIPS

A. Some of our interpersonal relationships arise from circumstances while others arise purely out of choice to interact.
B. Relationships can be further examined along three dimensions that are always present: trust, intimacy, and power.
C. Interpersonal attraction often sparks new relationships. Attraction can be based on physical attraction, credibility, competence, charisma, proximity, similarity, complementary needs, relationship potential, and reciprocation of liking. Some strategies for communicating attraction include nonverbal cues and verbally inclusive and informal language, affinity-seeking strategies, and self-disclosure.
D. Self-disclosure fuels our relationships by building intimacy, reducing uncertainty, enhancing trust, increasing vulnerability, and increasing potential benefits for the relationship while minimizing costs.
E. To better understand self-disclosure, two models are developed. The social penetration model illustrates how much and what kind of information we disclose at various stages of our relationships. The Johari window model illustrates how self-disclosure varies from relationship to relationship and over time.

DETAILED CHAPTER OUTLINE

I. An interpersonal relationship is an ongoing connection we make with another person that we carry in our minds (and metaphorically, in our hearts), whether the other person is present or not.
   A. Relationships of circumstance form simply because our lives overlap with those of others in some way.
   B. When we seek out and intentionally develop a relationship with someone, that is a relationship of choice.
   C. We act and communicate differently in these two types of relationships because the stakes are different.
   D. The effect of the same interpersonal communication behavior on different relationships can be dramatic.
   E. These categories are not mutually exclusive—relationships of circumstance can also be relationships of choice.
II. We can further examine interpersonal relationships along three dimensions that are always present in varying degrees: trust, intimacy, and power.
   A. Interpersonal trust is the degree to which we feel safe in disclosing personal information to another person.
      1. We exhibit a variety of trusting behaviors: revealing intimate information about ourselves; displaying vulnerability to another; displaying confidence in him or her.

2. As a relationship develops, we look for proof that our partner is trustworthy.
3. We look for behaviors to assure us that he or she accepts our feelings and won't exploit them, and that he or she will protect our vulnerability and remain in the relationship.
4. These behaviors include such things as not cheating, protecting information we have disclosed about ourselves, and continuing to show affection and closeness even when we reveal negative or threatening information.
5. The more we trust, the more information we are willing to share about ourselves, and the closer the relationship becomes.
6. Sometimes this sharing is selective.

B. Intimacy is the degree to which we can be ourselves in front of another person and still be accepted by him or her.
1. We can measure intimacy by the extent to which other people let us know that they see us the same way we see ourselves and express positive feelings about who we are.
2. We depend upon intimate relationships to bolster our self-confidence.
  a. The more intimate the relationship, the more the individuals depend upon each other for acceptance and confirmation of their self-image.
  b. During periods when we might not have very intimate relationships, it is sometimes hard to maintain a strong self-image.
3. We communicate our sense of intimacy directly and indirectly, verbally and nonverbally.
4. The more intimate a relationship, the stronger the emotional bond and the greater the mutual trust in relational commitment.
5. Because we are placing confirmation of our self into another person's hands, there is a great deal of emotionality associated with developing and ending intimacy.
  a. The feeling of "being in love" can create a variety of emotional responses, depending upon the way we have been raised to deal with emotions, our emotional experiences, and our emotional self-image.
  b. Emotions sometimes fly in the face of reason, which is why we say that people are "blinded by love."
  c. The roles that different emotions play in the development of intimacy are so many and varied that researchers and scholars have achieved little understanding of them.

d. There is evidence that sharing and discussing emotions leads to a healthier life.
e. Generally, it is a good idea to talk about emotions with your partner as you attempt to understand and respect one another's needs and preferences.

C. Interpersonal power is the ability to influence another in the direction you desire.
1. All interactions involve power.
2. Every relationship you have with another person falls on the continuum between you having more power than your partner and your partner having more power than you.
  a. In some relationships, there is a predefined imbalance of power.
  b. In complementary relationships, one partner willingly hands over power to the other.
  c. In parallel relationships, power continually shifts from one partner to the other, depending upon the nature of the interaction or the situation.
    1) When we try to equalize power in our relationships, we attempt to make them symmetrical.
    2) Although this may seem like an ideal to strive for, such attempts often backfire.
    3) When partners feel as if they have equal power over every decision, they sometimes compete with one another.
3. In all of these relationships, the balance of power affects how we talk and what we talk about.
4. When we communicate, we also affect the balance of power by exchanging information, which is a source of power.
5. When we trust another person enough to disclose information about ourselves, we give up control of that information, and empower the other person.
6. Typically, however, as relationships move toward intimacy, both partners share information with the other in a fairly equal manner, which gives both power over one another.
7. Nonverbal behaviors and speech patterns also reflect an individual's perception of his or her power relative to the person with whom he or she interacts.
  a. Traditionally, American cultural norms classify men's speech patterns as more powerful than women's.
    1) To be masculine is to be loud and forceful, to speak in deeper tones, to swear often, and to be authoritarian and blunt.

2) Feminine speech is gentle, smooth, friendly, warm, quick, gossipy, high-pitched, nonverbally expressive, and frequent.

    b. In truth, however, individuals of both sexes are apt to adopt either style.

III. Interpersonal attraction is the degree to which you desire to form or maintain an interpersonal relationship with a person.

    A. Interpersonal attraction occurs in the early stage of relational development as short-term initial attraction: the degree to which we sense a potential for developing an interpersonal relationship.

    B. Long-term maintenance attraction is the type that sustains relationships and is the level of liking or positive feeling that motivates us to maintain or escalate a relationship.

IV. Researchers have identified seven elements that influence our feelings of attraction.

    A. The degree to which we find another person's physical self appealing represents our physical attraction to him or her.

        1. Each culture has its own definition of the physical ideal, which it teaches and perpetuates.

        2. Physical attractiveness acts as a convenient filter to reduce relationship possibilities.

        3. In general, we tend to seek out individuals who represent the same level of physical attractiveness as ourselves.

        4. To a certain degree, the physical image a person presents can reflect more substantive qualities.

    B. Most of us are also attracted to individuals who seem competent, credible, and charismatic.

        1. We assume people are competent if they seem skilled, knowledgeable, and experienced.

        2. We find people credible if they display a blend of enthusiasm, trustworthiness, competence, and power.

        3. Competence, credibility, and sometimes physical attractiveness are all important elements in the composite quality we call charisma.

    C. We are more likely to be attracted to people who are physically close to us—who are in proximity to us—because it increases communication opportunities.

    D. In general, we are attracted to people whose personality, values, upbringing, personal experiences, attitudes, and interests are similar to ours.

        1. We seek them through shared activities.

        2. In the initial stages of a relationship, we try to emphasize positive information about ourselves to create a positive and attractive image.

        3. Yet we save our revelations about important attitudes and issues for a later stage in the relational development process.

        4. Attitude similarity is more likely to be a source of long-term maintenance attraction than of short-term initial attraction.

    E. Although we like people with whom we have much in common, most of us look for someone with complementary needs.

        1. Most of us wouldn't find it very exciting to be stuck for the rest of our lives with someone who had identical attitudes, needs, values, and interests.

        2. Schutz identified three interpersonal needs that motivate us to form and maintain relationships with others.

            a. Inclusion represents the need to include others in your activities, or to be included in theirs.

            b. Control represents the need to make decisions and take responsibility, or the willingness to accept others' decision making.

            c. Affection represents the need to be loved and accepted by others, or the willingness to give love and acceptance to others.

    F. We are attracted to others with whom we believe there may be high relationship potential.

        1. We need interpersonal relationships to confirm our self-image.

        2. Predicted Outcome Value theory claims that we assess the potential for any given relationship to meet this relational need and then weigh that assessment against the potential costs.

        3. Most of us begin predicting outcome values in initial interactions and continually modify our predictions as we learn more and more about the other person.

    G. We like people who like us, or who reciprocate liking.

        1. One way to get other people to reciprocate is to show that we like them.

        2. However, in initial interactions we are often reluctant to let other people know that we are attracted to them.

        3. We may hold back from showing our interest because we fear rejection or fear that we may give the other person a certain amount of power over us.

        4. Even in long-term relationships, people sometimes hold back in expressing their continued attraction for their friends or mates.

V. In general, the more we are attracted to someone, the more we attempt to communicate with him or her, although sometimes circumstances limit our ability to act upon our attraction.

   A. Communication is one of the ways we indicate our attraction.

   B. Usually, the amount of communication and interaction we have with a person indicates the level of attraction in the relationship.

   C. When we are attracted to people, we use a number of strategies to communicate our liking.

      1. First, we communicate our level of attraction through nonverbal cues, especially immediacy cues.

      2. We also use courtship readiness behaviors, preening behaviors, positional cues, and appeals to invitation.

      3. In addition, we communicate our attraction through language such as informal and personal language, addressing the person by his or her first name and often referring to "you," "I," and "we."

      4. Finally, sometimes we simply tell other people we like them.

   B. We also use affinity-seeking strategies to get people to like us.

      1. Often the methods just described to communicate attraction double as affinity-seeking strategies.

      2. In addition, we often try to establish mutual trust, be polite, show concern and caring, and involve others in our activities.

      3. Research suggests these strategies do work.

   C. We communicate with those to whom we are attracted in order to reduce uncertainty.

      1. Meeting strangers and starting relationships is rarely easy.

      2. We all seem to share a fear of the unknown, and this includes interactions with strangers whose behavior we cannot predict.

      3. Berger, Calabrese, and Bradac (1975) developed a theory based upon basic cause-effect assumption: We like to have control and predictability in our lives, and we are driven to gain information to reduce uncertainty.

      4. We are most comfortable in predictable situations, because we can call upon familiar strategies to handle the situation.

      5. In initial interactions we often follow predictable, scripted behavior that reduces uncertainty and may even stop interacting if the other person's responses do not follow the normal initiation script.

      6. Usually, however, we reduce uncertainty by gathering either cognitive or behavioral information about others.

         a. Cognitive information relates to thoughts, attitudes, and opinions.

         b. Behavioral information relates to reactions and remarks in various situations.

      7. We are particularly motivated to gain information early in a relationship when uncertainty is highest.

      8. We also are likely to seek out information if others behave in an unexpected way.

VI. Self-disclosure is the fuel for a relationship.

   A. When we self-disclose, we provide information that others would not learn if we did not tell them.

   B. Self-disclosure serves a relational function.

      1. We develop relationships through self-disclosure.

      2. We define relationships by their degree of mutual self-disclosure.

   C. Because self-disclosure plays such an important role in our relationships, we will examine its functions in more detail.

      1. Self-disclosure is a building block for intimacy.

         a. As relationships move toward intimacy, they typically include periods of high self-disclosure early in the relationship.

         b. However, the amount of information that is disclosed decreases as the relationship becomes more and more intimate.

         c. The more intimate the relationship becomes, the more intimate the information that is disclosed.

         d. Generally, a dramatic increase or decrease in self-disclosure reflects some significant change in the relationship.

         e. Without true self-disclosure, we form only superficial relationships.

      2. We expect self-disclosure to be reciprocal and appropriate.

         a. This cultural rule allows us to use disclosure as a strategy for gaining information and reducing uncertainty.

         b. If the other person does not reciprocate, both people might feel resentful.

            1) Sharing information about yourself gives others a certain amount of power over you.

            2) If one person shares information and the other doesn't, the resulting imbalance causes discomfort.

            3) Sometimes unwanted disclosures occur because one person misjudges the nature of the relationship.

      3. We assess self-disclosure risks differently.

         a. In judging what and when to disclose, you need to realize that different people have different standards.

         b. Be sensitive to the other person when you choose what and when to disclose.

c. Avoid stereotyping individuals and expecting them to behave in a certain way because of their sex.
4. We base self-disclosure on an analysis of costs and rewards.
   a. When we disclose, we make ourselves vulnerable and we risk damaging the relationship.
   b. In each stage of relational development, there is an optimum level of self-disclosure with which the individuals are comfortable.
   c. In general, we make disclosure because we believe that the benefits will be greater than the costs, even if the benefits are not immediate.
C. Two models help us to examine self-disclosure.
   1. Altman and Taylor (1973) developed a model of social penetration to illustrate how much and what kind of information we reveal in various stages of a relationship.
      a. The model starts with a circle that represents all the potential information about yourself that you could disclose to someone.
      b. The circle is divided like a pie into many pieces, with each piece representing a particular aspect of your self.
      c. Additional concentric circles in the pie represent the depth of information.
      d. Each of your relationships represents a degree of social penetration, or the extent to which the other person has penetrated your concentric circles (depth) and shared pieces of your pie (breadth).
   2. In the Johari Window model, the window represents your self.
      a. One axis is divided into what you have come to know about your self and what you don't yet know about your self.
      b. The other axis represents what some particular person knows about you and doesn't know about you.
      c. The intersection of these categories creates a four-paned window.
         1) The open quadrant represents that part of your self that you know and which you have revealed to the other person.
         2) The hidden quadrant is information you know about your self but have not shared with the other person.
         3) The information in the unknown quadrant is that part of your self which you have yet to discover or realize.
         4) The blind quadrant includes aspects of ourselves that we fail to recognize, while others do recognize it.

5) A change in any one quadrant will affect a change in other quadrants.

ACTIVITY 9.1

DISCOVERING SELF-DISCLOSURE NORMS

Objective

To allow students to participate in the discovery of safe and appropriate disclosures.

Directions

1. Explain that students will work in pairs on self-disclosing from a list of topics.
2. Divide the class into pairs.
3. Give disclosure topics (on the next page of the IRM) to each student.
4. Instruct students to take turns self-disclosing on each topic in sequential order on the list.
5. Observe the interactions. As they either dwindle or stray from the topic list, ask each pair to describe areas of difficulty they encountered.
6. You may link their experiences to:
   a. Topic areas (such as body, bodily functions, sex, religion, politics, money, or personality).
   b. Reciprocation expectations.
   c. Expectations for disclosure of little negative information in early interaction.
   d. Expectations for ritualistic communication in early interaction.

Disclosure Topics

Disclose to your partner:

1. Your name.
2. Your major field of study.
3. Your classification.
4. Your hometown.
5. Your age.
6. Where you live.
7. Why you are in this class.
8. Something for which you have a talent.
9. Something at which you would like to do better.
10. What you believe to be your best physical feature.
11. What you believe to be your worst physical feature.
12. A law you have broken.
13. Something you have done of which you are ashamed.
14. The things you fear.
15. What your political beliefs are.
16. How much money you and/or your parents make.
17. A lie you have recently told.
18. Your affection needs.
19. Your first sexual encounter—past or future.
20. Your last visit to the lavatory.

CHAPTER 10 Developing Interpersonal Relationships

INSTRUCTIONAL OBJECTIVES

After studying this chapter, students should be able to:

1. Explain the model of the stages of relational development.
2. Discuss the skills for starting relationships.
3. Identify and describe effective interpersonal communication skills for escalating and maintaining relationships.
4. Discuss some of the signals for identifying trouble in a relationship.
5. Describe three paths that relationships follow when coming to an end.
6. Identify direct and indirect strategies for ending relationships.
7. Explain three major causes of breakups.
8. Identify and explain the four elements of a model of ending relationships.

LEARNING TOOLS

TOOLS	TEXT PAGES
Building your skills activities	332, 335, 354
Chapter glossary	362
Considering others	334, 343, 345
Discussion and review questions	360
Journal entry guidelines	361
Key term recaps	355
Learning with others activities	361
Understanding diversity	351, 353

CHAPTER OVERVIEW

CHAPTER TEN: DEVELOPING INTERPERSONAL RELATIONSHIPS

A. Relationships proceed in discernible and predictable stages while escalating or de-escalating. The escalation process involves the stages of pre-interaction awareness, initiation, exploration, intensification, and individualization, separation, and post-interaction effects.

B. There are several suggestions for starting a relationship. We can gather information to reduce uncertainty, adopt an other-oriented perspective, observe and act upon approachability cues, use conversation starters, follow initiation norms, provide information about yourself, present yourself in a positive way, ask questions, and set realistic expectations for initial encounters.

C. Escalating and maintaining relationships requires a specific set of skills. By using skills such as being open and self-disclosing appropriately, expressing emotions, engaging in relationship talk, monitoring perceptions, listening actively and responding confirmingly, decentering and adapting, showing tolerance and restraint, managing conflict well, and seeking compliance, you can help sustain the forces that hold a relationship together.

D. Identifying and acting upon trouble signs can repair a relationship or end the relationship altogether. Repair involves applying the maintenance skills suggested earlier. Ending the relationship calls for considering your goals, such as preserving your partner's self-esteem, potential for future reconciliation, and so on.

E. Relationships de-escalate and can even end by descending through de-escalation stages. When an end to the relationship is desired by one or both partners, indirect or more direct and explicit strategies may be used. Causes for ending a relationship are varied and may be linked to "costs" outweighing "rewards." Most people attribute breakups to one of three reasons: personality or behavior faults in one partner, an unwillingness to compromise, or feeling constrained by relational commitments. One model for the ending process points to four phases that most often accompany breakups: the intrapsychic phase, the diadic phase, social phase, and the grave-dressing phase.

DETAILED CHAPTER OUTLINE

I. The process of relationships going through discernible stages as they move toward and away from greater intimacy is referred to as *relational development*.
   A. Understanding these stages is important to your studies because interpersonal communication is affected by the stage of the relationship.

B. We use interpersonal communication to move a relationship forward as we proceed from acquaintances, to friends, to lovers.

C. As a relationship moves from stage to stage, we use markers to indicate a change in the definition of the relationship.

   1. Often these markers signify turning points—specific events or interactions that are associated with positive or negative changes in a relationship.

   2. A pair of researchers found that 55 percent of the time these turning points inspired a discussion about the nature of a relationship.

D. We can think of the stages, from first meeting to intimacy, as the floors in a high-rise.

E. Relational escalation occurs in five stages.

   1. The first stage is the pre-interaction awareness stage.

     a. In this stage, you might observe someone or even talk with others about him or her without having any direct interaction.

     b. Gaining information about others without directly interacting with them is a passive strategy for acquiring knowledge.

   2. You might proceed to the initiation stage, one of the first turning points in a relationship.

     a. In this stage, interaction is typically routine.

     b. Once you make an initial contact though, you have created a relational history on which you will continue to build.

   3. The next stage is exploration.

     a. Here you will begin to share more in-depth information about yourselves.

     b. But you will have little physical contact, maintain your social distance, and limit the amount of time you spend together.

   4. If you proceed to the intensification stage, you will start to depend upon each other for self-confirmation and engage in more risky self-disclosure.

     a. You will spend more time together, increase the variety of activities you share, adopt a more personal physical distance, engage in more physical contact, and personalize your language.

     b. Also, you may discuss and redefine the relationship often in this stage.

   5. The top floor of the high-rise is the intimacy stage.

     a. In this stage the two partners turn to each other for confirmation and acceptance of their self-concept.

     b. Their communication is highly personalized and synchronized.

     c. They talk about anything and everything.

     d. There is a free flow of information and self-disclosure.

     e. There is a commitment to maintaining the relationship that might even be formalized.

     f. The partners share an understanding of one another's language and nonverbal cues, and have a great deal of physical contact.

     g. They use fewer words to communicate effectively, and they have a clearer definition of their roles and of the relationship.

F. Relational de-escalation is a process that is not a simple reversal of the formation stage.

   1. When an intimate relationship is not going well, it usually enters the turmoil or stagnation stage.

     a. Turmoil involves increase in conflict.

       1) There is an increase in one or both partners finding more faults in the other.

       2) The definition of the relationship seems to lose its clarity, and mutual acceptance declines.

       3) The communication climate is tense and exchanges become difficult.

     b. Stagnation occurs when the relationship loses its vitality and the partners become complacent.

       1) Communication and physical contact between the partners decrease.

       2) They spend less time together, but do not necessarily fight.

       3) Partners in a stagnating relationship tend to go through the motions of an intimate relationship without the commitment.

   2. Individuals might move down to the de-intensification stage, decreasing their interactions; increasing their physical, emotional, and psychological distance; and decreasing their dependence upon the other for self-confirmation.

   3. On the next floor down, the individualization stage, the partners tend to define their lives more as individuals and less as a couple.

   4. In the separation stage, individuals make an intentional decision to eliminate further interpersonal interaction.

   5. Although interaction may cease, you arrive at and remain in the post-interaction stage.

     a. This floor represents the lasting effects the relationship has on your self, and therefore on your other interactions and relationships.

    b. Duck (1982) claims that in this stage of terminating relationships we engage in "grave dressing": creating a public statement for people who ask why we broke up and also come to grips with losing the relationship.

II. There are several suggestions for getting started on initiating a relationship.

  A. Adopt an other-oriented perspective: Try to apply all the information you have and that you observe about the other person to make decisions about your own behavior.

  B. Observe and act upon approachability cues.

    1. Ways we can signal approachability include sustaining eye contact, turning toward another person, smiling, being animated, taking an open body posture, winking, and waving.

    2. Be aware that sometimes circumstances prevent us from exchanging approachability cues.

  C. Identify and use conversation starters.

    1. We all give off a certain amount of "free" information that others can easily observe.

    2. You can use that information as a starting point for a conversation.

      a. You will probably want to incorporate a greeting into your conversation starter.

      b. You might also want to include an open question.

  D. Follow initiation norms.

    1. Many of the early interactions in a relationship are almost ritualistic, or at least scripted.

    2. Following the script provides some comfort and security.

    3. As you follow the script, however, you should take advantage of opportunities to expand and develop the conversation in safe ways.

  E. Provide information about yourself.

    1. This allows the other person to make an informed decision about whether or not to continue the relationship.

    2. Both of you need to be in a position to make such a decision.

    3. However, you still need to be careful not to violate the script or cultural expectations about what is appropriate to disclose in an initial conversation.

  F. Present yourself in a positive way.

    1. We tend to find people attractive who have positive self-images.

    2. It is also against our cultural norms to disclose negative information early in a relationship.

    3. Yet do not act cocky or provide false information about yourself.

    4. Finally, keep in mind that we all have weaknesses and foibles, so the person interacting with you is probably also attempting to present a positive image.

  G. Ask questions.

    1. It will help you learn about the other person and it will let the person know that you are interested in her or him.

    2. Keep your questions open and noninvasive.

    3. Focus on things you know you have in common and that are safe.

  H. Don't put too much into the initial interaction.

    1. Initial interactions do not necessarily determine the future of the relationship.

    2. It will probably take a few interactions before you can make a sound cost-benefit analysis of the relationship.

III. To maintain a relationship, we must sustain the forces that hold a relationship together.

  A. The best tool we have for doing this is talk.

    1. Talk allows partners to verify that they share a common appreciation of the relationship.

    2. They generally do this through day-to-day small talk.

    3. Talk also lets us know if the relationship is in trouble.

  B. Every sustained relationship requires maintenance activity by both partners.

    1. The amount required depends upon the nature of the relationship.

    2. Usually, the more intimate the relationship, the more effort we are willing to put into maintaining it.

    3. We will continue to put forth effort as long as we reap appropriate benefits.

  C. Sometimes external factors prevent us from maintaining relationships effectively.

  D. One researcher found that people respond to the challenge of maintaining relationships in three ways.

    1. Some people are avoiders, who deal with fear that the relationship might change by systematically ignoring or avoiding opportunities to discuss or redefine it.

    2. Other people are more direct—they come out and say that they want things to stay the same.

    3. Some people use the third approach—to strive for balance in the relationship.

      a. They make an effort to understand their partner's moods and maintain a constant level of emotional support.

      b. They also do favors for the other person without trying to escalate the relationship.

c. This approach tends to be the most successful because the person derives rewards from his or her own behavior without depending heavily on what the partner does or does not do.

E. Other researchers note that people who are successful in maintaining relationships share certain behavioral patterns.

1. They set a positive tone by being cheerful and noncritical.

2. They provide assurances of their continued involvement and caring.

3. They share tasks to show their commitment.

4. They have supportive networks of family and friends who reinforce the value of the relationship.

F. In general, however, different stages of the relationship require different degrees of maintenance and different strategies.

G. We mix and match elements of the three strategies—avoidance, directness, and balance—to suit each situation.

H. Relational maintenance often requires conflict management skills.

I. The needs of a given relationship are a product of each partner's unique qualities.

J. The most successful friendships are maintained by choosing strategies that match specific characteristics of the relationship and partners.

IV. You can apply many of the interpersonal skills you have already learned, as well as others you will learn, as you escalate and maintain relationships.

A. Try to identify areas for your own skill improvement, but remember that you can also form satisfying relationships by seeking people with skill levels similar to your own.

B. It is important to remember that we all operate at less than the ideal level, and that many of us do it quite successfully.

C. The following skill suggestions present ideals for communication and relationships.

1. Monitor your perceptions, listen actively, and respond.

a. If you can consciously attend to more of the cues you receive from others, you can learn more about how they react to different situations and then shape your relationship maintenance behaviors accordingly.

b. By becoming more sensitive to your biases and working to counterbalance them, you can avoid overreacting to things your partner does.

c. If you make a practice of checking the accuracy of your perceptions of others,

you can avoid stewing and fretting over imagined slights and misunderstandings.

d. Listening skills are also crucial for developing and maintaining relationships.

e. Listening cues you into others' needs, wants, and values, and it enables you to respond to them in appropriate ways.

1) In the initial stages of a relationship, partners share a great deal of information.

2) The natural tapering off of the amount of information creates the illusion that you don't have to listen as much or as well as you did early on.

3) However, listening is a way to demonstrate ongoing interest in another person.

f. You also need to listen actively and provide confirming responses.

2. Be open and express emotions.

a. For a relationship to develop, both partners have to self-disclose.

1) Both must be sensitive to the timing and appropriateness of the disclosure.

2) Failing to disclose or disclosing something at the wrong time can damage a relationship.

b. In committed relationships, partners generally want to know how the other person is feeling, especially, if those feelings are negative.

1) However, many of us have difficulty expressing emotions.

2) Some people equate expressing emotions with being weak or being made vulnerable.

3) Even if we are willing to share positive feelings with others, we might feel it is risky to share negative ones.

4) Too much negative disclosure can reduce satisfaction in a relationship.

3. Empathize and adapt.

a. Decentering and empathizing allow you to select the most effective strategies to help you accomplish your communication goals—to adapt.

1) To adapt means to adjust your behaviors in accord with the relationship or situation.

2) When you modify your behavior in anticipation of an event, you adapt predictively.

3) When you modify your behavior after an event, you adapt reactively.

b. Adaptation behaviors are extremely beneficial to the development of a strong relationship and they require a lot of effort.

    1) It is challenging to consciously consider each message we send.

    2) Normally, we use scripts and rituals to communicate mindlessly.

    3) We have a natural tendency to be egocentric, to focus on ourselves instead of others.

  c. You need to adapt if a person is from another culture, when your partner cannot understand your messages, and when you are trying to gain something from another person.

4. Develop and apply communication sensitivity.

  a. Communication sensitivity requires an awareness and appreciation of all the dynamics of an interpersonal interaction.

  b. A willingness and ability to adapt, combined with sensitivity and perceptiveness about yourself, the situation, and the other, is called *rhetorical sensitivity*.

  c. A rhetorically sensitive person:

    1) Draws from a repertoire of roles or selves in response to different situations without losing sight of his or her "core."

    2) Avoids stylized behavior.

    3) Has an ability to handle the strain involved in adapting.

    4) Has an interaction consciousness about when to say things, when not to say things, and when to use placating comments.

    5) Appreciates the multiple ways ideas and feelings can be communicated.

  d. In contrast to rhetorically sensitive individuals are the noble self and the rhetorical reflector.

    1) Noble selves are inflexible and refuse to adapt—they believe that any departure from their true self or personal norms would be hypocritical.

    2) Rhetorical reflectors mold themselves to whatever the situation dictates or the other person wants—they do not have a strong "core" self.

  e. Rhetorically sensitive people are usually conversationally sensitive—they are able to pick up meanings in what people say, remember what has been said, and compose multiple ways of saying the same thing.

  f. Nonverbal sensitivity is the ability to pick up and accurately interpret the variety of nonverbal cues that we display in interactions.

5. Be tolerant and show restraint.

  a. The most satisfying relationships are those in which both partners refrain from continually disagreeing, criticizing, and making negative comments to the other.

  b. Both individuals learn to accept the other and do not feel compelled to continually point out flaws or failures.

  c. Maintaining a relationship requires tolerance.

  d. You must also be selective about disclosing your negative feelings about your partner.

6. Manage conflict cooperatively.

  a. Conflicts are inevitable in interpersonal relationships.

  b. As relationships develop, the individuals share more personal information and spend more time together, so the likelihood for conflict increases.

  c. The key to successful relational development and maintenance is not to avoid conflict, but to manage it.

  d. Using a cooperative management style can actually transform conflict into an experience that strengthens a relationship.

7. Gain compliance.

  a. To gain compliance is to use persuasive strategies to accomplish your personal goal.

  b. You need compliance-gaining strategies if you encounter resistance to fulfilling your goal.

  c. The strategy you choose will depend upon your skill level, the nature of the relationship, the amount of interaction time that is available, the likelihood of future interaction, opportunities for interaction, and concern for the relationship.

  d. Many of the communication skills that we have already discussed will play a role in your compliance-gaining attempts.

  e. Seeking to gain compliance from another person raises a number of ethical concerns.

V. How may we identify and act upon trouble signs in relationships?

  A. Because each stage in a relationship has unique communication qualities, specific verbal and nonverbal cues can tip us off when a relationship begins to de-escalate.

  B. When you pick up signals of relational problems, you have choices: just wait and see what happens; make a decision to end the relationship; or try to repair the relationship.

1. Repairing the relationship involves applying all the maintenance skills we previously discussed.
   a. The nature of the problem, the stage of the relationship, and the commitment and motivation of the partners all affect the success of repair efforts.
   b. Professional counseling might be an important option.
2. If you do choose to end the relationship, consider your goals.
   a. For example, do you want to continue the relationship at a less intimate level or terminate it altogether?
   b. Do you care enough about the other person to want to preserve his or her self-esteem?
   c. You can practice the effective relational management skills such as decentering and empathy, adaptation, and compliance-gaining.
3. The final issue to consider is how to deal with someone who wants to end his or her relationship with you.
   a. If possible, try to have a focused discussion on what has contributed to his or her decision.
   b. You might get information you need to repair the relationship or that will help you in future relationships.

VI. Relational de-escalation involves a reduction in the level of intimacy commitment, self-disclosing, and general resources necessary to hold a relationship together.
A. A relationship can descend through several stages before it reaches termination, or the end of interpersonal communication.
B. The more intimate a relationship becomes, the greater the impact.
C. The de-escalation and termination of a relationship is not inherently bad.
   1. Not all relationships are meant to endure.
   2. Ending a relationship can be a healthy move if the relationship is harmful, or if it no longer provides confirmation of the self or satisfies interpersonal needs.
   3. It also can open the door to new relationships.
   4. We also may choose to de-escalate to a less intimate stage where there is a better balance of benefits and costs.
D. Breaking up an intimate relationship is hard because of the degree to which we become dependent upon the other person to confirm our sense of self.

E. The process of ending a relationship is considerably different when only one party wants out of the relationship (unilateral) than when both parties are agreeable to it (bilateral).
   1. In unilateral dissolutions, the person who wants to end the relationship must use compliance-gaining strategies to get his or her partner to agree to the dissolution, or he or she must simply walk out of the relationship.
   2. In bilateral dissolutions, the parties simply need to sort out the details such as timing, dividing possessions, and defining conditions for the contact after the breakup.
F. A declining relationship usually follows one of several paths.
   1. Sometimes a relationship fades away—the two partners just drift farther and farther apart.
   2. Some relationships end in sudden death, frequently due to a single precipitating event.
   3. In between fading away and sudden death lies incrementalism—the process by which conflicts and problems continue to accumulate in the relationship until they reach a critical mass that leads to the breakup, or until the relationship becomes intolerable or too costly.
G. Partners use both indirect and direct strategies when they wish to end a relationship.
   1. Indirect strategies represent attempts to break up a relationship without explicitly stating the desire to do so.
      a. Withdrawal involves reducing the amount of contact and interaction without any explanation.
      b. In pseudo-de-escalation one partner claims that he or she wants to redefine the relationship at a lower level of intimacy, but in reality, he or she wants to end the relationship.
      c. Cost escalation is an attempt to increase the costs associated with the relationship in order to encourage the other person to terminate it.
   2. Direct strategies involve explicit statements.
      a. Negative identity management is a direct statement of the desire to terminate the relationship that does not take into account the other's feelings and may include criticisms.
      b. Justification is a clear statement of the desire to end the relationship accompanied by an honest explanation of the reasons.
         1) It may still hurt the other's feelings.

2) But a person who uses justification does not fault the other and attempts to protect both parties' sense of self.

3) One researcher found that most people on the receiving end like this strategy the best.

c. De-escalation is an honest statement of a desire to redefine the relationship at a lower level of intimacy or to move toward ending the relationship.

d. In using the direct strategy of positive tone, the initiator tries to affirm the other's personal qualities and worth at the same time that he or she calls a halt to the relationship.

H. The reasons for ending an interpersonal relationship are as varied as relationships themselves.

1. In general, we end relationships when they cost us more than they reward us.

a. Relationships are somewhat like savings accounts.

b. If the relationship is profitable, you deposit your excess rewards into an emotional savings account, from which you draw if there are times when relational costs are exceeding rewards.

c. Your savings account may run out, at which time you would have the choice of closing the account or keeping it open if you can foresee more benefits in the future.

2. One researcher found that most people attribute breakups to one of three main causes.

a. "Faults" are problems with personality traits or behaviors that one partner dislikes in the other and are the most commonly named cause.

b. "Unwillingness to compromise" represents a variety of failings on the part of one or both partners, including failure to put enough effort into the relationship, a decrease in effort, or failure to make concessions for the good of the relationship.

c. "Feeling constrained" reflects one partner's desire to be free from the commitments and constraints of a relationship.

I. Duck (1982) developed a model to show stages in ending a relationship.

1. In the first phase, the intrapsychic phase, one partner reaches a threshold of dissatisfaction and focuses on evaluating the other's behaviors, often fixing on the reasons to justify withdrawing.

2. In the dyadic phase, we move from internal contemplations about the relationship to confronting our partner.

3. If you and your partner agree to end the relationship, you enter the social phase and begin making the information public.

4. In the grave-dressing phase, one or both partners may attempt to place flowers on the grave of their relationship to cover up the hurt and pain associated with its death.

a. They tell a public, often self-enhancing, story about what happened.

b. Most importantly, they go through an internal stage of coming to acceptance of the end of the relationship.

ACTIVITY 10.1

RELATIONSHIP MAINTENANCE

Think about three specific relationships you have that are fairly stable, vary in their level of intimacy, and with which you feel satisfied. What behaviors do you engage in to keep the level of intimacy stabilized? How do you think the other person responds to your efforts to maintain the current level of intimacy? Have you or the other person ever tried to increase or decrease the level of intimacy? How did the other person respond?

ACTIVITY 10.2

SHARING EMOTIONS

How comfortable are you expressing your emotions to others?

Think of specific people for each of the following categories: an acquaintance of the same sex, an acquaintance of the opposite sex, a friend of the same sex, a friend of the opposite sex, a close friend of the same sex, a close friend of the opposite sex, a parent or relative of the same sex, and a parent or relative of the opposite sex.

Using a scale from 1 (most comfortable) to 10 (least comfortable), for each person, indicate how comfortable you would be about sharing the following feelings:

_____ liking for the other person
_____ love for the other person
_____ anger with the other person
_____ disappointment with the other person
_____ liking for a third person
_____ love for a third person
_____ anger toward a third person
_____ disappointment with a third person
_____ anger toward yourself
_____ disappointment in yourself
_____ embarrassment
_____ your fears
_____ happiness
_____ enthusiasm
_____ pride
_____ uncertainty

Compare your scores for each person. With whom are you most comfortable sharing your emotions? Compare the emotions you are most open about with the emotions you are most closed about. What makes you uncomfortable about sharing certain emotions?

ACTIVITY 10.3

WAYS TO LEAVE YOUR LOVER

Objective

To give students the opportunity to identify relationship dissolution strategies.

Directions

Explain that students will work in small groups to correctly label specific relationship dissolution strategies. Divide the class into small groups and provide each group with one copy of the following strategies. Have the groups report their findings to the class.

Note that some of the strategies seem to be combinations of our categories. In some cases, understanding the relationship dimension of the message would be critical for determining its classification. Also ask students to consider whether a direct strategy could be a nonverbal one, if it provided a clear emblem.

Strategies

1. Tell your (heterosexual) partner that you think you are homosexual.

2. Tell the other that you are going into the army; then avoid going to the places to which he or she goes.

3. While your husband is away at a convention, move to a new residence, leaving no forwarding address.

4. Call your boyfriend and ask him to meet you at a restaurant or club; then show up with a date and pretend to not know your boyfriend.

5. Go to your girlfriend's house and request that she return all of the things you have ever given to her. When she gives them to you, throw them into the street and repeatedly run over them with your car.

6. Tell your significant other that you are not good enough for him. Stress that you love him so much, you want him to find someone better than you.

7. Stop taking the other's calls. If you accidentally answer the telephone when he or she calls, act like there is trouble on the line and hang up the phone.

8. Purposefully invite your girlfriend out for a big evening and do not show up for the date.

9. Tell your wife that you think you should get divorced, while you're still friends, emphasizing what a good friend she is.

10. Throw your engagement ring at your fiancee's car, as he is pulling away from the curb, in front of your home.

CHAPTER 11 Relating to Family, Friends, and Colleagues

INSTRUCTIONAL OBJECTIVES

After studying this chapter, students should be able to:

1. Define the term *family* and describe four types of families.
2. Describe the cohesion and adaptability model of family functioning.
3. Identify and describe the communication characteristics of a healthy family.
4. Identify characteristics of childhood, adolescent, and adult friendships as well as friendships of the elderly.
5. List and describe strategies for making and losing friends.
6. Describe principles of upward, downward, horizontal, and outward communication.
7. Identify the characteristics of an effective leader and follower in an organization.
8. Describe the role and effects of technology upon interpersonal relationships in the workplace.

LEARNING TOOLS

TOOLS	TEXT PAGES
Building your skills activities	396
Chapter glossary	410
Considering others	373
Discussion and review questions	406
Electronic connections	404
Journal entry guidelines	407
Key term recaps	374, 379, 384, 387
Learning with others activities	408
Understanding diversity	398

CHAPTER OVERVIEW

CHAPTER ELEVEN: RELATING TO FAMILY, FRIENDS, AND COLLEAGUES

A. Much of our time is occupied with interpersonal relationships with family, lover and friend, and colleagues. For each of these specific types of relationships, many of the principles discussed earlier in the text apply.

B. Defining a family today can be challenging. One approach is to consider the various types of family: traditional, blended, single-parent, or extended. Family interaction can be characterized according to three concepts: adaptability, cohesion, and communication. Skillful family communication might involve making time to talk, active listening, supportiveness, and conflict management skills.

C. Friendships develop into mutually dependent relationships. Reasons for friendships might include needs for affection, inclusion, and control, help with coping and avoiding isolation, helping improve self-esteem, and managing the mundane. Our need for intimacy changes from childhood to adolescent to adulthood to elderly, and so does the nature of our friendships. Making friends involves communicating to others that you want a friendship, and understanding how friendships develop and grow. Losing friends is unfortunate. One researcher isolated ten common reasons for the loss of a friendship. Regardless of the reason, the more emotionally involved the relationship is, the more likely an ending would be abrupt rather than gradual.

D. Effective communication at work is necessary to navigate the all-too-common "people problems." Business communication competence begins with an understanding of how to relate appropriately to your boss, subordinates, peers, and customers. Leadership at work is any behavior that influences, guides, controls, or inspires others. Followership skills include active listening, providing feedback and suggestions, offering supportive evidence for your positions, and not sacrificing your ethics. Changes in technology requires learning new skills and etiquette.

DETAILED CHAPTER OUTLINE

I. Considerable controversy exists as to what constitutes a family unit.
   A. Traditional definitions of a family focus on the roles of husbands, wives, and children who all live together under one roof.
   B. For our purposes in this chapter, we define the family as a unit made up of any number of

persons who live in relationship with one another over time in a common living space, who are usually, but not always, united by marriage and kinship.

C. Within this definition, there are many family types.

1. The traditional family—a mother and father and their biological children—is often considered to be the natural family, or the nuclear family.

2. Increasingly common today is the blended family—two adults and their (not necessarily biological) children.

3. The single-parent family is self-explanatory and represents the fastest growing type of family unit in the United States today.

4. The extended family typically refers to the relatives—aunts, uncles, cousins, or grandparents—who are part of the family unit.

5. No matter what type your family is, it is your family of origin—the family in which you learned the rules and skills of interpersonal communication and developed your basic assumptions about relationships.

II. Is there a model for family interaction?

A. Recently, a pair of family therapists observed that unhappy people came from families where there were a lot of other unhappy people.

B. A few years later, another pair of researchers developed a model called the circumplex model of family interaction, based on three basic dimensions.

1. Adaptability, ranging from chaotic to rigid, refers to the family's ability to modify and respond to changes in its own power structure and roles.

2. Cohesion refers to the emotional bonding and feelings of togetherness that families experience and ranges from enmeshed to disengaged.

3. The third key element in the model is communication.

a. It is not labeled as a separate component in the model because it affects everything in the model.

b. Communication determines whether families are cohesive or adaptive.

C. However, research suggests that there is no single best way to be a family.

1. At some stages of family life, the balanced ideal of the circumplex model may not apply.

2. Only one thing is constant as we go through family life: Effective communication skills play an important role in helping families change their levels of cohesiveness or adaptability.

III. Several communication-related behaviors are very useful as skills.

A. Take time to talk about relationships and feelings.

1. Healthy families talk.

2. Healthy families have topics of conversation about things other than functional tasks.

3. Their communication reflects other-oriented messages about family members and family relationships.

B. Listen actively and clarify the meaning of messages.

1. Good listening requires an other-orientation.

2. Try to understand the feelings behind another person's words—according to that person's code system, not your own.

3. Another research team identifies a listening technique called documentation, in which you describe the experiences that led you to attach a certain meaning to another person's statement.

C. Support and encourage one another.

1. A smoothly functioning family can be a supportive, encouraging sanctuary from everyday stresses.

2. Through communication, we can let others know that we support and value them.

3. Satir (1988) suggests that many, if not most, sources of dysfunction in families are related to feelings of low self-worth.

4. Healthy families take time to nurture one another, express positive feelings, and take a genuine interest in each person's unique contributions to the family.

5. Parents have a special obligation to disclose responsibly to their children.

a. Too much negative and controlling feedback can cause permanent damage.

b. Parents frequently deliver control messages that involve coercion or threat to get children to do what they want.

c. Control messages are effective up to a point, after which they often cause rebellion.

d. Children need a balance of control and support as they seek their independence from their parents.

D. Use productive strategies for managing conflict, stress, and change.

1. All too often parents resort to violence when their children balk at their orders.

2. Learning to manage conflict with siblings is also a challenge to many families.

3. Sibling conflicts, as well as other family conflicts, often have a special intensity.

a. Maybe this is because we drop our guard in the privacy and security of a family.

b. Another reason this happens is that we often communicate. with family members when we are tired and stressed.

4. In studying couples, one team of researchers found that couples who lack constructive argumentation skills are those who resort to verbal aggression and even physical violence.

5. Another researcher who studied couples relationships for over twenty years suggests that we be on the alert for four key warning signs in our communication behavior.
   a. Criticism.
   b. Contempt.
   c. Defensiveness.
   d. Stonewalling.

6. The same researcher offers the following suggestions for managing couples conflicts. (Many of them apply to parent-child and sibling conflicts as well.)
   a. Pick your battles carefully.
   b. Schedule discussions.
   c. Structure your conflicts: build the agenda, persuade and argue, resolve.
   d. Acknowledge your partner's viewpoint before expressing your own.
   e. Moderate your emotions.
   f. Trust your partner and communicate nondefensively.
   g. Soothe your partner; learn how to comfort and provide positive reinforcement.
   h. Take stock in your partnership.
   i. Find the glory in your story as a couple and enhance romance.
   j. Know when to get help or when to give up.

7. Couples who have a more volatile relationship, in which emotions override rational approaches, can try the following:
   a. Tell your partner what you can or won't do: set limits and develop rules.
   b. Offer sincere and positive appreciation.
   c. Express interest in your partner; avoid phony flattery.
   d. Choose to be polite, regardless of your partner's actions.
   e. Be direct and honest.
   f. Be careful about teasing.

8. Couples who have developed a pattern of avoiding conflict can try these suggestions:
   a. Get in touch with your feelings.
   b. Reaffirm your basic beliefs about your relationship.
   c. Learn to level with your partner when necessary.

d. Create strategies that function like "suggestion boxes" to express ideas and suggestions.
   e. Turn to other friends and professionals for support.

9. Developing strategies to negotiate conflict over family roles is especially important, since evidence suggests that the match between roles and expectations largely determines family satisfaction.
   a. Take responsibility.
   b. Describe the expected behaviors.
   c. Engage in mutual renegotiation.
   d. Establish a time frame for renegotiation.

10. No list of do's and don'ts will miraculously manage all differences—these suggestions provide a starting point.

IV. What is friendship?
   A. A friend is someone we like and who likes us.
   B. We expect self-sacrifice from our friends.
   C. A friend is someone whom we choose to be with.
   D. Friendship is a relationship that exists over time between people who share a common history.
   E. Friendship develops naturally into an interdependent relationship that is different from other interpersonal relationships.
   F. There are many reasons for friendship.
      1. We develop friendships because we need to.
         a. The need for inclusion suggests that each of us has a need to be included in the activities of others.
         b. The need for control suggests that we also need some degree of dominion over the relationships we establish with others.
         c. The need for affection suggests we need to give and receive love, support, warmth, and intimacy, although the amounts vary enormously from person to person.
      2. Social isolation can negatively affect our physical and mental health.
      3. Friends help us cope with stress, take care of physical needs, and even help in the development of our personality.
      4. Friends also shape our attitudes and beliefs.
      5. Friends help us cope with uncertainty and have a profound influence on our behavior.
      6. Friends also bolster our self-esteem.
      7. Friends provide material help when we need it.
      8. One of the most important functions that friends perform, however, is to help us manage the mundane.

V. We also have different needs for intimacy at various stages of our lives.
   A. At about the age of two we form our first friendships.

B. These friendships are usually self-centered and can be categorized into five, sometimes overlapping stages.
1. From ages three to seven, we have momentary playmates—we interact with those in our presence.
2. From ages four to nine, we have one-way-assistance—we still view friendships from a "take" perspective.
3. From ages six to twelve we experience the fair-weather friend stage.
4. From ages nine to fifteen we have mutual intimacy—relationships become more possessive.
5. The last stage (twelve through adulthood) allows more independence in friendships, as well as deepening interdependence.

C. During adolescence, we move away from relationships with parents and other adults and toward greater intimacy with our peers.
1. We develop cliques of friends and form friendship networks.
2. Friendship relationships usually peak in late adolescence and early adulthood, before we select a mate.

D. Adult friendships are our most valued relationships, yet they often dissolve during adulthood due to:
1. Physical separation.
2. New work or social groupings.
3. Discovering dislike for something a friend does.
4. Changes due to beginning the process of selecting a mate.

E. Although the elderly make new friends, they value the old ones most.

F. Despite the differences, there are also common behaviors across age groups.
1. One research team found that self-disclosure did not seem to change in either depth or amount from young adulthood through age ninety-one.
2. They did report, however, that as friends get older, we are more willing to tell our friends less positive things about ourselves.

VI. Dale Carnegie (1937) once said, "You can make more friends in two months by becoming interested in other people than you can in two years by trying to get other people interested in you."
A. Recognize, select, and make the most of friendship opportunities.
1. A friendship opportunity is a situation in which you are likely to meet other people who may become your friends.
2. Knowing your own interests, likes, and dislikes is a first step in choosing places to look.

B. Encourage others to be your friend—explicitly or implicitly.
1. Some explicit approaches include:
a. Volunteer your name or information about yourself followed by a question about the other person.
b. Make a comment about the other person or ask him or her a question.
c. Talk about something you are both observing.
d. Ask open-ended questions.
e. Be other-oriented.
f. Remember what you talk about.
g. Take turns initiating and responding.
h. Don't talk only about yourself.
i. Don't say or do something that will cause the other person to value himself or herself less.
j. Reveal information about yourself so that the other person can get to know you.
2. You can also communicate your desire to make friends and to be a friend to someone through your nonverbal cues that communicate a friendly attitude.
a. Move closer and lean forward if you are seated (proximity).
b. Sit directly in front of or closely beside the person (orientation).
c. Look the person in the eyes, especially when he or she looks at you (gaze).
d. Smile (facial expression).
e. Nod your head; use lively movements (gestures).
f. Keep an open posture, with your arms outstretched toward the other person, rather than placing your arms on your hips or folding them (posture).
g. Touch the person in a friendly, nonsexual way (touch).
h. Use higher pitch, rising inflection, and clear pure tone in your voice (tone of voice).

C. Understand how friendships grow.
1. This course may be your first formal education in how relationships develop.
2. You also learn about relationships through your experience and the tips of others.
3. Knowing these textbook principles can help make you a wiser friend.
4. What do friends talk about?
5. One study suggests friends' conversations involve:
a. Social talk about events, jokes, and just enjoyment of one another's company.
b. Gossip about others.

c. Common interests.
d. Sharing information and solving problems.
e. Support and encouragement in times of stress.

6. If you are focusing on one of these areas to the exclusion of others, you may want to assess where you are in the friendship.

7. Much of our conversation either remains at a very basic level or proceeds to the second level of conventional conversation that involves the exchange of other non-threatening information.

8. At level three the conversation becomes more personal.

9. At the fourth level—the "gut level"—usually reserved for good friends, you share your emotions and feelings.

10. Only with your most intimate friends or lovers do you self-disclose your most personal thoughts—peak communication.

11. The goal of interpersonal conversation is not to raise every friendship to level five.

12. A meaningful relationship unfolds.

VII. It is equally useful to know how friendships are lost.

A. Argyle and Henderson (1985) identified communication patterns that discouraged close personal relationships.

B. Listed in order of offensiveness, they are:

1. Acting jealous or being critical of your relationship.

2. Discussing with others what your friend said in confidence.

3. Not volunteering help in time of need.

4. Not trusting or confiding in your friend.

5. Criticizing your friend in public.

6. Not showing positive regard for your friend.

7. Not standing up for your friend in his or her absence.

8. Not being tolerant of your friend's other friends.

9. Not showing emotional support.

10. Nagging your friend.

C. Relationships sometimes become less intense in predictable stages.

D. Love relationships usually end more abruptly and with more emotional intensity than friendships.

E. Physical separation and replacement of friends with new friends were the top cited reasons for ending same-sex friendships, in one study.

F. Third, people often just grow to dislike a characteristic of the friend's behavior or personality.

G. Last, interference from dating or a couples relationship contributes to the decay of friendship.

VIII. Researchers who study how communication flows in the workplace perceive four directions: upward, downward, horizontal, and outward.

A. Upward communication involves the flow of communication from subordinates to superiors.

1. Even the boss, president, or chief executive officer usually answers to a governing board or to stockholders.

2. Yet effective upward communication is far from the norm.

3. If there is little upward communication, the organization may be in a precarious situation.

a. Those lower down in the organization are often the ones who make contact with the customer, make the product, or work most closely with the development and delivery of the product or service.

b. Upward communication helps managers to deal quickly with problems and to hear suggestions for improving processes and procedures.

4. Developing a positive relationship with your boss may help you succeed.

5. If you are a manager yourself, encourage your subordinates to share both good news and bad news.

B. Downward communication is the flow of information from those higher up in an organization to those of lower rank.

1. It can happen via memo, newsletters, posters, video, or, of course, face-to-face.

2. Often the best method is oral, with a written follow-up.

3. In all of these situations, the best managers take care to develop and send ethical, other-oriented messages.

4. The worst managers indulge in an egocentric abuse of the legitimate power that accompanies their rank within an organization.

5. There are two types of harassment.

a. The first is *quid pro quo,* which translates from Latin as, "you do something for me and I'll do something for you."

b. The second involves creating a hostile environment, in which an employee feels his or her rights are being violated because of working conditions or offensive behavior on the part of other workers.

6. A supervisor who either creates, or fails to change, work situations that are threatening to a subordinate, is a party to sexual harassment.

C. Horizontal communication refers to communication among coworkers at the same level within an organization.

1. It may occur between workers in different departments or divisions who perform similar jobs at a similar level.

2. Most often we communicate with colleagues to coordinate job tasks, share plans and information, solve problems, make sure we understand job procedures, manage conflict, or to get a bit of emotional support on the job.

3. Grapevine messages tend to circulate within groups and departments rather than across departmental lines.

   a. Although grapevine errors can cause problems for an organization, most continue to encourage coworker communication because it enhances teamwork and allows the work group to develop a certain degree of independence.

   b. Some organizations even try to formalize it by forming *quality circles*, or groups of employees who meet together on a regular basis to talk about such issues as how to improve the quality of services or products, reduce mistakes, lower costs, improve safety, or develop better ways of working together.

D. Outward communication is communication to those outside the organization.

   1. In addition to selling to customers, today's organizations are also asking customers what they think about the quality of the goods and services the organization produces.

   2. They focus on the needs of these they serve through outward communication.

   3. They are training their staffs to develop more empathy, better listening skills, and more awareness of nonverbal messages from customers.

IX. Leadership is behavior that influences, guides, controls, or inspires others to take action.

A. There are several approaches to leadership.

   1. Studies show that some leaders are task-oriented.

   2. Other leaders are more relationship-oriented.

   3. Both task-oriented and relationship-oriented leaders may use different methods to influence others.

      a. Authoritarian leaders assume primary responsibility for decisions and orders and seek to control others.

      b. Democratic leaders consult with workers rather than issuing edicts and orders.

      c. Laissez-faire leaders provide little, if any, direction over workers.

      d. Situational leaders respond to the conditions under which they must work.

   4. No single style works well in every situation.

   5. In general, the more structured the task, the more useful is a task-oriented approach.

B. Though the first qualification for leadership is skill and knowledge about the task at hand, you need the skills necessary to motivate, inspire, and instruct others in their work.

   1. Covey, in *Seven Habits of Highly Effective People,* suggests the following.

      a. Be proactive.

      b. Begin with the end in mind.

      c. Put first things first.

      d. Think win/win.

      e. Seek first to understand, then to be understood.

      f. Synergize.

      g. Sharpen the saw. (Enhance your skills.)

   2. The most effective leaders combine a task orientation with a relationship orientation.

      a. The task functions they perform are:

         1) Initiating new ideas or approaches.

         2) Providing information.

         3) Seeking information.

         4) Seeking opinions.

         5) Offering opinions.

         6) Elaborating on and amplifying ideas of others.

         7) Evaluating the advantages and disadvantages of issues, ideas, or proposed solutions.

         8) Energizing and motivating the group.

      b. The relationship functions they perform are:

         1) Encouraging others and offering praise and acceptance.

         2) Harmonizing and mediating disagreements.

         3) Compromising and seeking ways of finding common ground among members.

         4) Being a gatekeeper by encouraging less talkative members to participate and limiting lengthy orations from big talkers.

C. If you find yourself playing the role of follower in a group, remind yourself that you can still make an enormous contribution.

   1. Seek opportunities to provide input and suggestions to leaders.

   2. Listen well.

   3. Provide appropriate feedback and ask for clarification when uncertain.

   4. Support your suggestions with evidence rather than with off-the-cuff opinions.

   5. Don't abandon your own ethical principles.

X. As new technologies develop, they will have a potent effect upon the interactions we have with others.

A. Technology has an immediate impact on the workplace.
   1. The pace at which we use technology to help us do our work will quicken.
   2. A recent poll found that two-thirds of those surveyed are using computers.
      a. Workers from the top level on down use computers.
      b. A modem lets you connect your computer to other computers via a telephone line.
      c. A scanner lets you insert photographs or text into a computer which you can then incorporate into documents and reports or send to others over the phone lines.
      d. A facsimile machine (fax) makes it possible to transmit written documents via telephone lines anywhere in the world.
      e. Interactive TV broadcasting systems now permit you to talk to others face-to-face over great distances.
      f. Using electronic messaging, or e-mail, you can type a message on your computer to be read by anyone who is connected to your network.
B. What are the effects of technology on workplace communication?
   1. The net result of these technological advances is that your workplace is no longer confined to your own office, store, or plant, nor to people who work for your organization.
   2. Your home computer can help you to plow through routine correspondence more efficiently and may occasionally even permit you to avoid commuting.
   3. Will these new technologies replace the need for face-to-face interpersonal relationships?
      a. Early evidence suggests that the answer is no.
      b. A growing collection of research studies show that we still use electronic media selectively for workplace communication.
         1) The more positive the message, the more immediate the media we use to communicate it.
         2) We prefer mediated communication when we need to communicate data and content-rich messages, and we like face-to-face meetings for relationship messages.
         3) Mediated messages work best in the workplace if the task is highly structured or involves sequential steps, while less-structured tasks seem to be managed better face-to-face.
         4) Groups who use video conferences and e-mail messages are more likely to have polarized opinions than those who meet face-to-face.
         5) Groups and individuals will be more productive if they have someone to help them when they experience either hardware or software problems.
         6) The use of sophisticated technology does not necessarily result in improved quality. It may let us make mistakes faster.
         7) In the future, people will still solve complex issues and problems face-to-face rather than through mediated messages.

ACTIVITY 11.1

WHO DOES WHAT?

Indicate which of the behaviors listed below are the *primary* responsibility of the wife (W), the husband (H), or both (H/W). Discuss your reasons for responding as you do.

_____ taking out the garbage
_____ writing thank-you notes
_____ initiating sexual activity
_____ balancing the checkbook
_____ changing diapers
_____ bringing home a paycheck
_____ disciplining the children
_____ starting up the barbecue
_____ doing the laundry
_____ planning for retirement
_____ cooking
_____ cleaning the bathrooms
_____ changing the oil in the car
_____ driving children to school
_____ mending clothes
_____ maintaining gutters
_____ buying Mother's Day and birthday presents for parents

ACTIVITY 11.2

WHAT DO YOU TALK ABOUT?

One evening, between the time you get home from work or school and bedtime, make a log categorizing what you and the members of your household talk about. You don't need to record the actual subject matter, just the types of messages you used. Consider the following categories:

1. Topic messages: information about basic events, ideas, or tasks that need to be performed.

2. Individual feeling messages: any messages in which you or your family members verbalize a specific feeling (such as, I'm pleased or I'm exhausted). Be sure to record what feelings were verbalized.

3. Partner messages: Statements that focus on the nature of the relationship, such as "we have a lot of fun together" or "we always seem to fight a lot."

Write an essay or journal entry, if you keep a journal for class, in which you discuss what you learned from your analysis.

ACTIVITY 11.3

FAMILY PHOTO ASSESSMENT

Objective

To integrate family communication concepts in a discussion of students' own family communication.

Directions

1. Ask students to bring several family photos to class, for a day designated for this activity. Assure students who may not be able to access family photos that they will be able to participate. Be prepared to bring some family photos of your own to: (a) compensate for missing pictures and (b) eliminate any perceived threat.

2. On the assigned day, explain that students will work in groups to discuss their families or others' families.

3. Remind them that they will need their other-orientation skills.

4. Divide the class into groups and distribute your own photos if necessary.

5. Explain that one researcher found links between families' self-assessments and observers' analyses of the families' photos. Lynn Blinn (Spring 1988, "The family photo assessment process (FPAP): A method for validating cross-cultural comparisons of family social identities," *Journal of Comparative Family Studies,* Vol. XIX, No. 1) found confirmation for the ideas that:

   a. The greater the commitment to a role, the more pictures there will be that represent and reinforce that image (such as, mother, husband).

   b. The more individuals in a social setting have clearly defined and understood role expectations, the more homogenous the types of pictures in a family collection.

   c. Families may be motivated in the picture-taking process by the placement, at the moment, of a particular role (for example, who to include in the picture, how many of us to include in the picture).

6. Allow groups time to analyze photos for clues to family roles.

7. Lead an analysis discussion.

Discussion Suggestions

1. We must consider that families' assessments of themselves and families' photos may be presentations of their ideal identities. Yet, even understanding how they ideally define themselves can be useful.

2. What surprised you about people's analyses of the photos? Did others note aspects of your family that you had never considered?

3. On which types of clues did we make the most accurate predictions? Why?

4. Did discussion move to explanation of people or things that were not actually in the photos? Why?

Famous Sayings of Love and Friendship*

1. Love: a temporary insanity curable by marriage or by removal of the patient from the influences under which he incurred the disorder. (Ambrose Bierce, *The Devil's Dictionary*)

2. Heav'n has no rage like love to hatred turn'd Nor Hell a fury like a woman scorn'd. (William Congreve, *The Mourning Bride*)

3. Friendship is Love without his wings. (George Gordon Byron, 6th Lord Byron, *Hours of Idleness*)

4. A faithful friend is the medicine of life. (*Ecclesiasticus 6*)

5. Forsake not an old friend; for the new is not comparable to him; a new friend is as new wine; when it is old, though shalt drink it with pleasure. (*Ecclesiasticus 9*)

6. Friendship is a disinterested commerce between equals; love, an abject intercourse between tyrants and slaves. (Oliver Goldsmith, *The Good-Natured Man*)

7. Love, free as air, at sight of human ties, Spreads his light wings, and in a moment flies. (Alexander Pope, *Eloisa to Abelard*)

8. Love, an' please your Honour, is exactly like war, in this; that a soldier, though he has escaped three week complete o' Saturday night,—may, nevertheless, be shot through his heart on Sunday morning. (Laurence Sterne, *Tristram Shandy*)

9. But of all plagues, good Heaven, thy wrath can send, Save, save, oh save me from the candid friend! (George Canning, *New Morality*)

10. A friend is, as it were, a second self. (Marcus Tullius Cicero, *De Amicitia*)

---

*As cited in 1994, *Dictionary of Quotations*, London: Bloomsbury Books

ACTIVITY 11.4

MY BEST FRIEND

Who's your "best" friend? Write his or her name below and then use the questions to help you analyze your relationship.

My best friend is _____

How we met: _____

_____

_____

_____

_____

Why we became friends: _____

_____

_____

_____

_____

How my friend meets my needs: _____

_____

_____

_____

_____

How I meet my friend's needs: _____

_____

_____

_____

ACTIVITY 11.5

FRIENDS ACROSS YOUR LIFE-CYCLE

Make lists of the friends you had in childhood and during adolescence, and of those you have now in the columns below. Are any friends in all three columns? If so, why? If not, what changed?

My Childhood Friends	My Adolescent Friends	My Friends Today
_____	_____	_____
_____	_____	_____
_____	_____	_____
_____	_____	_____
_____	_____	_____

ACTIVITY 11.6

WHO ARE YOUR FRIENDS?

Who are the friends you would turn to for support or to celebrate a major event? Answer the questions to do a "friendship inventory."

1. You have an extra ticket to a concert or major sports event. List the three people you would call, in order of preference.

   1. _____
   2. _____
   3. _____

2. You have just learned of the unexpected death of a family member. Who would you call first? Second? Third?

   1. _____
   2. _____
   3. _____

3. You are going on a cruise and have learned that you can bring a friend along for free. List in order of preference the first three people you would invite to be your guest.

   1. _____
   2. _____
   3. _____

4. As you are driving through a small town, you get a traffic ticket and you don't have your car registration or driver's license with you. You are taken to jail. List in order the first three people you would call.

   1. _____
   2. _____
   3. _____

ACTIVITY 11.7

PRACTICING PERFORMANCE INTERVIEW SKILLS

Role-play a performance interview with one of your classmates. One of you should play the role of the employer or supervisor, the other the role of the employee. Select an employment situation that is meaningful to both of you. For example, if both you and your partner have worked at a fast-food restaurant or retail store,

held an office job, or worked on a farm or ranch, develop a similar work situation with which both of you can identify. Use the following checklist to evaluate the role-play. Check all of the behaviors that are illustrated in the role-play. If time permits, switch roles so that each of you plays the roles of both supervisor and employee.

Did the supervisor:

Offer specific rather than general feedback? _____

Present areas for improvement in a clear, straightforward way? _____

Offer feedback at the right times? _____

Focus on behavior rather than the employee's self-worth? _____

Give the employee time to respond? _____

Keep nonverbal behavior consistent with verbal behavior? _____

Focus on important rather than trivial information? _____

Use appropriate verbal and nonverbal emphasis for each issue? _____

Avoid threats and coercion? _____

Did the employee:

Ask what the supervisor perceived as his/her strengths and accomplishments? _____

Ask how his/her work could be improved? _____

Ask whether his/her work goals are perceived to be consistent with those of the organization? _____

Ask if he/she needs new skills to enhance job performance? _____

Use consistent verbal and nonverbal behavior during the interview? _____

Respond calmly if negative feedback about job performance was offered? _____

ACTIVITY 11.8

STUDENT-FACULTY COMMUNICATION

Working in a group with other classmates, facilitate a discussion on the following topic: How can we improve communication between students and faculty at our college or university? Have different members of the group take turns leading the discussion, deliberately using different leadership styles. One person could use an authoritarian style; another could use a democratic style or a laissez-faire style. Appoint someone in your group to make notes about the group interaction, recording both leader behaviors and group members' responses to their leader. After several members have led the group, discuss which style worked best and why.

PART II
● Annotated Text

Interpersonal Communication Foundations

The first four chapters present fundamental concepts that frame our study of interpersonal communication. In Chapter 1 you will learn answers to these questions: What is interpersonal communication? What is the connection between interpersonal communication and interpersonal relationships? Why is it important to study relationships? What can I do to improve my relationships with others? Chapter 2 offers concepts and skills to help you understand more about who you are and how your self-concept and sense of self-worth influence your relationships. In Chapter 3 you will learn that perception plays a key role in effective interpersonal communication. By recognizing the factors that influence your perceptions and actively analyzing the meaning of perceptual information, you can become more adept at sharing your sense of the world with others. Chapter 4 explores principles to help you better understand people who are different from you and explain how developing an other-oriented perspective helps bridge cultural differences.

1

Introduction to Interpersonal Communication

After studying this chapter, you should be able to:

1. Compare and contrast definitions of communication, human communication, and interpersonal communication.

2. Explain why it is useful to study interpersonal communication.

3. Compare and contrast communication as action, interaction, and transaction.

4. Describe the key components of the communication process.

5. Discuss five principles of interpersonal relationships.

6. Identify strategies that can improve your communication effectiveness.

nterpersonal communication is like breathing; it is a requirement for life. And, like breathing, it is inescapable. Unless you live in isolation, you communicate interpersonally every day. Listening to your roommate, talking to a teacher, meeting for lunch with a friend, or talking to your parents or your spouse are all examples of interpersonal communication.

It is impossible not to communicate with others. Even before we are born, we respond to movement and sound. With our first cry we announce to others that we are here. Once we make contact with others, we communicate, and we continue to do so until our last breath. Even though many of our messages are not verbalized, we nonetheless intentionally, and sometimes unintentionally, send messages to others. Without interpersonal communication, a special form of human communication that occurs as we manage our relationships, people suffer and even die. Recluses, hermits, and people isolated in solitary confinement dream and hallucinate about talking with others face-to-face.

Human communication is at the core of our existence. Think of the number of times you communicated with someone today, as you worked, ate, studied, shopped, or went about your other daily activities. Most people spend between 80 and 90 percent of their waking hours communicating with others.[1] It is through these interactions with others that we develop interpersonal relationships.

Because these relationships are so important to our lives, later chapters will focus on the communication skills and principles that explain and predict how we develop, sustain, and sometimes end them. We'll explore such questions as: Why do we like some people and not others? How can we interpret other people's unspoken messages with greater accuracy? Why do some relationships blossom and others deteriorate? How can we better manage disagreements with others? How can we better understand our relationships with our family, friends, and coworkers?

This chapter charts the course ahead, addressing key questions about what interpersonal communication is and why it is important. We will begin by seeing how our understanding of the interpersonal communication process has evolved. And we will conclude by examining how we initiate and sustain relationships through interpersonal communication.

TEACHING STRATEGY
If you were to view your semester-long interpersonal course as one long public presentation, this chapter would represent opportunity to attract your audience's attention and to persuade them that the coming information will be of value to them. Asking students to take a few minutes to think of at least one relationship they would like to improve may be helpful in focusing their attention.

Defining Interpersonal Communication

In order to understand interpersonal communication, we must begin by understanding how it relates to two broader categories: communication in general and human communication. Scholars have attempted to arrive at a general definition of communication for decades, yet experts cannot agree upon a single one. One research team counted more than 126 published definitions;[2] however, in the broadest sense, **communication** is the process of acting upon information.[3] Someone does or says something, and others think or do something in response to the action or the words as they understand them.

Communication is not unique to humans. It is possible, for example, for you to act on information from your dog. He barks; you feed him. This definition also suggests that your dog can act on information from you. You head for the cupboard to feed him; he wags his tail and jumps up in the air, anticipating his dinner. Researchers do study communication between species as well as communication systems within single animal species, but these fields of study are beyond the scope of this book. The focus of our study is upon a form of human communication: people communicating with other people.

To refine this definition, we can say that **human communication** is the process of making sense out of the world and sharing that sense with others.[4] We learn about the world by listening, observing, tasting, touching, and smelling; then we share our conclusions with others. Human communication encompasses many media: speeches, songs, radio and television broadcasts, e-mail, letters, books, articles, poems, advertisements.

In face-to-face encounters, we simultaneously exchange both verbal and nonverbal messages that result in shared meanings. Through this kind of inter-relation, we build relationships with others. (Bob Daemmrich/Stock Boston)

Interpersonal communication is a special form of human communication that occurs when we interact simultaneously with another person and mutually influence each other, usually for the purpose of managing relationships. Four essential elements of this definition determine the unique nature of interpersonal communication apart from other forms of human communication.

1. Interpersonal communication is a special form of human communication. For several years many scholars defined interpersonal communication simply as communication that occurs when two people interact face-to-face. This limited definition suggests that if two people are interacting, then they are interpersonally communicating. Today, interpersonal communication is defined not just by the number of people who communicate, but also by the quality of the communication. Interpersonal communication occurs not just when we interact with someone, but when we treat the other as a unique human being.

Think of all human communication as ranging on a continuum from impersonal to interpersonal communication. **Impersonal communication** occurs when we treat people as objects, or when we respond to their roles rather than who they are as unique people. Interpersonal communication describes a more intimate level of communication in which we disclose personal information that cannot be known by another unless we tell him or her. When you buy a pair of socks at a clothing store, you have a two-person, face-to-face, relatively brief interaction with someone. You communicate. Yet that interchange could hardly be described as intimate or personal. When you ask a waiter in a restaurant for a glass of water, you are interacting with the role, not with the individual. You know nothing personal about him, and he knows nothing personal about you (unless he eavesdrops by your table). Interpersonal communication occurs when we interact with another person as a unique, authentic individual rather than as an object or someone performing a role. The exchanges with the sock-seller or waiter have the potential to become true interpersonal communication exchanges if you begin to interact with them as unique individuals. If, for example, during your conversation with the waiter you discover you were born in the same town and develop other personal links, the impersonal, role-oriented communication becomes more personal, and the quality of the communication moves toward the intimate end of the continuum.

Although interpersonal communication is more intimate and includes revealing more of yourself than impersonal communication, not all interpersonal communication involves sharing closely guarded personal information. As we will discuss later in the book, there are degrees of intimacy when interacting with others.

2. Interpersonal communication involves simultaneous interaction between individuals. When you communicate with someone interpersonally, both participants are acting on information that has originated with the other person *at the same time*. This simultaneous interaction may or may not involve words. The interaction may be fleeting or enduring. While you are talking and your mother is listening, you are also observing your mother's nonverbal expression. Just because she is not speaking does not mean she is not communicating. A

INTERNET RESOURCES
Hot Link: Go to http://www.courses.bus.ualberta.ca/consumerbehavior/lectures/groups/indes.htm Download a powerpoint presentation and class discussions/lecture notes on dyadic and group communication and information diffusion in the business world.

INTERNET RESOURCES
Hot Link: Go to http://www.mhcollege.com/catalogs/0070707405.mhtml Dyadic communication in specific is explored in this book summary.

simultaneous exchange occurs as you talk and she listens. She not only hears what you have to say, but also observes how you say it. Or, suppose you catch someone's eye in a crowded bus and you both smile at each other at the same time. Without exchanging words, you have communicated simultaneously. Interpersonal communication is not a one-way process of sending information to others back and forth in a linear fashion, but a process in which both individuals simultaneously affect each other. Affecting each other points to the third element in our definition of interpersonal communication, mutual influence.

3. *Interpersonal communication involves mutual influence between individuals.* Mutual influence means that *both* partners are affected by the interactions, not just one person. Let's go back to the bus example. Suppose your bus traveling companion doesn't see you smile. This is not really interpersonal, because there is no mutual interaction; only you have been affected by the communication. Interpersonal communication is that special circumstance in which *both* individuals are affecting the other. When both you and the other bus passenger see and respond to each other, there is mutual influence; each of you is changed as a result of the other person's action. Interpersonal communication has occurred. The degree of mutual influence varies a great deal from interaction to interaction. You probably would not be affected a great deal by a brief smile from a bus traveling companion, but would be greatly affected by your lover telling you he or she is leaving you. Every interpersonal communication interaction influences us. Sometimes it changes our lives dramatically, sometimes in small ways. Long-lasting interpersonal relationships are sustained not by one person giving and another taking, but by mutually satisfying communication.

4. *Interpersonal communication is the fundamental means we use to manage our relationships.* An interpersonal relationship is the ongoing connection we make with others through interpersonal communication. Later in this chapter we describe fundamental principles of interpersonal relationships, and Chapters 9 and 10 more fully describe the nature and development of our relationships with others.

It is through our interpersonal contacts with others that our relationships go through a series of developmental stages. The initial stages of a relationship often involve sharing less intimate or personal information. Later stages evolve to include more intimate conversations and behaviors.

We initiate and form relationships by communicating with those whom we find attractive in some way. We seek to increase our interactions with those with whom we wish to further develop relationships, and we continually interpersonally communicate to maintain the relationship. We also use interpersonal communication to end relationships that we have decided are no longer viable.

We can usually identify the stage of a relationship by simply observing the interpersonal communication We interact differently as we move toward or away from intimacy. Your interactions with a new acquaintance are different from those with a close friend. When interacting with a stranger you stand farther apart, use different words, are more likely to feel awkward, and are less certain about how to interpret body language than when you interact with a good friend.

Most of our relational management through interpersonal communication occurs indirectly. We typically spend a small amount of time together talking directly about how we feel toward others or about the nature and quality of our relationships. When you go home at the end of the day and start talking to your roommate about what's planned for dinner, the topic of conversation is not your relationship. However, the very fact that you engage in this conversation reflects a desire to maintain a relationship and confirms the mutual acceptance that you each have for the relationship. What would happen if you asked your roommate about dinner and your roommate simply walked away from you and didn't respond? You would probably be disturbed. You might begin to wonder if something was wrong. If this were a recurring reaction, you might begin to question the viability of the relationship. We often draw conclusions about the quality of our relationship by noting how others respond to us, rather than by directly stating how great or poor the quality of the relationship is.

In this book we define interpersonal communication as a special form of human communication. There are other forms, as well. **Mass communication** occurs when someone communicates the same message to many people at once, but the creator of the message is usually not physically present, and there is virtually no opportunity for listeners to immediately respond to the speaker. Messages communicated via radio and TV are examples of mass communication. **Public communication** occurs when a speaker addresses a large audience in person. **Small group communication** occurs when a group of from three to fifteen people meet to interact with a common purpose and mutually influence one another. The purpose of the gathering could be to solve a problem, make a decision, learn, or just have fun. While communicating with others in a small group, it is also possible to interpersonally communicate with others—to communicate to manage our relationship with one or more individuals in the group. Finally, **intrapersonal communication** is communication with yourself. Thinking is perhaps the best example of intrapersonal communication. In our discussion of self and communication in Chapter 2, we will discuss the relationships between your thoughts and your interpersonal communication with others.

The Importance of Interpersonal Communication to Our Lives

Why learn about interpersonal communication? Because it touches every aspect of our lives. It is not only pleasant or desirable to develop quality interpersonal relationships with others, it is vital for our well-being. Learning how to understand and improve interpersonal communication can improve our relationships with family and loved ones, friends, and colleagues and can enhance the quality of our physical and emotional health.

1. Being skilled in interpersonal communication can improve relationships with our family. Virginia Satir calls family communication "the largest single

RESEARCH AND LITERATURE

Robert Bolton, author of *People Skills*, asserts that "80% of the people who fail at work do so for one reason: they do not relate well to other people." (Simon & Schuster, 1986, p. 7). Ask students to comment.

WEB ACTIVITY

Interpersonal Communication Is Valued in the Workplace. Instruct students to browse the Internet using a search engine and search the topic of "employment." Have them note any references to communication, communication skills, etc. In class, lead a discussion on the importance of competent communication in the workplace.

WEB ACTIVITY

Interpersonal Communication Is in My Employment Future. Instruct students that they are to locate a job listing on the Internet that they would be interested in if they were in the job market. Have them print out the job description summary. In class, have all those with printouts of jobs that didn't list communication skills as part of the job description stand up (there shouldn't be many). Have these students read their job summaries and determine for each one whether communication skills would be helpful.

For many of us, friendships are vital to our personal well-being. By improving our interpersonal communication skills, we can learn how to improve our friendships. (Ian Shaw/Tony Stone Images)

factor determining the kinds of relationships [we make] with others."[5] Learning principles and skills of interpersonal communication can give us insight as to why we relate to others as we do. Our interaction with our parents deeply affected our self-concept. Did they praise or ignore achievements and accomplishments? As we will learn in the next chapter, our self-concept plays a major role in determining how we interact with others.

2. Being skilled in interpersonal communication can improve relationships with our friends. We don't choose our biological families, but we do choose our friends. Friends are people we choose to be with because we like them and usually they like us. For unmarried people, developing friendships and falling in love are the top-rated sources of satisfaction and happiness in life.[6] Conversely, losing a relationship is among life's most stressful events. Most individuals between the ages of nineteen and twenty-four report that they have had from five to six romantic relationships and have been "in love" once or twice.[7] Studying interpersonal communication may not unravel all of the mysteries of romantic love and friendship, but it can offer insight into our behaviors.

3. Being skilled in interpersonal communication can improve our relationships with colleagues. In many ways, our colleagues at work are like family members. Although we choose our friends and lovers, we don't always have the same flexibility in choosing those with whom or for whom we work. Understanding how relationships develop on the job can help us avoid conflict and stress and increase our sense of satisfaction. In addition, our success or failure in a job often hinges on how well we get along with supervisors and peers.

4. Being skilled in interpersonal communication can improve our physical and emotional health. Research has shown that the lack or loss of a close relationship can lead to ill health and even death. Physicians have long observed that patients who are widowed or divorced experience more medical problems such as heart disease, cancer, pneumonia, and diabetes than do married people.[8]

Grief-stricken spouses are more likely than others to die prematurely, especially around the time of the departed spouse's birthday or near their wedding anniversary.[9] Being childless can also shorten one's life. One study found that middle-aged, childless wives were almost two-and-one-half times more likely to die in a given year than those who had at least one child.[10] Terminally ill patients with a limited number of friends or no social support die sooner than those with stronger ties.[11] Loneliness can kill.

RECAP	Comparing Key Definitions
Term	**Definition**
Communication	The process of acting upon information.
Human Communication	The process of making sense out of the world and sharing that sense with others.
Interpersonal Communication	The process of interacting simultaneously with another and mutually influencing each other, usually for the purpose of managing relationships.

An Evolving Model for Human and Interpersonal Communication

Interpersonal communication involves more than simply transferring or exchanging messages; it is a complex process of creating meaning in the context of an interpersonal relationship. To more fully understand this process, it is useful to see how our perspective on the human communication process has evolved over the past half century. We will begin with the simplest and oldest model of the human communication process and then discuss more contemporary models.

Human Communication as Action: Message Transfer

"Did you get my message?" This simple sentence summarizes the communication-as-action approach to human communication. Communication takes place when a message is sent and received. Period. It is a way of transferring meaning from sender to receiver. In 1942, Harold Lasswell summarized the process as follows:

Who (sender)

Says what (message)

In what channel

WEB ACTIVITY
Speak Up for Life. Have students search the Internet under the topics of health and communication (also try interaction, socializing, support systems, laughter, self-disclosure, loneliness, and isolation). Instruct students to make a list of all the health benefit claims they find in association with communication. In small groups, have students generate master lists of the health benefits of communication.

INTERNET RESOURCES
Hot Link: Go to http://cwis.ave.dk/phd/fulltext/axe/sea/html/node9.html An interesting discussion of the effects of inclusion on stress and interaction.

DISCUSSION AND WRITING
Ask your students how many have taken a communication course in the past. Invite them to assist you in distinguishing interpersonal communication from other types of communication, especially intrapersonal, small group communication, and public address. Note that the functions of each differ: interpersonal communication focuses on initiating, building, maintaining, and terminating *relationships*.

TEACHING STRATEGY
Models of human communication are complex. Often, students must learn new definitions for terms for which they had pre-existing definitions, and the components can seem overwhelmingly abstract. Illustrating the models visually can help students to comprehend and remember the components.

ACTIVITY
See Activity 1.1 in the Instructor's Guide.

To whom (receiver)

With what effect.[12]

Figure 1.1 shows a basic model formulated in 1949, seven years after Lasswell's summary, that depicts communication as a linear input/output process. Today, although they view the process differently, researchers still define most of the key components in this model in basically the same way.

■ INFORMATION SOURCE AND TRANSMITTER

The **information source** for a communication can be a thought or an emotion. The transmitter (nowadays called the **source**), the originator of that thought or emotion, puts it into a code that can be understood by a receiver. Translating ideas, feelings, and thoughts into a code is called **encoding**. Vocalizing a word, gesturing, or establishing eye contact are signals that we use to encode our thoughts into a message that can be **decoded** by someone. Decoding, the opposite process of encoding, occurs when the words or unspoken signals are interpreted by the receiver.

■ RECEIVER

The **receiver** is the person who decodes and attempts to make sense out of what the source encoded. Think of a radio station with a source broadcasting to a receiver that picks up the station's signal. In human communication, however, there is something in between the source and the receiver: We filter messages through past experiences, attitudes, beliefs, values, prejudices, and biases.

■ SIGNAL, RECEIVED SIGNAL, AND MESSAGE

Today, all of these components are simply called the message. **Messages** are the written, spoken, and unspoken elements of communication to which we assign meaning. You can send a message intentionally (talking to a professor

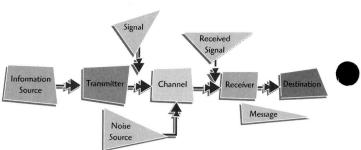

Figure 1.1

A Model for Communication as Action

From: *The Mathematical Theory of Communication* by Claude E. Shannon and Warren Weaver. Copyright 1949 by the Board of Trustees of the University of Illinois. Used by permission of the University of Illinois Press.

INTERPERSONAL COMMUNICATION FOUNDATIONS

Impersonal America

A few weeks back, I bought an upgrade card for my computer. Being inexpert at such things, I soon found myself out of my depth and placed a call to the company's technical-support line. After going through the menu of options offered by the machine that answered the phone, I was connected to a recorded voice that said I would be on hold for five or ten minutes before someone could help me.

I was actually on hold for about an hour, but my ordeal finally ended.

When the machine hung up on me.

Undaunted, I called the company back—did I mention that this was long-distance?—and spent another hour listening to the same three elevator tunes repeated endlessly. Fed up, I hung up, only to repeat the sequence over the next few days without getting even a smidgen of technical support from the technical-support line.

Which brings us to the question: Where have all the human beings gone?

You know, the people who used to answer your questions, explain your options . . . service with a smile and all that? What happened to them?

It's not just the computer company that makes me wonder. It's the utility company, the bank, the subscription department, the telephone operator and, yes, the automated phone system at my very own office.

It wasn't always like this. Remember when you took your questions to a human who gave you a human response? Now, you listen to a menu and input information. We live in Impersonal America, an acquaintance said the other day as he swiped his money card to buy gas at the pump. Not so long ago, he mused, filling the tank meant dealing with another human being. Maybe shooting the breeze for a moment or two. Now, we just pump and run. Granted, the new way is quicker and easier.

Less painful sometimes, too. Once, years ago, I needed to get an extension on a utility bill. I'm sitting there on hold, trying to frame a hard-luck tale for the clerk, when suddenly a machine picks up the phone. It instructs me to key in some information and quickly approves my request. Never even asks for my tale of woe. It seemed a good deal to me at the time. Only now do I find myself questioning whether the trade-off was worth it. Only now that humanity has been exchanged for cost-effectiveness and service swapped for speed.

And that's a term which seems especially apropos because I don't think this happened just because we were looking for greater efficiency. No, I think we also wanted greater uniformity. We wanted—and have made—our encounters sterile and personality-free. Know how bad it is? A cashier, an older woman who works in a cafeteria in Washington, got in hot water a while back for her habit of calling customers "honey" and "sweetie."

We wanted it to be like that. Wanted correctness over personality. Wanted one-size-fits-all customer service free from the messiness—bad moods, biases, idiosyncrasies, small talk—that characterizes human interaction. But I find that I miss the mess. Indeed, when I went through back channels and finally got a live human to answer my computer question, I was more pumped than an OPEC oil well. The guy even got snippy with me, and it was like hearing a favorite song for the first time in years.

It made me wonder: Are we really better off now than we were when human beings—snippy and otherwise—answered the phones and provided the service? OK, so maybe real live people aren't cost-effective. But I can tell you this: I wound up taking that upgrade card back to the store. Asked the clerk to recommend one from a company that could actually put a living, breathing human being on the line in a reasonable amount of time. The card he showed me costs about $100 more. And you know something? It's worth it.

Leonard Pitts, *Miami Herald*. Distributed by Knight–Ridder/Tribune Information Services.

RESEARCH AND LITERATURE

Investigate learning styles, using channel preferences. See Michael Brooks' *Instant Rapport* (Warner, 1989). Encourage students to discover their preferred learning style: Visual, auditory, kinesthetic/haptic, or a combination. Suggest that other-oriented communicators recognize their preferences but select channels that the recipient prefers for best results. For instance, when asking a "visual" boss for a raise, showing her/him a list of reasons for this pay boost may be more effective than a simple discussion. Likewise, an "auditory" friend may prefer a phone call to a Hallmark card.

DISCUSSION AND WRITING

Ask students to describe some common examples of external and psychological noise they encounter during class. Then discuss ways to minimize interfering stimuli.

MEDIA AND OUTSIDE RESOURCES

There are a number of situation comedies on television which rely upon semantic noise to create humor. "Three's Company" is a classic and nearly every "Seinfeld" portrays bypassing. Consider showing a portion of a show to illustrate how meanings are in people, not in words.

before class) or unintentionally (falling asleep during class); verbally ("Hi. How are you?"), nonverbally (a smile and a handshake), or in written form (this book).

◼ CHANNEL

A message is communicated from sender to receiver via some pathway called a **channel**. Channels correspond to your senses. When you call your mother on the telephone, the channel is an auditory one. When you talk with your mother face-to-face, the channels are many. You see her: the visual channel. You hear her: the auditory channel. You may smell her perfume: the olfactory channel. You may hug her: the tactile channel.

◼ NOISE

Noise is interference. Without noise, all of our messages would be communicated with sublime accuracy. But noise is always present. It can be literal—the obnoxious roar of a gas-powered lawn mower—or it can be psychological. Instead of concentrating on your teacher's lecture, you may start thinking about the chores you need to finish before the end of the day. Whichever kind it is, noise gets in the way of the message and may even distort it. Communicating accurate messages involves minimizing both external and psychological noise.

While the action approach is simple and straightforward, it has a key flaw: human communication rarely, if ever, is as simple and efficient as "what we put in is what we get out." Others cannot automatically know what you mean just because you think you know what you mean. Although by Lasswell's time, communication scholars had already begun identifying an array of key elements in the communication process, the action approach overlooked their complexity.

Although accurate communication can be difficult when there is noise interference, as in this steel mill, psychological noise may be even more difficult to overcome. (Carl Wolinsky/Stock Boston)

Human Communication as Interaction: Message Exchange

The next big leap in our understanding of human communication came in the late 1940s and early 1950s. The communication-as-interaction perspective used the same elements as the action models but added two new ones: feedback and context.

Think of a Ping-Pong game. Like a Ping-Pong ball, messages bounce back and forth. We talk; someone listens and responds; we respond to this response. This perspective can be summarized using a physical principle: For every action there is a reaction.

Feedback is the response to the message. Without feedback, communication is rarely effective. When you order your black olive pizza and the server says in response, "That's a black olive pizza, right?" he has provided feedback to ensure that he encoded the message correctly.

Feedback is really a response message. Like other messages, it can be intentional (applause at the conclusion of a symphony) or unintentional (a yawn as you listen to your uncle tell his story about bears again); verbal ("That's a black olive pizza, right?") or nonverbal (blushing after being asked to dance).

A second component recognized by the interaction perspective is **context**, the physical and psychological communication environment. All communication takes place in some context. As the cliché goes, "Everyone has to be somewhere." A conversation with your good friend on the beach would likely differ from one the two of you may have in a funeral home. Context encompasses not only the physical environment but also the number of people present and their relationship with the communicators, the communication goal, and the culture in which the communicators are steeped.

This perspective, as shown in Figure 1.2, is more realistic, but it still has limitations. Although it emphasizes feedback and context, it does not quite capture the complexity of the interpersonal communication process if the communication takes place simultaneously. The interaction model of communication still views communication as a linear, step-by-step process. But in interpersonal situations, both the source and the receiver send and receive messages at the same time.

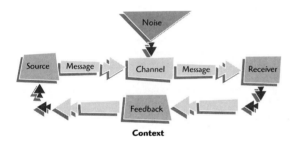

Figure 1.2

A Model for Communication as Interaction Interaction models of communication include feedback as a response to a message sent by the communication source.
From: *Invitation to Effective Speech Communication*, by John T. Masterson, Steven A. Beebe and Norman H. Watson, Scott, Foresman and Company, 1989.

Point out that, unlike the ping pong game, communication messages are being sent and received simultaneously and multidimensionally. Several balls are being played at once and from many planes. Ask students to identify the "balls" in your classroom at a given moment.

ACTIVITY
See Activity 1.2 in the Instructor's Guide.

DISCUSSION AND WRITING
Stress to students that we cannot have transactional meaning between ourselves and objects. The experience of persons is transactional; this is not so between a person and a machine. Computers offer interactions but not transactions. Ask students whether they believe that E-mail can be used to engage in interpersonal communication. Is the interaction simultaneous? Does it effect mutual influence?

Human Communication as Transaction: Message Creation

The communication-as-transaction perspective, developed in the 1960s, acknowledges that when we talk to another, we are constantly reacting to what our partner is saying. Most scholars today view it as the most realistic model for interpersonal communication. Although it uses such components as action and interaction to describe communication, in this model all of the interaction is simultaneous. As Figure 1.3 indicates, we send and receive messages concurrently. Even as we talk, we are also interpreting our partner's nonverbal and verbal responses. Transactive communication also occurs within a context; and noise can interfere with the quality and accuracy of the meaning of messages.

As we send messages, we monitor the degree to which the other person understands each message. We mutually define the symbols we use. If one partner misunderstands a message, both can work to clarify the meaning. For example, if I ask you to hand me the book off my desk and you hand me a pad of paper, we have failed to create a shared meaning. I might then say, "No, not the pad of paper, the red book next to the phone"; you then would hand me the book. Your action would require me to explain and be more specific. We would not simply transfer or exchange meaning; we would create it during a communication transaction.

One researcher says that interpersonal communication is "the coordinated management of meaning" through **episodes**, during which the message of one person influences the message of another.[13] Technically, only the sender and receiver of those messages can determine where one episode ends and another begins.

Figure 1.3

A Model for Communication as Simultaneous Transaction

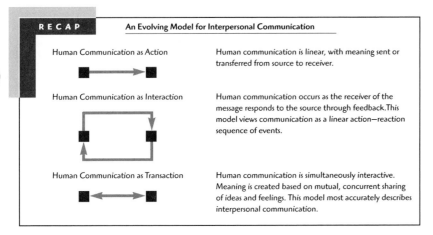

RECAP

An Evolving Model for Interpersonal Communication

Human Communication as Action

Human communication is linear, with meaning sent or transferred from source to receiver.

Human Communication as Interaction

Human communication occurs as the receiver of the message responds to the source through feedback. This model views communication as a linear action—reaction sequence of events.

Human Communication as Transaction

Human communication is simultaneously interactive. Meaning is created based on mutual, concurrent sharing of ideas and feelings. This model most accurately describes interpersonal communication.

Mediated Interpersonal Communication: A New Frontier

Today's technology allows us to expand our definition of interpersonal communication. Instead of having to rely on face-to-face contact for our interpersonal exchanges, we can now use various types of media to carry our interpersonal messages: Telephones, faxes, e-mail, and electronic chat rooms are among the sometimes bewildering assortment of devices through which we can interact, exercise mutual influence, and develop interpersonal relationships. When we use one of these media to carry the message, we are using **mediated interpersonal communication**. But as Leonard Pitts suggests in Electronic Connections: Impersonal America, mediated interpersonal communication may sometimes be less satisfying than a face-to-face encounter. Even in our electronic age, interacting with machines instead of humans is uncomfortable for some people.

At present, the most effective interpersonal communication, especially for expressing feelings, occurs when there are no media filters to interfere with clarity of the message or to delay feedback from the receiver of the message. For this reason, our key focus in this book will be on unmediated interaction between people.

But we will also begin to explore the new frontier in interpersonal communication. Can you communicate interpersonally with someone on the Internet? Can relationships be developed with another without meeting others face-to-face? There is evidence that people can and do develop meaningful relationships with others without meeting them in person. If you are attending a college or univer-

INTERNET RESOURCES
Hot Link: Go to http://www.city.ac.uk/csd/network/guide/
The Internet Facilities and Computer Communications Guide is a great site. It offers answers to miscellaneous questions pertaining to electronic communication and computer jargon.

"Gene, e-mail the kids and tell them to come downstairs for dinner."

sity away from family, friends, or loved ones, you may have found that sending e-mail messages can help keep you in touch with others who are important to you. College freshmen and their parents report e-mail connections reduce homesickness and the sadness parents often feel as their son or daughter leaves home. The past few years have seen an increase in the number of people who meet in a chat room on the Internet and eventually develop a real-time relationship. In special Electronic Connections features throughout the text we will highlight the ways that today's technology is affecting our relationships. As Electronic Connections: An Electronic Relationship illustrates, e-mail allows intimate relationships to develop between people who are separated by thousands of miles.

We have even developed new ways to communicate the feelings, emotions, and other responses that make it possible to communicate nonverbally. Some people use emoticons (keyboard symbols typed sideways, like :-O. Note several

ELECTRONIC CONNECTIONS

An Electronic Relationship

Today's technology makes it possible for people to develop relationships with others without meeting face-to-face. He was in Australia. She was in New York. They had never met. Their only contact was through an electronic bulletin board on the Internet. At first it was just a few e-mail messages a week. But as their relationship developed, they were soon communicating at least twenty times a day. As is the case with most face-to-face encounters, their early messages were about mundane topics such as the weather and daily activities. Eventually, their electronic correspondence became more personal. Then, nine months after they first logged on, Robert popped the question to his cyberspace sweetheart, Charlene. "We are having some difficulty in getting people to understand that we know all about one another," newlywed Robert told the *Buffalo News*. "But e-mail is the resurgence of correspondence—which has essentially died out. It was the way many people used to get to know one another." The difference, of course, is that partners can measure the intervals between these "letters" in nanoseconds instead of days or weeks. Although such exchanges are not simultaneous, they certainly can have the kind of spontaneity that we usually associate with interpersonal communication.

other emoticons identified in the following Electronic Connections box. We can also communicate emotions via e-mail by "screaming," TYPING IN ALL CAPITAL LETTERS TO SHOUT THE MESSAGE. In still other situations, we might respond to someone by verbally describing nonverbal behaviors: "I am frowning right now as I read what you are sending me."

Of course, just as not all face-to-face communication is interpersonal communication, not all mediated communication results in unique relationships with others. One of the key differences in these mediated communication situations is the reduced level of nonverbal cues. Even if you use emoticons, when you can't see the other person's facial expression, amount of eye contact, or whether they seem interested in what you are saying, accurately communicating your meaning, especially your feelings and emotions, can be more challenging.

One research team suggests that the richness of a communication channel can be measured using four criteria: (1) the amount of feedback that the communicators are able to receive; (2) the number of cues the channel is able to convey and that can be interpreted by a receiver; (3) the variety of language communicators use; and (4) the potential to express emotions and feelings.[14] Using these four criteria, researchers have developed a continuum of communication channels that are media rich to media lean. The model presented in Figure 1.4 illustrates this continuum.

ELECTRONIC CONNECTIONS

Emoticons

A kiss is just a : *, a sigh is just a : - (

Electronic-mail writers have adopted a lighthearted system of shorthand known as "emoticons." These clever combinations of keyboard characters punctuate a message with just the right spirit. To read them, simply look at the line with your head tilted slightly to the left.

For example, in the most basic emoticon, the smiley face, a colon, hyphen, and a right parenthesis become the eye, nose, and mouth of glee : -).

Here's a sample of some frequently used emoticons that will help you get across the nuances of your message:

: - |)	smiley with a mustache	| -)	hee hee
: D	big smile	| - D	ho ho
; -	wink	: /	not funny
: - @	scream	: - }	smirk
: X	keeping mouth shut	: - o	shocked (or singing the national anthem)
: - &	tongue-tied	: I	bored
: -J	tongue in cheek or joking	> : - <	angry
: p	sticking out tongue or giving a raspberry	< : -)	dumb question or dumb person
: *	kiss	(: - $	sick person or person is sick
: * * :	returning kiss	: - (	sad
( )	hug	: -	really sad
(((())))	lots of hugs	:' (	crying
: -)8	sharply dressed person	; - ?	licking your lips
: - >	hey hey		

From: Charles Bowen, *HomePC*, (January 1995), 109.

Figure 1.4

A Continuum of
Communication-Rich and
Communication-Lean
Channels of
Communication
Adapted from: L. K.
Trevino, R. L. Draft, and R.
H. Lengel, "Understanding
Managers' Media Choices:
A Symbolic Interactionist
Perspective." In
*Organizations and
Communication
Technology,* edited by
J. Fulk and C. Steinfield
(Newbury Park, CA: Sage,
1990), 71–94.

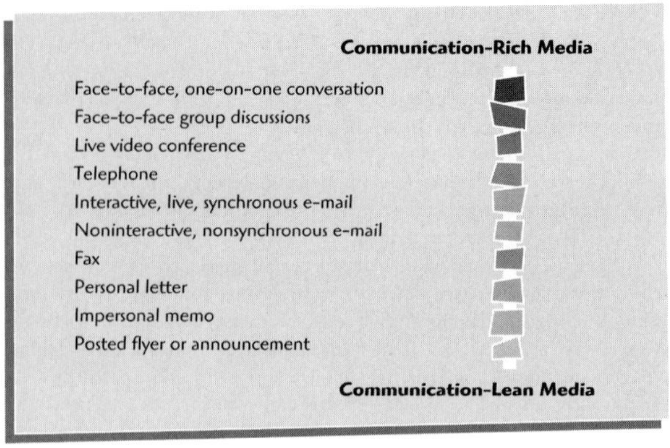

Communication-Rich Media

Face-to-face, one-on-one conversation
Face-to-face group discussions
Live video conference
Telephone
Interactive, live, synchronous e-mail
Noninteractive, nonsynchronous e-mail
Fax
Personal letter
Impersonal memo
Posted flyer or announcement

Communication-Lean Media

UNDERSTANDING DIVERSITY

The World Is Here

One of our most visionary politicians said that he envisioned a time when the United States could become the brain of the world, by which he meant the repository of all the latest advanced information systems. I thought of that remark when an enterprising poet friend of mine called to say that he had just sold a poem to a computer magazine and that the editors were delighted to get it because they didn't carry fiction or poetry. Is that the kind of world we desire? A humdrum homogenous world of all brains but no heart, no fiction, no poetry; a world of robots with human attendants bereft of imagination, or culture. Or does North America deserve a more exciting destiny? To become a place where the cultures of the world crisscross. This is possible because the United States is unique in the world: The world is here.[15]

These words from Ishmael Reed's essay, "The World Is Here," remind us that America is not a one-dimensional culture. We need not travel to far-off places to develop interpersonal relationships with people from other cultures, races, or ethnic backgrounds. America has long been known as a melting pot—a place where people from a variety of cultures and traditions have come together to seek their fortunes. Others think America is more like a tossed salad than a melting pot—in a salad each ingredient retains its essential character rather than melting together to form a united whole. Focusing on communication and diversity means much more than focusing on cultural differences. Culture consists of the learned values, behaviors, and expectations shared by a group of people. We need skill and sensitivity to develop quality interpersonal relationships with others whose religion, race,

ethnicity, age, gender, or sexual orientation are different from our own. Throughout the text, we will include boxes like this one to help you develop your sensitivity to important issues related to cultural diversity. As we embark on our study of interpersonal communication, consider these questions either individually or with a group of your classmates:

1. What are the implications of our melting-pot or tossed salad culture for our study of interpersonal communication?

2. Is there too much emphasis on being politically correct on college campuses today? Support your answer.

3. What specific interpersonal skills will help you communicate effectively with others from different cultural and ethnic traditions?

As we noted earlier, an **interpersonal relationship** is the ongoing connection we make with another person through interpersonal communication. We carry that connection in our minds (and metaphorically, in our hearts), whether the other person is present or not. One of the main purposes of this book is to explore that connection in depth. We agree with H. D. Duncan, who said, "We do not relate and then talk, but relate in talk." Close relationships are one of the most important reasons for being. They serve as our compass as we navigate our way through the world; they are critical to maintaining good health and happiness.

As we have seen, the process of meeting, talking, listening, responding, and reacting to others results in more than information exchange or sharing; it enables you to form relationships with others. In some relationships the emotional connection is minimal; if you are waiting for a bus with a stranger, you may simply be aware of another's presence. Your relationship with the person who delivers your mail or waits on you each morning when you order breakfast at your local fast-food restaurant may hold no deep emotional attachment or commitment. But your relationships with your mother, father, spouse, child, colleagues, and best friends are emotionally rich. To understand and improve these relationships is to make your life more worthwhile.

As our definition of interpersonal communication suggests, interpersonal communication and interpersonal relationships are connected in a number of ways. Each interpersonal interaction adds to the interpersonal relationship. We begin to communicate at ground zero, with no relationship. Over time, if we continue to interact, the relationship evolves. Each time we communicate, we

Once words are spoken, they cannot be taken back, even after an apology or explanation. Think about the situations in your life when you may have damaged an interpersonal relationship with words you spoke and later regretted. (Bob Daemmrich/Stock Boston)

21

add richness to the relationship, sometimes by great amounts and sometimes by infinitesimal amounts. The five principles that follow serve as a foundation for our discussion of the interpersonal relationships throughout the book.

Principle 1: Interpersonal Relationships Are Both Systems and Processes

A **system** is a set of interconnected elements; a change in one element affects all the other elements. For example, a change in the mood of one of your friends may affect your feelings and your interactions with him or her. In a close relationship, you may actually feel the same emotional response as a friend does in response to his or her situation. Viewing interpersonal relationships as systems affirms the process nature of relationships. Relationships are processes in the sense that they are constantly changing; they are not static. Your relationship with your parents is not the same as it was when you were seven. Even your relationship with your roommate changes from day to day, depending on what else is happening in your lives. If an external influence affects your roommate's self-concept, that change will in turn alter the nature of your relationship, and that alteration will in turn further affect both your and your roommate's self-concepts.

The systems/process nature of relationships also means we depend on knowledge we gain from prior relationships to help define expectations and behaviors in our current and future relationships. If your most recent first date was successful, you probably will act the same way again. If it was a disaster, you probably will use the knowledge gained in that experience to modify your behavior the next time. Although every relationship is unique, each provides us with a better understanding of relationships and helps us to improve our ability to manage them. This text and the course you are taking are based on this premise.

Because interpersonal communication is a process, it also follows that once you utter something, you can't "take it back." Our communication with others is irreversible.

"Disregard that last statement made by the witness," instructs the judge. Yet the clever lawyer knows that once her client has told the jury that her husband gave her a black eye during an argument, the client cannot really "take it back." This principle applies to all forms of oral communication. We may try to modify the meaning of a spoken message by saying something like, "Oh, I really didn't mean it." But in most cases, the damage has been done. Once created, communication has the physical property of matter; it can't be uncreated. As the helical model in Figure 1.5 suggests, once interpersonal communication begins, it never loops back on itself. Instead, it continues to be shaped by the events,

Figure 1.5

Interpersonal Communication Is Irreversible
This helical model shows that interpersonal communication never loops back on itself. It begins at the bottom and expands infinitely as the communication partners contribute their thoughts and experiences to the exchange. Copyright © F.E.X. Dance in *Human Communication Theory* (Holt, Rinehart and Winston, 1967) 294. Reprinted with permission.

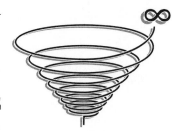

INTERPERSONAL COMMUNICATION FOUNDATIONS

DISCUSSION AND WRITING
Ask students to consider situations in which they are not engaged in communication. Under what conditions might people not be experiencing simultaneous contact? Consider sleeping, a coma, etc. Often a student will be able to relate an experience in which she or he was unconscious, but still aware of others' attempts to communicate. Ask your students whether they are communicating with one of their parents right now. Without mutual awareness, people are not communicating with one another. Stress that mutual awareness makes communication inevitable.

experiences, and thoughts of the communication partners. A Russian proverb nicely summarizes the point: "Once a word goes out of your mouth, you can never swallow it again."

Yet another impact of the systems/process nature of our relationships is the energy required to continually change the nature of our relationships—even old ones. For example, your relationship with your best friend probably has changed, or will change, when one of you gets married. You and your friend must renegotiate the nature of the relationship in light of the new circumstances.

Finally, the systems/process nature of interpersonal relationships can result in misunderstandings and complications. When we humans communicate, we interpret information from others as symbols. A **symbol** is merely a representation of something else, and it can have various meanings and interpretations. Language is a system of symbols. In English, our symbols do not resemble the words they represent. The word (symbol) for *cow* does not look at all like a cow; someone, somewhere decided that *cow* should mean a beast that chews a cud and gives milk. Our reliance upon symbols to communicate poses a communication challenge; we are often misinterpreted. Sometimes we don't know the code. Only if you are up-to-date on contemporary slang will you know that "home-skillet" means a good friend, "circle of death" means a lousy pizza, and "moma-flauge" means you are hiding something from your mother.

"I'm afraid you misunderstood . . .
I said I'd like a mango."

Messages are not always interpreted as we intend them. Osmo Wiio, a Scandinavian communication scholar, points out the messiness of communicating with others when he suggests the following maxims:

- If communication can fail, it will.

- If a message can be understood in different ways, it will be understood in just that way which does the most harm.

- There is always somebody who knows better than you what you meant by your message.

- The more communication there is, the more difficult it is for communication to succeed.[16]

While we are not as pessimistic as Professor Wiio, we do suggest that the task of understanding each other is challenging.

23

Principle 2: Interpersonal Relationships Emphasize Both Message Content and Personal Feelings

The emotional aspect of a message, often embodied in the nonverbal cues that accompany the verbal message, provides information about the content of the message. Communication scholars call this type of communication **meta-communication,** literally, communication about communication. What you say and how you say it—your tone of voice, amount of eye contact, facial expression, and posture—can reveal a great deal about the emotional makeup of a relationship.[17] Interpersonal exchanges provide clues about how intimate a relationship is, and also about the power structure within the relationship. When your mother yells, "CLEAN YOUR ROOM NOW!" and your father says gently, "Would you please clean your room?" both are delivering a message with the same goal. But the emotional tones of the two messages provide different relationship cues. The first message suggests that your mother sometimes resorts to exerting power and control. The second message suggests that your father tries to treat you more as an equal.

Principle 3: Interpersonal Relationships Are Defined by the Roles We Assume

A **role** is a set of expected behaviors associated with a particular situation. These sets of behaviors reflect how we are expected to behave toward others. The relationship between you and your instructor is defined by the situational context of the classroom. If that instructor also happens to be your adviser, then when you go into his or her office to discuss your future, you both adjust your roles to suit the new relationship. And if your instructor–adviser is also your father, that role—and the set of behaviors associated with being a son or daughter—also affects the relationship. In our more intimate relationships, we play several roles, depending on the demands of the situation. We might play counselor, companion, adviser, substitute parent, lover, helper, problem solver, or leader.

The role we assume in a relationship at any given time is also influenced by our own perceptions of who we think we are and who others think we are. Dean Barnlund has noted that whenever we communicate with another person, there are really at least six "people" involved: (1) who you think you are; (2) who you think the other person is; (3) who you think the other person thinks you are; (4) who the other person thinks he or she is; (5) who the other person thinks you are; and (6) who the other person thinks you think he or she is.[18] Whew! And when you add more people to the interaction, it becomes even more involved.

The varied number of roles we assume in a given relationship adds to the potential for the different perceptions we have of our partners. However, as relationships become more successful and more intimate, the partners spend more time aligning their perspectives. Research suggests that a couple's ability to share the same perceptions of their relationship determines how successful the relationship will be.[19]

Principle 4: Interpersonal Relationships Are Governed by Social Rules

According to Susan Shimanoff, a rule is "a followable prescription that indicates what behavior is obligated, preferred, or prohibited in certain contexts."[20] These rules, which help define appropriate and inappropriate communication in any given situation, may be explicit or implicit. For this class, explicit rules are probably spelled out in your syllabus. But your instructor has other rules that are more implicit. They are not written or verbalized because you learned them long ago: Only one person speaks at a time; you raise your hand to be called; you do not pass notes.

Interpersonal relationships are also shaped by both explicit and implicit rules. You may explicitly ask your friend not to phone you after 9:00 P.M. But you also have implicit expectations of others. In an early stage of a relationship, for example, you do not expect to learn private family secrets. At a later stage, you might be offended if an intimate friend does *not* reveal such secrets. Understanding rules helps you understand what is expected in a relationship.

Rules are developed both by those involved in the interaction and by the culture in which individuals are interacting. Michael Argyle and his colleagues asked individuals to identify general rules for relationship development and maintenance and then rate their importance. Here are the most important rules:[21]

■ Partners should respect the other's privacy.

■ Partners should not reveal each other's secrets.

■ Partners should look the other person in the eye during conversation.

■ Partners should not criticize the other person publicly.

Although we may modify rules to achieve the goals of our relationships, these general rules remain fairly constant. In fact, it is interesting to note how little they different from the social rules of George Washington's day, listed below.

In almost all interpersonal relationships the rules of a relationship are mutually defined and agreed on. Most of us don't like to be told what to do or how to behave all the time. The expectations and rules are continually renegotiated as the relationship unfolds.

Few of us learn relationship rules as Washington did, by copying them from a book. Most of us learn these rules from experience, by observing and interacting with family members and friends. Individuals who grow up in environments in which these rules are not observed may not know how to behave in close relationships.

Rule Breaker! Your authors suggest that interpersonal communication is governed by rules, and that these rules can be extended to the new media as well. Have students select a chat room and log on to observe for a while. When they are comfortable with the particulars of that environment, they should look for evidence of a social rule. Next, they should enter the chat and get involved. After some time, the student should create an opportunity to break the rule they had observed. Have students relate their experiment to the class. Help students make clear what the rule was that they broke, whether it was explicit or implicit, whether the reaction, if any, was explicit or implicit, and what, if any, punishing behaviors were evident. Point out that rules are developmental, socially constructed, and enforced with both explicit and implicit messages of approval/disapproval.

Principle 5: Interpersonal Relationships May Be Complementary, Symmetrical, or Parallel

Interpersonal interaction involves give-and-take, speaking and responding, influencing and being influenced. These patterns of interaction may be **complementary**. The partners' styles may fit together in a compatible way because one partner usually dominates and the other usually submits: One likes to listen and the other likes to talk; one likes someone to dictate a schedule and the other likes to control the agenda. Although these patterns of interaction complement each other, their inherent imbalance of power or influence may be unacceptable to some couples.

TEACHING STRATEGY

To illustrate complementary (versus symmetrical or parallel relationships, share the following passages from Marabel Morgan's 1973 bestseller *The Total Woman* (Old Tappan, New Jersey: Fleming H. Revell Company).

> What causes most of the problems in your marriage? I find that the conflict between two separate egos is usually the culprit. . . .The biblical remedy for conflict is stated, "You wives must submit to your husbands' leadership in the same way you submit to the Lord" (6). God planned for woman to be under her husband's rule (pp. 68–69).

During disagreements, like this one between supporters and protesters of the U.S. involvement in the Persian Gulf, people tend to exhibit dominating behaviors. (Jim Corwin/Stock Boston)

In a **symmetrical relationship,** both partners behave in similar ways.[22] In a **competitive symmetrical relationship,** each partner seeks to dominate the other. For example, each may try to control which TV programs the partners watch together or insist on participating in every spending decision. When both partners are consistently competing for equal power, they are bound to clash.

In contrast, some partners have **submissive symmetrical relationships,** in which each tries to relinquish control. The following snatch of conversation illustrates submissive symmetry:

Bea: What movie do you want to rent?

Vic: Oh, I don't care. You decide.

Bea: No, you decide. I don't care either.

Most relationships, however, are neither purely complementary nor purely symmetrical; they are **parallel.** In a **parallel relationship,** the partners' styles allow them to shift power back and forth in accordance with the situation or interaction. For example, if one partner knows a great deal about cars, then the other may be willing to bow out of the decision about which car to purchase. But that same partner may take the upper hand when it comes to discussing restaurants, and the other partner may defer to his or her judgment.

How To Improve Your Own Interpersonal Communication

Now that we have previewed the study of interpersonal communication and interpersonal relationships, you may be asking yourself, "Well, that's all well and good, but what do I have to do to improve my own interpersonal communication?" We suggest a five-part strategy.

DISCUSSION AND WRITING
Ask students to write for five minutes about whether they believe there are any sure-fire strategies for interacting with others. For instance, is honesty always the best policy? If you can't say something nice, should you refrain from saying anything at all? Invite students to consider other proverbs. Following the writing exercise, invite students to comment on the need for flexibility in communication.

INTERNET RESOURCES
Hot Link: Go to http://www.benton.org/
The Benton Foundation works to realize the social benefits made possible by the public interest in and use of communication.

INSTRUCTIONAL GOALS AND TIPS

Preview Maslow's stages of skill development (see Chapter 5). Describe how unconscious competence is the goal, but that awareness, awkwardness, and experimentation are necessary prerequisites for skill development. Remind students that "communication is risky business," and that the greater the need to communicate well, the harder it is to do.

Be Knowledgeable

By reading this chapter, you have already begun improving your communication skills. Competent communicators are knowledgeable. They know how communication works. They understand the components, principles, and rules of the communication process. As you read on in this book, you will learn theories, principles, concepts, and rules that will permit you to explain and predict how humans communicate.

Understanding these things is a necessary prerequisite for enhancing your interpersonal effectiveness, but this kind of knowledge alone does not make you competent. You would not let someone fix your car's carburetor if he or she had only read a book. Knowledge must be coupled with skill. And we acquire skill through practice.

Be Skilled

Competent communicators know how to translate knowledge into action. You can memorize the characteristics of a good listener but still not listen well. To develop skill requires practice and helpful feedback from others who can confirm the appropriateness of your actions.

Learning a social skill is not that different from learning how to drive a car or operate a computer.[23] To learn any skill, you must break it down into subskills that you can learn and practice. "Hear it, see it, do it, correct it" is the formula that seems to work best for learning any new behaviors. In this book we will examine the elements of complex skills such as listening, offer activities that will let you practice the skills, and provide opportunities for you to receive feedback and correct your application of the skills.

Be Motivated

Practicing skills requires work. You need to be motivated to use your information and skill. You must want to improve, and you must have a genuine desire to connect with others if you wish to become a competent communicator. You may know people who understand how to drive a car and have the skill to drive, yet are reluctant to get behind the wheel. Or maybe you know someone who took a course in public speaking but is still too frightened to stand in front of a crowd. Similarly, someone may pass a test about interpersonal communication principles with flying colors, but unless that person is motivated to use those newfound skills, his or her interactions with others may not improve.

Be Flexible

In this book we do not identify tidy lists of sure-fire strategies that you can use to win friends and influence people. The same set of skills is not effective in every situation, so competent communicators do not assume that "one size fits all." Rather, they assess each unique situation and adapt their behavior to achieve the desired outcome. They examine the context, the situation, and the needs, goals, and messages of others to establish and maintain relationships.

Be Other-Oriented

Most of us are egocentric—self-focused; our first inclination is to protect ourselves. Scholars of evolution might argue that it is our tendency to look out for number one that ensures the continuation of the human race.

Yet when we focus *exclusively* on ourselves, it is difficult to communicate effectively. If we fail to adapt our message to our listener, we may not be successful in achieving our intended communication goal. Adapting messages to others does not mean that we tell them only what they want to hear; that would be unethical. Nor does being considerate of others mean we abandon all concern for our own interests. Other-oriented communication suggests that we consider the needs, motives, desires, and goals of our communication partners while still maintaining our own integrity. The choices we make in forming the message and selecting the time and place to deliver it should consider the other person's thoughts and feelings.

How do you become other-oriented? Being other-oriented is really a collection of skills rather than a single skill. We will devote considerable discussion throughout the book to developing this collection of essential communication skills.[24]

Focusing on others begins with an accurate understanding of your self-concept and self-esteem; we will discuss these foundation principles in the next chapter. As you will learn in Chapter 3, developing an accurate perception of both yourself and others is an important element of effectively relating to others.

BUILDING YOUR SKILLS

Role Play: Other-Oriented or Self-Focused

With a communication partner, role-play the following interpersonal situations in two ways. First, role-play the scene with communicators who are not other-oriented—they are self-focused. Then, role-play the same scene with communicators who are other-oriented—they consider the thoughts and feelings of the other person.

Suggested situations:

- Try to return a broken VCR to a department store salesperson.
- Correct a grocery store cashier who has scanned an item at the wrong price.
- Meet with a teacher who gave your son or daughter a failing grade.
- Ask your professor for a one-day extension on a paper that is due tomorrow.
- Ask someone for a donation to a worthy cause.
- Ask a professor for permission to get into a class that has reached its maximum enrollment.
- Accept an unappealing compact disc as a gift from a friend.
- Remind your son or daughter that he or she needs to practice the piano.

SKILL DEVELOPMENT
Procedure: This role-play invites partners to negotiate eight different real-life scenarios that have the potential to create tension. Have students play each situation twice, the first time being self-oriented and the second time being other-oriented.

Variations: Consider having some same-sex dyads and other mixed-sex dyads. Consider encouraging intercultural and interracial dyads as well. After the role-plays, discuss how other-orientation can assist us in cross-gender, interracial, and intercultural communication effectiveness.

Assign several dyads to "float" around the room and record examples of specific behaviors that communicate either self-focus or other-orientation. Have the floaters post the list on the board and lead the class in a discussion of verbal and nonverbal messages that communicate other-orientation or self-focus.

Share with students these words by John Luther: "Natural talent, intelligence, a wonderful education—none of these guarantees success. Something else is needed: the sensitivity to understand what other people want and the willingness to give it to them. Worldly success depends on pleasing others. No one is going to win fame, recognition, or advancement just because he or she thinks it's deserved. Someone else has to think so too." (From *Bits & Pieces,* The Economics Press, 1992, Vol M, No. 1.)

Becoming other-oriented also involves adapting to those who may be considerably different from you. Your communication partner may have a different cultural background, be of the opposite sex, or be older or younger than you. In Chapter 4 we will explore some of these differences, especially cultural differences, that can sometimes challenge effective and appropriate communication with others; we will also suggest specific strategies to help you adapt to others who are different from yourself.

Being other-oriented is more than just having a set of skills or behaviors. It also includes developing positive, healthy attitudes about others. In 1951, Carl Rogers wrote a pioneering book called *Client-Centered Therapy*, which transformed the field of psychotherapy. In it Rogers explains how genuine positive regard for another person and an open and supportive communication climate lay the foundation for trusting relationships. Rogers emphasizes the importance of listening in connection to another human being, which we will explore in depth in Chapter 5.

We gain insight about others' feelings by being sensitive to nonverbal messages as well as the explicit verbal statements they make. We will discuss verbal communication skills in Chapter 6 and nonverbal communication skills in Chapter 7. The skills and principles of managing conflict presented in Chapter 8 provide tools and ideas for understanding others when we disagree.

Chapters 9 and 10 build upon the principles of interpersonal relationships introduced in this chapter to help you understand how relationships evolve, are maintained, and sometimes end. The final chapter applies our discussion of other-oriented interpersonal communication to various contexts such as families, friends, and colleagues. Our goal is to help you both to better understand how you relate to others and to develop enhanced interpersonal skill.

RECAP	How Can You Improve Your Communication Effectiveness?
BE KNOWLEDGEABLE	Learn principles, concepts, and ideas.
BE SKILLED	Translate knowledge into action.
BE MOTIVATED	Resolve to use your knowledge and skill.
BE FLEXIBLE	Select the right behavior; one size does not fit all.
BE OTHER-ORIENTED	Focus on others rather than only on your needs.

Summary

Communication is the process of acting on information. Human communication is the process of making sense out of the world and sharing that sense with others. Interpersonal communication is the process of developing a unique relationship with another person by interacting simultaneously and sharing mutual influence. Early models viewed human communication as a simple message-transfer process. Later models evolved to view communication as interaction and then as transaction. Contemporary approaches to interpersonal communication emphasize the simultaneous nature of influencing others. They identify seven key components in the interpersonal communication process: source, receiver, message, channel, noise, context, and feedback. Electronic media may encourage further evolution of our models for interpersonal communication.

The goal of this book is to help you improve your interpersonal skills and relationships. Interpersonal relationships range from impersonal to intimate, are complementary or symmetrical, are governed by rules, and evolve in stages. The most effective interpersonal communicators are knowledgeable, skilled, motivated, flexible, and other-oriented. Learning to connect with others is the key to establishing satisfying relationships.

For Discussion and Review

■ FOCUS ON COMPREHENSION

1. Discuss key differences among the communication as action, interaction, and transaction models.

2. Define communication, human communication, and interpersonal communication. Discuss the differences among them.

3. Identify the characteristics of interpersonal relationships.

4. Explain how to improve your interpersonal communication.

■ FOCUS ON CRITICAL THINKING

5. Analyze a recent interpersonal exchange that did not go well. Write down some of the dialogue. Did the other person understand you? Did your communication have the intended effect? Was your message ethical?

INTERNET RESOURCES

Hot Link: Go to http://www.fww.org/mission.htm Families Worldwide promotes those values and strengths which develop happy and lasting family relationships, including communication.

FOCUS ON COMPREHENSION

1. Communication as action suggests that a message is merely transferred from one person to another. Communication as interaction incorporates the exchange of messages between people. Finally, communication as transaction recognizes the creation of messages in the episodic act of communicating.

2. Interpersonal communication is a specific type of human communication in which people interact simultaneously and share mutual influence.

3. Communication is inevitable whenever there is mutual awareness between people. Because communication is a transactional process, it cannot be undone or redone. Finally, interpersonal communication is complex and made up of symbols which are ambiguous and often difficult to interpret.

4. Interpersonal relationships are varied and affected by the complexity of communication. Relationships may be personal or impersonal, complementary or symmetrical, self-oriented or other-oriented. Relationships evolve in stages and are governed by norms; they are affected by context and the emphasis we place upon the meaning dimensions of messages.

DISCUSSION AND WRITING

Ask students to form buzz groups (3–5 people) and complete exercise #6, in the "Focus on Critical Thinking" section, at the end of this chapter. To minimize students' discomfort with disclosure, suggest that they refrain from using proper names and use more general terms, including classmate, dentist, cashier, mother, or neighbor. Following the exercise, note that our more intimate relationships require greater amounts of time and trust to develop and maintain.

DISCUSSION AND WRITING
Stress the importance of communication ethics in your class. Include this expectation in your syllabus. Ask students to form groups of 3–4 and ask them to discuss Question #9 in the "Focus on Ethics" section at the end of this chapter. After 10 minutes, discuss these answers with the whole class.

6. Make a relationship scale on a piece of paper and label it "impersonal" at one end and "intimate" at the other. Place your family members and closest friends on the scale; then compare and discuss your entries with your class-mates.

7. What rules govern your relationship with your mother? Your father? Your communication teacher? Your roommate or spouse?

■ FOCUS ON ETHICS

8. Think about your primary goal for this course. Is it to develop strategies to achieve your own personal goals? Is it to develop sensitivity to the needs of others? What is behind your desire to achieve your goal? Is your purpose ethical?

9. Your parents want you to visit them for the holidays. You would rather spend the time with a friend. You don't want to hurt your parents' feelings, so you tell them that you have an important project that you are working on; you won't be able to come home for the holidays. Your message is understood. It achieves the intended effect; you don't go home. Explain why you think your message is ethical or unethical.

For Your Journal

1. Try to identify at least three personal goals for improving your interpersonal relationships. Write several specific objectives that you hope to accomplish by the end of this course.

2. Briefly describe a recent communication exchange that was not effective. Perhaps you or your communication partner did not understand the message, or the message may not have achieved its intended goal, or it may have been unethical. Analyze the communication exchange, applying the components of communication discussed in this chapter. For example, what was the communication context? What were sources of internal and external noise? Did you have problems encoding and decoding? Were there problems with the communication channel?

3. Keep a one-day log of your electronically mediated interactions, such as phone calls, e-mail messages, fax messages. Describe each one, noting whether there was a greater emphasis on the content or emotional elements of the messages you exchanged during the interaction.

1. Working with a group of your classmates, develop a five-minute lesson to teach one of the following concepts to your class:

   A. Human communication as action

   B. Human communication as interaction

   C. Human communication as transaction

   D. Differences between complementary and symmetrical relationships

   E. How interpersonal relationships are governed by rules

   F. How interpersonal relationships range from impersonal to intimate

   G. How to improve communication effectiveness

2. Working with a group of your classmates, develop your own model of interpersonal communication. Include all of the components that are necessary to describe how communication between people works. Your model could be a drawing or an actual object (like a Slinky toy) that symbolizes the communication process. Share your model with the class, describing the decisions your group made in developing it. Illustrate your model with a conversation between two people, pointing out how elements of the conversation relate to the model.

■ GLOSSARY

COMMUNICATION: Process of acting upon information.

HUMAN COMMUNICATION: Process of making sense out of the world and attempting to share that sense with others.

INTERPERSONAL COMMUNICATION: Process of interacting simultaneously with another person and mutually influencing each other, usually for the purpose of managing relationships.

IMPERSONAL COMMUNICATION: Communication that occurs when we treat people as objects, or when we respond to their role rather than who they are as a unique person.

MASS COMMUNICATION: Type of communication that occurs when one person issues the same message to many people at once; the creator of the message is usually not present and there is virtually no opportunity for listeners to respond to the speaker.

MEDIA AND OUTSIDE RESOURCES

There is a fun board game called, "I Think, You Think, I Think" (M. Boggs and Co., 1988) which employs the IPM (metaperspectives) theory. It can be adapted to a class if you do away with the board and the competitive aspect of the game. The game is available through TSR Inc., P.O. Box 756, Lake Geneva, WI 53147.

PUBLIC COMMUNICATION: Type of communication that occurs when a speaker addresses a large audience in person.

SMALL GROUP COMMUNICATION: Type of communication that occurs when a group of from three to fifteen people meet to interact with a common purpose and mutually influence one another.

INTRAPERSONAL COMMUNICATION: Communication with yourself; thinking.

INFORMATION SOURCE: Thought or emotion that triggers communication.

SOURCE: Originator of a thought or emotion who puts it into a code that can be understood by a receiver.

ENCODE: To translate ideas, feelings, and thoughts into a code.

DECODE: To interpret ideas, feelings, and thoughts that have been translated into a code.

RECEIVER: Person who decodes a message and attempts to make sense out of what the source has encoded.

MESSAGE: Written, spoken, and unspoken elements of communication to which people assign meaning.

CHANNEL: Pathway through which messages are sent.

NOISE: Information, either literal or psychological, that interferes with the accurate reception of the communication of the message.

FEEDBACK: Response to a message.

CONTEXT: Physical and psychological communication environment.

EPISODE: Sequence of interaction between individuals during which the message of one person influences the message of another.

MEDIATED INTERPERSONAL RELATIONSHIP: Communication with others established or maintained by using media (such as e-mail, telephone, or a fax) rather than a face-to-face encounter.

INTERPERSONAL RELATIONSHIP: Connection we forge with another human being through interpersonal communication.

SYSTEM: A set of interconnected, interrelated elements in which the whole is greater than the sum of the parts.

SYMBOL: Representation of something else.

METACOMMUNICATION: Communication about communication; information in one communication channel provides information about another aspect of a message, such as when nonverbal expressions provide clues about the meaning of a spoken message.

ROLE: Set of expected behaviors that are associated with a person in a specific situation.

COMPLEMENTARY RELATIONSHIP: Relationship in which the partners' communication styles fit together in a compatible way, one willingly turning over power to the other (for example, one person likes to talk, the other person likes to listen).

SYMMETRICAL RELATIONSHIP: Relationship in which both partners behave in similar ways while striving for equal power when they communicate.

COMPETITIVE SYMMETRICAL RELATIONSHIP: Relationship in which each partner seeks to dominate and control the other (for example, both individuals like to talk and monopolize the conversation).

SUBMISSIVE SYMMETRICAL RELATIONSHIP: A relationship in which each partner strives to relinquish control (for example, each may try to convince the other person to make a decision about something that affects both people—such as which TV program to watch).

PARALLEL RELATIONSHIP: A relationship in which the partners are willing to shift power back and forth in accordance with the communication situation or interaction.

Communication and Self

After studying this chapter, you should be able to:

1. Define, compare, and contrast the meanings of self-concept and self-esteem.

2. Identify factors that shape the development of your self-concept.

3. Describe how your self-concept affects your relationships with others.

4. Identify the effects of your communication style on your relationships with others.

5. List and describe strategies for improving your self-esteem.

*There's only one corner of the universe
you can be certain of improving,
and that's your own self.*
— ALDOUS HUXLEY

Philosophers suggest that there are three basic questions to which we all
seek answers: (1) "Who am I?" (2) "Why am I here?" and (3) "Who are
all these others?" In this chapter we will focus on these essential questions
about the **self.** We view them as progressive. Grappling with the question
of who we are and seeking to define a purpose for our lives are essential
to understanding others and becoming other-oriented in our interpersonal
communication and our relationships.

Fundamentally, all of your communication starts or ends with you. When you
are the communicator, you intentionally or unintentionally code your thoughts
and emotions to be interpreted by another. When you receive a message, you
interpret the information through your own frame of reference. Your self-image
and self-worth, as well as your needs, values, beliefs, and attitudes, serve as
filters for your communication with others. As you develop and establish relationships, you may become more aware of these filters, and perhaps want to alter
them. A close relationship often provides the impetus for change.

To better understand the role that self-concept plays in interpersonal communication, we will explore the first two basic questions, "Who am I?" and "Why
am I here?" by trying to discover the meaning of self. We will examine the
multifaceted dimensions of our self-concept, learn how it develops, and compare
self-concept to self-esteem. Then we will move to the third basic question,
"Who are all these others?" We will discuss the effect of our self-concept on our
communication with others, focusing on how our individual communication
styles affect our interpersonal relationships.

Self-Concept: Who Are You?

You can begin your journey of self-discovery by doing the exercise in
Building Your Skills: Who Are You?

How did you answer the question, "Who are you?" Perhaps with activities
in which you participate, or groups and organizations to which you belong. You
may have listed some of the roles you assume, such as student, child, or parent.
All of these things are indeed a part of yourself, the sum total of who you are.
Psychologist Karen Horney defines self as "that central inner force, common to
all human beings and yet unique in each, which is the deep source of growth."[1]

37

Have students complete this exercise in class. Next, have students volunteer to introduce themselves by reading and explaining each "I am" statement. Have the class provide feedback as to which statement was the most surprising, and which was the least. The discussions that follow will naturally bridge the material from chapter two to chapter three dealing with perceptions.

INSTRUCTIONAL GOALS AND TIPS

Prepare a poster board with ten answers to the "Communication Experience" about you. Share this with your students. Be sure to include entries about the roles you assume, your affiliations, talents, aspirations, accomplishments, and emotions, as well as your Wilson communication style. Demonstrate how multifaceted you are. Include some weaknesses to demonstrate that you've balance and a healthy self-concept. (Don't focus solely upon work-related roles/accomplishments. If you are unwilling to disclose, your students will follow suit.)

DISCUSSION AND WRITING

Ask students to break into groups of 3–4. Take five minutes to individually complete the rankings for Exercise 1 in the "Learning with Others" section at the end of the chapter. Then ask students to spend 10–15 minutes discussing their rankings. Ask students to be mindful of allowing each member the opportunity to speak and to be listened to.

BUILDING YOUR SKILLS

Who Are You?

Consider this question: Who are you? More specifically, ask yourself this question ten times. Write your responses in the spaces provided here or on a separate piece of paper. It may be challenging to identify ten aspects of yourself. The Spanish writer Cervantes said, "To know thyself . . . is the most difficult lesson in the world." Your answers will help you begin to explore your self-concept and self-esteem in this chapter.

I am _____   I am _____

I am _____   I am _____

I am _____   I am _____

I am _____   I am _____

I am _____   I am _____

Your answers are also part of your **self-concept**. Your self-concept is your subjective description of who you *think* you are—it is filtered through your own perceptions. For example, you may have great musical talent, but you may not believe in it enough to think of yourself as a musician. We can view self-concept as the labels we consistently use to describe ourselves to others.

Who you are is also reflected in the attitudes, beliefs, and values that you hold. These are learned constructs that shape your behavior and self-image. An **attitude** is a learned predisposition to respond to a person, object, or idea in a favorable or unfavorable way. Attitudes reflect what you like and what you don't like. If you like school, butter pecan ice cream, and your mother, you hold positive attitudes toward these things. You were not born with a fondness for butter pecan ice cream; you learned to like it just as some people learn to enjoy the taste of snails, raw fish, or pureed turnips.

Beliefs are the way in which you structure your understanding of reality— what is true and what is false. Most of your beliefs are based on previous experience. You trust that the sun will rise in the morning and that you will get burned if you put your hand on a hot stove.

How are attitudes and beliefs related? They often function quite independently of each other. You may have a favorable attitude toward something and still believe negative things about it. You may believe, for example, that your school football team will not win the national championship this year, although you may be a big fan. Or you may believe that God exists, yet not always like what God does. Beliefs have to do with what is true or not true, while attitudes reflect likes and dislikes.

Values are enduring concepts of good and bad, right and wrong. Your values are more resistant to change than either your attitudes or your beliefs. They are also more difficult for most people to identify. Values are so central to who you are that it is difficult to isolate them. For example, when you go to the supermarket, you may spend a few minutes deciding on whether to buy regular or cream-style corn, but you probably do not spend much time deciding whether you will steal the corn or pay for it. Our values are instilled in us by our earliest interpersonal relationships; for almost all of us, our parents shape our values. The model in Figure 2.1 illustrates that values are central to our behavior and concept of self, and that what we believe to be true or false stems from our values. Attitudes are at the outer edge of the circle because they are the most likely to change. You may like your coworker today but not tomorrow, even though you *believe* the person will come to work every day and you still *value* the concept of friendship.

Figure 2.1

Values, Beliefs, and Attitudes in Relation to Self

RECAP	Who You Are Is Reflected in Your Attitudes, Beliefs, and Values		
	Definition	**Dimensions**	**Example**
ATTITUDES	Learned predispositions to respond favorably or unfavorably toward something.	Likes–Dislikes	You like ice cream, incense, and cats.
BELIEFS	The way in which we structure reality.	True–False	You believe your parents love you.
VALUES	Enduring concepts of what is right and wrong.	Good–Bad	You value honesty and truth.

One or Many Selves?

Shakespeare's famous line, "To thine own self be true," suggests that you have a single self to which you can be true. But do you have just one self? Or is there a more "real you" buried somewhere within? "I'm just not myself this morning," sighs Sandy, as she drags herself out the front door to head for her office. If she is not herself, then *who is she*? Most scholars conclude that we have a core set of behaviors, attitudes, beliefs, and values that constitutes our self—the sum total of who we are. But our *concept* of self can and does change, depending on circumstances and influences.

In addition, our self-concepts are often different from the way others see us. We almost always behave differently in public than we do in private. One sociologist suggests that, like actors and actresses, we have "on-stage" behaviors when others are watching and "backstage" behaviors when they are not.

INTERNET RESOURCES
http://www.yahoo.com/society_and_culture/religion/faiths_andpractices/Christianity/organizations/ Explore different religious, culture, sex, faith, and other topics of different value systems.

INTERNET RESOURCES
For interesting alternatives to "Family Values" See Gay and Lesbian Parents' Family Values http://www.angelfiere.con/co/GayFamilyValues/index.html

DISCUSSION AND WRITING
Distribute copies of a blank shield to each student. Ask them to follow the directions for Exercise 2 in the "Learning with Others" section at the end of this chapter. Next, ask students to work in groups of 3–4 and share their shields with one another. Ask students to record their thoughts about this exercise in their journals. What did they learn about themselves? What were some of the reactions they received from their classmates? Were there any surprises about one another's shields?

As this sculpture implies, each of us dons a series of masks for our "on stage" interactions with others throughout the day. (Sandra Rice)

Perhaps the most enduring and widely accepted framework for describing who you are was developed by the philosopher William James. He identified three components of the self: the material self, the social self, and the spiritual self. We will continue our exploration by examining these components.

■ THE MATERIAL SELF

Perhaps you've heard the statement, "You are what you eat." The **material self** goes a step further by suggesting, "You are what you have." The material self is a total of all of the tangible things you own: your body, your possessions, your home. As you examine your list of responses to the question, "Who are you?" note whether any of your statements refers to one of your physical attributes or something you own.

One element of the material self gets considerable attention in our culture: the body. Do you like the way you look? Most of us, if we're honest, would like to change something about our appearance. When there is a discrepancy between our desired material self and our self-concept, we may respond to eliminate the discrepancy. We may try to lose weight, change the shape of our nose, or acquire more hair. The multibillion-dollar diet industry is just one of many that profit from our collective desire to change our appearance.

We also attempt to keep up with the proverbial Joneses by wanting more expensive clothes, cars, and homes. By extension, what we own becomes who we are. The bigger, better, and more luxurious our possessions, we may subconsciously conclude, the better *we* are.

■ THE SOCIAL SELF

Look at your "Who are you?" list once more. How many of your responses relate to your **social self**, the part of you that interacts with others? William

James believed that you have many social selves—that depending on the friend, family member, colleague, or acquaintance with whom you are interacting, you change the way you are. A person has, said James, as many social selves as there are people who recognize him or her.

For example, when you talk to your best friend, you are willing to "let down your hair" and reveal more thoughts and feelings than you would in a conversation with your communication professor, or even your parents. Each relationship that you have with another person is unique because you bring to it a unique social self.

Peter Blake sought to explore his self-dimensions by painting his self-portrait. What qualities does this self-portrait reveal about the artist? (Tate Gallery, London/Art Resources)

■ THE SPIRITUAL SELF

Your **spiritual self** consists of all your internal thoughts and introspections about your values and moral standards. It is not dependent on what you own or with whom you talk; it is the essence of who you *think* you are, and of your *feelings* about yourself, apart from external evaluations. It is an amalgam of your religious beliefs and your sense of who you are in relationship to other forces in the universe. Your spiritual self is the part of you that answers the question, "Why am I here?"

RECAP	William James's Dimensions of Self	
	Definition	**Examples**
MATERIAL SELF	All of the physical elements that reflect who you are.	Body, clothes, car, home.
SOCIAL SELF	The self as reflected through your interactions with others; actually, a variety of selves that respond to changes in situations and roles.	Your informal self interacting with your best friend; your formal self interacting with your professors.
SPIRITUAL SELF	Introspections about values, morals, and beliefs.	Belief or disbelief in God; regard for life in all its forms.

The text authors suggest that the spiritual self is the part of you that answers the question, "Why am I here?" Ask students to formulate a response to this question. Difficulty responding can be addressed with discussion of whether they are centered: whether they already have a well-defined sense of self.

MEDIA AND OUTSIDE RESOURCES
There are a number of video clips which might be useful to use as launching pads for excellent discussions about the spiritual self. Consider showing Joe Pesci's discussion of the importance of dignity in *With Honors*, and the discussion of the meaning of life between actors Kevin Kline and Danny Glover at the gas station in *Grand Canyon*.

Ask students to complete the Building Your Skills activity on page 38 if they haven't already. Go around the room in a systematic way and ask students to select one "I am" statement to read to the class. Introduce James's categories and ask which was most commonly cited by the class and which was least disclosed. Which category is the easiest to hide? Which category is the most obvious? Which category is most central to each student? Next, have students reflect on which category is most central to their self-concept.

TEACHING STRATEGY

Tap your students' strengths. Majors in Psychology, Elementary Education, and Childhood Development usually are able to contribute illustrations of the importance of children's interactions with others in the development of their self-concepts.

RESEARCH AND LITERATURE

Consider Thomas Moore's words from *Care of the Soul: A Guide for Cultivating Depth and Sacredness in Everyday Life:* "We know we are well on the way toward soul when we feel attachment to the world and the people around us and when we live as much from the heart as from the head. Soul is interested in the differences among cultures and individuals, and within ourselves it wants to be expressed in uniqueness if not in outright eccentricity." (HarperCollins, 1992, pp. 304–305)

BUILDING YOUR SKILLS

Dimensions of Your Self

Take another look at your responses to the question "Who are you?" Divide your list according to James's description of self-concept as material, social, or spiritual self. If, for example, nothing on your original list relates to your spiritual self, make an entry here so that you have a response for each of the three "selves."

Material Self	Social Self	Spiritual Self
References to physical elements that reflect who you are.	References to interactions with others that reflect who you are.	References to your reflections about values, morals, and beliefs.
Example:		
I collect antiques.	I am a member of the Chess Club.	I believe the *Book of Mormon* is an inspired book.
_____	_____	_____
_____	_____	_____
_____	_____	_____
_____		
_____		

How Your Self-Concept Develops

James's three elements define the dimensions of the self, but they do not tell us where our "Who am I?" responses come from. In truth, we can only speculate about their origins. But some psychologists and sociologists have advanced theories that suggest we learn who we are through four basic means: (1) our interactions with other individuals, (2) our association with groups, (3) roles we assume, and (4) our own labels. Like James's framework, this one does not cover every base in our study of self, but its constructs can provide some clues about how our own self-concepts develop.

■ INTERACTION WITH INDIVIDUALS

In 1902, Charles Horton Cooley first advanced the notion that we form our self-concepts by seeing ourselves in a kind of figurative **looking glass:** We learn who we are by interacting with others, much as we look into a mirror and see our reflection. Like Cooley, George Herbert Mead also believed that our sense of who we are is a consequence of our relationship with others. And Harry Stack Sullivan theorized that from birth to death our self changes primarily because of how people respond to us. One sage noted, "We are not only our brother's keeper; we are our brother's maker."

The process begins at birth. Our names, one of the primary ways we identify ourselves, are given to us by someone else. During the early years of our lives, our parents are the key individuals who reflect who we are. If our parents encouraged us to play the piano, we probably play now. As we become less dependent on our parents, our friends become highly influential in shaping our

Being Other-Oriented in Other Cultures

How we view others is an extension of how we view ourselves. Most religions of the world emphasize a common spiritual theme known in Christianity as the Golden Rule: Do unto others what you would have others do unto you. This "rule" is the basis for most ethical codes throughout the world. This fundamental principle of other-orientation is expressed in similar ways among the world's people:

HINDUISM	This is the sum of duty: Do nothing to others which would cause pain if done to you.
BUDDHISM	One should seek for others the happiness one desires for one's self.
TAOISM	Regard your neighbor's gain as your own gain, and your neighbor's loss as your loss.
CONFUCIANISM	Is there one principle which ought to be acted upon throughout one's whole life? Surely it is the principle of loving-kindness: do not unto others what you would not have them do unto you.
ZOROASTRIANISM	The nature alone is good which refrains from doing unto another whatsoever is not good for itself.
JUDAISM	What is hateful to you, do not do to others. That is the entire law: all the rest is but commentary.
ISLAM	No one of you is a believer until he desires for his brother that which he desires for himself.
CHRISTIANITY	Do unto others what you would have others do unto you.

Adapted from: Wayne Ham, *Man's Living Religions* (Independence, MO: Herald Publishing House, 1966), 39–40.

attitudes, beliefs, and values. And friends continue to provide feedback on how well we perform certain tasks. This, in turn, helps us shape our sense of identity as adults—we must acknowledge our talents in math, language, or art in our own minds before we say that we are mathematicians, linguists, or artists.

Fortunately, not *every* comment affects our sense of who we think we are. We are likely to incorporate the comments of others into our self-concept under three conditions:

First, we are more likely to believe another's statement if he or she repeats something we have heard several times. If one person casually tells you that you have a good ear for singing, you are not likely to launch a search for an agent and a recording contract. But if several individuals tell you on many different occasions that you have a talent for singing, you may decide to do something about it.

Second, we are more likely to value another's statements if he or she has already earned our credibility. If we believe the individual is competent, trustworthy, and qualified to make a judgment about us, then we are more likely to believe it. You would be more likely to think you were a talented singer if you heard it from opera star Luciano Pavarotti rather than your Aunt Sally. Again, while we are very young, our parents are the dominant voices of credibility and authority. If they tell us repeatedly that we are spoiled and sloppy, then we will probably come

DISCUSSION AND WRITING
Ask students to gather into groups of 4–5 and to share their answers to the following question: Which would you prefer to be: popular, honorable, or wealthy?

to view ourselves that way. If they tell us we are loving, gifted, and charming, we are likely to believe it.

Third, we are likely to incorporate another's comments into our own concept of self if the comments are consistent with other comments and our own experience. If your boss tells you that you work too slowly, but for years people have been urging you to slow down, then your previous experience will probably encourage you to challenge your boss's evaluation.

■ ASSOCIATION WITH GROUPS

I'm a Democrat. I'm a Girl Scout. I'm a rabbi. I'm a coach. I'm a member of the Marching Mules Band. Each of these self-descriptive statements has something in common. Each one answers the "Who are you?" question by providing identification with a group or organization. Reflect once more on your responses to the "Who are you?" question. How many associate you with a group? Religious groups, political groups, ethnic groups, social groups, study groups, and occupational and professional groups play important roles in determining our self-concept. Some of these groups we are born into; others we choose on our own. Either way, these group associations are significant parts of our identities.

As we have already noted, peer pressure is a powerful force in shaping attitudes and behavior, and adolescents are particularly susceptible to it. But adolescents are not alone in allowing the attitudes, beliefs, and values of others to shape their expectations and behavior. Most adults, to varying degrees, ask themselves, "What will the neighbors think? What will my family think?" when they are making choices.

Associating with groups is especially important for people who are not part of the dominant culture. Gays and lesbians, for example, find the support provided by associating with other gays and lesbians to be beneficial to their well-being. The groups we associate with not only provide information about our identify but also provide needed social support.

■ ROLES YOU ASSUME

Look again at your answers to the "Who are you?" question. Perhaps you see words or phrases that signify a role you often assume. Father, aunt, sister, uncle, manager, salesperson, teacher, and student are labels that imply certain expectations for behavior, and they are important in shaping self-concept. Couples who live together before they marry often report that marriage alters their relationship. Before, they may have shared domestic duties such as doing dishes and laundry. But when they assume the labels of "husband" and "wife," they slip into traditional roles. Husbands don't do laundry. Wives don't mow the grass. These stereotypical role expectations that they learned long ago may require extensive discussion and negotiation. Couples who report the highest satisfaction with marriage have similar role expectations for themselves and their spouses.

One reason we assume traditional roles automatically is that our gender group asserts a powerful influence from birth on. As soon as parents know the sex of

their child, many begin placing their children in the group by following cultural rules. They paint the nursery pink for a girl, blue for a boy. Boys get a catcher's mitt, a train set, or a football for their birthdays; girls get dolls, frilly dresses, and tea sets. These cultural conventions and expectations play a major role in shaping our self-concept and our behavior. We describe male babies as strong, solid, and independent; little girls are cute, cuddly, and sweet.[2] Recent research suggests that up until the age of three, children themselves are not acutely aware of sex roles. Between the ages of three and five, however, masculine and feminine roles begin to emerge,[3] and they are usually solidified between the ages of five and seven.

Although it is changing, American culture is still male-dominated. What we consider appropriate and inappropriate behavior is often different for males than it is for females. For example, in group and team meetings, task-oriented, male-dominated roles are valued more than feminine, relationship-building roles.[4] We applaud fathers who work sixty hours a week as "diligent and hard-working," but criticize mothers who do the same as "neglectful and selfish." The list "Stereotypical Labels for Males and Females" illustrates more of these contrasts.

Although our culture defines certain roles as masculine or feminine, we still exercise individual choices about our gender roles. One researcher developed an inventory designed to assess whether we play traditional masculine, feminine, or androgynous roles.[5] Because an **androgynous** role is both masculine and feminine, this role encompasses a greater repertoire of actions and behaviors.

■ SELF-LABELS

Although our self-concept is deeply affected by others, we are not blank slates for them to write on. The labels we use to describe our own attitudes, beliefs, values, and actions also play a role in shaping our self-concept.

DISCUSSION AND WRITING
Ask students to comment upon the following statement by Robert Anthony: "We move towards what we picture in our mind."

From where do we acquire our labels? We interpret what we experience; we are self-reflexive. **Self-reflexiveness** is the human ability to think about what we are doing while we are doing it. We talk to ourselves about ourselves. We are both participants and observers in all that we do. This dual role encourages us to use labels to describe who we are.

When you were younger, perhaps you dreamed of becoming an all-star basketball player or a movie star. Your coach may have told you that you were a great player or a terrific actor, but as you matured, you probably began observing yourself more critically. You scored no points; you did not get the starring role in the local production of *Annie*. So you self-reflexively decided that you were not, deep down, a basketball player or an actor, even though others may have labeled you as "talented." But sometimes, through this self-observation, we discover strengths which encourage us to assume new labels. One woman we know never thought of herself as "heroic" until she went through seventy-two hours of labor before giving birth and then nursed her baby right after delivery.

Self-Esteem: Your Self-Worth

Your **self-esteem** is closely related to your self-concept. Through your self-concept you *describe* who you are. Through your self-esteem, you *evaluate* who you are. The term **self-worth** is often used interchangeably with *self-esteem*. We derive our sense of self-worth from comparing ourselves to others, a process

RESEARCH AND LITERATURE
For more practical application of life positions, read Jess Lair's *I Ain't Much, Baby, But I'm All I've Got* (Fawcett Crest, 1969) or *Ain't I a Wonder . . . And Ain't You a Wonder Too!* (Fawcett Crest, 1976).

FRANK & ERNEST reprinted by permission of NEWSPAPER ENTERPRISE ASSOCIATION, INC.

LOW SELF-ESTEEM CLINIC

COME ON IN—IT'S OKAY, REALLY

www.frankandearnest.com
E-mail: FandEBobT@AOL.COM

THAVES 7-7

called **social comparison.** I'm good at playing soccer (because I beat others); I can't cook (because others cook better than I do); I'm not good at meeting people (most people I know seem to be more comfortable interacting with others); I'm not handy (but my brothers and sisters can fix a leaky faucet). Each of these statements implies a judgment about how well or badly you can perform certain tasks, with implied references to how well others perform the same tasks. A belief that you cannot fix a leaky faucet or cook like a chef may not in itself lower your self-esteem. But if there are *several* things you can't do well, or *many* important tasks that you cannot seem to master, these shortcomings may begin to color your overall sense of worth.

One of the powerful ways our self concept is formed is by comparing ourself to others. This process of **social comparison** helps us measure how well we think we are doing compared to others. You are more likely to compare yourself to your friends and neighbors, people you know and who are similar to you in many ways, than to people who are obviously not like you. You don't expect to be as wealthy as Microsoft Chairman Bill Gates so you don't compare your income to his. You might, however, compare how much you make at your job with the incomes of others who have similar positions. Our sense of self-worth stems from the conclusions we draw from such comparisons. Perhaps you thought your B+ on your algebra exam was a good score until you found out that over 80 percent of the class got an A on the test. How you think your abilities and resources stack up compared to others influences your sense of both who you are and your worth or value.

In the 1960s psychologist Eric Berne developed the concept of a **life position** to describe our overall sense of our own worth and that of others.[6] He identified four life positions: (1) "I'm OK, you're OK," or positive regard for self and others; (2) "I'm OK, you're not OK," or positive regard for self and low regard for others; (3) "I'm not OK, you're OK," or low self-regard and positive regard for others; and (4) "I'm not OK, you're not OK," or low regard for both self and others. Your life position is a driving force in your relationships with others. People in the "I'm OK, you're OK" position have the best chance for healthy relationships because they have discovered their own talents and also recognize that others have been given talents different from their own.

TEACHING STRATEGY
Ask students to describe typical communication behaviors for someone of low self-esteem. You might enhance their brainstorming by sharing and discussing the following passage from J. P. Hewitt (1991, *Self & Society: A Symbolic Interactionist Social Psychology (5th ed.),* Boston, MA: Allyn and Bacon).

Anxiety is an important motivational state. As a derivative of low self-esteem, it sensitizes the individual to others in a particularly painful way, making the person more vulnerable to the negative judgments of others as they verbalize them and more likely to see others in positive ways and to judge self negatively. Indeed, a vicious cycle can be found: the person approaches contact with others with a high level of anxiety; he or she is likely to be more vulnerable to their criticism and to make condemnations of self; and thus each social encounter produces an incremental reduction in overall self-esteem. (p. 143)

Show a clip from the movie
Rudy, in which Rudy defies
his coaches, family, and
friends' feedback to prove
himself worthy of playing
for Notre Dame's football
team. Next, discuss the
issue of anorexia nervosa
and how victims of this disease worry that they are fat
despite obvious starvation.
Ask students to write for
five minutes about the importance of agreement be-
tween the "I" and "Me"
perspectives.

**INSTRUCTIONAL GOALS
AND TIPS**

When gesturing to illustrate
a movement from left to
right, or from beginning
to end, try to get into the
habit of gesturing from
right to left so that your
audience sees it from their
perspective.

How Self-Concept and Self-Esteem
Affect Interpersonal Communication and Relationships

Your self-concept and self-esteem act as filters in every interaction with others. They determine how you approach, respond to, and interpret messages. Specifically, your self-concept and self-esteem affect your ability to be sensitive to others, your self-fulfilling prophecies, your interpretation of messages, and your typical communication style.

Self and Others

We have suggested the importance of becoming other-oriented—being sensitive to the thoughts and feelings of others—as a requisite for developing quality interpersonal relationships with others.

To become other-oriented involves recognizing that your "self" is different from others. As the Peanuts cartoon reminds us, the world does not revolve around our solitary selves. Others influence our actions and our self-image. George Herbert Mead suggests that we develop an "I," which is based upon our own perspective of ourselves, and a "Me," which is an image of ourselves based upon the collective responses we receive and interpret from others. Being aware of how your concept of self ("I") differs from the perceptions others have of you ("Me") is an important first step in developing an other-orientation.

When we begin the decentering process, we often interpret our assumptions about others using our own selves as a frame of reference, especially if we do not know the other person well.[7] For example, if you are nervous and frightened when you have to take a test, you might assume that your friend will react the same way. You may need to remind yourself that the other person is separate from you and has a different set of responses.

When you use a **specific-other perspective,** you rely on information that you have observed or that you can imagine about a particular person to predict his or her reactions. For example, if you know firsthand that your sister hates to have someone eat off her plate during dinner, you may use that experience to conclude that she would dislike sharing a bag of popcorn at the movies.

Sometimes a **generalized-other perspective** will be more useful. When you think about and respond to others, you can apply knowledge and personal theories that you have about people in general or about specific subgroups to the person with whom you are interacting. For example, you might think that your economics professor, who holds a Ph.D., would prefer to be addressed as *Doctor* rather than as *Mister* because almost all of your other professors with doctorates prefer to be called *Doctor.*

Your ability to predict how others will respond to you is based upon your ability to understand how your sense of the world is similar to, and different from, their own. First you must know yourself well. Then you can know and

INTERPERSONAL COMMUNICATION FOUNDATIONS

PEANUTS reprinted by permission of
UFS Inc.

understand others. One of the best ways to improve your ability to be other-oriented is to notice how others respond when you act on the predictions and assumptions you have made about them. You may discover that you have not moved out of your own frame of reference enough to make an accurate prediction about another person.

Self-Fulfilling Prophecy

While you are considering whether a person's behavior matches the predictions that you make about him or her, it is also important to remember that people interpret messages in ways that confirm what they already think of themselves. For example, suppose you think of yourself as an overly controlling person. If your brother surprises you by agreeing to lend you the twenty dollars you asked him for, you may feel guilty and wonder if he is just giving in to your bullying, instead of assuming that he is expressing affection for you. This extends into the realm of action as well. What we believe about ourselves often comes true because we expect it to come true. We refer to this as **self-fulfilling prophecy**. If you think you will fail the math quiz because you have labeled yourself inept at math, then you must overcome not only your math deficiency, but also your low expectations of yourself. As

As professor Henry Higgins said about Eliza Doolittle, "If you treat a girl like a flower girl, that's all she will ever be. If you treat her like a princess she may be one." (Shooting Star)

ACTIVITY
See Activity 2.1 in the Instructor's
Guide.

TEACHING STRATEGY
To illustrate self-fulfilling prophecy, ask students to describe how they feel about the probability of their success in a course when an instructor begins the semester with an introduction like the following one:

> I do not believe in "A" work. There is no such thing as a perfect paper. Look to your right; look to your left; one of those two people will not be here by the end of the semester. My job is to weed out those of you who do not really belong here.

INTERNET RESOURCE
Can self-fulfilling prophecy make you a better painter? See site: www.artsbusiness. com/banktwentysix.html

INTERNET RESOURCE
Pygmalion Effect
http://www.okstate.edu/osu. ag/agedcm4h/academic/ aged3103/reinforce/tsld001. htm
Download a slide presentation on the how's and why's of reinforcing positive behavior.

Professor Henry Higgins argues in George Bernard Shaw's *Pygmalion*, "If you treat a girl like a flower girl, that's all she will ever be. If you treat her like a princess, she may be one." Your attitudes, beliefs, and general expectations about your performance have a powerful and profound effect on your behavior.

The medical profession is learning the power that our attitudes and expectations have over healing. Dr. Bernard Siegel, in his book *Love, Medicine, and Miracles*,[8] provides convincing evidence that patient attitudes about the healing process have a direct effect upon their recovery. Patients who have a positive, cooperative spirit are more likely to recover from illness more quickly than those who assume the worst. As the article "Don't Worry, Be Happy" illustrates, your state of mind may influence your state of health.

Don't Worry, Be Happy: Study Shows Optimism Helps Fight Heart Disease

BOSTON—A healthy outlook helps heal the heart, scientists say in a study that found pessimism can be a killer.

The study identified optimism as a powerful predictor of who will live and who will die after the diagnosis of heart disease. It is the most recent in a series of recent reports showing that people's emotions and friendships play a critical role in recovery.

"Optimism is a good thing," Dr. Daniel Mark said. "When people give up and feel they are not going to make it, it's usually a self-fulfilling prophecy."

Mark, a heart specialist at Duke University, based his findings on a follow-up on 1,719 men and women who had undergone heart catheterization, a common procedure used to check the arteries for clogging. He outlined the results at a meeting of the Society of Behavioral Medicine in Rockville, Maryland.

The patients typically underwent the test because of chest pain, and all had heart disease. When interviewed, 14 percent said they doubted they would recover enough to resume their daily routines. After one year, 12 percent of these pessimists had died, compared with 5 percent of those who were optimistic about getting better.

Even when the severity of people's conditions was taken into account, outlook was a crucial factor in survival. In fact, optimism often seemed to have little bearing on how sick people were. In his study, pessimism appeared to be even more damaging to recovery than depression, which is also shown to be bad for heart patients.

Dr. Nancy Frasure-Smith of the Montreal Heart Institute presented follow-up data on the effect of negative emotions on 222 patients, most of them in their sixties, who were recovering from heart attacks.

They were given a psychological test that measures feelings of sadness and depression. Those who scored high on this were eight times more likely than more upbeat folks to die during the following eighteen months. Feeling anxious tripled the risk, as did holding in anger.

TEACHING STRATEGY

Review the article excerpt "Don't Worry, Be Happy" from chapter two. The claim is that positive emotions decrease the likelihood of a fatal heart attack. Ask students to work in groups and develop a list of "positive emotional states" and another list of "ways to create positive emotional states" based upon their own experiences. Have each group report to the class and combine ideas on the board.

Less clear, however, is what to do about these black moods in heart patients.

"We don't know how to change negative emotions," Frasure-Smith said. "And if we try to intervene, we don't know if we will change the prognosis."

How emotions harm the heart is unclear. Heart attacks usually occur when a bit of fatty buildup, called plaque, breaks in a heart artery. A blood clot sticks to this wound, plugging the artery and choking off the heart's oxygen supply. Researchers speculate that emotions may increase levels of hormones that put strain on the artery walls or make the blood more likely to clot.

—DANIE Q. HANEY

Cox News Service. Reprinted by permission.

Self and Interpretation of Messages

Do you remember Eeyore, the donkey friend of Winnie-the-Pooh and his friends? Eeyore lived in the gloomiest part of the Hundred Acre Wood and had a self-image to match. In one story all of the animals congregate on a stormy night to check on Eeyore:

> . . . they all came to the part of the forest known as Eeyore's gloomy place. On this stormy night it was terribly gloomy indeed—or it would have been were it not for Christopher Robin. He was there with a big umbrella.
> "I've invited Eeyore to come and stay with me until the storm is over," said Christopher Robin.
> "If it ever is," said Eeyore, "which doesn't seem likely. Not that anybody asked me, you understand. But then, they hardly ever do."[9]

Perhaps you know or have known an Eeyore—someone whose low self-esteem colors how he or she interprets messages and interacts with others. According to research, such people are more likely to have the following traits:[10]

- Be more sensitive to criticism and negative feedback from others.
- Be more critical of others.
- Believe they are not popular or respected by others.
- Expect to be rejected by others.
- Prefer not to be observed when performing.
- Feel threatened by people who they feel are superior.
- Expect to lose when competing with others.
- Be overly responsive to praise and compliments.
- Evaluate their overall behavior as inferior to that of others.

The Pooh stories offer an antidote to Eeyore's gloom in the character of the optimistic Tigger, who assumes that everyone shares his exuberance for life:

> . . . when Owl reached Piglet's house, Tigger was there. He was bouncing on his tail, as Tiggers do, and shouting to Piglet. "Come on," he cried. "You can do it! It's fun!"[11]

If, like Tigger, your sense of self-worth is high, research suggests you will

- Have higher expectations for solving problems.
- Think more highly of others.
- Be more likely to accept praise and accolades from others without feeling embarrassed.
- Be more comfortable having others observe you when you perform.
- Be more likely to admit you have both strengths and weaknesses.
- Prefer to interact with others who view themselves as highly competent.
- Expect other people to accept you for who you are.
- Be more likely to seek opportunities to improve skills that need improving.
- Evaluate your overall behavior more positively than would people with lower self-esteem.[12]

Reflecting the assumption that our self-concept influences our behavior is the principle of **selective exposure**, which suggests that we tend to place ourselves in situations consistent with who we think we are. Whom do you usually find at a Baptist church on Sunday morning? Baptists. Who are the attendees at a Democratic convention? Democrats. If you view yourself as a good student who wants an A in the class, where are you likely to be during class time? We behave in ways that reinforce our perception of self, both in our interpretation of messages and in our behavior.

Self and Interpersonal Needs

According to social psychologist Will Schutz, our concept of who we are, coupled with our need to interact with others, profoundly influences how we communicate with others. Schutz identifies three primary social needs that affect the degree of communication we have with others: the need for inclusion, the need for control, and the need for affection.[13] The **need for inclusion** suggests that each of us has a need to be included in the activities of others. We all need human contact and fellowship. We need to be invited to join others, and perhaps we need to invite others to join us. Of course, the level and intensity of this need differs from person to person, but even loners desire some social contact. Our need to include others and be included in activities may stem, in part, from our concept of ourselves as either a "party person" or a loner.

The second need, the **need for control**, suggests that we also need some degree of influence over the relationships we establish with others. We may also have a need to be controlled because we desire some level of stability and comfort in our interactions with others. If we view ourselves as people who are comfortable being in charge, we are more likely to give orders to others rather than take orders from them.

And finally, we each have a **need for affection**. We need to give and receive love, support, warmth, and intimacy, although the amounts we need vary enormously from person to person. If we have a high need for affection, we will more likely place ourselves in situations where that need can be met. The greater our inclusion, control, and affection needs are, the more likely it is that we will actively seek others as friends and initiate communication with them.

Self and Communication Style

Our self-concept and self-esteem affect not only the way we feel about ourselves, the way we interpret messages, and our personal performance; they also influence the way we *deliver* messages and treat other people. Each of us has a **communication style** or **social style** that is identifiable by the habitual ways in which we behave toward others. The style we adopt helps others interpret our messages. As they get to know us, other people begin to expect us to behave in a certain way, based on previous associations with us.

The Wilson Learning Corporation classifies our communication styles by the degree to which we display assertive and responsive behaviors.[14] **Assertiveness** refers to efforts to control others and direct their behavior. Tell-assertive individuals tend to tell others what to do; ask-assertive people are more likely to ask for directions or information. **Responsiveness** refers to our efforts to place the feelings of others above our own. A people-responsive individual is more other-oriented and emotionally expressive. A task-responsive person (responsive more to the task than to people) is less emotional and more reserved in communicating with others.

Figure 2.2 illustrates a grid of four basic social styles. Each of the four styles—driver, expressive, amiable, and analytical—is based on a different combination of assertiveness and responsiveness. **Drivers** are highly assertive and less responsive to others. **Analyticals** are low on both assertive and responsive behaviors. **Expressives** are both highly assertive as well as responsive. **Amiables** are responsive to others but less assertive. Let's take a closer look at each of these four social styles.

Because Drivers are highly assertive but less responsive, they tend to be more aloof, cool, abrupt, and highly task-oriented; they control their emotions and even design their living space to focus on work and accomplishment, displaying awards and plaques that symbolize achievement. They strive for efficiency. When you visit a Driver's office, you will probably sit across from the Driver, with a desk or table between you, rather than face-to-face without a barrier.

Analyticals, low on both assertiveness and responsiveness behaviors, tend to be highly task-oriented and focus on the job to be done rather than on relationships. Analyticals like structures and systems, so their offices and homes may have lots of cubbyholes and be highly organized. Analyticals are more comfortable accomplishing tasks than working with others.

WEB ACTIVITY

Personality Tests   Have students assess their personality types on-line. Taking personality tests can be interesting, enlightening, and fun. There are many available on the web and here are some locations:

http://www.freshy.com/personality/index.shtml/

http://www.yahoo.com/science/psychology/

http://www.yahoo.com/science/psychology/teset_and_experiments/

http://www.users.dircon.co.uk/~sandi/

http://www.platinumrule.com

http://www.scientology.org/oca.htm

http://www.ns.net/cash/selftestselftest.html

http://www.uscu.colorado.edu/~doyler/psych.html

http://www.goofiness.com/personality.phtml

http://www.occpsy.demon.co.uk/test.htm

http://admin.acadiv.ca/counsel/testing.htm

Ask students to develop role-play demonstrations of interactions between two people with low self-esteem and then between two people with high self-esteem. Using Wilson's terms, ask the audience to comment upon the portrayed communication styles.

The training video *How to Deal with Difficult People,* narrated by Rick Kirschner and Rick Brinkman, describes and illustrates these four communication styles. It also provides some tips on how to improve communication, including some related to pacing, and to developing an other-orientation. This video is available from Career Track Publications.

Figure 2.2

Four Primary Communication Styles
(Copyright 1982 by Wilson Learning Corporation)

Task–Unresponsive to Others
· Reserved, unresponsive.
· Wants facts and details.
· Eyes serious.
· Limited gestures.
· Limited exposure of personal feelings, story-telling, or small talk.
· Preoccupied or vigilant.

Ask–Unassertive
· Little use of voice to express ideas.
· Deliberate, studied, or slow in speech.
· Indifferent handshake.
· Asks questions more often than makes statements.
· Vague about what is wanted.
· Tends to lean backwards.

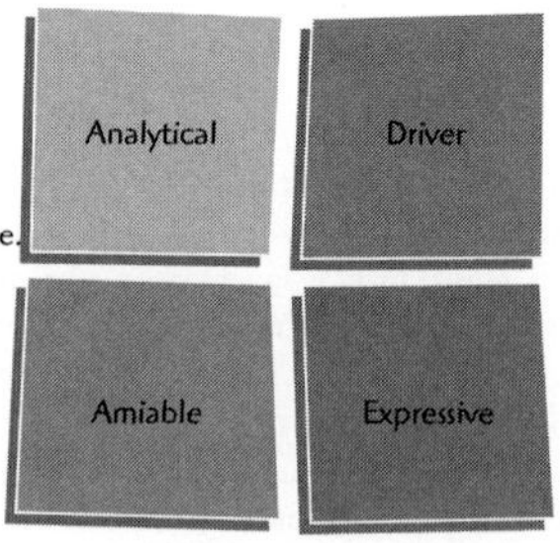

Tell–Assertive
· Emphasizes ideas by tone change.
· Quick, clear, or fast paced.
· Firm handshake.
· Makes statements more often than asks questions.
· Lets others know what is wanted.

Analytical | Driver

Amiable | Expressive

People–Responsive to Others
· Animated, uses facial expressions.
· Actions open or eager.
· Little effort to push for facts.
· Friendly gaze.
· Varied gestures.
· Shares personal feelings.
· Attentive, responsive, enjoys the relationship.

The Expressive social style is characterized by people who are both assertive and responsive toward others. While they often feel a need to control relationships, they may also be emotive and impulsive. Expressives tell and/or show others how they feel. Their offices and homes may be more disheveled and disorganized than a driver's. Expressives may communicate their feelings with signs, slogans, and bumper stickers. Expressives, like Drivers, want to get the job done, but they go about it in a more emotional way.

Amiables are the most responsive and emotive toward others, but the least assertive. They are more concerned with relationships than work; they want to meet people's social needs. They have high needs for inclusion and affection. Their goal is to make others feel welcome and comfortable. Amiables are likely to converse with others while seated at a round table or in chairs without a table; they don't like barriers between people.

According to the Wilson learning model, each of us has a predominant communication style, and we tend to interact most effectively with others who have a similar style. But we also have a **backup communication style** that we may

What's Your Communication Style?

1. Determine your communication style using the Wilson Learning Corporation model. For each of the scales below, place an X on the scale nearest the description that best fits you.

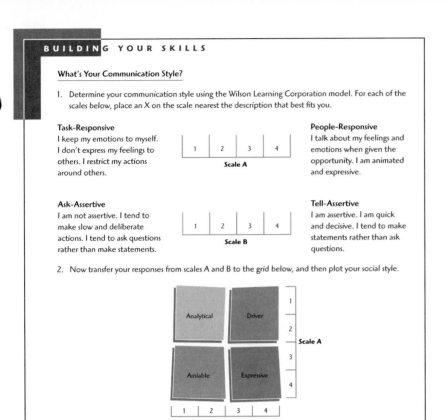

Task-Responsive
I keep my emotions to myself. I don't express my feelings to others. I restrict my actions around others.

| 1 | 2 | 3 | 4 |
Scale A

People-Responsive
I talk about my feelings and emotions when given the opportunity. I am animated and expressive.

Ask-Assertive
I am not assertive. I tend to make slow and deliberate actions. I tend to ask questions rather than make statements.

| 1 | 2 | 3 | 4 |
Scale B

Tell-Assertive
I am assertive. I am quick and decisive. I tend to make statements rather than ask questions.

2. Now transfer your responses from scales A and B to the grid below, and then plot your social style.

Analytical   Driver
Scale A
1
2
3
4
Amiable   Expressive
| 1 | 2 | 3 | 4 |
Scale B

use under stress if our primary style does not achieve the desired results. Under pressure, an amiable may become more assertive and move toward an expressive style. If a driver is unsuccessful in directing others, he or she may become less assertive and move closer to an analytical style. Cultivating this kind of flexibility in responding to others can enhance the effectiveness of communication.

The Wilson communication style model helps us see how our interaction with others is based on learned assumptions that are closely tied to our self-concept and self-esteem. Recognizing the styles that you and others use will help you adapt your messages to others. We are not suggesting that you should, or even that you *can,* completely forsake the style that comes naturally to you. You can, however, develop flexibility and sensitivity to feedback, using it to enhance your self-concept and learn more about your own behavior.[15]

Have students complete this activity and then form four groups based upon each of the four social styles. Next, ask each group to generate lists of adjectives describing their group (happy, bossy, insightful, etc.) Give the groups a problem or puzzle to solve. Upon completion by all groups, have each group explain how they communicated to complete the task. See whether the admitted style matches the group's defining communication style. Discuss how these style traits transcend all aspects of communication life, including intrapersonal, interpersonal, group, public, and mass communication contexts.

**How Self-Concept and Self-Esteem Affect
Interpersonal Communication and Relationships**

	Definition	Examples
MESSAGE INTERPRETATION AND INTERACTION	Feelings of high or low self-esteem affect how you understand and react to messages.	If you have high self-esteem, you are more likely to accept praise without embarrassment.
SELF-FULFILLING PROPHECY	What you believe about yourself will come true because you expect it to come true.	You expect to have a rotten time at a party so you behave in ways that guarantee you won't enjoy the party.
COMMUNICATION STYLE	Your self-concept and self-esteem contribute to habitual ways of responding to others.	Your image of yourself influences your responsive or assertive behavior toward others.

There are several songs that emphasize the need for high self-esteem. Consider playing Whitney Houston's "Greatest Love of All" or show a clip from "Mister Roger's Neighborhood," "Barney and Friends," or "Sesame Street." These television shows focus on the uniqueness and value of each viewer.

TEACHING STRATEGY

Any segment of the popular movie *Forrest Gump* complements Chapter 2. Gump—a man with very real handicaps—continuously engages in positive visualization and self-talk and maintains high self-esteem.

Improving Your Self-Esteem

We have already seen how low self-esteem can affect our own communication and interactions. In recent years teachers, psychologists, ministers, rabbis, social workers, and even politicians have suggested that many of our societal problems as well stem from our collective feelings of low self-esteem. Our feelings of low self-worth may contribute to our choosing the wrong partners, to becoming dependent on drugs, alcohol, or other substances, and to experiencing problems with eating and other vital activities. So we owe it to society, as well as ourselves, to maintain or develop a healthy sense of self-esteem.

While no simple list of tricks can easily transform low self-esteem into feelings of being valued and appreciated, you can make improvements in the ways you think about yourself and interact with others. We'll explore seven proven techniques that have helped others.

Self-Talk

Intrapersonal communication is communication within yourself—self-talk. Your level of self-esteem influences the way you talk to yourself about your abilities and skills. Perhaps you remember the children's story, *The Little Engine That Could*, in which the pint-sized hero repeated, "I think I can. I think I can," to overcome a seemingly impossible challenge. Although becoming your own cheerleader may not enable you to climb your own metaphorical mountains quite so easily, there is evidence that self-talk, both positive and negative, does in fact influence behavior. Realistic, positive self-talk can have a reassuring effect upon your level of self-worth and therefore your interactions with others. Conversely, repeating negative messages about your lack of skill and ability can keep you from trying and achieving.

For example, imagine that you have a biology test coming up. If you are not optimistic about your performance on the test, you may be tempted to let your self-fulfilling prophecy come true by not studying. But by reminding yourself (talking to yourself) about the importance of study and effort, you may be able to change your defeatist outlook. If you tell yourself, "I won't fail if I study," or "If I seek help from the teacher and spend more time on biology, I can be successful," you may motivate yourself to improve your performance. Improved performance can enhance your confidence and self-worth. Of course, blind faith without hard work won't succeed. Self-talk is not a substitute for effort; it can, however, keep you on track and help you ultimately to achieve your goal.

Visualization

Visualization takes the notion of self-talk one step further. Besides just telling yourself that you can achieve your goal, you can actually try to "see" yourself conversing effectively with others, performing well on a project, or exhibiting some other desirable behavior. Recent research suggests that an apprehensive public speaker can manage his or her fears not only by developing skill in public speaking, but also by visualizing positive results when speaking to an audience. If you are one of the many people who fears speaking in public, try visualizing yourself walking to the lectern, taking out your well-prepared notes, and delivering an interesting, well-received speech. This visualization of positive results enhances confidence and speaking skill. The same technique can be used to boost your sense of self-worth about other tasks or skills. Visualizing yourself performing well can yield positive results in changing long-standing feelings of inadequacy. Of course, your visualization should be realistic and coupled with a plan to achieve your goal.

DISCUSSION AND WRITING
If you have athletes in the class, ask them to relate their experiences of using positive imagery/visualization in their training regimes. There are a number of books and tapes on this topic as well.

MEDIA AND OUTSIDE RESOURCES

Having Our Say is a delightful book to read. You'll probably find several other excerpts from this book which effectively illustrate concepts for this course. An audiotape is available as well.

Avoiding Comparisons

Even before we were born, we were compared with others. The latest medical technology lets us see sonograms of fetuses still in the womb, so parents may begin comparing children with other babies before birth. For the rest of our lives we are compared with others, and rather than celebrating our uniqueness, comparisons usually point up who is bigger, brighter, and more beautiful. Many of us have had the experience of being chosen last to play on a sports team, passed over for promotion, or standing unchosen against the wall at a dance.

In North American culture we may be tempted to judge our self-worth by our material possessions and personal appearance. If we know someone who has a newer car (or simply a car, if we rely on public transportation), a smaller waistline, or a higher grade point average, we may feel diminished. Comparisons such as, "He has more money than I have," or "She looks better than I look," are likely to deflate our self-worth. Centenarians Sadie and Bessie Delaney, sisters who endured racial prejudice, inspired many by their refusal to let what they didn't have deter their sense of personal accomplishment. In their bestseller, *Having Our Say*, these two family matriarchs write of the value of emphasizing what we have, rather than comparing our lack of resources with the abundance of others who have more.

Rather than finding others who seemingly are better off, focus on the unique attributes that make you who you are. Avoid judging your own value in comparison to that of others. A healthy, positive self-concept is fueled not by judgments of others, but by a genuine sense of worth that we recognize in ourselves.

Reframing

Reframing is the process of redefining events and experiences from a different point of view. Just as reframing a work of art can give the picture a whole new look, reframing events that cause us to devalue our self-worth can change our perspective. Research suggests that in times of family stress, individuals who are able to engage in self-talk and describe the event from someone else's perspective manage stress more successfully. For example, if you get a report from your supervisor that says you should improve one area of your performance, instead of listening to the self-talk that says you're bad at your job, reframe the event within a larger context: tell yourself that one negative comment does not mean you are hopeless as a worker.

Of course, all negative experiences should not be lightly tossed off and left unexamined, because you can learn and profit from your mistakes. But it is important to remember that our worth as human beings is not contingent on a single letter grade, a single response from a prospective employer, or a single play in a football game. Looking at the big picture—what effect this small event will have on your whole life, on society, on history—places negative experiences that we all have in a realistic context. The reading that follows is a good reminder to maintain this longer perspective.

Einstein was four years old before he could speak and seven before he could read. Isaac Newton did poorly in grade school, and Beethoven's music teacher once said of him, "As a composer he is hopeless." When Thomas Edison was a boy, his teachers told him he was too stupid to learn anything. F. W. Woolworth got a job in a dry goods store when he was twenty-one, but his employers would not let him wait on a customer because he "didn't have enough sense." A newspaper editor fired Walt Disney because he had "no good ideas." Caruso's music teacher told him, "You can't sing. You have no voice at all." The director of the Imperial Opera in Vienna told Madame Schuman-Heink that she would never be a singer and advised her to buy a sewing machine. Leo Tolstoy flunked out of college; Wernher von Braun flunked ninth-grade algebra. Admiral Richard E. Byrd had been retired from the Navy as "unfit for service" until he flew over both Poles. Louis Pasteur was rated as "mediocre" in chemistry when he attended the Royal College. Abraham Lincoln entered the Black Hawk War as a captain and came out as a private. Louisa May Alcott was told by an editor that she could never write anything that had popular appeal. Fred Waring was once rejected for high school chorus. Winston Churchill failed the sixth grade.

From Milton E. Larson, "Humbling Cases for Career Counselors," *Phi Delta Kappan* 54, no. 6 (February 1973): 374.

Developing Honest Relationships

Having at least one other person who can help you objectively and honestly reflect on your virtues and vices can be extremely beneficial in fostering a healthy, positive self-image. As we noted earlier, other people play a major role in shaping our self-concept and self-esteem. The more credible the source of information, the more likely we are to believe it. Having a trusted friend, colleague, clergyperson, or counselor who can listen without judging you and give you the straight scoop about yourself can help you avoid "pity parties." Prolonged periods of self-pity left unchecked and unconfirmed can lead to feelings of inferiority. Later in the book we will discuss how honest relationships are developed through the process of self-disclosure. As the author of the essay "All The Good Things" learned, honest, positive support can provide encouragement for a lifetime.

Letting Go of the Past

Your self-concept is not a fixed construct. It was not implanted at birth to remain constant for the rest of your life. Things change. You change. Others

RESEARCH AND LITERATURE
Several of these and similar stories are available in the book *Chicken Soup for the Soul: 101 Stories to Open the Heart and Rekindle the Spirit.* Jack Canfield and Mark Victor Hansen wrote and compiled this Health Communications book in 1993.

TEACHING STRATEGY
Discussion of self spurs some students to defensiveness. You can do some prevention of this by carefully noting that we all have parts of ourselves we would like to improve. Giving an example of your own can defuse the perceived separation that allows for defensiveness.

All the Good Things

He was in the first third-grade class I taught at Saint Mary's School in Morris, Minnesota. All thirty-four of my students were dear to me, but Mark Eklund was one in a million. Very neat in appearance, he had that happy-to-be-alive attitude that made even his occasional mischievousness delightful.

Mark also talked incessantly. I had to remind him again and again that talking without permission was not acceptable. What impressed me so much, though, was his sincere response every time I had to correct him for misbehaving—"Thank you for correcting me, Sister!" I didn't know what to make of it at first, but before long I became accustomed to hearing it many times a day.

One morning my patience was growing thin when Mark talked once too often, and then I made a novice-teacher's mistake. I looked at Mark and said, "If you say one more word, I am going to tape your mouth shut!"

It wasn't ten seconds later when Chuck blurted out, "Mark is talking again." I hadn't asked any of the students to help me watch Mark, but since I had stated the punishment in front of the class, I had to act on it.

I remember the scene as if it had occurred this morning. I walked to my desk, very deliberately opened the drawer and took out a roll of masking tape. Without saying a word, I proceeded to Mark's desk, tore off two pieces of tape and made a big X with them over his mouth. I then returned to the front of the room.

As I glanced at Mark to see how he was doing, he winked at me. That did it! I started laughing. The entire class cheered as I walked back to Mark's desk, removed the tape, and shrugged my shoulders. His first words were, "Thank you for correcting me, Sister."

At the end of the year I was asked to teach junior-high math. The years flew by, and before I knew it Mark was in my classroom again. He was more handsome than ever and just as polite. Since he had to listen carefully to my instruction in the "new math," he did not talk as much in ninth grade as he had in third.

One Friday, things just didn't feel right. We had worked hard on a new concept all week, and I sensed that the students were growing frustrated with themselves—and edgy with one another. I had to stop this crankiness before it got out of hand. So I asked them to list the names of the other students in the room on two sheets of paper, leaving a space between each name. Then I told them to think of the nicest thing they could say about each of their classmates and write it down.

It took the remainder of the class period to finish the assignment, but as the students left the room, each one handed me the papers. Charlie smiled. Mark said, "Thank you for teaching me, Sister. Have a good weekend."

That Saturday, I wrote down the name of each student on a separate sheet of paper, and I listed what everyone else had said about that individual. On Monday I gave each student his or her list. Some of them ran two pages. Before long, the entire class was smiling. "Really?" I heard whispered. "I never knew that meant anything to anyone!" "I didn't know others liked me so much!"

No one ever mentioned those papers in class again. I

never knew if they discussed them after class or with their parents, but it didn't matter. The exercise had accomplished its purpose. The students were happy with themselves and one another again.

That group of students moved on. Several years later, after I returned from a vacation, my parents met me at the airport. As we were driving home, Mother asked the usual questions about the trip—the weather, my experiences in general. There was a slight lull in the conversation. Mother gave Dad a sideways glance and simply said, "Dad?" My father cleared his throat as he usually did before saying something important. "The Eklunds called last night," he began.

"Really?" I said. "I haven't heard from them for several years. I wonder how Mark is."

Dad responded quietly. "Mark was killed in Vietnam," he said. "The funeral is tomorrow, and his parents would like it if you could attend." To this day I can still point to the exact spot on I-494 where Dad told me about Mark.

I had never seen a serviceman in a military coffin before. Mark looked so handsome, so mature. All I could think at that moment

was, *Mark, I would give all the masking tape in the world if only you could talk to me.*

The church was packed with Mark's friends. Chuck's sister sang "The Battle Hymn of the Republic." Why did it have to rain on the day of the funeral? It was difficult enough at the graveside. The pastor said the usual prayers, and the bugler played taps. One by one those who loved Mark took a last walk by the coffin and sprinkled it with holy water.

I was the last one to bless the coffin. As I stood there, one of the soldiers who had acted as a pallbearer came up to me. "Were you Mark's math teacher?" he asked. I nodded as I continued to stare at the coffin. "Mark talked about you a lot," he said.

After the funeral, most of Mark's former classmates headed to Chuck's farmhouse for lunch. Mark's mother and father were there, obviously waiting for me. "We want to show you something," his father said, taking a wallet out of his pocket. "They found this on Mark when he was killed. We thought you might recognize it."

Opening the billfold, he carefully removed two worn pieces of notebook paper that

had obviously been taped, folded and refolded many times. I knew without looking that the papers were the ones on which I had listed all the good things each of Mark's classmates had said about him. "Thank you so much for doing that," Mark's mother said. "As you can see, Mark treasured it."

Mark's classmates started to gather around us. Charlie smiled rather sheepishly and said, "I still have my list. It's in the top drawer of my desk at home." Chuck's wife said, "Chuck asked me to put his in our wedding album." "I have mine too," Marilyn said. "It's in my diary." Then Vicki, another classmate, reached into her pocketbook, took out her wallet and showed her worn and frazzled list to the group. "I carry this with me at all times," Vicki said without batting an eyelash. "I think we all saved our lists."

That was when I finally sat down and cried. I cried for Mark and for all his friends who would never see him again.

—HELEN P. MROSLA

© Proteus, Shippensburg University

Show a clip from the film *Ordinary People* in which Conrad's psychiatrist, Dr. Berger, demonstrates his unconditional support and willingness to understand Conrad's pain. He encourages him to forgive himself and to let go of the past.

INSTRUCTIONAL GOALS AND TIPS

Remind students as the course progresses that courage, persistence, and perseverance worked for Lincoln and are essential for growth. As Beverly Sills said, "You may be disappointed if you fail, but you are doomed if you don't try."

change. Individuals with low self-esteem may be locking on to events and experiences that happened years ago and tenaciously refusing to let go of them. Someone wrote, "The lightning bug is brilliant, but it hasn't much of a mind; it blunders through existence with its headlight on behind." Looking back at what we can't change only reinforces a sense of helplessness. Constantly replaying negative experiences in our mental VCR only serves to make our sense of worth more difficult to change. Becoming aware of the changes that have occurred and can occur in your life can assist you in developing a more realistic assessment of your value. If you were overweight as a child, you may have a difficult time accepting that your worth does not hinge upon pounds you carried years ago. Being open and receptive to change in self-worth is important to developing a healthy self-concept. Longfellow's advice to let go of the past remains wise advice today: "Look not mournfully into the past. It comes not back again. Wisely improve the Present. It is thine. Go forth to meet the shadowy future, without fear. . . ." As the following chronology of Abraham Lincoln's life suggests, letting go of the past, coupled with reframing, persistent effort, and talent, served Abraham Lincoln well.

Abraham Lincoln Didn't Quit

The sense of obligation to continue is present in all of us. A duty to strive is the duty of us all. I felt a call to that duty.

—ABRAHAM LINCOLN

1816	His family was forced out of their home. He had to work to support them.
1818	His mother died.
1831	Failed in business.
1832	Ran for state legislature—*lost.*
1832	Also lost his job—wanted to go to law school but couldn't get in.
1833	Borrowed some money from a friend to begin a business and by the end of the year he was bankrupt. He spent the next 17 years of his life paying off this debt.
1834	Ran for state legislature again—*won.*
1835	Was engaged to be married, sweetheart died and his heart was broken.
1836	Had a total nervous breakdown and was in bed for six months.
1838	Sought to become speaker of the state legislature—*defeated.*
1840	Sought to become elector—*defeated.*
1843	Ran for Congress—*lost.*
1846	Ran for Congress again—*this time he won*—went to Washington and did a good job.
1848	Ran for re-election to Congress—*lost.*
1849	Sought the job of land officer in his home state—*rejected.*
1854	Ran for Senate of the United States—*lost.*

1856	Sought the Vice-Presidential nomination at his party's national convention—got less than 100 votes.
1858	Ran for U.S. Senate again—*again he lost.*
1860	*Elected president of the United States.*

The path was worn and slippery. My foot slipped from under me, knocking the other out of the way, but I recovered and said to myself, "It's a slip and not a fall."

—ABRAHAM LINCOLN
(After losing a senate race)

From: J. Canfield and M.V. Hansen, Eds., *Chicken Soup for the Soul* (Health Communications, Inc.), 1995.

Seeking Support

Some of your self-image problems may be so ingrained that you need professional help. A trained counselor, clergy member, or therapist can help you sort through them. Therapists traditionally take a psychoanalytic approach, inviting you to search for experiences in your past that may help you first to understand your feelings and then to change them. Other counselors use different techniques. If you are not sure to whom to turn for a referral, you can start with your school

BUILDING YOUR SKILLS

Assessing Your Skills for Enhancing Your Self-Esteem

Evaluate your skill for improving your self-esteem using the scales below. Scores of 35–25 suggest that you have skills which can help you improve your self esteem. Scoring 25–15 means you may have some skill or you may be uncertain as to whether you possess these skills. A score below 15 suggests that you are not confident of your skills for enhancing your self-esteem.

	Highly Skilled	Somewhat Skilled	Uncertain of Skill	Little Skill	No Skill
Self-Talk	5	4	3	2	1
Visualization	5	4	3	2	1
Avoiding Comparisons	5	4	3	2	1
Reframing	5	4	3	2	1
Developing Honest Relationships	5	4	3	2	1
Letting Go of the Past	5	4	3	2	1
Seeking Support	5	4	3	2	1

SKILL DEVELOPMENT
Summarize each of the seven methods for increasing self-esteem offered in the text (See Recap Box, page 64). Have students complete the activity on page 63 but assure them that all responses will be confidential and will not be shared with the class or the instructor. Next, explain that we learn these skills by having them modeled for us. Have students find out which of the skills they rated highest for themselves. Break the class into seven groups that reflect the seven skills such that students go to a group whose skill is their strongest or second strongest. Have each group decide on one clear, detailed example that best represents the skill. Each group should report to the class.

WEB ACTIVITY
Social Psychology Research Online
http://home.earthlink.net/
~joannmooney/psyc.html
Excellent jump point for Social Psychology. "Social psychologists study how an individual's thoughts, feelings, and behaviors are influenced by actual or implied presence of other people." Many related web site links offered. Have students select a topic and prepare a brief oral report to the class.

counseling services. Or, if you are near a medical school teaching hospital, you can contact the counseling or psychotherapy office there for a referral.

Because you have spent your whole lifetime developing your self-esteem, it is not easy to make big changes. But as we have seen, talking through our problems can make a difference. As communication researchers Frank E. X. Dance and Carl Larson see it, "Speech communication empowers each of us to share in the development of our own self-concept and the fulfillment of that self-concept."[16]

RECAP — Strategies for Improving Your Self-Esteem

SELF-TALK	If you're having a bad hair day, tell yourself that you have beautiful eyes and lots of friends who like you anyway.
VISUALIZATION	If you feel nervous before a meeting, visualize everyone in the room congratulating you on your great ideas.
AVOID COMPARISON	Focus on what you can do to enhance your own talents and abilities.
REFRAME	If you experience one failure, keep the larger picture in mind rather than focusing on that isolated incident.
DEVELOP HONEST RELATIONSHIPS	Cultivate friends in whom you can confide and who will give you honest feedback for improving your skills and abilities.
LET GO OF THE PAST	Talk yourself out of your "old tapes"; focus on ways to enhance your abilities in the future.
SEEK SUPPORT	Talk with professional counselors who can help you identify your gifts and talents.

Summary

We all seek answers to three questions: "Who am I?" "Why am I here?" "Who are all these others?" William James answered the first question by dividing the self into three parts. The material self includes our bodies and those tangible possessions that give us identity. The social self is the part that engages in interaction with others. The spiritual self consists of thoughts and assumptions about values, moral standards, and beliefs about forces that influence our lives. Other theorists conclude that our self-concept develops through interaction with other people. The groups we belong to also give us identity. Our roles as sister, brother, student, and parent are important in how we view who we are; the roles we assume provide labels for who we are. We also self-reflexively make our own observations about ourselves apart from others, and about groups or roles we assume. Our gender plays a key part in affecting our view of who we are in relationship to others.

Your self-concept and self-esteem affect how you interact with others. Self-concept is who you think you are; self-esteem is your evaluation of your self-worth. Your life position—whether you view yourself as okay or not okay in relationship to others—is a reflection of your self-worth. Our self-labels are powerful influences upon our actions, and our self-understanding also affects how we send and receive interpersonal messages. Our personality and style of relating to others are also influenced by our concept of self. One model, called social styles, identifies our communication styles based on varying degrees of assertiveness and responsiveness: Driver, Expressive, Amiable, and Analytical. Few of us adopt the same style in all situations.

It is difficult to alter your self-esteem, but seven techniques have been helpful to others: engaging in positive self-talk, visualizing success, avoiding comparisons with others, reframing events and relationships from a different perspective, developing honest relationships with others, letting go of the past, and seeking professional help.

For Discussion and Review

■ FOCUS ON COMPREHENSION

1. List and describe the three selves identified by William James.

2. Define, compare, and contrast the terms self-concept and self-esteem.

3. Identify and describe four factors that explain how our self-concept develops.

■ FOCUS ON CRITICAL THINKING

4. Joel, who is thirty years old, married, and has two children, suffers from feelings of low self-esteem. Although he has many friends and a wife who loves him, he feels that others perform much better than he does at work. What strategies would help Joel enhance his self-esteem?

5. Make a list of all of the groups, clubs, and organizations to which you belong. Rank order them from most important to least important. What does your rank ordering tell you about these groups in reference to your self-concept?

6. Provide an original example of how visualization might help you enhance your self-esteem. Describe the positive scene.

■ FOCUS ON ETHICS

7. Discuss the ethical implications of using untrue flattery to enhance a friend's self-esteem.

8. There are many self-help books on the market that claim to enrich your social life by providing sure-fire techniques for enhancing self-esteem. Do you think these claims are ethical? Why or why not?

9. Aelish has long planned to attend a top-notch Ivy League college. Her grades, however, are only in the C and B range. Her SAT scores are average. Should she try to reframe this factual information or deal with her problem in another way?

For Your Journal

1. Record goals for your self-talk and note your self-talk messages day by day. You might want to organize your journal around specific topics such as academic achievement, personal appearance, or social skills. Under academic achievement you could write: "I will monitor my self-talk messages to keep myself on track while I study for two hours each day." Your personal appearance self-talk goal may be to tell yourself something positive about your appearance instead of only thinking about what you don't like.

2. In your journal, write the ten responses you wrote for Building Your Skills: Who Are You? at the beginning of this chapter. At the end of the course, again write ten responses to the "Who are you?" question without looking at your earlier responses. What are the differences in your responses? How do you explain them?

3. If someone were to walk into one of your favorite rooms in your home, dorm, or apartment, what conclusions might he or she draw about your social style? Are you neat and well-organized? Or does your room have the characteristics of an expressive personality? Write a brief description of who you are from a social style perspective based upon the clues in your room.

Learning with Others

1. Place the following list of values in rank order from one to twelve. In a group with other students, compare your answers. Discuss how your personal ranking of these values influences your interaction with others.

_____	Honesty	_____	Justice
_____	Salvation	_____	Wealth
_____	Comfort	_____	Beauty
_____	Good health	_____	Equality

INTERPERSONAL COMMUNICATION FOUNDATIONS

_____ Human rights _____ Freedom

_____ Peace _____ Mercy

2. You are going to make a shield of your life. Draw a large outline of a shield that fills up an entire sheet of paper. Divide your shield into four equal sections. In the upper right-hand section of your shield, draw or symbolize something at which you have skill or talent. In the upper left-hand section draw or symbolize something you are trying to improve or a new skill you are learning. In the lower right-hand section, draw or symbolize your most prized material possession. Finally, in the lower left-hand section, write three words that you hope someone would use to describe you.

Share your shield with other students. Tell your classmates why you drew what you did. Discuss how your shield reflects your attitudes, beliefs, and values.

3. Go through your personal music library of tapes or CDs and identify a selection that best symbolizes you. Your selection may be based upon either the lyrics or the music. Bring your selection to class and play it for your classmates. (Your instructor will bring a tape or CD player.) Tell why this music symbolizes you. Discuss with classmates how today's music provides a glimpse of our culture and a vehicle for self-expression.

■ GLOSSARY

SELF: The sum total of who a person is; a person's central inner force.

SELF-CONCEPT: A person's subjective description of who he or she is.

ATTITUDES: Learned predispositions to respond to a person, object, or idea in a favorable or unfavorable way.

BELIEFS: The ways in which you structure your understanding of reality—what is true and what is false.

VALUES: Enduring concepts of good and bad, right and wrong.

MATERIAL SELF: Your concept of self as reflected in a total of all the tangible things you own.

SOCIAL SELF: Your concept of self as developed through your personal, social interactions with others.

SPIRITUAL SELF: Your concept of self based upon your thoughts and introspections about your values and moral standards.

LOOKING-GLASS SELF: A concept that suggests we learn who we are based upon our interactions with others, which are reflected back to us.

ANDROGYNOUS ROLE: A gender role that includes both masculine and feminine qualities.

SELF-REFLEXIVENESS: The human ability to think about what we are doing while we are doing it.

SOCIAL COMPARISON: Process of comparing yourself to others to measure your worth and value in relationship to others who are similar to you.

SELF-ESTEEM (SELF-WORTH): Your evaluation of your worth or value as reflected in your perception of such things as your skills, abilities, talents, and appearance.

LIFE POSITIONS: Your feeling of being either "OK" or "Not OK" as reflected in your sense of worth and self-esteem.

SPECIFIC-OTHER PERSPECTIVE: Process of relying upon information that a person observes or imagines about another person that is used to predict a person's behavior.

GENERALIZED-OTHER PERSPECTIVE: Process of relying upon observed or imagined information about many people or people in general that is used to predict a person's behavior.

SELF-FULFILLING PROPHECY: Notion that predictions about your future actions are likely to come true because you believe that they will come true.

SELECTIVE EXPOSURE: Principle that suggests we tend to place ourselves in situations that are consistent with our self-concept and self-esteem.

NEED FOR INCLUSION: Interpersonal need to be included and to include others in social activities.

NEED FOR CONTROL: Interpersonal need for some degree of domination in our relationships as well as the need to be controlled.

NEED FOR AFFECTION: Interpersonal need to give and receive love, personal support, warmth, and intimacy.

INTRAPERSONAL MESSAGES: Self-talk; thoughts and ideas that you "say" to yourself.

COMMUNICATION STYLE (SOCIAL STYLE): Your consistent way of relating to others based upon your personality, self-concept, and self-esteem.

ASSERTIVENESS: Dimension of the Wilson Learning Corporation social style model that describes a personal quality that refers to an individual's effort to control others.

RESPONSIVENESS: Dimension of the Wilson Learning Corporation social style model that describes a personal quality of placing the feelings of others above our own and expressing those feelings.

DRIVER STYLE: Communication style characterized by high achievement, assertiveness, and controlled emotions.

ANALYTICAL STYLE: Communication style characterized by high assertiveness and low expressiveness, considerable attention to detail, and task achievement.

EXPRESSIVE STYLE: Communication style characterized by a high degree of expressiveness and assertiveness; there is a tendency both to control others and to respond emotionally or impulsively.

AMIABLE STYLE: Communication style characterized by a high degree of expressiveness and sensitivity toward others and a minimum of assertiveness.

BACKUP COMMUNICATION STYLE: Communication style we often use when we are under stress or when our primary style does not achieve the desired results.

INTRAPERSONAL COMMUNICATION: Communication within yourself that includes your self-talk.

VISUALIZATION: Technique of imagining that you are performing a particular task in a certain way. Positive visualization can enhance your self-esteem.

REFRAMING: Process of redefining events and experiences from a different point of view.

Interpersonal Communication and Perception

After studying this chapter, you should be able to:

1. Define perception and interpersonal perception.

2. Identify and explain the three stages of interpersonal perception.

3. Describe the relationship between interpersonal communication and interpersonal perception.

4. Explain the interpersonal perception processes of impression formation, implicit personality theory, attribution theory, and constructs.

5. Identify the ten factors that distort the accuracy of our interpersonal perceptions.

6. Identify seven suggestions for improving your interpersonal perceptions.

- UNDERSTANDING THE INTER-
  PERSONAL PERCEPTION
  PROCESS

- PERCEPTION AND INTERPER-
  SONAL COMMUNICATION

- HOW WE ORGANIZE AND
  INTERPRET INTERPERSONAL
  PERCEPTIONS

- BARRIERS TO ACCURATE
  PERCEPTIONS

- IMPROVING YOUR
  PERCEPTUAL SKILLS

ook at the picture in Figure 3.1. What is happening and what has happened? What is the relationship among the individuals in the painting? You probably have deduced that the boy was running away from home, the policeman found him, and then he took the boy into the local coffee shop for ice cream or some other treat. Perhaps you think that the counterman is wistfully recalling his own days of running away as a child. What are your feelings about the policeman? Do you see him as a friendly and caring person who has a good understanding of kids?

As human beings we interpret and attribute meaning to what we observe or experience, particularly if what we are observing is other people. We tend to make inferences about their motives, personalities, and other traits based on their physical qualities and behaviors. The types of conclusions we draw from observing the picture in Figure 3.1 exemplify the process we call interpersonal perception. Through interpersonal perception we piece together various bits of information about other people and draw conclusions that may or may not be accurate. Because our feelings and responses to other people are based on our perceptions, those who are skilled at making observations and interpretations have a head start in developing effective interpersonal relationships.

Most of the time, we are unaware of our own perception process. For example, you may not have realized that you were drawing conclusions about the painting until you read the questions above. But we may become aware of the process when differences in perception cause a conflict or disagreement. For example, at the end of the movie *Thelma and Louise,* the two main characters drive off the edge of the Grand Canyon. The scene sparked a lot of arguments between friends because some people perceived it as a tragic ending, whereas others perceived it as an uplifting one because the two characters maintained the freedom they had finally come to realize. In truth, no two individuals ever perceive the same thing in exactly the same way. Fortunately, communication tools such as conversation allow us to create shared meanings despite the differences in our perceptions.

Figure 3.1

The Runaway. Original oil painting for a *Saturday Evening Post* cover, September 20, 1958. Old Corner House Collection, Stockbridge, Massachusetts.

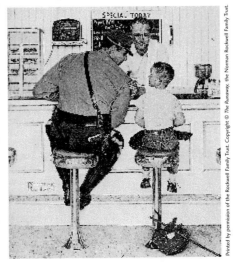

Perceptual Differences

Think of two instances in which you and a friend had a very similar perception of something—perhaps of the food in a restaurant, a scene in a movie, or of some behavior you observed in another person.

How did you know that you and your friend had similar perceptions? What factors in your backgrounds influenced the way you each perceived the experience?

Now think of two instances in which you and a friend had different perceptions of the same thing. How did you

discover that you and your friend had different perceptions? To what factors in each of your backgrounds do you attribute these different perceptions? What effects did the differences in perception have upon your interactions?

Our perceptions are influenced by who we are, including the accumulation of our experiences. If you have had several bad experiences with the police, for example, you may not view the policeman in Figure 3.1 as a friendly person. Or if you know something about the life and work of Norman Rockwell, the illustrator who painted the picture, you may view all his works as representations of an idyllic American culture and society that existed only in his mind. As we saw in Chapter 2, everything we perceive is filtered through our self-concept.[1] It is important to recognize and examine factors that might distort the accuracy of our interpretations. We can also reduce inaccuracies by applying an other-oriented approach as we interact with people. By focusing on how others perceive the world, we can reduce the amount of distortion that our own self-concepts impose on our perceptions.

Before we turn to the role that perception plays in interpersonal communication, let's first take a closer look at the interpersonal perception process itself.

Understanding the Interpersonal Perception Process

What is perception? On the most general level, **perception** is simply the arousal of any of our senses. A sound travels through the air, vibrates in our eardrum, activates the nerves, and sends a signal to the brain. A similar sequence of events takes place when we see, smell, feel, or taste something. The process of perception also includes organizing and interpreting information provided by the senses. You come out of a building and see wet pavement and puddles of water, hear thunder, smell a distinct odor caused by ions, and observe drops of water falling in front of you. You integrate all those bits of information and conclude that it is raining, and has been for a while.

Our perceptions of people, however, include analysis and interpretation that goes beyond simple interpretation of sensory information. **Interpersonal perception** is the process by which we decide what people are like and give meaning to their actions. It includes making judgments about personality and drawing inferences from what we observed.[2] When you meet someone new, you *select* certain information to attend to: You note whether the person is male or female, has an accent, smiles, uses a friendly tone of voice, as well as particular personal information (she is from Boone, Iowa). You then *organize* the information under some category that is recognizable to you, such as "a friendly Midwesterner." Then you *interpret* the organized perceptions: This person is trustworthy, honest, hardworking, and likable.

In our discussion we will focus on this kind of interpersonal perception, which relates to understanding our observations of other people. We will begin by examining the three stages of the interpersonal perception process that we described above: selecting, organizing, and interpreting what we observe.

A cab driver's ability to make a living can be enhanced by his or her ability to use selective perception to find fares among the passers-by on a busy street. (David Simson/Stock Boston)

Stage One: Selecting, Simplifying, and Categorizing the Stimuli

■ SELECTING

Sit for a minute after you read this passage and try to tune in to all the sensory input you are receiving: Consider the feel of your socks against your feet, the pressure of the floor on your heels, the pressure of the piece of furniture against your body as you sit, the buzzing sounds from various sources around you—this "white noise" might come from a refrigerator, personal computer, fluorescent lights, water in pipes, voices, passing traffic, or your own heartbeat or churning stomach. What do you smell? What do you see? Without moving your eyes, turn your awareness to the images you see in the corner of your vision. What colors do you see? What shapes? What taste is in your mouth? How do the pages of this book feel against your fingertips? Now stop reading and consider all these sensations. Try to focus on all of them at the same time. You can't.

The number of sensations we can attend to at any given time is limited. Therefore, we are selective about which sensations make it through to the level of awareness. Perhaps you close your eyes or sit in the dark as you listen to music. This allows you to select more auditory sensations because you are eliminating visual ones. Individuals who have an impaired sense often become more tuned in to input from other senses because they have fewer sensations vying for their attention.

This selectivity can also cause us to fail to perceive information that is important. Imagine that you are standing with your back to an open hallway door talking to a friend and complaining about your roommate or spouse just as that roommate or spouse walks in the door. Your friend tries to signal with her hand that the other person has just entered, but you miss this cue and go on to say things that you later wish your roommate or spouse had not heard. You missed the signal because you failed to perceive the gesture. Because you were simplifying the stimuli to which you attended, you did not process the hand gesture.

■ SIMPLIFYING

During the selection stage, we attempt to simplify the stimuli that flood in through our senses, using various techniques. We use perceptual filters to screen out constant sensations that we have learned are unimportant, such as the sensations of our clothes against our skin and the surrounding white noise and smells. However, we do attend to the sensation of the elastic bands of our underclothes if they pull too tight, because a threshold of arousal is crossed, forcing the brain to attend to that stimulus. Each of our senses has such a threshold.

Directing our attention to specific stimuli and consequently ignoring others is called **selective perception**. In our interactions with others we may choose to focus on specific cues such as gestures or foot movement. What specific qualities or features do you tend to focus on when you first meet others? Do you pay particular attention to handshakes, smiles, eye contact, body posture, gestures, or tone of voice? Sometimes we exercise selective perception when we are listening for a specific piece of information. As in the example above of missing your friend's hand signal, our selective focus might prevent us from perceiving other important cues.

■ CATEGORIZING

We also simplify stimuli by categorizing information and inventing stereotypes. We create categories to reduce the amount of information to which we have to attend to or remember. If you learn that your communication partner is a parent, you may put him or her into a "mother" or "father" category that contains stored information, which you then could apply to this person. You may automatically attribute qualities to this person that you typically associate with parenthood: being loving, responsible, committed, and tired. This saves you the trouble of selecting and perceiving the individual pieces of information that you would otherwise need to draw these conclusions. This automatic attribution of qualities based on a person's membership in some category is known as **stereotyping**. Try to think about some of the categories into which you place people: jocks, teachers, partyers, high school students, women, and men. The more we interact with a variety of individuals, the greater the number of categories we can potentially create and use in this simplification process.

Despite its efficiency, however, this simplification process can create significant problems. We easily may attribute inaccurate qualities to an individual because of these stereotypes. The word *stereotype* was originally a printing term; it refers to a metal plate that was cast from type set by a printer. The plate would print the same page of type over and over again. When we stereotype people, we place them into inflexible, all-compassing categories. We "print" the same judgments on anyone placed into a given category. We may even choose to ignore contradictory information that we receive directly from the other person. Instead of adjusting our conception of that person, we adjust our perception. That is, we see what we want to see, rather than seeing what is really there.

Categorizing individuals is not an inherently bad thing to do, but it is harmful to hang on to a stereotypical image of another person in the face of contradictory information. For example, not all mothers are responsible or loving. Because American culture reveres motherhood, we may not process easily our perceptions of a mother who is abusive or negligent.

Stage Two: Organizing and Imposing Structure on What We Observe

Look at the four items in Figure 3.2. What does each of them mean to you? If you are like most people, you will perceive item A as a rabbit, item B as a telephone number, and item C as the word *interpersonal*, and item D as a circle. Strictly speaking, none of those perceptions is correct. We'll discuss why after we explore the second stage of perception: organization.

■ PATTERNING

After we select what stimuli we are going to attend to and process, we start to organize them into convenient, understandable, and efficient patterns that allow us to make sense of what we have observed. Organizing makes it easier for us to process complex information because it allows us to impose the familiar onto the unfamiliar, and because we can easily store and recall simple patterns. For example, when you looked at item A in Figure 3.2, you saw the pattern of dots that you label a rabbit because a rabbit is a concept you know and to which you attach various meanings. The set of dots would not have meaning for you in and of itself, nor would it be meaningful for you to attend to each particular dot or to the dots' relationships to one another. It would be possible to create a mathematical model of the dots indicating their placement on an X-Y grid, but such a model would be extremely complex and difficult to observe and remember. It's much easier to organize the dots in a way that refers to something stored in your memory: a rabbit. For similar reasons, we organize patterns of stars in the sky into the various constellations with shapes like the bear, the crab, and the Big and Little Dippers. As we do for the pattern of dots making up the rabbit, we search for and apply patterns to our perceptions of people. You might have a friend who jogs and works out at a gym. You put these together and label the friend "athletic." That label represents a pattern of qualities you use in relating to your friend that will be discussed later in the chapter.

■ PUNCTUATING

The way we organize information depends partly on the way we punctuate it. Item B in Figure 3.2 looks like a telephone number because it has three numbers followed by four numbers. You might also remember that *555* is the prefix you use for calling information. However, the digits could just as easily represent two totally independent numbers: five hundred and fifty-five followed by the number four thousand, four hundred and thirty-three. How we interpret the numbers depends on how we punctuate[3] or separate them. When we record

A.

B. **5 5 5   4 4 3 3**

C. **N T R P R S N L**

D.

Figure 3.2

What Do You See?

information, we use commas, periods, dashes, and colons to signal meanings and interpretations. In our minds we sometimes impose punctuation marks where we believe they should be. For example, we put a dash between 555 and 4433 even though no dash appeared there.

When it comes to punctuating relational events and behaviors, we each develop our own separate set of standards. You will sometimes experience difficulties and disagreements because of differences in how you and your partner choose to punctuate a conversational exchange or shared sequence of events.[4] For example, suppose you and a friend have been talking about her recent school problems. After a few moments of silence, you assume that your conversation on that topic has ended, so you start talking about your recent job interview. Later on, you find out that you offended your friend because she had not punctuated the conversation the same way. She believed that her problems should still have been the focus of the conversation. One classic example of relational problems resulting from differences in punctuation involves a husband who displays withdrawal behaviors and a wife who nags.[5] The husband punctuates their interactions such that he sees his withdrawal behavior as a reaction to her nagging. The wife, on the other hand, punctuates their interactions differently. She sees herself nagging her husband because he keeps withdrawing. The husband and wife punctuate their perceptions differently because they each perceive different starting points for their interactions. Resolution of such conflicts involves having the parties describe how they have punctuated the event, and agreeing on a common punctuation.

■ SUPERIMPOSING

Looking again at Figure 3.2, you can see that our inclination to superimpose structure and consistency on what we observe also leads us to create a familiar word from the meaningless assemblage of letters in item C, and to label the figure in item D a circle, even though circles are continuous lines without gaps on the right side. This process of filling in missing information is called **closure.** We apply the same principles in our interactions with people. When we have an incomplete picture of another human being, we impose a pattern or structure, classify the person on the basis of the information we do have, and fill in gaps. Perhaps you've played the game where you sat in an airport waiting area or in a busy shopping mall watching people and tried to guess what they did for a living, what their personalities were like, or what their backgrounds were. Maybe you saw people you guessed were a teacher, a banker, a rebel, a housewife, a loser, a loner, a psychotic. As you looked at people's clothing and the manner in which they walked or behaved, you made inferences about them. You superimposed some structure by using a general label and filling in gaps for information you didn't have through closure to reach your conclusions.

Stage Three: Interpreting or Attributing Meaning to What We Observe

Once we have organized the stimuli, we are ready to interpret what they mean. We attach meaning to all that we observe. We learn through socialization and our own recurring experiences to attribute particular meaning to particular

INTERPERSONAL COMMUNICATION FOUNDATIONS

stimuli. In some cases the meanings are fairly standardized, as they are for language, for example. But others are much more personalized. As the excerpt from "The Greek Interpreter" shows, the fictional detective Sherlock Holmes was noted for his ability to apply exacting interpretations to what he observed. In general, the heroes in mysteries usually excel in their ability to observe, organize, and interpret the stimuli around them. Sherlock and Mycroft Holmes possess an ability to attend to specific cues that you and I may miss. They also are able to organize the cues to create a unique meaning and interpretation. Seeing that the man in dark mourning clothes is carrying a baby's toy and picture-book takes on special meaning when the two clues are combined.

Sherlock Holmes and His Brother Mycroft Make Some Observations

In this excerpt Sherlock Holmes is visiting his brother Mycroft. Both are looking out a window when Mycroft asks Sherlock what he makes of a very small, dark fellow with his hat pushed back and several packages under his arm standing on the street corner. Dr. Watson records their conversation:

"An old soldier, I perceive," said Sherlock.

"And very recently discharged," remarked his brother.

"Served in India, I see."

"And a non-commissioned officer."

"Royal Artillery, I fancy," said Sherlock.

"And a widower."

"But with a child."

"Children, my dear boy, children."

"Come," said I, laughing, "this is a little too much."

"Surely," answered Holmes, "it is not hard to say that a man with that bearing, expression of authority, and sun-baked skin, is a soldier, is more than a private, and is not long from India."

"That he has not left the service long is shown by his still wearing his ammunition boots, as they are called," observed Mycroft.

"He had not the cavalry stride, yet he wore his hat on one side, as is shown by the lighter skin on that side of his brow. His weight is against his being a sapper [army engineer]. He is in the artillery."

"Then, of course, his complete mourning shows that he has lost someone very dear. The fact that he is doing his own shopping looks as though it were his wife. He has been buying things for children, you perceive. There is a rattle, which shows that one of them is very young. The wife probably died in childbed. The fact that he has a picture-book under his arm shows that there is another child to be thought of."

From: Sir Arthur Conan Doyle, The Greek Interpreter.

Although all of us may not possess Sherlock Holmes's perceptual talents, we do all attribute meaning to what we observe. If you shake someone's hand and it feels like a wet, dead fish, what is your reaction and interpretation? If you notice someone you don't know winking at you from across a room, what do you

DISCUSSION AND WRITING
Have a volunteer read (or distribute copies of) Lewis Carroll's "Jabberwocky." This nonsense poem is fun to interpret. Ask students what occurred in this story and on what they based their perceptions.

Divide the class into groups of 3 people. Have them read the Building Your Skills exercise and then send them out on campus to investigate. Give the teams 15 minutes to complete the task. When finished, have each triad explain what they found. Lead a discussion over perceptual accuracy and the factors that may account for it (See text, pages 79–97).

think? If a toddler is crying in a room full of people and a woman comes over and picks the child up, what do you assume about the woman? If you see a student glance over at another student's exam paper and then record an answer, what do you think the student has done? All of these are examples that show we impose meaning on what we observe to complete the perceptual process.

BUILDING YOUR SKILLS

Perceptual Interpretations

Find a place where you can sit and watch people for a while. Write down as many observations as you can about the people that pass by or that are seated nearby. Try to make some interpretations based upon your observations, just as Sherlock Holmes might have. What do you notice about their clothing, their shoes, the manner in which they walk? What are they carrying with them? Do they seem to be in a hurry? Can you tell which are students, teachers, or members of other professions? If you are watching other students, can you tell what their majors are?

If you get the chance, you might approach some of these people and see how accurate your observations are. People are generally open to hearing positive perceptions about themselves. You may want to hold back on sharing negative perceptions.

RECAP — The Interpersonal Perception Process

Term	Explanation	Examples
Perception	The arousal of any of our senses.	Hearing a car horn, smelling roses, or tasting saltwater.
Interpersonal Perception	The process of piecing together information about people and drawing conclusions about them.	Turning toward the sound of a car horn and noticing it is someone you know, therefore deciding the car horn was meant to convey a greeting.
Selection	The first stage in the perceptual process, in which we select sensations for our awareness.	Sitting in your apartment where you hear lots of traffic sounds and car horns, but attending to a particular rhythmic car honking that seems to be right outside your door.
Organization	The second stage in the perceptual process, in which we assemble stimuli into convenient and efficient patterns.	Putting together the car honking with your anticipation of a friend's arrival to pick you up in her car to drive to a movie that starts in five minutes.
Interpretation	The final stage in perception, in which we assign meaning to what we have observed.	Deciding the car honking must be your friend signaling you to come out to the car quickly because she's running late.

Perception and Interpersonal Communication

Interpersonal perception is a two-way street. Our perceptions of others affect the ways in which we communicate with them, and their perceptions of us affect the way they communicate with us.

We continually modify the topics, the language, and the manner in which we communicate according to the perceptions we have of others. For example, if you observe a woman in a tracksuit running in a park, you may conclude that she is a physical fitness fanatic. Then, if you strike up a conversation with her, you may bring up topics such as physical fitness, sports, and diet. But if she informs you that she knows nothing about those things and has just started jogging to offset the time she spends watching videos and eating potato chips, then you would probably shift your focus according to a revised perception. You might start talking about movies and the relative merits of rippled versus plain potato chips. Similarly, if you were talking to a child, you would probably use simple language rather than complex technical terminology. If you were talking to a person who is hearing impaired, you might slow down your speech and raise your speaking volume.

The way that others talk and behave also tells us a great deal about how they perceive us. Maybe you can remember the first time someone younger than you called you Mister, Ms., Mrs., or Miss (if it hasn't happened yet, it will). It probably surprised you to realize that someone perceived you as "old," or as someone with authority. We also analyze others' reactions to us for clues about their conception of who we are. For example, suppose your new college friends go out to play basketball, your favorite sport, but do not invite you. When you later ask them why, they say they always thought of you as the unathletic, studious type. Sometimes others' perceptions of us are surprising. If we never ask, we may never discover that they are inaccurate. The degree to which others have a conception of us that is different from our own is often a measure of the quality of the relationship. The stronger the interpersonal relationship, the closer our self-perceptions are to the perceptions others have of us.[6]

How much we notice about another person's communication behavior relates to our level of interest and need. Perception can be either a passive or an active process. **Passive perception** occurs simply because our senses are in operation. We see, hear, smell, taste, and feel things around us without any conscious attempt to do so. We've all heard noises that startle us and make us wonder, "What was that?" We then try to recall the sound and identify it, or we might investigate—seek out additional information. We are constantly bombarded by stimuli to our senses. Think of all the things you potentially could select for your awareness while interacting with a friend: words you hear with variations in the tone, rate, and so forth; behaviors you see with variations in eye contact, gestures, body movement, and facial expressions. As we have seen, because of the overwhelming amount of potential information that is available to our senses, we usually don't catch it all.

INSTRUCTIONAL GOALS AND TIPS
Monitor your own perceptions of students. Be careful not to label students during the first couple of weeks of class as "average" or "troublemakers" and the like. Use the pygmalion effect to students' advantage.

DISCUSSION AND WRITING
Tell students that they will be given five minutes to write about your appearance. Leave the classroom for this time, then return and read these interpretations aloud. Emphasize the different perceptions, attributes, and impressions students noted. Restate the principle that meanings are in people.

If we feel uncertainty about a given situation or interaction, we become motivated to select particular information through **active perception**. If you need to know whether someone is lying to you about why he was late for a meeting, you might watch his eyes, look for nervous body movements, and listen for hesitation in his voice. We try to reduce uncertainty because we want to control and predict the world around us in order to accomplish our personal goals, and we need accurate and complete information to make plans and develop strategies toward that end.[7] If you can gain information about others, then you can predict their reactions and behaviors, adapt your behaviors and strategies, and therefore maximize the likelihood of fulfilling your social needs. Although this might sound calculating, it really isn't. If you enjoy outdoor activities such as camping and hiking, one of your goals in establishing social relationships is probably to find others who share your interest. So observing, questioning, and processing information to determine a potential friend's interests can help you assess whether the relationship will meet your goals. In Chapter 5 we will discuss ways to improve your ability to gain information through more effective listening.

How We Organize and Interpret Interpersonal Perceptions

As we collect information about others, we organize and interpret that information in various ways. Interpersonal perception involves three processes: forming impressions of others; applying implicit personality theories and the use of mental constructs, which we use to organize information about people; and finally, developing attribution theories, which help us explain why people behave the way they do.

Impression Formation and Management

Impressions are collections of perceptions about others that we maintain and use to interpret their behaviors. Impressions tend to be very general: She seemed nice, he was very friendly, or what a nerd. We form these impressions through perceptions of physical qualities and behavior, information people disclose about themselves, and information that third parties tell us. We select, organize, and interpret all of these perceptions to create a general impression. We tend to form these impressions readily and part with them reluctantly. When we first meet someone, we form a first impression without having much information, and we often hold on to this impression throughout the relationship.

In one study conducted by Solomon Asch, individuals were asked to provide an evaluation of two people based on two lists of adjectives.[8] The list for the first person had the following adjectives: intelligent, industrious, impulsive, critical, stubborn, and envious. The list for the other person had the same adjectives, but in reverse order. Although the content was identical, respondents gave the first person a more positive evaluation than the second. One explanation for this is that the first words in each list created a first impression that respondents used

INTERPERSONAL COMMUNICATION FOUNDATIONS

Attempt to make your initial impression upon students a positive one each time you enter the classroom. Remember that you set the tone for each session. Consider smiling and making small talk with those students who are early for class.

ACTIVITY
See Activity 3.2 in the Instructor's Guide.

to interpret the remaining adjectives. In a similar manner, the first impressions we form about someone often affect our interpretation of subsequent perceptions of them.

This effect of attending to the first pieces of information that we observe is called the **primacy effect**. We also tend to put a lot of stock in the last thing we observed, which is called the **recency effect**.[9] For example, if you think for years that your friend is honest, but today you discover that she lied to you about something important, that lie will have a greater impact on your impression of her than the honest behavior she has displayed for years. The primacy and recency effects explain why you are more likely to remember information at the beginning or end of a paragraph than you are to remember information in the middle.

We also attempt to manage the impressions others form of us. We make implicit guesses about how other people will interpret our own physical displays and behaviors; as a result we attempt to manipulate those displays and behaviors to our advantage. Think about the first day of classes this semester. Did you think about what clothes you were going to wear to classes? Did you worry about how your hair looked, or your breath smelled? Most of us choose clothes that we think will create a positive statement and reflect who we are. In this way we attempt to manage the impressions others form of us. Our ability to effectively manage such impressions is dependent upon our ability to socially decenter (that will be discussed in the next chapter) by looking at ourselves from other people's perspectives. The more accurate you are at determining how others will react to people's looks and behaviors, the more potential you have for adapting your own looks and behaviors.

The impressions we form of others at our first meeting often stay with us throughout our relationship. Following this introduction, will all the participants remember the winning smiles or the fact that the young man failed to stand up during the introduction? (Bob Daemmrich/Stock Boston)

Implicit Personality Theory

Which of the following characteristics would you associate with someone who is "warm": happy, insincere, vain, helpful, honest, boring? You probably chose happy, helpful, and honest. Most of us have developed an **implicit personality theory**, a pattern of associated qualities that we attribute to people which allows us to understand other people.[10] Implicit personality theory provides a way of organizing the vast array of information we have about people's personalities. Implicit personality theories are essentially stereotypes that we apply to people in general. We accomplish perceptual closure through the use of implicit personality theory; that is, we are able to fill in the blanks about a person's personality without actually having to observe additional qualities. Once you have determined that someone is a "warm" person, you automatically associate the related terms. Your implicit personality theory may be similar to that held by

81

SKILL DEVELOPMENT
Ask five volunteers to play the "Telephone Game" (sometimes called "Gossip"). Explain that you will start the message which is to be whispered down the line. After passing the message to the next listener, each volunteer should return to his/her seat and record the message. The message you'll send? "Peter Piper packed a pack of peppered pickles." When the last student says the message aloud, discuss with students what went wrong. Consider the problem of assimilation to a prior message as one constraint to perception.

others in your culture, but each of us forms our own individual theory. There is more consistency between the personality framework you would use to judge two strangers than there is between the personality frameworks you use and the one another person uses to describe the same stranger.

Implicit personality theories allow us to effectively manage a lot of information, but they also can lead us to incorrect conclusions about other people. How accurately does "happy" actually describe a "warm" person? There are probably unhappy warm people. In assuming a connection between these two concepts, you might have reached an erroneous conclusion about the other person. As mentioned in the beginning of this section, your interactions with other people are based on your perception and conceptions of them. When you assume the warm person is happy, you might not perceive the person's need for support and nurturing. As a result, your responses will be inappropriate and lead to ineffective interpersonal communication.

One feature common to most of our implicit personality theories is the tendency to put people into one of two categories: those we like and those we don't like. Categorizing people as those we "like" often creates a **halo effect** in which we attribute a variety of positive qualities to them without even personally confirming the existence of these qualities. If you like me, you will put a halo around your impression of me, and then apply those qualities from your implicit personality theory that apply to people you like; such as, being considerate of other people, warm, caring, and fun to be with, and having a great sense of humor. On the other hand, if you don't like me, you might think of me more as a devil, attributing a variety of negative qualities from your implicit personality theory. This is called the **horn effect**.

Constructs

While implicit personality theory reflects how we organize our perceptions of people's personalities in general, constructs explain how we organize our perceptions of a specific person. **Constructs** were originally conceived of by George Kelly as bipolar qualities that are associated with how we conceptualize people: good or bad, athletic or nonathletic, warm or cold, funny or droll, selfish or generous, and so on. Think about a close friend of yours. What qualities or constructs would you use to describe that person? What qualities differentiate that person from others? What qualities does that person share with others? These are personal constructs. People who are able to develop a long list of constructs to describe people are said to be **cognitively complex**. Cognitive complexity varies in terms of differentiation, elaboration, and integration. Differentiation is the development of more and more constructs from which to draw in describing and differentiating among people. Elaboration is how abstract or refined each of your set of constructs becomes. Integration is how well you organize your constructs. Each of these constructs becomes further developed as we move from childhood to adulthood.

Cognitive complexity affects and is affected by our perception. People with less developed sets of constructs see the world in simpler terms; they do not differentiate among people as well as a highly cognitively complex person would. A person with a highly developed set of constructs is aware of the

motives and causes of people's actions and is able to pick up on their emotional states. Our sensitivity and perceptiveness provide us with the information we need to develop the construct systems we use to describe those people with whom we interact. Most importantly, a highly developed construct system enables us to take on another person's perspective, to empathize, and to orient toward the other person. Let's look at how this could potentially affect interpersonal communication. Jake, Miranda, and Daphne are all friends. Jake has two constructs to describe Daphne: shy and scatterbrained. Miranda has a highly developed set of constructs she associates with Daphne, including shy, scatterbrained, courageous, self-reliant, independent, dependable, troubled, and overwhelmed. Daphne shows up late to meet her two friends and apologizes. Jake sees her tardiness as typical "scatterbrain" behavior and says, "I suppose you forgot to look at your watch." Miranda is able to better understand Daphne's situation, which results in a more other-centered statement: "It's okay Daphne, don't worry about it. I know you've got a lot of things on your mind lately. I'm just glad you could come." Miranda's more developed construct system allowed her to better explain and respond to Daphne's behavior. Explaining behavior is part of the next process to be discussed, attribution theory.

Attribution Theory

Attribution theory relates to the third stage of the perception process: interpreting. We attribute specific motives and causes to the behaviors we observe. For example, suppose the student sitting next to you in class gets up in the middle of the lecture and walks out. Why did the student leave? Did the student become angry at something the instructor said? No, the lecturer was simply describing types of cloud formations. Was the student sick? You remember noticing that the student looked a little flushed and occasionally winced. Maybe

INTERNET RESOURCE
http://www.swin.edu.au/ aare/conf91/BORNL91.029 Download the student paper "Perceptions of Achievement—Compared to Whom?" and read about social comparison processes.

Another way we seek to understand our perceptions of people is by attributing the behavior to a specific cause. We might decide, for instance, when we see the behavior in this photo, that this woman is preparing for a swinging lesson with her grandchild. (Zigy Kaluzny/Tony Stone Images)

MEDIA AND OUTSIDE RESOURCES
Show the film *The Eye of the Beholder* or excerpts from the movie *He Said, She Said* to illustrate how perceptions affect our communication behaviors. Both films point out the need for an other-orientation to communication.

the student has an upset stomach. Or maybe the student is just a bit of a rebel, and often does strange things like leaving in the middle of a class.

Fritz Heider said that we are "naive psychologists,"[11] because we all seek to explain the motives people have for their actions. We are naive because we do not create these explanations in a systematic or scientific manner, but rather by applying common sense to our observations. Developing the most credible explanation for the behavior of others is the goal of the **attribution process**. According to one attribution theory, **correspondent inference theory**, we try to determine the intentionality of the person in causing the effect.[12] In determining how intentional the act was, we may take into account what other choices the person had available to him or her, how desirable the action was, and whether we believe the person changed his or her behavior in an attempt to impress us. What did the student intend to accomplish in leaving the class?

Causal attribution theory identifies three potential causes for any person's action: circumstance, a stimulus, or the person herself or himself.[13] Attributing to *circumstance* means that you believe a person acts in a certain way because the situation leaves no choice. This way of thinking places responsibility for the action outside of the person. You would be attributing to circumstance if you believed the student quickly left the classroom because of an upset stomach. Concluding that the student left because the instructor said something inappropriate would be attributing the student's action to the *stimulus* (the instructor). But if you knew the instructor hadn't said anything out of line, and that the student was perfectly healthy, you would place the responsibility for the action on the student. Attributing to the *person* means that you believe there is some quality about the person that caused the observed behavior. Attributions to the person are the ones we are most concerned with in this text because they are factors in our impressions of others.

A number of factors affect the accuracy of our attributions: our ability to make effective and complete observations; the degree to which we are able to directly observe the cause and the effect; the completeness of our information;

and our ability to rule out other causes. It is also helpful to know how unique the person's response is to the particular stimulus, to compare the person's response to how other people typically respond, and to know whether the person usually responds each time in the same way to the stimulus. Even with the most complete information, however, we can never completely understand another person's action because we cannot become the other person. Fortunately, we can improve our level of understanding by using decentering and by becoming more sensitive to the assumptions or theories we use to make attributions.

RECAP	How We Organize and Interpret Interpersonal Perceptions		
Term	**Definition**		**Examples**
Impression Formation	We form global perspectives of others based upon general physical qualities, behaviors, and disclosed information.		Categorizing people as nice, friendly, shy, or handsome.
Implicit Personality Theory	We develop a set of relationships among personality characteristics.		"If she is intelligent, then she must be caring, too."
Personal Constructs	We associate specific qualities or attributes with each person we know.		"My friend Fred is caring, smart, strong, and devoted."
Attributions	We develop reasons to explain the behaviors of others. We attribute others' actions to the circumstance, a stimulus, or to the person.		"I guess she didn't return my call because she doesn't like me." "He's just letting off steam because he had a bad week of exams."

Barriers to Accurate Perceptions

Think about the most recent interaction you have had with a stranger. Do you remember the person's age, sex, race, or body size? Did the person have any distinguishing features, such as a beard, wild clothing, or a loud voice? The qualities you recall will most likely serve as the basis for attributions you make about that person's behavior. But these attributions, based upon your first impressions, might be highly inaccurate. We each see the world from our own unique perspective. That perspective is clouded by a number of distortions and barriers that contribute to inaccurate interpersonal perception. We'll examine these barriers next.

Ignoring Details

We give too much weight to information that is obvious and superficial.[14] We tend to explain the motives for a person's actions on the basis of the most obvious information rather than on in-depth information we might have. This means we tend to lump people into general categories and make biased statements about them: "He acts that way because he's a man"; "I guess you can expect that behavior from someone his age"; and "Of course, it was a woman driver." When meeting someone new, we perceive his or her physical qualities first: color of skin, body size and shape, age, sex, and other obvious physical characteristics. We overattribute to these qualities because they are so vivid and available. We have all been victims of these kinds of attributions, some of us more than others. Often we are unaware that others are making biased attributions because they do not express them openly. But sometimes we can tell by the way others react to us and treat us.

One female student described a job interview in which the male interviewer talked at her for fifteen minutes and then abruptly dismissed her without asking a single question. A male friend of hers with less distinguished academic qualifications and work experience spent forty minutes fielding questions from this same interviewer. Did the interviewer have a sex bias? Probably. Looking only at the female student's gender, he attributed qualities to her that he decided would make her unsuitable for the job. Instead of looking at the more specific information her résumé provided, he simply disregarded it. As discussed earlier, this tendency reflects our desire to simplify stimuli, but it can be dangerous and unfair.

Overgeneralizing

We treat small amounts of information as if they were highly representative.[15] This tendency also leads us to draw inaccurate, prejudicial conclusions. For example, your authors may talk to two students from your school, and then generalize the impression we have of those two students to the entire student population. In a similar way, we tend to assume that the small sampling we have of another person's behavior is a valid representation of who that person is. As we saw in Figure 3.2, we create a rabbit even when we have only a few dots on which to base our perception.

Holding on to Preconceptions and Stereotypes

We distort or ignore information that violates our expectations, preconceptions, or stereotypes.[16] We see what we want to see, hear what we want to hear. Earlier in this chapter we talked about how we develop impressions and constructs. Once we develop them, we have preconceptions about what we expect from another person. These preconceptions and stereotypes can be so strong that we will distort the way we process our perceptions in order to remain constant to them. The halo and horn effects discussed earlier are reflections of this tendency. For example, if an instructor gets an excellent paper from a student who she has concluded is not particularly bright or motivated, she may tend to find errors and shortcomings that are not really there, or she may even accuse the student of plagiarism.

Reference the different perceptions people have had concerning the content or efficacy of political debates, including the Nixon-Kennedy, Lincoln-Douglas, or Bush-Ferraro events. What preconceptions do many audience members have which bias their perceptions?

Imposing Consistency

We overestimate the consistency and constancy of others' behaviors. When we organize our perceptions, we also tend to ignore fluctuation in people's behaviors, and see them as consistent. We believe that if someone acted a certain way one day, he or she will continue to act that way in the future. Perhaps you have embarrassed yourself in front of a new acquaintance by acting foolish and silly. At another encounter with this new acquaintance, you realize that the person is continuing to see your behavior as foolish, even though you don't intend it to be seen that way. The other person is imposing consistency on the perception of your inconsistent behavior.

In fact, everyone's behavior varies from day to day. Some days we are in a bad mood, and our behavior on those days does not represent what we are generally like. As intimacy develops in relationships, we interact with our partners in a variety of activities that provide a more complete picture of their true nature.

Preconnecting Causes and Effects

We rely on preexisting ideas about underlying causes and what we observe. We've already seen how preconceptions about a person can shape our attributions. We also develop a particular type of preconception that reflects both our implicit personality theory and our personal constructs. We create beliefs about what particular causes are linked to what particular effects. This keeps us from investigating and collecting additional information to explain an individual's action. For example, suppose you take a two-hour lunch one day because your child falls off the monkey bars at school and you have to rush her to the doctor. You return to work and your boss screams that people who take long lunches (effect) are lazy, irresponsible, or alcoholic (cause), and refuses to listen to your explanation. To avoid imposing your own preconceptions on others, you must be ready to listen to alternative explanations.

BUILDING YOUR SKILLS

Preconceived Explanations

Think about your own preconceptions about cause–effect relationships. For each of the following, think about what your first explanation of the cause would be:

- A person not calling back after a first date.

- A waitress giving you lousy service.

- Your car not being repaired after you paid a high service fee.

- A teacher being late for class.

- A child who beats up on other kids.

- A student who copies test answers from the student next to him.

- A mother who refuses to let her teenage son drive the car on Friday nights.

Now go back and generate as many alternative explanations for each behavior as you can. How can you be sure which explanation is correct?

Have students brainstorm a top ten list (like David Letterman's) which describes the ten barriers to perception in interpersonal relationships. Encourage students to be creative! Next, analyze these reasons in light of the barriers described in this chapter.

SKILL DEVELOPMENT

Prepare each of the seven scenarios on separate note cards. Divide the class into seven groups and have a representative from each group select a scenario. Have each group list the most obvious cause and then brainstorm for "wacky alternatives." Allow each group to report to the class and have a vote for the most creative and wacky report. You might provide a reward (candy, bonus points, etc.) for the winning group.

SKILL DEVELOPMENT
Suggest that students audio-tape their side of a telephone conversation with a friend. Then ask them to re-play it and decide how valuable each of the comments was in terms of content and relationship. How might these comments have been misinterpreted if taken out of context?

Preferring Simple Explanations

We prefer simple explanations to complex ones. When Imelda picks you up late to go to a movie, she says, "Sorry, I lost track of the time." The next day, Mary also picks you up late to go to a movie. She says, "Sorry. You wouldn't believe how busy I've been. I ran out of hot water when I was showering and my hair dryer must be busted. It kept shutting off. Then I stopped to get something to eat and it took forever to get my order. And then it turned out they had it all messed up and had to redo it." Whose explanation can you accept more easily, Imelda's or Mary's?

Usually we prefer simple explanations; they tend to be more believable and easier to use in making sense of another's actions. But in reality our behaviors are affected by a multitude of factors, as Mary's explanation indicates. Unfortunately, it takes a lot of effort to understand what makes another person do what he or she does—more effort than we are typically willing to give.

Ignoring Circumstances

We diminish the effect of external circumstances on another's behavior.[17] Although we tend to explain our own negative actions in terms of circumstances, we tend to attribute others' actions to their personality. If we are late for an appointment, it is because of traffic or the need to wrap up a project, and so on. But if others are late, it is because they are unpunctual and have intentionally chosen to treat us rudely. Again, this tendency represents our desire for simplification. We are often unaware of the circumstances that affect others, and we do not want to take the trouble to investigate them.

We also fail to compare one person's behavior with that of others under the same circumstances. Suppose you have a close friend who has flunked out of school because of personal problems, financial difficulties, and insufficient college preparation. You gain many insights into his motives and emotions as you spend time providing support. However, if you meet someone else who flunked out of school, you may not compare this other person's situation with your friend's. Usually, we come to appreciate the effect of circumstances on the behaviors of those we know intimately, but we discard that knowledge when we encounter it in someone else, preferring to attribute the behavior to the person.

Crediting Irrelevant Information

We treat irrelevant information as if it were relevant. Have you ever sat and analyzed a conversation after it was finished, considering what each word, gesture, and intonation really meant? In truth, most exchanges are filled with irrelevant information, and it requires skill and experience to separate the irrelevant information from information that really does help explain another's actions. Imagine eating at a restaurant where the waiter seems rude and impatient. Later you may ask yourself, "Why was that waiter so rude to me? Did I take too long in placing my order? Was he upset when I asked for a second order of fries? Maybe he thinks I'm not going to leave a tip? Didn't he realize I was joking around when I placed my order for 'ground cow on a wheat bun'?" Such questions relate to information that may have nothing to do with his behavior. The waiter may have worked a double shift, had problems with the kitchen staff, or had personal problems at home.

Focusing on the Negative

We give more weight to negative information than to positive information.[18] Job interviewers often ask interviewees to describe their strengths and weaknesses. If you describe five great strengths and one weakness, it is likely that the interviewer will attend more to the one weakness you mention than to the strengths. We seem to recognize this bias and compensate for it when we first meet someone by sharing only positive information about ourselves.

In another of the Solomon Asch experiments on impression formation, participants heard one of the following two lists of terms describing a person: (1) intelligent, skillful, industrious, warm, determined, practical, cautious; or (2) intelligent, skillful, industrious, cold , determined, practical, cautious.[19] The only difference in these two lists is the use of "warm" in the first list, and "cold" in the second. Despite the presence of six other terms, those with the "cold" list had a much more negative impression of the person than those with the "warm" list. One piece of negative information can have a disproportionate effect on our impressions and negate the effect of several positive pieces of information.

Seeing Good or Bad

We distort our attributions to match our like or dislike for someone. A small dog comes running up to a person. The person kicks the dog, sending it yelping away. The person is someone you don't like. Why do you think he or she behaved this way? You would probably say something like, "That person is mean." You would attribute the behavior to an internal cause. But what if that person was a close friend whom you liked a lot? Then you would probably say, "My friend is afraid of dogs," or "That dog was about to bite her—what else could she do?" You relieve your friend of responsibility by attributing her action to external causes. By the same token, if someone we like does something positive, we attribute it to his or her personality, but when those we dislike do something positive, we attribute it to external reasons or to some darker motivation.

We explain our own behavior in a similar way: the things we do that people like about us are because of who we are; the things we do that are undesirable, we attribute to circumstance. For example, if you fail an exam, you are likely to blame some external cause—the exam was unfair, you had to work, or your roommates were noisy when you were studying. But if you ace the exam, it is because you are smart and studious.

INSTRUCTIONAL GOALS AND TIPS
This is also the case for students who are listening to teachers' feedback. Sandwich constructive criticism between positive comments whenever possible.

INSTRUCTIONAL GOALS AND TIPS
This self-serving bias is both necessary and desirable. Notice this when students make excuses for their behavior.

WEB ACTIVITY
What's Your VALS Type?
http://future.sri.com/vals/ivals/ ques-nt.html/
Complete the questionnaire to identify your psychological profile. This test captures a cluster of values to represent your lifestyle. Ask students if their perception of the VALS Type is accurate.

IGNORING DETAILS	We give too much weight to information that is obvious and superficial.
OVERGENERALIZING	We treat small amounts of information as if they were highly representative.
HOLDING ON TO PRECONCEPTIONS	We distort or ignore information that violates our expectations or preconceptions.
IMPOSING CONSISTENCY	We overestimate the consistency and constancy of others' behaviors.
PRECONNECTING CAUSES AND EFFECTS	We rely on preexisting ideas about the underlying causes for what we observe.
PREFERRING SIMPLE EXPLANATIONS	We prefer simple explanations to complex ones.
IGNORING CIRCUMSTANCES	We diminish the effect of external circumstances on another's behavior. We fail to compare one person's behavior with that of others under the same circumstances.
CREDITING IRRELEVANT INFORMATION	We treat irrelevant information as if it were relevant.
FOCUSING ON THE NEGATIVE	We give more weight to negative information than to positive information.
SEEING GOOD OR BAD	We distort our attributions to match our like or dislike for someone.

Improving Your Perceptual Skills

With so many barriers to perceiving and interpreting other people's behavior accurately, what can you do to improve your perceptual skills? Increasing your awareness of the factors that lead to inaccuracy will help initially, and you will find further suggestions in this section. Ultimately, your improvement will depend upon your willingness to grow as you expand your experiences, to communicate about your perceptions with others, and to seek out and consider others' perceptions of you. Realize that you have had a lifetime to develop these barriers and that it will take time, commitment, and effort to overcome their effects.

Increase Your Understanding of the Perceptual Process

Study this chapter well because it will help you to understand many of the elements that affect your perception. You need to understand the process through which you make sense of the world and other people. Don't take your conclusions about others for granted. Question your perceptions and analyze the process through which you arrive at perceptual conclusions. Emulate Sherlock

---

INSTRUCTIONAL GOALS AND TIPS

Write two letters of recommendation, one simplistic and equivocal, the other specific and clear. Have students describe which recommendation they would prefer to receive and why this is so. Use the Recap as a reference for this discussion.

DISCUSSION AND WRITING

Consider these statistics: "Over 50% agreed . . ." or "Nearly 30% disagreed . . ." How might each be interpreted? Recommend that positive feedback be introduced before negative feedback is offered.

Holmes: use your knowledge of the perceptual process to sharpen your own perceptions and conclusions.

Increase Your Observational Acuity

Your senses are constantly bombarding you with information, much of which you ignore. You can increase the amount of information that you process from your senses by consciously attending to the input. When you interact with others, try to identify one new thing each time to focus on and observe. Watch their gestures, their eyes, the wrinkles around their eyes, their foot movements; listen to their tone of voice. Each observation will provide information that potentially can improve the quality of your interactions. You may create additional problems, however, if you focus so narrowly on one element that you miss others or overestimate the meaning of irrelevant information. Try to notice as much detail as possible, but keep the entire picture in view.

Recognize the Elements to Which You Attribute Meaning

As we have seen, the third stage in the perception process involves attributing meaning to what we perceive. We do this so automatically that we often fail to realize that we have attributed meaning to something. Therefore, we also fail to recognize the effect it might have on what we do and say. Try to become aware of the stimuli to which you attribute meaning. For instance, if you shake a man's hand that is weak and clammy, you might quickly withdraw your hand and form an impression of the man as wimpy and aloof without realizing that you have attributed meaning to the handshake. Take an inventory of your own perceptual tendencies. Do you pay particular attention to eye contact, gestures, facial expressions, clothing, accents, or vocal intonations? When you become more aware of what you attend to and when you are attributing meaning, you can then decide whether you are giving proper weight to the elements you are perceiving.

Check Your Perceptions

You can check out the accuracy of your perceptions and attributions indirectly and directly. **Indirect perception checking** involves seeking additional information through passive perception to either confirm or refute your interpretations. If you suspect someone is angry at you but is not admitting it, for example, you could look for more cues in his or her tone of voice, eye contact, and body movements to confirm your suspicion. You could also ask questions or listen more intently to the person's words and language.

Direct perception checking involves asking straight out whether your interpretations of a perception are correct. This often is not easy to do for several reasons: We don't like to admit uncertainty or suspicions to others; we might not trust that they will respond honestly; if our interpretations are wrong, we might suffer embarrassment or anger. But asking someone to confirm a perception shows that you are committed to understanding his or her behavior. If your friend's voice sounds weary and her posture is sagging, you may assume that she

---

SKILL DEVELOPMENT
Ask five volunteers to line up and repeat a story or describe their perceptions of a picture down the line. Again each should record his or her transmission. Discuss the changes down the line.

SKILL DEVELOPMENT
Then, have students form diads, introduce themselves, and shake hands. Next, ask them to turn around so that they cannot see one another. Instruct them to silently make three changes in their appearance. Have them turn face to face and identify the changes made by their partner. Repeat this exercise with three additional changes. Discuss students' observational acuity following the exercise.

DISCUSSION AND WRITING
Ask students to take five minutes and write a summary of the main points covered in this class session so far. Next, have students exchange summaries and edit these for accuracy. Discuss the value of perception checking.

ACTIVITY
See Activity 3.3 in the Instructor's Guide.

is depressed or upset. If you ask, "I get the feeling from your tone of voice and the way you're acting that you are kind of down and depressed; what's wrong?" your friend can then either provide another interpretation: "I'm just tired; I had a busy week"; or expand on your interpretation: "Yeah, things haven't been going very well. . . ." Your observation might also be a revelation: "Really? I didn't realize I was acting that way. I guess I am a little down."

Increase Your Awareness of Perceptual Inaccuracies and Compensate for Them

As you read through the list of distorting factors earlier in this chapter, some of them should have struck a familiar chord. Keep in mind which distortions tend to color your perceptions of others and be aware of their effect. For example, if you know that you are likely to interpret the behavior of people you don't like in a negative way, regardless of their intent, then you can question your interpretations and correct them if necessary.

Increase Your Awareness of Others' Perceptions of You, and Seek Honest and Constructive Feedback

The best athletes don't avoid hearing criticisms and observations from their coaches. Instead, they seek out as much feedback as they can about what they are doing right and wrong. Olympic training often involves the use of videotaped replays and computer analysis so that athletes can see themselves as others see them and use that perspective to improve their performance. It is difficult to be objective about our own behavior, so feedback from others can help us with our self-perceptions. The strongest relationships are those in which the partners are both willing to share and be receptive to the perceptions of the other.

MEDIA AND OUTSIDE RESOURCES

Show scenes from the movie *White Christmas,* in which Betty Hayes misattributes Bob Wallace's motives for appearing on "The Ed Harris Show." Discuss the dangers of perceptual inaccuracies. How might Betty have clarified her misperception?

Identifying Your Bias

Write down a list of some recent interpretations you've made about others' behaviors. Identify the specific behavior or quality that you have observed and the resulting inter-

pretation. For example, Joe is a really big man (quality); therefore, he must be a football player (interpretation).

Identify which interpretations might have been affected by any of the biases we've talked about (for example, giving

weight to information that is obvious and superficial).

See if you can find out the validity of those interpretations by collecting additional information. Ask Joe if he plays football, or look on the football roster for his name.

Develop Social Decentering, Empathy, and Other-Orientation

Effective interpersonal perception depends upon our ability to understand where others are coming from, to get inside their heads, to see things from their perspectives. We have already introduced the importance of social decentering and empathy in interpersonal communication. They enable us to increase our understanding of others, and they improve our ability to predict and adapt, to increase our communication effectiveness, and to achieve our interpersonal goals.[20] To improve your ability to decenter (to focus on the thoughts of others), strive for two key goals: (1) gather as much knowledge about the circumstances that are affecting the other person as possible; and (2) gather as much knowledge about the other person as possible. We will discuss these skills in more detail in Chapter 4.

Ten Questions That Enhance Social Decentering:

How to Take the Perspective of Another Person

1. What factors or circumstances are affecting the person?
2. How can I determine whether there are factors I don't know about or don't fully understand?
3. What do I know about this person that explains his or her behaviors and feelings?
4. What is going through the other person's mind at this time?
5. What are the other person's feelings at this time?
6. What other explanations could there be for the person's actions?
7. What would I think if I were in the same situation?
8. How would I feel if I were in the same situation?
9. What would other people think if they were in that situation?
10. What would other people feel if they were in that situation?

TEACHING STRATEGY

You can expand this Building Your Skills activity to include seeking honest and constructive feedback by having students pass their anonymous lists of recent interpretations to you. Read several student lists to the class, asking the class to critique the interpretations.

TEACHING STRATEGY

To emphasize developing decentering, empathy, and other-orientation, ask students to name professions that would require these skills. Ask students whether you can effectively perform any job that affects other people without some degree of skill in these areas.

TEACHING STRATEGY

Some students may believe empathy—feeling what another person feels—sounds silly. To respond to this, ask the class whether they have ever cried, shouted, or clapped at a movie. You can argue that they needed to empathize in order to do these things.

TEACHING STRATEGY

Speaking about perception checking and developing empathy is guaranteed to be easier than doing. The "Impression Formation in the Classroom" activity (Activity 3.2 in the Instructor's Guide) could be used for an expanded version of the text's "Learning with Others" idea on page 96.

Summary

Interpersonal perception is a fundamental element of interpersonal communication. Our communication and interpersonal relationships are affected by the way we perceive those with whom we interact. Interpersonal perception is more than just the arousal of the senses; it also involves selecting, organizing, and interpreting what we observe in order to decide what people are like and give meaning to their actions.

Our perceptions of others affect how we communicate, and how others perceive us affects how they communicate with us. Interpersonal perception can be a passive or active process. It is passive when only our senses are in operation; it is active when we feel a need for information and intentionally seek it. We are motivated to seek information in situations that have high amounts of uncertainty. Perception of information helps reduce uncertainty and provides us with more control of the situation.

Interpersonal perception affects and is affected by the development of impressions, our own implicit personality theories, constructs, and attributions. Our general impressions of individuals are often affected by primacy and recency effects; we pay particular attention to the first things we notice and the most recent things we notice about others. In our interactions with others, we all seem to operate as "naive psychologists," developing and applying our own implicit personality theories. These implicit personality theories represent the general way we believe people behave. We develop specific personal constructs that represent the qualities we associate with specific people we know. Finally, we try to explain the actions and behaviors of others through the process of attribution. According to attribution theorists, we seek to find out the intent and cause of a person's action; we see a person's action as a response to a given circumstance, a particular stimulus, or the person's own personality. To make rational and accurate attributions, we must overcome perceptual barriers. We can identify ten specific tendencies that distort the accuracy of our attributions, such as focusing on obvious or negative information.

The following suggestions will help you to improve your interpersonal perception: (1) increase your understanding of the perceptual process; (2) increase your observational acuity; (3) recognize the elements to which you are attributing meaning; (4) check out your perceptions directly and indirectly; (5) increase your awareness of perceptual biases and compensate for them; (6) increase your awareness of others' perceptions of you and seek honest and constructive feedback; and (7) develop your ability to decenter and empathize.

For Discussion and Review

■ FOCUS ON COMPREHENSION

1. In what ways does interpersonal perception affect our interpersonal communication and relationships?

2. Identify and describe the three stages of the interpersonal perception process.

3. Explain the relationships among impressions, implicit personality theory, constructs, and attribution theory.

4. Identify and explain three barriers to accurate perception.

5. How can you improve your perceptual skills?

■ FOCUS ON CRITICAL THINKING

6. Think about some of your recent interpersonal conflicts. How would you describe your perception of the problem? How do you think the others would describe their perceptions of it? What role did perception play in contributing to or resolving the conflict?

7. What do you think contributes to the development of the tendencies that cause us to perceive people inaccurately? How might the effects of those factors be minimized or eliminated?

■ FOCUS ON ETHICS

8. Do you have a right in an intimate relationship to expect your partner to share his or her perceptions of you, whether those perceptions are positive or negative? Explain your reasoning.

9. If you are aware of how you are distorting your own perceptions and attributions, should you try to change them? Is it a moral obligation? Explain your reasoning.

For Your Journal

1. As you interact with a friend, try to assess your awareness level of the cues that are being communicated. Ask your friend to confirm your interpretation of the cues that you have observed. How effective and accurate were you at picking up information?

FOCUS ON COMPREHENSION

1. Interpersonal perception is the process of interpreting and attributing meaning to our observations and experiences. When we perceive others in relationships, we ascribe meanings and motives to their appearance and behaviors. This directly affects the way that we respond and communicate with others.

2. The three stages of the perceptual process include the selection, organization, and interpretation of stimuli. First, we focus on or simplify the stimuli being received. Next we impose structure on what we observe or select. Finally, we attribute or assign meaning to these observations.

3. Impressions are collections of perceptions about others that we maintain and use to interpret their behaviors. We organize these impressions by developing our own implicit theories and hypotheses to explain how people behave. Attributes are traits we assign to people and their circumstances; a set of these is called a construct. We use constructs to categorize people into groups that help us develop reasons to explain others' behaviors.

4. Barriers to accurate perception include the following:

• ignoring details,

• overgeneralizing,

• having preconceptions,

• imposing consistency,

• using causation,

• preferring simplification,

• ignoring circumstances,

• treating irrelevant information as relevant,

• focusing on negative information, and

• distorting attributions to match our opinions of others.

5. Perceptual skills can be improved by doing the following:

• increasing your understanding of the perceptual process;

• increasing your observational acuity;

• recognizing the elements to which you are attributing meaning;

• checking your perceptions;

• increasing your awareness of perceptual inaccuracies and compensating for them; and

• developing decentering, empathy, and an other-orientation.

2. Use the list of barriers to accurate perception to do a self-analysis. Which barriers influence your perceptions the most? What problems do those distortions create in your interactions with others?

3. Choose two of the suggestions for improving your perceptions. Develop a plan for what you will do in your next interaction to apply that suggestion. Try the suggestion; then write an evaluation of how well you applied the suggestion, how well the suggestion worked, and how you might modify your plan to apply the suggestion in the future.

Learning with Others

1. Choose an advertisement, magazine illustration, photograph, or painting that shows a group of people and bring it to class. In groups of four or five, pass around the pictures. For each picture, write down a few words to describe your perceptions about what you see in the picture. What are the people doing? What is their relationship to one another? What is each one like? How is each one feeling? Why are they doing what they are doing? After you have finished, share with one another what you wrote down. Try to determine why there were differences. What factors influenced your perceptions?

2. Pair up with someone in class who you do not know and have not interacted with before. Without saying anything to each other, write down the words from the following list that you think apply to the other person. Now converse for five minutes. In a separate section of your paper, write down any additional words that you believe apply to the person. You can go back and put a line through any of the words in the first list that you now think are inaccurate. Share with your partner what words you put down before and during the conversation, and what words you changed. Have your partner share his or her perceptions of you. Discuss, as best you can, the reasons you chose each word.

Intelligent	Athletic	Artistic	Studious
Nice	Funny	Conceited	Friendly
Introvert	Extrovert	Hard worker	Shy
Talented	Popular	Inquisitive	Moody
Emotional	Happy	Brave	Responsible
Leader	Follower	Uncertain	Confused

■ GLOSSARY

PERCEPTION: The arousal of any of our senses.

INTERPERSONAL PERCEPTION: The process of selecting, organizing, and interpreting our observations of other people.

SELECTIVE PERCEPTION: Directing our attention to specific stimuli and consequently ignoring other stimuli.

STEREOTYPE: A set of qualities that we attribute to a person because of the person's membership in some category.

CLOSURE: The process of filling in missing information.

PASSIVE PERCEPTION: Perception that occurs because our senses are in operation.

ACTIVE PERCEPTION: Seeking out specific information through intentional observation and questioning.

IMPRESSION: A general collection of perceptions about people that we maintain and use to interpret their behaviors.

PRIMACY EFFECT: Placing heavy emphasis upon the first pieces of information that we observe about another to form an impression.

RECENCY EFFECT: Placing heavy emphasis on the most recent information we have observed about another to form or modify our impression.

IMPLICIT PERSONALITY THEORY: Our own set of beliefs and hypotheses about what people are like.

HALO EFFECT: Attributing a variety of positive qualities to those we like.

HORN EFFECT: Attributing a variety of negative qualities to those we dislike.

CONSTRUCTS: Bipolar qualities that we associate with people as we conceptualize them.

COGNITIVE COMPLEXITY: The level of ability to develop a sophisticated set of personal constructs.

ATTRIBUTION PROCESS: The process whereby we generate explanations for people's behaviors.

CORRESPONDENT INFERENCE THEORY: One theory of attribution that is based on determining how intentional a person's actions are.

CAUSAL ATTRIBUTION THEORY: One theory of attribution that is based upon determining whether a person's actions are caused by circumstance, a stimulus, or the person.

INDIRECT PERCEPTION CHECKING: Seeking additional information to confirm or refute interpretations you are making through passive perception.

DIRECT PERCEPTION CHECKING: Asking for confirmation or refutation from the observed person of an interpretation or a perception about him or her.

4

Interpersonal Communication and Cultural Diversity: Adapting to Others

After studying this chapter, you should be able to:

1. Define culture.

2. Identify cultural elements, values, and contexts.

3. Discuss differences and similarities in verbal and nonverbal communication in different cultures.

4. Discuss barriers that inhibit effective intercultural communication.

5. Identify strategies for developing knowledge, motivation, and skills that can improve intercultural competence.

■ THE NATURE OF CULTURE

■ BARRIERS TO EFFECTIVE INTERCULTURAL COMMUNICATION

■ IMPROVING INTERCULTURAL COMPETENCE

Perhaps you've heard the saying, "Everyone's a little strange except you and me, and I'm not so sure about you." There is a kernel of truth in that sentiment. The simple fact is there is no one else exactly like you, which means that others can seem strange or different from you.

One of life's unprofound principles with profound implications for interpersonal communication is this: We each have different backgrounds and experiences. And, as we learned in the last chapter, we each perceive the world differently. To some degree, we are each estranged from others. There are differences between you and your best friend, even if you grew up together and lived in the same neighborhood.

The greater the difference in background, experience, and the manner in which you perceive others, the more challenging it can be to develop quality relationships with others. A central goal of our study of interpersonal communication is to learn how to better relate to others. Some of the differences that contribute to our diversity and thus interfere with developing relationships include differences in age, learning style, gender, religion, ethnicity, sexual orientation, social class, race, and culture.

In the first three chapters we acknowledged the influence of diversity on our interpersonal relationships. In this chapter we will examine in more detail the impact that our differences have on our lives and suggest some communication strategies for bridging those differences in interpersonal relationships. Specifically, we will focus on the nature of cultural difference, identify barriers that result from those differences, and suggest strategies that can help you better understand, appreciate, and adapt to people who are different from you. Our premise for this discussion of diversity is that in order to live comfortably in the twenty-first century, we must learn ways to appreciate and understand cultural differences instead of ignoring them, suffering because of them, or wishing that they would disappear.

Some people believe that diversity, especially cultural diversity, is overemphasized. One student overheard before class exclaimed, "I've had it with all this cultural diversity stuff. It seems like every textbook in every class is obsessed with it. My history textbook talks about all these obscure people I've never heard of before. In English lit all we're reading is stuff by people from different cultures. I'm tired of all this politically correct nonsense. I mean, we're all Americans. We're not all going off and live in China. Why don't they just teach us what we need to know and cut all this diversity garbage?"

Perhaps you've encountered this kind of "diversity backlash" among some of your classmates, or you may hold this attitude yourself. It may seem unsettling

99

DISCUSSION AND WRITING
Some cultual diversity experts argue that we've a tossed salad America rather than a melting pot America. Ask students to comment upon the communication effects of each perspective. Furthermore, comment upon the value of treating each student exactly the same versus differently by equally. To illustrate the need for interpersonal sensitivity, you might use the analogy of the gardener who treats each plant differently but devotes equal energy to each for optimal growth.

INSTRUCTIONAL GOALS AND TIPS
Conduct the "Diversity Bingo" exercise in the "Learning with Others" section at the end of the chapter. Consider doing some additional research on those topics you know little about so that you can debrief with confidence.

that our textbooks are changing, and that educators are concerned with cultural diversity. But these changes are not motivated by an irrational desire to be politically correct. They are taking place because the United States is changing. As the statistics in the Diversity Almanac below suggest, the United States is becoming an increasingly culturally diverse country. With this growing diversity comes a growing awareness that learning about cultural differences can affect every aspect of our lives in positive ways. You may not plan to travel the world, but the world is traveling to you. Your boss, teacher, religious leader, best friend, or marriage partner may have grown up with different cultural traditions than your own. Our textbooks and courses are reflecting the change, not initiating it.

Diversity Almanac

■ Two-thirds of the immigrants on this planet come to the United States.[1]

■ By the year 2000 white males are expected to become a minority in a work force that is likely to be 12 percent African American, 11 percent Hispanic, 8 percent Asian American, and 43 percent female.[2]

■ Estimates show that by the year 2000, more than 40 million U.S. residents will have a non-English first language—including 18 million people for whom Spanish is a first language.[3]

■ Almost one-third of U.S. residents under the age of thirty-five are members of minority groups, compared with one-fifth of those aged thirty-five or older. According to U.S. Census Bureau population projects, by the year 2025, nearly half of all young adults in this country will come from minority groups.[4]

- If the current trend continues, by the year 2050 the population of U.S. white ethnics will decrease to 60 percent, down from a current 80 percent, while Asians increase to 16 percent, up from 1.6 percent, Hispanics triple their numbers to over 19 percent, up from just over 6.5 percent, and African Americans increase their proportion slightly from the current 12 percent.[5]

- Persons from co-cultures within the United States consume more goods and services than do any of America's trading partners, and constitute 25 percent of the U.S. economic market at the turn of the century.[6]

Guo-Ming Chen and William Starosta argue that the "political and economic effectiveness of the United States in the global arena will depend on individual and collective abilities to communicate competently with people from other cultures."[7] To support this claim they note:

- Thirty-three percent of corporate profits in the United States stem from international trade.

- Half of the total profits from the twenty-three largest U.S. banks are derived from overseas.

- Foreign trade helps to generate four out of five of every new job in the United States.

- The United States has over $300 billion invested abroad.

- Foreign individuals and corporations have invested over $1.5 trillion in the United States in the last twenty-five years.[8]

As noted by one statistician, if the world was a village of 1,000 people, in the village would be: 590 Asians, 123 Africans, 96 Europeans, 84 Latin Americans, 55 Former Soviet Union members and 53 North Americans.[9] Clearly, a global economy increases the likelihood that you will communicate with people from many of these different cultures. And you need not travel the world to communicate with people from other cultures. As noted in the Diversity Almanac, two-thirds of all immigrants on this planet come to the United States.[10]

Even though you may not have traveled to the four corners of the world, today's economical and swift transportation system increases the likelihood that you will travel abroad. As Peace Corps volunteer Charles Larson discovered when he traveled abroad, becoming immersed in a new culture has positive benefits. His Peace Corps opportunity was a transforming experience.

> *I saw ways of life I would never have seen had I remained within the comfortable domain of my provincial Midwestern upbringing. For the first time, I learned to think of someone besides myself, to consider that there is no single way of observing a problem or answering a troubling question. I discovered that without the mutual tolerance and respect of other people's cultures, there is no possibility for harmony in our world.*[11]

His experience helped him become more other-oriented, a quality we will discuss later in the chapter.

INSTRUCTIONAL GOALS AND TIPS
Be certain to focus your discussions upon communication issues rather than cultural values and differences (i.e., anthropology).

Assign the "Intercultural Scavenger Hunt" (exercise 4 in the "Learning with Others" section at the end of this chapter). Develop a handout of some key items to find or discover that include a souvenir from the international student affairs office or whatever is the equivalent on your campus.

DISCUSSION AND WRITING
Ask students whether they believe that political ideology (e.g., liberal or conservative) might be appropriately included in this list. Consider the work of University of Michigan political scientist Michael Bennett who estimates that less than a third of Americans have anything other than a rudimentary understanding of political ideology. For instance, half of those he interviewed believed that the national Democratic Party was more conservative than the GOP or said they didn't know. Bennett said, "When people don't understand the language of politics, they lose out in their ability to control their political leaders."

Given the importance of culture and cultural differences, we will first turn our attention to defining the nature of culture, then we will identify barriers to effective intercultural communication, and finally, we will identify strategies that can improve your intercultural competence.

The Nature of Culture

Exactly what is culture? **Culture** is a learned system of knowledge, behaviors, attitudes, beliefs, values, and norms that is shared by a group of people.[12] In the broadest sense, culture includes how people think, what they do, and how they use things to sustain their lives. Geert Hofstede describes culture as the "mental software" that touches every aspect of how we make sense out of the world and share that sense with others.[13] Cultural diversity results from the unique nature of each culture. The elements, values, and context of each culture distinguish it from all others.

When we speak of culture, we may be referring to a **co-culture**. A co-culture is a cultural group within a larger culture. Many communication researchers consider gender as one of the most important co-cultures that has a significant effect on our communication with others. Gays and lesbians constitute another important co-culture in our society. Understanding Diversity: Our Range of Differences describes both cultural and co-cultural variables that affect our interpersonal relationships with others.

Cultural Elements

Categories of things and ideas that identify the most profound aspects of cultural influence are known as **cultural elements**. According to one research team, cultural elements include the following:

- Material culture: things and ideas

- Social institutions: schools, governments, religious organizations

- Individuals and the universe: system of beliefs

- Aesthetics: music, theater, art, dance

- Language: verbal and nonverbal communication systems[14]

As we grow, we learn to value these cultural elements. You were not born with a certain taste in music, clothes, and automobiles. Through **enculturation**, the process of communicating a group's culture from generation to generation, you learned what you liked by choosing from among the elements that were available within your culture. Your friends, colleagues, the media, and most importantly, your family, communicate information about these elements and advocate choices for you to make.

INTERNET RESOURCE
Enculturation
http://www.wsu.edu:8001/vcwsu
/commons/topics/culture/glossary/
reproduction.html
Defines and provides examples.

http://www.uta.edu/huma/
enculturation/splash.html
Enculturation in today's society.

http://www.stewart.cs.sdsu.edu/
ernestboyer/oneil_noframes...

Cultures are not static; they change as new information and new influences penetrate their stores of knowledge. We no longer believe that bathing is unhealthy, or that we can safely use makeup containing lead. These changes resulted from scientific discoveries. But other changes take place through **acculturation**; we acquire other approaches, beliefs, and values by coming into

The enculturation these women received growing up in Koreatown in Los Angeles was quite different from what they would have received had they lived in another neighborhood. (A. Ramey/Woodfin Camp & Associates)

BUILDING YOUR SKILLS

Assessing Your Communication with Strangers

Your comfort level in communicating with strangers is related to your ability to communicate with people from other cultures. Respond to each statement by indicating the degree to which it is true of your communication with strangers: Always False (answer 1), Usually False (answer 2), Sometimes True and Sometimes False (answer 3), Usually True (answer 4), or Always True (answer 5).

_____ 1. I accept strangers as they are.

_____ 2. I express my feelings when I communicate with strangers.

_____ 3. I avoid negative stereotyping when I communicate with strangers.

_____ 4. I find similarities between myself and strangers when we communicate.

_____ 5. I accommodate my behavior to strangers when we communicate.

To find your score, add the numbers you wrote next to each statement. Scores range from 5 to 25. The higher your score, the greater your potential for developing a strong relationship with someone from a different background.

From: William B. Gudykunst, *Bridging Differences: Effective Intergroup Communication* (Newbury Park: Sage, 1991), 143.

Ask students to describe in writing how members of their family show interest, act polite, indicate disapproval, and greet one another. Next, have students compare their answers in small group discussions.

contact with other cultures. Today, acupuncture, yoga, t'ai chi, and karate studios are commonplace in most cities across America. Taco shells are available in every supermarket, salsa sales now surpass ketchup sales, and Dunkin' Donuts sells bagels. In less obvious ways, "new" perspectives from other cultures have also influenced our thoughts, actions, and relationships.

Cultural Values

Identifying what a given group of people values or appreciates can provide insight into the behavior of an individual raised within that group. Although there are great differences among the world's **cultural values**, one researcher identified four variables for measuring values that are significant in almost every

UNDERSTANDING DIVERSITY

Our Range of Differences

Cultural diversity includes more than differences in ethnic background or gender. To become other-oriented is to consider a range of differences that affect how we communicate and respond to others. Note the following differences that affect our interactions with others.

AGE Different generations, because they share different cultural and historical events, often view life differently. If your grandparents experienced the Great Depression of the 1930s, they may have different attitudes about savings accounts than you or even your parents. Today's explicit song lyrics may shock older Americans who grew up with such racy lyrics as "makin' whoopee." The generation gap is real.

RELIGION Eating habits and attitudes toward abortion and use of alcohol are just a few of the factors in a person's religious beliefs and traditions that can

affect relationships. Although most people in the United States are Christians, there is great diversity in the beliefs and practices of different denominations. Here is a breakdown of the top ten denominations by percent of total U.S. population:

Percent of population

1.	Roman Catholic	26.2%
2.	Baptist	19.4%
3.	Protestant (nondenomination)	9.8%
4.	Methodist	8.0%
5.	Lutheran	5.2%
6.	Christian	4.8%
7.	Presbyterian	2.8%
8.	Pentecostal	1.8%
9.	Episcopalian/Anglican	1.7%
10.	Mormon/Latter Day Saint	1.4%

The top five other religions in the United States are:

Percent of population

1.	Judaism	1.8%
2.	Islam	.5%
3.	Buddhism	.4%
4.	Hinduism	.2%
5.	Bahaism	.01%

DISABILITY Although you may not think of the disabled as part of the cultural diversity equation, there is evidence that we unconsciously alter our communication style when we converse with disabled people. For example, we make less eye contact with people who are in wheelchairs; we also afford them more personal space when conversing. We often speak more loudly and more slowly to those who are blind. Many disabled people find these behaviors insulting.

SOCIAL CLASS The Constitution declares that all people are created equal, but there is dramatic evidence that class culture.[15] According to Geert Hofstede, each culture places varying degrees of value upon masculine and feminine perspectives, avoidance of uncertainty, distribution of power, and individualism. Hofstede's research conclusions for ten countries on these four dimensions are reflected in Table 4.1. High scores indicate greater value for the dimension; low scores suggest that less value is placed on the dimension.

■ MASCULINE VERSUS FEMININE PERSPECTIVES

Some cultures emphasize traditional male values, whereas others place greater value on female perspectives. These values are not really about biological sex differences but over-arching approaches to interacting with others.

differences exist and affect communication patterns. Social psychologist Michael Argyle reports that the cues we use to make class distinctions are: (1) way of life, (2) family, (3) job, (4) money, and (5) education. Class differences influence whom we talk with, whether we are likely to invite our neighbors over for coffee, and whom we choose as our friends and lovers. Most of us must make a conscious effort if we want to expand beyond our class boundaries.

GENDER In this book we emphasize how gender affects the way we listen, use words, and send and interpret nonverbal messages. Sex differences are biological differences between males and females: only men can impregnate, only women can menstruate, gestate, and lactate. But gender differences focus on learned behavior that is culturally associated with being a man or a woman. Gender role definitions are flexible: a man can adopt behavior that is associated

with a female role definition in a given culture and vice versa.

SEXUAL ORIENTATION During the past decade gays and lesbians have become more assertive in expressing their rights within American society. Issues such as whether gays belong in the military, in the clergy, and in the teaching professions have stirred the passions of many. Being gay has become a source of pride for some, but it is still a social stigma for others. The incidence of suicide among gay teenagers is significantly higher than among nongay teens. Although gay people are gaining legal rights and protections, they are still subject to discriminatory laws and social intolerance. The gay and lesbian community functions as a co-culture or a culture within the larger U.S. culture.

RACE According to the dictionary, race is based upon the genetically transmitted physical characteristics of a group of people classified together on the basis of a common history,

nationality, or geographical location. Skin color and other physical characteristics affect our responses and influence the way people of different races interact. Racial prejudice still has a devastating effect upon interpersonal communication patterns and relationships.

ETHNICITY Ethnicity refers to a social classification based upon a variety of factors such as nationality, religion, language, or ancestral heritage. Nationality and geographical location are especially important in defining an ethnic group. Those of Irish ancestry are usually referred to as an ethnic group rather than as a race. The same could be said of Britons, Norwegians, and Spaniards. Ethnicity, like race, fosters common bonds that affect communication patterns. On the positive side, ethnic groups bring vitality and variety to American society. On the negative side, members of these groups may experience persecution or rejection from members of other groups in our society.

DISCUSSION AND WRITING
Ask students to define the terms "tomboy" and "sissy." What do these terms say about enculturation?

INTERNET RESOURCE
Gender Roles
http://osu.orst.edu/~huj/512
Discover how "going beyond pink and blue" can influence gender roles in American society.

Masculine cultures value achievement, assertiveness, heroism, and material wealth. **Feminine cultures** value relationships, caring for the less fortunate, and overall quality of life.[16] Of course, rarely is a culture on the extreme end of the continuum; many are somewhere in between. For centuries most countries in Europe, Asia, and the Americas have had masculine cultures. Men and their conquests dominate history books; men have been more prominent in leadership and decision making than women. But today many of these cultures are moving slowly toward the middle—legal and social rules are encouraging more gender balance and greater equality between masculine and feminine roles.

■ TOLERANCE OF UNCERTAINTY VERSUS AVOIDANCE OF UNCERTAINTY

Sven works for the phone company as a customer service representative. He grew up in Finland where there is sometimes a higher tolerance for bureaucratic uncertainty than there is in the United States. Jake is from Long Island, New York; he expects (sometimes demands) that his problems be resolved quickly. Sven's higher tolerance for uncertainty and Jake's desire for straight, prompt answers to questions created an oil-and-water confrontation. Jake phoned Sven to complain about the slow response to his request to have a new phone line installed for his fax machine. Sven tried to be reassuring, but Jake got the distinct impression that Sven was not sympathetic and thought that a week's wait for a new line was perfectly reasonable. Jake expected his new line within

Table 4.1

A Comparison of Cultural Values Across Ten Countries

Country	Masculinity	Uncertainty Avoidance	Distribution of Power	Individualism
Costa Rica	21 L	86 H	35 L	15 L
France	43 M	86 H	68 H	71 H
Germany	66 H	65 M	35 L	67 H
Great Britain	66 H	35 L	35 L	89 H
Indonesia	46 M	48 L	78 H	14 L
Japan	95 H	92 H	54 M	46 M
Netherlands	14 L	53 M	38 L	80 H
USA	62 M	46 L	40 L	91 H
Russia	40 L	90 H	95 H	50 M
China	50 M	60 M	80 H	20 L

L = Low; M = Medium; H = High

Data from: G. Hofstede, *Cultures and Organizations* (London: McGraw Hill, 1991) and G. Hofstede, "Cultural Constraints on Management Theories," *Academy of Management Executive* 7 (1993) and summarized by P. Salem in "Learning to Learn: The Challenges in Russia," *Intercultural Communication Studies* (1994): 34.

twenty-four hours. Both had difficulty tuning in to the cultural difference in their expectations about how quickly a bureaucracy should respond to an individual request.

Some cultures tolerate more ambiguity and uncertainty than others. Those in which people need certainty to feel secure are more likely to have and enforce rigid rules for behavior and develop more elaborate codes of conduct. People from cultures with a greater tolerance for uncertainty have more relaxed, informal expectations for others. "Go with the flow" and "It will sort itself out" are phrases that describe their attitudes. Sven and Jake's experience is explained by a study showing that people from Portugal, Germany, Peru, Belgium, and Japan have high certainty needs, but people from Scandinavian countries tend to tolerate uncertainty.[17]

■ CONCENTRATED VERSUS DECENTRALIZED DISTRIBUTION OF POWER

Some cultures value an equal or decentralized distribution of power, whereas others accept a concentration of hierarchical power in a centralized government and other organizations. In the latter, hierarchical bureaucracies are common, and people expect some individuals to have more power than others. Russia, France, and China are all high on the concentrated power scale. Those that often strive for greater equality and distribution of power and control include many (but not all) citizens of Australia, Denmark, New Zealand, and Israel. People from these latter countries tend to minimize differences in power between people.

■ INDIVIDUAL VERSUS GROUP ACHIEVEMENT

Cealy: We've got this group project to do. Let's divvy up the work and then meet back here next week to see what each of us has done.

Ayako: Wait a minute, Cealy. It might seem to be more efficient to divide up the work into little separate pieces, but in the end we'll have a better report if we all work on every section.

Cealy: Are you kidding? We'll be here all night! Josh, you take the history of the problem. Bert, you look at problem causes and effects. Ayako, why don't you do a literature search on the CD-ROM in the library and start looking up articles.

Ayako: All right. But I still think it would be better to go to the library together. I think we'd have better luck if we worked on each aspect of the problem as a team.

Cealy and Ayako clearly have different strategies for working together. Cealy approaches the project from an individualistic perspective; Ayako prefers a collective or group strategy to achieve the goal. Traditionally, North Americans

MEDIA AND OUTSIDE RESOURCES
Ask students to discuss the cultural goals depicted in movies such as *Rocky* or *Mr. Smith Goes to Washington*. Consider Emerson's quote, "All great men are nonconformists."

champion individual accomplishments and achievements. People from Asian backgrounds often value collective or group achievement more highly. One researcher summed up the American goal system this way:

> Chief among the virtues claimed . . . is self-realization. Each person is viewed as having a unique set of talents and potentials. The translation of these potentials into actuality is concurred the highest purpose to which one can devote one's life.[18]

In a collectivistic culture, conversely, people strive to attain goals for all members of the family, group, or community. In Kenyan tribes, for example:

> . . . nobody is an isolated individual. Rather, his [or her] uniqueness is secondary fact.
> . . . In this new system group activities are dominant, responsibility is shared, and accountability is collective. . . . Because of the emphasis on collectivity, harmony and cooperation among the group tends to be emphasized more than individual function and responsibility.[19]

Individualistic cultures tend to be more loosely knit socially; individuals feel responsible for taking care of themselves and their immediate families.[20] In collectivistic cultures, individuals expect more support from others, also more loyalty to and from the community. Because collectivistic cultures place more value on "we" than "I," teamwork approaches usually succeed better in their workplaces. U.S. businesses have tried to adopt some of Japan's successful team strategies for achieving high productivity.

RECAP	Dimensions of Cultural Values
Masculine versus Feminine	Does the culture place the highest value on assertiveness, heroism, and wealth or on relationships, caring for others, and overall quality of life?
Tolerance of Uncertainty versus Avoidance of Uncertainty	Does the culture value or appreciate ambiguity and uncertainty or does it hold more rigid and explicit behavioral expectations?
Concentrated versus Decentralized Power	Does the culture tolerate or accept hierarchical power structures or does it favor a more equal distribution of power?
Individual versus Group Achievement	Does the culture value individual achievement more than collective group accomplishments or vice versa?

Cultural Contexts

Individuals from different cultures use **cultural contextual** cues in varying degrees to enhance messages and meaning. This led Edward T. Hall to categorize cultures as either high- or low-context.[21] As shown in Figure 4.1 below, in **high-context cultures** nonverbal cues are extremely important in interpreting messages. **Low-context cultures** rely more explicitly on language, and use fewer contextual cues to send and interpret information. Individuals from high-context cultures may perceive persons from low-context cultures as less attractive, knowledgeable, and trustworthy, because they violate unspoken rules of dress, conduct, and communication. Individuals from low-context cultures often are not skilled in interpreting unspoken, contextual messages.[22]

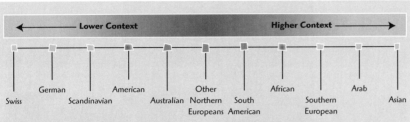

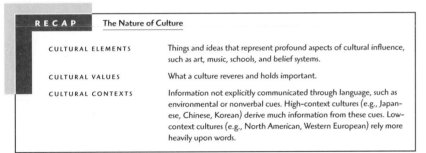

Low-Context Cultures
(Information must be provided explicitly, usually in words.)
· Less aware of nonverbal cues, environment, and situation
· Lack well-developed networks
· Need detailed background information
· Tend to segment and compartmentalize information
· Control information on a "need to know" basis
· Prefer explicit and careful directions from someone who "knows"
· Knowledge is a commodity

High-Context Cultures
(Much information drawn from surroundings. Very little must be explicitly transferred.)
· Nonverbal important
· Information flows freely
· Physical context relied upon for information
· Environment, situation, gestures, mood all taken into account
· Maintain extensive information networks

RECAP   The Nature of Culture

CULTURAL ELEMENTS	Things and ideas that represent profound aspects of cultural influence, such as art, music, schools, and belief systems.
CULTURAL VALUES	What a culture reveres and holds important.
CULTURAL CONTEXTS	Information not explicitly communicated through language, such as environmental or nonverbal cues. High-context cultures (e.g., Japanese, Chinese, Korean) derive much information from these cues. Low-context cultures (e.g., North American, Western European) rely more heavily upon words.

INTERNET RESOURCE
High/Low-Context Cultures
http://www.sin.edu/-ekachai/dimensions.html
Illustrates Hall's high/low-context culture and Hofstede's individual/collectivist culture.

Barriers to Effective Intercultural Communication

Sari, an urban planner who had recently moved from New York to New Orleans, couldn't understand it. The meeting was supposed to start at 4:00 P.M., but she was the only person present. She felt frustrated and began mumbling to herself that she'd never worked with a more discourteous bunch of people. Finally, after about twenty minutes, another committee member straggled in. Then another. By 4:40 P.M. almost everyone was present and the meeting began. What Sari didn't understand was that most of her colleagues came from a cultural background where a half-hour slippage in starting time was normal. Sari expected punctuality, but most of the committee members assumed that the meeting would just start when everyone was ready. She became so incensed by their failure to apologize for being late that she was unable to conduct the meeting with her usual cool competence.

Intercultural communication occurs when individuals or groups from different cultures communicate. The transactional process of listening and responding to people from different cultural backgrounds can be challenging. The greater the difference in culture between two people, the greater the potential for misunderstanding and mistrust.

Misunderstanding and miscommunication occur between people from different cultures because of different coding rules and cultural norms, which play a major role in shaping our patterns of interaction. The greater the difference between the cultures, the more likely it is that they will use different verbal and nonverbal codes. When you encounter a culture that has little in common with your own, you may experience **culture shock,** or a sense of confusion, anxiety, stress, and loss. If you are visiting or actually living in the new culture, your uncertainty and stress may take time to subside as you learn the values and codes that characterize the culture. But if you are simply trying to communicate with someone from a background very different from your own—even on your home turf—you may find the suggestions in this section helpful in closing the communication gap.[23]

The first step to bridging differences between cultures is to find out what hampers effective communication. What keeps us from connecting with people from other cultures? Sometimes it is different meanings created by different languages or by different interpretations of nonverbal messages. Sometimes it is our inability to stop focusing on ourselves and begin focusing on the other. We'll examine some of these barriers first, then discuss strategies and skills for overcoming them.

Ethnocentrism

Marilyn had always been intrigued by Russia. Her dream was to travel the country by train, spending time in small villages as well as exploring the cultural riches of Moscow, Pyatigorsk, and St. Petersburg. Her first day in Russia was a disappointment, however. When she arrived in Moscow, she joined a tour touting the cultural traditions of Russia. When the tour bus stopped at Sparrow Hills, affording the visitors a breathtaking hilltop view of the Moscow skyline, she was perplexed and mildly shocked to see women dressed in elegant wedding gowns mounted on horseback and galloping through the parking lot. Men in suits were cheering them on as a crowd of tipsy revelers set off fireworks and danced wildly to a brass band. "What kind of people are these?" sniffed Marilyn.

"Oh," said the tour guide, "it is our custom to come here to celebrate immediately following the wedding ceremony."

"But in public with such raucousness?" queried Marilyn.

"It is our tradition," said the guide.

"What a backwards culture. They're nothing but a bunch of peasants!" pronounced Marilyn, who was used to more refined nuptial celebrations at a country club or an exclusive hotel.

For the rest of the tour Marilyn judged every Russian behavior as inferior to those of Westerners. That first experience colored her perceptions, and her ethnocentric view served as a barrier to effective interpersonal communication with the Russian people she met.

Ethnocentrism stems from a conviction that our own cultural traditions and assumptions are superior to those of others. In short, it is the opposite of an other-orientation that embraces and appreciates the elements that give another culture meaning. This kind of cultural snobbism is one of the fastest ways to create a barrier that inhibits rather than enhances communication.

4   INTERPERSONAL COMMUNICATION AND CULTURAL DIVERSITY

DISCUSSION AND WRITING
Assign exercise 3 in the "Learning with Others" section at the end of this chapter.

TEACHING STRATEGY
To illustrate ethnocentrism, ask students to consider whether U.S. citizens often visit other countries, expecting people who value tourist business to speak English. Next, ask them whether we feel compelled to be fluent in the languages of visitors to the United States. Point out that many other countries have English-language proficiency requirements at high-school levels.

You are on your first trip to Los Angeles. As you step off the bus and look around for Hollywood Boulevard, you realize that you have gotten off at the wrong stop. You see what looks like an old-fashioned corner grocery store with "Bodega" painted on a red sign. So you walk in and ask the man behind the counter, "How do I get to Hollywood Boulevard, please?"

"*No hablo Ingles,*" smiles the man, shrugging his shoulders. But he points to a transit map pasted onto the wall behind the counter.

Today, even when you travel within the United States, you are likely to encounter people who do not speak your language. Obviously, this kind of intercultural difference poses a formidable communication challenge. And even when you do speak the same tongue as another, he or she may come from a place where the words and gestures have different meanings. Your ability to communicate will depend upon whether you can understand each other's verbal and nonverbal codes.

In the example above, although the man behind the counter did not understand your exact words, he noted the cut of your clothing, your backpack, and your anxiety, and he deduced that you were asking directions. And you could understand what his gesture toward the transit map meant. Unfortunately, not every communication between the users of two different languages is this successful.

Even when language is translated, there can be missed or mangled meaning. Note the following examples of mistranslated advertisements:

- A General Motors auto ad with "Body by Fisher" became "Corpse by Fisher" in Flemish.

- A Colgate-Palmolive toothpaste named "Cue" was advertised in France before anyone realized that *Cue* also happened to be the name of a widely circulated pornographic book about oral sex.

- Pepsi-Cola's "Come Alive With Pepsi" campaign, when it was translated for the Taiwanese market, conveyed the unsettling news that "Pepsi brings your ancestors back from the grave."

- Parker Pen could not advertise its famous "Jotter" ballpoint pen in some languages because the translation sounded like "jockstrap" pen.

- One American airline operating in Brazil advertised that it had plush "rendezvous lounges" on its jets, unaware that in Portuguese (the language of Brazil) "rendezvous" implies a special room for making love.[24]

Stereotyping and Prejudice

All Europeans dress fashionably.

All Asians are good at math.

All Americans like to drive big cars.

INSTRUCTIONAL GOALS AND TIPS

Consider the Spanish phrases "Te quiero" (I love you) and "Quiero te" (I want tea.) Compare this with the English "blind Venetian" and "venetian blind." Point out the universal lesson that each culture is complex and challenging.

These statements are stereotypes. They are all inaccurate. To **stereotype** someone is to push him or her into an inflexible, all-encompassing category. In Chapter 3, you saw how our tendency to simplify sensory stimuli can lead us to adopt stereotypes as we interpret the behavior of others. When we do so, we "print" the same judgment over and over again, failing to consider the uniqueness of individuals, groups, or events. This becomes a barrier to effective intercultural communication. Two anthropologists suggest that every person is, in some respects, (1) like all other people, (2) like some other people, and (3) like no other people.[25] Our challenge when meeting others is to sort out how they are alike and how they are unique.

Can stereotypes play a useful role in interpersonal communication? It may sometimes be appropriate to draw on stereotypes, or generalizations drawn from limited instances. If, for example, you are alone and lost in a large city at two o'clock in the morning and another car repeatedly taps your rear bumper, it would be prudent to try to drive away as quickly as possible rather than to hop out of your car to make a new acquaintance. You would be wise to prejudge that the other driver might have some malicious intent. In most situations, however, **prejudice**—prejudging someone on the basis of stereotypes or before you know all the facts—inhibits effective communication, especially if your labels are inaccurate or assume superiority on your part.

Certain prejudices are widespread. Although there are more females than males in the world, one study found that even when a male and a female hold the same type of job, the male's job is considered more prestigious than the female's.[26] Today, gender and racial discrimination in hiring and promotion is illegal in the United States. But some personal opinions have not kept pace with the law. In 1997 a University of Texas professor created a firestorm of controversy with his remarks that certain minorities "come from cultures in which failure is not looked upon in disgrace" and thus cannot compete at selective colleges and universities.[27] Outraged university officials feared that the professor's inflammatory stereotyping would hamper their efforts to attract and retain minority students. The professor's comments resulted in a renewed focus on affirmative action programs and college admissions policies.

Assuming Similarity

Just as it is inaccurate to assume that all people who belong to another social group or class are worlds apart from you, it is usually erroneous to assume that others act and think just as you do. Even if they appear to be like you, all people are not alike. While this statement is not profound, it has profound implications. Like Sari, who *assumed* that others would value punctuality as she did, we often make the mistake of assuming that others value the same things we do, maintaining a self-focused perspective instead of an other-oriented one. As you saw in Chapter 3, focusing on superficial factors such as appearance, clothing, and even a person's occupation, can lead to false impressions. Instead, we must take the time to explore the person's background and cultural values before we can determine what we really have in common.

RESEARCH AND LITERATURE

More than 100 years ago, the artificial international language Esperanto was introduced by Dr. L. L. Zamenhof. There are still about 1.5 million people in the world who use it. Put the following sentence on the board and ask students to translate, "Persono lernas la lingvon Esperanto facile kaj rapide." ("People learn the Esperanto language easily and quickly.") Discuss with the class whether they would favor a single universal language.

RESEARCH AND LITERATURE

Consider this quote by Gordon Allport (from his book *The Nature of Prejudice*):

"See that man over there;
I hate him.
But you don't know him.
That's why I hate him."

114

Improving Intercultural Competence

Eleanor Roosevelt once said, "We have to face the fact that either all of us are going to die together or we are going to live together, and if we are to live together we have to talk."[28] In essence, she was saying that to overcome our differences we need effective communication skills. It is not enough to just point to the barriers to effective intercultural communication and say, "Don't do that." Although identifying the causes of misunderstanding is a good first step to becoming interculturally competent, most people need help with specific strategies to help them overcome these barriers. In this book and in this chapter, we want to focus attention on the interpersonal communication strategies that can lead to intercultural communication competence.

The remaining portion of this chapter presents three sets of strategies to help you bridge differences between yourself and people who come from a different cultural background. These three strategy sets—appropriate knowledge, motivation, and skill—are based on our understanding of how to be a competent communicator.

Our suggestion to enhance your understanding or **knowledge** of others is based on the assumption that knowing more about others is important in quality relationships. One of the barriers to effective intercultural communication is having different communication codes. Improving your knowledge of how others communicate can reduce the impact of this barrier. We offer strategies to help you learn more about other cultures by actively pursuing information about others.

CONSIDERING OTHERS

Ethnocentric Thinking

All good people agree,
And all good people say,
All nice people like Us,
are We,
And everyone else is They.

In a few short lines, Rudyard Kipling captured the essence of what sociologists and anthropologists call ethnocentric thinking. Members of all societies tend to believe that "All nice people like Us, are We . . ." They find comfort in the familiar and often denigrate or distrust others. Of course, with training and experience in other climes, they may learn to transcend their provincialism, placing themselves in others' shoes. Or, as Kipling put it,

> *. . . if you cross over the sea,*
> *Instead of over the way,*
> *You may end by (think of it!)*
> *looking on We*
> *As only a sort of They.*

In a real sense, a main lesson of the sociology of intergroup relations is to begin to "cross over the sea," to learn to understand why other people think and act as they do and to be able to empathize with their perspectives.

Adapted from: Faun B. Evans, Barbara Gleason, and Mark Wiley, *Cultural Tapestry: Readings for a Pluralistic Society* (HarperCollins, 1992).

INTERPERSONAL COMMUNICATION FOUNDATIONS

INTERNET RESOURCE
See how intercultural communication varies in time, space, and context.
http://www3.soc.hawaii.edu/css/dept/com/resources/Intercultural/Hall.html
Also includes a selected bibliography at the end of reading.

RESEARCH AND LITERATURE
The Dictionary of Cultural Literacy (Houghton Mifflin, 1988, Introduction) states that thoughtful communication depends on our knowledge of a common stock of people, places, sayings, and happenings.

INTERNET RESOURCE
Journal on Intercultural Relations is online at:
http://kumo.swcp.com/bus/theedge/spring98.html

INTERNET RESOURCE
Good jump point for intercultural links.
http://www.rc.kyushu-u.ac.jp/-michel/serv/intcult/links.html

ACTIVITY
See Activity 4.1 in the Instructor's Guide

A second set of strategies focuses on becoming motivated to improve our intercultural communication knowledge and skills. **Motivation** is an internal state of readiness to respond to something. A competent communicator wants to learn and improve; an incompetent communicator is not motivated to develop new skills. Technically, no one can motivate you to do something; motivation comes from within. But developing strategies to appreciate others who are different from yourself may help you appreciate different cultural approaches to communication and relationships. We suggest you endeavor to be more tolerant of uncertainty and to avoid knee-jerk negative evaluations of others.

The final set of strategies, developing **skill** in adapting to others, focuses on specific behaviors that can help overcome the barriers and cultural differences we have discussed. Here, to address the barrier of ethnocentrism, we will identify the advantages of becoming a more flexible communicator. We will also describe the essential competence of becoming other-oriented—focusing on the needs, goals, and values of others instead of only on yourself. As we discussed in Chapter 1, becoming other-oriented is critical to the process of relating to others.

Developing Knowledge: Strategies to Understand Others Who Are Different from Us

Knowledge is power. To increase your knowledge of others who are different from you, we suggest that you actively seek information about others, ask questions and listen for the answers, and establish common ground. Let's discuss these strategies in more detail.

■ SEEK INFORMATION ABOUT THE CULTURE

Prejudice stems from ignorance. Learning about another person's values, beliefs, and behaviors can help you understand his or her messages and their meaning. Every person has a **world view** based on cultural beliefs about the universe and key issues such as death, God, and the meaning of life.[29] According to Carley Dodd, "A culture's world view involves finding out how the culture perceives the role of various forces in explaining why events occur as they do in a social setting."[30] These beliefs shape our thoughts, language, and behavior. Only through intercultural communication can we hope to understand how each individual views the world. As you speak to a person from another culture, think of yourself as a detective, watching for implied, often unspoken messages that provide information about the values, norms, roles, and rules of that person's culture.

You can also prepare yourself by studying the culture. If you are going to another country, courses in the history, anthropology, art, or geography of that place can give you a head start on communicating with understanding. Learn not only from books and magazines, but also from individuals whenever possible. Even in a high-context culture, no one will fault you for asking directly for help if you show a sincere desire to learn. If you are trying to communicate with someone closer to home who is from a different background, you can study

ACTIVITY
See Activity 4.2 in the Instructor's Guide.

The members of the rodeo co-culture are likely to develop friendships that they may or may not carry to their lives outside the rodeo. What happens when an unexpected member, such as the woman in this group, joins such a co-culture? (Joe Bensen/Stock Boston)

magazines, music, food, and other readily available sources of information about his or her culture. Or exchange visits to one another's homes or hangouts to observe and learn more about the person.

Given the inextricable link between language and culture, the more you learn about another language, the more you will understand the traditions and customs of the culture. Politicians have long known the value of using even a few words of their constituents' language. President Kennedy impressed and excited a crowd in Berlin by proclaiming "Ech Bien In Berliner." Even though his pronunciation was less than perfect, he conveyed the message that he identified with his listeners. Speaking even a few words can signify your interest in learning about the language and culture of others.

As we noted at the beginning of this chapter, when we speak of culture we are also referring to co-cultures. A co-culture is a cultural group within a larger culture. Learning how men and women, each a separate co-culture, communicate differently can help us improve our communication with the opposite gender. Men, for example, are more likely to develop friendships through participating in common activities with other men (playing on a baseball team, working together).[31] Women are more likely to develop friendships through talking together rather than working together.

Reading books about differences between the way men and women communicate is one strategy to help both sexes improve understanding and develop insight into different approaches to communication. Deborah Tannen's book *You Just Don't Understand* and John Gray's bestseller *Men Are From Mars, Women Are From Venus* are popular books that can help create a dialogue between men and women about communication differences and thus promote greater knowledge about how to improve communication.

As you read about other cultures or co-cultures, it is important not to develop rigid categories or stereotypes for the way others may talk or behave. Proclaiming, "Oh, you're just saying that because you're a man" or "You women always say things like that" can increase rather than decrease communication barriers. Throughout this book we will discuss research-based gender differences in the way men and women communicate to enhance your understanding and improve communication with members of the opposite sex. But we don't recommend that you treat men and women as completely separate species from different planets and automatically assume you will immediately misunderstand the opposite sex.

◼ ASK QUESTIONS AND LISTEN EFFECTIVELY

When you encounter a person from another background, asking questions then pausing to listen is a simple technique for gathering information and also for confirming the accuracy of your expectations and assumptions. Some cultures, such as the Japanese, have rigid expectations regarding gift giving. It is better to ask what these expectations are than to assume that your good old down-home manners will see you through.

When you ask questions, be prepared to share information about yourself, too. Otherwise, your partner may feel as if you are interrogating him or her as a way to gain power and dominance rather than from a sincere desire to learn about cultural rules and norms.

Communication helps to reduce the uncertainty that is present in any relationship.[32] When you meet people for the first time, you are highly uncertain about who they are and what they like and dislike. When you communicate with someone from another culture, the uncertainty level is particularly high. As you begin to interact, you exchange information that helps you develop greater understanding. If you continue to ask questions, eventually you will feel less uncertain about how the person is likely to behave.

Just asking questions and sharing information about yourself is not sufficient to bridge differences in culture and background. It is equally important to listen to what others share. In the next chapter we will provide specific strategies for improving your listening skills.

◼ DEVELOP A "THIRD CULTURE"

Several researchers suggest that one of the best ways to enhance understanding when communicating with someone from a different cultural background is to develop a **third culture.** This is created when the communication partners join aspects of separate cultures to create a third, "new" culture that is more comprehensive and inclusive than either of the two separate cultures.[33] The goal of developing a third-culture mentality is to reduce our tendency to approach cultural differences as an "us" versus "them" point of view. Rather than trying to eliminate communication barriers stemming from two different sets of experiences, adopting a third culture framework seeks to create a new understanding of both participants for each other.[34]

Consider the example of Marsha, a business woman from Lincoln, Nebraska, and Tomiko, a business woman from Tokyo, Japan. In the context of their business relationship, it would be difficult for them to develop a comprehensive understanding of each other's cultural traditions. However, if they open-

WEB ACTIVITY
IC Conferences
www.rit.edu
This site gives a couple of options for viewing two intercultural conferences, one in 1996, and one in 1997. Have students view and take notes on one of the conferences. Next, have students organize their notes into the categories of what was accomplished, what needs to be done, and what issues were raised. Create a master list based on student results.

Have students complete this activity before class. In class, discuss the results with the class. Explain that rules are in every communication context, and are often invisible to us until we change cultures. Have the class break into four groups and have each group make a list of Do's and Don'ts Rules for someone unfamiliar with our culture. Have each group focus on one of the following four contexts: classroom etiquette, dating etiquette, buying/selling etiquette, automobile etiquette.

BUILDING YOUR SKILLS

Identifying Rules

What are typical rules and manners for most people native to the United States? Try to identify generally held rules of etiquette in the following situations.

Expectations regarding punctuality at meetings: _____
_____

Greetings between good friends: _____
_____

Greetings between business or professional colleagues: _____

Gift giving and receiving among friends: _____
_____

Gift giving and receiving among business associates: _____
_____

Typical times for daily meals: _____
_____

Appropriate use of someone's first name: _____
_____

Inappropriate use of someone's first name: _____
_____

Share your answers with your classmates. Note similarities and differences in your responses. If you and your classmates have different expectations in these situations, what does this suggest about how reliable the suggestions are for other countries listed in Understanding Diversity: Mind Your Manners—and Theirs?

ly acknowledged the most significant of these differences and sought to create a third culture by identifying explicit rules and norms for their interaction, they might be able to develop a more comfortable relationship with each other.

As described by Benjamin Broome, the third culture "is characterized by unique values and norms that may not have existed prior to the dyadic [two-person] relationship."[35] Broome labels the essence of this new relationship **relational empathy**, which permits varying degrees of understanding rather than requiring complete comprehension of another's culture or emotions.

One of the barriers to effective intercultural communication is having different communication codes. In seeking a third culture, you are seeking a way to develop a common code or framework to enhance understanding. Developing such a code that both individuals can understand may include each party's learning the language of the other. It can also include discussing meanings of nonverbal communication so that misunderstandings can be reduced. Further, it involves using the perception check skill we discussed in the previous chapter.

The cultural context includes all of the elements of the culture (learned behaviors and rules or "mental software") that affect the interaction. Do you come from a culture that takes a tea break each afternoon at 4:00 P.M.? Does your culture value hard work and achievement, or relaxation and enjoyment? Creating a third culture acknowledges the different cultural contexts and interactions participants have experienced and seeks to develop a new context for future interaction.

RECAP	Develop Knowledge to Enhance Understanding
SEEK INFORMATION ABOUT THE CULTURE	Learn about a culture's world view.
ASK QUESTIONS AND LISTEN	Reduce uncertainty by asking for clarification and listening to the answer.
DEVELOP A THIRD CULTURE	Create common ground.

Developing Motivation: Strategies to Accept Others Who Are Different from Us

To be motivated is to want to do something. One of the elements of a competent communicator is that the communicator has developed a positive mindset for enhancing his or her ability to relate to others and to also accept others as they are. A key to accepting others is to develop a positive attitude of tolerance and acceptance of those who are different from us. We suggest three strategies to help improve your acceptance and appreciation of others who are different from you: tolerate ambiguity, develop mindfulness, and avoid negative judgments about others.

■ TOLERATE AMBIGUITY

Communicating with someone from another culture produces uncertainty. It may take time and several exchanges to clarify a message. Be patient and try to expand your capacity to tolerate ambiguity if you are speaking to someone with a markedly different world view.

When Ken and Rita visited Miami, they asked their hotel concierge to direct them to a church of their faith, and they wound up at one with a predominantly Haitian congregation. They were not prepared for the exuberant chanting and verbal interchanges with the minister during the sermon. They weren't certain whether they should join in or simply sit quietly and observe. Ken whispered to Rita, "I'm not sure what to do. Let's just watch and see what is expected of us." In the end, they chose to sit and clap along with the chanting rather than to become actively involved in the worship. Rita felt uncomfortable and conspicuous, though, and had to fight off the urge to bolt. But after the service, several members of the congregation came up to greet Ken and Rita, invited them to lunch, and expressed great happiness in their visit. "You know," said Rita later in the day, "I'm so grateful that we sat through our discomfort. We might never have met those terrific people. Now I understand why their worship is so noisy—they're just brimming over with joy."

■ DEVELOP MINDFULNESS

"Our life is what our thoughts make it," said Marcus Aurelius in *Meditation*s. To be **mindful** is to be consciously aware of cultural differences, to acknowledge that there is a connection between thoughts and deeds when you interact with a person from a background different from your own. William Gudykunst suggests that being mindful is one of the best ways to approach any new cultural encounter.[36] Remember that there are and will be cultural differences, and try to keep them in your consciousness. Also try to consider the other individual's frame of reference or world view and to use his or her cultural priorities and assumptions when you are communicating.[37] Adapt your behavior to minimize cultural noise and distortion.

BUILDING YOUR SKILLS

Can You Tolerate Ambiguity?

Respond to each statement with a number from 1 to 5: (1) Always False, (2) Usually False, (3) Sometimes False and Sometimes True, (4) Usually True, or (5) Always True.

_____ 1. I am comfortable in new situations.

_____ 2. I deal with unforeseen problems successfully.

_____ 3. I experience little discomfort in ambiguous situations.

_____ 4. I am relaxed in unfamiliar situations.

_____ 5. I am not frustrated when things do not go the way I expected.

To find your score, add the numbers you wrote next to each statement. Scores range from 5 to 25. The higher your score, the greater your tolerance for ambiguity.

From: William B. Gudykunst, *Bridging Differences: Effective Intergroup Communication* (Newbury Park: Sage, 1991), 121.

You can become more mindful through self-talk, something we discussed in Chapter 2. Self-talk consists of rational messages you tell yourself to help you manage your emotions or discomfort with a certain situation. Imagine that you are working on a group project with several of your classmates. One classmate, Suji, was born in Iran. When interacting with you, he consistently gets about a foot away, whereas you are more comfortable with three or four feet between you. When Suji encroaches on your space, you could "be mindful" of the difference by mentally noting, "Suji sure likes to get close to people when he talks to them. This must represent a practice in his culture." This self-talk message makes you consciously aware that there may be a difference in your interaction styles. If you still feel uncomfortable, instead of blurting out, "Hey, man, why so close?" you could express your own preferences with an "I" message: "Suji, I'd prefer a bit more space between us when we talk."

BUILDING YOUR SKILLS

Measuring Mindfulness

Respond to each statement with a number from 1 to 5: (1) Always False, (2) Usually False, (3) Sometimes False and Sometimes True, (4) Usually True, or (5) Always True.

_____ 1. I pay attention to the situation and context when I communicate.

_____ 2. I can describe others with whom I communicate in great detail.

_____ 3. I seek out new information about the people with whom I communicate.

_____ 4. I try to find rational reasons why others may behave in a way I perceive negatively.

_____ 5. I recognize that the person with whom I am communicating has a different point of view than I do.

To find your score, add the numbers you wrote next to each statement. Scores range from 5 to 25. The higher your score, the more mindful you are when you communicate.

From: William B. Gudykunst, *Bridging Differences: Effective Intergroup Communication* (Newbury Park: Sage, 1991), 120.

■ AVOID NEGATIVE JUDGMENTS ABOUT ANOTHER CULTURE

American tourist on her first visit to France:

Can you believe it. How repulsive! These people actually eat horse meat and think it's a delicacy.

Black teenager watching his white classmates dance:

Man, they don't know anything about good music! And those dances are so dumb. I don't call this a party.

Japanese businessperson visiting Argentina:

These people are never on time. No wonder they can never catch up to us.

German student, after watching a documentary about life in Japan:

No wonder they work so hard. They have dinky little houses. I'd work long hours too if I had to live like that.

MEDIA AND OUTSIDE RESOURCES
Invite an expert in foreign-exchange programs to discuss with the class ways to enculturate and to manage culture shock.

The kind of ethnocentrism that underlies judgments like these is a communication barrier. It is also an underlying cause of suspicion and mistrust and, in extreme cases, a spark that ignites violence. Instead of making judgments about another culture, try simply to acknowledge differences and to view them as an interesting challenge rather than as an obstacle to be eradicated.

RECAP	Develop Motivation to Accept Others
TOLERATE AMBIGUITY	Take your time and expect some uncertainty.
DEVELOP MINDFULNESS	Be conscious of cultural differences rather than ignoring the differences.
AVOID NEGATIVE JUDGMENTS	Resist thinking your culture has all of the answers.

Developing Skill: Strategies to Adapt to Others Who Are Different from Us

To be skilled is to be capable of putting what you know and want to achieve into action. The underlying skill in being interculturally competent is the ability to be flexible and adapt to others. We discuss these crucial skills as an introduction to the communication skills that we will present in the next four chapters.

■ DEVELOP FLEXIBILITY

When you interact with someone from another background, your responding skills are crucial. You can only learn so much from books; you must be willing to learn as you communicate. Every individual is unique, so cultural generalizations that you learn from research may not always apply. It is not accurate to assume, for example, that *all* French people are preoccupied with food and fashion. Many members of minority groups in the United States find it draining to correct these generalizations in their encounters with others. Pay close attention to the other person's nonverbal cues when you begin conversing; then adjust your communication style and language if necessary to put the person at ease. And avoid asking questions or making statements based on generalizations.

■ BECOME OTHER-ORIENTED

Throughout the book we have emphasized the importance of becoming other-oriented—focusing on others rather than yourself—as an important way to enhance your interpersonal competence. We have also discussed the problems ethnocentrism can create when you attempt to communicate with others, especially with those whose culture is different from your own. We now offer three

Ask students to prepare exercise 2 from the "Learning with Others" section at the end of this chapter. Compare these with North American stories. You might consult texts such as Bruno Bettelheim's *The Uses of Enchantment: The Meaning and Importance of Fairy Tales* (Random House, 1975).

INTERPERSONAL COMMUNICATION FOUNDATIONS

Predicting How Others Feel

Look at the descriptions below and rank order them from 1 (highest) to 6 (lowest) in terms of how readily you think you could predict each person's reactions to finding out his or her mother or other close relative has just died.

_____ A. A close friend of yours of the same sex, age, race, and culture.

_____ B. A sixty-year-old male Chinese farmer.

_____ C. A college student who is twenty years older than you but of the same race, sex, and culture.

_____ D. A ten-year-old California girl who is the child of Asian and Hispanic parents.

_____ E. A college student of a different race than you but the same age, culture, and sex.

_____ F. A college student of the opposite sex than you but the same age, race, and culture as you.

What qualities do you feel provide you the best information on which to base your judgments? Why? What would you need to know about each person to feel comfortable in making a prediction? How can you get that information?

---

specific ways to increase your other-orientedness: social decentering, empathy, and adaptation.

Although our focus in this discussion will be on how to increase other-orientation in intercultural interactions, the principles apply to *all* interpersonal interactions. The major difference between intercultural interactions and those that occur within your own culture is primarily the obviousness of the differences between you and the other person.

1. SOCIAL DECENTERING. **Social decentering**, the first strategy, is a *cognitive process* in which we take into account the other person's thoughts, feelings, values, background, and perspectives. This process involves viewing the world from the other person's point of view. The greater the difference between ourselves and the other person, the more difficult it is to accomplish social decentering. In doing the Building Your Skills: Predicting How Others Feel exercise you may find it easier to judge your close friend than any of the other relationships that are described.

The rest of your rankings depend on the various experiences you have had. Your interactions with members of the opposite sex, or with someone from another race, or of a different age are probably the next most frequent, and next highest ranked. Interactions with people from other cultures are probably the most difficult because your experiences in such interactions are often limited. It is easier to socially decenter about someone who is similar in culture and background to you.

There are three ways to socially decenter or take another's perspective: (1) develop an understanding of another, based upon how you have responded

Have students complete this exercise and compare results in informal groups. Next, place a series of eight to ten pictures of faces selected from magazines. The pictures should reflect a variety of cultures, ages, backgrounds, and so on. Have each group file past the pictures and get a good look at each one. Next, have groups select which of the people's faces are the happiest/saddest, the most excited/least excited, the most dominant/least dominant. Question the results and point out that such emotions are expressed in terms relative to a particular culture. Finally, ask students which person they would have the most difficulty relating to. Most students will select someone very foreign from American culture. Point out that a lack of ability to relate to those different from us can have negative consequences. Ask students what things they might do to try to increase their ability to relate to the person. Compile the list on the board and compare the class findings to the suggestions in the text beginning on page 123.

when something similar has happened to you, (2) base your understanding of others upon the knowledge you have about a specific person, or (3) make generalizations about someone, based upon your understanding of how you think most people would feel or behave.[38]

When you draw upon your direct experience, you use your past knowledge of what happened to you to help you guess how someone else may feel. To the degree that the other person is similar to you, your reactions and theirs will match. For example, suppose you are talking to a student who has just failed a midterm exam in an important course. You have also had this experience. Your reaction was to discount it because you had confidence you could still pull a passing grade. You might use this self-understanding to predict your class-mate's reactions. To the degree that you are similar to the classmate, your prediction will be accurate. But suppose your classmate comes from a culture with high expectations for success. Your classmate might feel upset over having dis-honored his family by his poor performance. In this situation, understanding your own reaction needs to be tempered by your awareness of how similar or dissimilar the other person is to you. Recognition of differences should lead you to recognize the need to socially decenter in another way.

The second way we socially decenter—or take the perspective of another—is based on specific knowledge we have of the person with whom we are interacting. Drawing on your memory of how your classmate reacted to a previous failed midterm gives you a basis to more accurately predict his reaction. Even if you have not observed your classmate's reaction to the same situation, you project how you think he or she would feel based on similar instances. As relationships become more intimate, we gain more information to allow us to more readily socially decenter. Our ability to accurately predict and understand our partners usually increases as relationships become more intimate. In intercultural interactions, the more opportunity you have to interact with the same person and learn more about the person and his or her culture, the more your ability to socially decenter will increase.

The third way we socially decenter is to apply our understanding of people in general, or of categories of people from whom we have gained some knowledge. Each of us develops implicit personality theories, constructs, and attributions of how people act, as discussed in Chapter 3. You might have a general theory to explain the behavior of men and another for women. You might have general theories about Mexicans, Japanese, Canadians, Slovenians, Texans, or Iowans. As you meet someone who falls into one of your categories, you draw upon that conceptualization to socially decenter. The more you can learn about a given culture, the stronger your general theories can be, and the more effectively you can use this method of socially decentering. The key, however, is to avoid developing inaccurate, inflexible stereotypes of others and basing your perceptions of others only on those generalizations.

2. EMPATHY. Besides *thinking* about how another may feel (socially decentering), we can have an *emotional* reaction to what others do or tell us. We feel empathy for another. **Empathy,** a second strategy for becoming other-oriented, is an *emotional reaction* that is similar to the one being experienced by another person, as compared to social decentering, which is a *cognitive reaction*.

INTERPERSONAL COMMUNICATION FOUNDATIONS

Empathy is feeling what another person feels. Our emotional reaction can be either similar to or different from the emotions the other person is experiencing. You might experience mild pity for your classmate who has failed the midterm, in contrast to his stronger feeling of anguish and dishonor. On the other hand, you might share his same feelings of anguish and dishonor.

Some emotional reactions are almost universal and cut across cultural boundaries. You might experience empathy when seeing photos or videos depicting emotional scenes occurring in other countries. Seeing a mother crying while holding her sick or dying child in a refugee camp might move you to cry and feel a deep sense of sadness or loss. You empathize with the woman. You might also experience empathy for your brother, who has just received the devastating news that his best friend has been killed in an automobile accident. You grieve with him. Empathy can enhance interpersonal interactions in a number of ways: it can provide a bond between you and the other person; it is confirming; it is comforting and supportive; it can increase your understanding of others; and it can strengthen the relationship. We can empathize most easily with those who are similar to us, and in situations with which we have had a similar emotional experience.

Developing empathy is different than sympathizing with others. When you offer **sympathy,** you tell others that you are sorry that he or she feels what he or she is feeling. Here are examples and statements of sympathy: "I'm sorry your Uncle Joe died," or "I'm sorry to hear you failed your test." When you sympathize with others, you acknowledge their feelings. But, when you empathize, you experience an emotional reaction that is similar to the other person's; you, too, feel grief or sadness. We will discuss strategies for developing empathic listening skills in the next chapter.

3. ADAPTATION. Social decentering and empathy are two processes that give us insight into what other people are thinking or feeling; in addition, they

provide a base from which to make strategic communication decisions. A third way to become other-oriented is to adapt and respond to what you learn about others. **Adaptation** means adjusting our behaviors in accord with the individual, the relationship, and the situation. When you modify your behavior in anticipation of an event, you **adapt predictively**. For example, you might decide to buy a friend flowers to soften the news about breaking a date because you know how much your friend likes flowers. When you modify your behavior after an event, you **adapt reactively**. For example, you might buy your friend flowers to apologize for a fight.

There are a number of reasons we adapt our communication to the other person. We often adapt our messages in an attempt to make them more understandable. For instance, in talking to an individual with limited understanding of English, you would probably choose simple words and phrases (we have a tendency to make our voices louder in these situations under the false assumption that the other person isn't "hearing" what we say). We also adapt our messages in order to accomplish our goals more effectively. In our intercultural interactions, we frequently adapt our communication behavior in response to the feedback or reactions we are receiving. Table 4.2 lists a variety of ways we adapt our verbal messages to others.

We also adapt our nonverbal cues. Many times we raise or lower the volume of our voices in response to the volume of our partner, or we lean forward toward people in response to their leaning toward us. We'll talk more about such nonverbal cues in Chapter 7.

Adaptation across intercultural contexts is usually more difficult than within your own culture. Imagine shaking hands with a stranger, and having the stranger hold on to your hand as you continue to talk. In the United States, hand-holding between strangers is a violation of our nonverbal norms. But in some cultures maintaining physical contact while talking is expected. Pulling your hand away from this person would be rude. As illustrated in Understanding Diversity: Mind Your Manners—and Theirs, what may be mannerly in one culture is not always acceptable in another. Adapting to these cultural differences means developing that "third" culture that we talked about earlier in the chapter.

Taking an other-oriented approach to communication means considering the thoughts, feelings, background, perspectives, attitudes, and values of your interpersonal partners and adjusting your interaction with them accordingly. Other-orientation leads to more effective interpersonal communication, regardless of whether you are dealing with someone in your family or from another country.

By careful analysis of the factors that affect our communication partners, we can develop understanding and empathy. That understanding and empathy can then help us make the most effective strategic communication choices as we adapt our messages and responses.

In an effective interpersonal relationship, your partner is also orienting him- or herself to you. A competent communicator has knowledge of others, is motivated to enhance the quality of communication and possesses the skill of being other-oriented.

Table 4.2

Communication Adaptation Behaviors

Type	Examples
TOPICAL: Choosing a topic or issue to discuss because you know it will interest the other person.	Talking about a mutual friend, talking about a party you both went to, asking if he or she saw a particular play that was in town.
EXPLANATORY/ELABORATION: Providing additional information or detail because you recognize that the other person does not know it.	Explaining your mother's eating habits to a new friend, explaining to a neighbor who has squirrel problems how you keep them away from your bean plants.
WITHHOLDING EXPLANATION OR INFORMATION: Not providing explanation because your partner already knows the information; because it might hurt or anger your partner; because of fear of how the other person might misuse it; or to avoid violating a confidentiality.	Not elaborating on the parts of an auto engine when you describe a car problem because you know the listener is knowledgeable about cars; not telling a friend you saw his or her lover with another person because he/she would be hurt; not telling someone about your interest in a mutual friend because you are afraid that person would blab about it to the mutual friend.
EXAMPLES/COMPARISONS/ANALOGIES: Choosing examples that you know your partner will find relevant.	Explaining roller blading by comparing it to ice skating, something your partner knows how to do.
PERSONAL REFERENCING: Referring to your partner's specific attitudes, interests, personality, traits, ethnic background, etc.	"I've got something to tell you I think you'll find funny." "Could you help me balance my checkbook; you're so good at math." "That's a behavior I'd expect from you, given the way your parents raised you."
VERNACULAR/LANGUAGE: Choosing or avoiding certain words because of their potential effect on the receiver. Using words that have a unique meaning for you and your partner. Using words that you think are appropriate to the other person's level of understanding.	A wife asking her husband if he was catching flies during a movie, meaning he was asleep with his mouth wide open. A father telling his child that a criminal is someone who does bad things. Two computer jocks talking about "bytes," "ram," and "chips."
DISCLOSURE: Consciously deciding to share information about yourself that the other does not know about you.	Telling your lover about your sexual fantasies. Telling your instructor about family problems.
IMMEDIATE FOLLOW-UP QUESTIONING: Seeking additional information from the other person about information he or she shares during the interaction.	"So, what was it like growing up in small town Iowa?" "Tell me more about your vacation in Florida." "Where are you going on your date?"
DELAYED FOLLOW-UP QUESTIONING: Seeking additional information from the other person about previous information he or she shared.	"How's your mother doing after her operation yesterday?" "How was your date Saturday night?"
ADAPTING TO IMMEDIATE REACTION/FEEDBACK: Modifying your words or behavior because of your partner's reaction.	If your friend starts to cry when you talk about her mother's death, you might quickly change the topic.

If you learn the skills and principles we have presented here, will it really make a difference in your ability to relate to others? Recent evidence suggests the answer is "yes." A study by Lori Carell found that students who had been exposed to lessons in empathy linked to a study of interpersonal and intercultural communication improved their ability to empathize with others.[39] There is evidence that if you master these principles and skills, you will be rewarded with greater insight and ability to relate to others who are different from you.

TEACHING STRATEGY
Students may have difficulty seeing the importance of intercultural communication in their own lives. Ask students to carefully consider the "co-cultures" presented in the Understanding Diversity box. Remind them that a culture is simply a learned system of knowledge, behavior, attitudes, beliefs, and values. Thus, opportunities and challenges for intercultural communication surround us.

Ask students to identify other groups who seem to share cultural characteristics different from their own. For example, nonmajors in Speech Communication often testify that Speech Communication classes, students, and faculty are of a culture different from their own.

UNDERSTANDING DIVERSITY

Mind Your Manners —and Theirs

If it be appropriate to kiss the Pope's slipper, by all means do so.

—Lord Chesterfield, founder of modern etiquette, in 1750

The saying "When in Rome do what the Romans do" suggests that international travelers should adopt an other-oriented approach to the host country's manners and customs. After interviewing hundreds of international businesspersons, Roger Axtell offers the following tips on etiquette when visiting with people from other countries or traveling to international destinations.[40] Realize, of course, that these observations are not true of all individuals. As in the United States, in many of these countries there are dozens of different cultural groups with their own sets of values and customs.

Austrians
- Are punctual
- Use a firm handshake (both men and women)
- Consider keeping their hands in their lap when dining to be impolite
- Are uncomfortable with first names until a friendship is established

English, Scots, Welsh
- Tend to use understatement in business matters
- Value punctuality
- Are accustomed to cooler room temperatures than Americans
- Call a Scot a Scotsman, not a Scotchman or Scottish

French
- Rarely use first names, even among colleagues
- Frequently shake hands but their grip is less firm than most

- Eat their main meal of the day usually at midday
- Make decisions after much deliberation

Irish
- Are not overly conscientious about time and punctuality
- Do not typically give business gifts
- Regard refusing a drink or failing to buy your round as bad manners

Italians
- Use strong and frequent hand and body gestures
- May grasp your elbow as they shake hands
- Do not consider punctuality a virtue, at least for social events
- Do not talk business at a social event

Russians
- Want to know what Americans really think

- When greeting, shake hands and announce their name
- Among friends, some give "bear hugs" and kiss cheeks

Egyptians
- Like all Muslims, rest on Friday
- Regard friendship and trust as a prerequisite for business
- Social engagements usually held late in the day

Zambians
- Often shake hands with the left supporting the right
- When dining, may ask for food; it is impolite not to
- Consider it improper to refuse food

Australians
- Speak frankly and directly; they dislike pretensions
- Will not shy away from disagreement
- Appreciate punctuality

- Have good sense of humor, even in tense situations

Indians
- When greeting a woman, they put palms together and bow slightly
- Do not eat beef and regard the cow as a sacred animal
- Show great respect to elders

Japanese
- Exchange business cards before bowing or shaking hands
- Consider it impolite to have long or frequent eye-to-eye contact
- Rarely use first names
- Avoid the word "no" to preserve harmony

Thais (Thailand)
- Regard displays of either temper or affection in public as unacceptable
- Have a taboo against using

your foot to point, or showing your sole
- Don't like pats on the head

Brazilians
- Like long handshakes
- Like to touch arms, elbows, and backs
- When conversing, view interruption as enthusiasm
- Attach a sexual meaning to the OK hand signal

Mexicans
- Are not rigidly punctual
- Take their main meal at about 1:00 or 4:00 P.M.
- Refrain from using first names until they are invited to do so
- Consider hands in pockets to be impolite

Adapted from: Roger E. Axtell, *Do's and Taboos of Hosting International Visitors* (New York: John Wiley & Sons, 1989).

DISCUSSION AND WRITING
Invite students to add to these lists or to modify them.

Summary

A culture is a system of knowledge that is shared by a larger group of people. It includes cultural elements, values, goals, and contexts. Cultural elements are categories of things and ideas that identify key aspects of cultural influence. Cultural values reflect how individuals regard masculine and feminine behaviors and individual and collective achievements. They also reflect whether individuals can tolerate ambiguity or need a high degree of certainty, and whether they believe in concentrated or decentralized power structures. The goals of a culture depend upon the way it values individual versus group achievement. In high-context cultures, the meaning of messages depends heavily upon nonverbal information; low-context cultures rely more heavily upon words than upon context for deriving meaning.

Intercultural communication occurs when individuals or groups from different cultures communicate. There are several barriers that inhibit effective intercultural communication. Ethnocentrism is the belief that our own cultural traditions and assumptions are superior to those of others. Differences in language and the way we interpret nonverbal messages also interfere with effective intercultural communication. We stereotype by placing a group or a person into an inflexible, all-encompassing category. A related barrier is prejudice—we often prejudge someone before we know all of the facts. Stereotyping and prejudice can keep us from viewing people as unique individuals and therefore hamper effective, honest communication. Finally, assuming that we are similar to others can also be a barrier to intercultural communication. All humans have some similarities, but our cultures have taught us to process the world differently.

Although it is reasonably easy to identify cultural differences, it is more challenging to bridge those differences. To enhance understanding between cultures, we suggest the following: Develop knowledge by seeking information about the culture, ask questions and listen, and develop a "third culture." Increase your motivation to appreciate others who are different from you by tolerating ambiguity, developing mindfulness, and avoiding negative judgments about another culture. Finally, enhance your skill by becoming flexible. Be other-oriented by socially decentering, becoming more empathic, and adapting your verbal and nonverbal behavior to others.

■ FOCUS ON COMPREHENSION

1. What is culture?

2. What are four contrasting cultural values?

3. What are the differences between high-context and low-context cultures?

4. What are the differences between individualistic and collectivistic cultures?

5. What is ethnocentrism?

■ FOCUS ON CRITICAL THINKING

6. Jonna, an American, has just been accepted as a foreign exchange student in Germany. What are potential cultural barriers that she might face? How should she manage these potential barriers?

7. What's the problem in assuming that other people are like us? How does this create a barrier to effective intercultural communication?

8. If you were to design a lesson plan for elementary age students about how to deal with racial and ethnic stereotypes, what would you include?

9. What are appropriate ways to deal with someone who consistently utters racial slurs and evidences prejudice toward racial or ethnic groups?

■ FOCUS ON ETHICS

10. Marla is the director of the campus multicultural studies program. She wants to require all students to take at least four courses in a four-year degree program that focus on multicultural issues. Is it appropriate to force students to take such a concentration of courses?

11. When Wayne, a Polish American, went to visit Dave, who was from an old Southern Baptist family, Dave's dad made a bigoted statement about African Americans. This upset Wayne, and he wondered whether Dave's father was prejudiced against Catholics, too. Should Wayne have spoken up and told Dave's dad that he did not like the remark?

12. Is it ethical or appropriate for someone from one culture to attempt to change the cultural values of someone from a different culture? For example, culture A practices polygamy: one husband can be married to several wives. Culture B practices monogamy: one husband can be married to only one wife. Should a person from culture B attempt to make someone from culture A change his or her ways?

4 INTERPERSONAL COMMUNICATION AND CULTURAL DIVERSITY

131

FOCUS ON COMPREHENSION

1. Culture is defined as the knowledge, behavior, beliefs, attitudes, values, and norms that a group of people share.

2. Geert Hofstede argued that "each culture places varying degrees of value upon gender roles, individualism, tolerance of uncertainty, and the use of power."

3. High-context cultures rely heavily on verbal and nonverbal cues to interpret information, whereas low-context cultures depend more heavily upon language.

4. In a collectivist culture, members place a higher value on "we" than "I." They give and receive more loyalty from their extended families, communities, and employers. In an individualist culture, people think their primary responsibility is to themselves and to their immediate families.

5. Ethnocentrism is the attitude that one's own culture, traditions, and assumptions are superior to others'.

1. Describe your perceptions of your cultural values, based upon the discussion of cultural values beginning on page 104 in this chapter. On a scale of 1 to 10, rate yourself in terms of the value of masculine versus feminine perspective, individual versus group achievement, tolerance of uncertainty versus need for certainty, and centralized versus decentralized power. Provide an example of your reaction to an interpersonal communication encounter to illustrate each of these values.

2. Write a journal entry discussing how you have experienced one of the barriers to effective intercultural communication described in this chapter. Have you been ethnocentric in your thoughts or behavior or a victim of ethnocentrism? Describe a situation in which communication was difficult because you and your communication partner spoke different languages. Have you been a victim of stereotyping or prejudice? Have you assumed someone was similar to yourself and later found that there were more differences than you suspected?

3. This chapter presented eight specific strategies or skills to help bridge differences in background and culture. Rank order these skills and strategies in terms of what you need to improve in your interactions with people from different backgrounds. Give a rank of 1 to the skill or strategy that you most need to develop, a rank of 2 to the next area you feel you need to work on, and so on. Rank yourself on all eight strategies.

Seek information about the culture _____

Be other-oriented _____

Ask questions of others _____

Be mindful _____

Be flexible _____

Tolerate ambiguity _____

Avoid negative judgments about another culture _____

Develop a "third culture" _____

Based upon the areas in which you need greatest improvement, write a journal entry about how you will develop skill in these areas. How will you put what you have learned in this chapter into practice?

Learning with Others

1. Your instructor will guide you in playing Diversity Bingo to help you get better acquainted with the international and intercultural experiences of your classmates.

■ DIVERSITY BINGO

Your assignment is to locate people who have either done or know about the things listed in the boxes below, and then to obtain their autographs. You must first introduce yourself and share two personal things not listed in any of the boxes. After the introduction, the person may autograph the appropriate boxes for you. The person who collects the most autographs wins. You may not go back to the same person twice.

Was born outside the United States	Has attended a Native American powwow	Knows the significance of Angel Island	Is a morning person	Is a vegetarian	Has worked outside the United States
Has been to Austria	Can communicate in American Sign Language	Has attended a Cinco de Mayo celebration	Has never watched a Super Bowl	Knows the significance of the Stonewall Riots	Knows which tribal government the U.S. Constitution was modeled after
Has traveled outside the United States	Celebrates Hanukkah	Has had his or her last name mispronounced	Is a late night person	Knows who Rosa Parks is	Knows the opening date of the deer hunting or fishing season
Can name at least two traditionally black U.S. colleges	Has been a student for more than five years	Has a lesbian, gay, or bisexual friend	Has a Native American ancestor	Worked while going to high school	Has been to Europe
Is bilingual or multi-lingual	Knows what Kwanzaa is	Knows the meaning of Juneteenth	Knows the meaning of Jeri Curl	Has danced to Tex-Mex music	Can name the books of the Old or New Testament
Is an avid country music fan	Has been to a long-house	Knows his or her Chinese birth sign	Has danced to Zydeco music	Knows why many Irish people immigrated to the United States in the 1880s	Is an avid Dilbert fan

Adapted from: 3M, Austin, Texas, Diversity Seminar, 1994.

2. Bring to class a fable, folktale, or children's story from a culture other than your own. As a group, analyze the cultural values implied by the story or characters in the story.

3. Working with a group of your classmates, develop an ideal culture based upon the combined values and elements of people in your group. Develop a name for your culture. Suggest foods, recreational activities, and other leisure pursuits. Compare the culture your group develops with those that other groups in your class develop. How would the communication skills and principles discussed in this chapter help you bridge differences between those cultures?[41]

4. As a group, go on an intercultural scavenger hunt. Your instructor will give you a time limit. Scavenge your campus or classroom area to identify influences of as many different cultures as you can find. For example, you could go to the cafeteria and make note of ethnic foods that you find. Identify clothing, music, or architecture that is influenced by certain cultures.

5. In small groups, identify examples from your own experiences for each barrier to effective intercultural communication discussed in the text. Use one of the examples to develop a skit to perform for the rest of the class. See if the class can identify which intercultural barrier your group is depicting. Also suggest how the skills and principles discussed in the chapter might have improved the communication in the situation you roleplay.

	A powow is a Native American celebration.	Angel Island is where Chinese immigrants disembarked to enter the United States.			
	American Sign is used by the hearing impaired to communicate.	Cinco de Mayo celebrates the Mexican victory over the French in 1862.		A 1969 police raid on a bar in NY started the gay rights movements.	
	Hanukkah is a Jewish holiday celebrating rededication of the temple in 165 B.C.			Rosa Parks is a Black woman who refused to sit down in the back of a bus in Montgomery, Alabama.	
Howard, Hampton, Tuskegee, and Spelman are among notable black colleges.					
	Kwanzaa is an African American holiday.	Juneteenth celebrates the freeing of slaves in Texas in 1865.	Jeri Curl is a hair treatment used by African Americans.	Tex-Mex music is a country swing style that originated in southern Texas.	
	A longhouse is a Native American meeting place.	Chinese birth signs: Rat, Ox, Tiger, Rabbit, Dragon, Snake, Horse, Sheep, Monkey, Rooster.		There was a devastating potato famine in Ireland in the 1880s.	

■ GLOSSARY

CULTURE: A learned system of knowledge, behavior, attitudes, beliefs, values, and norms that is shared by a group of people.

CO-CULTURE: A culture that exists within a larger cultural context (e.g., the gay and lesbian culture).

CULTURAL ELEMENTS: Categories of things and ideas that identify the most profound aspects of cultural influence (e.g., schools, governments, music, theater, language).

ENCULTURATION: Process of communicating a group's culture from generation to generation.

ACCULTURATION: Process through which an individual acquires new approaches, beliefs, and values by coming into contact with other cultures.

CULTURAL VALUES: What a given group of people values or appreciates.

MASCULINE CULTURAL VALUES: Achievement, assertiveness, heroism, and material wealth.

FEMININE CULTURAL VALUES: Relationships, caring for the less fortunate, and overall quality of life.

CULTURAL CONTEXT: Information not explicitly communicated through language, such as environmental or nonverbal cues.

HIGH-CONTEXT CULTURE: Culture that derives much information from nonverbal and environmental cues.

LOW-CONTEXT CULTURE: Culture that derives much information from the words of a message and less information from nonverbal and environmental cues.

INTERCULTURAL COMMUNICATION: Communication between or among people who have different cultural traditions.

CULTURE SHOCK: Feeling of stress and anxiety a person experiences when encountering a culture different from his or her own.

ETHNOCENTRISM: Belief that your cultural traditions and assumptions are superior to others.

STEREOTYPE: To place a person or group of persons into an inflexible, all-encompassing category.

PREJUDICE: Prejudging someone before you know all of the facts or background of that person.

KNOWLEDGE: One of the elements of becoming a competent communicator; information that enhances understanding of others.

MOTIVATION: Internal state of readiness to respond to something. An element of interpersonal competence.

SKILL: Behavior that improves the effectiveness or quality of communicating with others.

WORLD VIEW: Perception shared by a culture or group of people about key beliefs and issues, such as death, God, and the meaning of life, which influences interaction with others.

THIRD CULTURE: Establishing common ground by joining separate cultures to create a third, "new," more comprehensive and inclusive culture.

SOCIAL DECENTERING: Cognitive process in which we take into account another person's thoughts, feelings, values, background, and perspectives.

MINDFULNESS: Awareness of cultural differences and the connection between thoughts and deeds when interacting with someone from a background different from your own.

EMPATHY: Process of developing an emotional reaction that is similar to the reaction being experienced by another person. Feeling what another person is feeling.

SYMPATHY: To acknowledge that someone may be feeling bad; to be compassionate toward someone.

ADAPTATION: Adjusting behavior in accord with what someone else does. We can adapt based upon the individual, the relationship, and the situation.

ADAPT PREDICTIVELY: Modifying or changing behavior in anticipation of an event.

ADAPT REACTIVELY: Modifying or changing behavior after an event.

Interpersonal Communication Skills

People judge you by your behavior, not by your intentions. The following four chapters focus on research-based communication skills that will help you monitor and shape your behavior to improve the quality of your relationships. Chapter 5 offers tips and strategies for listening to others and confirming your understanding of what you hear. Chapter 6 explores how the words we use and misuse affect our relationships with others. Meanings, as we'll learn, are in people, not in words themselves. Becoming other-oriented involves both listening to the words and reading the behavior cues of others. Chapter 7 focuses on the scope and importance of unspoken messages. We will explore the implications of the adage, "Actions speak louder than words." Chapter 8 will present principles and skills to help you manage conflict and disagreements with others.

Listening and Responding

After studying this chapter, you should be able to:

1. Describe four elements of the listening process.

2. Understand why we listen and list several important barriers to effective listening.

3. Identify ways to improve your other-orientation and listening skills.

4. Identify responding skills and understand strategies for improving them.

- LISTENING DEFINED

- WHY YOU LISTEN

- LISTENING BARRIERS

- IMPROVING YOUR LISTENING SKILLS

- RESPONDING WITH EMPATHY

- IMPROVING YOUR RESPONDING SKILLS

onversation overheard at Jimmie's Bar and Grill last Thursday:

Terry: So, let's get down to the details. Where are we gonna hold this party?

Bonnie: I can't think about it now, Terry. I'm too upset over a fight I had with Alex this morning.

Terry: Why don't you get rid of that husband, kiddo? You're always fighting. Find someone who treats ya with more respect. Now come on, just think about the best place—here at Jimmie's or over at Nate and Carmen's house?

Roseanne: What did you fight about, Bonnie?

Bonnie: He wants me to quit my job—which I don't like so much anyway—and have a baby. But I'm not sure I feel ready for such a big move, although I'd love to stop working there.

Roseanne: So you're feeling torn because you'd like to quit your job, but not to have a baby.

Bonnie: Well, I don't know. But if I did decide to have a baby, I wouldn't want to do it just to please him .

Terry: Don't give in to him, Bonn. He'll never stop pushing you around. I think maybe Nate and Carmen's. They've got that big barbeque pit.

Roseanne: Let's go over to my house where there's no jukebox and talk this over, Bonnie. It sounds like you're not really dismissing the idea, are you?

Bonnie: No. I would like to talk.

Can you identify the skilled listener in this snatch of conversation? Probably. Can you describe the skills that she is using? Probably not. But you will be able to by the time you finish this chapter.

You spend more time listening to others than almost anything else you do. Typical Americans spend more than 80 percent of an average day communicating with other people, and, as the pie chart in Figure 5.1 shows, they spend 45 percent of that communication time listening to others.[1] Ironically, most people's formal communication training focuses

Figure 5.1

What You Do With Your Communication Time

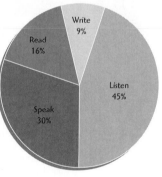

Write 9%

Read 16%

Listen 45%

Speak 30%

141

INSTRUCTIONAL GOALS AND TIPS

Rather than lecturing, consider focusing upon role-playing and listening-skill development for this topic. Provide immediate and descriptive feedback to role-play participants. Role-model these skills and encourage students to offer their feedback as well.

WEB ACTIVITY

Take a virtual tour of the ear. http://ctl.augie.edu/perry/ar/speech.htm
This and other tours related to communication such as speech perception are available at this site along with lesson plans. Download and take your class into the hearing process, literally.

DISCUSSION AND WRITING

Discuss the value of selecting more than sound when listening. How might we listen with our eyes, our skin, and our other senses? You might suggest Helen Keller's interaction with Anne Sullivan as an illustration.

on writing, the activity to which we devote the least amount of communication time. Chances are that up until now, you have had no formal training in listening. In this chapter, we will focus on this often neglected, yet quintessential, skill for developing quality interpersonal relationships. Listening is the process by which we learn the most about other people. In addition, we will explore ways to respond appropriately to others.

Listening Defined

"**D**id you hear what I said?" demanded a father who had been lecturing his teenage son on the importance of hanging up his clothes. In fact, his son did *hear* him, but he may not have been *listening*. **Listening** is a complex process we use to make sense out of what we hear. **Hearing** is the physiological process of decoding sounds. You hear when sound vibrations reach your eardrum and buzz the middle ear bones: the hammer, anvil, and stirrup. Eventually, these sound vibrations are translated into electrical impulses that reach the brain. In order to listen to something, you must first select that sound from competing sounds. Listening involves four activities—selecting, attending, understanding, and remembering. We confirm that listening occurs, by responding.

Selecting

To **select** a sound is to focus on one sound as you sort through the various sounds competing for your attention. As you listen to another in an interpersonal context, you focus on the words and nonverbal messages of your partner. Even now, as you are reading this book, there are undoubtedly countless noises within earshot. Stop reading for a moment and sort through the various sounds around you. Do you hear music? Is there noise from outside? How about the murmur of voices, the tick of a clock, the hum of a computer, the whoosh of an air conditioner or furnace? To listen, you must select which of these sounds will receive your attention.

Even in the din of a noisy train station, we can hold a meaningful conversation by selecting just the voice we want to hear. (Paul Chesley/Tony Stone Images)

Attending

After selecting a sound, you then focus on it. Attention can be fleeting. You may **attend** to the sound for a moment and then move on or return to other thoughts or other sounds. Typically, you attend to those sounds and messages that meet your needs or are consistent with what you think you should be focusing on. If you are hungry, you may select and then attend to a commercial for a sizzling burger or a crispy-crust pizza. Information that is novel, intense, or that

Reprinted with special permission of King Features Syndicate.

somehow relates to you also may capture your attention. And conflict, humor, new ideas, and real or concrete things command your attention more easily than abstract theories that do not relate to your interests or needs.

In addition, when someone invites you to participate or respond, you listen much more attentively than you do when someone just talks at you. One of your authors recently attended a daylong series of lectures at Oxford University on life in England during the Middle Ages. As a paleoanthropologist droned on about femur measurements and Harris lines, I struggled to stay awake. But when the lecturer produced several recently unearthed skeletons and invited the audience to participate in drawing conclusions about their lives and environment, I was all ears.

Understanding

Whereas hearing is a physiological phenomenon, **understanding** is the process of assigning meaning to the sounds you select and to which you attend. There are several theories about how you assign meaning to words you hear, but there is no universally accepted notion of how this process works. We know that people understand best if they can relate what they are hearing to something they already know. A well-advertised series of commercial foreign language tapes bases its guarantees of success on this principle, claiming that speakers of English can quickly learn to speak Spanish like a native by using mnemonic devices—for example, using the word *S-O-C-K-S* to remember the Spanish phrase *"Eso si, que es?"*

A second basic principle about how people understand others is this: The greater the similarity between individuals, the greater the likelihood for more accurate understanding. Individuals from different cultures who have substantially different religions, family lifestyles, values, and attitudes often have difficulty understanding each other, particularly in the early phases of a relationship. In a scene from her novel *The Joy Luck Club*, Amy Tan describes a culturally based misunderstanding between Jing-mei's Chinese mother and American boyfriend:

> As is the Chinese cook's custom, my mother always made disparaging remarks about her own cooking. That night she chose to direct it toward her famous steamed pork and preserved vegetable dish, which she always served with special pride.
>
> "Ai! This dish not salty enough, no flavor," she complained, after tasting a small bite. "It is too bad to eat."

5 LISTENING AND RESPONDING

DISCUSSION AND WRITING
Tell me, show me, involve me. . . . How does each method of instruction employ various channels of communication? Assess which individuals prefer which method.

TEACHING STRATEGY
The text author's suggestion that the greater the similarity between individuals, the greater the likelihood for more accurate understanding in listening leads to interesting discussion of similarity versus complementarity in interpersonal attraction. Ask students to consider whether individuals who are dissimilar may have difficulty in immediate understanding, but may have greater opportunity to reach understanding of new perspectives.

MEDIA AND OUTSIDE RESOURCES
It would be useful to show the clip from this movie. Several other scenes also provide excellent examples of listening, including a poignant scene between a separated husband and wife who strive to reconcile.

This was our family's cue to eat some and proclaim it the best she had ever made. But before we could do so, Rich said, "You know, all it needs is a little soy sauce." And he proceeded to pour a riverful of the salty black stuff on the platter, right before my mother's horrified eyes.[2]

You understand best that which you also experience. Perhaps you have heard the Montessori school philosophy: I hear, I forget; I see, I remember; I experience, I understand. Hearing alone does not provide us with understanding. We hear over 1 billion words each year, but we understand a fraction of that number. In Chapter 3 we discussed the processes involved in perception and observed that different people can reach dramatically different conclusions about the same events and messages, based on their previous experiences. A key to establishing relationships with others is trying to understand those differences in experience in order to arrive at a common meaning for the messages we exchange.

Remembering

To **remember** is to recall information. Some researchers theorize that you store every detail you have ever heard or witnessed; your mind operates like a video camera. But you cannot retrieve or remember all of the tapes. Sometimes you are present, yet you have no recollection of what occurred.

Our brains have both short-term and long-term memory storage systems. Short-term memory is where you store almost all the information you hear. You look up a phone number in the telephone book, mumble the number to yourself, then dial the number, only to discover that the line is busy. Three minutes later you have to look up the number again because it did not get stored in your long-term memory. Our short-term storage area is very limited. Just as airports have just a few short-term parking spaces, but lots of spaces for long-term parking, our brains can accommodate a few things of fleeting significance, but acres of important information. Most of us forget hundreds of snips and bits of insignificant information that pass through our brains each day.

The information we store in long-term memory includes events, conversations, and other data that are significant for us. We tend to remember dramatic and vital information, as well as seemingly inconsequential details connected with such information. Most people over the age of forty today know exactly where they were on November 22, 1963, the day President Kennedy was assassinated. Many over the age of sixty can also recall where they were on December 7, 1941, Pearl Harbor Day. Do you remember what you were doing on April 19, 1995, when you heard the news that the Alfred P. Murrah Federal Building in Oklahoma City had been bombed? Or, do you recall that Saturday evening or Sunday morning in late August 1997 when you first heard that Princess Diana had been killed in an automobile accident? Information makes it to long-term memory because of its significance to us.

Responding

Interpersonal communication is transactive; it involves both talking and responding. You **respond** to people to let them know you understand their messages. Responses can be nonverbal; direct eye contact and head nods let your partner know you're tuned in. Or you can respond verbally by asking questions to confirm the content of the message: "Are you saying you don't want us to spend as much time together as we once did?" or by making statements that reflect the feelings of the speaker: "So you are frustrated that you have to wait for someone to drive you where you want to go." We will discuss responding skills in more detail later in the chapter.

RECAP	What Is Listening?
SELECTING	Sorting through various sounds that compete for your attention.
ATTENDING	Focusing on a particular sound or message.
UNDERSTANDING	Assigning meaning to messages.
REMEMBERING	Recalling information that has been communicated.
RESPONDING	Confirming your understanding of a message.

Why You Listen

Why do you listen to others? As the great explorer Sir Edmund Hillary replied when asked why he climbed Mount Everest—because it's there. You listen because words are there. But you also listen because you have a need to connect with other humans; it is through listening that you develop and maintain relationships. You listen to enjoy, to learn, to evaluate, and to empathize with others.

Listening to Enjoy

Often, you listen to others just for the fun of it. Perhaps one of the reasons your friends are your friends is that they are entertaining storytellers or clever wisecrackers. You select TV programs, movies, music, and other forms of entertainment for the same reason. Listening is part of the pleasure of being with others. You enjoy going to parties, dining with friends, and getting together just to hang out because you can share the joys and humorous events of life by listening and being listened to.

Listening to Learn

Not all listening is for pleasure. Nothing snaps a class to attention more quickly than a professor's proclamation that "This next point will be covered on the test." Another key reason you listen is to learn. Since the days you began watching *Sesame Street* (if you grew up in America during or after the 1970s)

5   LISTENING AND RESPONDING

SKILL DEVELOPMENT

Ask students to role-play a dialogue in which one partner describes a frustrating event in his/her week and the other refrains from responding in ANY WAY. Instruct the speakers to do their best to encourage listening and advise the listeners to resist the speakers' pleas. After 2 minutes, debrief with the class.

INSTRUCTIONAL GOALS AND TIPS

Because the single most important word for listening is one's name, be sure to use your students' names whenever possible.

MEDIA AND OUTSIDE RESOURCES

Play some of the Orson Wells radio broadcast of *War of the Worlds* which triggered a public panic. Discuss the importance of distinguishing between entertainment and news. How does this translate to current radio programming (such as Rush Limbaugh's talk show)?

MEDIA AND OUTSIDE RESOURCES

The U.S. National Archives and Records Administration has several audio tapes that are useful for listening skills improvement. Consider, "Sounds of History," for example, which features recordings of people who made history.

until now, as you pursue a degree, you have been challenged to understand and remember what you hear. The more motivated you are to learn, the more likely it is that you listen.

You do most of your listening and learning outside the classroom, though. In interpersonal situations, you listen for everyday information, such as who will pick up the kids after school and where and when to pick up the laundry. You also listen to find out about the daily activities of others. Your phone calls to family members when you are separated by distances are often motivated by wanting to find out what's happening. It is through listening that we learn.

Listening to Evaluate

Besides listening to accumulate information, you also listen to acquire information that you can then use to solve problems and to make critical decisions and judgments. The job interview is a classic situation in which both people listen to gather information to make a critical decision. The interviewer listens to the applicant's responses to determine whether the person can do the job well and get along with others. The applicant also seeks information and listens to evaluate whether the work will be suitable and the boss a reasonable manager for him or her. As we saw in Chapter 3, because of the barrage of information coming at us each day, we often make snap judgments. These first impressions are based upon information we hear, and upon our own biases and backgrounds. As the saying goes, you never get a second chance to make—or to form—a first impression.

We use critical thinking skills to evaluate the messages of others. If we are adept at separating facts from inferences, identifying fallacies in reasoning, and analyzing evidence, then our evaluations of others' messages can be reasonably accurate.

One of our best motivations for listening is to accurately evaluate information we hear. Both parties in the interview situation are motivated to gain as must information as they can from the interaction. (Bob Daemmrich/Stock Boston)

Listening to Empathize

The word *empathy* comes from a Greek word for "passion" and is related to the German word, *Einfuhling*, which means "to feel with." Empathy involves emotions. As we discussed in Chapter 4, to **empathize** with someone is to try to feel what he or she is feeling, rather than just to think about or acknowledge the feelings.

Sympathy versus Empathy

Most card shops have a sympathy card section. Such cards let people know you realize they are feeling bad about the death of someone close to them. To **sympathize** is to say you are sorry—that you want to offer your support and acknowledge that someone is feeling bad. Empathy goes one step further than sympathy. Empathy means that you try to perceive the world from another's perspective; you attempt to feel what someone else feels.

Respond to the sample situations below both with sympathy and with empathy.

1. A good friend of yours just phoned to tell you that her dog, a well-loved fourteen-year-old pet, has just died.

Respond with sympathy: _____

_____

Respond with empathy: _____

_____

2. Your older brother comes to visit you and tells you that he and his wife are getting a divorce after twenty years of marriage.

Respond with sympathy: _____

_____

Respond with empathy: _____

_____

3. A friend tells you that she just got fired from her job.

Respond with sympathy: _____

_____

Respond with empathy: _____

_____

From William Gudykunst, *Bridging Differences*, 2d ed. (Thousand Oaks, CA: Sage Publications, 1994). Reprinted by permission of Sage Publications, Inc.

When your friends have "one of those days," perhaps they seek you out to talk about it. They may not have any real problems to solve—perhaps it was just a day filled with miscommunication and squabbles with their partners or co-workers. But they want to tell you the details. Do you listen empathically, without giving advice? Often that is what they are seeking—a listener who focuses attention on them and understands what they are saying. We are willing to listen empathically for the same reasons that we like to give our friends gifts. It makes us feel good to show others that we value them. Carl Rogers summarized the value of empathy when he said, "A high degree of empathy in a relationship is possibly the most potent factor in bringing about change and learning."

5 LISTENING AND RESPONDING

Encourage students to consider phoning a general hotline that specializes in Rogerian listening. Instruct students to have an actual issue to speak about when they phone. Of what value is this style of listening for solving problems? Students will undoubtedly have positive feelings about the compassion and empathy this listening creates.

SKILL DEVELOPMENT

Have the class take this exercise-test. Next, divide the class into three roughly equal groups based on the results: a higher scoring group, a middle scoring group, and a lower scoring group. In each group, have students write their approximate Grade Point Average (GPA) on a slip of paper. Collect the slips of paper and pass them to another group which will calculate the average GPA for that group. Upon completion, see whether there is a relationship between listening and good or bad grades. As a variation to this activity, keep students in the three groups and lecture over chapter four. Next, distribute a short quiz on your lecture. Have students grade one another's quizzes and calculate a quiz average for each group. Did their scores reflect their group's location on the listening skills exercise?

Listening Barriers

Even though we spend so much of our communication time listening, most of us don't listen as well as we should. Twenty-four hours after we hear a speech, a class lecture, or a sermon, we forget more than half of what was said. And it gets worse. In another twenty-four hours we forget half of what we remembered, so we really remember only a quarter of the lecture.

Our interpersonal listening skills are not much better. If anything, they may be worse. When you listen to a speech or lecture, you have a clearly defined listening role; one person talks and you are expected to listen. But in interpersonal situations, you may have to alternate quickly between speaking and listening. This takes considerable skill and concentration. Often you are thinking of what you want to say next rather than listening.

One study found that even in the most intimate relationships, our listening skills are not highly developed. Couples who had been married for at least five years were placed in separate rooms, and researchers asked the wives, "During the last six months have you and your spouse talked about who would be responsible for some of the household chores such as taking out the garbage and other domestic responsibilities?" "Yes," recalled at least 71 percent of the wives. Interestingly, when the same question was put to their husbands, only 19 percent recalled a discussion of domestic duties. Intrigued, the researchers next asked a more personal question of the wives: "In the last six months have you and your spouse discussed the possibilities of increasing the size of your family? Have you talked about having children?" An overwhelming majority, 91 percent, of the wives responded affirmatively. Curiously, only 15 percent of the husbands recalled having a conversation about having more children. While one anecdotal study does not prove conclusively that all intimate relationships suffer from listening lapses, it does illustrate the problem. And as Understanding Diversity: Who Listens Better, Men or Women? reiterates, often the problem is gender related.

Another surprising study found that we sometimes pay more attention to strangers than to intimate friends or partners. Married couples in the study tended to interrupt each other more often and were generally less polite to each other than were strangers involved in a decision-making task.[3] Apparently, we take listening shortcuts when communicating with others in close relationships.

Most interpersonal listening problems can be traced to a single source—ourselves. While listening to others, we also "talk" to ourselves. Our internal thoughts are like a play-by-play sportscast. We mentally comment on the words and sights that we select and to which we attend. If we keep those comments focused on the message, they may be useful. But we often attend to our own internal dialogues instead of others' messages. Then our listening effectiveness plummets.

Inattentive listening is a bit like channel surfing when we watch TV—pushing the remote control button to switch from channel to channel, avoiding commercials and focusing for brief periods on attention-grabbing program "bites." When we listen to others, we may fleetingly tune in to the conversation for a moment, decide that the content is uninteresting, and then focus on a personal thought. These thoughts are barriers to communication, and they come in a variety of forms.

5 LISTENING AND RESPONDING

SKILL DEVELOPMENT
Suggest to students that they discuss with their significant others their strengths and weaknesses as listeners. Then have them compare the feedback to these research findings.

UNDERSTANDING DIVERSITY

Who Listens Better: Men or Women?

Research provides no definitive answer to this question. There is evidence that men and women listen somewhat differently and have different expectations about the role of listening and talking. Deborah Tannen suggests that one of the most common complaints wives have about their husbands, is "He doesn't listen to me anymore" along with, "He doesn't talk to me anymore." Another scholar noted that complaints about lack of communication were usually at the top of women's lists of reasons for divorce but mentioned much less often by men. Since both men and women are participating in the same conversation, why are women often more dissatisfied with the listening and talking process than men? Tannen's explanation: women expect different things from conversations than men do.

One researcher suggests that men and women may have different attention styles. When men listen, they may be looking for a new structure or organizational pattern, or to separate bits of information they hear. They continually shape, form, observe, inquire, and direct energy toward a chosen goal. Men's attention style is reported to be more emotionally controlled than women's attention style. Women are described as more subjective, empathic, and emotionally involved as they listen. They are more likely to search for relationships among parts of a pattern and to rely upon more intuitive perceptions of feelings. They are also more easily distracted by competing details. Females may hear more of the message because they reject less of it. These differences in attention styles and the way men and women process information, suggests the researcher, can potentially affect listening, even though we have no direct evidence linking attention style to listening skill.

Another researcher suggests that when men listen, they listen to solve a problem; men are more instrumental and task oriented. Women listen to seek new information to enhance understanding. There is additional evidence that men may be more goal oriented when they listen. What are the implications of these research studies? It may mean that men and women focus on different parts of messages and have different listening objectives. These differences can affect relationship development. Males may need to recognize that while they are attending to a message and looking for new structure to solve a problem or achieve a goal, they may hear less of the message and therefore listen less effectively. And even though many females may hear more of the message, they may need to make connections between the parts of the information they hear to look for major ideas, rather than just focus on the details. In any case, gender-based differences in attention style and information processing may account for some of the relational problems that husbands and wives, lovers, siblings, and male-female pairs experience.[4]

INTERPERSONAL COMMUNICATION SKILLS

150

Barrier: Focusing on a Personal Agenda

Most of us have had the experience of waiting our turn in a conversation, formulating what we were going to say next. This focus on an internal message can keep us from selecting and attending to the other person's message. If you are supposed to be listening to Aunt Mae tell about her recent trip to the Buckner County Fair, but you are eager to hit her up for a loan, your personal agenda will serve as a barrier to your listening ability. Or you may simply decide that Aunt Mae's monologue is boring and unimportant and give yourself permission to tune out as she drones on. Like humorist James Thurber's famous daydreamer, Walter Mitty, you may eventually find yourself unable to respond cogently, lost in your own world:

"Not so fast! You're driving too fast!" said Mrs. Mitty. "What are you driving so fast for?"

"Hmmm?" said Walter Mitty. He looked at his wife, in the seat beside him, with shocked astonishment. She seemed grossly unfamiliar, like a strange woman who had yelled at him in a crowd.[5]

How do you short-circuit this listening problem? First, diagnose it. Note consciously when you find yourself drifting off, thinking about your agenda rather than concentrating on the speaker. Second, throttle up your powers of concentration when you find your internal messages are distracting you from listening well. If you notice that you are "telling" yourself that Aunt Mae's anecdote is boring, you can also mentally remind yourself to listen with greater energy and focus.

Barrier: Emotional Noise

Words are powerful symbols that affect our attitudes, our behavior, and even our blood pressure. Words arouse us emotionally. **Emotional noise** occurs when our emotional arousal interferes with communication effectiveness. If you grew up in a home in which R-rated language was never used, then four-letter words may be distracting to you. Words that insult your religious or ethnic heritage can also be fighting words. Most of us respond to certain trigger words like a bull to a waving cape; we want to charge in to correct the speaker or perhaps even do battle with him or her.

Sometimes it is not specific words, but rather concepts or ideas that cause an emotional eruption. Some talk-radio hosts try to boost their ratings by purposely using demagogic language that elicits passionate responses. Although listening to such conflict can be interesting and entertaining, when your own emotions become aroused, you may lose your ability to converse effectively. Strong emotions can interfere with focusing on the message of another.

The emotional state of the speaker may also affect your ability to understand and evaluate what you hear. If you are listening to someone who is emotionally distraught, you will be more likely to focus on his or her emotions than on the content of the message.[6] R. G. Owens advises that when you are communicating

MEDIA AND OUTSIDE RESOURCES

To learn more about gender communication, consider seeing comedian Rob Becker's "Defending the Caveman." This is an entertaining, respectful one-man show which encourages tolerance and an other-orientation.

TEACHING STRATEGY

Give an example of a word or concept that is likely to spur emotional noise in you. Then ask students to silently, anonymously, record words or concepts that trouble them. Collect the writings and read them to the class. This may serve not only as a concrete illustration of emotional noise, but also as a reminder of Chapter 3 material on perception.

MEDIA AND OUTSIDE RESOURCES

Encourage students to use the scan button on their radios to listen to deejays and radio personalities like Howard Stern, G. Gordon Liddy, or Rush Limbaugh. How are their communication styles similar? How do they differ? Most students will perceive more similarities than differences.

TEACHING STRATEGY

Challenge students' ability to listen without criticizing a speaker based on superficial factors, by wearing something very unusual to class when you cover this material.

with someone who is emotionally excited, you should remain calm and focused, and try simply to communicate your interest in the other person.[7]

Your listening challenge is to avoid emotional sidetracks and keep your attention focused upon the message. When your internal dialogue is kicked into high gear by objectionable words or concepts, or by an emotional speaker, make an effort to quiet it down and steer back to the subject at hand.

BUILDING YOUR SKILLS

Identifying Emotional "Hot Buttons"

Following are some listening situations and phrases that may cause you to be emotional. Check those that are "hot buttons" for you as a listener, and add others that strongly affect you, positively or negatively.

_____ "You never/always . . ."

_____ Know-it-all attitudes

_____ Individuals who smoke cigarettes or cigars while talking to you

_____ "Shut up!"

_____ Being ignored

_____ Bad grammar

_____ "You never listen."

_____ Obscene language

_____ Whining

_____ "What you should do is . . ."

_____ Being interrupted

Others:

_____

_____

_____

Knowing what your emotional hot buttons are can help prevent your overreacting when they are pushed.

Adapted from Diane Bone, *The Business of Listening* (Crisp Publications, 1995), p. 52.

Barrier: Criticizing the Speaker

The late Mother Teresa once said, "If you judge people, you have no time to love them." Being critical of the speaker may distract us from focusing on the message. As you learned in Chapter 3, most people are especially distracted by appearances, forming impressions of others based solely on nonverbal information. Superficial factors such as clothing, body size and shape, age, and ethnicity all affect our interpretation of a message. In his essay "Black Men and Public Space," journalist Brent Staples provides this account of an incident that made communication impossible because of the way a woman reacted to his appearance:

On assignment for a local paper and killing time before an interview, I entered a jewelry store on the city's affluent Near North Side. The proprietor excused herself and returned with an enormous red Doberman pinscher straining at the end of a leash. She stood, the dog extended toward me, silent to my questions, her eyes bulging nearly out of her head.[8]

Again, it is important to monitor your internal dialogue to make sure you are focusing on the message rather than criticizing the messenger. Good listeners say to themselves, "While it may be distracting, I am simply not going to let the appearance of this speaker keep my attention from the message."

Barrier: Speech Rate vs. Thought Rate

Your ability to think faster than people speak is another listening pitfall. The average person speaks at a rate of 125 words a minute. Some folks talk a bit faster, others more slowly. You, on the other hand, have the ability to process up to 600 or 800 words a minute. The difference between your mental ability to handle words and the speed at which they arrive at your cortical centers can cause trouble, giving you time to daydream, tune the speaker in and out, and give you the illusion that you are concentrating more attentively than you actually are.[9]

You can turn your listening speed into an advantage if you use the extra time instead to summarize what a speaker is saying. By periodically sprinkling in mental summaries during a conversation, you can dramatically increase your listening ability and make the speech-rate/thought-rate difference work to your advantage.

Barrier: Information Overload

We live in an information-rich age. We are all constantly bombarded with sight and sound images, and experts suggest that the volume of information competing for our attention is likely to become even greater in the future. Fax machines, car phones, audio Internet messages, and other technological devices can interrupt conversations and distract us from listening to others.

Be on the alert for these information interruptions when you are talking with others. Don't assume that because you are ready to talk, the other person is ready to listen. If your message is particularly sensitive or important, you may want to ask your listening partner, "Is this a good time to talk?" Even if he or she says yes, look for eye contact and a responsive facial expression to make sure the positive response is genuine.

Barrier: External Noise

As you will recall, all of the communication models we saw in Chapter 1 include the element of noise—distractions that take your focus away from the message. Many households seem to be addicted to noise. Often there is a TV on (sometimes more than one), a computer game beeping, and music emanating from another room. These and other sounds compete with your attention when you are listening to others.

Besides literal noise, there are other potential distractors. A headline in your evening paper about the latest details in a lurid sex scandal may "shout" for your attention just when your son wants to talk with you about his latest science fiction story. A desire to listen to your new compact disk of "Pacific Overtures" may drown out your spouse's overtures to a heart-to-heart about your family's budget problems. The lure of music, TV, books, or your computer can all distract you from your listening task.

Distractions make it difficult to sustain attention to a message. You have a choice to make. You can attempt to listen through the labyrinth of competing

MEDIA AND OUTSIDE RESOURCES
Listen to John Moschitta's work on tape. For instance, "Mighty Mouth" Moschitta's "Ten Classics in Ten Minutes" (Workman Publishing, 1986) is very entertaining. Encourage students to listen carefully and report their ability to listen at these increased rates.

SKILL DEVELOPMENT
Using a "fishbowl" exercise, have students role-play doing this face-to-face and by telephone. In some cases, have them say "yes," and in others, "no." Then debrief with the class. [Note: fishbowl exercises involve putting the role-players in the middle of the room with classmates encircling them.]

TEACHING STRATEGY
When you discuss external noise as a barrier, pause for a minute and then ask students to list the sources of external noise they find in your classroom environment.

DISCUSSION AND WRITING
Suggest that students take
an inventory of their family
room (or living room) to
determine how the furniture
arrangement allows conversation. Where is conversation easiest?

TEACHING STRATEGY
Reinforce Maslow's four
levels of skill by asking students to give examples of
skills other than listening
that they have performed at
each of these levels.

distractions, or you can modify the environment to reduce them. Turning off the stereo, setting down the paper, and establishing eye contact with the speaker can help to minimize the noise barrier.

RECAP   **Overcoming Barriers to Listening**

Listening Barriers	To Overcome the Barrier
Focusing on Our Personal Agenda	Consciously become aware of the self-focus and shift attention.
Emotional Noise	Use self-talk to manage emotions.
Criticizing the Speaker	Focus on the message, not the messenger.
Information Rate	Use the difference between speech rate and thought rate to mentally summarize the message.
Information Overload	Realize when you or your partner is tired or distracted and not ready to listen.
External Noise	Take charge of the listening environment by eliminating the distraction.

Improving Your Listening Skills

Many of the listening problems we have identified stem from focusing on ourselves rather than on the messages of others. You can begin improving your listening skills by following three steps you probably first encountered in elementary school: (1) stop, (2) look, and (3) listen. Simple as they may seem, these steps can provide the necessary structure to help you refocus your mental energies and improve your listening power. Let's consider each step separately.

Stop

In order to select and attend to the messages of others, we must tap into our internal dialogue and stop our own running commentary about issues and ideas that are self-focused rather than other-focused. To tune out distracting internal noise and focus on the present moment may take considerable effort. It is a learned skill.

A model of how we learn any skill, attributed by many to Abraham Maslow, suggests that we operate at one of four skill levels:

- Unconscious incompetence

- Conscious incompetence

- Conscious competence

- Unconscious competence

The first level—*unconscious incompetence*—means we are unaware of our own incompetence. We don't know what we don't know. In this case, before you read this chapter, you may simply not have been aware that you are distracted by your internal dialogue when you interact with others.

The second level is *conscious incompetence*. Here we become aware or conscious that we are not competent; we know what we don't know. You may now be aware that you are an easily distracted listener, but you do not know how to solve the problem.

Level three is *conscious competence*; we are aware that we know something, but it has not yet become an integrated habit. You might have to work at decentering when you first begin using it as you listen.

The final level of skill attainment is *unconscious competence*. At this level your skills become second nature to you. After the age of six, most people are unconsciously competent at tying their shoes; it is automatic. In the same way, you may become so skilled in the decentering process that you do it as the rule rather than as an exception. At this level you will also probably have the capacity to empathize, or "feel with" others as you listen. Considering Others: Doctors Must Address More Than Physical Complaints points out that some doctors, despite their high level of professional training, do not always have highly developed listening skills. If they took time to *stop* and listen, says the writer, they would be far more effective at treating their patients. As a wise person once said, "Take a tip from nature—your ears aren't made to shut, but your mouth is."

Look

Nonverbal messages are powerful. As the primary ways we communicate feelings, emotions, and attitudes, they play a major role in the total communication process, particularly in the development of relationships. Facial expressions and vocal cues, as well as eye contact, posture, and use of gestures and movement, can dramatically color the meaning of a message. When the nonverbal message contradicts the verbal message, we almost always believe the nonverbal message. In listening to others, it is vital that you focus not only on the words, but also on the nonverbal messages. Listen with your eyes as well as your ears.

Another reason to look at another person is to establish eye contact, which signals that you are focusing your interest and attention on him or her. If your eyes are darting over your partner's head, looking for someone else, or if you are constantly peeking at your watch, your partner will rightfully get the message that you're not really listening. J. Harrigan found that we telegraph our desire to change roles from listener to speaker by

Nonverbal messages can be a powerful part of interpersonal communication. What message does the look in this woman's eyes send as she listens to the speaker? (Bob Daemmrich/Stock Boston)

Skill Levels

	Unconscious	Conscious
Incompetent	1	2
Competent	3	4

TEACHING STRATEGY
Reinforce the importance of looking while listening by having pairs of students create and role-play conversations in which the speaker's nonverbal message contradicts his or her verbal message.

RESEARCH AND LITERATURE
In 1995, the Speech Communication Association hosted a summer conference on the topic of health communication. Consider requesting transcripts from these sessions.

increasing our eye contact, using gestures such as a raised finger, and shifting our posture.[10] So it is important to maintain eye contact and monitor your partner's nonverbal signals when you are speaking as well as listening.

It is important, however, not to be distracted by nonverbal cues that may prevent us from interpreting the message correctly. A research team asked one group of college students to listen to a counselor, and another group to both view and listen.[11] The students then rated the counselor's effectiveness. Students who both saw and heard the counselor perceived him as *less* effective because his distracting nonverbal behaviors affected their evaluations. We will provide more information about how to enhance your skill in interpreting the nonverbal messages of others in Chapter 7.

Listen

After making a concerted effort to stop distracting internal dialogue and to look for nonverbal cues, you will then be in a better position to understand the verbal messages of others. To listen is to do more than focus on facts; it is to search for the essence of the speaker's thoughts. We recommend the following strategies to help you improve your listening skill.

1. *Determine your listening goal.* As we saw earlier in this chapter, you listen to other people for several reasons—to learn, to enjoy yourself, to evaluate, or to provide support. With so many potential listening goals and options, it is useful to decide consciously what your listening objective is.

    If you are listening to someone give you directions to the city park, then your mental summaries should focus on the details of when to turn left and how many streets past the courthouse you go before you turn right. The details are critical to achieving your objective. If, on the other hand, your neighbor is telling you about her father's triple bypass operation, then your goal is to empathize. It is probably not important that you be able to recall when her father checked into the hospital or other details. Your job is to listen patiently and to provide emotional support. Clarifying your listening objective in your own mind can help you use appropriate skills to maximize your listening effectiveness.

2. *Transform listening barriers into listening goals.* If you can transform the listening barriers you read about earlier into listening goals, you will be well on your way to improving your listening skill. Make it a goal not to focus on your personal agenda. Make it a goal to use self-talk to manage emotional noise. Set a goal not to criticize the speaker. Remind yourself before each conversation to do mental summaries that capitalize on the differences between your information processing rate and the speaker's verbal delivery rate. And make it your business to choose a communication environment that is free of distraction from other incoming information or noise.

3. *When your listening goal is to remember a message, mentally summarize the details of the message.* This suggestion may seem to contradict the suggestion to avoid focusing only on facts; but if your goal is to be able to recall infor-

ACTIVITY
See Activity 5.2 in the Instructor's Guide.

Doctors Must Address More Than Physical Complaints

What's wrong with this picture: An eighty-year-old woman visits her doctor, the same one she has been seeing for a long time. He asks about her health, and she starts talking about not being happy in her new apartment after forty-one years living in the same house.

The apartment is in a different part of town and she misses her former neighbors, who used to pick up items for her at the grocery store. Buying furniture has posed a problem, especially because her failing eyesight makes it difficult to drive places. She also worries about making her retirement money stretch as far as she needs. She says she is so lonely.

The doctor says "Mmm-hmm" and "That's too bad" at the appropriate times during her story. Then he steers the conversation toward the woman's heart condition and whether she has been experiencing any pain or other symptoms.

Stop right there, says Dr. Howard Waitzkin, an internal-medicine physician and sociologist at the University of California at Irvine. He says the doctor is focused on the physical symptom (a weak heart) and not listening to what is really disrupting this woman's life (the loss of community).

"Social problems almost always come up when doctors and patients are talking," Waitzkin says, "but they tend to be marginalized in the conversation."

This added work [of taking more time to listen] may seem a burden for busy doctors, but Waitzkin insists such careful listening has long-term benefits: it helps address patients' underlying concerns in one visit rather than let a stressful situation linger at the potential expense of the patient's health.

mation, it is important to grasp the details your partner provides. As we noted earlier, you can process words much more quickly than a person speaks. So periodically summarize the names, dates, and locations in the message. Organize the speaker's factual information into appropriate categories or try to place events in chronological order. Without a full understanding of the details, you will likely miss the speaker's major point.

4. *Mentally weave these summaries into a focused major point or series of major ideas.* Facts usually make the most sense when we can use them to help support an idea or major point. So, as you summarize, try to link the facts you have organized in your mind with key ideas and principles. Use facts to enhance your critical thinking as you analyze, synthesize, evaluate, and finally summarize the key points or ideas your listening partner is making.[12]

5. *Practice listening to challenging material.* To improve or even maintain any skill, you need to practice it. Listening experts suggest that our listening skills deteriorate if we do not practice what we know. Listening to difficult, challenging material can sharpen our listening skills, so good listeners practice by listening to documentaries, debates, and other challenging material rather than mindless sitcoms and other material that entertains but does not engage them mentally.

Listening Skills	Definition	Action
Stop	Tune out distracting, competing messages.	Become conscious of being distracted; use self-talk to remain focused.
Look	Become aware of the speaker's non-verbal cues; monitor your own nonverbal cues to communicate your interest in the speaker.	Establish eye contact; avoid fidgeting or performing other tasks when someone is speaking to you. Listen with your eyes.
Listen	Comprehend the meaning of facts and details in your partner's message.	Mentally summarize details; link these details with main ideas.

Responding with Empathy

Above all, good listening is an other-oriented ability. Good listening is active, not passive. To listen passively is to avoid displaying any behavior that lets the speaker know we are listening.[13] Passive listeners sit with a blank stare or a frozen facial expression. Their thoughts and feelings could be anywhere, for all the speaker knows. **Active listeners**, in contrast, respond mentally, verbally, and nonverbally to a speaker's message. Responding serves several specific functions. First, it can be a measure of how accurately you understood the message. If you burst out laughing as your friend tells you about losing his house in a flood, he'll know you misunderstood what he was saying. Second, your responses indicate whether you agree or disagree with the comments others make. If you tell your friend that you do not approve of her comments on abortion, she'll know your position on the information she shared. Finally, your responses tell speakers how they are affecting others. When you get tears in your eyes as you listen to your friend describe how lonely he has felt since his father died, he will know that you are affected by the pain he is feeling. Like radar that guides high-tech weapons, your feedback provides information to help others decide whether or not to correct the course of their messages.

As you can see, responding is something we do for others that also holds out great benefits for us. It is the key to exchanging mutually understood, emotionally satisfying messages. Responding is especially critical if you are listening to provide support. Of course, listening to empathize is only one of the possible listening goals you may have. We are not suggesting that ferreting out someone's emotions is the goal of every listening encounter. That would be tedious for both you and your listening partners. But when you do want to listen empathically and respond, you must shift the focus to your partner and try to understand the message from his or her perspective.[14]

Empathy is not a single skill but a collection of skills that help you predict how others will respond. Daniel Goleman's book *Emotional Intelligence* is an

Ask students to describe verbal listening/attending behaviors. Put these on the board:

- paraphrases
- back channeling cues
- open-ended questions
- summaries
- attentive silence
- eye contact

ACTIVITY
See Activity 5.3 in the Instructor's Guide.

outstanding resource that discusses the role and importance of our emotions in developing empathy with others.[15] Goleman has found evidence that people who are emotionally intelligent—sensitive to others, have empathy, and are other-oriented—have better interpersonal relationships. Goleman summarizes the centrality of emotions in developing empathy by quoting Antoine De Saint-Exupery: "It is with the heart that one sees rightly; what is essential is invisible to the eye."[16]

The quiz in Considering Others: Test Your Empathy Ability can help you determine how effectively you empathize with others. We then will discuss four strategies you can use to enhance your empathy skills.

INSTRUCTIONAL GOALS AND TIPS
Another response skill is to use back channel cues. These are described in Chapter 7.

INSTRUCTIONAL GOALS AND TIPS

Distinguish between projection and listening for empathy.

INSTRUCTIONAL GOALS AND TIPS

Compare open-ended questions to closed-ended questions. Suggest that open-ended questions such as "How?" and "What?" invite talk, whereas "Why?" tends to invite defensiveness.

SKILL DEVELOPMENT

Assign students to role-play discussions in which the listener asks loaded questions: "Don't you think that? . . ." and "Did you consider? . . ." and "Why did you? . . ." It will quickly become apparent how these diminish rapport.

We can better understand our partner's feelings—empathize with him or her—if we listen and try to recall how we might have felt in similar situations. (Gerard Loucel/Tony Stone Images)

Understand Your Partner's Feelings

If your goal is to empathize or "feel with" your partner, you might begin by imagining how you would feel under the same circumstances. If your spouse comes home dejected from being hassled at work, try to recall how you felt when that happened to you. If a friend calls to tell you his mother is ill, try to imagine how you would feel if the situation were reversed. Of course, your reaction to these events might be different from your spouse's or your friend's. You may need to decenter and remember how your partner felt in other similar situations, to understand how he or she is feeling now.

Ask Questions

Sometimes when others share a momentous occurrence, the story may tumble out in a rambling, disorganized way. You can help sort through the story if you ask questions to identify the sequence of events. "What happened first?" and "Then what happened?" can help both you and your partner clarify what happened.

If your partner is using words or phrases that you don't understand, ask for definitions. "He's just so lackadaisical!" moans Mariko. "What do you mean by lackadaisical? Could you give me an example?" asks Reggie. Sometimes asking for an example helps the speaker sort through the events as well.

Of course, if you are trying to understand another's feelings, you can ask how he or she is feeling, or how the event or situation made him or her feel. Often, however, nonverbal cues are more revealing than a verbal disclosure about feelings and emotions.

Reflect Content by Paraphrasing

After you try to imagine how you would feel under similar circumstances and to make sure you have an accurate understanding of the events that occurred, you need to check your understanding of the facts. Respond with a statement such as:

"Are you saying . . . ."

"You seem to be describing . . . ."

"So the point you are making seems to be . . . ."

II   INTERPERSONAL COMMUNICATION SKILLS

"Here is what I understand you to mean . . . ."

"So here is what seemed to happen . . . ."

Then summarize the events, details, or key points you think the speaker is trying to convey. This is not a word-for-word repetition of what the speaker has said, nor do you need to summarize the content of *each* phrase or minor detail. Rather, it is a **paraphrase** to check the accuracy of your understanding. Here is an example:

Juan: This week I have so much extra work to do. I'm sorry if I haven't been able to help keep this place clean. I know it's my turn to do the dishes tonight, but I have to get back to work. Could you do the dishes tonight?

Brigid: So you want me to do the dishes tonight and for the rest of the week. Right?

Juan: Well, I'd like you to help with the dishes tonight. But I think I can handle it for the rest of the week.

Brigid: OK. So I'll do them tonight and you take over tomorrow.

Juan: Yes.

Research conducted in clinical counseling settings found that when a listener paraphrases the content and feelings of a speaker, the speaker is more likely to trust and value the listener.[17] Remember the conversation at the beginning of this chapter? Roseanne cultivates trust by paraphrasing, whereas Terry focuses on her own issues and dispenses unsolicited advice. Paraphrasing to check understanding is also a vital skill to use when you are trying to reconcile a difference of opinion. Chapter 8 will show you how to use it in that context.

Reflect Feelings by Paraphrasing

The bottom line in empathic responding is to make certain that you accurately understand how the other person is feeling. Again, you can paraphrase, beginning with such phrases as:

"So you are feeling . . . ."

"You must feel . . . ."

"So now you feel . . . ."

"Emotionally, you must be feeling . . . ."

In the following example of empathic responding, the listener asks questions, summarizes content, and summarizes feelings.

David: I think I'm in over my head. My boss gave me a job to do and I just don't know how to do it. I'm afraid I've bitten off more than I can chew.

Mike: (Thinks how he would feel if he were given an important task at work but did not know how to complete the task, then asks for more information.) What job did she ask you to do?

DISCUSSION AND WRITING

Display the following paragraph on an overhead projector, or distribute as a handout:

I have the worst class in the world! My teacher is a real jerk. We just sit there watching Dr. Roberts read to us from the book. The professor never looks up. Whenever I ask a question, Dr. Roberts gets mad at me for not already knowing the answer. Everybody in the class feels the same way. I'm thinking about withdrawing from the class but I need the credit to graduate.

Have one student read this paragraph aloud. Next, ask students to construct appropriate reflections.

David: I'm supposed to do an inventory of all of the items in the warehouse on the VAX computer system and have it finished by the end of the week. I don't have the foggiest notion of how to start. I've never even used that system.

Mike: (Summarizing feelings.) So you feel panicked because you may not have enough time to learn the system *and* do the inventory.

David: Well, I'm not only panicked, I'm afraid I may be fired.

Mike: (Summarizing feelings.) So your fear that you might lose your job is getting in the way of just focusing on the task and seeing what you can get done. It's making you feel like you made a mistake in taking this job.

David: That's exactly how I feel.

Note that toward the end of the dialogue Mike has to make a couple of tries to summarize David's feelings accurately. Also note that Mike does a good job of just listening and responding without giving advice. Just by being an active listener, you can help your partner clarify a problem.

We have discussed responding and the active listening process from a tidy step-by-step textbook approach. In practice, you may have to back up and clarify content, ask more questions, and rethink how you would feel before you attempt to summarize how someone else feels. Conversely, you may be able to summarize feelings *without* asking questions or summarizing content if the message is clear and it relates to a situation with which you are very familiar. Overusing this skill can slow down a conversation and make the other person uncomfortable or irritated. But if you use it judiciously, paraphrasing can help both you and your partner keep focused on the issues and ideas at hand.

Reflecting content or feeling through paraphrasing can be especially useful in the following situations:

- Before you take an important action.

- Before you argue or criticize.

- When your partner has strong feelings or wants to talk over a problem.

- When your partner is speaking "in code" or using unclear abbreviations.

- When your partner wants to understand *your* feelings and thoughts.

- When you are talking to yourself.

- When you encounter new ideas.[18]

Sometimes, however, we truly don't understand how another person really feels. At times like this, be cautious of telling others "I know just how you feel." It may be more important simply to let others know that you care about them than to grill them in search of "their feelings."

If you do decide to use reflecting skills, researchers suggest you keep the following guidelines in mind:

- Use your own words.
- Don't go beyond the information communicated by the speaker.
- Be concise.
- Be specific.
- Be accurate.

Do *not* use reflecting skills if you aren't able to be open and accepting; if you do not trust the other person to find his or her own solution; if you are using these skills as a way of hiding yourself from another; or if you feel pressured, hassled, or tired.[19] And as we have already discussed, overuse of paraphrasing can be distracting and unnatural.

Don't be discouraged if your initial attempts to use these skills seem awkward and uncomfortable. Any new skill takes time to learn and use well. The instructions and samples you have seen here should serve as a guide, rather than as hard-and-fast prescriptions to follow during each conversation.

BUILDING YOUR SKILLS

Listening and Reflecting Content and Emotion

Working in groups of three, ask person A to briefly identify a problem or conflict that he or she is having (or has had) with another person (coworker, supervisor, spouse, or family member). Person B should use questioning, content paraphrasing, and emotion paraphrasing skills to explore the problem. Person C should observe the discussion and evaluate person B's listening and reflecting skills, using the Observer Checklist. Make a check mark next to all of the skills that person B uses effectively.

Observer Checklist

Nonverbal Skills		Verbal Skills	
Direct Eye Contact	_____	Effective and Appropriate Questions	_____
Open, Relaxed Body Posture	_____	Accurate Paraphrase of Content	_____
Uncrossed Arms	_____	Accurate Paraphrase of Emotion	_____
Uncrossed Legs	_____	Timely Paraphrase	_____
Appropriate Hand Gestures	_____	Didn't Interrupt the Speaker	_____
Reinforcing Nods	_____		
Responsive Facial Expression	_____		
Appropriate Tone of Voice	_____		
Appropriate Volume	_____		

Listen

When I ask you to listen to me and you start giving advice,
you have not done what I asked.
When I ask you to listen to me and you begin to tell me why I shouldn't feel that way
you are trampling on my feelings.
When I ask you to listen to me and you feel you have to do something
to solve my problems, you have failed me, strange as that may seem.
Listen! All I asked, was that you listen. Not talk or do—just hear me.
Advice is cheap: 50 cents will get you both Dear Abby and Billy Graham
in the same newspaper.
And I can do for myself; I'm not helpless. Maybe discouraged and faltering,
but not helpless.
When you do something for me that I can and need to do for myself, you contribute
to my fear and weakness.
But when you accept as a simple fact that I do feel what I feel,
no matter how irrational, then I quit trying to convince you
and can get about the business of understanding what's behind this irrational feeling.
And when that's clear, the answers are obvious and I don't need advice.
Irrational feelings make sense when we understand what's behind them.
Perhaps that's why prayer works, sometimes, for some people
because God is mute, and doesn't give advice or try to fix things,
God just listens and lets you work it out for yourself.
So, please listen and just hear me, and, if you want to talk,
wait a minute for your turn: and I'll listen to you.

—ANONYMOUS

Improving Your Responding Skills

Even if providing support is not your main goal, responding skills are crucial to the success of most interactions. Here are some additional suggestions for becoming an active listener.

Provide Well-Timed Responses

Feedback is usually most effective when you offer it at the earliest opportunity, particularly if your objective is to teach someone a skill. For example, if you are teaching your friend how to make your famous egg rolls, you provide a step-by-step commentary as you watch your pupil. If he makes a mistake, you don't wait until the egg rolls are finished to tell him that he left out the cabbage. He needs immediate feedback to finish the rest of the sequence successfully.

Sometimes, however, if a person is already sensitive and upset about something, delaying feedback can be wise. Use your critical thinking skills to analyze when feedback will do the most good. Rather than automatically offering immediate correction, use the just-in-time (JIT) approach, and provide feedback just before the person might make another mistake. If, for example, your daughter typically rushes through math tests and fails to check her work, remind her right before her next test to double-check her answers, not immediately after the one she just failed. To provide feedback about a relationship, select a mutually agreeable place and time when both of you are rested and relaxed; avoid hurling feedback at someone "for his own good" immediately after he offends you.

When you are teaching someone a new skill, the timing of your feedback is just as important as what you say. When should this grownup tell the child he is helping how to improve his handstand? (Robert Harbison)

Provide Usable Information

Perhaps you've heard this advice: Never try to teach a pig to sing. It wastes your time. It doesn't sound pretty. And it annoys the pig. When you provide information to someone, be certain that it is useful and relevant. How can you make sure your partner can use the information you share? Put yourself in your partner's mind-set. Ask yourself, "If I were this person, how would I respond to this information? Is it information I can act on? Or is it information that may make matters worse?" Under the guise of effective feedback, we may be tempted to tell others our complete range of feelings and emotions. But research suggests that selective feedback is best. In one study,

SKILL DEVELOPMENT
Reference Maslow's skill development stages here. Role-play empathic listening and ask students to focus on identifying feelings and reflecting these to their partner before sharing their evaluations.

married couples who practiced selective self-disclosure were more satisfied than couples who told everything they knew or were feeling.[20] Immersing your partner in information that is irrelevant or that may be damaging to the relationship may be cathartic, but it may not enhance the quality of your relationship or improve understanding.

Avoid Unnecessary Details

When you are selecting meaningful information, also try to cut down on the volume of information. Don't overwhelm your listener with details that obscure the key point of your feedback. Hit only the high points that will benefit the listener. Be brief.

Be Descriptive Rather Than Evaluative

"You're an awful driver!" shouts Doris to her husband Frank. While Doris may feel she has provided simple feedback to her spouse about his skills, Frank will probably not respond warmly or even listen closely to her feedback. If Doris tries to be more descriptive and less evaluative, then he might be inclined to listen: "Frank, you are traveling seventy miles an hour in a fifty miles an hour zone" or "Frank, I get very nervous when you zigzag so fast through the freeway traffic" is a less offensive comment. They describe Frank's behavior rather than render judgments about him that are likely to trigger a defensive, passive listening reaction.

Suggestions for Improving Responding Skills

Provide Well-Timed Responses	Sometimes immediate feedback is best; at other times provide a just-in-time (JIT) response when it will do the most good.
Provide Meaningful Information	Select information that your partner can act on rather than making vague comments or suggestions that are beyond his or her capabilities.
Avoid Unnecessary Details	Avoid information overload; don't bombard the listener with too much information; keep your comments focused on major points.
Be Descriptive	Don't evaluate your listening partner; focus on behavior rather than personality.

DISCUSSION AND WRITING
Develop and distribute a worksheet of problematic statements and encourage students to rephrase them for more constructive conversation. E.g., "You don't know what you're talking about" might be rephrased, "I don't agree with that conclusion."

Summary

Listening effectively to others is the quintessential skill required for establishing other-oriented relationships. Listening, the process of making sense out of what we hear, includes selecting, attending, understanding, remembering, and responding to others. Most of us listen for a variety of reasons: to enjoy, to learn, to evaluate, and to empathize with and support others.

Most of us don't listen effectively because we are self-oriented instead of other-oriented. Barriers to effective listening include focusing on our personal agendas, being distracted by emotional noise, criticizing the speaker, daydreaming, and being distracted by information overload and external noise.

To become better listeners, we can pursue three seemingly simple steps: stop, look, and listen. To stop means to avoid tuning in to our own distracting messages and to become mindful of what others are saying. To look is to observe and interpret unspoken messages. Nonverbal communication skills and principles will be discussed in greater detail in the next chapter. After stopping and looking, we can then listen more effectively to others by focusing on details and the speaker's key ideas. Being other-oriented does not mean you should abandon your own convictions or values, but that you should make a conscious effort to pay attention to the needs and concerns of others.

We can check the accuracy of our listening skill by reflecting our understanding of what our partner has said. Responding skills are especially important if our goal is to empathize with and support others. These skills include understanding the feelings of others, asking questions, and reflecting the message's content and the speaker's feelings through paraphrasing. Responding effectively does not mean consistently parroting or repeating what the speaker has said. Instead, judicious use of responding skills can enhance our understanding of the message, and tell the speaker whether he or she is communicating the intended message. The most effective responses to others are carefully timed, provide usable information, avoid unnecessary details, and are descriptive rather than evaluative.

For Discussion and Review

■ FOCUS ON COMPREHENSION

1. What are some differences between hearing and listening?

2. What are key listening barriers that keep people from listening well?

3. What strategies can we follow to respond with empathy?

FOCUS ON COMPREHENSION

1. Hearing is a physiological process of decoding sounds which can then be used to listen; that is, to make sense out of what we hear. Hearing is a component of the listening process.

2. Listening with empathy involves striving to fully experience the emotions of another and respond with understanding.

3. Common listening barriers include the following:

- focusing on our personal agenda;
- experiencing emotional and external noise;
- criticizing the speaker;
- failing to use the thought/speak difference well; and
- experiencing information overload.

4. An effective way to reflect understanding of the content of an interpersonal message is to paraphrase. This involves putting the other's message into your own words. Summarizing the essence of the information also provides a perception check, as recommended in Chapter 3.

4. What are suggestions for effectively reflecting the content of interpersonal messages?

■ FOCUS ON CRITICAL THINKING

5. Identify two situations during the past twenty-four hours in which you were an effective or ineffective listener. What factors contributed to your listening skill (or lack of skill)?

6. Miranda and Salvador often disagree about who should handle some of the child-rearing tasks in their home. When they have discussions on these issues, what are some effective listening skills and strategies that they could use to make sure they understand one another?

7. Jason and Chris are roommates. They both work hard each day and come home exhausted. What suggestions would you offer to help them listen effectively even when they are tired?

■ FOCUS ON ETHICS

8. Is it possible for paraphrasing and active listening to become a way to manipulate others? Support your answer.

9. Your friend asks you how you like her new dress. You really feel it is a bit too revealing and may embarrass your friend. But it is time to leave for your evening activity. Should you respond honestly even though it may mean that you and your friend will be late for important engagements?

10. Your roommate wants to tell you about his day. You are tired and really don't want to hear all of the details. Should you fake attention so that you won't hurt his feelings or should you simply tell your roommate that you are tired and would rather not hear about the details of his life?

For Your Journal

1. Keep this checklist, first published in the *International Listening Association Newsletter*, with you one full day to monitor your listening problems.

A CHECKLIST FOR LISTENERS

Today I . . .

Interrupted other people _____ times.

Misunderstood other people _____ times.

Lost track of a conversation _____ times.

Stopped making eye contact with a speaker _____ times.

Asked someone to repeat himself/herself _____ times.

Let my mind wander while listening to someone _____ times.

Changed the subject in the middle of a conversation _____ times.

Jumped to a conclusion about what someone was going to say _____ times.

Reacted emotionally to what someone was saying before he or she finished _____ times.

After keeping track of your personal listening statistics, what changes would you like to make in your listening behavior?

2. Monitor and then jot down notes about your own self-talk during a conversation with another person. What competing thoughts and ideas occurred to you while you were conversing with your partner? What did you do to refocus on the message?

Learning with Others

1. Place a check mark beside all of the communication barriers that affect you. Identify the action you will take to manage the barrier. Discuss your results with your classmates.

HOW WILL YOU OVERCOME LISTENING BARRIERS?

Barrier	Action
Focusing on a Personal Agenda	_____ _____
Emotional Noise	_____ _____
Criticizing the Speaker	_____ _____
Speech Rate vs. Thought Rate	_____ _____
Information Overload	_____ _____
Outside Distractions	_____ _____

2. Charting Your Listening Cycle

Are you a morning person or an evening person? Use the chart shown here to plot your listening energy cycle. Draw a line starting at 6:00 A.M. showing the highs and lows of your potential listening effectiveness. For example, if you are usually still asleep at 6:00 A.M., your line will be at 0 and start upward when you awake. If you are a morning person, your line will peak in the morning. Or perhaps your line will indicate that you listen best in the evening.

After you have charted your typical daily listening cycle, gather in small groups with your classmates to compare listening cycles. Identify listening strategies that can help you capitalize on your listening "up" periods. Also, based upon the chapter and your own experiences, identify ways to enhance your listening when you traditionally have low listening energy.

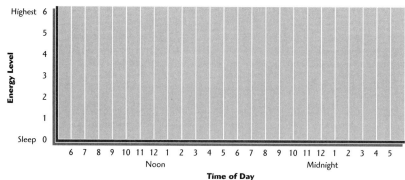

Your Listening Energy Cycle

3. Assign one student from a group to speak very slowly on a difficult subject. Have the other members of the group write down short summaries during pauses in the speech, then compare their summaries.

4. Make a list of "red-flag" word that have derailed your listening ability in the past. Ask another student to make up a paragraph about an important issue, using these words, and read it aloud to you. Monitor your reactions to the words and see whether you can steer your internal conversations back to the issue. Also notice how you begin to feel about the speaker and what you do about those feelings.

LISTENING:	Process of selecting, attending, understanding, remembering, and responding to sounds and messages.
HEARING:	Physiological process of decoding sounds.
SELECTING:	Process of sorting through various sounds competing for your attention.
ATTENDING:	Process of focusing on a particular sound or message.
UNDERSTANDING:	Assigning meaning to messages.
REMEMBERING:	Recalling information that has been communicated.
RESPONDING:	Confirming your understanding of a message.
EMPATHIZE:	To feel what others are feeling, rather than just to acknowledge that they are feeling a certain way.
SYMPATHIZE:	To acknowledge that someone may be feeling bad.
EMOTIONAL NOISE:	Form of communication caused by emotional arousal.
ACTIVE LISTENING:	Interactive process of responding mentally, verbally, and nonverbally to a speaker's message.
PARAPHRASING:	Checking the accuracy of your understanding by offering a verbal summary of your partner's message

Communicating Verbally

A fter studying this chapter, you should be able to:

1. Describe the relationship between words and meaning.

2. Understand how words influence us and our culture.

3. Identify word barriers and know how to manage them.

4. Discuss how the words we use affect our relationships with others.

5. Understand supportive approaches to relating to others.

6. Understand how to confirm other people's sense of themselves.

- WORDS AND MEANING

- WORDS HAVE POWER

- WORD BARRIERS

- USING WORDS TO ESTABLISH SUPPORTIVE RELATIONSHIPS

- USING WORDS TO VALUE OTHERS

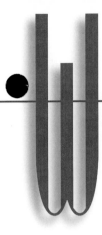

ords are powerful. Those who use them skillfully can exert great influence with just a few of them. Consider these notable achievements:

Lincoln set the course for a nation in a 267-word speech: the Gettysburg Address.

Shakespeare expressed the quintessence of the human condition in Hamlet's famous "To be, or not to be" soliloquy—363 words long.

Several of our great religions adhere to a comprehensive moral code expressed in a mere 297 words: The Ten Commandments.

Words have great power in our private lives as well. In this chapter we will examine ways to use them more effectively in interpersonal relationship. We'll investigate how to harness the power that words have to affect your emotions, thoughts, and actions, and we'll describe links between language and culture. We will also identify communication barriers that may keep you from using words effectively and note strategies and skills for managing those barriers. Finally, we will examine the role of speech in establishing supportive relationships with others. In one of his pessimistic moments, the poet Robert Frost said, "Half the world is composed of people who have something to say and can't, and the other half who have nothing to say and keep on saying it." This chapter is designed to help you prove him wrong, to help you become a person who has something to say and can say it well.

Words and Meaning

As you read the printed words on this page, how are you able to make sense out of these black marks? When you hear words spoken by others, how are you able to interpret those sounds? Although there are several theories that attempt to explain how we learn language and ascribe meaning to both printed and uttered words, there is no single universally held view that neatly clarifies the mystery. We can, however, better understand the nature of words by taking a closer look at what words are and how they function.

173

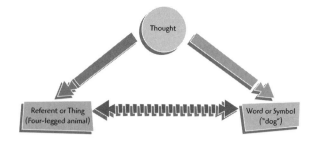

Figure 6.1

Triangle of Meaning

Thought

Referent or Thing
(Four-legged animal)

Word or Symbol
("dog")

Words Are Symbols

As we noted in Chapter 1, words are symbols that represent something else. A printed or spoken word triggers an image, sound, concept, or experience. Take the word *cat*, for instance. The word may conjure up in your mind's eye a hissing creature with bared claws and fangs. Or perhaps you envision a cherished pet curled up by a fireplace.

The classic model in Figure 6.1 was developed by Ogden and Richards to explain the relationships between *referents*, *thoughts*, and **symbols**.[1] **Referents** are the things the symbols (words) represent. **Thought** is the mental process of creating a category, idea, or image triggered by the referent or the symbol. So these three elements, referents, thoughts, and symbols, become inextricably linked. Although some scholars find this model too simplistic to explain how we link all words to a meaning, it does illustrate the process for most concepts, people, and tangible things.

Words Are Arbitrary

In English, words arbitrarily represent something else. The word *dog*, for example, does not *sound* like a dog or *look* at all like a dog. There is no longer a logical connection between the beast and the symbol. Figure 6.2 shows the language tree that charts the evolution of, and links among, human languages. As you can see, the English language evolved from a mixture of Indo-European tongues. It will continue to evolve as we develop the need to name and describe new phenomena. Electronic Connections: Cyber Shorthand illustrates how our use of "words" continues to evolve.

Words Are Context Bound

Your English or speech communication teacher has undoubtedly cautioned you that taking something out of context changes its meaning. Symbols derive their meaning from the situation in which they are used. The phrase *old man* could refer to a male over the age of seventy, your father, your teacher, your principal, or your boss. We would need to know the context of the phrase in order to decipher its specific meaning.

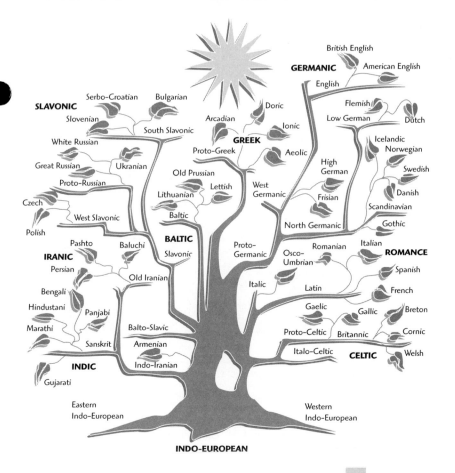

Figure 6.2
The "Language Tree"
Copyright © 1994 by Allyn and Bacon. Adapted by permission.

Words Are Culturally Bound

As we learned in Chapter 4, culture consists of the rules, norms, values, and mores of a group of people, which have been learned and shaped from one generation to the next. The meaning of a symbol such as a word can change from culture to culture. To a European, for example, a "Yankee" is someone from

INSTRUCTIONAL GOALS AND TIPS
Also consider the terms, "blind Venetian" and "venetian blind."

ACTIVITY
See Activity 6.1 in the Instructor's Guide.

America; to a player on the Boston Red Sox, a "Yankee" is an opponent; and to someone from the South, a "Yankee" is someone from the North. A few years ago, General Motors sold a car called a Nova. In English, *nova* means bright star—an appropriate name for a car. In Spanish, however, the spoken word *nova* sounds like the words "no va," which translates, "It does not go." As you can imagine, this name was not a great sales tool for the Spanish-speaking market.

Although the arbitrary printed or spoken word "dog" does not sound like or look like a dog, English-speaking people have no trouble connecting the word and image. (Donald Johnston/Tony Stone Images)

ELECTRONIC CONNECTIONS

Cyber Shorthand

People who connect online have developed a host of verbal shortcuts to save time and keystrokes when communicating with others. Here's a list of some popular cyber shorthand that reflects our evolving use of language.

PPL	=	people	J/K	=	just kidding
LOL	=	laughing out loud	S2S	=	skin to skin
ROLF	=	rolling on the floor laughing	IMHO	=	in my humble opinion
AFK	=	away from the keyboard	OIC	=	oh, I see
			TTYL	=	talk to you later
BAK	=	back at the keyboard	GMTA	=	great minds think alike
BRB	=	be right back	TTFN	=	ta ta for now
BBL	=	be back later (logging off)	ISO	=	in search of
BTW	=	by the way			

The study of words and meaning is called semantics. One important body of semantic theory known as **symbolic interaction** suggests that as a society we are bound together because of our common use of symbols. Originally developed by sociologists as a way of making sense out of how societies and groups are linked together,[2] the theory of symbolic interaction also illuminates how we use our common understanding of symbols to form interpersonal relationships. Common symbols foster links in understanding and therefore lead to satisfying relationships. Of course, even within a given culture we misunderstand each other's messages. But the more similar the cultures of the communication partners, the greater the chance for a meeting of meanings.

UNDERSTANDING DIVERSITY

High-Context and Low-Context Cultures

As we learned in Chapter 4, some cultures place great emphasis on the verbal context—the explicit importance of words—in a message. Others place more emphasis on the nonverbal context. Renowned anthropologist Edward T. Hall categorized these distinctions as **high context** (emphasis on the nonverbal) and **low context** (emphasis on the verbal).[3] The chart in Figure 6.3 depicts cultures arranged along a continuum from high to low context.[4]

Individuals from high-context cultures find nonverbal cues extremely important in helping them interpret the messages of others. Consequently, individuals from high-context cultures are usually more skilled at decoding nonverbal messages than individuals from low-context cultures. In addition, because context plays a major role in communicating meaning, they may use fewer words and spend less time speaking than do individuals from low-context cultures.

Larry Samovar and Richard Porter found that individuals from high-context cultures often perceive those from low-context cultures as less attractive, knowledgeable, and trustworthy. They find typical low-context requests such as, "Say what you mean," "Don't beat around the bush," and "Tell it to me straight" particularly annoying because they expect others to be as skilled as they are in interpreting unspoken, contextual cues.

Novelist Amy Tan notes:

I try to explain to my English-speaking friends that Chinese language is more strategic in manner, whereas English tends to be more direct; an American business executive may say, "Let's make a deal," and the Chinese manager may reply, "Is your son interested in learning about your widget business?" Each to his or her own purpose, each with his or her own linguistic path.[5]

High-Context Cultures

Japanese
Arab
Greek
Spanish
Italian
English
French
American
Scandinavian
German
German-Swiss

Low-Context Cultures

Figure 6.3

Cultures arranged along the high-context/low-context dimension. Figure from Larry Samovar and Richard Porter, *Communication Between Cultures* (Belmont, CA: Wadsworth, 1991), p. 235.

MEDIA AND OUTSIDE RESOURCES

Two excellent films which focus on language skills are *Children of a Lesser God* and *Nell*. Both describe how language is used to build trust and intimacy. Consider showing either of these. An alternative is a scene from the movie *Four Weddings and a Funeral*, in which a woman is attracted to a man who is deaf. She decides to learn to sign in order to communicate with him more effectively. Although she uses the wrong signs, she is understood and appreciated by the man.

DISCUSSION AND WRITING
Working in groups, have students construct lists of words which have different meanings than those found in the dictionary. Or ask students to define terms such as the following: culture, class, hit, peck, noise, bun, flamed, or chair.

Words Have Denotative and Connotative Meaning

Language is the vehicle through which we share our sense of the world with others. Through language we transfer our experience into symbols and then use the symbols to share our experience. But as we learned in Chapter 1, the process of symbol sharing through language is not just a simple process of uttering a word and having its meaning clearly understood by another. Messages convey both content and feelings. So our language conveys meaning on two levels: the denotative and the connotative.

The **denotative** level conveys content. The denotation of a word is its restrictive or literal meaning. For example, here is one dictionary definition for the word *school*:

> An institution for the instruction of children; an institution for instruction in a skill or business; a college or a university.[6]

This definition is the literal or denotative definition of the word *school*; it describes what the word means in American culture.

The **connotative** level of language conveys feelings. Words also have personal and subjective meanings for us. The word *school* to you might mean a wonderful, exciting place where you meet your friends, have a good time, and occasionally take tests and perform other tasks that keep you from enjoying fellowship with your chums. To others, *school* could be a restrictive, burdensome obligation that stands in the way of making money and getting on with life. The connotative meaning of a word is more individualized. While the denotative or objective meaning of the word *school* can be found in your *Webster's*, *Funk and Wagnalls*, or *American Heritage* dictionary, your subjective response to the word is probably not contained there.

RECAP	Denotative and Connotative Meaning	
Level	**Definition**	**Examples**
DENOTATIVE	Literal, restrictive definition of a word.	Mother: the female person who gave birth to you.
CONNOTATIVE	Personal, subjective reaction to a word.	Mother: the warm, caring woman who nurtured and loved you; or the cold, distant woman who always implied that you were not measuring up to her standards.

Words Communicate Concrete or Abstract Meaning

Words can be placed along a continuum from abstract to concrete. We call a word concrete if we can experience its referent with one of our senses; if we can

ACTIVITY
See Activity 6.2 in the Instructor's Guide.

see it, touch it, smell it, taste it, or hear it, then it's concrete. If we cannot do these things with the referent, then the word is abstract. We can visualize the continuum from abstract to concrete as a ladder:

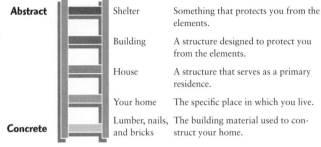

Abstract		
	Shelter	Something that protects you from the elements.
	Building	A structure designed to protect you from the elements.
	House	A structure that serves as a primary residence.
	Your home	The specific place in which you live.
Concrete	Lumber, nails, and bricks	The building material used to construct your home.

In general, the more concrete the language, the easier it is for others to understand.

Words Have Power

> Sticks and stones may break my bones,
> But words can never hurt me.

This old schoolyard chant may provide a ready retort for the desperate victim of name-calling, but it is hardly convincing. With more insight, the poet Robert Browning wrote, "Words break no bones; hearts though sometimes." And in his book *Science and Sanity*, mathematician and engineer Alfred Korzybski argued that the words we use (and misuse) have tremendous effects upon our thoughts and actions.[7] Browning and Korzybski were right. As we said at the beginning of this chapter, words have power.

Words Have Power to Create

"To name is to call into existence—to call out of nothingness,"[8] wrote French philosopher Georges Gusdorff. Words give us a tool to create our world by naming and labeling what we experience. You undoubtedly learned in your elementary science class that Sir Isaac Newton discovered gravity. Perhaps it would be more accurate to say that he labeled rather than discovered it. His use of the word *gravity* gave us a cognitive category; we now converse about the pull of the earth's forces that keeps us from flying into space. Words give us the symbolic vehicles to communicate our creations and discoveries to others.

When you label something as "good" or "bad," you are using language to create your own vision of how you experience the world. If you tell a friend that

MEDIA AND OUTSIDE RESOURCES

Bring in the game, "Taboo" (Milton Bradley, 1989). This highly interactive and entertaining game demands that players use concrete language.

INSTRUCTIONAL GOALS AND TIPS

Be sure to use language to invoke trust and to demonstrate respect for students, avoiding terms such as "kids" or "girls" and "boys." If you are treating students respectfully, you can demand that they do the same with one another.

TEACHING STRATEGY

To illustrate the idea that words have the power to create our world, have students consider whether we suddenly see certain phenomena frequently occurring as soon as we name and define them. Discussion examples might include:

- reverse discrimination
- sexual harassment
- codependency
- dysfunctional families
- attention deficit disorder

DISCUSSION AND WRITING

Ask students to consider the many different terms they use to describe their best friend or mate. Discuss the implications of pet names and terms of endearment. Compare the intended meaning when a parent says, "Robert Joseph" as opposed to the usual "Bob."

ACTIVITY

See Activity 6.3 in the Instructor's Guide

Words have the power to affect our thoughts and actions. What thoughts might come to your mind as you pass this car on the highway? (Bill Gallery/Stock Boston)

the movie you saw last night was vulgar and obscene, you are not only providing your friend with a critique of the movie; you are also communicating your sense of what is appropriate and inappropriate.

As we noted in Chapter 2, you create your self-worth largely with self-talk and with the labels you apply to yourself. One theorist believes that you also create your moods and emotional state with the words you use to label your feelings.[9] If you get fired from a job, you might say that you feel angry and helpless, or you might declare that you feel liberated and excited. The first response might lead to depression, and the second to happiness. One fascinating study conducted over a thirty-five-year period found that people who described the world in pessimistic terms when they were younger were in poorer health during middle age than those who had been optimistic.[10] Your words and corresponding outlook have the power to affect your health. The concept of reframing that we discussed in Chapter 2 as a way to improve our self-concept is based on the power of words to "call into existence" that which we create with words.

Words Have Power to Affect Thoughts and Actions

How about some horse meat for supper tonight? Most of us find such a question disgusting. Why? Horse meat is not something we typically eat. One theorist argues that horse meat is not a featured delicacy at the local supermarket simply because we have no other word for it. Your butcher does not advertise pig meat or cow meat; labeling the meat as pork chops, ham, and sausage, or as steak and ribs, makes it sound more appetizing. Advertisers have long known that the way a product is labeled affects our propensity to purchase it.

Words also have power to affect policy and procedures. Consider the unsubstantiated story about a young FBI man who was put in charge of the supply

II   INTERPERSONAL COMMUNICATION SKILLS

department. In an effort to save money, he reduced the size of memo paper. One of the smaller sheets ended up on J. Edgar Hoover's desk. The director didn't like the small size and wrote on the narrow margin of the paper, "Watch the borders." For the next six weeks, it was extremely difficult to enter the United States from Canada or Mexico.

In the late 1960s a California sociology professor conducted an experiment to demonstrate that words have power to affect behavior.[11] He divided his class into two groups. To one group, he distributed a bumper sticker that boldly displayed the words, "I support the Black Panthers." At that time, many members of the students' local community thought the Panthers were using unnecessary force to promote their agenda. Students in this first group had to drive around for a week with the stickers on their cars. The other group drove around as usual, without stickers.

It took only a few hours to prove the professor's point: words do affect attitudes and behavior. Students who had the stickers were harassed by other motorists and issued traffic tickets at an alarming rate. The other group had no increase in hassles. By the end of the study, seventeen days later, the "Panther" group had received thirty-three traffic citations.

Words Have Power to Affect and Reflect Culture

About a decade before the sociology professor's bumper sticker experiment, anthropologists Benjamin Whorf and Edward Sapir simultaneously began to refine a theory called **linguistic determinism**, which had originated in the nineteenth century.[12] Their version is based on a hypothesis of reciprocity: Language shapes your culture and culture shapes your language. To understand your culture, theorize these anthropologists, you should study the words you use. If an impartial investigator from another culture were to study a transcript of all of your spoken utterances last week, what would he or she learn about you and the culture in which you live? If you frequently used words like *CD* and *rollerblades*, the investigator would know that these things are important to you. But he or she might not know what they mean if they are not also part of his or her culture.

Words not only reflect your culture; there is evidence that they mold it. When a speech therapist noticed that very few Indians in a certain tribe stuttered, he also found that their language had no word for stuttering. He concluded that few people had this affliction because it never entered their minds as a possibility. Perhaps you've heard that Eskimos have twenty-three different words for snow. As the article "The Melting of a Mighty Myth" points out, even though they really don't have quite that many, there is evidence that they have more words for snow than someone native to Miami, Florida.

These examples also show that the words we use and listen to affect our **world view**—how we interpret what we experience. If you were to don someone else's prescription glasses, the world would literally look different to you, and the glasses would either enhance or inhibit your ability to see the world around

DISCUSSION AND WRITING

Ask students to brainstorm with you synonyms for the concept, "human female." Write these on the board as students share them. Include vulgar terms. Expect to brainstorm about 50 terms. Next, do the same for "human male." Then discuss which words have positive, negative, or neutral connotations. What general patterns do you see? You will probably note many more negative terms than positive ones. Since male-bashing became popular in the 1980s, there are many new derogatory terms for males, particularly gay men. Discuss how this mix reflects linguistic determinism.

you. In a sense, your world view is your own set of prescription glasses, which you formulate over time, based upon your experiences, attitudes, beliefs, values, and needs. The words you use to describe your view of the world reflect and further shape your perspective. And you, in turn, help to shape your culture's collective world view through your use of language.

The Melting of a Mighty Myth

Guess What: Eskimos Don't Have Twenty-Three Words for Snow

Once in a while science makes a breakthrough so revolutionary that it changes forever the way we think about reality, like the discovery that hay fever usually isn't caused by hay. To the great iconoclasts of science, one can add anthropologist Laura Martin of Cleveland State University, who has had the audacity to assert that *Eskimos don't actually have any more words for "snow" than anyone else.*

This will be shattering news to millions of people who attended college after about 1958, when the theories of the great amateur linguist Benjamin Lee Whorf began to appear in college psychology texts. Whorf held that Eskimos—living in daily contact with snow in its variously slushy, dry, powdery, or crusty forms—use different words for substances that English speakers call just "snow." (Whorf didn't specify how many words, but he implied there were around seven.) It is not hard to see why this mundane observation should have emerged as one of the handful of facts most liberal-arts majors retained from their educations. Simple to grasp, it had implications so profound that anyone who stayed awake through his introductory psychology course could feel like another Descartes. For if the Eskimos use many different words for things that English speakers lump into one category, does it not follow that they actually perceive the world differently? That Eskimos do not grasp the unity among all forms of frozen precipitation, while non-Eskimos do not see the differences, at least until they try to lift a shovelful of slush? Like, is that heavy—the idea, not the shovel—or what?

It would be, if only it were true. Martin, along with the linguist Geoffrey K. Pullum, author of *The Great Eskimo Vocabulary Hoax,* has traced the story's progress from learned exotica to the world of Sunday-Supplement Astounding Facts, showing how it became more incredible along the way. Most of the references Martin found put the number of Eskimo snow words at seventeen to twenty-three, but the *New York Times* once casually referred to 100. The misunderstanding seems to have arisen because Eskimos do indeed have more than one word for snow and snow-related phenomena. Anthony Woodbury of the University of Texas at Austin puts the number at around a dozen. But, he adds, the proper comparison to English is not with the single noun "snow," but a list of at least ten words, including "blizzard," "dusting," and "avalanche." Martin admits that her efforts are unlikely to get the public to drop such a charming myth. But she was disappointed in the reaction of her colleagues when she pointed out the fallacy; most, she says, took the position that true or not, "It's still a great example."

Well, so it is. To play Descartes for a minute, does it perhaps provide an example of how language can be used to change how we perceive reality? If a lack of vocabulary can cause us to overlook the differences between kinds of snow, then maybe we could learn to ignore the differences between human races by unlearning the names for them. Just a thought: We are all, after all, much more alike than, say . . . powder, hardpack, and slush.

Word Barriers

According to theologian and educator Ruel Howe, a communication barrier is "something that keeps meaning from meeting."[13] Words have the power to create monumental misunderstandings as well as deep connections. Let's identify some of the specific barriers to understanding that we can create through language.

Bypassing: One Word, Two Thoughts

A student pilot was on his first solo flight. When he called the tower for flight instructions, the control tower said, "Would you please give us your altitude and position?"

The pilot said: "I'm five feet ten inches, and I'm sitting up front."

Bypassing occurs when the same words mean different things to different people.

In another amusing example of this phenomenon, an Englishwoman who was looking for permanent accommodations in a Swiss town asked the schoolmaster if he could recommend any rooms. He took her to see several. When everything was arranged, the woman returned to her home to make final preparations for the move. On arriving home, she suddenly realized that she had not seen a water closet (a toilet). She immediately wrote a note to the school master, asking him if there was a W.C. around the place. Knowing only limited English, the schoolmaster asked the parish priest if he could help out in this matter. Together they tried to discover the meaning of the letters W.C. The only solution they could come up with was "Wayside Chapel." The schoolmaster wrote the following letter to the woman:

> Dear Madam:
> I take great pleasure in informing you that a W.C. is situated nine miles from your house, in the center of a beautiful grove of pine trees, surrounded by lovely grounds.
> It is capable of holding two hundred and twenty-two persons and is opened on Sundays and Thursdays only. As there are a great number of

INSTRUCTIONAL GOALS AND TIPS

Notice how puns, jokes, and riddles depend upon bypassing for success. Ask students to share some of their favorites.

people expected during the summer months, I would advise you to come early. Although there is usually plenty of standing room, this is an unfortunate situation, particularly if you are in the habit of going regularly.

You will no doubt be glad to hear that a great number of people bring their lunch and make a day of it, while others who can afford to, go late and arrive just in time. I would especially advise your ladyship to go on Thursday when there is an organ accompaniment. The acoustics are excellent, and often the most delicate sounds can be heard everywhere.

It may interest you to know that my daughter was married in the W.C. It was there she met her husband. I can remember the rush there was for seats. There were ten people to seats usually occupied by one. It was wonderful to see the expressions on their faces.

The newest attraction is the bell donated by a wealthy resident of the district. It rings every time a person enters. A bazaar is to be held to provide the plush seats for all, since the people believe it is a long-felt need.

My wife is rather delicate so she cannot attend regularly. It is almost a year since she last went. Naturally, it pains her very much not to be able to go more often. I shall be delighted to reserve the best seat for you if you wish, where you will be seen by all. For the children there is a special time and place so they will not disturb the elders.

Hoping to have been of service to you.

> *Sincerely yours,*
> *Father Franz*

Meaning is fragile. And the English language is imprecise in many areas. One researcher estimated that the 500 words we use most often in our daily conversations with others have over 14,000 different dictionary definitions. And this number does not take into account personal connotations. So it is no wonder that bypassing is a common communication problem.

We all know that Pavlov's dog salivated when he heard the bell that he learned to associate with food. Sometimes we respond to symbols the way Pavlov's dog did to the bell, forgetting that symbols (words) can have more than one meaning.

Bafflegab: High-Falutin' Use of Words

Do you suffer from bafflegab? Here is an example of it: Bafflegab is multiloquence characterized by consummate interfusion of circumlocution or periphrasis, inscrutability, incognizability, and other familiar manifestations of abstruse expatiation commonly used for promulations implementing procrustean determinations by governmental bodies. Whew! What a mouthful. Why do some people use such highly abstract language? Perhaps they are just trying to dazzle their listener with evidence of their education, or they may simply not be other-oriented. Bafflegabbers may be focused on impressing the receiver rather than on conveying meaning. Other-oriented speakers use clear words that the listener can understand: They adapt their choice of words to their listener.

INSTRUCTIONAL GOALS AND TIPS

Before the lecture begins, consider writing the following statement on the board: "Are you as erudite as you'd like to be?" Wait to discover whether students pretend to understand, ask for clarification, or have a clever comeback such as "Well, I'm at least as erudite as you, dear Pedagogue!"

ACTIVITY

See Activity 6.5 in the Instructor's Guide.

Lack of Precision: Uncertain Meaning

Alice Roosevelt Longworth writes about a merchant seaman who was being investigated under the McCarran Act. "Do you," asked the interrogator, "have any pornographic literature?"

"Pornographic literature!" the sailor burst out indignantly. "I don't even have a pornograph!"

At a ceremony in the Princeton University chapel, an old lady buttonholed an usher and commanded, "Be sure you get me a seat up front, young man. I understand they've always had trouble with the agnostics in the chapel!"

Each of these examples, along with the Far Side cartoon here, illustrates a **malapropism**—a confusion of one word or phrase for another that sounds similar to it. You have probably heard people confuse such word pairs as *construction* and *instruction*, and *subscription* and *prescription*. Although this confusion may at times be humorous, it may also result in failure to communicate clearly. So, too, can using words out of context, using inappropriate grammar, or putting words in the wrong order. Confusion is the inevitable result, as these sentences taken from a letter to the Philadelphia welfare department illustrates:

Ha ha ha, Biff. Guess what? After we go to the drugstore and the post office, I'm going to the vet's to get tutored.

> I want my money as quickly as I can get it. I've been in bed with the doctor for two weeks, and it didn't do me any good. If things don't improve, I will have to send for another doctor.

And the following statements appeared in church bulletins:

> The eighth-graders will be presenting Shakespeare's Hamlet in the church basement on Friday at 7:00 P.M. The congregation is invited to attend this tragedy.

> This afternoon there will be meetings in the North and South ends of the church—Children will be baptized on both ends.

These are funny examples, but in fact, incorrect or unclear language can launch a war or sink a ship. It is vital to remember that *meanings are in people, not in words*. We give symbols meaning; we do not receive inherent meaning *from* symbols. If you are other-oriented, you will assess how someone else will respond to your message and try to select those symbols that he or she is most likely to interpret as you intend.

For most communication, the object is to be as correct, specific, and concrete as possible. Vague language creates confusion and frustration. Consider this example:

Derrick: Where's the aluminum foil?

SKILL DEVELOPMENT

Have students write directions on how to get from the classroom to your office. Next, have them exchange papers and decide whether a new classmate would be able to follow them. What details or general statements were missing? Did students provide an overview (preview) first? How could this help?

Pam: In the drawer.

Derrick: What drawer?

Pam: In the kitchen.

Derrick: But where in the kitchen?

Pam: By the fridge.

Derrick: But which one? There are five drawers.

Pam: Oh, the second one from the top.

Derrick: Why didn't you say so in the first place?

Is it possible to be too precise? It is if you use a restricted code that has a meaning your listener does not know. A **restricted code** involves the use of words that have a particular meaning to a subgroup or culture. Sometimes we develop abbreviations or specialized terms that make sense and save time when we speak to others in our group. Musicians, for example, use special terms that relate to reading and performing music. Most computer hackers know that "a screamer" is someone who sends messages in cyberspace in ALL CAPITAL LETTERS. Ham radio operators use codes to communicate over the airwaves. Yet, in each instance this shorthand language would make little sense to an outsider. In fact, groups that rely upon restricted codes may have greater cohesiveness because of this shared "secret" language or **jargon**. Whatever your line of work, guard against lapsing into phrases that can only be interpreted by a few.

When people have known one another for a long time, they may also use restricted codes for their exchanges. The Blondie cartoon is an example of how married couples can communicate using a code that no outsider could ever interpret.

Allness: The Language of Generalization

The tendency to use language to make unqualified, often untrue generalizations is called **allness**. Allness statements deny individual differences or variations. Statements such as "All women are poor drivers" and "People from the South love iced tea" are generalizations that imply that the person making the

Reprinted with special permission of King Features Syndicate.

pronouncement has examined all the information and has reached a definitive conclusion. Although our world would be much simpler if we *could* make such statements, reality rarely, if ever, provides evidence to support sweeping generalizations.

For example, although research conclusions document differences between the way men and women communicate, it is inaccurate to say that all women are more emotional and that all men are task-oriented. Empathic, other-oriented speakers avoid making judgments of others based only upon conventional wisdom or traditionally held attitudes and beliefs. If you respond to others (of a different gender, sexual orientation, or ethnicity) based on stereotypical concepts, you will diminish your understanding and the quality of the relationship.

One way to avoid untrue generalizations is to remind yourself that your use and interpretation of a word is unique. Saying the words "to me" either to yourself or out loud before you offer an opinion or make a pronouncement can help communicate to others (and remind yourself) that your view is uniquely yours. Rather than announcing, "Curfews for teenagers are ridiculous," you could say, "To me, curfews for teenagers are ridiculous."

Indexing your comments and remarks is another way to help you avoid generalizing. To index is to acknowledge that each individual is unique. Rather than announcing that all doctors are abrupt, you could say, "My child's pediatrician spends a lot of time with me, but my internist never answers my questions." This helps you remember that doctor number one is not the same as doctor number two.

Static Evaluation: The Language of Rigidity

You change. Your world changes. An ancient Greek philosopher said it best: "You can never step in the same river twice." A **static evaluation** is a statement that fails to recognize change; labels in particular have a tendency to freeze-frame our awareness. Ruby, known as the class nerd in high school, is today a successful and polished businessperson; the old label does not fit.

In addition, some of us suffer from hardening of the categories. Our world view is so rigid that we can never change or expand our perspective. But the world is a technicolor moving target. Just about the time we think we have things neatly figured out and categorized, something moves. Our labels may not reflect the buzzing, booming, zipping process of change. It is important to acknowledge that perception is a process, and to avoid trying to nail things down permanently into all-inclusive categories.

General semanticists use the metaphorical expression "the map is not the territory" to illustrate the concept of static evaluation. Like a word, a map symbolizes or represents reality. Yet our road system is constantly changing. New roads are built, old ones are closed. If you were to use a 1949 map to guide you on your cross-country tour from Washington, D.C., to Kansas City, Missouri, the interstate highway system would not even be on it, and you would probably lose your way. Similarly, if we use old labels and do not adjust our thinking to accommodate change, we will be semantically lost.

What can this woman do to avoid using a static evaluation with these children, rigid language that fails to recognize that the world changes? (Kevin Horan/Tony Stone Images)

DISCUSSION AND WRITING

In 1952, when Lucille Ball became pregnant in real life, the producers incorporated her pregnancy into the storyline of "I Love Lucy." But network censors would not allow the word "pregnant" to be used on the air. Ask students to brainstorm euphemisms for the term "pregnant."

DISCUSSION AND WRITING

Ask students to analyze political campaign ads which strive to polarize public opinions. Suggest ways to use critical thinking when watching or reading these messages.

INTERNET RESOURCE

Fear Appeals
http://carmen.artsci. washington.edu/ propaganda/fear.htm
Defines fear appeals as a form of propaganda. Fear appeal is discussed in terms of a four-step process.

Perhaps you have a parent who still uses "old maps" when you come home to visit, expecting that you will be there for dinner each night and will still eat four helpings at every meal. Your parent may not understand that you have changed, and his or her old map does not function well in your new territory. You may have to help construct a new one.

To avoid static evaluation yourself, try dating your observations and indicate to others the time period from which you are drawing your conclusion. If your second cousin comes to town for a visit, say, "When I last saw you, you loved to listen to Patti Smith." This allows for the possibility that your cousin's tastes may have changed during the last few years. But most importantly, try to observe and acknowledge changes in others. If you are practicing what you know about becoming other-oriented, you are unlikely to erect this barrier.

Polarization: The Language of Extremes

Describing and evaluating what we observe in terms of extremes, such as good or bad, old or new, beautiful or ugly, brilliant or stupid is known as **polarization**. General semanticists remind us that the world in which we live comes not in black and white but in a variety of colors, hues, and shades. If you describe things in extremes, leaving out the middle ground, then your language does not accurately reflect reality. And because of the power of words to create, you may believe your own pronouncements.

"You either love me or you don't love me," says Jerome.

"You're either for me or against me," replies Lisa.

188

INTERPERSONAL COMMUNICATION SKILLS

188

Both people are overstating the case, using language to polarize their perceptions of the experience.

Family counselors who listen to family feuds find that the tendency to see things from an either-or point of view is a classic symptom of a troubled relationship. Placing the entire blame on your partner for a problem in your relationship is an example of polarizing. Few relational difficulties are exclusively one-sided.

Fact-Inference Confusion: Jumping to Conclusions

Imagine this scene. You are a detective investigating a death. You are given the following information: (1) Leo and Moshia are lying together on the floor; (2) Leo and Moshia are dead; (3) they are surrounded by water and broken glass; (4) on the sofa near Leo and Moshia is a cat with its back arched, apparently ready to defend itself. Given these sketchy details, do you, the detective assigned to the case, have any theories about the cause of Leo and Moshia's demise? Perhaps they slipped on the water, crashed into a table, broke a vase, and died (that would explain the water and broken glass). Or maybe their attacker recently left the scene, and the cat is still distressed by the commotion. Clearly, you could make several inferences (conclusions based upon partial information) as to the probable cause of death. Oh yes, there is one detail we forgot to mention: Leo and Moshia are fish. Does that help?

We often spin grand explanations and hypotheses based upon sketchy details. Acting upon inferences, we may act as though the "facts" clearly point to a specific conclusion. Determining the difference between a fact and an inference can help us more accurately use language to reach valid conclusions about what we see and experience.

What makes a fact a fact? Most students, when asked this question, respond by saying, "A fact is something that has been proven to be true." If that is the case, *how* has something been proven to be true? In a court of law, a fact is something that has been observed or witnessed. Anything else is speculation or inference.

"Did you see my client in your house, taking your jewelry?" asks the wise attorney.

"No," says the plaintiff.

"Then you do not know for a fact that my client is a thief."

"I guess not," the plaintiff admits.

The semantic problem occurs when we respond to something as if it were a fact (something observed), when in reality it is an inference (a conclusion based upon speculation):

"It's a fact that your mother doesn't like me."

"It's a fact that you will be poor all of your life."

"It's a fact that you will fail this course."

Each of these statements, although it might very well be true, misuses the term *fact*. If you cannot recognize when you are making an inference instead of stating a fact, you may give your judgments more credibility than they deserve.

INTERNET RESOURCE
Lists fallacies to arguments, including a discussion on how fear in people does not constitute evidence for a claim.
http://www.nizkor.org/features/fallacies/appeal-to-fear.html

Biased Language: Insensitivity Toward Others

Using words that reflect your biases toward other cultures or ethnic groups, or someone's gender, can create a word barrier for your listeners. Although TV, radio, and magazine articles may debate the merits of political correctness, it is clear that sexist or racially stereotypical language can offend others. In addition, such language ignores the fact that the world is constantly changing. Sexist language can reflect stereotypical attitudes or describe roles in exclusively male or female terms. Words such as Congress*man*, mail*man*, and *man*kind ignore the fact that women are part of the workforce and the human race. Contrast these with member of congress, letter carrier, and humankind, which are gender neutral and allow for the inclusion of both men and women. Or, rather than eliminating the word *man* from your vocabulary, try to use appropriate labels when you know the gender of the subject. A male police officer is a policeman; a female police officer is a policewoman. Rather than salesperson, you could say salesman or saleswoman, depending upon the gender of the seller.

O'Donnell found that even dictionaries fall into patterns of describing men and women with discriminatory language.[14] Included in the *Oxford English Dictionary* definition for *woman* are (1) an adult female being, (2) female servant, (3) a lady-love or mistress, and (4) a wife. Men are described in more positive and distinguished terms: (1) a human being, (2) the human creation regarded abstractly, (3) an adult male endowed with many qualities, and (4) a person of importance of position.

Many of our social conventions also diminish or ignore the importance of women:

Sexist	Unbiased
I'd like you to meet Dr. and Mrs. John Chao.	I'd like you to meet Dr. Sue Ho and Dr. John Chao. They are husband and wife.
	or
	I'd like you to meet John Chao and Sue Ho. They're both doctors at Mercy Hospital.
Let me introduce Mr. Tom Bertolone and his wife Beverly.	Let me introduce Beverly and Tom Bertolone.

We have, however, made more substantial progress in reflecting changes and changed attitudes toward women in the professional arena. Compare the terms we use to describe workers now with those used in the 1950s:

Terms Used Today	Terms Used in 1950s
Flight attendant	Stewardess
Fire fighter	Fireman
Police officer	Policeman

Terms Used Today (con't)	Terms Used in 1950s(con't)
Physician	Female doctor
Women at the office	Girls at work
Ms.	Miss/Mrs.
People/humans	Mankind

Consciously remembering to use nonsexist language will result in several benefits.[15] First, nonsexist language reflects nonsexist attitudes. Your attitudes are reflected in your speech and your speech affects your attitudes. Monitoring your speech for sexist remarks can help you monitor your attitudes about sexist assumptions you may hold. Second, using nonsexist language will help you become more other-oriented. Monitoring your language for sexist remarks will reflect your sensitivity to others. Third, nonsexist language will make your speech more contemporary and unambiguous. By substituting the word *humankind* for *mankind*, for example, you can communicate that you are including all people, not just men, in your observation or statement. And finally, your nonsexist language will empower others. By eliminating sexist bias from your speech, you will help confirm the value of all the individuals with whom you interact.

In addition to monitoring your language for sexual stereotypes, avoid racial and ethnic stereotypes. Using phrases such as "She's an Indian giver," or "I jewed him down" (to negotiate a price for goods or services), or "He doesn't have a Chinaman's chance" demonstrates an insensitivity to members of other cultural groups. Monitor your speech so that you are not, even unconsciously, using phrases that depict a racial group or ethnic group in a negative, stereotypical fashion.

Is Supreme Court justice Clarence Thomas Black or African American? Is someone from Mexico Hispanic or Latina? Given the power of words, the terms we use to label ethnic groups have a direct reflection upon perceptions of culture and identity. Using the wrong word can result in someone's being labeled "politically incorrect" or worse, "bigot." Just a few years ago, the U.S. Bureau of Labor Statistics surveyed 60,000 households, asking what ethnic label they like best. More than 44 percent of households then called "Black" by the government preferred the term "Black," while 28 percent preferred "African American." Twelve percent preferred "Afro-American" and a little over 9 percent had no preference. In another ethnic category, "Hispanic" was the choice of 58 percent of those currently labeled "Hispanics," rather than terms like "Latino" or the generic "of Spanish origin." Over 10 percent had no preference. The survey also reported that the label "American Indians" was the term of choice for slightly less than half of the respondents, while 37 percent preferred "Native American." Most of those currently designated "White" preferred that term, although 16 percent liked the term "Caucasian" and a very small percentage liked the term "European American."[16] Some of these preferences may surprise you, in that they may have changed in just the few years since this survey was conducted. A sensitive, other-oriented communicator

TEACHING STRATEGY

Consider synonyms for ethnic or racial minorities in United States culture. Robin Lakoff (1975; *Language and Woman's Place*, New York: Harper & Row, p. 21) suggests that for an ethnic group popularly perceived as unrespectable, there is a much greater incidence of derogatory epithets for that group and that there concurrently exist more euphemisms for those derogatory epithets.

INTERNET RESOURCE
Racism
http://www.users.interport.net/~heugene/race_racism.html
Collection of articles and essays on racism.

INTERNET RESOURCE
http://wwww.wsu.edu:8080/~burnsa/race.html
This site targets the ways to interpret racism, the traits and characteristics of racism, and the groups most susceptible.

INTERNET RESOURCE
http://rtpnet.org/~jacobs/generations/g_invisible.html
This site deals with the fact that some people no longer feel that racism is an issue. A closer examination of the environment of racism reveals otherwise.

INTERNET RESOURCE
Racism and Intercultural Communication
http://peace.ml.org/race/racism.
This site describes communication tensions between ethnic groups. Offers communication techniques for healing inequalities among different cultures.

keeps abreast of such changes and adopts the designations currently preferred by members of the ethnic groups themselves.

RECAP	Word Barriers	
Barrier	**Definition**	**Examples**
Bypassing	Misinterpreting a word that evokes different meanings for different people.	W. C. might mean wayside chapel to a Swiss and water closet to someone from England.
Bafflegab	Unnecessary use of many abstract words.	"Please extinguish all smoking materials" instead of "No Smoking."
Lack of Clarity	Words used inappropriately or in imprecise ways.	Sign in Acapulco hotel: The manager has personally passed all the water served here.
Allness	Lumping things or people into all-encompassing categories.	All Texans drive pickup trucks and hang a rifle in their back windows.
Static Evaluation	Labeling people, objects, and events without considering change.	You call your twenty-eight-year-old nephew a juvenile delinquent because he spray-painted your fence when he was eleven.
Polarization	Description in either-or terms— good or bad, right or wrong.	You're either for me or against me.
Fact-Inference Confusion	Pronouncing something as a fact without directly observing it or verifying it through the authority of an expert's research or observation.	It is a fact that cats are smarter than dogs.
Biased Language	Language that reflects gender, racial, or ethnic biases.	My mom is a mailman.

Using Words to Establish Supportive Relationships

Imagine that you are a corporate manager attending a professional meeting. A counterpart from another company approaches you and says, "I'm Harvey Michaels. I read your letter to the editor of the *Daily Mirror* yesterday, and I don't think you understand the first thing about the future of our industry." This stranger's critique more than likely makes you feel defensive: You want to protect yourself or strike back. Or you want to run away. The climate is not conducive to developing a quality relationship.

For more than three decades, Jack Gibb's observational research has been used as a framework for both describing and prescribing verbal behaviors that contribute to feelings of either supportiveness or defensiveness.[17] Gibb spent several years listening to and observing groups of individuals in meetings and conversations, noting that some exchanges seemed to create a supportive climate, whereas others created a defensive one.

Words and actions, he concluded, are tools we use to let someone know whether we support them or not. Now let's consider how you can use words to create a supportive climate rather than an antagonistic one.

Describe Your Own Feelings Rather Than Evaluate Others

Most of us don't like to be judged or evaluated. Criticizing and name-calling obviously can create relational problems, but so can our attempts to diagnose others' problems or win their affection with insincere praise. In fact, any form of evaluation creates a climate of defensiveness. As Winston Churchill declared, "I am always ready to learn, although I do not always like being taught." Correcting others, even when we are doing it "for their own good" can raise their hackles.

One way to avoid evaluating others is to eliminate the accusatory *you* from your language. Statements such as, "You always come in late for supper," or "You need to pick up the dirty clothes in your room," attack a person's sense of self-worth and usually result in a defensive reaction.

Instead, use the word *I* to describe your own feelings and thoughts about a situation or event: "I find it hard to keep your supper warm when you're late," or "I don't enjoy the extra work of picking up your dirty clothes." When you describe your own feelings instead of berating the receiver of the message, you

An essential skill in being supportive rather than defensive is describing what you want with "I" language rather than "you" language. Could the use of "I" language help this couple? (Chip Henderson/Tony Stone Images)

MEDIA AND OUTSIDE RESOURCES
Reginald Rose's *12 Angry Men* is an excellent film/play which depicts the problems of defensive communication and the value of supportive communication. Suggest that students compare the communication behaviors of juror #8 (Henry Fonda) to that of #10 (Ed Begley). In addition, notice how juror #7 (Jack Warden) tells Fonda, "You do-gooders are all alike. Why don't you stop wasting our time?" (allness and polarization). Notice how Fonda uses empathy and provisionalism with statements such as: "I just think we owe him a few words," or "I keep putting myself in the kid's place."

Using I language is one of the most important skill-building exercises you can do in this course. Do spend time on this Building Your Skills box.

RESEARCH AND LITERATURE

Robert Bolton, author of *People Skills* (Simon and Schuster, 1979), asserts that genuineness has three ingredients: self-awareness, self-acceptance, and self-expression. Bolton argues that the children's story *The Velveteen Rabbit* (Margery Williams, Avon, 1975) describes the development of genuineness. Consider reading the skin horse's speech (pp. 16–17) to the rabbit aloud in class for illustration.

ACTIVITY

See Activity 6.6 in the Instructor's Guide.

194

BUILDING YOUR SKILLS

Practice Using *I* Language

An essential skill in being supportive rather than defensive is describing what you want with *I* language rather than *you* language. Rephrase the following *you* statements into *I* statements.

You Language	*I* Language
1. You are messy when you cook.	_____
2. Your driving is terrible.	_____
3. You never listen to me.	_____
4. You just lie on the couch and never offer to help me.	_____
5. You always decide what movie we see.	_____

are in essence taking ownership of the problem. This approach leads to greater openness and trust because your listener is less likely to feel rejected or as if you are trying to control him or her. Also, when you express your emotions, make sure you choose the right words to communicate your feelings. Building Your Skills: Practice Using *I* Language will help you practice your skill in accurately expressing your feelings.

Solve Problems Rather Than Control Others

When you were younger, your parents gave you rules to keep you safe. Even though you may have resented their control, you needed to know what was hot, when not to cross the street, and not to stick your finger in a light socket. Now that you are an adult, when people treat you like a child, it often means they are trying to control your behavior, to take away your options. In truth, we have little or no control over someone else's behavior.

Most of us don't like to be controlled against our will. Someone who presumes to tell us what's good for us, instead of helping us puzzle through issues and problems, is likely to engender defensiveness. Open-ended questions, such as, "What seems to be the problem?" or "How can we deal with the issue?" create a more supportive climate than critical comments, such as, "Here's where you are wrong" or commands such as, "Don't do that!"

Be Genuine Rather Than Manipulative

To be genuine means that you honestly seek to be yourself rather than someone you are not. It also means taking an honest interest in others and considering the uniqueness of each individual and situation, avoiding generalizations or strategies that focus only on your own needs and desires. A manipulative person has hidden agendas; a genuine person uses words to discuss issues and problems openly and honestly.

Empathize Rather Than Remain Detached from Others

Empathy is one of the hallmarks of supportive relationships. As we learned earlier, empathy is the ability to understand the feelings of others and to predict the emotional responses they will have to different situations. The opposite of empathy is neutrality. To be neutral is to be indifferent or apathetic toward another. Even when you express anger or irritation toward another, you are investing some energy in the relationship.

After an unsuccessful attempt to persuade his family to take a trip to Yellowstone National Park, Preston declared, "I don't care what you think; that's where we're going." His proclamation reflects a disregard for the feelings of others in his family. This insensitivity is self-defeating. The defensive climate Preston creates with his words will probably prevent the whole family from enjoying the vacation.

Be Flexible Rather Than Rigid Toward Others

Most people don't like someone who always seems certain that he or she is right. A "you're wrong, I'm right" attitude creates a defensive climate. This does not mean that you should have no opinions and go through life blithely agreeing to everything. And it doesn't mean that there is *never* one answer that is right and others that are wrong. But instead of making rigid pronouncements, you can use phrases such as, "I may be wrong, but it seems to me . . ." or "Here's one way to look at this problem." This manner of speaking gives your opinions a softer edge that allows room for others to express a point of view.

Present Yourself as Equal Rather Than Superior

You can antagonize others by letting them know that you view yourself as better or brighter than they are. You may be gifted and intelligent, but it's not necessary to announce it. And although some people have the responsibility and authority to manage others, "pulling rank" does not usually produce a cooperative climate. With phrases such as "Let's work on this together" or "We each have a valid perspective," you can avoid erecting walls of resentment and suspicion.

Also, avoid using bafflegab to impress others. Keep your messages short and clear, and use informal language. When you communicate with someone from

RESEARCH AND LITERATURE
John Gray, author of *Men Are from Mars, Women Are from Venus* (HarperCollins, 1992) argues that when men and women are able to respect and love their differences, then love has a chance of blooming.

BUILDING YOUR SKILLS

Expressing Your Emotions

Communication is enhanced if you can clearly express the emotions you are feeling to others. One way to communicate your emotions is to describe how you are feeling with a well-chosen word or phrase. The following list gives you several options for expressing your feelings in positive, neutral, or negative terms.

Positive:

calm
cheerful
comfortable
confident
content
delighted
ecstatic
elated
enthusiastic
excited
flattered
free
friendly
glad
grateful
happy
high
hopeful
hysterical
interested
joyful
loving
optimistic
passionate
peaceful
playful
pleased
refreshed
romantic
sexy
tender
warm
willing
wonderful

Neutral:

amazed
ambivalent
apathetic
bashful
bored
detached
hurried
lukewarm
numb
possessive
sentimental
vulnerable

Negative:

afraid
angry
annoyed
alone
bitter
confused
defeated
defensive
depressed
devastated
disappointed

another culture, you may need to use an **elaborated code** to get your message across. This means that your messages will have to be more explicit, but they should not be condescending. Two of your authors remember vividly trying to explain to a French exchange student what a fire ant was. First, we had to translate *ant* into French, and then we had to provide scientific, descriptive, and narrative evidence to help the student understand how these tiny biting insects terrorize people in the Southern part of the United States.

disgusted
disturbed
empty
exhausted
fearful
frustrated
furious
guilty
helpless
horrible
humiliated
intimidated
listless
mad
mean
miserable
paranoid
rebellious
regretful
resentful
restless
shocked
suspicious
terrified
ugly
sad

To practice expressing your emotions, consider using some of the words listed here to respond to the following situations. Write your response for each situation. Consider describing your response using either a single word or short phrase such as "I feel angry" or express your feelings in terms of what you'd like to do such as "I'd be so embarrassed I would sink through the floor," or "I would feel like leaving and never coming back to this house."

1. You have several thousand dollars charged to your credit cards, and you get fired from your job.

2. Your best friend, with whom you spend a lot of time, is moving to another country.

3. You have just learned that your Aunt whom you adored died and left you a $35,000 inheritance.

4. Even though you do your best to keep your room clean, your roommate is complaining again about how you are a slob.

5. You have brought your two-year-old son to a worship service but he continues to talk, and run around during the service, and will not sit still. Other worshipers are looking at you with disapproval.

6. You arrive at your vacation hotel only to discover that they do not have a reservation for you and you do not have your room confirmation number.

RECAP   **Use Words to Create a Supportive Climate**

Describe your feelings instead of evaluating the behavior of others.

Keep the focus on problem solving, not control.

Be genuine rather than manipulative in your approach.

Show that you understand another person's point of view instead of ignoring feelings.

Make it clear that you do not have all the answers rather than be perceived as a know-it-all.

Present yourself as an equal rather than as a superior.

Using Words to Value Others

I just don't feel appreciated any more," confides Tynisha during her counseling session. "My husband Patrick just doesn't let me know he cares for me." One of the key skills in maintaining a long-term relationship is to know how to demonstrate that you value the other person. It's not just *nice* to know that someone cares about us; it is vital that we know others have genuine feelings of concern for us. In addition to acts of kindness, it is our words that let others know we appreciate them.

ELECTRONIC CONNECTIONS

The Power of Confirming Responses

A Disabled Writer Finds a Friend Along the Information Superhighway

To Chris Young, e-mail is the great equalizer. Nearly ten years ago, my wife, Pamela, "met" Chris through the engaging messages he'd posted in CompuServe's Issues Forum. Chris's thoughts and writing style caught Pamela's eye; she happened to mention how much she enjoyed the postings to forum administrator Georgia Griffith, who, in turn, relayed her compliments to Chris.

"When Georgia wrote [via e-mail] to tell me, I laughed out loud," Chris recalls today. That was partly because he'd never thought of himself as a writer, but it was also because he knew Pamela had no idea what a physical challenge each of his messages posed. Chris was born with a congenital neuromuscular disease similar to muscular dystrophy and he spends his days in a motorized wheelchair. He has never walked, has limited use of his right hand and types by poking the computer keys, one laborious letter at a time, with a wooden pointer.

"Years ago," he says, "when I first started using e-mail, I was shocked when I realized that some of my on-line acquaintances didn't know about my disability. For the first time in my life, people had the opportunity to meet the real me before seeing my disability, which doesn't happen when I meet someone face to face." Often, however, Chris chooses to tell people on-line about his disability. "I'm not fully myself without my disability," says Chris. "It gives me a unique perspective on life that I can share with others."

Chris and Pamela began a regular e-mail correspondence. In Chris's messages—each are thousands of words long and represent hours of painstaking labor—the young Indianapolis computer programmer shared his life stories with the grace, insight, and humor of a seasoned writer.

"Where some people spill their guts onto blank pages starting with the words 'Dear Diary,' my personal journals have been in the form of e-mail that begins 'Dear Pamela,'" Chris says. "It's somehow more significant to me knowing a real live human being is on the other end of the line than it would be pouring my soul onto pages that might never see the light of day. Also the distance between us provides some safety. Pamela will likely never meet most of the characters in my life, so I am totally free to speak my mind about them."

Chris credits Pamela's support for inspiring him to pursue his writing professionally. Over the past few years, several of his articles have appeared in technical computer magazines. His first book, *Ray Tracing Creations*, about computer graphics, was recently published by The Waite Group; the dedication reads, "To my friend, Pamela, who convinced me I could write."

Researchers have identified ways we use language to confirm or disconfirm others.[18] A **confirming response** is a statement that causes others to value themselves more. Conversely, a **disconfirming response** is one that causes others to value themselves less.

The words we select to communicate our feelings *do* affect our relationships with others. Electronic Connections: The Power of Confirming Responses illustrates how confirming responses can bolster another person's self-esteem and lead to a meaningful relationship.

Confirming Responses

The adage, "People judge us by our words and behavior rather than by our intent" summarizes the underlying principle of confirming responses. Those who receive your messages determine whether they have the effect you intended. Formulating confirming responses requires careful listening and attention to the other person. We will describe several kinds of confirming responses here:

■ DIRECT ACKNOWLEDGMENT

When you respond directly to something another person says to you, you are acknowledging not only the statement, but also that the person is important.

Joan: It certainly is a nice day for a canoe trip.

Mariko: Yes, Joan, it's a great day to be outside.

■ AGREEMENT ABOUT JUDGMENTS

When you confirm someone's evaluation of something, you are also affirming that person's sense of taste and judgment.

Nancy: I think the steel guitar player's riff was fantastic.

Victor: Yes, I thought it was the best part of the performance.

■ SUPPORTIVE RESPONSE

When you express reassurance and understanding, you are confirming a person's right to his or her feelings.

Lionel: I'm disappointed that I only scored a 60 on my interpersonal communication test.

Sarah: I'm sorry to see you so sad, Lionel. I know that test was important to you.

■ CLARIFYING RESPONSE

When you seek greater understanding of another person's message, you are confirming that he or she is worth your time and trouble. Clarifying responses also encourage the other person to talk in order to explore his or her feelings.

Larry: I'm not feeling very good about my family situation these days.

Tyrone: Is it tough with you and Margo working different shifts?

■ EXPRESSION OF POSITIVE FEELING

We feel confirmed or valued when someone else agrees with our expression of joy or excitement.

Lorraine: I'm so excited! I was just promoted to associate professor.

Dorette: Congratulations! I'm so proud of you! Heaven knows you deserve it.

■ COMPLIMENT

When you tell people you like what they have done or said, what they are wearing, or how they look, you are confirming their sense of worth.

Jean Christophe: Did you get the invitation to my party?"

Manny: Yes! It looked so professional. I didn't know you could do calligraphy. You're a talented guy.

In each of these examples, note how the responder provides comments that confirm the worth or value of the other person. But we want to caution that confirming responses should be sincere. Offering false praise is manipulative, and your communication partner will probably sniff out your phoniness.

Complimenting someone for a job well done is a powerful way to confirm that person's self worth. (Jeff Persons/Stock Boston)

INTERPERSONAL COMMUNICATION SKILLS

BUILDING YOUR SKILLS

Using Word Pictures to Express Your Feelings

A word picture is a short statement or story that dramatizes an emotion you experience. Using a visual image can add extra power in expressing your feelings where a simple descriptive word may not suffice.[19] Word pictures can be used to clarify how you feel, to offer praise or correction, as well as develop greater intimacy. A key goal of a word picture is to communicate your feelings and emotions. An effective way to express your emotions through a word picture is to use a simile. A simile, as you may remember from your English class, is a comparison that uses the words

like or as to clarify the image you want to communicate. "When you forgot my birthday, I felt like crumbs that had been swept from the table," exclaimed Marge to her forgetful husband. Or, after a hard day's work, Jeff told his family, "Have you seen a worn-out punching bag? That's just how I feel. I've been pounded time and time again and now I feel torn and scuffed. I need a few minutes of peace and quiet before I join in the family conversation." His visual image helped communicate how exhausted he really felt. The best word pictures use an experience or image to which the listener can relate. To practice your skill, try to develop word pictures for the following situations to

express your feelings in a powerful and memorable way.

1. You have just learned that a cherished family pet has died.

2. You want to tell your friends how happy you are when you learn you received an "A" in a difficult course.

3. You've asked your sister not to leave an empty milk carton in the refrigerator, but you discover another empty carton in the fridge.

4. Your family is planning a vacation but didn't ask you to be involved in the planning.

ELECTRONIC CONNECTIONS

Netiquette Guidelines

Netiquette is the practice of being thoughtful when communicating online. Here are some simple netiquette rules to help you avoid cyberspace gaffes when communicating with others.

1. Help others understand what you mean. Use symbols or emoticons (described in Chapter 1) to communication emotions —like <g> for

grin; or simply set clear boundaries as to what you will and will not do on or off line. Since you don't have nonverbal cues to help interpret what you mean, use extra diligence to clarify your meaning.

2. Don't use vulgar or profane language in chat rooms. Be polite—especially when you are in a chat room, where others can see your messages.

3. Keep track of the people you meet online. You can meet a host of people in a chat room. Keep a list of the people you meet. In real time people like to be remembered; so do people in cyberspace.

4. Be yourself. Honesty is the best policy in cyberspace, just as it is live and in person. Don't tell your cyberfriends you are someone you are not; be authentic.

INTERNET RESOURCE

Gossip

http://www.calvarychapel.
org/se-portland/gossip.htm
Gossip is defined and
placed in a Judeo-Christian
context of sinful behavior.
Strategies for managing
and minimizing gossip are
offered.

Ambiguity

http://crl.nmsu.edu/users/
mabesh/thesis-tr/node49.
html
Discusses two types of ambiguities: global and local.

See http://crl.nmsu.edu/
users/mabesh/thesis-tr/
node93.html for more on
local ambiguities.

See http://crl.nmsu.edu/
users/mabesh/thesis-tr/
node169.html for more on
structural ambiguities and
phase boundary ambiguity.

SKILL DEVELOPMENT

Ask students to provide
better responses to each
of the initial statements, opposite. Next, ask students
to role-play responses to
the secondary comments
by Harvey, Sharon, Peter,
Samantha, Bill, George, and
Steve. Debrief these with
the class, asking students to
provide specific, descriptive
feedback that employs I-
Language. (E.g., "I liked the
way you smiled at Rosa,
Harvey. I noticed that she
sat straighter and smiled in
return.")

RECAP | **Responses That Confirm Another Person's Self-Worth**

Directly acknowledge something someone has said.

Agree with the person's judgments.

Be supportive; let the other person know you are trying to understand how he or she feels.

Ask questions to help clarify another person's statements if you are not sure you understand.

Express positive feelings to echo those of the other person.

Compliment the person if you can be sincere.

Disconfirming Responses

Some statements and responses can undermine another person's self-worth. We offer these categories so that you can avoid using them and also recognize when someone is trying to chip away at your self-image and self-esteem.

■ IMPERVIOUS RESPONSE

When a person fails to acknowledge your statement or attempt to communicate, even though you know he or she heard you, you may feel a sense of awkwardness or embarrassment.

Rosa: I loved your speech, Harvey.

Harvey: (No response, verbal or nonverbal.)

■ INTERRUPTING RESPONSE

When people interrupt you, they may be implying that what they have to say is more important than what you have to say. In effect, they could also be implying that they are more important than you are.

Anna: I just heard on the news that . . .

Sharon: Oh yes. The stock market just went down 100 points.

■ IRRELEVANT RESPONSE

An irrelevant response is one that has nothing at all to do with what you were saying. Chances are your partner is not listening to you at all.

Arnold: First we're flying down to Rio, and then to Quito. I can hardly wait to . . .

Peter: They're predicting a hard freeze tonight.

The real message Peter is sending is, "I have more important things on my mind."

Supportive–Defensive Communication Charades

Divide into groups of two to four people. Each team or group should prepare a short play depicting one of the supportive or defensive communication responses described in this chapter. Perform your play for the class or another team to see if they can identify the type of supportive or defensive communication behavior your team is portraying. Consider one of the following situations or develop one of your own:

Speaking with a professor about a grade.

Returning a broken item to a store.

Talking with your child about his or her grades.

Responding to a telemarketing salesperson who calls you during dinner.

Talking with one of your employees who made a work-related mistake.

Re-booking a flight because your flight was canceled by the airline.

Taking an order from a customer at a fast-food restaurant.

Receiving a complaint from a customer about poor service.

Talking with someone who has knocked on your door inviting you to his or her church.

Asking someone to turn down the stereo or TV while you are trying to study.

Variation: Instead of illustrating supportive and defensive communication, roleplay an example of one of the confirming or disconfirming communication behaviors discussed in this chapter.

Essential Guidelines

The key to shared understanding is to focus on the needs, goals, and mind-set of your communication partner. Throughout this chapter we have emphasized how to develop an other-oriented approach to communicating verbally. You can use a few slogans to remind yourself of what you have read:

Slogan # 1: *Meanings are in people not in words.*

Words are arbitrary, contextually and culturally bound symbols that can have denotative and connotative, concrete or abstract meaning. Focus on what the words may mean to your partner.

Slogan # 2: *Think before you speak.*

Words have power to create and affect feelings and actions, as well as to affect and reflect culture. Before you speak, consider the impact your words will have on others. Remember that words can hurt—and once spoken, words cannot be taken back.

Slogan # 3: *Say what you mean and mean what you say.*

Given the complexity of the meaning creation process, it is a wonder that we communicate as accurately as we do. When speaking with others, be mindful of the potential for miscommunication and misunderstanding. Use precise language and be accurate in conveying your true feelings. Remember that you are responsible for what you communicate. The spoken word belongs half to the person who speaks and half to the person who understands.

Slogan # 4: *Speak to others as you wish to be spoken to.*

Our words can engender a supportive communication climate or create defensiveness, which can lead to misunderstanding. Always try to put yourself in your partner's place.

INSTRUCTIONAL GOALS AND TIPS

Point out that in a high-context environment, these slogans would not be as valuable or necessary as they are in the United States.

■ TANGENTIAL RESPONSE

A tangential response is one that acknowledges you, but that is only minimally related to what you are talking about. Again, it indicates that the other person isn't really attending to your message.

Richard: This new program will help us stay within our budget.

Samantha: Yeah. I think I'll save some bucks and send this letter by regular mail.

■ IMPERSONAL RESPONSE

A response that intellectualizes and uses the third person distances the other person from you and has the effect of trivializing what you say.

Diana: Hey, Bill. I'd like to talk with you for a minute about getting your permission to take my vacation in July.

Bill: One tends to become interested in recreational pursuits about this time of year, doesn't one?

■ INCOHERENT RESPONSE

When a speaker mumbles, rambles, or makes some unintelligible effort to respond, it may leave you wondering if what you said was of any value or use to the listener.

Paolo: George, here's my suggestion for the merger deal with Antrax. Let's make them an offer of forty-eight dollars a share and see how they respond.

George: Huh? Well . . . So . . . Well . . . hmmm . . . I'm not sure.

■ INCONGRUOUS RESPONSE

When a verbal message is inconsistent with nonverbal behavior, we usually believe the nonverbal message, but we usually feel confused as well. An incongruous response is like a malfunctioning traffic light with flashing red and green lights—you're just not sure whether the speaker wants you to go or stay.

Sue: Honey, do you want me to go grocery shopping with you?

Steve: (Shouting) OF COURSE I DO! WHY ARE YOU ASKING?

Although it may be impossible to eliminate all disconfirming responses from your repertoire, becoming aware of the power of your words and monitoring your conversation for offensive phrases may help you avoid unexpected and perhaps devastating consequences.

Summary

The words we use have great power to affect our self-image and to influence the relationships we establish with others. English words are symbols that refer to objects, events, people, and ideas. They are arbitrary. We interpret their meaning through the context and culture to which they belong. Communication is complex because most words have both denotative (literal) meanings and connotative (subjective) meanings, and because words range from concrete to abstract.

The power of words stems from their ability to create images and to influence our thoughts, feelings, and actions. There is also an important link between the words we use and our culture. Language shapes culture and culture shapes language. Our view of the world is influenced by our vocabulary and the categories we have created with words.

Several word barriers can contribute to misunderstanding in interpersonal communication. Bypassing occurs when a word means one thing to one person and another to someone else. Our verbal expressions may lack clarity, either because we make language errors or because the meaning we want to convey is not clear to us. Allness statements can mislead and alienate listeners because the speaker falsely implies that he or she knows all there is to know about something. Another barrier, static evaluation, fails to take changes into account and uses outdated labels and categories. Polarization is the language of extremes; when someone thinks in black and white, many shades of meaning disappear. Confusing facts with inferences results in jumping to conclusions that are not based upon direct observations. Finally, biased language that is insensitive to others creates noise that interferes with the meaning of a message.

The words you use can enhance or detract from the quality of relationships you establish with others. Supportive communication is descriptive rather than evaluative, problem oriented rather than control oriented, genuine rather than contrived or manipulative, empathic rather than neutral, flexible rather than rigid, and equal rather than superior. The words we use can either confirm or undermine another's sense of self-worth. If you directly acknowledge people, agree with their judgments, voice support when they feel bad, ask them to clarify their messages, affirm their positive feelings, and compliment them sincerely, then you may help them boost their self-images. Conversely, our responses can be disconfirming if we are impervious, interrupt someone, or use irrelevant, tangential, impersonal, incoherent, or incongruous messages.

1. Through classical conditioning, we assign meanings to words and respond to them. Therefore the word "good" might trigger feelings of happiness.

2. Common barriers include bypassing (using terms which have multiple meanings), equivocation (using ambiguous and vague terms), allness (making generalizations), static evaluation, polarization, assumptions (confusing inferences with facts), and biased language (which provoke defensiveness).

3. Supportive communicators are rhetorically sensitive to the arbitrary and changing nature of language. Supportive communicators seek to clarify meanings with perception checks, paraphrases, and confirmation. In addition, these communicators use language responsibly to describe their thoughts and feelings and to seek to understand others.

4. A confirming response is feedback which seeks to support the other. (In Transactional Analysis, this is called a "warm fuzzy.") Confirming responses are positive, expressive, clear, employ I-language, and are genuine.

5. Disconfirming responses demonstrate a lack of respect or regard for the other. (In Transactional Analysis, these are called "cold pricklies.") Disconfirming responses are marked by evaluation, directiveness, neutrality, or dogmatism.

For Discussion and Review

■ FOCUS ON COMPREHENSION

1. How do words create meaning for others?

2. What are some barriers to effective understanding, and what are strategies for overcoming these barriers?

3. What are the characteristics of a supportive communicator?

4. What are confirming communication responses? Describe a few.

5. What are disconfirming communication responses? Describe a few.

■ FOCUS ON CRITICAL THINKING

6. Marge and Paul are having an argument. Paul shouts, "You're constantly criticizing me! You don't let me make any important decisions!" How could Paul communicate how he feels in a more supportive way?

7. Alan asked Jessie to pick him up after work at the circle drive at 5:30 P.M. Jessie waited patiently at the circle drive on the other side of campus and finally went home at 6:30 P.M., having seen no sign of Alan. Alan was waiting at the circle drive behind his office rather than at the one on the other side of the campus. What word barriers do you think led to this misunderstanding?

8. Rephrase the following statements to use less biased language:

   A. I'd like to introduce Mr. Russell Browne and his wife, Muriel.

   B. In an office memo: "Several gals have been leaving their purses at their desks."

9. Rephrase the following statements, using the skill of indexing.

   A. All politicians want power and control over others.

   B. All teachers are underpaid.

   C. All Texans like to brag about how great their state is.

■ FOCUS ON ETHICS

10. If you really don't want to listen to your coworker go into detail about her latest vacation trip or provide details about the recent escapades of her children or grandchildren, is it appropriate to tell her that you'd rather not hear her "news"? Support your response.

11. Is it ethical to correct someone when he or she uses sexist language or makes a stereotypical remark about someone's race, gender or sexual orientation? What if that person is your boss or your teacher? Explain your answer.

12. Is it ethical to mask your true feelings of anger and irritation with someone by using supportive statements or confirming statements when what you really want to do is tell him or her "the truth" in no uncertain terms?

For Your Journal

1. Keep a log of examples of word barriers you experience or encounter. Note examples of bypassing, lack of precision in language, bafflegab, and other uses of words that inhibit communication. The examples could come from your own verbal exchanges or those that you observe in the conversations of others.

2. Make a list of words that are in your vocabulary today that were not in your vocabulary five years ago. Include new vocabulary words that you may have learned in school as well as words that were not generally used or that have been coined in the last half-decade (for example, CD-ROM, homepage).

3. Record a sample dialogue between you and a good friend that illustrates some of the confirming responses described on pages 191-193.

Learning With Others

1. Think of a bypass miscommunication that you've experienced. Share your recollection with a small group and compare your feelings and responses with those of others.

2. In your group, choose one person to play a recently divorced person whose spouse is not abiding by a child custody agreement and insists on seeing the children at odd hours. Another person should play the role of a trusted friend who only listens and responds. Ask the trusted friend to use the skills he or she learned in this chapter along with effective listening skills presented in Chapter 4. Then do a group evaluation of his or her response.

3. To practice separating facts from inferences, read each of the following stories. Assume that all the information presented is accurate, and refer to the story whenever you wish.

   Next read the statements and mark whether the statement is definitely true on the basis of the information in the story (T) or definitely false (F). And ? means that you cannot be certain on the basis of the information in the story; mark this if any part of a statement is doubtful.

Story A

As you step onto your front porch from your living room, you observe a delivery truck approaching along the street. You see that your next-door neighbor is backing her car from her garage into the street in the path of the approaching truck. You see the truck swerve, climb over the curb, and come to a stop against a tree, which crumples one of the truck's front fenders.

■ STATEMENTS ABOUT STORY A

1. Your next-door neighbor was backing her car into the street in the path of an approaching truck.   **T**   **F**   **?**

2. The delivery truck was traveling at a reasonable speed.   **T**   **F**   **?**

3. The only damage resulting from the incident was to the truck's fender.   **T**   **F**   **?**

4. You saw the truck swerve and climb over the curb.   **T**   **F**   **?**

5. Your neighbor across the street was backing her car out of the garage.   **T**   **F**   **?**

6. The truck suffered no damage.   **T**   **F**   **?**

7. You saw the truck approaching as you stepped onto your front porch from your living room.   **T**   **F**   **?**

8. The man who drove the delivery truck swerved and ran his truck up over a curb.   **T**   **F**   **?**

9. The delivery truck driver swerved in order to miss a child playing in the street.   **T**   **F**   **?**

Story B

A husband, wife, and their sons ages eleven and fourteen drove cross-country on a vacation trip in their three-year-old automobile. They started the trip on a Friday, the thirteenth of the month. The wife said she did not like the idea of leaving on that day and the man laughed at her statement. In the course of the trip the following mishaps occurred:

The automobile radiator sprang a leak.
The eleven-year-old boy became carsick for the first time in his life.
The wife was badly sunburned.
The husband lost his fishing rod.

■ STATEMENTS ABOUT STORY B

1. There were fewer than two children in the family.   **T**   **F**   **?**

2. The sedan's radiator sprang a leak.   **T**   **F**   **?**

■ INTERPERSONAL COMMUNICATION SKILLS

3. The wife really didn't mind leaving on Friday the thirteenth. **T   F   ?**

4. A fishing reel was lost. **T   F   ?**

5. The family's trip began on Friday the thirteenth. **T   F   ?**

6. The eleven-year-old boy lost his fishing rod. **T   F   ?**

7. The story mentions the name of the family taking the trip. **T   F   ?**

8. The make of the automobile in which the family made the trip was not mentioned in the story. **T   F   ?**

9. The husband laughed at his wife's fears of Friday the thirteenth. **T   F   ?**

Story C

John and Betty Smith are awakened in the middle of the night by a noise coming from the direction of their living room. Smith investigates and finds that the door opening into the garden, which he thought he had locked before going to bed, is standing wide open. Books and papers are scattered all over the floor around the desk in one corner of the room.

■ STATEMENTS ABOUT STORY C

1. Mrs. Smith was awakened in the middle of the night. **T   (F)   ?**

2. Smith locked the door from his living room to his garden before going to bed. **T   (F)   ?**

3. The books and papers were scattered between the time Mr. Smith went to bed and the time he was awakened. **T   (F)   ?**

4. Smith found that the door opening into the garden was shut. **T   (F)   ?**

5. Mr. Smith did not lock the garden door. **T   (F)   ?**

6. John Smith was not awakened by a noise. **(T)   F   ?**

7. Nothing was missing from the room. **T   (F)   ?**

8. Mrs. Smith was sleeping when she and Mr. Smith were awakened. **T   (F)   ?**

9. The noise did not come from their garden. *came from the direction of the living room.* **(T)   F   ?**

10. Smith saw no burglar in the living room. **T   (F)   ?**

11. Mr. and Mrs. Smith were awakened in the middle of the night by a noise. **T   (F)   ?**

Developed by T. Richard Cheatham and Robert Sherman for *Oral Communication Handbook* (Warrensburg, MO: Central Missouri State University, 1972).

SYMBOL: Word, sound, or visual device that represents a thought, concept, or object.

REFERENT: Thing that a symbol represents.

THOUGHT: Mental process of creating a category, idea, or image triggered by a referent or symbol.

HIGH-CONTEXT CULTURE: Culture in which the meaning of messages is highly dependent upon context and nonverbal cues.

LOW-CONTEXT CULTURE: Culture that relies primarily on language to communicate messages.

SYMBOLIC INTERACTION: Theory that suggests societies are bound together through common use of symbols.

DENOTATIVE MEANING: Restrictive or literal meaning of a word.

CONNOTATIVE MEANING: Personal and subjective meaning of a word.

LINGUISTIC DETERMINISM: Theory that describes how use of language determines or influences thoughts and perceptions.

WORLD VIEW: Culturally acquired perspective for interpreting experiences.

BYPASSING: The same words mean different things to different people.

MALAPROPISM: Confusion of one word or phrase for another that sounds similar to it.

RESTRICTED CODE: Using words that have meaning to a person, group, or culture.

JARGON: Another name for restricted code; specialized terms or abbreviations whose meaning is known only to members of a specific group.

ALLNESS: Tendency to use language to make unqualified, often untrue generalizations.

INDEXING: Way of avoiding allness statements by separating one situation, person, or example from another.

STATIC EVALUATION: Pronouncing judgment on something without taking changes into consideration.

POLARIZATION: Describing and evaluating what we observe in terms of extremes such as good or bad, old or new, beautiful or ugly.

ELABORATED CODE: Using many words and various ways of describing an idea or concept to communicate its meaning.

CONFIRMING RESPONSE: Statement that causes another person to value himself or herself more.

DISCONFIRMING RESPONSE: Statement that causes another person to value himself or herself less.

WORD PICTURE: Short statement or story that illustrates or describes your emotions; word pictures often use a simile (a comparison using the word "like" or "as") to clarify the image.

7

Communicating Nonverbally

After studying this chapter, you should be able to:

1. Explain why nonverbal communication is an important and challenging area of study.

2. Describe the functions of nonverbal communication in interpersonal relationships.

3. Summarize research findings that describe codes of nonverbal communication behavior.

4. Describe three bases for interpreting nonverbal behavior.

5. Formulate a strategy for improving your ability to interpret nonverbal messages accurately.

■ WHY LEARN ABOUT NON-VERBAL COMMUNICATION?

■ THE CHALLENGE OF INTERPRETING NONVERBAL MESSAGES

■ NONVERBAL COMMUNICA-TION CODES

■ INTERPRETING NONVERBAL COMMUNICATION

■ IMPROVING YOUR ABILITY TO INTERPRET NONVERBAL MESSAGES

> *Eddie: Lisa, will you get the telephone?*
> *Lisa: Get it yourself!*
> *Eddie: Hey! Why so testy? All I asked you*
> *to do was answer the phone!*

f we could view a videotape of Eddie and Lisa's interaction, we could more clearly see the source of the conflict. Eddie's tone of voice and his scowling facial expression made his simple request seem more like an order.

As we noted in Chapter 1, communication has both content and emotional dimensions. Our tone of voice, eye contact, facial expressions, posture, movement, vocal cues, appearance, use of personal space, manipulation of the communication environment, and other nonverbal clues reveal how we feel toward others. We can define **nonverbal communication** as behavior other than written or spoken language, that creates meaning for someone. In this chapter we will focus on how nonverbal communication affects the quality of our interpersonal relationships. As we identify the functions and codes of nonverbal cues, we will also explore ways to improve our skill in interpreting the nonverbal messages of others.

Why Learn about Nonverbal Communication?

When you are sitting in a public place such as a shopping mall, airport, or bus stop, do you make assumptions about what other people might be like as you observe their nonverbal behavior? Most of us are people watchers, and we rely on nonverbal communication clues to predict how others may feel about and react to us. Nonverbal communication plays a major role in relationship development because it is also the main channel we use to communicate our feelings and attitudes toward others. But because much of our nonverbal communication behavior is unconscious, most of us have limited awareness or understanding of it. We can begin examining nonverbal communication by looking at the ways we use it.

Nonverbal Messages Communicate Our Feelings and Attitudes

Daryl knew that he was in trouble the moment he walked into the room. His wife Sandra gave him a steely stare. Her brow was furrowed and her arms were crossed. On the table was a dish of cold lobster Newburg, extinguished candles burnt to nubs, and dirty dishes in all but one spot: his. Daryl was in the doghouse for forgetting the special meal his wife had prepared, and he needed no words to sense the depth of her displeasure.

213

INTERNET RESOURCE

Nonverbal Communication Online Join in on the online discussion group at: http://maine.maine.edu/~zubrick/tren5.html

MEDIA AND OUTSIDE RESOURCES

Consider showing a clip from the movie *Ferris Bueller's Day Off*, in which Bueller is lying to an authority figure. Ask students to use Zuckerman, et al.'s list of nonverbal cues to detect deception.

RESEARCH AND LITERATURE

Milo Frank's bestselling book *How to Get Your Point Across in Thirty Seconds or Less* (Simon and Schuster, 1985) is a good reference. Frank provides several examples to reinforce this point.

The nonverbal message this boy gives is far more believable than any words he might have spoken to his brother. (Bob Daemmrich/Stock Boston)

Albert Mehrabian concluded that as little as 7 percent of the emotional meaning of a message is communicated through explicit verbal channels.[1] The most significant source of emotional communication is our face—according to Mehrabian's study, it channels as much as 55 percent of our meaning. Vocal cues such as volume, pitch, and intensity, communicate another 38 percent of our emotional meaning. In all, we communicate approximately 93 percent of the emotional meaning of our messages nonverbally. Although these percentages do not apply to every communication situation, the results of Mehrabian's investigation do illustrate the potential power of nonverbal cues in communicating emotion.

When we interact with others, we base our feelings and emotional responses not on what our partner says, but rather on what he or she does. We also alter our nonverbal communication to suit different relationships. With good friends you let down your guard; you may slouch, scratch, and take off your shoes to show you trust them. But if you were interviewing for a job or meeting your fiancé's parents for the first time, your posture would probably be stiffer and your smiles more carefully controlled as you tried to convey the impression that you are mature, competent, and respectable.

Nonverbal Messages Are More Believable

"Honey, do you love me?" asks Brenda.

"OF COURSE I LOVE YOU! HAVEN'T I ALWAYS TOLD YOU THAT I LOVE YOU? I LOVE YOU!" shouts Jim, keeping his eyes glued to his morning newspaper.

Brenda will probably not be that reassured by Jim's pledge of affection. The contradiction between his spoken message of love and his nonverbal message of irritation and disinterest will leave her wondering about his true feelings.

Actions speak louder than words. This cliché became a cliché because nonverbal communication is more believable than verbal communication. Nonverbal messages are more difficult to fake. One research team concluded that North Americans use the following cues, listed in order of most to least important, to help us discern when a person is lying.[2]

- Greater time lag in response to a question
- Reduced eye contact
- Increased shifts in posture

INTERPERSONAL COMMUNICATION SKILLS

- Unfilled pauses

- Less smiling

- Slower speech

- Higher pitch in voice

- More deliberate pronunciation and articulation of words

It is difficult to manipulate an array of nonverbal cues, so a skilled other-oriented observer can see when our true feelings leak out. Paul Ekman and Wallace Friesen have identified the face, hands, and feet as key sources of nonverbal leakage cues.[3] Are you aware of what your fingers and toes are doing as you are reading this book? Even if we become experts at masking and manipulating our faces, we may first signal disinterest or boredom with another person by finger wiggling or toe wagging. Or we may twiddle a pen or pencil. When we become emotionally aroused, the pupils of our eyes dilate, and we may blush, sweat, or change our breathing patterns.[4] Lie detectors rely on these unconscious clues. A polygraph measures a person's heart and breathing rate, as well as the electrical resistance of the skin (called galvanic skin response), to determine whether he or she is giving truthful verbal responses.

Nonverbal Communication Plays a Major Role in Interpersonal Relationships

As we learned in Chapter 1, you cannot *not* communicate; one researcher suggests that as much as 65 percent of the social meaning in our messages is based upon nonverbal communication.[5] Of course, the meaning that others interpret from your behavior may not be the one you intended, and the inferences they draw based on nonverbal information may be right or wrong.

We learned in Chapter 3 that we begin making judgments about strangers just a fraction of a second after meeting them, based upon nonverbal information. Within the first four minutes of interaction we scope the other out and draw conclusions about him or her.[6] Another research team found that you may decide whether a date is going to be pleasant or dull during the first thirty seconds of meeting your partner, before your partner has had time to utter more than "Hello."[7] Nonverbal cues are the ones that form first impressions, accurate or not.

Portrait artists play close attention to nonverbal cues such as posture, facial expression, and gesture to capture their subjects' personalities. What do the nonverbal cues reveal about this Spanish dancer? (John Singer Sargeant, "Belle Epoque." Erich Lessing/Art Resource)

Nonverbal cues are important not only when we initiate relationships, but also as we maintain and develop mature relationships with others. In fact, the more intimate the relationship, the more we use and understand the nonverbal cues of our partners. Long-married couples spend less time verbalizing their feelings and emotions to each other than they did when they were first dating; each learns how to interpret the other's subtle nonverbal cues. If your spouse is silent during dinner, you may know that the day was a tough one, and you should give her a wide berth. And if, when you put on your new kelly green pants, your husband grimaces as he asks, "New pants?" you may understand that he does not love them. In fact, all of us are more likely to use nonverbal cues to convey negative messages than to explicitly announce our dislike of something or someone. We also use nonverbal cues to signal changes in the level of satisfaction with a relationship. When we want to cool things off, we may start using a less vibrant tone of voice and cut back on eye contact and physical contact with our partner.

Judee Burgoon and her colleagues have concluded that nonverbal cues play a key role in how we adapt to others.[8] If, for example, your friend leans forward to tell a story, you may reciprocally lean forward to listen. Or, if during a meeting you sit with folded arms, unconvinced of what you are hearing, you look around the conference table and find others with similarly folded arms. Like an intricate dance, when we communicate, we relate to others by responding to movement, eye contact, gestures, and other nonverbal cues to relate to others. Sometimes we relate by mirroring the posture or behavior of others. Or we may find ourselves gesturing in sync with someone's vocal pattern. The rhythm of life is often conveyed as we respond and adapt to others through our nonverbal behavior.

Although we rely heavily on nonverbal messages, they do not operate independently of spoken messages in our relationships. Instead, verbal and nonverbal cues work together in two primary ways to help us make sense of others' messages.

First, nonverbal cues substitute for, repeat, contradict, or regulate verbal messages. An extended thumb signals that a hitchhiker would like a ride. A circle formed by the thumb and index finger can either signal that everything is A-OK or convey an obscene message. When someone asks, "Which way did he go?" we can silently point to the back door. In these instances, we are substituting nonverbal cues for a verbal message.

We can also use nonverbal cues to repeat or reinforce our words. "Where is the personnel department?" asks a job applicant. "Three flights up. Take the elevator," says the security guard, pointing to the elevator. The guard's pointing gesture repeats her verbal instruction and clarifies the message.

"Sure, this is a good time to talk about the Henrikson merger," says the business executive, nervously looking at her watch, stuffing papers into her attaché case, and avoiding eye contact with her coworker. In this instance, the nonverbal cues contradict the verbal ones. And as we learned earlier, the nonverbal message is almost always the one we believe.

We also use nonverbal cues to regulate our participation in verbal exchanges. In most informal meetings it is not appropriate or necessary to signal your desire

INSTRUCTIONAL GOALS AND TIPS
This is also the ASL sign for the letter "F."

to speak by raising your hand. Yet somehow you are able to signal to others when you'd like to speak and when you'd rather not talk. How does this happen? You use eye contact, raised eyebrows, an open mouth, or perhaps a single raised index finger to signal that you would like to make a point. If your colleagues do not see these signals, especially the eye contact, they know you are not interested in talking.[9]

The second way in which nonverbal cues work together with verbal ones is in accenting and complementing emotional messages. "Unless we vote to increase our tax base," bellows Mr. Coddlington, "we will not have enough classroom space to educate our children." While delivering his impassioned plea to the school board, Mr. Coddlington also loudly slaps the lectern to accent his message and reinforce its intensity. A scolding mother's wagging finger and an angry supervisor's raised voice are other nonverbal cues that accent verbal messages.

Complementary nonverbal messages that we deliver simultaneously with a verbal message can also help to color the emotion we are expressing or the attitude we are conveying. The length of a hug while you tell your son you are proud of him provides additional information about the intensity of your pride. The firmness of your handshake when you greet a job interviewer can confirm your verbal claim that you are eager for employment.

RECAP   Reasons to Study Nonverbal Communication

1. Nonverbal communication is the primary way in which we communicate feelings and attitudes toward others.

2. Nonverbal messages are usually more believable than verbal messages.

3. Nonverbal communication plays a major role in relationship development.

   - Nonverbal cues substitute for, repeat, contradict, or regulate verbal messages.

   - Nonverbal cues accent and complement emotional messages.

The Challenge of Interpreting Nonverbal Messages

Even though we have made great claims for the value of studying nonverbal behaviors, it is not always easy to decipher unspoken messages. We have dictionaries to help us interpret words, but we have no handy reference book to help us decode nonverbal cues. To help you with the decoding process, we are going to attempt to classify some common types of nonverbal behaviors. But first, you should be aware of some of the difficulties inherent in attempting a classification.

7 COMMUNICATING NONVERBALLY

217

INSTRUCTIONAL GOALS AND TIPS
Consider asking students to play a round of the game "Charades." This is a popular class participation exercise, which can also fulfill an individual presentation assignment in this course.

DISCUSSION AND WRITING
Ask students to brainstorm with you possible ways to write a love letter. Consider such writing implements as crayon, blood, laser ink, purple marker, etc. Next, consider types of paper (e.g., card stock and construction paper) and penmanship (written, printed, typed, etc.). Nonverbal communication serves to accent and complement emotional messages.

To illustrate the ambiguity of nonverbal communication, point out nonverbal behaviors of students in the classroom and ask the class whether we can state that these behaviors "mean" what the research in the text says they often imply. Examples of behaviors to cite and corresponding questions to ask might include:

a. all students folding their arms across their bodies
"Are all of these people 'cold' in personality or might they be physically cold?"

b. all students demonstrating a backward lean in their chairs
"Are all of these people uninterested in class?"
"Are these people more dominant or of higher status than are the rest of us?"

c. all students commanding more space relative to the class norms
"Are these people powerful?"

INSTRUCTIONAL GOALS AND TIPS

Ask students to freeze their bodies and to become aware of their posture and body placement. What nonverbal messages are they conveying to others?

TEACHING STRATEGY

Tap the insights of students who hail from other national cultures by asking them to give examples of cross-cultural discrepencies in nonverbal communication behaviors. Students born of different geographic regions within the United States often notice dissimilarities as well.

Nonverbal Messages Are Often Ambiguous

Most words carry a meaning that everyone who speaks the same language can recognize. But the meaning of nonverbal messages may be known only to the person displaying them. Perhaps even more importantly, that person may not intend for the behavior to have any meaning at all. And some people have difficulty expressing their emotions nonverbally. They may have a frozen facial expression or a monotone voice. Or they may be teasing you, but their deadpan expressions lead you to believe that their negative comments are heartfelt. Often it is tough to draw meaningful conclusions about another person's behavior, even if we know him or her quite well.

Nonverbal Messages Are Continuous

Words are discrete entities; they have a beginning and an end. You can point to the first word in this sentence and underline the last one. Our nonverbal behaviors are not as easily dissected. Like the sweep of a second hand on a watch, nonverbal behaviors are continuous. Some, such as a slap or a hand clap, have definite beginnings and endings. But more often than not, your nonverbal behavior unfolds without clearly defined starting and stopping points. Gestures, facial expressions, and even eye contact can flow from one situation to the next with seamless ease. Researchers have difficulty studying nonverbal cues because of this continuous stream, so trying to categorize and interpret them will be challenging for us as well.

Nonverbal Cues Are Multichanneled

Have you ever tried to watch two or more TV programs at once? Some televisions let you see as many as eight programs simultaneously so that you can keep up with three ball games and two soap operas and view commercials on the three other channels. Like the multichannel TV, nonverbal cues come to our perception center from a variety of sources simultaneously. And just as you can really watch only one channel at a time on your multichannel television—although you can move among them very rapidly—so too can you actually attend to only one nonverbal cue at a time. One researcher suspects that negative nonverbal messages (frowns, grimaces, lack of eye contact) command attention before positive messages when the two compete.[10] Moreover, if the nonverbal message contradicts the verbal message, then we may have trouble interpreting either one correctly.[11]

Nonverbal Interpretation Is Culture Based

There is some evidence that humans from every culture smile when they are happy and frown when they are unhappy.[12] We also all raise or flash our eyebrows when meeting or greeting others, and young children in many cultures wave to signal they want their mothers, raise their arms to be picked up, and

UNDERSTANDING DIVERSITY

Cultural Differences in Interpreting Nonverbal Messages

Research investigating nonverbal communication in a variety of cultures confirms that individuals interpret nonverbal messages from their unique cultural perspective. Note the following conclusions:[13]

FACIAL EXPRESSIONS One research team found that some facial expressions such as happiness, sadness, anger, disgust, and surprise were the same in 68 to 92 percent of the cultures examined. All humans probably share the same neurophysiological basis for expressing emotions, but we learn different rules for sending and interpreting the expressions. For example, the Japanese culture does not reinforce the show of negative emotions; it is important for Japanese to "save face" and to help others save face as well.

EYE CONTACT There seems to be more eye contact in interpersonal interactions between Arabs, South Americans, and Greeks than between people from other cultures. There is evidence that some African Americans look at others less than do whites when sending and receiving messages. One of the most universal expressions among cultures appears to be the eyebrow flash (the sudden raising of the eyebrows when meeting someone or interacting with others).

GESTURES Hand and body gestures with the most shared meaning among Africans, North Americans, and South Americans include pointing, shrugging, head nodding, clapping, thumbs down, waving hello, and beckoning. There are, however, regional variations within cultures; it is not wise to assume that all people in a given culture

share the same meaning for certain gestures. The "okay" gesture made by forming a circle with the thumb and finger has sexual connotations for some South American and Caribbean countries. In France the okay sign means worthless.

SPACE Arabs, Latin Americans, and Southern Europeans seem to stand closer to others than people from Asia, India, Pakistan, and Northern Europe. If you have been to Britain you know that people queue or wait for buses in orderly straight lines. In France, however, queuing is less orderly, and individuals are more likely to push forward to be the next customer or get the next seat on the bus. As with gestures, however, there are regional variations in spatial preferences.

suck their thumbs for comfort.[14] All this suggests that there is some underlying basis for expressing emotion. Yet each culture may develop unique rules for displaying and interpreting these gestures and expressions.

There is no common cross-cultural dictionary of nonverbal meaning. Consider the case of the Muslim woman who was arrested in St. Paul, Minnesota, by suspicious policemen, when she strolled through a downtown skywalk. Her crime? She was wearing a veil. Revealing her face in public would violate her religious beliefs. If you grew up in a Seattle suburb, you might be startled when on a visit to New Orleans you stumble upon a handkerchief-waving, dancing, exuberantly singing crowd, and discover that it is an African-American jazz funeral. What to the uninformed may seem like disrespect for the dead, others recognize as a joyous send-off to a better world. An American tourist in Russia might be puzzled to hear an audience break out in synchronized rhythmic hand clapping to express its appreciation of an act at the Moscow Circus.

7 COMMUNICATING NONVERBALLY

219

Nonverbal Communication Codes

Keeping all of these challenges to our understanding in mind, we can begin looking at the categories of nonverbal information that researchers have studied: movement and gestures, eye contact, facial expressions, use of space and territory, touch, and personal appearance.[15] Although we will concentrate on the codes that fall within these categories in mainstream Western culture, we will also look at codes for other cultures and subcultures.

Body Movement, Posture, and Gestures

In 1771, when English explorer Captain Cook arrived in the New Hebrides, he didn't speak the language of the natives. His only way of communicating was sign language. Through gestures, pointing, and hand waving, he established contact with the natives. There is evidence that people have used gestures to communicate since ancient times—especially to bridge cultural and language differences. The first record of using sign language to communicate is found in Xenophon's *The March Up Country*, in which unspoken gestures were used to help the Greeks cross Asia Minor in about 400 B.C. Even when we do speak the same language as others, we use gestures to help us make our point.[16]

Kinesics is the study of human movement and gesture. It was Francis Bacon who noted, "As the tongue speaketh to the ear, so the hand speaketh to the eye." We have long recognized that the movement and gestures we exhibit provide valuable information to others. Various scholars and researchers have proposed paradigms for analyzing and coding these movements and gestures, as we do for spoken or written language.[17]

One paradigm identifies four stages of "quasi-courtship behavior."[18] The first stage is *courtship readiness*. When we are attracted to someone, we may suck in our stomach, tense our muscles, and stand up straight. The second stage includes *preening behaviors*: We

Can you identify the quasi-courtship behavior in this painting?

Printed by permission of the Norman Rockwell Family Trust. Copyright © *Soda Jerk*, The Norman Rockwell Family Trust.

manipulate our appearance by combing our hair, applying makeup, straightening our tie, pulling up our socks, and double-checking our appearance in the mirror. In stage three we demonstrate *positional cues*, using our posture and body orientation to be seen and noticed by others.

One researcher recently found fifty-two gestures and nonverbal behaviors that women use to signal an interest in men. Among the top unspoken flirting cues were: smiling and surveying a crowded room with the eyes, and moving closer to the object of our affection.[19] We intensify these cues in the fourth stage, *appeals to invitation*, using close proximity, exposed skin, open body positions, and eye contact to signal our availability and interest. The classic Norman Rockwell painting at left shows teenagers illustrating typical appeals to initiation. Subjects in one study reported that they were aware of using all these techniques to promote an intimate relationship. In fact we use these quasi-courtship behaviors to some extent in almost any situation in which we are trying to gain favorable attention from another.

Another team of researchers focused on nonverbal behaviors that make us label a person warm and friendly or cold and distant.[20] They found that "warm" people face their communication partners directly, smile more, make more direct eye contact, fidget less, and generally make fewer unnecessary hand movements. "Cold" people make less eye contact, smile less, fidget more, and turn away from their partners.

Posture and body orientation reveal important information. Open body posture (uncrossed arms and legs) communicates that we are receptive and responsive listeners. When we are trying to decrease our contact with someone, say at a party or family gathering, we are likely to turn away from the individual we want to avoid. As you will find when you participate in Building Your Skills: Communicating Interest, your body orientation and posture provide important cues as to your interest and willingness to continue or end communication with someone.

Albert Mehrabian has identified the nonverbal cues that contribute to perceptions of liking.[21] He found that an open body and arm position, a forward lean, and a more relaxed posture communicate liking. When we are attempting to persuade someone, we typically have more eye contact and a more direct body orientation; we are more likely to lean forward and closer to others.

Ekman and Friesen classified movement and gestures according to their function. They identified five categories: emblems, illustrators, affect displays, regulators, and adaptors.[22]

■ EMBLEMS

Nonverbal cues that have specific, generally understood meanings in a given culture and may actually substitute for a word or phrase are called **emblems**. When you are busy typing a report that is due tomorrow and your young son bounces in to ask for permission to buy a new computer game, you turn from your computer and hold up an open palm to indicate your desire for uninterrupted quiet. To communicate your enthusiastic enjoyment of a violin soloist at a concert, you applaud wildly. You want your children to stop talking in the library, so you put an index finger up to your pursed lips.

7 COMMUNICATING NONVERBALLY

DISCUSSION AND WRITING
Athletes in your class might enjoy discussing referees' signals. Musicians and vocalists can speak of conductors' and choral directors' emblems.

SKILL DEVELOPMENT
Using this Building Your
Skills box, ask students to
provide feedback to one another as a perception check.

BUILDING YOUR SKILLS

Communicating Interest

Nonverbally play the roles of both a good listener and a bad listener. First, imagine that you are listening to some-one talk. As a good listener, how would you communicate your interest in what the person is saying without uttering a word? Note your posture, eye contact, presence or lack of hand move-ment. Are your arms and legs crossed?

Now roleplay a poor listener—someone who appears to be bored or even irritated by what a speaker is saying. What are the differences in the cues you use? Use the space below or write your responses on a sheet of paper to describe the differences.

Nonverbal Behaviors of a Good Listener	Nonverbal Behaviors of a Poor Listener
Posture: _____	Posture: _____
_____	_____
_____	_____
Body Orientation: _____	Body Orientation: _____
_____	_____
_____	_____
Eye Contact: _____	Eye Contact: _____
_____	_____
_____	_____
Gestures: _____	Gestures: _____
_____	_____
_____	_____
Movement: _____	Movement: _____
_____	_____
_____	_____

■ ILLUSTRATORS

We frequently accompany a verbal message with **illustrators** that either contradict, accent, or complement the message. Slamming a book closed while announcing, "I don't want to read this anymore" or pounding a lectern while proclaiming, "This point is important!" are two examples of nonverbal behav-iors that accent the verbal message. Typically, we use nonverbal illustrators at the beginning of clauses or phrases.[23] TV newscasters, for example, turn a page to signal that they are moving to a new story or topic. Most of us use illustra-tors to help us communicate information about the size, shape, and spatial rela-tionships of objects. You probably even use them when you talk on the phone, although probably not as many as you use in face-to-face conversation.[24]

■ AFFECT DISPLAYS

Nonverbal movements and postures used to communicate emotion are called **affect displays**. As early as 1872, when Charles Darwin systematically studied the expression of emotion in both humans and animals,[25] we recognized that nonverbal cues are the primary ways we communicate emotion. Our facial

DISCUSSION AND WRITING
Ask students to write about
and then discuss their per-
ceptions of a "poker face."
In the movie *Maverick*, Bret
Maverick talks of telltale
signs made by card players.
Discuss these.

expressions, vocal cues, posture, and gestures convey the intensity of our emotions.[26] If you are happy, for example, your face will telegraph your joy to others. The movement of your hands, the openness of your posture, and the speed with which you move will tell others *how* happy you are. Similarly, if you are feeling depressed, your face will probably reveal your sadness or dejection, while your slumped shoulders and lowered head will indicate the intensity of your despair. When we are feeling friendly, we use a soft tone of voice, an open smile, and a relaxed posture.[27] When we feel neutral about an issue, we signal it by putting little expression on our face or in our voice. When we feel hostile, we use a harsh voice, frown with our teeth showing, and keep our posture tense and rigid.

■ REGULATORS

We use **regulators** to control the interaction or flow of communication between ourselves and another person. When we are eager to respond to a message, we make eye contact, raise our eyebrows, open our mouth, raise an index finger, and lean forward slightly. When we do not want to be part of the conversation, we do the opposite: we avert our eyes, close our mouth, cross our arms, and lean back in our seats or away from the verbal action.

■ ADAPTORS

When we are cold, we reach for a sweater or wrap our arms around our chests to keep warm. When it's 102 degrees Fahrenheit in the shade without a breeze, we reach for a fan to make our own breeze. These behaviors are examples of **adaptors**—nonverbal behaviors that help us to satisfy a personal need and adapt to the immediate situation. When you adjust your glasses, scratch a mosquito bite, or comb your hair, you are using movement to help you manage your personal needs.

■ THE FIVE CATEGORIES AND INTERPERSONAL COMMUNICATION

How will understanding these five categories of nonverbal behavior help you understand interpersonal communication? They give you a new and more precise way to think about your own behavior. By noting how often you use emblems instead of words to communicate a message, you can recognize how important emblems are in your relationships with others. The more you rely on emblems that have unique meanings for you and your partner, the more intimate the interpersonal relationship. Also start to notice whether your nonverbal behavior contradicts what you say. Monitoring your use of illustrators can help you determine whether you are sending mixed signals to others. Be aware of how you display affect. Knowing that your face and voice communicate emotion, and that posture and gesture indicate the intensity of your feelings, can help you understand how others make inferences about your feelings and attitudes. If other people have difficulty interpreting your emotional state, you may not be projecting your feelings nonverbally. And finally, notice how you use adaptors. Individu-

Consider this: Marriage counselors advise couples to hold hands while discussing contentious issues. Suggest this tip to students and ask them to report the results.

TEACHING STRATEGY
Ask students to help you brainstorm a master list of rules pertaining to nonverbal behavior.

a. "Never raise your hand to ask a question during the last three minutes of class time." (regulators: movement and gestures)
b. "If the instructor asks for a volunteer, lower your head and stare at your desk." (regulators: movement, gestures, and posture)
c. "If you win first runner-up in a competition, smile and pretend to be happy that someone else won." (affect displays: facial expression)

Students do not seem to tire of the classic, breaking nonverbal rules activity. Give your students ten minutes to leave the classroom and break nonverbal rules. When they return, have them report on: the rule violation they performed, the response they received from the recipient of the violation, and any interesting implications of their experiment.

INTERNET RESOURCE
Pupil Dilation
http://www.nfobbs.com/
txt2/1478.ufo
Investigates pupil dilation
as a function of conversation, thought, and talk
activities.

www.opt.indiana.edu/vily/
HomePage/Pupil_Abnormal/
2Pupil-Abnormal.
This site contains several
links describing the relationship between tensions,
feelings, and pupil dilation.
In addition, one link de-
scribes pupil dilation in relation to feelings and
nonverbal communication
between men and women.

**INSTRUCTIONAL GOALS
AND TIPS**
As you discuss this area
with students, refrain from
making any eye contact
with them. Look at the
clock, at your notes, and at
students' feet. Still, without
looking, ask them to pro-
vide you with feedback. (If
they didn't notice, you're
not making enough contact
normally!)

als who do not learn the cultural norms of displaying adaptors can have a difficult time socially. For example, if you were never taught not to comb your hair
or belch at the table, you may find you receive few dinner invitations.

Since nonverbal cues are ambiguous, it's not a good idea to use them to
achieve a specific objective. But as you have seen, people are more likely
to respond in predictable ways if you use behaviors they can recognize and
interpret easily.

RECAP Categories of Movement and Gestures

Category	Definition	Examples
Emblems	Behaviors that have specific, generally understood meaning.	A hitchhiker's raised thumb.
Illustrators	Cues that accompany verbal messages and provide meaning for the message.	A public speaker's pounding the podium to emphasize a point.
Affect Displays	Expressions of emotion.	Hugging someone to express love.
Regulators	Cues that control and manage the flow of communication between others.	Looking at someone when you wish to speak.
Adaptors	Behaviors that help you adapt to your environment.	Scratching, combing your hair.

Eye Contact

Subtle power. Whether you choose to look at someone or avert your gaze has
an enormous impact on your relationship with that person. Kendon has identified four functions for eye contact in interpersonal interactions.[28]

First, it serves a *cognitive* function because it gives you information about
another person's thought processes. For example, if your partner breaks eye
contact after you ask him or her a question, you will know that he or she is
probably thinking of something to say.

Second, we use eye contact to *monitor* the behavior of others. We receive a
major portion of the information we obtain through our eyes. We look at others
to determine whether they are receptive to our messages. In fact, this search for
feedback is implicit in the word for the center part of the eye, pupil, which
comes from the Latin word *pupilla* or "little doll." When you look into someone's eyes, you can see a miniature reflection of yourself.[29]

Third, eye contact is one of the most powerful *regulatory* cues we use to
signal when we want to talk and when we don't want to communicate. Your
authors have noticed that when they ask questions such as, "Who can tell me
the four functions of eye contact?" students quickly yet unobtrusively avert their
eyes to signal, "Don't call on me." When we do want to communicate with
others, say when we're standing in line at the bakery, we fix our eyes on the
clerk to signal, "My turn next. Please wait on me."

Finally, the area around our eyes serves an *expressive* function. The eyes have been called the "mirror of the soul" because they reveal our emotions to others. We may cry, blink, and widen or narrow our gaze to express our feelings.

What are the reasons we look or don't look at others? The following list from nonverbal communication scholar Mark Knapp provides some insight.[30]

You are most likely to look at your partner when you:

- are physically distant from him or her

- are discussing easy, impersonal topics

- have nothing else to look at

- are interested in your partner's reactions—that is, you are interpersonally involved

- are interested in your partner—that is, like or love your partner

- are trying to dominate or influence your partner

- are from a culture that emphasizes visual contact in interaction

- are an extrovert

- have high affiliative or inclusion needs

- are dependent on your partner (and the partner has been unresponsive)

- are listening rather than talking

- are female

You are less likely to look at your partner when you:

- are physically close

- are discussing difficult, intimate topics

- have other relevant objects, people, or backgrounds to look at

- are not interested in your partner's reactions

- are talking rather than listening

- are not interested in your partner—that is, you dislike him or her

- are from a culture that imposes sanctions on visual contact during interaction

- are an introvert

- are low on affiliative or inclusion needs

- have a mental disorder like autism, schizophrenia, or the like

- are embarrassed, ashamed, sorrowful, sad, submissive, or trying to hide something

When we do establish eye contact with others, it may seem that our gaze is constant. Yet research suggests that we actually spend the majority of our time looking at something other than the person's eyes. One research team found that we focus on something else, including our partner's mouth, 57 percent of the time.[31] Not surprisingly then, facial expressions are another rich source of information in our communication with others.

RECAP	Functions of Eye Contact
COGNITIVE FUNCTION	Provides cues about our thinking and thought processes.
MONITORING FUNCTION	Provides information about how others are responding to us; we monitor to seek feedback.
REGULATORY FUNCTION	Manages the flow of communication; we use eye contact to signal when we do and do not want to interact with another person.
EXPRESSIVE FUNCTION	Provides information about feelings, emotions, and attitudes.

Facial Expressions

You tell your parents that you will not be able to spend the holidays with them because you have decided to take your children skiing. You present your fiancée with a new abstract art painting that you would like to hang in your bedroom after you are married. As the personnel director reviews your résumé, you sit in silence across from her desk. In each of these situations you would be eagerly awaiting some reaction from your partner. And what you would be scanning is his or her face. The face is the exhibit gallery for our emotional displays. And although we often try to manipulate our facial cues to project a premeditated feeling, our faces may still betray our true emotions to others.[32]

To interpret our partner's facial expressions accurately, we need to put our other-orientation skills to work, focusing on what the other person may be thinking or feeling. It helps if we know the person well, can see his or her whole face, have plenty of time to watch it, and understand the situation that prompted the emotion.[33] But it is also helpful to know the cues for "reading" facial expressions.

Your face is versatile. According to Ekman and Friesen, it is capable of producing over 250,000 different expressions.[34] Research suggests that women have greater variety in their emotional expressions and spend more time smiling than men.[35] But all of our expressions can be grouped under six primary emotional categories; the following list describes the changes that occur on our faces for each one.[36]

Surprise: Wide-open eyes; raised and wrinkled brow; open mouth.

**Japanese Turn
E-mail "Smiley Faces"
Right Side Up**

TOKYO—When Yukihiro Furuse first began prowling international computer networks in the mid-1980s, he was perplexed to encounter emoticons, the strange combinations of punctuation and accent marks and letters that Westerners used in electronic mail to indicate happiness, sadness and other emotions.

But when Furuse and other network pioneers tried to incorporate symbols such as :-) into their domestic e-mail, their Japanese correspondents found the Western smiley—dare we say it—inscrutable.

"We had to write many times, 'If you tilt your head, you will see the face,'" said Furuse, who is director of the publications department at the Center

for Global Communications, a research institute affiliated with International University of Japan.

So in the latest example of Japan seizing upon a Western idea, adapting it to their culture and improving upon it, Japanese computer users have evolved a unique set of emoticons. The Japanese smileys are intricate in their design, somewhat ambiguous in their expression and, in what many here would argue is a

big advance, are right side up instead of sideways.

The basic smiley in Japan, (^_^), is much easier to recognize as a face than the Western version, but since the mouth doesn't curl upward (no character on the keyboard can do that), the Japanese smiley is somewhat harder to understand without knowing the context.

Andrew Pollack, The New York Times

Japanese emoticons

Regular smile:	(^_^) (caret underscore caret)
Girl's smile:	(^.^) (caret . caret)
Banzai smiley:	\(^_^)/ backslash (caret underscore caret) /
Cold sweat:	(^^;) (caret caret ;)
Excuse me:	(^o^;>) (caret o caret ; greater than symbol)
Double-byte smiley:	(^__^) (caret long underscore caret)
Exciting:	(*^o*^) (asterisk caret o caret asterisk)

Facial Expression Quiz

Divide into teams of two people. Person A should select one of the six primary emotions communicated by the face and attempt to display the emotion to person B. The six primary emotions are happiness, sadness, surprise, disgust, anger,

and fear. Communicate all six emotions *in random order.*

Person B should attempt to identify the emotions expressed by person A and list them in order below.

When person A has communicated all six emotions, he or she can reverse roles with person B.

1. _____
2. _____
3. _____
4. _____
5. _____
6. _____

SKILL DEVELOPMENT
This exercise lends itself naturally to class interaction. This exercise can be easily adapted to illustrate our ability to accurately decode paralanguage. Have students stand back-to-back and have them say something neutral such as, "Hi, how are you today?" Each time they say the phrase, they should communicate an emotional state. Students are often amazed to discover how much of the emotional content of a message is carried by nonverbals in general, and facial expressions and paralinguistic cues in specific.

Fear: Open mouth; tense skin under the eyes; wrinkles in the center of the forehead.

Disgust: Raised or curled upper lip; wrinkled nose; raised cheeks; lowered brow; lowered upper eyelid.

Anger: Tensed lower eyelid; either pursed lips or open mouth; lowered and wrinkled brow; staring eyes.

Happiness: Smiling; mouth may be open or closed; raised cheeks; wrinkles around lower eyelids.

Sadness: Lip may tremble; corners of the lips turn downward; corners of the upper eyelid may be raised.

You are undoubtedly familiar with emoticons, the computer "smiley faces" and other combinations of keyboard characters designed to communicate facial expression via e-mail. As Electronic Connections: Japanese Turn E-mail "Smiley Faces" Right-Side Up shows, the Japanese have adapted the use of emoticons to express emotions appropriate for their culture.

How accurately do we interpret emotions expressed on the face? Several studies have attempted to measure subjects' skill in identifying emotional expressions of others. They have found that reading facial expression is a tricky business. According to Eckman and Friesen, even though our faces provide a great deal of information about emotions, we have learned how to control our facial expressions.[37] In addition, our facial expressions also seem to be contagious. One researcher who showed his subjects video clips of President Reagan giving speeches discovered that they were likely to smile when Reagan smiled and frown when Reagan appeared angry or threatening.[38]

The face is an exhibit gallery for our emotions. The messages we convey through thousands of different expressions are usually more powerful and direct than verbal ones. (Bob Daemmrich/Stock Boston)

INTERPERSONAL COMMUNICATION SKILLS

Vocal Cues

Try this. Say "John" to communicate the following emotions: anger, sadness, disgust, happiness, fear, surprise. If you are reading this in a public place, stop reading for a moment and give it a try even if you have to whisper. What happened to your voice? Like your face, your voice is a major vehicle for communicating your emotions. The pitch, rate, and volume at which we speak, and our use of silence, all provide important clues to our feelings.

Your voice is a primary tool for communicating information about the nature of relationships between you and others.[39] We use our voices to present one message on the surface (with words) and usually a more accurate expression of our feelings with our vocal quality. Say the following sentence out loud: "This looks great." Now say it sarcastically; you really don't think it looks great: "This looks great." Clearly, your vocal cues provide the real meaning.

Some vocal expressions of emotion are easier to identify than others. Expressions of joy and anger are obvious ones, whereas shame and love are the most difficult emotions to identify based on vocal cues alone.[40] We are also likely to confuse fear with nervousness, love with sadness, and pride with satisfaction. As an example of how the intonation of a single word can convey rich meaning, read the excerpt below from *A Lesson Before Dying*. In this story, a black schoolteacher is collecting money to buy a radio for a black man unfairly condemned to death by a white jury in Louisiana in the late 1940s.

I ate the food hungrily because I had not had dinner, and I sopped up the gravy with the light bread. Thelma watched me all the time. When I was finished, she put a wrinkled ten-dollar bill on the counter by my plate.

"Here."

It was the kind of "here" your mother or your big sister or your great-aunt or your grandmother would have said. It was the kind of "here" that let you know this was hard-earned money but, also, that you needed it more than she did, and the kind of "here" that said she wished you had it and didn't have to borrow it from her, but since you did not have it, and she did, then "here" it was, with a kind of love. It was the kind of "here" that asked the question, "When will all this end? When will a man not have to struggle to have money to get what he needs 'here'? When will a man be able to live without having to kill another man 'here'?"

I took the money without looking at her. I didn't say thanks. I knew she didn't want to hear it.

—ERNEST J. GAINES,
A Lesson Before Dying

Our voices also provide information about our self-confidence and our knowledge of the subject matter in our messages. Most of us would conclude

Ask several students to play the role of observer during this exercise. Request that they observe whether men or women are better at accurately identifying emotions. Following the exercise, ask the observers to discuss their observations.

INTERNET RESOURCE
Paralanguage
http://www.byu.edu/tmcbucs/arts-ed/9–12/c2.ab/para.html
This is an experimental study on paralanguage and related concepts.

http://www2.gol.com/users/rsdavis/cyberlab/para.html
This site offers many samples of paralanguage.

DISCUSSION AND WRITING
Write the following statement on the board: I DIDN'T SHARE A BED WITH YOUR SISTER. Next, ask six students to take turns reading this statement aloud. Have each punctuate a different word in the statement. Paraphrase the statement to prove that, "It's not what you say, but how you say it."

DISCUSSION AND WRITING
Invite a discussion of the social meanings of silence during a first date. Show some funny scenes from the movie *Annie Hall*, which depict this.

INSTRUCTIONAL GOALS AND TIPS
Assign students the task of monitoring their use of positive silences in their personal relationships.

that a speaker who mumbles, speaks slowly, consistently mispronounces words, and uses "uhs" and "ums" is less credible and persuasive than one who speaks clearly, rapidly, and fluently.[41] Even though mispronunciations and vocalized pauses ("ums" and "ahs") seem to have a negative effect on credibility, they do not seem to be a major impediment to attitude change. People may, for example, think that you are less knowledgeable if you stammer, but you may still be able to get your persuasive message across.

In addition to providing information about emotions, self-confidence, and knowledge, vocal cues also serve a regulatory function in interpersonal situations, signaling when we want to talk and when we don't. When we are finished talking, we may lower the pitch of our final word. When we want to talk, we may start by interjecting sounds such as "I . . . I . . . I . . ." or "Ah . . . Ah . . . Ah . . ." to interrupt the speaker and grab the verbal ball. We also may use more cues such as, "Sure," "I understand," "Uh-huh," or "Okay" to signal that we understand the message of the other person and now we want to talk or end the conversation. These *back channel* cues are particularly useful in telephone conversations when we have no other nonverbal cues to help us signal that we would like to get off the phone.

Sometimes it is not what we say, or even how we say it, that communicates our feelings. Being silent may communicate volumes. One researcher, in commenting about the importance of silence in speech, said: "Silence is to speech as white paper is to this print. . . . The entire system of spoken language would fail without [people's] ability to both tolerate and create sign sequences of silence-sound-silence units."[42]

Why are we sometimes at a loss for words? There are many possible reasons. We may simply not know what to say. Or, there is evidence that when someone tells a lie, he or she may need a few moments to think of a credible ruse. We may be silent because we want to distance ourselves from those who are around us; we want to communicate that we really don't want to be involved in the conversation. Or perhaps we just need some time to think about what we want to contribute to the conversation. Silence, too, may be a sign of respect. Some children were raised with the message, Be seen and not heard. They were taught that those in authority should maintain control of the talking process. At other times you are silent with someone because words would diminish the experience you are sharing. Walking hand-in-hand on the beach, watching the sun set, or sitting on a balcony overlooking a spectacular mountain vista may call for silence; trying to translate the experience into words would diminish it.

Would you be comfortable just sitting silently with a good friend? Sidney Baker's theory of silence suggests that the more at ease we are when we share a silence with a close friend, the more comfortable we are with just being together and enjoying each other's companionship. People need to talk until there is nothing left to say; the uncertainty has been managed. In most long-term relationships, partners may not feel a need to fill the air with sound. Just being together to enjoy each other's company may be most fulfilling. Baker calls such moments "positive silence."[43]

Personal Space

Imagine that you are sitting alone in a booth at your local pizza parlor. As you sit munching your thin-and-crispy pepperoni pizza, you are startled when a complete stranger sits down in your booth directly across from you. With several empty tables and booths in the restaurant, you feel very uncomfortable that this unknown individual has invaded "your" area.

Normally, we do not think much about the rules we observe regarding personal space, but in fact every culture has fairly rigid ways of regulating space in social interactions. Violations of these rules can be alarming and, as in the preceding scenario, even threatening. How close we are willing to get to others relates to how well we know them and to considerations of power and status.

One of the pioneers in helping us understand the silent language of personal space was Edward T. Hall. His study of **proxemics** investigated how close or how far away we arrange ourselves around people and things.[44] Hall identified four spatial zones that we unconsciously define for ourselves, as shown in Figure 7.1. When we are between zero and one-and-one-half feet from someone, we are occupying **intimate** space. This is the zone in which the most intimate interpersonal communication occurs. It is open only to those with whom we are well acquainted, unless we are forced to stand in an elevator, a fast-food line, or some other crowded space.

The second zone, which ranges from one-and-one-half to four feet, is called **personal space**. Most of our conversations with family and friends occur in this zone. If someone we don't know well invades this space on purpose, we may feel uncomfortable.

Zone three, called **social space**, ranges from four to twelve feet. Most group interaction, as well as many of our professional relationships, take place in this zone. The interaction tends to be more formal than that in the first two zones.

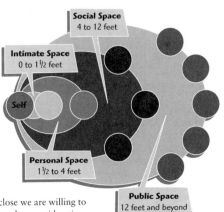

Figure 7.1

Edwin T. Hall's Four Zones of Space

RECAP	Edward T. Hall's Classification of Spatial Zones	
	Definition	**Examples**
ZONE ONE	Intimate space	Zero to one-and-one-half feet
ZONE TWO	Personal space	One-and-one-half to four feet
ZONE THREE	Social space	Four to twelve feet
ZONE FOUR	Public space	Twelve feet and beyond

INTERNET RESOURCE
Proxemics
http://www.unm.edu/
~yimou/proxemics.htm
This site describes different cultures and the distances they stand away from other people.

SKILL DEVELOPMENT
Ask two students to come to the front of the room. (It's most interesting to select a tall man and a petite woman for this exercise.) Instruct the audience to observe the kinesthetic behavior of the two as they walk toward one another. Have the audience applaud the actors and discuss their nonverbal behaviors as they approached one another's intimate space.

DISCUSSION AND WRITING
Ask students to compare their personal space in the classroom with yours. Discuss how space is used to send messages of status and power. If you have time, ask students to move into small groups and discuss implicit rules of elevator etiquette.

Public space, the fourth zone, begins at twelve feet. Interpersonal communication does not usually occur in this zone, and many public speakers and teachers position themselves even more than twelve feet from their audience.

The specific space that you and others choose depends upon several variables.[45] The more you like someone, the closer you will stand. We allow individuals with high status to surround themselves with more space than we allow for people with lower status. Large people also usually have more space around them than smaller ones, and women stand closer to others than men do.[46] All of us tend to stand closer to others in a large room than we do in a small room.

In a group, who's in charge, who's important, and who talks to whom are reflected by the spatial arrangement we self-select. The more dominant group members tend to select seats at the head of a table, while shyer individuals often select a corner seat at a rectangular table.[47]

Territory

Territoriality is the study of how animals use space and objects to communicate occupancy or ownership of space. You assumed "ownership" of the booth in the pizza parlor and the accompanying "right" to determine who sat with you, because you and your pizza were occupying the booth. In addition to invading your personal space, the intrusive stranger broke the rules that govern territoriality.

We announce our ownership of space with territorial markers—things which signify that the area has been claimed—much as explorers once planted a flag claiming uncharted land for the king. When you are studying at the library, for example, and need to hop up and check a reference at the computerized card catalog, you might leave behind a notebook or a pencil. In rural areas, landowners post signs at the borders of their property to keep hunters off their territory. Signs, locks, electronic security systems, and other devices secure our home and office territories.

We also use markers to indicate where our space stops and someone else's starts. "Good fences make good neighbors," wrote the poet Robert Frost. When someone sits too close, we may try to erect a physical barrier, such as a stack of books or a napkin holder, or we might use our body as a shield by turning away. If the intruder does not get the hint that "this land is our land," we ultimately resort to words to announce that the space is occupied.

Touch

Standing elbow to elbow in a crowded elevator, you may find yourself in physical contact with total strangers. As you stiffen your body and avert your eyes, a baffling sense of shame floods over you. If you are sitting at a conference table and you accidentally brush the toes of your shoes against your colleague's ankle, you may jerk away and even blush or apologize. Why do we react this way to unpremeditated touching? Normally, we touch to express intimacy. When intimacy is not our intended message, we instinctively react to modify the impression.

INTERPERSONAL COMMUNICATION SKILLS

DISCUSSION AND WRITING
Ask students to justify their seat selection in this classroom. Do they select the same seat for each session of class? Are they creatures of habit when they park their car at the shopping mall? For those who have a sleeping partner, do they sleep on the same side of the bed each night? Why?

INTERNET RESOURCE
Haptics
http://haptic.mech.nwu.edu/
An excellent starting point for research dealing with haptics.

Countless studies have shown that intimate touching is vital to our personal development and well-being.[48] Infants and children need it to confirm that they are valued and loved. Many hospitals invite volunteers in to hold and rock newborns whose mothers cannot do it themselves. Advocates of breastfeeding argue that the intimate touching it entails strengthens the bond between mother and child.[49]

The amount of touch we need, tolerate, receive, and initiate depends upon many factors. The amount and kind of touching you receive in your family is one big influence. If your mom or dad greets you with hugs, caresses, and kisses, then you probably do this to others. If your family is less demonstrative, you may be restrained yourself. Studies by Nancy Henley show that most of us are more likely to touch people when we are feeling friendly, or happy, or under other specific circumstances:[50]

- when we ask someone to do something for us

- when we share rather than ask for information

- when we try to persuade someone to do something

- when we are talking about intimate topics

- when we are in social settings that we choose rather than in professional settings that are part of our job

- when we are thrilled and excited to share good news

- when we listen to a troubled or worried friend

Appearance

In all of our interactions with others, appearance counts. American culture places a high value upon how much we weigh, the style of our hair, and the clothes we wear; these things are particularly important in the early stages of relationship development. Attractive females have an easier time persuading others than do those who are perceived as less attractive. In general, we think attractive people are more credible, happier, more popular, more sociable, and even more prosperous than less attractive people.[51]

In Chapter 2 we discussed the link between our self-concept and personal appearance. The shape and size of your body also affects how others perceive you. Heavier and rounder individuals are often perceived to be older, more old-fashioned, less good-looking, more talkative, and more good-natured than thin people, who are perceived to be more ambitious, more suspicious of others, more uptight and tense, more negative, and less talkative. Muscular and athletically fit folks are seen as better looking, taller, and more adventurous. These perceptions are, in fact, so common that they have become easily recognizable stereotypes on which casting directors for movies, TV shows, and plays rely in selecting actors and actresses.

Aside from keeping us warm and within the legal bounds of decency, our clothes also affect how others perceive us. One classic study found that a man who jaywalked while dressed in nice clothes attracted more fellow violators than he could when he was shabbily attired.[52] Although studies have attempted to identify a "power" look and magazines are constantly giving us prescriptions for ways to be attractive and stylish, the fact is that there is no formula for dressing for success.[53] Styles and expectations about appearances change. We have only to look at the clothing norms of the 1950s, 1960s, or 1970s to note how they are different from those of today.

RECAP	Codes of Nonverbal Communication
MOVEMENTS AND GESTURES	Communicate information, status, warmth, credibility, interest in others, attitudes, liking.
EYE CONTACT	Serves cognitive, monitoring, regulatory, and expressive functions.
FACIAL EXPRESSIONS	Express emotions.
VOCAL CUES	Communicate emotion through pitch, rate, volume, and quality, and modify the meaning of messages.
PERSONAL SPACE	Provides information about status, power, and intimacy.
TERRITORY	Provides cues to use, ownership, or occupancy of space.
TOUCH	Communicates intimacy, affection, or rejection.
APPEARANCE	Influences perceptions of credibility and attraction.

Interpreting Nonverbal Communication

So what does it all mean? How do we make sense out of the postures, movements, gestures, eye contact, facial expressions, uses of space and territory, touch, and appearance of others? Albert Mehrabian has found that we synthesize and interpret nonverbal cues along three primary dimensions: *immediacy*, *arousal*, and *dominance*.[54] These three dimensions provide a useful way to summarize how nonverbal cues may be interpreted.

Immediacy

Sometimes we are not able to put our finger on the precise reason we find a person likable or unlikable. Mehrabian believes that **immediacy** cues are a likely explanation. Immediacy cues are behaviors that communicate liking and engen-

Gender Differences and Nonverbal Communication

There is evidence that men and women display and interpret nonverbal cues differently.[55]

EYE CONTACT:	Women usually have a more prolonged gaze with others than do men. Women, however, are less likely to just stare at someone; they break eye contact more frequently than men. In general, women receive more eye contact from others than do men.
SPACE:	Men tend to have more space around them than do women. Women both approach and are approached more closely than men. And when conversing with others, women seem to prefer side-by-side interactions.
FACIAL EXPRESSION:	Research suggests that women smile more than men. It is also reported that women tend to be more emotionally expressive with their faces than men; this is perhaps related to the conclusion that women are more skilled at both sending and interpreting facial expressions.
GESTURE AND POSTURE:	Overall, women appear to use fewer and less expansive gestures than men. Women are more likely, for example, to rest their hands on the arms of a chair while seated; men are more likely to use gestures. Men and women cross their legs differently: women cross their legs at the knees or ankles while men are more likely to sit with their legs apart.
TOUCH:	Men are more likely to initiate touch with others than are women. Women are touched more than men. Men and women also attribute different meaning to touch; women are more likely to associate touch with warmth and expressiveness than are men.
VOCAL CUES:	Vocal patterns may be more related to biological differences in the vocal register than other nonverbal behaviors. Women speak in both higher and softer tones than do men. Women also use their voice to communicate a greater range of emotions than do men. Women are also more likely to raise their pitch when making statements; some people interpret the rising pattern (as in asking a question) as an indication of greater uncertainty.

der feelings of pleasure. The principle underlying immediacy is simple: we move toward persons and things we like and avoid or move away from those we dislike. Immediacy cues increase our sensory awareness of others.

Our use of space and territory is not the only cue that contributes to positive or negative feelings. Mehrabian has noted several other nonverbal cues that increase immediacy. One of the most powerful is touch; others include a forward lean, increased eye contact, and an open body orientation. The meaning of these behaviors is usually implied rather than explicitly spelled out in words.

To increase students' interest in observing their own nonverbal behaviors, ask them to consciously alter one of their nonverbal behaviors for the rest of the day, noting differences in reactions they receive from others.

ACTIVITY

See Activity 7.2 in the Instructor's Guide.

In brief, to communicate that we like someone, we use these cues:[56]

Proximity:	Close, forward lean
Body Orientation:	Direct, but could be side-by-side
Eye Contact:	Eye contact and mutual eye contact
Facial Expression:	Smiling
Gestures:	Head nods, movement
Posture:	Open, arms oriented toward others
Touch:	Cultural- and context-appropriate touch
Voice:	Higher pitch, upward pitch

Arousal

The face, voice, and movement are primary indicators of **arousal**. If we see arousal cues, we conclude that another person is responsive to and interested in us. If the person acts passive or dull, we conclude that he or she is uninterested.

When you approach someone and ask whether he or she has a minute or two to talk, that person may signal interest with a change in facial expression and more animated vocal cues. People who are aroused and interested in you show animation in their face, voice, and gestures. Forward lean, a flash of the eyebrows, and a nod of the head are other cues that implicitly communicate arousal. Someone who says, "Sure, I have time to talk with you," in a monotone and with a flat, expressionless face is communicating the opposite. Think of arousal as an on-off switch. Sleeping is the ultimate switched-off state.

Dominance

The third dimension of Mehrabian's framework for implicit cues communicates the balance of power in a relationship. **Dominance** cues communicate status, position, and importance. A person of high status tends to have a relaxed body posture when interacting with a person of lower status.[57] When you talk to a professor, she may lean back in her chair, put her feet on the desk, and fold her hands behind her head during the conversation. But unless your professor is a colleague or a friend, you will maintain a relatively formal posture during your interaction in her office.

Another dominance cue is the use of space. High-status individuals usually have more space around them; they have bigger offices and more "barriers" protecting them. A receptionist in an office is usually easily accessible, but to reach the president of the company you may have to navigate through several corridors, past several secretaries and administrative assistants who are "guarding" the door.

Other power cues that communicate feelings of dominance include our use of furniture, clothing, and locations. You study at a table in the library; the college president has a large private desk. You may wear jeans and a T-shirt to class; the head of the university wears a business suit. Your dorm may be surrounded by other dorms; the president's residence may be a large house surrounded by a lush, landscaped garden in a prestigious neighborhood. We use space, territory, posture, and artifacts such as clothing and furniture to signal feelings of dominance or submissiveness in the presence of others.

Michael Argyle summarizes the nonverbal cues that communicate dominance:[58]

Use of Space:	Height (on a platform or standing) Facing a group More space
Eye Contact:	More when initially establishing dominance More when staring to establish power More when talking
Face:	No smile, frown, mature adult features
Touch:	Initiating touch
Voice:	Loud, low pitch, greater pitch range Slow, more interruptions, more talk Slight hesitation before speaking
Gesture:	Pointing at the other or at his or her property
Posture:	Standing, hands on hips, expanded chest, more relaxed

RECAP **Dimensions for Interpreting Nonverbal Behavior**

Dimension	Definition	Nonverbal Cues
Immediacy	Cues that communicate liking and pleasure.	Eye contact, touch, forward lean, close distances.
Arousal	Cues that communicate active interest and emotional involvement.	Eye contact, varied vocal cues, animated facial expressions, forward lean, movement.
Dominance	Cues that communicate status and power.	Protected space, relaxed posture, status symbols.

Improving Your Ability to Interpret Nonverbal Messages

As we have already cautioned, there are no universal dictionaries to which we can turn for help in interpreting specific nonverbal behaviors. There are some principles and key skills, however, that we can use to enhance our interpretive ability.

7 COMMUNICATING NONVERBALLY

237

DISCUSSION AND WRITING

Fold your arms across your chest and ask students to decode this message. Consider possible answers:

- defensive or angry
- hiding a missing button
- cold or tired
- nervous or uncomfortable
- comfortable
- sick

ACTIVITY

See Activity 7.3 in the Instructor's Guide.

INSTRUCTIONAL GOALS AND TIPS

Do model this listening skill whenever possible. Many of your students' movements are not intended to be a message for you. Clarify which ones *are* meant for you. At the end of a class session observe, "I see that many of you are gathering your books. Are you hoping that I'll stop talking so that you may leave or are you concerned about being tidy?" Mention that they are demonstrating "leave-taking behavior."

Consider Nonverbal Cues in Context

Just as quoting an expert out of context can change the meaning of a statement, trying to draw conclusions from an isolated snatch of behavior or a single cue can lead to misinterpretations. Beware of looking at someone's folded arms and concluding that he or she does not like you or is not interested in what you are saying. It could be that the air conditioner is set too low and the person is just trying to keep warm.

Look for Clusters of Nonverbal Cues

Instead of focusing on a specific cue, look for corroborating cues that can lead you to a more accurate conclusion about the meaning of a behavior. Is the person making eye contact? Is he or she facing you? How far away is he or she standing from you?

Always consider nonverbal behaviors in conjunction with other nonverbal cues, the environment, and the person's verbal message.

Consider Past Experiences When Interpreting Nonverbal Cues

Familiarity may breed contempt, but it also increases our ability to interpret another's nonverbal behavior. You may have learned, for example, that when your mother started crying when you played the piano, it meant she was proud of you, not melancholy. Family members can probably interpret one another's nonverbal cues more accurately than can those from outside the family. But after knowing someone over a period of time, you begin to increase your sensitivity to certain glances, silences, movements, and vocal cues that might be overlooked or misunderstood by others.

Check Your Perceptions with Others

You judge others by their behavior, not by their intent. The only way to know what people intend is to ask them whether you have interpreted their behavior correctly. But before you blurt out a hunch, first consider the context and confirming cues; think about this person's previous behavior. Then, if you are still confused or uncertain about the meaning of a behavior, ask for clarification.

For example, if you receive a tremendous job offer that requires you to move to a new state, and your spouse greets your enthusiastic announcement with silence, you could ask, "Does your silence mean that you're opposed to the move, or are you speechless with excitement?" Then wait for a response.

Or suppose you work in the kitchen all day to make fish stew for your friend from Iowa. After her first bite you see her eyes open wide and her lips purse up. So you ask, "Does that mean you don't like it, or did you taste something new and different?"

This key skill is called **perception checking**. As we saw in Chapter 3, you can follow three steps to check someone's perception. First, observe the nonverbal cues, making a point to note such variables as amount of eye contact, posture, use of gestures, facial expression, and tone of voice. Second, try to interpret what the individual is expressing through his or her nonverbal behavior. Finally, check your perception by asking him or her if it is accurate. Of course, we are not suggesting that you need to go through life constantly checking everyone's nonverbal cues. Overusing this skill would be irritating to most people. We are suggesting, however, that when you are uncertain of how someone feels, and it is important to know, a perception check may be in order. Consider this example:

Deonna: Hi Mom. I'm sorry Erik and I missed the family reunion last week. It's been a hectic week. The kids had something goin' on every night and we just needed to rest.

Muriel: (Frowns, has little eye contact, folds her arms, and uses a flat voice.) Oh, don't worry about it.

Deonna: I know you said don't worry about it, Mom, but it looks like you are still upset. I know that look of yours. I also hear in your voice that you are not really pleased. Is it really OK, or are you still a little miffed?

Muriel: Well, yes, to be honest, Dad and I were really looking forward to getting all of the kids together.

Deonna: I'm sorry, Mom. We will make an effort to be at the next one. Thanks for sharing with me how you really felt.

Addressing your question to a specific nonverbal cue will help you interpret your partner's behavior in future interactions as well. As we noted earlier, evidence suggests that the longer couples are married, the more they rely upon nonverbal behavior to communicate. One study claims that most couples spend less than eleven minutes a week in sustained conversation.[59] Even in marriages of fifty years, however, conversation is still required occasionally to clarify nonverbal responses.

RECAP	How to Check Your Perceptions of Others' Nonverbal Cues
Steps	**Consider**
1. Observe their nonverbal behavior.	Are they frowning? Do they have eye contact? Are their arms crossed? What is their tone of voice? What is their posture?
2. Form a mental impression of what you think they mean.	Are they happy, sad, angry? Is the nonverbal message contradicting the verbal message?
3. Ask to check whether your perception is accurate.	"Are you upset? You look angry." "Your expression and your voice suggest you don't believe me. Do you think I'm lying?" "The look on your face tells me you really like it. Do you?"

INSTRUCTIONAL GOALS AND TIPS

Toward the end of the session, you might discuss chronemics (the study of time). Ask students how long they would be willing to wait for class to start. Discuss how long they'd be willing to stay in class. Suggest that you'll teach for another 15 minutes (at no additional charge!) if they'd like it. This is often a fun way to end the session.

SKILL DEVELOPMENT

Once students have completed this activity and you are confident in their ability to successfully formulate a perception-checking message, send students out on campus in pairs. Instruct the pairs to find opportunities to check perceptions of individuals they encounter. For example, students might see someone in the library who is quickly scanning a hefty pile of notes. One student should approach, apologize for the brief interruption, and offer the perception check, "You seem very busy with your notes, are you cramming for an exam?" Have each person in the team continue to engage others until they are satisfied that they have succeeded in accurately and effectively wording a perception check. Upon returning to class, solicit examples of the perception checks that were attempted.

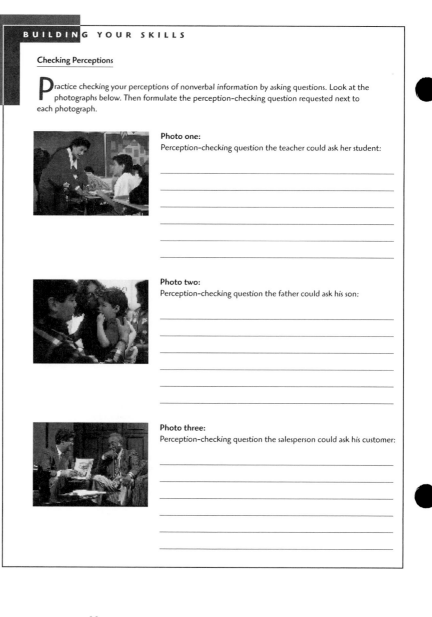

Checking Perceptions

Practice checking your perceptions of nonverbal information by asking questions. Look at the photographs below. Then formulate the perception-checking question requested next to each photograph.

Photo one:
Perception-checking question the teacher could ask her student:

_____

_____

_____

_____

_____

Photo two:
Perception-checking question the father could ask his son:

_____

_____

_____

_____

_____

Photo three:
Perception-checking question the salesperson could ask his customer:

_____

_____

_____

_____

_____

Summary

Unspoken messages have a major effect on interpersonal relationships. The primary way in which you communicate feelings, emotions, and attitudes is through nonverbal cues. When there is a contradiction between your
verbal and nonverbal messages, others almost always believe the nonverbal
one. But nonverbal messages are usually more ambiguous than verbal
messages. While some nonverbal messages have a definite beginning and
ending, most are part of a seamless flow of movement, gestures, glances, and
inflections. Also, there are culture-based differences in the way we learn and
interpret unspoken messages.

Nonverbal cues can be categorized and studied to reveal the codes to our
unspoken communication. Movement, posture, and gestures communicate
both content and expressive information when we use them as emblems,
illustrators, affect displays, regulators, and adaptors. Eye contact is an important code for regulating interaction in interpersonal exchanges. Facial expressions and vocal cues provide a wealth of information about our emotions.
Our use of personal space and territory communicates a variety of messages
relating to power, status, and other relational concerns. Touch is one of the
most powerful cues to communicate liking; and our appearance telegraphs to
others how we wish to be treated and how we perceive our role in relation
to them.

One of the prime fascinations with nonverbal messages is the potential to
understand hidden meaning communicated through unspoken codes. It is difficult to read nonverbal cues as easily as reading the words on this page, but
there is a general framework that can help you assess the nonverbal messages
of others, as well as your own nonverbal expressions. Researchers have identified three primary dimensions for interpreting nonverbal messages: Immediacy
cues provide information about liking and disliking. Arousal cues tip others off
as to our interest and level of engagement with them; and position, power, and
status are often communicated through dominance cues.

To enhance your skill in interpreting nonverbal messages, always consider
the context in which you observed the cues and look for clusters of nonverbal
behaviors. The longer you have known someone, the easier it is to interpret his
or her unspoken messages. But in order to verify whether you understand
someone's nonverbal behavior, you should ask whether your interpretation is
accurate.

FOCUS ON
COMPREHENSION

1. Nonverbal communication is nonlinguistic (involving neither written nor spoken language) behavior that creates meaning for someone.

2. Nonverbal communication is important to study for three reasons:

- It is the primary way we communicate feelings and attitudes toward others;

- These messages are usually more believable than verbal messages; and

- It plays a major role in interpersonal relationships.

3. Nonverbal emblems, illustrators, affect displays, regulators, and adapters are categories of movement and gestures which create meaning. They are particularly useful to emphasize, punctuate, and represent feelings and attitudes.

4. The nonverbal communication codes discussed in this chapter include kinesics (body movement, posture, gestures, eye contact, and facial expression), vocal cues, personal space and territory, touch, and appearance.

5. We synthesize and interpret nonverbal cues along three primary dimensions: immediacy (the degree of liking); arousal (the degree of interest and responsiveness); and dominance (the degree of power and status).

For Discussion and Review

FOCUS ON COMPREHENSION

1. What is nonverbal communication?

2. Why is it important to study nonverbal communication?

3. Describe nonverbal emblems, illustrators, affect displays, regulators, and adaptors.

4. What are the nonverbal communication codes presented in this chapter?

5. What are the nonverbal cues that communicate immediacy, arousal, and power?

FOCUS ON CRITICAL THINKING

6. Sasha has had difficulty getting hired as a manager. One of her best friends suggested that she pay more attention to her nonverbal behavior when she is interviewed for a job. What advice would you give Sasha to ensure that she monitors her nonverbal interview behavior?

7. Greg has been told that he sometimes comes across as cold, aloof, and stand-offish. What could Greg do to communicate his sincere desire to be interpersonally warm and approachable?

FOCUS ON ETHICS

8. Donald really wants to be hired as a salesperson. He hires a fashion consultant to recommend what he should wear and determine how he should look when he interviews for a job. In general, is it ethical to manipulate your appearance so that you can impress others?

9. Is it appropriate to draw definitive conclusions about another's personality and attitudes based only upon a "reading" of his or her other nonverbal cues? Support your answer.

10. Is it ethical for salespersons, politicians, and others who wish to make favorable impressions to alter their nonverbal messages to get you to like them, vote for them, or buy their products? Explain your answer.

1. Videotape fifteen minutes of a TV drama or situation comedy. View the program with the sound turned off. Using the four principles of interpreting nonverbal messages, describe the meaning of the nonverbal messages you watch. After you have made written observations in your journal, view the program with full sound and determine how accurate your interpretations were.

2. Mehrabian has suggested that we convey 55 percent of our emotional meaning through facial expressions, 38 percent through vocal cues, and only 7 percent through verbal statements. Spend thirty minutes observing four or five people in a public place, such as a mall, airport, or student center, and attempt to prove or disprove Mehrabian's conclusions. Before you begin your people watching, design a method for recording your observations in your journal.

Learning with Others

1. Go on a nonverbal communication scavenger hunt. Your instructor will ask you to observe your family members and friends to find one or more of the following sets of nonverbal communicators:

   A. Examples of emblems, illustrators, affect displays, regulators, and adaptors.

   B. Examples of how people use the four zones of personal space.

   C. Examples of pleasure, arousal, and dominance.

   D. Examples of the cognitive, monitoring, regulatory, and expressive functions of eye contact.

   E. Examples of clothing that reveals intentions or personality traits.

2. Divide into groups of three or four people. Use the following evaluation form to evaluate a room or public space. Each person in your group should evaluate the same room. It could be your own room, a cafeteria, classroom, fast-food restaurant, or even a hotel lobby. Compare your answers with other group members. You could also give a report to the class on your results.

SKILL DEVELOPMENT
These are both terrific exercises. Assign one or both for opportunities to apply theory directly and immediately.

7 COMMUNICATING NONVERBALLY

3. Spend some time observing people in a public place, such as a restaurant, airport terminal, your student center, or bar, and write examples of quasi-courtship behavior as discussed in this chapter. List the four phases we described (courtship readiness, preening, positional cues, appeals to invitation) on a sheet of paper, and describe several examples to illustrate each of these phases.

Environment Analysis

Use the following guide to help you analyze a communication environment.

1. Briefly describe the environment you analyzed. Describe the size, furniture or other movable objects, predominant colors, lighting, sounds, decor.

2. Rate the room you observed using the following scales:

formal   __ __ __ __ __ __ __   informal

warm   __ __ __ __ __ __ __   cold

pleasant   __ __ __ __ __ __ __   unpleasant

useful   __ __ __ __ __ __ __   not useful

beautiful   __ __ __ __ __ __ __   ugly

3. Describe the probable effects the room design has upon communication interaction patterns (for example, does it encourage or discourage communication?).

_____

_____

_____

_____

4. Based on your observations, is the room appropriately designed for its intended use? Explain.

_____

_____

_____

_____

NONVERBAL COMMUNICATION: Behavior other than written or spoken language that creates meaning for someone.

KINESICS: Study of human movement and gestures.

EMBLEMS: Nonverbal cues that have specific, generally understood meanings in a given culture and may substitute for a word or phrase.

ILLUSTRATORS: Nonverbal behaviors that accompany a verbal message and either contradict, accent, or complement it.

AFFECT DISPLAY: Nonverbal behavior that communicates emotions.

REGULATORS: Nonverbal messages that help to control the interaction or level of communication between people.

ADAPTORS: Nonverbal behaviors that help satisfy a personal need and help a person adapt or respond to the immediate situation.

PROXEMICS: Study of how close or far away from people and objects we position ourselves.

INTIMATE SPACE: Zone of personal space most often used for very personal or intimate conversation, ranging from zero to eighteen inches.

PERSONAL SPACE: Zone of personal space most often used for conversation, ranging from one-and-one-half to four feet.

SOCIAL SPACE: Zone of personal space most often used for group discussion, ranging from four to twelve feet.

PUBLIC SPACE: Zone of personal space most often used by public speakers or one speaking to many people, ranging beyond twelve feet.

TERRITORIALITY: Study of how animals and humans use space and objects to communicate occupancy or ownership of space.

IMMEDIACY: Feelings of liking, pleasure, and closeness communicated by such nonverbal cues as eye contact, forward lean, touch, and open body orientation.

AROUSAL: Feelings of interest and excitement communicated by such nonverbal cues as vocal expression, facial expressions, and gestures.

DOMINANCE: Feelings of power, status, and control communicated by such nonverbal cues as a relaxed posture, greater personal space, and protected personal space.

PERCEPTION CHECK: Skill of asking someone whether your interpretation of his or her nonverbal behavior is accurate.

Conflict Management Skills

A fter studying this chapter, you should be able to:

1. Define conflict.

2. Compare and contrast three types of interpersonal conflict.

3. Identify commonly held myths about interpersonal conflict.

4. Describe differences between destructive and constructive approaches to managing conflict.

5. List and describe five stages of conflict.

6. Describe three types of conflict management styles.

7. Identify and use conflict management skills to help manage emotions, information, goals, and problems when attempting to resolve interpersonal differences.

■ WHAT IS CONFLICT?

■ TYPES OF CONFLICT

■ MYTHS ABOUT CONFLICT

■ CONFLICT IN OUR RELATIONSHIPS

■ UNDERSTANDING CONFLICT AS A PROCESS

■ CONFLICT MANAGEMENT STYLES

■ CONFLICT MANAGEMENT SKILLS

■ WHEN OTHERS AREN'T OTHER-ORIENTED: HOW TO BE ASSERTIVE

his house stinks," said Paolo, wrinkling up his nose. "It smells like day-old garbage."

"Take it out yourself. It's your job," said Anya, turning her back on him to scrub furiously at an imaginary morsel of food on a frying pan that was already polished clean.

"Hey, hey," said Paolo, holding up both hands in front of him, "I wasn't accusing you. I just said it smelled bad in here. Don't be so touchy."

"Oh, no? Well, you're always criticizing me. You think just because you have a big important job that you can come in here and say anything you like. And I come home from work feeling tired, too, you know, but you don't do anything to help, not even the things you agree to!" shouted Anya, turning around to confront her mate, planting her soapy hands on her hips.

"Well, you're always hocking me for no reason. I'm not putting up with this bad treatment from you anymore," snarled Paolo. As he turned on his heel to stalk out of the kitchen, Anya burst into tears.

Does this conflict have a ring of familiarity? Do you know why Paolo and Anya reached an impasse in their attempt to communicate? If you answered yes and then no, read on.

Eventually, all relationships experience conflict. Paolo and Anya's exchange is complicated, seething with conflicting goals and underlying resentments. How do we avoid the same kind of outcome in our own complicated exchanges?

Conflict management is not a single skill but a set of skills. But to manage conflict effectively involves more than learning simple techniques.

The best route to success in resolving conflict effectively is acquiring knowledge about what conflict is, what makes it happen, and what we can do about it. We will begin by defining conflict, then examine some of the myths about it and focus on some of its constructive functions. We will also discuss the relationship among conflict, power, and conflict management styles.

In addition, we will discuss how learning about our typical style of managing conflict can give us insight into managing interpersonal differences. And finally, we will build on the skills of listening and verbal and nonverbal communication that we discussed in the previous chapters, to help manage the inevitable interpersonal conflicts that arise in the best of relationships.

247

Explore Keltner's defini-
tions of these terms more
fully. Be prepared for questions from students about
the term *fight*.

Ask students to consider
how goals may be similar
but methods of achieving
them may differ. For in-
stance, if the shared goal is
to have a fun evening to-
gether, two people may
have very different ideas
about what constitutes
"fun." Discuss the impor-
tance of clear and descriptive language.

What Is Conflict?

Simply stated, **interpersonal conflict** is a struggle that occurs when two people cannot agree on a way to meet their needs. When the needs are incompatible, if there are too few resources to satisfy them, or if the individuals opt to compete rather than cooperate to achieve them, then conflict occurs. The intensity level of a conflict usually relates to the intensity of the unmet needs. Sam Keltner developed the "struggle spectrum," shown in Figure 8.1, to describe conflicts ranging from mild differences to fights.[1] But at the bedrock of all conflict are differences—different goals, experiences, genders, cultures, and other factors.

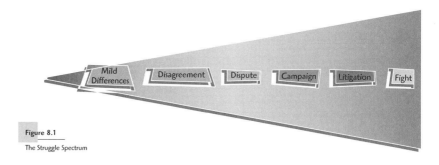

Figure 8.1

The Struggle Spectrum

Goals and Conflict

Psychologists agree that we are need-driven, goal-oriented individuals. Since most of what we do is based on achieving a desirable goal, it is not surprising that most conflict is goal driven. You want something; your partner wants something else. If your partner interferes with your achievement of your goal, there may be a fight.

Suppose you are trying to find a parking spot in a busy shopping center. Just as you find one, another shopper zips into "your" space. Your blood boils, and you get out of your car fighting mad. Or suppose you have had a difficult day at work. All you want to do is hunker down with a bowl of popcorn and watch MTV. But your spouse announces that a friend and his six-year-old son are coming over for dinner. "That's not what *I* feel like doing tonight. Why didn't you ask *me* before you invited them?" you shout. In both instances, your goals are colliding head on with someone else's, and you feel as if you have lost control of the situation.

Experiences and Conflict

Our inherent differences, coupled with our experiences, provide fuel for conflict. Consider the conflict that newlyweds Christy and Matt are having about how to celebrate the upcoming winter holidays. They have only two days to spend in their parents' town before returning to their new home in another city. Christy's family always exchanges presents and has a huge gathering on Christmas Eve and a family dinner on Christmas Day. Matt's family is Jewish. They celebrate Hanukkah quietly and do not feel comfortable trying to fit in at someone else's traditional celebration. Matt would like to celebrate Hanukkah at his parents' house, but Christy cannot understand why his family does not want to join her family's festivities. The conflict between Christy and Matt is not based upon different goals: they both want to see each set of parents and both want to celebrate the holidays. The conflict stems from their different backgrounds and experiences.

Types of Conflict

At some time or another, many close relationships go through a conflict phase. "We're always fighting," complains a newlywed. But if she were to analyze these fights, she would discover important differences among them. According to Miller and Steinberg, most conflicts fit into three different categories: (1) **pseudo conflict**—triggered by a lack of understanding; (2) **simple conflict**—stemming from different ideas, definitions, perceptions, or goals; and (3) **ego conflict**—which occurs when conflict gets personal.[2]

Gender and Conflict

Throughout our discussion of interpersonal relationships we have noted that men and women are often socialized to learn different ways of relating to others. Research suggests that women are more likely to focus on relationship issues, whereas men typically focus on tasks.[3] Women often interact with others to achieve intimacy and closeness, but men interact to get something done or to accomplish something apart from the relationship. Men are often more aggressive and assertive than women when pursuing a goal or conquest.[4] The following list summarizes key differences that researchers have observed between some men's and women's responses to conflict.

Perceived Gender Differences in Responding to Conflict[5]

Females	Males
Concerned with equity and caring; connect with and feel responsible to others.	Concerned with equality of rights and fairness; adhere to abstract principles, rules.
Interact to achieve closeness and interdependence.	Interact for instrumental purposes; seek autonomy and distance.
Attend to interpersonal dynamics to assess relationship's health.	Are less aware of interpersonal dynamics.
Encourage mutual involvement.	Protect self-interest.
Attribute crises to problems in the relationship.	Attribute crises to problems external to the relationship.
Are concerned with the impact of the relationship on personal identity.	Are neither self- nor relationship-centered.
Respond to conflict by often focusing mainly on the relationship.	Respond to conflict by often focusing on rules and being evasive until a unilateral decision is reached.

DISCUSSION AND WRITING
Ask students to comment upon these gender differences. How might age, socioeconomic, and partnership perspectives affect approaches to conflict?

Pseudo Conflict

Will: Meet me at the fountain.

Sean: No, that's too far. Meet me by the administration building.

Will: The fountain is closer and more convenient.

Sean: No it's not.

Will: Yes it is. It's just off Market Street.

Sean: Oh, you mean the fountain by the administration building.

Will: Sure, that's exactly what I mean.

Sean: Oh, no problem. That's the place I had in mind.

Although these findings provide a starting point for analyzing our conflicts with members of the opposite sex, we caution you against lapsing into "allness" statements such as, "Oh, you're just like all women. That's why you disagree with me." Or, "You're just like all men. You never want to focus on how I feel." Even thinking in these ways can prevent you from listening to what your partner is saying.

The most recent perspective on analyzing gender differences is called the *partnership perspective*. Rather than viewing gender differences as a gulf between people who live on different planets, this perspective suggests that men and women are not locked into particular styles or approaches.[5] The partnership approach emphasizes the importance of keeping channels open and avoiding the tendency to stereotype communication styles by gender.

Culture and Conflict

An individual's culturally learned assumptions influence his or her conflict behavior. In some cultures, most of the conflict is **expressive**; it focuses on the quality of relationships, and on managing interpersonal tension and hostility. In other cultures, conflict is more **instrumental**. It centers less on relationships and more on achieving a specific goal or objective.[6] One researcher noted that for people from low-context cultures, (those who derive more meaning from words than from the surrounding context), conflicts are most often instrumental.[7] Most North Americans come from low-context cultures. Many Asian cultures, on the other hand, are high-context cultures. They are also collectivist: they value group effort over individual achievement.[8] For people from these cultures, conflicts often center on expressive, rela-

tional concerns. Keeping peace in the group or saving face is often a higher priority than achieving a goal.

Managing culture-based conflict requires a strong other-orientation. One research team suggests that Anglo-Americans of European descent receive little training in how to develop solutions to problems that are acceptable to an entire group.[9] They are often socialized to stick up for their own rights at any cost, and they approach conflict as a win-lose situation. In contrast, people from collectivist cultures approach conflict management situations from a win-win perspective; it is important that both sides save face and avoid ridicule. Such differences in approaches provide a double challenge. In addition to disagreeing over the issue at hand, people from different cultures may also have different strategies for reaching agreement.

Pseudo means false or fake. Pseudo conflict occurs when we simply miss the meaning in a message. But unless we clear up the misunderstanding by asking for more information, a real conflict might ensue. Note that in this example, Will offers helpful information ("It's just off Market Street") and Sean checks it with feedback ("Oh, you mean the fountain by the administration building").

Listening well and testing your understanding of a message with questions and feedback can help you keep these kinds of conflicts from escalating.

Simple Conflict

Simple conflict stems from differences in ideas, definitions, perceptions, or goals. You want to go to Disney World for your vacation; your spouse wants to go to Washington, D.C. Your spouse wants to fly; you would rather take the train. You understand each other, but you disagree.

A key to unraveling a simple conflict is to keep the conversation focused on the issues at hand so that the expression of differences does not deteriorate into a battle focusing on personalities.

The following exchange between Mark and Nick illustrates a conflict over a simple difference of opinion; notice how both partners stick to the issues and figure out a way to resolve their differences.

Mark: I want to watch *The Simpsons* tonight. It's their Christmas show.

Nick: No way, man. I have to watch a documentary about textiles for my history class. It's an assignment.

Mark: But I've worked all weekend. I'm beat. The last thing I want to watch is some stuffy old documentary on the history of weaving.

Nick: Tell you what. Go ahead and watch *The Simpsons*. I'll videotape the documentary and watch it later. Deal?

Mark: Okay. Thanks. And I'll go grill some burgers so we can have supper together first.

This next exchange between Sue and Nadiya is a bumpier one. What starts as a simple conflict deteriorates into a series of personal attacks.

Nadiya: Sue, can I borrow your skirt? I have a date tonight. It would look great with my new jacket.

Sue: Sorry, Nadiya. I'm going to wear it tonight. I've got to give a presentation to the school board about our new mentor program.

Nadiya: In case you don't remember, when you brought it home you said I could borrow it anytime. Besides, you haven't paid back the twenty bucks I loaned you to buy it.

Sue: Yes, but I bought the skirt especially for this occasion.

Nadiya: Well, don't ask to borrow anything from me ever again. You're just plain selfish.

Sue: Oh, yeah? Well *you're* the one who hogs all the space in the refrigerator. Talk about someone who's selfish. If that's not the pot calling the kettle black!

Nadiya: All right, now that we're being honest about who hogs what, *you're* the one who monopolizes the bathroom in the morning.

And so it escalates. The original disagreement about the skirt is forgotten and egos become attacked and bruised.

Ego Conflict

As you can see from the preceding example, a personal attack puts your partner on the defensive, and many people behave according to the adage, "The best defense is a good offense." When you launch a personal attack, you are

"picking a fight." And as Sue and Nadiya's exchange illustrates, fights that begin as pseudo or simple conflicts can easily lapse into more vicious ego conflicts. Here's another example:

Michael: I don't think you should allow students to wear Halloween costumes to school. What can I do with a bunch of monsters and witches in P.E. class?

Anita: Well, all the parents are calling me up about it, and the kids are excited.

Michael: Is that how you make decisions? By responding to pressure from parents and kids?

Anita: You're just disagreeing with me because you wanted to be chair of this committee.

Michael: Not true! I just don't think *you* have the ability to chair it!

Note that as each person in the conflict becomes more defensive about his or her position, the issues become more tangled.

Remember Paolo and Anya's argument at the beginning of this chapter? It started with what was probably an offhand remark and escalated into a major argument because both participants began attacking each other and bringing up other sensitive issues instead of focusing on the original comment.

If you find yourself involved in ego conflict, try to refrain from hurling personal attacks and emotional epithets back and forth. Instead, take turns expressing your feelings without interrupting each other, then take time to cool off. It is difficult to use effective listening skills when your emotions are at a high pitch.

RECAP	Types of Conflict
PSEUDO CONFLICT	Individuals misunderstand each other.
SIMPLE CONFLICT	Individuals disagree over which action to pursue to achieve their goals.
EGO CONFLICT	Individuals feel personally attacked.

SKILL DEVELOPMENT
Ask students to develop role-plays which demonstrate different types of conflict and discuss ways to effectively manage each.

Myths About Conflict

Although not all conflict is destructive to our relationships, many cultures have taboos against displaying it in public. According to one researcher, many of us were raised with five **conflict myths** that contribute to our negative feelings about conflict.[10] As you read the following sections, you may shake your head and say, "That's not where I came from." In some American families, conflict is expressed openly and often. But even if your experience has been different, reading about these prevailing myths may help you understand your emotional responses to conflict or your partner's response when conflict occurs.

Myth 1: Conflict Can Always Be Avoided

"If you can't say anything nice, don't say anything at all." Many of us learned early in our lives that conflict is unnatural and that we should eliminate it from our conversations and relationships. Yet evidence suggests that conflict arises in virtually every relationship. Because each of us has a unique perspective on our world, it would be extraordinary for us *always* to see eye-to-eye with another person. Research suggests that contentment in marriage relates not to the amount of conflict, but to the way in which partners manage it.[11] Conflict is also a normal and productive part of interaction in group deliberations.[12] It is a myth that we should view conflict as inherently unproductive and something to be avoided. It happens, even in the best of relationships.

Myth 2: Conflict Always Occurs Because of Misunderstandings

"You just don't understand what my days are like. I need to go to sleep!" shouts Janice as she scoops up a pillow and blanket and stalks off to the living room. "Oh yeah? Well, you don't understand what will happen if I don't get this budget in!" responds Ron, who is hunched over the desk in their bedroom. It is clear that Ron and Janice are having a conflict. They have identified the cause of their problem as a lack of understanding between them, but in reality they *do* understand each other. Ron knows that Janice wants to sleep; Janice knows he wants to stay up and work. Their problem is that they disagree about whose goal is most important. Conflicts do sometimes flare up because of a lack of understanding or empathy for the other person, but there are times when individuals simply have different needs or goals. These differences, not lack of understanding, are the source of the conflict.

Myth 3: Conflict Is Always a Sign of a Poor Interpersonal Relationship

It is an oversimplification to assume that all conflict is rooted in underlying relational problems. Although it is true that constant bickering and sniping can be symptomatic of deeper problems, disagreements do not necessarily signal

|| INTERPERSONAL COMMUNICATION SKILLS

that the relationship is on the rocks. Overly polite, stilted conversation is more likely to signal a problem than are periodic disagreements. In fact, the free expression of honest disagreement is a hallmark of a healthy relationship.

Myth 4: Conflict Can Always Be Resolved

Consultants and corporate training experts often offer advice about how to eliminate conflict so that all will be well and harmony will prevail. Some people claim that with the application of a few skills and how-to techniques, conflicts can disappear, much like a stain from a shirt laundered with the right kind of detergent. This is simply not true. Not all differences can be resolved by listening harder or paraphrasing your partner's message. Some disagreements are so intense and the perceptions so fixed that individuals may have to agree to disagree and live with it.

Myth 5: Conflict Is Always Bad

It's a common fantasy to dream of eliminating all interpersonal conflict from our relationships. It would be bliss, we think, if we could live without disagreement, hassle, haggling, and tension. But conflict is a healthy component of our relationships. In fact, if a relationship is conflict-free, the individuals are probably not being honest with each other. Although it can be destructive, conflict can also help us identify issues that need further discussion and lead to negotiations that give us fresh insights into the relationship.

RECAP	Conflict Myths
MYTH 1:	Conflict can always be avoided.
MYTH 2:	Conflict always occurs because of a misunderstanding.
MYTH 3:	Conflict is always a sign of a poor interpersonal relationship.
MYTH 4:	Conflict can always be resolved.
MYTH 5:	Conflict is always bad.

Conflict in Our Relationships

Constructive Conflict

To construct something is to build or make something new. Characterized by greater cooperation in dealing with differences, **constructive** conflict helps build new insights and establishes new patterns in a relationship. The airing of differences can lead to a more satisfying relationship in the long run.

INSTRUCTIONAL GOALS AND TIPS
Ask students to consider the quotation by Eugene Debs: "Intelligent discontent is the mainspring of civilization."

Conflict can suggest which elements of a relationship need to change or be improved. Here's an example:

Jenni: You know, I'm so tired of talking about what we're going to buy, what we're going to eat, where we're going next weekend. It's been weeks since we've had a real conversation.

Rex: What do you mean? We talk all the time.

Jenni: Yes, but that's just the point. We talk about everyday concerns, nothing else.

Rex: I don't know what you want, Jenni. But let's get a baby-sitter and go have dinner tomorrow night so we can talk. If I can figure out what's bothering you, maybe I can do something about it.

Note that Rex recognizes the need for further dialogue about Jenni's complaint. He transforms the issue of disagreement into a topic for discussion and relational adjustment. If Jenni had not expressed her dissatisfaction, the issue might have assumed larger proportions.

A well-managed disagreement that includes sharing personal needs or revising goals can lead couples or friends to first examine and then repledge their commitment to one another. It can revitalize the relationship, enabling both people to view its elements from different perspectives, even if the information shared seems negative at first.

Destructive Conflict

Destructive conflict dismantles relationships without restoring them. If both individuals are dissatisfied with the outcome of the conflict, then it has been more destructive than constructive. The hallmark of destructive conflict is a lack

---

TEACHING STRATEGY

You can use the popular movie *The War of the Roses* to recap relational de-escalation stages and to illustrate destructive conflict, controlling conflict style, and aggressiveness. The movie is a humorous saga of the relational de-escalation of a married couple, the Roses, illustrated in continual, destructive conflict. Other favorites include:

- *Who's Afraid of Virginia Woolf?*
- *Scenes from a Mall*
- *Cat on a Hot Tin Roof*

of flexibility in responding to others.[13] Conflict can become destructive when people view their differences from a win–lose perspective, rather than looking for solutions that allow each individual to gain. If the combatants assume that one person will lose, the resulting competitive climate precludes cooperation and flexibility.

A rapidly spiraling conflict can be as destructive as a tornado churning through a trailer park. As with the conflict between Paolo and Anya at the beginning of this chapter, it may start over a seemingly small issue, but it increases in intensity as other issues and differences are brought into the discussion. Such destructive escalation reduces flexibility, blocks off options for managing differences, and makes a win–win solution more elusive. One way to minimize destructive conflict cycles is to understand the sequence of conflict-triggering causes so you can stop them at an early stage.

Understanding Conflict as a Process

Cathy was reading the Sunday paper, enjoying a second cup of coffee, and listening to her favorite classical music station. All seemed well. Suddenly, for no apparent reason, her roommate Barb brusquely stormed into the room and shouted, "I can't stand it anymore! We have to talk about who does what around here." Cathy was taken completely off guard. She had no idea her roommate was upset about the division of household chores. To her, this outburst seemed to come out of the blue; in reality, however, several events led up to it.

Most relational disagreements have a source, a beginning, a middle, an end, and an aftermath.[14] Let's find out how they function.

Source: Prior Conditions

The first phase in the conflict process is the one that sets the stage for disagreement; it begins when you become aware that there are differences between you and another person. The differences may stem from role expectations, perceptions, goals, or resources. In the previous example, Barb perceived that she and Cathy played different roles in caring for the household.

In interpersonal relationships, *many* potential sources of conflict may be smoldering below the surface. It may take some time before they flare up into overt conflict. Moreover, they may be compounded with other concerns, making them difficult to sort out.

Beginning: Frustration Awareness

At this stage, at least one of you becomes aware that the differences in the relationship are increasingly problematic. You may begin to engage in self-talk, noting that something is wrong and creating frustration. Perhaps you realize that you won't be able to achieve an important goal or that someone else has

INTERNET RESOURCE
Rejection
http://www.bcx.net/
hypnosis/rejectn.htm
This sight offers several explanations for a self-driven need for rejection, and considers a case of overweight people.

DISCUSSION AND WRITING
Michele Weiner-Davis, author of *Divorce Busting* (Simon & Schuster, 1992), asserts that "Having unreasonable expectations about marriage is high on the list of things that destroy otherwise healthy relationships." Ask students to write about their expectations and to share these with their spouses (or relationship partners).

Encourage students to refer
to the "Fighting Fairly" tips
box found on page 283 in
this chapter. Discuss these
suggestions.

INTERNET RESOURCE
Conflict Resolution and
Negotiation
www.gmu.edu/department/
icar/
This site provides a background on the Institute for
Conflict Analysis, which
deals with conflict intervention methods in community,
national, and international
settings.

INTERNET RESOURCE
www.martin.uidaho.edu
This is the Martin Institute
for Peace Studies and Conflict Resolution home page.
Case studies and research
on successful conflicts
abound here.

SKILL DEVELOPMENT
Hold a contest and offer a
reward to the top three entries for the best "Thanks
for the Fair Fight" card design and inscription.

resources you need to achieve it. Or you may become aware of differences in perceptions. Barb knew that Cathy's family always used weekends for relaxation. In Barb's family, on the other hand, everyone pitched in on weekends to get household chores done for the week. She may have recognized that difference, even as her frustration level rose.

Becoming aware of differences in perception does not always lead to increased frustration. But when the differences interfere with something you want to accomplish, then your frustration level rises. In Barb's case, she wanted to get the house clean so she could turn her attention to studying for a test she had the next day. Cathy's apparent indifference to helping Barb achieve that goal was a conflict trigger.

Middle: Active Conflict

When you bring your frustration to the attention of others, a conflict becomes an active, *expressed struggle*.[15] If frustrations remain only as thoughts, the conflict is passive, not active. Active conflict does not necessarily mean that the differences are expressed with shouting or emotional intensity. An expression of disagreement may be either verbal or nonverbal. Calmly asking someone to change an attitude or behavior to help you achieve your goal is a form of active conflict; so is kicking your brother under the table when he starts to reveal your secret to the rest of the family.

Cathy was not aware of the division of labor problem until Barb stormed into the room demanding a renegotiation of roles. Barb had been aware of her frustration for some time, yet had not acted on it. Many experts advocate that you do not wait until your frustration level escalates to peak intensity before you approach someone with your conflict. Bottled-up frustration tends to erupt like soda in a bottle that has just been shaken. Intense emotions can add to the difficulty of managing a conflict.

End: Resolution

When you begin to try to manage the conflict, it has progressed to the resolution stage. Of course, not all conflicts can be neatly resolved. Couples who divorce, business partners who dissolve their corporation, or roommates who go their separate ways have all found solutions, even though they may not be amicable.

After Barb's outburst, she and Cathy were able to reach a workable compromise about the division of their household labor. Cathy agreed to clean the house every other week; Barb promised not to expect her to do it on weekends.

Aftermath: Follow-Up

As Yogi Berra once said, "It ain't over 'til it's over." After a conflict has been resolved, the follow-up stage involves dealing with hurt feelings or managing simmering grudges, and checking with the other person to confirm that the

Analyzing Conflicts

Think about a recent conflict that you have had or are having with someone and trace its development through the stages of conflict escalation. Perhaps it is a conflict that hasn't yet been resolved. Plot the evolution of the conflict to its current state. If no resolution has occurred, consider some possible solutions. Share your analysis of your conflict with one of your classmates.

1. Prior conditions: What is the source of the conflict?

    _____
    _____
    _____
    _____

2. Frustration awareness: When did you become aware of the conflict?

    _____
    _____
    _____
    _____

3. Active conflict: When and why did the conflict become an active conflict?

    _____
    _____
    _____
    _____

4. Resolution: Is there a resolution? If so, what is it? If not, what are some ways the conflict could be managed?

    _____
    _____
    _____
    _____

5. Follow-up: Is the conflict over? Do you still harbor some resentment? If so, what are strategies to help you manage the resentment?

    _____
    _____
    _____
    _____

SKILL DEVELOPMENT

Having students share their answers to this exercise is particularly helpful if you can allow time in class for each diad to report their results. As an alternative to this assignment, or perhaps a graded paper, instruct students to interview a manager or teacher about a recent conflict. Have them lead the interview through the stages of conflict escalation, taking careful notes of the details. When the interview gets to steps four and five, students have the opportunity to demonstrate an understanding of the material in this chapter and others. In addition to being a "capstone" exercise for this chapter, students get to experiment with the consultant role during the interview when they investigate possible resolutions and follow-up strategies.

conflict has not retreated into the frustration awareness stage. As we noted in Chapter 1, interpersonal relationships operate as interactive processes rather than as linear, step-by-step functions. Conflict does progress in stages, but your resolutions can backslide unless you confirm your understanding of the issues with your partner.

The Friday after their discussion, Cathy proudly showed off a spotless apartment to Barb when she came home from class. Barb responded with a grin and a quick hug and privately resolved to get up early on Sunday morning so that she could go out to get Cathy pastries and the Sunday papers before she awoke. This kind of mutual thoughtfulness exemplifies a successful follow-up in a conflict.

RECAP	Understanding Conflict as a Process
PRIOR CONDITIONS STAGE	The stage is set for conflict because of differences in the individuals' actions or attitudes.
FRUSTRATION AWARENESS STAGE	One individual becomes aware that the differences are problematic and becomes frustrated and angry.
ACTIVE CONFLICT STAGE	The individuals communicate with each other about the differences; the conflict becomes an expressed struggle.
RESOLUTION STAGE	The individuals begin seeking ways to manage the conflict.
FOLLOW-UP STAGE	The individuals check with themselves and each other to monitor whether both are satisfied with the resolution.

Conflict Management Styles

What's your approach to managing interpersonal conflict: fight or flight? Do you tackle conflict head-on or seek ways to remove yourself from it? Most of us do not have a single way of dealing with differences, but we do have a tendency to manage conflict following patterns that we have used before. The pattern we choose depends on several factors: our personality, the individuals with whom we are in conflict, the time and place of the confrontation, and other situational factors. For example, if your boss gives you an order, you respond differently than if your spouse gives you an order. Virginia Satir, author of *Peoplemaking*, a popular book about family communication, suggests that we learn conflict response patterns early in life.[16]

Several researchers have attempted to identify the patterns or styles of conflict. One model distinguishes only two dimensions: (1) how concerned you are for others and (2) how concerned you are for yourself.[17] Another more widely accepted approach organizes conflict styles into three types: (1) non-confrontational (avoiding, withdrawing, being indirect); (2) confrontational (attempting to use power strategies to control or manipulate outcomes); and

INTERPERSONAL COMMUNICATION SKILLS

INSTRUCTIONAL GOALS AND TIPS
Reference Chapter 3 here and consider different communication styles (e.g., driver vs. amiable) for managing conflict.

ACTIVITY
See Activity 8.1 in the Instructor's Guide.

(3) cooperative (seeking a solution that both individuals will find acceptable).[18] Before you read the following sections, try the Communication Experience on page 262 to see what style you typically use in managing conflict.

Nonconfrontational Style

One approach to handling conflict is to back off, either avoiding the conflict or giving in to the other person. Placating, distracting, computing, withdrawing, and giving in are responses that typify a **nonconfrontational style**.

A *placating* response is an attempt to please; generally placaters are uncomfortable with negative emotions and may adopt this approach because they fear rejection if they rock the boat. Typically, they seek approval and try to avoid threats to their self-worth. Placaters never seem to get angry, are so controlled that they seem unresponsive to the intensity of the situation, quickly agree with others to avoid conflict, and try to avoid confrontation at all costs. They appear to be other-oriented, but in fact they are simply seeking self-protection. Satir describes them as "syrupy, martyrish, and bootlicking." In the following exchange, note Hillary's placating response to Leslie's complaint:

Leslie: Hillary, I'm not in agreement with you on the QCN merger. I think the merger should be called off.

Hillary: Okay. Whatever you think is best. I just want you to feel good about your decision.

Another nonconfrontational style that Satir identifies is *distracting*. Distracters attempt to change the subject and avoid conflict or stress, rather

MEDIA AND OUTSIDE RESOURCES
Show scenes from the film *Joy Luck Club,* in which a wife agrees to pay for cat bills and for half of an ice cream purchase to avoid conflict with her stingy husband. Discuss how this couple can demonstrate equality in more constructive ways.

COMMUNICATION EXPERIENCE

Identifying Your Conflict Management Style

Different people learn different ways of managing conflict. This exercise gives you an opportunity to increase your awareness of what strategies you use and how they compare with strategies of others.

1. With your classmates, form groups of six. Make sure you know the other members of the group; do not join a group of strangers.

2. Working by yourself, respond to the twenty-four state-ments under How You Act in Conflicts, below.

3. Still working by yourself, read the descriptions of the conflict styles on the Scoring portion of this exercise. Then make five slips of paper. Write the names of the other five members of your group on the slips of paper, one name to a slip.

4. On each slip of paper, iden-tify that person's conflict strategy.

5. After all group members are finished, pass out your slips of paper to the people whose names are on them. Each member of your group should end up with five slips of paper describing his or her conflict strategy.

6. Score your questionnaire, using the table that follows the discussion of conflict strategies. Rank the five conflict strategies from the one you use the most to the one you use the least.

7. After drawing names to see who goes first, ask one member to describe the results of his or her own self-assessment. Then ask him or her to read off the strategies on each of the five slips of paper. He or she should ask other group members what specific examples led to their conclusions, and group members should use the rules for constructive feedback. The person to the left of the first member should then repeat this procedure, and so on around the group.

8. Each group should discuss the strengths and weaknesses of each of the conflict strategies.

How You Act in Conflicts

The proverbs listed below can be thought of as descriptions of different strategies for resolv-ing conflicts. Read each one carefully. Using the following scale, indicate how typical each proverb is of your actions in a conflict.

5 = very typical of the way I act in a conflict
4 = frequently typical of the way I act in a conflict
3 = sometimes typical of the way I act in a conflict
2 = seldom typical of the way I act in a conflict
1 = never typical of the way I act in a conflict

_____ 1. Smooth words make smooth ways.
_____ 2. If you cannot make a person think as you do, make him or her do as you think.
_____ 3. Soft words win hard hearts.
_____ 4. Come now and let us reason together.
_____ 5. When two quarrel, the person who keeps silent first is the most praise-worthy.
_____ 6. Might overcomes right.
_____ 7. He hath conquered well that hath made his enemies flee.
_____ 8. You can catch more flies with honey than vinegar.
_____ 9. A fair exchange brings no quarrel.
_____ 10. No person has the final answer, but every person has a piece to contribute.
_____ 11. Fields are won by those who believe in winning.
_____ 12. Tit for tat is fair play.

_____ 13. Only the person who is willing to give up his or her monopoly on truth can ever profit from the truths that others hold.

_____ 14. Kind words are worth much and cost little.

_____ 15. One gift for another makes good friends.

_____ 16. Bring your conflicts into the open and face them directly; only then will the best solution be discovered.

_____ 17. The best way of handling conflicts is to avoid them.

_____ 18. Put your foot down where you mean to stand.

_____ 19. Getting part of what you want is better than not getting anything at all.

_____ 20. Frankness, honesty, and trust will move mountains.

_____ 21. There is nothing so important that you have to fight for it.

_____ 22. There are two kinds of people in the world, winners and losers.

_____ 23. When someone hits you with a stone, hit him or her with a piece of cotton.

_____ 24. When both give in halfway, a fair settlement is achieved.

SCORING: Next to the proverb number, fill in the rating you gave yourself in the How You Act in Conflicts section. Then total each column.

Nonconfrontational Style	**Confrontational Style**	**Cooperative Style**
Avoids conflict or minimizes differences. Is uncomfortable facing conflict directly. Tries to make everyone happy or uses distracting nonconfrontational style.	Tries to blame, coerce, or threaten to manage differences and resolve conflicts.	Seeks a win–win solution by separating people from the problem, focusing on common goals, generating multiple solutions, and basing decisions on objective criteria.
1. _____	2. _____	4. _____
3. _____	6. _____	9. _____
5. _____	7. _____	10. _____
8. _____	11. _____	13. _____
14. _____	12. _____	15. _____
17. _____	16. _____	19. _____
21. _____	18. _____	20. _____
23. _____	22. _____	24. _____
Total _____	Total _____	Total _____

The higher the total score for each conflict strategy, the more frequently you tend to use that strategy. The lower the total score for each conflict strategy, the less frequently you tend to use that strategy.

Adapted from: David W. Johnson and Frank P. Johnson, *Joining Together: Group Theory and Group Skills* (Englewood Cliffs, NJ: Prentice-Hall, 1987), 270.

Confrontational people use a win-lose philosophy to manage their conflict. What happens when two confrontational people meet over a disagreement? (Christopher Bissel/Tony Stone Images)

than face issues directly. They hope that eventually the problem will just go away if it can be put off long enough.

A third nonconfrontational style is called *computing*; computers remove themselves from conflict by remaining aloof and cool. They avoid emotional involvement and refuse to be provoked or ruffled, even under intense pressure. This detachment allows them to avoid expressing genuine feelings about issues and ideas. Instead, they respond to emotional issues with impersonal words and phrases, such as "One would tend to become angry when one's car is dented, wouldn't one?" The computing style is characterized by low empathy and minimal involvement with the issues at hand.

Withdrawing from conflict, either physically or psychologically, is another nonconfrontational approach. "I don't want to talk about it," "It's not my problem," "Don't bother me with that now," or "I'm not interested in that" are typical responses from someone who uses this style.

Finally, some people consistently *give in* when faced with conflict. They are so uncomfortable that they surrender before the conflict escalates. Reggie hates westerns. Yet when Pam wants to rent *How the West Was Won*, Reggie says, "Okay, fine," just to avoid a confrontation.

Confrontational Style

"You're wrong!" shouts Ed. "Here's how to get our project in on time. We can't waste time in the library. We just have to write up what we have."

"But Ed," suggests Derrick, "the assignment calls for us to have three library sources."

"No. We just don't have time. Just do it," argues Ed.

INTERNET RESOURCE
Argumentativeness
http://www.as.wvu.edu/
~mmb/teaching/traits.htm
This site defines and characterizes verbal aggressiveness, introversion, extroversion, and argumentativeness, among other related concepts.

Ed wants to control, not collaborate.

Each of us has some need to control and be controlled by others. But some people almost always want to dominate and make sure that their objectives are achieved. In managing conflict, **confrontational** people have a win–lose philosophy. They want to win at the expense of the other person, to claim victory over their opponents. They want to control others. They are focused on themselves and usually ignore the needs of others. Confronters often resort to *blaming*, or seeking a scapegoat, rather than assuming responsibility for a conflict. "I didn't do it"; "Don't look at me"; and "It's not my fault" are typical controlling statements.

If this strategy does not work, confronters may try hostile name-calling, personal attacks, or threats and warnings. Threats refer to actions they can actually carry out.[19] Warnings are negative prophecies they cannot actually control. The boyfriend who says, "If you don't stop calling me names, I'm going to leave you," has issued a threat; he has the power to leave. If he were to say, "Don't call your parents names or they'll write you out of their will," that would be a warning. In reality, he has no control over his girlfriend's parents.

Obviously, threats are more powerful than warnings in changing behavior, and then only if the other person would genuinely find the threatened actions punishing or disruptive. If a parent threatens a spanking, a child will take the threat seriously only if he or she knows the parent will carry it out. If the parent has administered only light raps on the wrist in the past, the child will probably not pay much attention to the threat.

Cooperative Style

Those who take a **cooperative** approach to conflict management view conflicts as a set of problems to be solved, rather than games in which one person wins and another loses. They use other-oriented strategies and foster a win-win climate by using the following techniques:[20]

Separate the people from the problem. They leave personal grievances out of the discussion, describing problems without making judgmental or evaluative statements about personalities.

Focus on shared interests. They ask questions such as: What do we both want? What do we both value? Where are we already agreeing? to emphasize common interests, values, and goals.

Generate many options to solve the problem. They use brainstorming and other techniques to generate alternative solutions. (You will learn more about problem-solving techniques later in this chapter.)

Base decisions on objective criteria. They try to establish standards for an acceptable solution to a problem—these standards may involve cost, timing, and other factors. Suppose, for example, that you and your neighbor are discussing possible ways to stop a nearby dog from barking endlessly into the night. You decide upon these criteria: the solution must not harm the dog; it must be easy for the owner to implement; the owner must agree to it; it should

INTERNET RESOURCES
Dogmatism
www.math.ku.dk/~buhl/
library/sangerHow_To_
Avoid_Dogmatism.
An excellent discussion of
how we come to hold beliefs and when they become
dogmatic and/or dangerous.

**INSTRUCTIONAL GOALS
AND TIPS**
Ask students to consider
this quotation from Indira
Gandhi: "You cannot shake
hands with clenched fists."

not cost more than fifty dollars; and it must keep the dog from disturbing the sleep of others. Your neighbor says, "Maybe the dog can sleep in the owner's garage at night." This solution meets all but one of your criteria, so you call the owner, who agrees to put the dog in the garage by 10:00 P.M. Now everyone wins because the solution meets a sound, well-considered set of objective criteria.

RECAP	**Conflict Management Styles**
NONCONFRONTATIONAL STYLE	Avoids conflict by placating (agreeing), distracting, computing (becoming emotionally detached), or withdrawing from the conflict.
CONFRONTATIONAL STYLE	Wants to manipulate others by blaming and making threats; sets up win-lose framework.
COOPERATIVE STYLE	Seeks mutually agreeable resolutions to manage differences. Works within an other-oriented, win-win framework: • Separates people from the problem. • Focuses on shared interests. • Generates many options to solve problems. • Bases decisions upon objective criteria.

Conflict Management Skills

As we saw in the previous section, the nonconfrontational and confrontational styles of conflict management do not solve problems effectively, nor do they foster healthy long-term relationships. The skills we will review here are those we touched on in our discussion of the cooperative style.[21]

Managing conflict, especially emotion-charged ego conflict, is not easy. Even with a fully developed set of skills, you should not expect to melt tensions and resolve disagreements instantaneously. The following skills can, however, help you generate options that promote understanding and provide a framework for cooperation.

Manage Your Emotions

For weeks you have been working on a brochure with a tight deadline. You turned it over to the production department with instructions two weeks ago. Today you call to check on its progress, and you discover that it is still sitting on the production coordinator's desk. You feel angry and frustrated. How should

RESEARCH AND LITERATURE

Reference Stephen Covey's *The Seven Habits of Highly Effective People* (Simon & Schuster, 1989) for more information on how habits four, five, and six inspire a cooperative style.

Empathy Can Span the Abyss

Intergenerational conflicts and misunderstandings can cause pain and emotional bruises. Instead of finding nurturing and love within the family circle, some people encounter exactly the opposite.

For example, a Nebraska man writes: "I don't look forward to family gatherings because I come back with my self-esteem reduced to zero and feeling like a stereotypical old geezer. I'm rebuffed by my own children, giggled at, and made to feel my thoughts aren't important."

An Indiana reader describes in detail a truly unhappy situation. "I gave my money to my children, trusting them to take care of my needs when I grew older. But now that I have no money left, they have discarded me. How stupid I was not to take care of my security! I'm alone now, really alone. I need to understand what I did wrong. I guess I gave too much, cared too much."

Many letters from elderly people tell similar stories. I also hear from their sons and daughters, members of the so-called sandwich generation, whose reports have a different focus. A fifty-four-year-old woman writes from New York about the "hard burden" she bears in caring for her eighty-eight-year-old mother: "I'm angry that I am increasingly having to be a parent to someone whose self-centeredness and narcissism made her unable to be a mother to me. The simple, awful fact is that I respect my mother and love her as my flesh and blood, but I don't like her

and I wish she weren't in my life. My fear is that she's going to live on and on, growing more and more needful of my 'parenting,' and that I won't be free of her presence until I'm approaching seventy myself."

Another letter from a member of the sandwich generation comes from Arizona: "My challenge involves my relationship with my mother-in-law of twenty-nine years. She's eighty-nine. She has lost all semblance of a positive outlook. She speaks only of her aches and pains and the bleakness of her life. I cannot deal with this negative approach to living. Whatever I try to do for her, nothing is ever right."

Reflecting on these letters, I find the key word for what *both* sides need is empathy—which the dictionary defines as identification with and understanding of the situation, feelings, and motives of another person. Without this empathy, a great abyss can exist where there should be communication. Can we overemphasize that there's no substitute for honest communication between people? *Tell* others what you feel! Try to explain *why* you feel as you do. This can lead to real understanding.

A woman in New Jersey offers a promising, creative role model for others: "Sometimes I'm not delighted to hear what my mother needs and wants because it impinges on my time and energy. However, I prefer to know what she's thinking and feeling, even if it results in conflict. The resolution of such conflicts has strengthened our friendship and the community that is our family. Love, I believe,

is being open and seeking a resolution that may require mutual sacrifice."

An extremely helpful, sound definition. Speaking of love, a Florida reader writes: "Many years ago my mother gave me a book that set my life on a self-respecting, self-valuing course. It says it's quite okay to love yourself. If you don't, how can anyone else love you? If you think you're not worth loving, then, by cracky, you're not. If you think you're not worth much, you will always be a problem—if not a pain—to be around. Is that what you want for yourself? Not I."

A final intergenerational note from Florida: "My life was lonely after I lost my husband," a woman writes. "I volunteered at the hospital, bowled twice a week, was active at my church and kept my home. But there was still a terrible void in my life. Then my 23-year-old granddaughter told me to keep Wednesday evenings open for her. We take turns cooking, or sometimes we go out. You have no idea what this has done for me. We share a meal, talk, and just enjoy our friendship. Our talk may be about her work or what I've done the past week—just nice conversation. We sometimes cry together. But we laugh together as well."

This grandmother and granddaughter have found a happy way to bridge the generation gap. Others could profit from their example.

From: Malcolm Boyd, *Modern Maturity*. Reprinted with permission from *Modern Maturity*. Copyright 1992, American Association of Retired Persons.

RESEARCH AND LITERATURE
For more information, consider reading Hocker and Wilmot's *Interpersonal Conflict* (William C. Brown, 1991).

INSTRUCTIONAL GOALS AND TIPS
As much as possible, give students opportunities to work together to develop constructive conflict role-plays. Stress to students that they have developed some ineffective strategies over the years and that these habits are difficult but not impossible to change. Reference Maslow's stages of skill development from Chapter 5.

you respond? You may be tempted to march into her office and scream at her, or to shout at her supervisor.

Try to avoid taking action when you are in such a state. You may regret what you say, and you will probably escalate the conflict.

Often the first sign that we are in a conflict situation is a feeling of anger, frustration, fear, or even sadness, which sweeps over us like an ocean wave. If we feel powerless to control our own fate, then we will have difficulty taking a logical or rational approach to managing the conflict. Expressing our feelings in an emotional outburst may make us feel better for the moment, but it may close the door to logical, rational negotiation.

When we are emotionally charged, we experience physical changes as well. One researcher found that

> . . . our adrenaline flows faster and our strength increases by about 20 percent. The liver, pumping sugar into the bloodstream, demands more oxygen from the heart and lungs. The veins become enlarged and the cortical centers where thinking takes place do not perform nearly as well. . . . the blood supply to the problem-solving part of the brain is severely decreased because, under stress, a greater portion of blood is diverted to the body's extremities.[22]

Such changes fuel our fight-flight responses. If we choose to stay, verbal or physical violence may erupt; if we flee from the conflict, we cannot resolve it. Until we can tone down (not eliminate) our emotions, we will find it difficult to apply other skills. Let's look at some specific strategies that you can draw upon when an intense emotional response to conflict clouds your judgment and decision-making skills.[23]

■ SELECT A MUTUALLY ACCEPTABLE TIME AND PLACE TO DISCUSS A CONFLICT

If you are upset, or even tired, you are at risk for an emotion-charged shouting match. If you ambush someone with an angry attack, don't expect him or her to be in a productive frame of mind. Instead, give yourself time to cool off before you try to resolve a conflict. In the case of the lapsed deadline, for example, you could call both the production coordinator and her boss and schedule an appointment to meet with them later in the day. By that time you could gain control of your feelings and also think the issue through. Of course, sometimes issues need to be discussed on the spot; you may not have the luxury to wait. But whenever it is practical, make sure the other person is ready to receive you and your message.

■ PLAN YOUR MESSAGE

If you are approaching someone to discuss a disagreement, take care to organize your message. Identify your goal and determine what outcome you would like; do not barge in and pour out your emotions.

II   INTERPERSONAL COMMUNICATION SKILLS

Managing Anger During Conflict

One of the most typical emotional responses you may experience during conflict is anger. Anger occurs when we feel someone is keeping us from what we want, someone is unjustly blaming us for something we didn't do, or someone is attacking us. Some people may tell you it is a good idea to express your anger to the person who is making you angry; get your anger out; don't keep it bottled up. There are times when expressing your anger is appropriate. Being assertive in expressing what bothers you is appropriate when the other person is not aware of what is bothering you. But uncensored angry words can escalate the anger you feel and also increase others' anger.[24] One research team offers these prescriptions for helping you manage your anger during conflict.[25]

1. *Determine not to get angry yourself.* If you know you are going to face someone who is likely to tick you off, prepare yourself before you meet with them. Assertively express your feelings but make yourself promise not to "lose it" by degenerating into a loud shout fest.

2. *Get on the same physical level as the other person.* One person should not be standing and the other sitting. Try to face each other eye-to-eye. You can also build rapport by trying to mirror the posture of the other person. We're not suggesting that you mimic your partner (this would probably make him or her more angry), but try to adopt a similar communication position.

3. *Be silent.* If you are angry and afraid you might say something you'll regret, just be quiet and listen.

4. *Express your concern nonverbally.* Since much of the emotional message is communicated nonverbally, use your facial expression and eyes to let the other person know you care about him or her. Your communication partner will believe what you do more than what you say.

5. *Make an appropriate empathic statement.* Saying, "I would probably feel angry if I had experienced what you experienced" or "I think I can see why you are so upset" may help. But be careful not to say, "I know just how you feel, or I know where you're coming from." For many people, those statements can seem patronizing.

6. *Remind yourself that no one can make you angry.* You control your own emotions. Even though others may do and say things that can upset you, you are the only person who can control you and your response to others. Try to respond to others rather than just emotionally react to them.

7. *Recognize that angry emotional outbursts rarely change someone's mind.* Exploding in an angry tirade may make you feel better for a moment by getting it "off your chest" but it usually does little to advance understanding and manage the issues at hand.

You might also consider talking with a trusted friend or colleague first. A good friend with empathic listening skills can help you clarify the issues in the conflict. If you don't talk with a friend, consider writing down the key ideas you want to express to help you prepare for your face-to-face discussion. The purpose of the notes is not to deliver a speech when you meet your conflict partner. But taking time to plan your message with a friend or in writing can help you frame the issues of the disagreement.

What strategies does it appear that this mother and daughter have drawn upon to manage their conflicts? (Bruce Ayres/ Tony Stone Images)

INTERNET RESOURCE
What Is Your Verbal Aggressiveness?
http://www.adm.uwaterloo.ca/infoipa/Gazette/1996/Gazette,%20January%2018,%201995/Student%20looks%20at%20conversational%20styles
This site offers an interactive scale to measure verbal aggressiveness. Stories and examples of high and low aggressiveness are offered.

See also: http://scils.rutgers.edu/~whitew/EX2_Models.htm

■ MONITOR NONVERBAL MESSAGES

As you learned in Chapter 7, your actions play a key role in establishing the emotional climate in any relationship. Monitoring your nonverbal messages can help to de-escalate an emotion-charged situation. Speaking calmly, using direct eye contact, and maintaining a natural facial expression will signal that you wish to collaborate rather than control. Your nonverbal message should also support your verbal response. If you say you are listening to someone, but you continue to read the paper or work on a report, you are communicating a lack of interest in the speaker and the message.

■ AVOID PERSONAL ATTACKS, NAME-CALLING, AND EMOTIONAL OVERSTATEMENT

Using threats and derogatory names can turn a simple conflict into an ego conflict. When people feel attacked, they will respond by protecting themselves. Also try to avoid exaggerating your emotions. If you say you are irritated or annoyed rather than furious, you can still communicate your feelings, but you will take the sting out of your description.

Avoid the bad habit of gunny sacking. This occurs when you dredge up old problems and issues from the past, like pulling them out of an old bag or gunny sack, to use against your partner. Keep your focus on the issues at hand, not old hurts from the past. Gunny sacking usually succeeds only in increasing tension, escalating emotions and reducing listening effectiveness. See the list of "fair fighting" strategies on page 283 to help keep your discussions productive rather than allow them to degenerate into emotional shouting matches.

‖ INTERPERSONAL COMMUNICATION SKILLS

When Tom was chairing the committee meeting, Monique accused him of falsifying the attendance numbers at the last fine arts festival. Instead of lashing back at Monique, he paused, took a slow, deep yet unnoticed breath, and thought, "I'm tired. If I snarl back, all we will do is escalate this issue out of proportion. I'll talk with Monique later after we have both cooled down." Perhaps you think that talking to yourself is an eccentricity. Nothing could be further from the truth. As you saw in Chapter 2, thoughts are directly linked to feelings,[26] and the messages we tell ourselves play a major role in how we feel and respond to others. Ask yourself whether an emotional tirade and an escalating conflict will produce the results you want. When Eleanor Roosevelt noted that "No one can make you feel inferior without your consent," she was acknowledging the power of self-talk in affecting our emotional response to what others say and do.

Manage Information

Because uncertainty, misinformation, and misunderstanding are often byproducts of conflict and disagreement, skills that promote mutual understanding are an important component of cooperative conflict management. Based on the describing, listening, and responding skills discussed in Chapter 5, the following specific suggestions can help you reduce uncertainty and enhance the quality of communication during conflict.

■ CLEARLY DESCRIBE THE CONFLICT-PRODUCING EVENTS

Instead of just blurting out your complaints in random order, think of delivering a brief, well-organized minispeech. When Marsha almost had a car accident, she came home and told her husband, "Last week you said you would get the brakes fixed on the car. On Monday, when you still hadn't taken the car in, you said you would do it on Wednesday. Now it's Friday and the brakes are in even worse shape. I had a close call this afternoon when the car almost wouldn't stop. We've got to get those brakes fixed before anyone drives that car again."

Public speaking teachers recommend that you describe events in chronological order. Use the same technique when describing a conflict. Offer your perspective on what created the conflict, sequencing the events like a well-organized story. Think of yourself as a journalist who is reporting on a news event. Your job is to describe the events dispassionately so that the other person shares your understanding of the problem.

■ "OWN" YOUR STATEMENTS BY USING DESCRIPTIVE "I" LANGUAGE

"I feel upset when you post the week's volunteer schedule without first consulting with me," reveals Katrina. Her statement describes her feelings as

8 CONFLICT MANAGEMENT SKILLS

her own. If she had said, "You always prepare a schedule without telling anyone first. All of us who volunteer are mad about that," her statement would have had an accusatory sting. Beginning the statement with "you" sets the listener up for a defensive response. Also, notice that in the second statement, the speaker does not take responsibility for the problem; she suggests that it belongs to several unidentified people as well. If you narrow the issue down to a conflict between you and the other person, you put the conflict into a more manageable framework.

■ USE EFFECTIVE LISTENING SKILLS

Managing information is a two-way process. Whether you are describing a conflict situation to someone, or that individual is bringing a conflict to your attention, good listening skills will be invaluable.

Give your full attention to the speaker and make a conscious point of tuning out your internal messages. Sometimes the best thing to do after describing the conflict-producing events is simply to wait for a response. If you don't stop talking and give the other person a chance to respond, he or she will feel frustrated, the emotional pitch will go up a notch, and it will become more difficult to reach an understanding.

Finally, focus not only on the facts or details, but also analyze them so you can understand the major point the speaker is making. Try to use your understanding of the details to interpret the speaker's major ideas. Remember to stay other-oriented and "seek to understand rather than to be understood."[27]

■ CHECK YOUR UNDERSTANDING OF WHAT OTHERS SAY AND DO

Respond clearly and appropriately. Your response and that of your conflict partner will confirm that you have understood each other. Checking perceptions is vital when emotions run high.

Reprinted with permission of King Features Syndicate

If you are genuinely unsure about facts, issues, or major ideas addressed during a conflict, ask questions to help you sort through them instead of barging ahead with solutions. Then summarize your understanding of the information; do not parrot the speaker's words or paraphrase every statement, but check key points to ensure that you have understood the message. Note how Ted adeptly paraphrases to check his understanding:

Maggie: I don't like the conclusion you've written to the conference report. It doesn't mention anything about the ideas suggested at the symposium. I think you have also misinterpreted the CEO's key message.

Ted: So, if I understand you, Maggie, you're saying the report missed some key information and may also include an inaccurate summary of the CEO's speech.

Maggie: Yes, Ted. Those are the concerns I have.

Manage Goals

As we have seen, conflict is goal-driven. Both individuals involved in an interpersonal conflict want something. And for some reason, be it competition, scarce resources, or lack of understanding, the goals appear to be in conflict. To manage conflict, it is important to seek an accurate understanding of these goals and to identify where they overlap.

■ IDENTIFY YOUR GOAL AND YOUR PARTNER'S GOAL

After you describe, listen, and respond, your next task should be to identify what you would like to have happen. What is your goal? Most goal statements can be phrased in terms of wants or desires. Consider the following examples:

Problem	Goal
Your boss approaches you and wants you to work overtime; you need to pick up your son from day care.	You want to leave work on time; your boss wants the work completed ASAP.
Your spouse wants to sleep with the window open; you like a warm room and sleep better with the window closed.	You want a good night's rest; your spouse wants a good night's rest.

Problem	Goal
Your six-year-old son wants to go to a swim party with no lifeguards.	You want your son to be safe; your son wants to have a good time.

Often in conflicts you will be faced with balancing the achievement of your goal against the goal of maintaining the relationship that you have with your

MEDIA AND OUTSIDE RESOURCES

Consider this excerpt from Gregory Godek's book *Romance 101* (Casablanca Press, 1993, p. 7):

Arguing about money is rarely about money. It's about power. Arguing about chores is rarely about the chores. It's about fairness. Arguing about jealousy is rarely about fidelity. It's about maturity. Arguing about work is rarely about the work. It's about time.

Encourage students to develop some more of these.

partner. Eventually, you may decide that the latter goal is more important than the substantive conflict issue.

Next, it is useful to identify your partner's goal. In each of the problems in the preceding list, you would need to know what the other person wants in order to manage the conflict. Use effective describing, listening, and responding skills to determine what each of you wants and to verbalize your goals. Obviously, if you both keep your goals hidden, it will be difficult to manage the conflict.

■ IDENTIFY WHERE YOUR GOALS AND YOUR PARTNER'S GOALS OVERLAP

Roger Fisher and William Ury stress the importance of focusing on shared interests when seeking to manage differences.[28] Armed with an understanding of what you want and what your partner wants, you can then determine whether the goals overlap. In the conflict over whether the window should be open or closed, the goal of both parties is the same: each wants a good night's sleep. Framing the problem as "how can we achieve our mutual goal" rather than arguing over whether the window should be up or down, moves the discussion to a more productive level.

If you focus on shared interests (common goals) and develop objective, rather than subjective, criteria for the solution, there is hope for finding a resolution that will satisfy both parties.

Manage the Problem

If you can structure conflicts as problems to be solved rather than battles to be won or lost, you are well on your way to seeking strategies to manage the issues that confront you and your partner. Of course, as we have stressed earlier, not all conflicts can be resolved. But approaching the core of a conflict as a problem to be managed can provide a constructive way of seeking resolution. Structuring a conflict as a problem also helps to manage the emotion and keeps the conversation focused on issues (simple conflict) rather than personalities (ego conflict). The problem-solving structure we suggest here is straightforward: Define the problem, analyze the problem causes and effects, determine the goal you and your partner seek, generate many possible options, then select the option that best achieves the goals of both you and your partner.

■ DEFINE THE PROBLEM

You can apply all of the skills described so far to pursue a proven method for problem solving, which is shown in Table 8.1. First, *define the problem*. Most problems boil down to something you want more or less of.

Cara and Vaughn have been going together for over a year. Lately they have been fighting over small issues, so they decide to spend some time talking about

Table 8.1

Solving Problems: One Method of Organizing Problem-Solving Discussions

1. Define the Problem	What's the issue?
2. Analyze the Problem	What are the causes, symptoms, effects, and obstacles?
3. Determine the Goals	What do you want? What does your partner want? How do the goals overlap?
4. Generate Many Solutions	List many options rather than debating one or two strategies for achieving the goal.
5. Select the Best Solution and Try It	Eliminate options that are not mutually agreeable. If possible, take the best ideas from several generated to reach an amicable resolution.

what is wrong and trying to understand one another. At the root of their conflicts, they discover, is a basic problem: Cara wants to get married to Vaughn now. Vaughn wants to stay with Cara, but he wants to wait until he feels ready for marriage. He also wants to feel financially secure before he marries.

■ ANALYZE THE PROBLEM

Next, *analyze the problem*. To analyze is to break something down into its components. With your partner, begin by describing the conflict-producing events in chronological order (see page 271). Then decide whether it is a pseudo conflict, a simple conflict, or an ego conflict (see page 249). Attempt to ferret out symptoms, effects, and obstacles; decide whether the conflict stems from several subproblems or from one major issue. As you proceed with your analysis, you and your partner may decide that you need more information to help clarify the issues.

After some discussion, Cara and Vaughn analyze the problem. They realize they come from different family backgrounds and have different expectations about marriage. Cara's folks were high school sweethearts and got married when they were eighteen. Vaughn's parents are older; they met after each of them had been divorced, and they married after a long, slow-paced relationship. Cara and Vaughn's different frames of reference help explain their feelings about the timing of marriage.

■ DETERMINE THE GOALS

The next step in managing the problem is to *determine the goals* of you and your partner, following the suggestions on page 273. Also, generate objective criteria for a solution (see page 265). The more measurable, verifiable, and objective the criteria, the greater the likelihood that you and your partner will be able to agree when the criteria have been met. Cara and Vaughn decide that, ultimately, they have the same goal: to get married. The issue boils down to timing. So they decide to seek a course of action that will make them both feel secure.

■ GENERATE MULTIPLE SOLUTIONS

Their next step is to *generate multiple solutions*. Simply understanding the issues and the causes, effects, symptoms, and history of a problem will not enable you to manage a conflict. It takes time and creativity to find mutually satisfactory solutions to most problems. It stands to reason that the more solutions you generate, the greater the probability that you can manage the conflict constructively. One way to generate options is through brainstorming. To use brainstorming, try the following suggestions:

1. Make sure the problem and the goals are clear to both of you.

2. Try to temporarily suspend judgment and evaluation; do not censor your thoughts.

3. Specify a certain time period for brainstorming.

4. Consider having each partner brainstorm ideas separately before a meeting, or write ideas down before verbalizing solutions.

5. Try to develop at least one unique or far-out idea. You can always tame wild ideas down later.

6. Piggyback off the ideas of your partner. Encourage your partner to use or modify your ideas.

7. Write down all of the ideas suggested.

8. Review each idea, noting ways to combine, eliminate, or extend them.

If the goal is to find the best way to manage the difficulty, it may take only one good idea to help move the conflict forward to a constructive resolution.

When they brainstorm, Cara and Vaughn generate the following options: save money for a year and then get married; take turns going to college; take turns working to support the family while the other gets a degree; get married now, get jobs, and postpone college; get married now and take out college loans.

■ SELECT THE BEST SOLUTION

Finally, they decide to *select the best solution*. Sometimes it may take several attempts at defining, analyzing, goal-setting, and generating multiple ideas before a mutually agreeable solution emerges. It is always appropriate to

Practicing Conflict Management Skills

In this activity you will be paired with another person and invited to roleplay a conflict that you have had with another person. A third person will observe and provide feedback about the communication skills you use to manage the conflict.

Person A.
Think about a recent incident in which someone offended you. Make a few notes about the conflict. Then approach person B, who will play the person who has offended you. Describe the conflict, remembering to manage your emotions.

Person B.
You have offended person A. Your job is to listen, reflect, and help to manage the conflict. Start a dialogue to identify each other's goals and see how they overlap; then try to generate strategies to achieve the goals.

Person C.
Your job is to observe the roleplay. Use the following checklist to help you evaluate the participants. When the roleplay is over, tell the participants what they did well. Ask them how they could improve, and offer suggestions as well.
If time permits, switch roles and conduct another roleplay.

Conflict Management Roleplay Checklist

	Person A	Person B
Managing Emotions		
Makes direct eye contact.	_____	_____
Maintains open body posture.	_____	_____
Uncrosses arms and legs.	_____	_____
Has a slight forward lean.	_____	_____
Uses a calm voice.	_____	_____
Uses reinforcing head nods.	_____	_____
Has appropriate facial expression.	_____	_____
Managing Information		
Paraphrases content accurately.	_____	_____
Paraphrases feelings accurately.	_____	_____
Clearly describes the problem.	_____	_____
Managing Goals		
States the goals clearly.	_____	_____
Identifies how goals overlap.	_____	_____
Managing the Problem		
Identifies several options.	_____	_____

SKILL DEVELOPMENT

Consider this activity and the one on page 281 for their potential as a graded skills assessment of your students. If you choose to try this, adapt the exercises such that you play the role of person C. In addition to directly assessing skills, you will have the option to coach students individually, which is usually an all-too-rare event.

SKILL DEVELOPMENT

Role-play as many of these as is possible. Ask students to complete the checklist and to offer constructive criticism to the players.

WEB ACTIVITY

Talk Group on Assertiveness

http://growthgroups.com/Assertiveness.htm

On this site, you can choose to be assertive in a number of situations. You become a member of an assertive group which involves 8–12 other participants. Experiences emphasize building assertiveness skills using model presentations, rehearsal, positive feedback, prompting, and homework assignments.

SKILL DEVELOPMENT

Ask students to develop and present realistic role-play scenarios that include dirty fighting tactics: sarcasm; the silent treatment; interrupting; and focusing on the past. Next, ask students to demonstrate assertiveness and cooperative communication to manage these conflicts.

---

recheck your understanding of the issues and goals. Cara and Vaughn decide to combine the best of several ideas. They agree to get engaged, but not to set a date. Instead, they set a financial goal of five thousand dollars in savings. When they hit that goal, they will set a wedding date. If they are both attending college, they will get part-time jobs so that they have income, and they will also apply for college loans.

If, after repeated attempts, you cannot arrive at a mutually acceptable solution, you may decide to keep trying. Or you may agree to take the issue to an impartial person who can help you identify conflict management strategies and solutions. At work, your immediate superior may be called in to help settle the matter. Or, occasionally, you may agree to disagree and drop it.

Even though we have presented these conflict management steps as prescriptive suggestions, it is important to remember that *conflict rarely follows a linear, step-by-step sequence of events*. These skills are designed to serve as a general framework for collaboratively managing differences. But if your partner does not want to collaborate, your job will be more challenging.

In reality, you don't simply manage your emotions and then move neatly on to developing greater understanding with another person. Sorting out your goals and your partner's goals is not something that you do once and then put behind you. It will take time and patience to balance your goal of maintaining a relationship with your immediate achievement goals. In fact, as you try to manage a conflict, you will more than likely bounce forward and backward from one step to another. This framework gives you an overarching perspective for understanding and actively managing disagreements, but the nature of interpersonal relationships means that you and your partner will respond—sometimes in unpredictable ways—to a variety of cues (psychological, sociological, physical) when communicating. Think of the skills you have learned as options to consider rather than as hard-and-fast rules to follow in every situation.

When Others Aren't Other-Oriented: How to Be Assertive

Even if you master collaborative conflict management skills, others may make irrational, inappropriate demands that create conflict and tension. In these instances, you will need to assert yourself, especially if someone has aggressively violated your rights.

Assertiveness Defined

To **assert** yourself is to let your communication partner know that his or her behavior or message is infringing on your rights. We each have rights. In interpersonal communication, you have the right to refuse a request someone makes of you, the right to express your feelings as long as you don't trample on the feelings of others, and the right to have your personal needs met if they don't infringe upon the rights of others.

Some people confuse the terms *assertiveness* and *aggressiveness*. **Aggressiveness** means pursuing your interests by denying the rights of others. Assertiveness is other-oriented; aggressiveness is exclusively self-oriented. Aggressive people are coercive. They blame, judge, and evaluate to get what they want. They use intimidating nonverbal cues such as steely stares, a bombastic voice, and flailing gestures. Assertive people can ask for what they want without judging or evaluating their partner.

In Chapter 5 we talked about using "I" messages to express your thoughts and feelings rather than "you" messages. "I" messages describe what you want by expressing your feelings and goals. "You" messages lead with an attack on the person. "You creep! You ate the last breakfast taco" is an aggressive "you" statement. "I asked you to save one taco for me; now I won't have anything to eat for breakfast" is an assertive statement that states your rights and describes the consequences of violating them.

INTERNET RESOURCE
http://www.nscee.edu/ unlv/Student_Services/ Student_Psychological_ Services/assert.htm
This article introduces the basics of assertiveness and offers strategies and tips for becoming more assertive.

RECAP   Assertiveness *versus* Aggressiveness

Assertiveness	Aggressiveness
Expresses your interests without denying the rights of others.	Expresses your interests and denies the rights of others.
Is other-oriented.	Is self-oriented.
Describes what you want.	Evaluates the other person.
Discloses your needs, using "I" messages.	Discloses your needs, using "you" messages.

How to Assert Yourself If You Are Sexually Harassed

What Is Sexual Harassment?

Any unwelcome sexual advances, requests for sexual favors, or other inappropriate verbal or physical behavior of a sexual nature may be classified as sexual harassment. Examples include:

- repeated and unwanted requests for dates, sexual flirtations, or propositions of a sexual nature;

- unwanted sexual remarks or questions about a person's clothing, body, or sexual activity;

- unnecessary touching, patting, hugging, or brushing against a person's body;

- direct or implied threats that failure to submit to sexual advances will affect employment, work status, grades, letters of recommendation, or residential choice;

■ physical assault;

■ a pattern of conduct that causes humiliation or discomfort, such as use of inappropriate terms of greeting; sexually explicit or sexist comments, questions, or jokes; or leering at a person's body.

What to Do if You Are Sexually Harassed

■ Be direct and candid with the person.

■ Use "I" messages (e.g., I don't like those kinds of jokes made about me).

■ Avoid being overly dramatic; remain confident that the incident will be dealt with.

■ If the incident happens at school or work, use the grievance procedure.

■ Report the harasser to your supervisor, department chair, or dean.

■ If the harasser is your supervisor or an administrative official, report the incident to his or her supervisor.

■ Report the harassment immediately after it occurs. The longer you wait, the less credible your story will be.

■ When the harassment occurs, write down important facts.

■ Report the incident as if you were a journalist: give the who, what, when, where, and how. Keep to the facts.

■ Be prepared to give the interviewer names of witnesses.

■ Put aside your anger and be thorough when telling the story.

Information adapted from Southwest Texas State University policy and procedure statement on sexual harassment and Vicki West, "Sexual Harassment: Identify, Stop, and Prevent" seminar.

Five Steps in Assertive Behavior

Many people have a tendency to withdraw in the face of controversy, even when their rights are being violated or denied. But you can develop skill in asserting yourself by practicing five key suggestions.[29]

■ DESCRIBE

Describe how you view the situation. To assert your position, you first need to describe how you view the situation. You need to be assertive because the other person has not been other-oriented. For example, Doug was growing increasingly frustrated with Maria's tardiness at the weekly staff meeting. He first approached Maria by describing his observation: "I have noticed that you

II   INTERPERSONAL COMMUNICATION SKILLS

INSTRUCTIONAL GOALS AND TIPS

Play the "Win as Much as You Can" game at the end of this chapter. This exercise will take approximately 45 minutes to play and debrief.

How to Assert Yourself

Working with a partner, describe a situation in which you could have been more assertive. Ask your partner to assume the role of the person toward whom you should have been more assertive. Now replay the situation, using the following skills:

1. Describe: Tell the other person that what he or she is doing bothers you. Describe rather than evaluate.

2. Disclose: Then tell the other person how you feel. For example, "I feel X, when you do Y . . ."

3. Identify Effects: Tell the other person the effects of his or her behavior upon you

or your group. Be as clear and descriptive as you can.

4. Wait: After you have described, disclosed, and identified the effects, wait for a response.

5. Reflect: Use reflective listening skills: question, paraphrase content, paraphrase feelings.

Observation of Assertiveness Skills

Ask your classmates to observe your roleplay and provide feedback, using the following checklist.

When you have finished asserting your point of view, reverse roles.

Clearly describes what the problem was.	_____
Effectively discloses how he or she felt.	_____
Clearly describes the effects of the behavior.	_____
Pauses or waits after describing the effects.	_____
Uses effective questions to promote understanding.	_____
Accurately paraphrases content.	_____
Accurately paraphrases feelings.	_____
Has good eye contact.	_____
Leans forward while speaking.	_____
Has an open body posture.	_____
Has appropriate voice tone and quality.	_____

are usually fifteen minutes late to our weekly staff meetings." A key to communicating your assertive message is to monitor your nonverbal message, especially your voice. Avoid sarcasm or excessive vocal intensity. Calmly yet confidently describe the problem.

■ DISCLOSE

Disclose your feelings. After describing the situation from your perspective, let the other person know how you feel.[30] Disclosing your feelings will help to build empathy and avoid lengthy harangues about the other person's unjust treatment. "I feel as if you don't take our weekly meetings seriously," continues Doug as he asserts his desire for Maria to be on time to the meeting. Note that Doug does not talk about how others are feeling ("Every member of our group is tired of you coming in late"); he describes how *he* feels.

■ IDENTIFY EFFECTS

Identify effects. Next, you can identify the *effects* of the other person's behavior upon you or others. "When you are late, it disrupts our meeting," says Doug.

■ BE SILENT

Wait. Then you can simply wait for a response. Nonassertive people find this step hard. Again, be sure to monitor your nonverbal cues. Make sure your facial expression does not contradict your verbal message. Delivering an assertive message with a broad grin might create a double bind for your listener, who may not be sure what the primary message is—the verbal one or the nonverbal one.

■ USE REFLECTIVE LISTENING

Reflect content and feelings. After the other person responds appropriately, reflect your understanding of both the content and feelings of the message. "Oh, I'm sorry. I didn't realize I was creating a problem. I have another meeting that usually goes overtime. It's difficult for me to arrive at the start of our meeting on time," says Maria. Doug could respond, "So the key problem is a time conflict with another meeting. That must make you feel frustrated to try to do two things at once."

If the other person is evasive, unresponsive, or aggressive, you'll need to cycle through the steps again: clearly describe what the other person is doing that is not acceptable; disclose how you feel; identify the effects; wait; then reflect and clarify as needed. A key goal of an assertive response is to seek an empathic connection between you and your partner. Paraphrasing feelings is a way of ensuring that both parties are connecting.

If you tend to withdraw from conflict, how do you become assertive? Visualizing can help. Think of a past situation in which you wished you had been more assertive and then mentally replay the situation, imagining what you might have said. Also practice verbalizing assertive statements. When you are appropriately assertive, consciously congratulate yourself for sticking up for your rights. To sharpen your assertiveness skills, try Building Your Skills: How to Assert Yourself.

Fighting Fairly

Consider the following suggestions to keep you focused on issues rather than personalities when you experience interpersonal conflict:

1. Be specific when you introduce a complaint.

2. Don't just complain; ask for a reasonable change that will make the situation better.

3. Give and receive feedback about the major points of disagreement to make sure you are understood by your partner.

4. Try tolerance. Be open to your own feelings, and equally open to your partner's feelings. Openness means that you accept change and can verbalize that attitude to your partner.

5. Consider compromise if appropriate. Many conflicts involve issues that are neither right nor wrong. Your partner may even have some good ideas.

6. Deal with one issue at a time.

7. Don't "mind rape." Don't assume to tell your partner what he or she knows or feels. Never assume you know what your partner thinks. Ask.

8. Attack the issue, not each other.

9. Don't call each other names or use sarcasm.

10. Don't "gunny sack." Just as farmers use a gunny sack to carry feed, many people carry past hurts into the conflict and then unleash them from the "gunny sack." Forget the past and stay with the issue at hand.

11. Don't burden your partner with too many issues.

12. Think about your thoughts and feelings before speaking.

Adapted from George R. Bach and Ronald M. Deutsch, *Pairing* (New York: Peter Wyden, 1970).

RECAP How to Assert Yourself

Step	Example
1. Describe	"I see that you haven't completed the report yet."
2. Disclose	"I feel that the work I ask you to do is not a priority with you."
3. Identify Effects	"Without that report, our team will not achieve our goal."
4. Be Silent	Wait for a response.
5. Use Reflective Listening	
Question	"Do you understand how I feel?"
Paraphrase content	"So, you were not aware that the report was late."
Paraphrase feelings	"Perhaps you feel embarrassed."

Make a copy of "Fighting Fairly" and suggest to students that they place it on their refrigerators. Be careful to employ these tips yourself in your interactions with students.

INTERNET RESOURCE
Mediation and Intercultural Communication
http://natlaw.com/pubs/spmxlb4.htm
This excellent paper considers explanations for failed negotiation attempts by examining tensions between cultures. A case of U.S. and Mexico is offered and analyzed.

FOCUS ON COMPREHENSION

1. Pseudo conflict is based upon misunderstanding and can generally be resolved by using effective listening skills, especially perception checking. Simple conflict is inevitable and often desirable. These disputes are based upon limited resources or incompatible goals. If managed well, these conflicts can become discussions and debates rather than disputes or worse. Ego conflict is dangerous and harmful to relationships because it is marked by pride and competition.

2. It is not true that conflict can be avoided, that it is bad, resolvable, or always based upon misunderstanding. Simple conflict is both inevitable and challenging, even for the best communicators.

3. Although conflict cannot always be resolved, it can be managed. Understanding the five phases of the process can be useful. These include recognizing the source of a problem; acknowledging the emotions associated with it; bringing these emotions into the open; and managing or resolving them. It is important to follow up on problem solving to ensure that the solutions or resolutions are effective.

4. There are five types of power: legitimate (elected); referent (attractiveness or fame); expert (knowledge); reward (control of resources); and coercive (abuse of authority or resources).

5. For effective conflict management, the authors recommend focusing on emotions, information, goals, and the problem.

Summary

Interpersonal conflict is an expressed struggle that occurs when two people cannot agree upon a way to meet their needs or goals. At the root of all conflicts are our individual perspectives, needs, and experiences.

Conflict can result from misunderstanding someone (pseudo conflict), or it can stem from a simple difference of opinion or viewpoint (simple conflict). Ego conflict occurs when personalities clash; the conflict becomes personal and you may feel a need to defend your self-image.

Myths about the conflict management process tell us that conflict should always be avoided; that conflict always occurs because of misunderstandings; that conflict always occurs because of a poor interpersonal relationship; and that conflict can always be resolved. But conflict in interpersonal relationships is not always destructive. It can actually play a constructive role by identifying areas that need attention and transformation.

Although conflict seems to erupt suddenly, it often originates in events that occur long before the conflict manifests itself. It evolves from these prior conditions into frustration awareness, active conflict, solution, and follow-up stages. Understanding conflict as a process also involves recognizing how people seek and are given control over others.

Nonconfrontational approaches to conflict include placating, distracting, computing, and withdrawing. Controlling approaches employ blaming and threats. Cooperative approaches involve separating the person from the problem, focusing on shared interests, generating many options to seek a solution, and basing the decision on objective rather than subjective criteria. Skills for managing conflict focus on managing emotions, information, goals, and ultimately on managing the problem.

The goal of this chapter is not to eliminate conflict from your interpersonal relationships; that would be unrealistic and even undesirable. But knowing principles and skills for bridging differences can give you greater flexibility in maintaining satisfying relationships with others.

For Discussion and Review

■ FOCUS ON COMPREHENSION

1. What are pseudo, simple, and ego conflict?

2. What are five myths about conflict?

3. What are the five stages of the conflict management process?

4. What are the four essentials skills of managing conflict?

5. Richard has an explosive temper. He consistently receives poor performance evaluations at work because he lashes out at those who disagree with him. What strategies might help him manage his emotional outbursts?

6. Melissa and Jake always seem to end up making personal attacks and calling each other names when they get into a disagreement. What type of conflict are they experiencing when they do this, and how can they avoid it?

7. Analyze the opening dialogue in this chapter. What are Anya and Paolo doing wrong in managing their differences? Are they doing anything right?

8. Is it ethical to mask your true emotions in order to get along with others? Is honesty in a relationship always the best policy? Explain your response.

9. When a conflict arises between two people, are certain types of power more ethical to draw upon than others? Explain your answer, describing conditions that would justify the use of certain types of power.

10. Are there situations when you should *not* assert your point of view? Provide an example to support your answer.

For Your Journal

1. Analyze several recent conversations in which you were trying to convince someone to do something. Discuss the types of power you used in your efforts.

2. Consider a recent conflict you have had with someone. Determine whether it was a pseudo, simple, or ego conflict. Describe the strategies you used to manage the conflict. Now that you have read this chapter, discuss the other strategies you could have used to help manage the disagreement.

3. Identify a current or recent conflict you are having or have had with a friend or acquaintance. Use the problem-solving steps presented in this chapter to seek a solution to the problem that is creating the conflict. Define the problem: Identify the issues. Analyze the problem: What are the causes, symptoms, effects, and obstacles that keep you from achieving

your goal? Determine your goal: What do you want? What does your partner want? Generate many possible solutions that would solve the problem. Finally, select the solution(s) that would permit each person to achieve his or her goal.

4. Briefly describe a conflict during which you did *not* do a good job of managing your emotions, that is, one in which you became angry and upset and lost your cool. Respond to the following questions: Why did you lose control of your emotions? If you could go back in time, what would you do differently to better manage your emotions before and during the conflict? Consider incorporating some of the suggestions discussed in this chapter.

Learning with Others

1. Win As Much As You Can[31]

This activity is designed to explore the effects of trust and conflict on communication. You will be paired with a partner. There will be four partner teams working in a cluster.

| 4 Xs: Lose $1 each |
| 3 Xs: Win $1 each
1 Y: Lose $3 |
| 2 Xs: Win $2 each
2 Ys: Lose $2 each |
| 1 X: Win $3
3 Ys: Lose $1 each |
| 4 Ys: Win $1 each |

Directions: Your instructor will provide detailed instructions for playing this game. For ten successive rounds you and your partner will choose either an X or a Y. Your instructor will tell all partner teams to reveal their choices at the same time. Each round's payoff will depend on the decision made by others in your cluster. For example, according to the scoring chart shown above, if all four partner teams mark X for round one of this game, each partner team loses $1. You are to confer with your partner on each round to make a joint decision. Before rounds 5, 8, and 10, your instructor will permit you to confer with the other pairs in your cluster. Keep track of your choices and winnings on the score sheet below. When you finish the game, compare your cluster's results with those of others. Discuss the factors that affected your balances. There are three key rules:

1. Do not confer with the other members of your cluster unless you are given specific permission to do so. This applies to nonverbal and verbal communication.

2. Each pair must agree on a single choice for each round.

3. Make sure that the other members of your cluster do not know your pair's choice until you are instructed to reveal it.

Round	Time Allowed	Confer with	Choice	$ Won	$ Lost	$ Balance	
1	2 min.	partner	_____	_____	_____	_____	
2	1 min.	partner	_____	_____	_____	_____	
3	1 min.	partner	_____	_____	_____	_____	
4	1 min.	partner	_____	_____	_____	_____	
5	3 min.	cluster					Bonus Round:
	1 min.	partner	_____	_____	_____	_____	Pay x 3
6	1 min.	partner	_____	_____	_____	_____	
7	1 min.	partner	_____	_____	_____	_____	
8	3 min.	cluster					
	1 min.	partner	_____	_____	_____	_____	Pay x 5
9	1 min.	partner	_____	_____	_____	_____	
10	3 min.	cluster					
	1 min.	partner	_____	_____	_____	_____	Pay x 10

2. Agree-Disagree Statements about Conflict

Read each statement once and mark whether you agree (A) or disagree (D) with it. Take five or six minutes to do this.

_____ 1. Most people find an argument interesting and exciting.

_____ 2. In most conflicts someone must win and someone must lose. That's the way conflict is.

_____ 3. The best way to handle a conflict is simply to let everyone cool off.

_____ 4. Most people get upset at a person who disagrees with them.

_____ 5. If people spend enough time together, they will find something to disagree about and will eventually become upset with one another.

_____ 6. Conflicts can be solved if people just take the time to listen to one another.

8   CONFLICT MANAGEMENT SKILLS

INSTRUCTIONAL GOALS AND TIPS

As a variation on this game, divide the class into four groups, each representing a different region: North, South, East, and West. Give each region some play money and change the earnings to millions of dollars. Make the cluster meetings diplomatic summits between regions. Watch students battle their desires to compete as they attempt to cooperate. During the debriefing, discuss the importance of interdependence among nations and the value of treaties and organizations such as the United Nations.

Invite an expert on sexual harassment to come and discuss this topic and to focus on ways to prevent harassment. The Center for Women Policy Studies (202-872-1770) produces publications addressing issues such as this.

_____ 7. If you disagree with someone, it is usually better to keep quiet than to express your personal difference of opinion.

_____ 8. To compromise is to take the easy way out of conflict.

_____ 9. Some people produce more conflict and tension than others. These people should be restricted from working with others.

After you have marked the above statements, break up into small groups and try to agree or disagree unanimously with each statement. Especially try to find reasons for differences of opinion. If your group cannot reach agreement or disagreement, you may change the wording in any statement to promote consensus. Assign one group member to observe your group interactions. After your group has attempted to reach consensus, the observer should report how effectively the group used the guidelines suggested in this chapter.

■ GLOSSARY

INTERPERSONAL CONFLICT: Struggle that occurs when two people cannot agree upon a way to meet their needs or goals.

PSEUDO CONFLICT: Conflict triggered by a lack of understanding and miscommunication.

SIMPLE CONFLICT: Conflict that stems from different ideas, definitions, perceptions, or goals.

EGO CONFLICT: Conflict that is based upon personal issues; conflicting partners attack one another's self-esteem.

EXPRESSIVE CONFLICT: Conflict that focuses on issues about the quality of the relationship and managing interpersonal tension and hostility.

INSTRUMENTAL CONFLICT: Conflict that centers on achieving a particular goal or task and less on relational issues.

CONFLICT MYTHS: Inappropriate assumptions about the nature of interpersonal conflict.

CONSTRUCTIVE CONFLICT: Conflict that helps build new insights and establishes new patterns in a relationship.

DESTRUCTIVE CONFLICT: Conflict that dismantles relationships without restoring the relationship.

NONCONFRONTATIONAL STYLE: Style of managing conflict that includes placating, distracting, computing, withdrawing, and giving in.

CONFRONTATIONAL STYLE: Style of managing conflict motivated by a desire to dominate. Behaviors include blaming, threatening, warning, and other forms of verbal abuse.

COOPERATIVE STYLE: Style of managing conflict that seeks win-win solutions to problems. Cooperative people separate the people from the problem, focus on shared interests, generate multiple solutions, and base decisions on objective criteria.

GUNNY SACKING: Dredging up old problems and issues from the past, like pulling them out of an old bag or gunny sack, to use against your partner.

ASSERTIVENESS: Pursuing your best interests without denying your partner's rights.

AGGRESSIVENESS: Expressing your interests while denying the rights of others by blaming, judging, and evaluating the other person.

Diana Ong/Superstock

Interpersonal Communication Relationships

Why do we like some people and not others? How do relationships begin and end? How can I enhance the quality of my relationships with family, friends, and colleagues? These are just some of the questions we will explore in this unit as we build upon our understanding of interpersonal communication skills and principles. Chapter 9 discusses some fundamental elements of interpersonal relationships such as how we reveal information about ourselves and develop relationships with others. Chapter 10 presents a model of relationship development, including specific skills about how to initiate, escalate, maintain, and if necessary, end interpersonal relationships. Chapter 11, our final chapter, applies relationship principles and skills to interactions with our families, friends, and colleagues.

291

Understanding Interpersonal Relationships

A fter studying this chapter, you should be able to:

1. Explain relationships of circumstance and relationships of choice.

2. Describe three dimensions of interpersonal relationships.

3. Explain what interpersonal attraction is.

4. Describe the elements that contribute to interpersonal attraction.

5. Explain the relationship between attraction and interpersonal communication.

6. Describe the principles of self-disclosure.

7. Construct two models of self-disclosure.

■ RELATIONSHIPS OF CIRCUM-STANCE AND RELATIONSHIPS OF CHOICE

■ TRUST, INTIMACY, AND POWER IN RELATIONSHIPS

■ INTERPERSONAL ATTRACTION: THE SPARK FOR A RELATIONSHIP

■ SELF-DISCLOSURE: A FOUNDA-TION FOR RELATIONAL ESCALATION

■ TWO MODELS FOR SELF-DISCLOSURE

Pat:	Hi, aren't you in my communication course?
Chris:	Oh, yeah, I've seen you across the room.
Pat:	What do you think about the course so far?
Chris:	It's okay but I feel a little intimidated by some of the class activities.
Pat:	I know what you mean. It gets kind of scary to talk about yourself in front of everyone else.
Chris:	Yeah. Plus some of the stuff you hear. I was paired up with this one student the other day who started talking about being arrested last year on a drug charge. It made me feel uncomfortable.
Pat:	Really? I bet I know who that is. I don't think you have to worry about it.
Chris:	Don't mention that I said anything.
Pat:	It's okay. I know that guy, and he just likes to act big.

This interaction between Pat and Chris illustrates the reciprocal nature of interpersonal communication and interpersonal relationships. As you learned in Chapter 1, **interpersonal relationships** are connections that we develop with other people as a direct result of our interpersonal communication with them. The character and quality of interpersonal communication is affected, in turn, by the nature of the relationship.

The conversation between Pat and Chris begins with a casual acknowledgment but quickly proceeds to a higher level of intimacy. Chris confides in Pat. Pat, an other-oriented listener, offers confirmation and support; this response encourages Chris to confide even more. In this brief encounter, Pat and Chris have laid the groundwork for transforming their casual acquaintanceship into an intimate relationship.

In the next two chapters, we will explore the dynamic link between interpersonal communication and interpersonal relationships. Drawing from the understanding of communication you have acquired from the first eight chapters, you will learn about the nature of relationships, their development from initiation to termination, and the specific communication skills you can apply to maintaining them.

In this chapter we will examine the nature of interpersonal relationships and the principles of how relationships work, building on the descriptions presented in Chapter 1.

293

**INSTRUCTIONAL GOALS
AND TIPS**

Draw on the board a long horizontal line that depicts the relationship continuum from impersonal to intimate. Working with students, plot types of relationships along this line and discuss the kinds of communication you would expect to experience in each. For instance, acquaintances are superficial relationships and require little time or energy. (Close friendships require a great deal of time, self-disclosure, and trust.)

**INSTRUCTIONAL GOALS
AND TIPS**

Point out to students that although we might choose to terminate a relationship of choice, it is more difficult to terminate one of circumstance (such as family). In the latter, the level of intimacy will change, but the relationship will continue.

DISCUSSION AND WRITING

Discuss with students how many superficial relationships they have as compared to intimate ones. [Expect the numbers will range from hundreds (for acquaintances) to a couple (for intimates).] Point out that the distinctions are generally a function of time and trust.

DISCUSSION AND WRITING

Ask students how many prefer to enroll in courses in which they know the instructor versus courses for which the instructor's name is not listed. Usually students feel greater levels of comfort and control if they can choose the instructor.

Relationships of Circumstance and Relationships of Choice

In Chapter 1 an interpersonal relationship is defined as an ongoing connection with another person that we carry in our minds (and metaphorically, in our hearts), whether the other person is present or not. These ongoing connections can be formed either because of unintentional circumstances or because of intentional choice. **Relationships of circumstance** form not because we choose them, but simply because our lives overlap with others' in some way. Relationships with family members, teachers, classmates, and coworkers fall into this category. In contrast, when we seek out and intentionally develop relationships, those are **relationships of choice**. These relationships might include friends, lovers, spouses, and counselors.

> It is chance that makes brothers but hearts that make friends.
>
> —VON GEIBEL

We act and communicate differently in these two types of relationships because the stakes are different. The effect of the same interpersonal communication behavior on different relationships can be dramatic. If we act in foolish or inappropriate ways, our friends might end the relationships. If we act the same way within the confines of our family, our relatives may not like us much, but we will still remain family.

Of course, these categories are not mutually exclusive. Relationships of circumstance can also be relationships of choice: Your brother or sister can also be your best friend. You can break off interacting with family members or quit your job to sever your relationships with fellow employees. In addition, the other individual can define and redefine the relationship. Your boss might fire you, a relative might cut you off, or a lover might desert you.

Trust, Intimacy, and Power in Relationships

We can further examine interpersonal relationships along three dimensions that are always present in varying degrees: trust, intimacy, and power. Although we have touched on these elements in other discussions, we will now examine more closely the role that they play in forming and maintaining relationships. You should recognize the importance interpersonal communication has in the development of these dimensions.

In an intimate, trusting relationship, we can feel safe in telling our deepest secrets to another person. (Peter Cade/Tony Stone Images)

Trust

Think about the kind of trust you have in people who are important to you. What does it mean to trust your doctor? Your lover or spouse? Your accountant? More than likely, each of these relationships involves a different kind of trust, as shown in Table 9.1.

In most interpersonal relationships, especially intimate ones, the last two types of trust listed in Table 9.1 are the most important. **Interpersonal trust** is the degree to which we feel safe in disclosing personal information to another person. We exhibit a variety of trusting behaviors: revealing intimate information

Table 9.1

Types of Trust

Types of Trust	Explanation	Example
Trust in someone's ability:	You believe that the person has the skill, knowledge, will, and ethical standards to do a good job or fulfill some role expectation.	Your accountant
Trust in someone's regard for your welfare:	You believe that this person will not cause you harm as you place your health, welfare, resources, and security in his or her hands.	Your doctor
Trust in someone's regard for privileged information:	You believe that the person to whom you have disclosed personal information will not use this information against you.	Your counselor or a friend
Trust in someone's relational commitment:	You believe that when you disclose personal information, the other will acknowledge your feelings and vulnerability, will not exploit you, and will remain in the relationship.	Your lover or partner

INTERNET RESOURCE
Trust:
Hot Link: http://pages. prodigy.net/liaisons/trusteln. htm
Power and Equality

DISCUSSION AND WRITING
Suggest that students reflect upon the different levels of trust they have in themselves, others, the world, or a higher power. This would also be an excellent journal entry. What are the implications of believing that oneself is more trustworthy than others?

RESEARCH AND LITERATURE
Hugh Prather, author of *Notes to Myself* (Real People Press, 1970), writes, "In order to see I have to be willing to be seen." Discuss the importance of self-disclosure for self-knowledge. Preview the Johari Window here (see page 320).

BUILDING YOUR SKILLS

Whom Do You Trust?

Create a list of names of those people with whom you have ongoing relationships: family members, coworkers, boss, friends, teachers, and so on. For each person on your list, write down the type of trust that char-

acterizes your relationship: trust in ability, trust in regard for your welfare, trust in protecting privileged information, or trust in commitment to the relationship. You can put down more than one type for each person. Next, assign a number from 1 to 10 for the amount of trust you have in

each person, with 1 being very little, and 10 being a lot.

Are your rankings consistently high or consistently low? What general observations can you make about how trusting you are of others?

CONSIDERING OTHERS

Who Trusts You?

So far we've been talking about how much trust you bestow on others. But how trustworthy are you? Use the list of names of those whom you trust to protect privileged information

and/or maintain a relational commitment. Using the same scale of 1 to 10, write down a number to indicate how much trust you believe the other person has in you.

How do your scores match up with those for the preceding

Building Your Skills? What are some of the reasons for the similarities and differences? In what kinds of relationships do you share a high degree of mutual trust? In what kinds is there a large imbalance in the levels of trust?

about ourselves; displaying our vulnerability to another; displaying confidence in him or her.[1] As a relationship develops, we look for proof that our partner is **trustworthy**. We look for behaviors to assure us that he or she accepts our feelings and won't exploit them, and that he or she will protect our vulnerability and remain in the relationship. These behaviors include such things as not cheating, protecting information we have disclosed about ourselves, and continuing to show affection and closeness even when we reveal negative or threatening information. Our partner, in turn, expects the same from us. To sustain a close interpersonal relationship, both participants need to exhibit and expect trusting and trustworthy behavior.[2]

There is a direct correlation between how much we trust someone and how much we can potentially gain from a relationship. The more we trust, the more information we are willing to share about ourselves, and the closer the relationship becomes. Sometimes this sharing is selective. Students may tell their professors about very personal family problems, yet they would never tell their professors if they cheated on an exam. You may tell your parents about your finances and your academic progress, but you may be reluctant to tell them about the development of each of your new intimate relationships.

INSTRUCTIONAL GOALS AND TIPS

Preview the Social Penetration Theory here (see page 318). Strive to whet your students' appetites for this information.

Intimacy

You have already seen that most relationships range from nonintimate to intimate. But what does *intimate* mean, exactly? Sometimes the term refers to the sexual activity in a relationship, but that is not the way we are using the term *intimacy* here. Instead, **intimacy** means the degree to which we can be ourselves in front of another person and still be accepted by him or her. We can measure intimacy by the extent to which other people let us know that they see us the same way we see ourselves and express positive feelings about who we are. We depend upon intimate relationships to bolster our self-confidence. The more intimate the relationship, the more the individuals depend upon each other for acceptance and confirmation of their self-image.[3] During periods when we might not have very intimate relationships, it is sometimes hard to maintain a strong self-image.

We communicate our sense of intimacy directly and indirectly, verbally and nonverbally. We might tell another person how we feel about him or her and how much we value the relationship. We might also use a variety of nonverbal cues, such as close physical proximity, eye contact, word selection, tone of voice, physical contact, and spending time together.

The more intimate a relationship, the stronger the emotional bond and the greater the mutual trust in relational commitment. Because we are placing confirmation of our self into another person's hands, there is a great deal of emotionality associated with developing and ending intimacy. The feeling of "being in love" can create a variety of emotional responses, depending upon the way we have been raised to deal with emotions, our emotional experiences, and our emotional self-image. We might welcome a growing sense of intimacy with excitement and enthusiasm, or turn away from it in fear.

Emotions sometimes fly in the face of reason. That is why we say that people are "blinded by love" or "infatuated." The roles that different emotions play in the development of intimacy are so many and varied that researchers and scholars have achieved little understanding of them. There is evidence that sharing and discussing emotions leads to a healthier life; generally, it is a good idea to talk about emotions with your partners as you attempt to understand and respect one another's needs and preferences.

As the following Arabian proverb so aptly puts it, intimacy is not simply a quality between lovers but also between good friends.

> A friend is one
> to whom one may pour
> out all the contents
> of one's heart,
> chaff and grain together
> knowing that the
> gentlest of hands
> will take and sift it,
> keep what is worth keeping
> and with a breath of kindness
> blow the rest away.

DISCUSSION AND WRITING

Ask students to write about the nature of intimacy for self-validation. How does dating or marriage confirm one's social standing? You might write the following statement on the board and ask students to reflect upon it: "Let's get married so we can be somebody."

TEACHING STRATEGY

The popular film *Fool for Love* casts a tale of brother and sister, raised in separate households, who meet and fall in love without awareness of their familial relationship. Their interaction is characterized by ongoing turmoil over their inability to clarify roles and define their relationship. While the story is an unorthodox one, it is worth consideration for its stark illustrations of chapter concepts. It also serves well for review of communication barriers, defensive climates, and disconfirming communication. Other student favorites include:

- *Singles*
- *Reality Bites*
- *Scenes from a Mall*

RESEARCH AND LITERATURE

M. Scott Peck, author of *The Road Less Traveled* (Simon & Schuster, 1978, Section II), asserts that "falling in love" is sexually motivated and invariably temporary. This is not genuine intimacy. Further, Peck defines love as the will to extend one's self for the purpose of nurturing one's own or another's spiritual growth (or evolution). Ask students whether people who are "in love" are capable of intimacy.

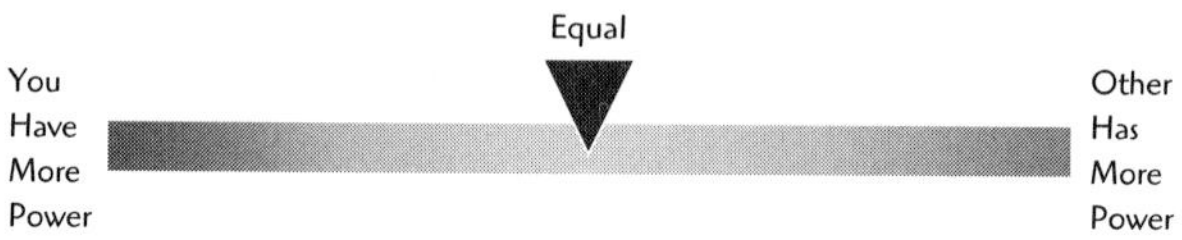

TEACHING STRATEGY

In discussing power, ask students to consider Waller's Principle of Least Interest: The person with the least invested in a relationship has the most power (as cited in J. L. Hocker and W. W. Wilmot, *Interpersonal Conflict (2nd ed.)*, Dubuque, Iowa: Wm. C. Brown Publishers, 1937). Ask students whether this seems to hold true in their interpersonal relationships. Discuss the "power source" that might be tapped by a person having and/or demonstrating "least interest."

- referent power (reducing the referent power of the other party)
- reward power (withholding the "reward" of concern and caring)
- coercive power (for example, punishing the other with "the silent treatment," communicating with "neutrality" rather than with "empathy")

INTERNET RESOURCE
Power
www.student.richmond.edu/~mgibbons/nc-reward.html
Power bases are defined and coercive power in particular is discussed.

http://www.theage.com.au/daily/971010/news/news21.html
In this article the use of legitimate power is discussed and exemplified.

TEACHING STRATEGY
Complementary relationships are discussed in this chapter as those in which "one partner willingly hands over power to the other." Ask students to consider whether we typically believe the lower-power party in an imbalanced-power relationship has chosen the lower-power

position. Again, the transactional model of communication recognizes mutual influence. Ask students to consider the abundance of television talk shows dedicating programs to portfolios on various types of victimization.

Power

The third dimension in interpersonal relationships, power, might be the most significant of all. We might not realize it, but distributing power between partners requires a lot of subtle negotiation. Furthermore, our ability to do it successfully is a major factor in relational development. Power and control have been defined in a variety of ways,[4] but for our purposes **interpersonal power** means the ability to influence another in the direction you desire—to get another person to do what you want.

All interactions involve power. If you ask some friends to go to the movies with you, you are attempting to influence them. If they say no, they are mustering resistance and, in essence, demonstrating their power over you. If you get upset by their rejection, you might offer to buy your friends' tickets, or to drive. We will discuss the issue of interpersonal persuasion (compliance gaining) in Chapter 10. We will also discuss power when we examine the nature of conflict in Chapter 10, because power negotiations often create or intensify conflict.

Every relationship you have with another person falls on the continuum shown in Figure 9.1. At one extreme you have more power than your partner; at the other, your partner has more power than you.

In some relationships, such as teacher to student or doctor to patient, there is a predefined imbalance of power. In Chapter 1 we referred to some relationships as complementary; in such relationships, one partner willingly hands over power to the other. For example, if one partner has trouble making decisions, he or she may feel comfortable letting the other partner make most of the purchases and plan most of the activities for the household. In a parallel relationship, power continually shifts from one partner to the other, depending upon the nature of the interaction or situation. For instance, if one partner is in charge of keeping the finances straight, he or she will have more power in budgetary decisions. If the other partner is a better cook, he or she probably will exert more power over decisions about diet and menus. When we try to equalize power in our relationships, we attempt to make them symmetrical. Although this might seem like an ideal to strive for, in fact, such attempts often backfire. When partners feel as if they have equal power over every decision, sometimes they compete with each other; neither one is willing to give in to the other person. The negotiation process can be time-consuming and ineffective when quick decisions are needed.

In all of these types of relationships, the balance of power affects how we talk and what we talk about; it is reflected in every message we convey. Read the sample interactions below to see if you can tell who has more power in each exchange.

Figure 9.1
Interpersonal Power

You Have More Power — Equal — Other Has More Power

■ INTERACTION ONE

Fong: Do you want me to sweep up the floor now?

Pearl: No, not yet. Go into the freezer and get me another container of fudge caramel.

Fong: Okay.

■ INTERACTION TWO

Mickey: So, do you want to go to a movie tonight, or just sit home and watch TV?

Sarah: I don't know. What movies are showing?

Mickey: Same old things. Nothing new has come out for a few weeks.

Sarah: Why don't we just stay home?

■ INTERACTION THREE

Al: I can't believe I failed that test. I don't think it was very fair. Should I go in and complain to the instructor?

Tika: Hey, you're the one who went out partying instead of studying.

Al: Don't remind me. Whose side are you on anyway? I don't need that kind of scolding.

Tika: You're always criticizing me for what I say to you. If you don't want my opinion, don't ask for it.

Al: Okay, I won't. Forget I said anything.

Interaction One is between an employee and a boss. Clearly, Pearl has more power than Fong in this situation. In Interaction Two the power tends to shift back and forth, but Sarah makes the final decision. In the third interaction the power balance is less obvious, but the last two statements seem to indicate that Tika has the upper hand. In all of these interactions, the messages have both an obvious meaning and a more subtle one that reflects the power-negotiation process. In the first interaction Pearl easily could have surrendered power by telling Fong, "You can decide if the floor needs to be swept." We can empower others by turning decision-making requests back to them.

When we communicate, we also affect the balance of power by exchanging information. Information is a source of power. Possessing special information or knowledge serves as the basis for expert power. In addition, when we trust another person enough to disclose information about ourselves, we give up control of that information, and empower the other person. If you reveal to a coworker at a bank that you were arrested at your last job for embezzlement, sharing that information gives your coworker a certain degree of power over you. He or she might threaten to tell your boss about your record in an attempt

Ask students to construct a list of dirty-fighting tactics: silent treatment, sarcasm, depersonalizing, hitting below the belt, and gunny-sacking. Next, ask students to explore suggestions for substituting constructive behaviors in place of these tactics.

DISCUSSION AND WRITING
Write the following phrases on the board: "Being taken of" and "Being taken." Ask students to write about how they view the roles of husbands and wives in terms of responsibilities. Is there a balance of power?

DISCUSSION AND WRITING
Ask students to form small groups to discuss the question of what kinds of marriages we should enter into and which ones we should leave. The debriefing will be very interesting!

INTERNET RESOURCE
Equality
www.umass.edu/soc/ncel/
This is the site of the National Coalition for Student Learning Equality. Issues of equality are raised and links are offered.

INTERNET RESOURCE
Symmetrical Relationships
http://www.si.dep.no/
k20–10–97/grunig.html
See how the Norwegian
government views symmet-
rical relationships.

DISCUSSION AND WRITING
Ask students to brainstorm
names of celebrities who
are able to use their referent
power to influence others in
public service announce-
ments and advertisements.
Consider Bill Cosby for
Jello, for instance.

DISCUSSION AND WRITING
M. Scott Peck argues that
"a good marriage can only
exist between two strong
and independent people"
(*The Road Less Traveled,*
Simon & Schuster, 1978,
p. 104). Encourage students
to discuss this assertion.

**RESEARCH AND
LITERATURE**
For further reading, con-
sider Regina Barreca's *Per-
fect Husbands and Other
Fairy Tales* (Harmony
Books, 1993).

to force you to comply with a request. Typically, however, as relationships move toward intimacy, both partners share information with the other in a fairly equal manner, which gives both power over each other. We will discuss the process of disclosing personal information later in this chapter.

Nonverbal behaviors and speech patterns also reflect an individual's percep-tion of his or her power relative to the person with whom he or she interacts. Traditionally, American cultural norms classify men's speech patterns as more powerful than women's. To be masculine is to be loud and forceful; to speak in deeper tones; to swear often; and to be authoritarian and blunt. Feminine speech, in contrast, is gentle, smooth, friendly, warm, quick, gossipy, high pitched, nonverbally expressive, and frequent. In truth, however, individuals of both sexes are apt to adopt either style. Table 9.2 lists behaviors that American culture classifies as "powerful" and "powerless."

One pair of researchers developed a classic framework for defining bases of power that has been tested in several communication contexts, including classrooms and small group communication settings. The framework includes five power sources that we use to influence others: legitimate power (or posi-tion power), referent power, expert power, reward power, and coercive power.[5] **Legitimate power** *is power that comes because of respect for a posi-tion that another person holds.* Teachers, parents, law officers, store man-agers, and company presidents all have power because of the position they hold relative to other people. When a police officer tells you to pull off to the side of the road you respond to this enactment of power by obeying the officer's command. **Referent power** *is power that comes from our attraction to another person, or the charisma a person possesses.* We let people we like influence us. We change our behavior to meet their demands or desires because we are attracted to them. **Expert power** *is based on the influence derived from a person's knowledge and experience.* We convey power on those who know more than we do, or have some expertise we don't possess. This knowledge can even include knowledge about how to manage a relationship effectively. We grant power to partners who have more experience in relation-ships. There were frequent episodes of the *Seinfeld* TV series in which the characters defer to the expertise of their friends when it came to how to handle various relational crisis. **Reward power** *is based on another person's ability to satisfy our needs.* There are obvious rewards, such as money and gifts, but most rewards are more interpersonal in nature. In Chapter 2 we talked about the interpersonal needs of control, affection, and inclusion. The degree to which another person is able to satisfy these needs gives them cer-tain power over us. For example, those people who are able to help us meet our need to be included in social activities have power over us. We will do what they ask if we see that our need will continue to be met. Reward power is probably the most common form of power in interpersonal relationships. Withholding rewards is actually a form of punishment, or what is called coer-cive power. **Coercive power** *involves the use of sanctions or punishment to influence others.* Sanctions include holding back or removing rewards. If you have a high need for physical affection, your partner might threaten to hold back that affection if you do not comply with a given request. We might

Table 9.2[6]

Cues that Indicate Powerful and Powerless Speech

"Powerful" Speaker	"Powerless" Speaker
Talks first	Talks last if at all
Dominates speaking time	Doesn't talk much
Initiates conversations	Lets others initiate
Makes longer statements	Makes short statements/replies
Talks over others	Makes frequent hedging statements (Ah . . . , Um . . .)
Interrupts	Adds qualifiers (. . .if that's okay. Maybe)
Asks questions	Uses disclaimers (I'm not very good at . . .)
Uses expletives	Makes nervous gestures
	Makes frequent gestures
	Uses overly formal grammar
	Uses polite language (Please, Thanks)

BUILDING YOUR SKILLS

Powerful and Powerless Cues

Form groups of three students.

1. Student A and student B will engage in a debate. Student A will argue that all eighteen- to twenty-year-olds should do compulsory government service for a year. Student B will argue against that proposal. Student C should carefully listen and watch the other two, recording powerful and powerless speech cues. After three to five minutes, stop, and trade roles.

2. Student A will record the power cues while student B argues that all incoming college students should be required to own a personal computer and student C argues against it. Again, stop after three to five minutes, and switch again.

3. Student B will record while students A and C take opposite sides to debate whether we should extend the length of the elementary and high school year by an additional month.

After you have completed all three debates, share your observations about power cues. Which powerful and powerless cues did people use most often? What effect did the topic have upon the use of these cues? What effect did switching roles have? To what degree was each of you affected by your partner's use of powerful or powerless speech?

RECAP Dimensions of Interpersonal Relationships

TRUST	The degree to which we are comfortable disclosing personal information about ourselves to another.
INTIMACY	The degree to which individuals depend upon each other for acceptance and confirmation of their self-image.
POWER	The ability to influence another person in a desired direction.

SKILL DEVELOPMENT
This exercise can be very helpful to those students with habitual powerless speech patterns. Variation: Instruct two student volunteers to conduct a mock employment interview in front of the class. You and the rest of the class will count examples of powerless speech. After the interviews, switch roles and do the exercise again. Process the exercise with the same questions offered on page 301. Additionally, you should impress upon students that employers are looking for powerful and productive employees during the employment interview.

Friendship and Culture

The following chart lists the qualities associated with friendship (and their importance) for three cultures. These qualities reflect inherent values of each culture, which, as you can see, vary widely.

United States	Korea	Nigeria
Trust (high)	Generosity (high)	Tolerance (high)
Respect (high)	Intelligence (high)	Honesty (high)
Authenticity (high)	Congeniality (moderate)	Caring (high)
Psychological support (low)	Sympathy (moderate)	Trust (high)
	Unselfishness (moderate)	Responsibility (moderate)
Responsibility (moderate)	Humor (low)	
Honesty (moderate)		

From A. M. Nicotera, "Summary of Studies on the Theory of Friendship and Consideration of Implications." In *Interpersonal Communication in Friend and Mate Relationships*, A. M. Nicotera and Associates (Albany, NY: State University of New York Press, 1993), 125–35.

threaten to end the relationship as a sanctioned form of power in order to accomplish a given goal. Punishment involves imposing something on another person that he or she does not want. Coercive power exists in relationships when one partner has the ability to impose the sanction or punishment on another. Your parents had the power to take away your allowance when you were younger, and therefore you did the chores they requested. However, once you have your own source of income, your parents no longer have this source of power over you.

Not for Love but Money

Money may not buy happiness, but it's a key ingredient in the potion of love.

A study suggests that women rank a man's "salary and earning potential" above attractiveness, education, or occupation as a key criterion for selecting a mate, researchers said in findings presented at the annual meeting of the American Psychological Association recently in Chicago.

Men favor attractiveness above all else, followed by income, the study found. Drs. Belinda Tucker and Saskia Karen Subramanian of University of California, Los Angeles, reached those conclusions after interviewing 3,407 adults between the ages of eighteen and fifty-five in twenty-one cities.

Tucker said it was striking that the surveys found men's economic concerns are almost as strong as women's—reflecting "the new reality that making it today requires two income-producing partners."

Some general trends emerged from the surveys:

- While money is the most important factor in mate selection for women, it's even more important for women in the South than in cities in other regions.
- Men and women who rate themselves as highly attractive are most demanding in requiring top income potential.
- Men and women living in cities with high unemployment or poverty rates were more likely to be attracted to potential mates with high earning potential.
- Money is as important as sex in maintaining a relationship, as well. "In general, it's the key factor before and during marriage," Tucker said.

The study also suggested that some men who lose their jobs may have reason to be concerned about the faithfulness of their wives, but men whose wives lose their jobs are only slightly less likely to stray.

Researchers were somewhat surprised that men as well as women believe "men have the obligation to provide" financially for the family.

Male or female, across ethnic group or race, one thing is clear, Tucker said:

"Satisfaction with your partner's financial contributions is strongly related to how you feel about your relationship, and whether you feel you will stay in the relationship."

From: Cox News Service (August 26, 1997).

Interpersonal Attraction: The Spark for a Relationship

Knowing the types and dimensions of relationships is helpful to our understanding of how relationships work, but it is not sufficient to explain how and why they begin. What does it mean to say that you are attracted to another person? **Interpersonal attraction** is the degree to which you desire to form or maintain an interpersonal relationship.

Attraction exists whenever we feel a positive regard for another person, or when we like someone; however, the intensity or strength of that attraction varies from relationship to relationship. Think about your feelings of liking for those people you regard as casual friends, and those you regard as best friends. You *like* your best friends more—you have greater attraction toward your best friends. There is a strong correlation between the level of intimacy in a relationship and our level of attraction. Our feelings of attraction continually change as relationships change.

Interpersonal attraction occurs in the early stages of relational development as short-term initial attraction, and in the later stages of relational development as long-term maintenance attraction. You can understand the difference between the two by looking at your own relationships. Think of the dozens of

INSTRUCTIONAL GOALS AND TIPS
Consider sharing with students the circumstances of your initial encounter with your spouse or best friend.

INTERNET RESOURCE
Attraction
www.sexinabottle.co.uk
This site claims to have a product that will make you irresistible to the opposite sex. Fact or fiction; you be the judge.

DISCUSSION AND WRITING
Ask students to write a description of the single person with whom they would most like to be stranded on a desert island. Give them choices: a farmer, a model, a minister, or a speech communication professor. Discuss these answers in small groups.

MEDIA AND OUTSIDE RESOURCES

Consider showing the complementary attraction of Cee Cee Bloom and Bertie Barron in Iris Rainer Dart's novel/film *Beaches*.

RESEARCH AND LITERATURE

For more information on this topic, reference Ellen Berscheid and Elaine Hatfield Walster's text *Interpersonal Attraction* (Addison-Wesley, 1978).

people whom you initially found attractive but with whom you never developed an intimate relationship. **Short-term initial attraction** is the degree to which we sense a *potential* for developing an interpersonal relationship. For instance, you might find one of your classmates to be physically attractive, but never move to introduce yourself. The information you gather in your first interaction with someone can also generate a short-term initial attraction for a relationship, which you may or may not pursue, depending upon the circumstances. **Long-term maintenance attraction**, on the other hand, is the type that sustains relationships like your best friendships. It refers to a level of liking or positive feeling that motivates us to maintain or escalate a relationship. Short-term attraction gives way to long-term attraction as a relationship develops through the stages we will discuss in Chapter 10.

Think about your best friend. How did that relationship start? Perhaps it was because he or she was physically attractive, or perhaps you observed your friend laughing and joking with others and found that quality attractive. Why are you still friends with this person? Rarely (except in movies or TV shows) do we commit to, and maintain, a long-term intimate relationship such as marriage solely because we find another person physically attractive.[7] Perhaps you have discovered that you and your friend have a lot in common, or that you complement each other's personalities. For instance, your friend's calm, even disposition might balance your fiery temper.

Elements of Interpersonal Attraction

Why do we feel attracted to some people and not to others? The explanations are complex, but researchers have identified seven elements that influence our feelings of attraction. As you read about them, try to analyze your own feelings about people you find attractive.

 PHYSICAL ATTRACTION

The degree to which we find another person's physical self appealing represents our **physical attraction** to him or her. That appeal might be based on size, height, clothing, hairstyle, makeup, jewelry, vocal qualities, gestures, and so forth. The old adage, "Beauty is in the eye of the beholder," is particularly true in terms of explaining physical attraction. Each culture has its own definition of the physical ideal, which it teaches and perpetuates. In the United States, for instance, advertisements and TV programs promote a slender ideal for both males and females. This certainly contributes to the American fixation on losing weight and staying fit. However, in some cultures, and at various times throughout history, physical attractiveness was synonymous with bulkiness.

Physical attractiveness acts as a convenient filter to reduce relationship possibilities.[8] In general, we tend to seek out individuals who represent the same level of physical attractiveness as ourselves. Suppose you are really into physical conditioning and have a personal philosophy about good eating habits, exercising, avoiding drugs, and not smoking. You will probably seek out and attract a physically fit person to be your partner. To a certain degree, the physical image a person presents can reflect more substantive qualities. For example, there is a good possibility that a physically fit individual's philosophy about eating and exercise would be similar to yours. That similarity might serve as the basis for a long-term maintenance attraction. As you learned in Chapter 3, we use superficial information to make inferences about personality with varying degrees of accuracy, but whether we decide to escalate a relationship depends upon what happens in the initial interaction and subsequent interactions.

■ CREDIBILITY, COMPETENCE, AND CHARISMA

Most of us are also attracted to individuals who seem competent and credible. We like those who are sure of themselves, but not full of themselves. We assume they are competent if they seem skilled, knowledgeable, and experienced. We find people credible if they display a blend of enthusiasm, trustworthiness, competence, and power. Competence, credibility, and sometimes physical attractiveness are all important elements in the composite quality we call *charisma*, which inspires strong attraction and allegiance. Political and other types of leaders often depend upon their charisma to attract supporters who are motivated to form relationships with them and willing to devote themselves to a chosen cause.

■ PROXIMITY

We are more likely to be attracted to people who are physically close to us than to those who are farther away. In this class, you are more likely to form relationships with classmates sitting on either side of you than with someone seated at the opposite end of the room. This is partly because physical **proximity** increases communication opportunities. We tend to talk with someone on a casual, offhand basis because he or she is right next to us. We are more likely to talk, and therefore to feel attracted to, neighbors who live right next door than those who live down the block. Any circumstance that increases the possibilities for interacting is also likely to increase attraction.

In impromptu surveys of students in our classes over the years, your authors have found that a high percentage form close friendships with dormitory roommates who were randomly assigned. There is a good chance that two individuals will become good friends simply because they share living accommodations. In one study on attraction, a researcher told pairs of people about each other, describing to each the other's dissimilar attitudes on a particular topic.[9] The participants were then asked to rate their attraction to the other person. All of the ratings were low. Then the partners were introduced to one another and allowed to interact. Even when they discussed only the attitude on which they disagreed, they had significantly more attraction for one another. Clearly, the information exchange that communication affords, increases our ability to make an informed decision about pursuing a relationship. In addition, in both of these examples, the interaction was

MEDIA AND OUTSIDE RESOURCES
Consider showing or discussing the relationships between characters in the films *The Breakfast Club*, *The Great Escape*, or nearly any other prison or military movie.

Physical proximity plays a pivotal role in interpersonal attraction. We are much more inclined to find our next-door neighbors to our liking than to be attracted to someone who lives a block away. (Catherine Karnow / Woodfin Camp & Associates)

between two college students—two individuals who already have a great deal in common. That commonality is the source of the next form of attraction.

■ SIMILARITY

In general, we are attracted to people whose personality, values, upbringing, personal experiences, attitudes, and interests are **similar** to ours. We seek them out through shared activities. For example, you may join a folk dance group because you know the members share a dance interest with you. Within the group, you would be especially attracted to those who have a similar sense of humor, who share the same attitudes on certain issues, or who enjoy some of the same additional activities that you do. As we interact, we discover both similarities and differences between ourselves and others. We assess the relative weight of those similarities and differences and arrive at a level of attraction that may change over time as we continue to discover more information.

In the initial stages of a relationship, we try to emphasize positive information about ourselves to create a positive and attractive image. We reveal those aspects of ourselves that we believe we have in common with the other person, and the other person does the same.[10] Think about your initial interactions with strangers; typically, you spend the first few minutes trying to find topics of mutual interest. You discover that the person is from a place near your hometown, has the same musical tastes, likes the same sports, frequents the same restaurants, has been to your favorite campground, has the same attitude about school, has had the same instructor for history class, and on and on. But the depth of this information is limited. You save your revelations about important attitudes and issues for a later stage in the relational development process.[11] Attitude similarity is more likely to be a source of long-term maintenance attraction than of short-term initial attraction.

■ COMPLEMENTARY NEEDS

You have heard the adage, "Opposites attract." Although we like people with whom we have much in common, most of us wouldn't find it very exciting to be stuck for the rest of our lives with someone who has identical attitudes, needs, values, and interests. Most of us look instead for someone with **complementary needs**. Schutz identified three interpersonal needs that motivate us to form and maintain relationships with others: inclusion, control, and affection. *Inclusion* represents the need to include others in our activities, or to be included in theirs. *Control* represents the need to make decisions and take responsibility, or the willingness to accept others' decision making. *Affection* represents the need to be loved and accepted by others, or the willingness to give love and acceptance to others.

If you have a high need to control and make decisions, and little respect for others' decision making, you will be more compatible with someone who does not have similar needs—someone who wants others to make decisions for him or her. In essence, we can view pairs of individuals as a team in which both sides complement the other side's weaknesses. If you're not very good at keeping track of your bills and balancing your checkbook, you might pair up with someone who is good at maintaining a budget to create a strong personal finance team. In reality, there are no "perfect" matches, only degrees of compatibility relative to needs.

■ RELATIONSHIP POTENTIAL

We need interpersonal relationships to confirm our self-image. **Predicted Outcome Value theory** claims that we assess the potential for any given relationship to meet this relational need and then weigh that assessment against the potential costs.[12] We are attracted to others with whom a relationship may yield a high outcome value (the rewards might exceed the costs). Over time, our assessments may change. In the movie *When Harry Met Sally*, for example, the main characters both thought initially that their relationship had little potential of meeting their needs. Over time, Harry and Sally developed a friendship that did meet certain needs. At that point they both thought the relationship had gone as far as it could. In the end, however, they discovered that they could have a more intimate relationship with a high outcome value.

Like Harry and Sally, most of us begin predicting outcome values in initial interactions and continually modify our predictions as we learn more and more about the other person. We pursue attractions beyond the initial interaction stage if we think they can yield positive outcomes, and generally avoid or terminate relationships for which we predict negative outcomes.[13]

■ RECIPROCATION OF LIKING

Reciprocation-linking simply means that we like people who like us. One way to get other people to reciprocate is to show that we like them. However, in initial interactions we are often reluctant to let other people know that we are attracted to them. We may hold back from showing our interest because we

MEDIA AND OUTSIDE RESOURCES
Ask your faculty resource administrator to purchase copies of Schutz' FIRO-B (the Fundamental Interpersonal Relationship Orientation-Behavior questionnaire). Administer this survey to your students and discuss the results.

MEDIA AND OUTSIDE RESOURCES
Robert Waller's novel and subsequent film *The Bridges of Madison County* (Warner, 1992) provides an alternate example of relationship potential.

RESEARCH AND LITERATURE
This principle is the basis of Dale Carnegie's advice in *How to Win Friends and Influence People* (Simon & Schuster, 1937). Reinforcement theorists and cognitive consistency theorists agree that we dislike those who dislike us.

SKILL DEVELOPMENT

As an alternative to this exercise, make copies of the questionnaire and provide students with four copies each. Tell students that they should select a significant other in their life and get them to participate in this exercise. Both parties should fill out two questionnaires, one for their own perceived levels of need and one for their perception of the other party's levels of need. As students compare findings, they are likely to have some distress over the gap between self-perceptions and those perceptions our significant others have of us. Warn students in advance to help them anticipate the stress and cope in a proactive manner. One example of a proactive response to such tension might include discussing the differing perceptions and together trying to isolate examples where these perceptions originate. Another approach might be to focus on steps that can be taken to close the gap between self and other perceptions with regard to needs.

fear rejection or fear that we may give the other person a certain amount of power over us.

A study conducted by one of your authors and a colleague found that we often underestimate how much a new acquaintance is attracted to us.[14] Pairs of male and female college students interacted for the first time and then indicated their level of attraction for their partner, as well as their perception of how attracted their partner was to them. Most of the students significantly underestimated the amount of attraction the other person felt for them. It is unclear whether we underestimate because we don't have much confidence that others will like us as much as we like them, or because we, as Americans, in general do not communicate effectively our level of attraction for others. Even in long-term relationships, people sometimes repress their continued attraction for their friends or mates. As you interact with new acquaintances, keep in mind that they probably are more attracted to you than you realize, so you might want to adapt your decision making accordingly.

Communication of Attraction

In general, the more we are attracted to someone, the more we attempt to communicate with him or her, although sometimes circumstances limit our ability to act upon our attraction. **Communicating attraction** is one of the ways we indicate our attraction. We avoid people we do not like and seek out those we do. Usually, the amount of communication and interaction we have with a person indicates the level of attraction in the relationship. We try to interact most often with people whom we find attractive.

■ STRATEGIES FOR COMMUNICATING ATTRACTION

When we are attracted to people, we use both indirect and direct strategies to communicate our liking, through nonverbal and verbal cues. Nonverbal cues are typically indirect and are often referred to as immediacy. For instance, we tend to reduce the physical distance between us; increase our eye contact and use of touch; lean forward; keep an open body orientation; and smile. We also use the courtship readiness behaviors, preening behaviors, positional cues, and appeals to invitation described in Chapter 7.

We also indirectly communicate our attraction verbally. We use informal and personal language, addressing the person by his or her first name and often referring to "you and I," and "we." We ask questions to show interest, probe for details when our partner shares information, listen responsively, and refer to information shared in past interactions. All of these are confirming behaviors that demonstrate that we value what the other person is saying.

We can also directly communicate our attraction verbally. Most of us don't do this very often. But think about how you feel when a friend tells you that he or

People use an array of nonverbal cues to let others know whether or not they want to make contact. Can you imagine what exchange of cues might have taken place before the photographer snapped this photo? (Bill Horsman/Stock Boston)

INTERNET RESOURCE
Spontaneity
http://www.fastcompany.com/online/06/burton3.html
This site develops the thesis that what we often consider to be spontaneous may be the result of structure. Spontaneity and teaching are examined in this light.

Attraction and the Development of Relationships

The following excerpt illustrates several principles that underlie attraction and the development of relationships. Through their interaction on a work project, two coworkers shared a growing attraction and began sharing personal information as well. Their attraction was based partially on complementary needs—she was impatient, he was easygoing. And it developed despite racial differences (she is white and he is black). Although the community's response to their developing intimacy forced them to move, the bond between them was strong enough to sustain the relationship.

When Karen, forty-three, first met Andrew, forty-five, they had work on their minds, not romance. They both were employed in Charlotte, North Carolina, he as an engineer and she as a systems troubleshooter.

"I was working on a difficult project, and he offered to help," says Karen. "I found out what an easygoing, understanding person he is. I'm very impatient, and he helped me stay focused. In a way, we're opposites—that's how it all began."

They started meeting in Karen's home to work on the project. When it was finally completed, she invited Andrew over for a celebratory dinner. "Sometime during that meal, I realized that our friendship had gone beyond the professional, but I wasn't ready to accept it," says Karen. "In the back of my mind, I was thinking, Oh my God, what have I done?"

Karen was so unnerved by her feelings that she took a three-week vacation to North Dakota to put some distance between herself and Andrew. Though she had never considered herself a prejudiced person, neither had she pictured herself being married to a black man. But, she says, "I just couldn't get him out of my mind." The day

she returned home, there were a dozen roses from him on her front step. "I knew right then that we were going to be together," she recalls.

After almost two months of dating, they sat down and talked about the problems they would face if they wed. Both had been married before within their respective races. Though they knew there would be difficulties, their love carried them forward. Their first joint decision: leave town. The atmosphere in Charlotte, as in many parts of the South, was just too charged, and the reactions they got walking down the street arm in arm were unsettling.

"I'm surprised people's heads didn't just whiplash off their necks," Karen says, "We could hear people whisper, 'Did you see that?' The first few times I was crushed, but after a while it didn't matter to me as much."

From: Lois Romano and Jacqueline Tescott, Redbook.

MEDIA AND OUTSIDE RESOURCES

Suggest that students explore a Hallmark card rack to note how some cards are designed to attend to immediacy needs. (There are lines of cards for parents to share with children, for instance.)

she likes you. It raises your self-esteem; you feel valued. You can make others feel that way by communicating your liking for them, although in the early stages of relational development, there are social mores against doing so. We verbally communicate liking in other, more subtle ways as well. We might tell someone that we like a particular trait or ability, such as the way she tells jokes, or the way he handled an irritating customer. Or we might compliment someone's outfit, hairstyle, or jewelry. Each of these messages communicates attraction for the other person and is likely to elicit a positive response from him or her.

We also use **affinity seeking** strategies to get people to like us. Table 9.3 summarizes the strategies that one research team identified.[15] Often, the methods just described to communicate attraction double as affinity-seeking strategies. In addition to using nonverbal immediacy cues and verbal self-concept confirmation, we often try to establish mutual trust, be polite, show concern

Table 9.3

Affinity-Seeking Strategies

1.	Control	Present yourself as in control, independent, free-thinking; show that you have the ability to reward the other person.	"I'm planning on going to grad school, and after that I'm going to Japan to teach English." "You can borrow my notes for the class you missed if you'd like."
2.	Visibility	Look and dress attractively; present yourself as an interesting, energetic, and enthusiastic person; increase your visibility to the other person.	"Wow, that was a great show about Chinese acrobats. I do gymnastics too. Would you like to come watch me next week in our dual meet?"
3.	Mutual Trust	Present yourself as honest and reliable; display trustworthy behaviors; show that you trust the other person by self-disclosing.	"That guy you're having problems with called me and asked about you. I told him I didn't have anything to say." "I've never told anyone this, but I'd really like to be an astronaut."
4.	Politeness	Follow appropriate conversational rules; let the other person assume control of the interaction.	"I'm sorry, I interrupted. I thought you were done. Please, go on." "No you're not boring me at all; it's very interesting. Please tell me more about it."
5.	Concern and Caring	Show interest in and ask questions about the other person; listen; show support and be sensitive; help the other person accomplish something or feel good about him- or herself.	"How is your mother doing after her operation?" "I'd like to help out at the benefit you're chairing this weekend." "That must have been really hard for you, growing up under those conditions."
6.	Other-Involvement	Put a positive spin on activities you share; draw the other person into your activities; display nonverbal immediacy and involvement with the other person.	"This is a great party, I'm glad you came along." "A group of us are going to get a midnight snack; how about coming along?"
7.	Self-Involvement	Try to arrange for encounters and interactions; engage in behaviors that encourage the other person to form a closer relationship.	"Oh hi! I knew your class ended at two, so I thought I'd try to catch you." "It would really be fun to go camping together this summer; I have this favorite place."
8.	Common-alities	Point out similarities between yourself and the other person; try to establish equality (balanced power); present yourself as comfortable and at ease around the other person.	"I've got that computer game too. Don't you love the robots?" "Let's both work on the project together. We're a great team." "It's so easy to talk to you. I really feel comfortable around you."

Adapted from R. A. Bell and J. A. Daly, "The Affinity Seeking Function of Communications," *Communication Monographs* 51 (1984): 91–115.

ELECTRONIC CONNECTIONS

Conversation with a Computer

Carrying on conversations is not an easy task. We must learn to adapt to the other person, to follow the flow of the interaction, to pick up cues from the other person and incorporate them into the exchange, and to achieve a balance between asking for and offering information. There are no hard-and-fast rules. In fact the task is so complex that computer programmers cannot replicate our ability to carry on conversations.

A 1994 annual contest at California State University at San Marcos again proved that making conversation is an art, not a science. The objective of the competition was for computer programmers to create a software program that would convince judges that they were communicating with another person. As in the past three years of the competition, the computers fooled no one. All of the judges correctly identified whether they were interacting with a computer or a person. The contest is structured so that ten judges have conversations with ten different computer terminals. Half of the judges were interacting with people; the other half were connected to computers programmed to respond to questions and statements from the judge. The computers were programmed to talk about such things as pets, the *Star Trek* television series, environmental issues, and the O. J. Simpson trial. The people who were interacting with the judges conversed about such things as American history, classical music, cryonics, comics, and the Rolling Stones. Artificial intelligence creators still have some work to do before they can emulate the complex and sometimes challenging process of talking with another human being.

Adapted from David L. Wilson, The Chronicle of Higher Education.

and caring, and involve others in our activities. Apparently, these strategies do work. The researchers found that individuals who seemed to use many affinity-seeking strategies were perceived by others as likable, socially successful, and satisfied with their lives.

Self-Disclosure: A Foundation for Relational Escalation

Self-disclosure occurs when we provide information to others that they would not learn if we did not tell them. People can learn our approximate age, height, and weight by just observing us. But they can't learn our exact age, height, or weight unless we disclose it. Disclosing personal information not only provides a basis for another person to understand us better, it conveys our level of trust and acceptance of the other person. In these ways, self-disclosure serves a relational function. We develop relationships through self-disclosure, and we define relationships by the degree of mutual self-disclosure. A distinguishing quality associated with your best friends is that you have shared your most personal information with them.

Because self-disclosure plays such an important role in our relationships, we will look at some of the ways it functions in more detail. Most of the principles

Rules for Self-Disclosing

Each culture has its own special rules about self-disclosure. In some cultures, individuals are open about sharing personal information, whereas in other cultures it is considered rude to even talk about yourself. Imagine that an individual from another country is coming to visit you and wants to know the "self-disclosure rules" in your culture. Write down as many rules as you can think of, including such things as the type of information that is appropriate to disclose in each of the relational escalation stages: initiation, exploration, intensification, and intimacy. What happens when the rules are violated? What are the exceptions to the rules?

discussed here have been identified in research on self-disclosure in the United States and are limited in their cross-cultural application. Before reading this section, be sure to read and think about Building Your Skills: Rules for Self-Disclosing.

Self-Disclosure Is a Building Block for Intimacy

As relationships move toward intimacy, they typically include periods of high self-disclosure early in the relationship. However, the *amount* of information that is disclosed decreases as the relationship becomes more and more intimate. In other words, there is generally more self-disclosing activity earlier in a relationship than later. As a relationship proceeds, we begin sharing low-risk information fairly rapidly, move on to share higher risk information, and then finally, to share our most intimate disclosures. The more intimate the relationship becomes, the more intimate the information that is disclosed. The sculpture below represents the way we reveal ourselves when we are with close friends.

As we develop a relationship we reveal more of ourselves, removing the masks that we routinely use with strangers. (Sandra Rice)

DISCUSSION AND WRITING
Try the first "Learning with Others" exercise at the end of this chapter. Are there differences for men and women, for adults and children, for professionals and unemployed?

TEACHING STRATEGY
For discussion, ask students to describe their methods for reducing uncertainty about the following types of interpersonal encounters:

- blind dates
- known, potential dates
- new neighbors
- job interviewers
- professors

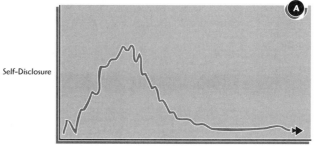

A long and intimate
relationship

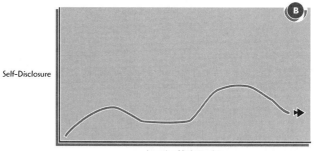

Two individuals who
started to get to know
each other, but were
interrupted before
finally becoming friends.

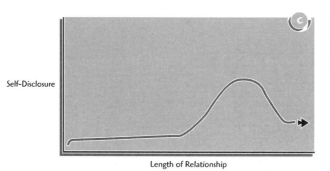

Two individuals who
knew each other as
acquaintances before
the relationship started
to escalate.

Figure 9.2

Self-Disclosure and
Relational Development

||| INTERPERSONAL COMMUNICATION RELATIONSHIPS

Self-Disclosure Patterns

Think about two of your current relationships and draw a graph like those in Figure 9.2 to show how the self-disclosure has progressed in each of them. How do the patterns compare? What do the differences or similarities reflect about the two relationships? What caused the peaks and valleys? Were there times when you or your partner tried to increase the rate of self-disclosure, and the other person rejected that attempt? What happened?

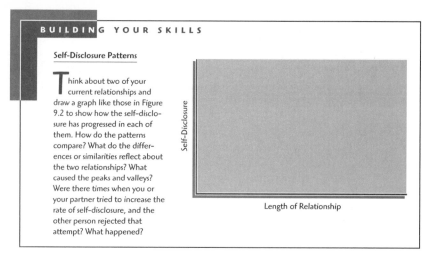

Length of Relationship

Holding back from sharing intimate information signals a reluctance to escalate the relationship. The amount of information that we have to share about ourselves is finite, so we slow down as we have less left to disclose.

Graph A in Figure 9.2 illustrates a typical disclosure pattern over the course of a long and intimate relationship. The peaks and valleys represent periods of variable disclosure. Note that most of the disclosure takes place in the beginning of the relationship. Not all relationships progress this way, however. The relationship in graph B represents two individuals who started to get to know each other but were interrupted before they became close friends. They might have stopped because of some conflict, indecisiveness about pursuing the relationship, or external circumstances that limited opportunities for interacting. When the disclosure resumed, it became more intense. Graph C represents two individuals who probably knew each other as acquaintances for some time but never really had the opportunity or inclination to self-disclose. Once they did begin to escalate the relationship, however, there was a steep rise in self-disclosure. This graph might represent two coworkers who eventually start dating, or two students who have shared a class or two together before striking up a friendship.

Generally, a dramatic increase or decrease in self-disclosure reflects some significant change in the relationship. Even long-term relationships have significant increases and decreases in disclosure that signify changes. Before the birth of a first child, for example, both parents might disclose their fears and expectations about child rearing, and the information might have a profound effect on the relationship.

Interpersonal relationships cannot achieve intimacy without self-disclosure. Without true self-disclosure, we form only superficial relationships. You can confirm another person's self-concept, and have your self-concept confirmed, only if both you and your partner have revealed yourselves to each other.

RESEARCH AND LITERATURE
Introduce students to the five levels of communication in John Powell's book, *Why Am I Afraid to Tell You Who I Am?* (Argus, 1969). The levels of communication are the phatic, factual, opinion, feelings, and communal levels.

INSTRUCTIONAL GOALS AND TIPS

Compare self-disclosure to balloon launching. When disclosing, we launch a trial balloon that is vulnerable to attack. We expect that it will not be shot down and that the other will launch a similar balloon (reciprocate).

INSTRUCTIONAL GOALS AND TIPS

Stress that disclosures are best done incrementally, as a function of time and trust. (This is congruent with Powell's levels of communication.)

INSTRUCTIONAL GOALS AND TIPS

Point out that we self-disclose to help ourselves, others, and the relationship. If disclosure does not do this, it is not appropriate.

We Expect Self-Disclosure to Be Reciprocal and Appropriate

One rule that you might have noted in Building Your Skills: Rules for Self-Disclosing, on page 315, is that in mainstream U.S. culture, when we share information about ourselves, we expect the other person to share similar information about her or himself. If you introduce yourself to someone, by giving your name, you expect that person to respond by telling you his or her name. This cultural rule allows us to use disclosure as a strategy for gaining information and reducing uncertainty.

If the other person does not reciprocate, however, both people might feel resentful. Sharing information about yourself gives others a certain amount of power over you. If the other person reciprocates and discloses similar information, it helps maintain an equal balance of power. But if one person shares information and the other doesn't, the resulting imbalance causes discomfort. Perhaps you can recall how you felt when an acquaintance chose to relate his or her troubles to you, a relative stranger. We do not necessarily want to know the deep dark secrets of those with whom we have a limited relationship.

Sometimes these unwanted disclosures occur because one person misjudges the nature of the relationship. In Building Your Skills: Rules for Self-Disclosing, you probably identified some kinds of information that are inappropriate to disclose at an early stage, but appropriate to disclose later on in a relationship. You must assess the relationship and situation to determine the appropriateness of any given disclosure.

We Assess Self-Disclosure Risks Differently

What is high self-disclosing for one person might be low self-disclosing for another and vice versa. In judging what and when to disclose, you need to realize that different people have different standards. For instance, some individuals are quite comfortable talking about their sex lives with relative strangers, whereas others find such discussions appropriate only in the most intimate relationships. The context in which the disclosure is made also affects the risk level. Giving your name and phone number to a stranger at a bar might be riskier than sharing that same information with a new member of your church group or a classmate needing an assignment.

Be sensitive to the other person when you choose what and when to disclose. Consider how the other person will react to the information. Although you may not feel certain information is intimate, the other person may. Conversely, when your partner reveals information, try to determine whether it is highly personal to her or him. You could upset the other person if you fail to treat the information appropriately. If you share that information with others, for example, your partner may feel betrayed.

The research findings about differences between male and female self-disclosure are contradictory. Some research shows that males give more information to strangers than females, but that the information is not very intimate. Females are reportedly more intimate in their disclosures with friends. Other studies found that both males and females prefer to disclose to females.[16] These findings are consistent with cultural stereotypes in the United States: both men and women perceive women as more sensitive, empathic, and supportive; whereas they consider men aggressive and control oriented. We perpetuate these stereotypes in our interactions when we expect someone to behave in a certain way because of his or her sex.

There is nothing inherent in men or women that leads them to self-disclose more or less. In truth, some men are highly self-disclosing and some women are quite closed. You will be most effective in your communication with others if you treat each person as an individual, putting aside stereotypical expectations about their self-disclosing behavior. If you find that someone is reluctant to disclose, don't attribute that behavior to his or her sex; look for an explanation in the person's background, upbringing, or past relationships.

We Base Self-Disclosure on an Analysis of Costs and Rewards

As we have seen, self-disclosure is not without its costs and risks. When we disclose, we make ourselves vulnerable, we forfeit control of information, we might hurt or insult the other by saying things he or she finds offensive, we risk signaling an unintended level of intimacy, and we risk damaging the relationship with ill-timed and inappropriate disclosures. Typically, we seek a balance between the potential risks and rewards. In each stage of relational development, there is an optimum level of self-disclosure with which the individuals are comfortable. As Figure 9.3 indicates, if we go beyond that level, one or both partners might become less satisfied.

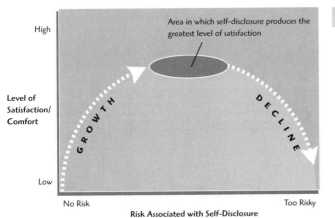

Figure 9.3

Too Much Disclosure Can Lower Satisfaction and Growth in New Relationships

How do we achieve a balance between rewards and costs? In general, we make disclosures because we believe that the benefits will be greater than the costs. The benefits might not be immediate. We might disclose some negative piece of information about ourselves that initially upsets our partner, but we do it because we believe that in the long run it will be better for the relationship. We trust that our partner will still accept us, even with the negative disclosure, and will eventually appreciate our honesty and openness. Relational development is filled with such judgments. We base our estimates of benefits and costs upon past and present relational experiences. You are likely to share information about yourself with someone if you have found it rewarding to do so in the past. You will be reluctant to self-disclose if you have been harmed, either in your relationship with him or her, or in other relationships.

Two Models for Self-Disclosure

We have already seen that we self-disclose in order to move a relationship toward intimacy. We will cover two models that illustrate the process by which this happens. The first model, Social Penetration, shows how self-disclosure involves revealing a broad range of information about ourselves as well as delving deeper into more personal information. The second model, the Johari Window, uses imaginary window panes that correspond to the information we know and don't know about ourselves, as well as panes for what personal information another person might or might not know about us.

Social Penetration Model

One pair of researchers, Irwin Altman and Dalmas Taylor, developed a model of **social penetration** to illustrate how much and what kind of information we reveal in various stages of a relationship.[17] Their model starts with a circle which represents all the potential information about yourself that you could disclose to someone (see Figure 9.4, circle A). This circle is divided like a

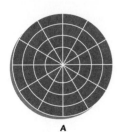

A

Your "self" with all its various dimensions. The pies represent the breadth of your "self", and the rings represent depth.

B

A limited relationship in which one dimension of your "self" has been disclosed to another person.

Figure 9.4

Social Penetration Models

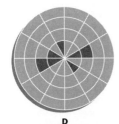

C

A relationship with greater breadth than B but with no intimacy.

D

A highly intimate, close relationship in which there has been extensive breadth and depth of disclosure.

pie into many pieces, with each piece of pie representing a particular aspect, construct, or dimension of yourself. For instance, some of the constructs in your personality pie might relate to athletic activities, religion, family, school, recreational activities, political interests, and fears. These pieces of pie represent the breadth of information available about you.

In addition, the concentric circles in the pie represent the depth of information. The smallest circle represents the most personal information. Each of your relationships represents a degree of social penetration, or the extent to which the other person has penetrated your concentric circles (depth) and shared pieces of your pie (breadth). For example, the shading on circle B shows a relationship that involves a high degree of penetration, but on only one aspect of yourself. Perhaps you have a good friend with whom you study and go to the library, but do not socialize. You might have disclosed a depth of information to that friend about your academic skills and weaknesses, but nothing about your family, hobbies, politics, or other aspects of yourself.

RESEARCH AND LITERATURE
Mark Feigen Festeau, author of "Friendship Among Men" (Evelyn Ashton-Jones and Gary Olson's *The Gender Reader,* Simon & Schuster, 1991) documents that women in a mixed group are usually the ones to make the first personal reference. Ask students to observe whether this is true in their encounters.

INSTRUCTIONAL GOALS AND TIPS

Point out that the open Johari Window is made possible by a willingness to disclose, and an openness to feedback.

Your relationships with your instructors probably look a little like circle B, with its limited breadth. In circle C, more pieces of the pie are shaded, but the information is all fairly safe, surface information about yourself. This would probably be the kind of disclosure associated with a new or limited friendship. Circle D represents almost complete social penetration, the kind we achieve in an intimate, well-developed relationship, in which a large amount of self-disclosure has taken place.

Johari Window Model

The **Johari Window** in Figure 9.5 is another model of how self-disclosure varies from relationship to relationship. It also reflects various stages of relational development, degrees of self-awareness, and others' perceptions of us. Its name comes from the first names of the two men who developed it (Joe and Harry) and from its windowlike appearance.[18] The window, like the circles in the social penetration model, represents yourself. This self encompasses everything about you, including things even you don't see or realize. One axis is divided into what you have come to know about yourself and what you don't yet know about yourself. The other axis represents what some particular person knows about you and doesn't know about you. The intersection of these categories creates a four-paned window.

The OPEN quadrant represents that part of yourself that you know and which you have revealed to the other person. As a relationship becomes more intimate, the OPEN quadrant grows larger. The HIDDEN quadrant is information you know about yourself but have not shared with the other person. This quadrant is fairly large initially, but as you disclose to another, it shrinks as the OPEN quadrant grows. The information in the UNKNOWN quadrant is that part of yourself which you have yet to discover or realize. As we learn and self-disclose more about ourselves, or as others learn more about us, this quadrant becomes smaller and smaller. Individuals who are not very intro-

Figure 9.5
———
Johari Window

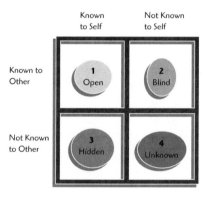

spective and do not have a very well-developed sense of self will have larger UNKNOWN areas than those who have made a concerted effort to come to know themselves.

Because we can never know ourselves completely, the UNKNOWN quadrant will always exist; we can only guess at its current size because the information it contains is unavailable to us. But sometimes our friends observe things about us that we don't realize or perceive about ourselves. This kind of unintentional self-disclosure is represented by the BLIND quadrant. This quadrant does not include misperceptions about us, but rather real aspects of ourselves that we fail to recognize. The BLIND quadrant is usually small when someone doesn't know us very well, and it grows larger as that person observes more and more information that is in our UNKNOWN quadrant. However, as the relationship becomes more intimate, the other person is more likely to reveal his or her perceptions of us, so the UNKNOWN and the BLIND quadrants

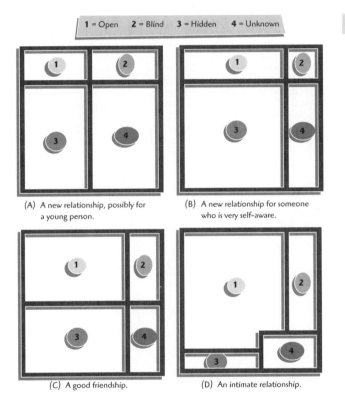

1 = Open   **2** = Blind   **3** = Hidden   **4** = Unknown

Figure 9.6

Variations on Johari Windows

(A) A new relationship, possibly for a young person.

(B) A new relationship for someone who is very self-aware.

(C) A good friendship.

(D) An intimate relationship.

INSTRUCTIONAL GOALS AND TIPS

Window B in Figure 9.6 illustrates "the interviewer," who is disinclined to share her or his self with others. Share with students the importance of self-disclosure for enhancing relationships.

INSTRUCTIONAL GOALS AND TIPS

Window D is considered "the ideal" window for an intimate relationship. Discuss with students whether this window would be appropriate in business or social relationships.

Share with students two other extreme Johari Windows: "the bull in the china shop" (a huge blind pane); and "the turtle" (a huge unknown pane). In both cases, the communicator needs to solicit and listen to feedback to learn more about him- or herself.

shrink as the information becomes known and accessible to us. As you can see, then, intimate relationships play an important role in the growth of self-knowledge.

As we did with the social penetration model, we can draw Johari Windows to represent each of our relationships (see Figure 9.6). Window A depicts a new or very restricted relationship for someone who is probably young or at least not very self-aware. Very little information has been disclosed or observed by the other, so the OPEN and BLIND quadrants are small. Window B also shows a new or restricted relationship for someone who knows him- or herself very well. Again, the OPEN and BLIND quadrants are small, but the UNKNOWN quadrant is also small. Window C represents a relationship that has evolved into a good friendship, and window D shows a very intimate relationship in which both individuals are open and disclosing.

By looking at a collection of your own Johari Windows, you can learn a great deal about your general approach to relationships. If you are reluctant to disclose information to others, and you do not reveal a great deal about yourself through your behaviors, your windows will consistently look like window A or window B in Figure 9.6. If you have a very outgoing and open personality, your windows will resemble window D. We can also examine the status of a particular relationship by drawing a window. Then we can see whether one member has disclosed more of him, or herself than the other (and has a larger OPEN quadrant) or whether one member has more complete self-knowledge (and a smaller UNKNOWN quadrant).

Johari Window

1. Make two Johari Windows for yourself, one that depicts one of your relationships two years ago, and one that shows the same relationship today. How much information has moved from your UNKNOWN quadrant to your HIDDEN quadrant? To your OPEN quadrant? What observations can you make about the relationship?

Your Window
Two Years Ago

Your Window
Today

2. Think of another relationship with a friend. Draw a window for yourself as it would appear in this relationship. Then draw a window for your partner (or have him or her draw it). Next, draw windows to reflect your relationship with a parent or other relative.

Your Window

Friend's Window

Your Window

Parent or Relative's
Window

What are the differences between your friend's window and your window? What effects do these differences have upon the relationship? How have the two windows changed most recently?

What are the differences between your parent's or relative's window and your window? How do these windows compare with the windows you drew for the friend relationship? How are the differences reflected in the way you communicate in these two relationships?

SKILL DEVELOPMENT

After students complete this activity, distribute slips of paper and pencils. Explain that people often hide information from others because they perceive the risk is too high if they make that information public. In some instances, people harbor secrets for a lifetime because they build up an irrational fear of disclosing it to others. Have students write on the slip of paper examples of information that they have kept as secrets. Assure students that any items will be anonymous. Collect the papers and pencils, and create a list of the responses you receive. Next, ask students either individually or in teams to rank-order the list from least to most risky. Discuss the results and point out that there could be someone in the class who is surprised to learn the relative low risk of their own secret. For example, a student may be surprised to learn that disclosing that they were adopted is relatively unrisky. With this new information, what might someone in that situation do? What course of action would the class recommend to someone like this? What precautions might they be wise to consider?

FOCUS ON COMPREHENSION

1. Relationships of circumstance depend upon the roles in which we allow ourselves to be cast (e.g., student, teammate, relative, patient, neighbor, or parishioner), whereas relationships of choice depend upon our selective decision to enter into a relationship with another individual (e.g., friend, housemate, lover).

2. Trust is the degree of confidence or faith we have in ourselves and others which affects self-disclosure and other relational risks.

Intimacy is the degree to which two or more people can be authentic and genuine with one another. Intimate relationships are characterized by strong physical, emotional, spiritual, and intellectual bonds.

Power is the degree to which one is able to influence another's feelings, beliefs, attitudes, or behaviors. It is important to consider ethics when exercising power.

3. When we share ourselves with others, we have the potential to build intimacy, but we are also vulnerable to rejection. Therefore, it is appropriate to disclose incrementally, to monitor whether that disclosure is reciprocated, and to evaluate whether the disclosure is helpful to ourselves, the other, and/or the relationship.

Summary

We can classify interpersonal relationships as relationships of circumstance—those that occur because the surrounding conditions cause us to interact with someone else; and relationships of choice—those that we seek out to establish and intentionally develop. We can also distinguish among relationships by looking at the degrees of trust, intimacy, and power in each one. Although there are many types of trust, interpersonal trust generally involves a belief that we can disclose information about ourselves to another person because he or she accepts who we are and is committed to the relationship. Intimacy is the degree to which our sense of self is accepted and confirmed by another person. Power is the degree to which we can influence another in the direction we desire.

Interpersonal attraction occurs in the early stages of relational development as short-term initial attraction, and in the later stages of relational development as long-term maintenance attraction. Elements that influence our feelings of attraction include physical appeal; credibility, competence, and charisma; proximity; similarity; complementary needs; relationship potential; and reciprocation of liking. Generally, the more we are attracted to someone, the more we try to communicate our attraction. To do so we use a number of verbal and nonverbal strategies, especially those that can be categorized as affinity-seeking strategies.

Often we know little about the individuals to whom we are attracted, and this uncertainty creates anxiety. We are motivated to reduce this uncertainty by finding out more about them. Part of the process of finding out about others involves self-disclosure, or sharing information that others would not learn if we did not tell them. The four principles of self-disclosure show that it is a building block for intimacy, that we expect it to be reciprocal in a relationship, that people have different standards for self-disclosing, and that we assess costs and benefits before we self-disclose. Two models relate self-disclosure to the development of relationships. The social penetration model shows the depth and breadth of what we disclose to different people. The four quadrants in the Johari Window (OPEN, HIDDEN, UNKNOWN, and BLIND), reflect how much information we and others know about ourselves. As we develop relationships, the sizes of these windows change relative to one another.

For Discussion and Review

■ FOCUS ON COMPREHENSION

1. Distinguish relationships of circumstance from relationships of choice.

2. Define trust, intimacy, and power.

3. List and explain the principles for self-disclosure.

4. Under what circumstances is it inappropriate for a person to use the power he or she has over another person to satisfy personal goals?

5. What is the relationship between interpersonal attraction and self-disclosure?

6. Under what circumstances in an intimate relationship might a person's OPEN quadrant in a relationship with another person actually become smaller?

7. How can you judge whether information that has been disclosed to you is privileged and private information not to be shared with others? When is it okay to tell other people what you know about someone?

8. Under what conditions is it ethical or unethical to approach (a) a coworker, (b) a subordinate, or (c) a superior for the purposes of developing an interpersonal relationship because you feel attracted to him or her?

For Your Journal

1. Monitor a face-to-face conversation between two or three of your friends that is at least four minutes long. You should play the role of a quiet observer. Write down all of the ways in which your friends attempted to gain or concede power during the interaction. Include examples of the language they used and the nonverbal cues they exchanged.

2. At the end of a day, reflect upon your interactions with others. For each interaction you can recall, write down what you disclosed. What factors affected what you chose to disclose? How did the differences in your relationships with the various people involved affect your decisions about self-disclosure?

Learning with Others

1. Create two lists of names: those people you regard as casual friends and those you regard as close friends. Identify what attracts you to the people on your list. Compare what attracts you to casual friends and close friends with

other students. How does your list fit with the categories for attraction identified in the text? What's different? What's the same?

2. In groups, combine your responses to the Building Your Skills: Rules for Self-Disclosing on page 315 into a "manual" that might be given to an international student. Discard any rules that don't seem valid or that are too specific. Prioritize the rules from the most important to the least important. How did the differences in your relationships with the various people involved affect your decisions about self-disclosure?

■ GLOSSARY

INTERPERSONAL RELATIONSHIPS: Those connections we make with other people through interpersonal communication.

RELATIONSHIPS OF CIRCUMSTANCE: Interpersonal relationships that exist because of the circumstances in which we are born, circumstances in which we work or study, and so on.

RELATIONSHIPS OF CHOICE: Interpersonal relationships we choose to initiate, maintain, and terminate.

INTERPERSONAL TRUST: A quality of a relationship represented by the degree to which the partners believe it is safe to disclose personal information.

TRUSTWORTHY: A quality we use to describe an individual who can be trusted to accept personal information without exploiting it, support vulnerabilities, and remain in a relationship.

INTIMACY: A quality of a relationship represented by the degree to which a person's sense of self is accepted and confirmed by another person.

INTERPERSONAL POWER: A quality of a relationship represented by the degree to which one person can influence another in the direction he or she desires.

LEGITIMATE POWER: A type of power that comes from respect for a position that another person holds.

REFERENT POWER: A type of power that comes from our attraction to another person, or the charisma a person possesses.

EXPERT POWER: A type of power based on a person's knowledge and experience.

REWARD POWER: A type of power based on a person's ability to satisfy our needs.

COERCIVE POWER: A type of power based on the use of sanctions or punishments to influence others.

INTERPERSONAL ATTRACTION: The degree to which you desire to form or maintain an interpersonal relationship.

SHORT-TERM INITIAL ATTRACTION: The degree to which we sense a potential for an interpersonal relationship.

LONG-TERM MAINTENANCE ATTRACTION: A liking or positive feeling that motivates us to sustain a relationship.

PHYSICAL ATTRACTION: The degree to which we find another person's physical self appealing.

PROXIMITY: That quality which promotes attraction because of being physically close to another and therefore in a position to communicate easily.

SIMILARITY: We are attracted to people whose personality, values, upbringing, personal experiences, attitudes, and interests are similar to ours.

COMPLEMENTARY NEEDS: We are attracted to those whose needs complement our own; one person's weakness is the other person's strength.

RELATIONSHIP POTENTIAL (PREDICTED OUTCOME VALUE THEORY): We are most attracted to those relationships that potentially have greater rewards or benefits than costs.

RECIPROCATION OF LIKING: We like people who like us.

COMMUNICATING ATTRACTION: We communicate our attraction toward other people by the use of nonverbal cues, language, and direct declarations.

AFFINITY SEEKING: Strategies used to get other people to like us.

SELF-DISCLOSURE: Providing information about ourselves that another person would not learn if we did not tell them.

SOCIAL PENETRATION: A model of self-disclosure and relational development that reflects sharing information that has both depth and breadth.

JOHARI WINDOW: A model of self-disclosure that reflects the movement of information about ourselves from BLIND and UNKNOWN quadrants to HIDDEN and OPEN ones.

Developing Interpersonal Relationships

A fter studying this chapter, you should be able to:

1. Explain the model of the stages of relational development.

2. Discuss the skills for starting relationships.

3. Identify and describe effective interpersonal communication skills for escalating and maintaining relationships.

4. Discuss some of the signals for identifying trouble in a relationship.

5. Describe three paths relationships follow when coming to an end.

6. Identify direct and indirect strategies for ending relationships.

7. Explain three major causes of breakups.

8. Identify and explain the four elements of a model of ending relationships.

■ STAGES OF INTERPERSONAL RELATIONSHIPS

■ SKILLS FOR STARTING RELATIONSHIPS

■ INTERPERSONAL COMMUNICATION SKILLS FOR ESCALATING AND MAINTAINING RELATIONSHIPS

■ IDENTIFYING AND ACTING ON TROUBLE SIGNS IN RELATIONSHIPS

■ DE-ESCALATING AND ENDING RELATIONSHIPS

Jean: Hi. It's Andy, isn't it? We met at Mary Lynn's party, remember? It's good to see you again.

Andy: Sure, sure. I was hoping we'd run into each other again. How are you?

Jean: I'm fine. I've really been busy, though. I have a new job, and my parents have been in town visiting.

Andy: You do sound busy. What's the new job?

Jean: I'm working on some web page development projects for the university. What have you been up to?

Andy: Not much. How was the visit with your parents?

Jean: It was great. I had the chance to show them some of my favorite parts of town, like places I like to take walks and little coffee houses. They even came and watched me bowl with my league team. How's your job?

Andy: About the same as always. Well, I need to head on; I'll catch you again some time.

This interaction is the second encounter between Andy and Jean. In this interaction who do you think is more interested in the other? How equal do you see the power between the two people? Who discloses the most?

In Chapter 9 we discussed why we are attracted to certain other people, how we communicate that attraction, and how we self-disclose to provide a foundation for greater intimacy. In Chapter 10 we will explore **relational development**, the discernible stages relationships go through as they move toward and away from intimacy.

Stages of Interpersonal Relationships

Although researchers use different terms and different numbers of stages, all agree that relational development does proceed in discernible stages. Understanding these stages is important to your studies because interpersonal communication is affected by the stage of the relationship. Individuals in an intimate stage discuss topics and display nonverbal behaviors that do not appear in

329

the early stages of a relationship. We use interpersonal communication to move a relationship forward as we proceed from acquaintances, to friends, to lovers. Outsiders usually can tell what stage a relationship is in by observing the interpersonal communication.

We can think of the stages, from first meeting to intimacy, as the floors in a high rise. Relational development is an elevator that stops at every floor. As you get to each floor, you might get off and wander around for a while before taking the elevator to the next floor (see Figure 10.1). Each time you get on, you don't know how many floors up the elevator will take you, or how long you will stay at any given floor. In fact, sometimes you will never get back on the elevator, electing instead to stay at a particular stage of relational development. But, if you fall head over heels in love, you might want to move quickly from floor to floor toward intimacy. Part of the time you share this elevator with your partner, and the two of you make decisions about how high you will ride the elevator, how long to stay at each floor, and when and whether to ride the down elevator.

Just as there are lights on a panel to let us know the elevator has moved from one floor to another, we have markers that signal a move from one stage to another. These markers are called turning points. **Turning points** are specific events or interactions that are associated with positive or negative changes in a relationship.[1] A first meeting, first date, first kiss, first sex, saying "I love you" for the first time, meeting a partner's family, going away together somewhere, making up after a conflict, moving in together, providing help in a crisis, or providing a favor or gift might all be turning points that indicate a relationship is moving forward. A pair of researchers found that 55 percent of the time, these turning points inspired a discussion about the nature of the relationship.[2] Such discussion helps the partners reach mutual agreement about the definition of the relationship.

Figure 10.1

Elevator Model of Relational Stages

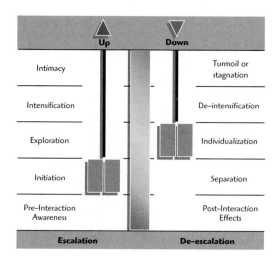

III   INTERPERSONAL COMMUNICATION RELATIONSHIPS

Relational Escalation

As you can see in the model in Figure 10.1, the first floor is the *pre-interaction awareness stage*. Here, you might observe someone or even talk with others about him or her without having any direct interaction. Gaining information about others without directly interacting with them is a *passive strategy* for acquiring knowledge.[3] Through your passive observations, you form an initial impression. You might not move beyond the pre-interaction awareness stage if that impression is not favorable or the circumstances aren't right.

If you are attracted to the other person and the circumstances are right, you might proceed to the *initiation stage*, one of the first turning points in a relationship. In this stage, the interaction typically is routine; you might each respond to a large number of standard questions during the first four minutes of conversation,[4] sticking to safe and superficial topics, and presenting a "public self" to the other person. Your partner is now riding on the elevator with you, and any decision about whether the elevator should go up, down, or nowhere is a mutual one for the rest of the ride. You can never return to the initiation stage. Once you make an initial contact, you have created a relational history on which you will continue to build.

If you decide to go to the next floor, *exploration*, you will begin to share more in-depth information about yourselves. But you will have little physical contact, maintain your social distance, and limit the amount of time you spend together. This stage can occur in conjunction with the initiation stage.

If you proceed to the *intensification stage*, you will start to depend upon each other for self-confirmation and engage in more risky self-disclosure. You will spend more time together, increase the variety of activities you share, adopt a more personal physical distance, engage in more physical contact, and personalize your language. Also, you

As couples proceed from exploration to intensification, they have more physical contact and begin sharing more activities and confidences. Does it seem as if this couple is heading into the intensification stage? (Sandra Rice)

Keep in mind that the stages of relationship growth are common to more than just romantic relationships; they also are relevant to friendships, and working relationships with colleagues, superiors, and subordinates. Have students complete this exercise first for their lover. Next have them repeat the exercise for a dear friend. Finally, have them repeat the exercise considering a coworker. What general trends in time spent can the class identify for each category? What are the major differences in where we spend our time for these types of interpersonal relationships? Is this always appropriate? When might it not be?

MEDIA AND OUTSIDE RESOURCES

Consider an alternative to this exercise to analyze the relational development of the main characters from the film *When Harry Met Sally.*

may discuss and redefine the relationship often in this stage, perhaps putting a turning-point label on yourselves, such as "going steady," "good buddies," or "best friends." Other turning points associated with this stage include decisions to date each other exclusively, to become roommates, or to spend time with each other's families.

The top floor in the building is the *intimacy stage.* In this stage the two partners turn to each other for confirmation and acceptance of their self-concept. Their communication is highly personalized and synchronized. They talk about anything and everything. There is a free flow of information and self-disclosure. There is a commitment to maintaining the relationship that might even be formalized through marriage or some other agreement. The partners share an understanding of each other's language and nonverbal cues, and have a great deal of physical contact. They use fewer words to communicate effectively, and they have a clearer definition of their roles and of the relationship. Reaching this stage takes time—time to build trust, time to share personal information, time to observe each other in various situations, and time to build a commitment and emotional bond.

BUILDING YOUR SKILLS

Graphing your Relationship Changes

Think of an interpersonal relationship that you have had for at least a year. On the graph at right, plot the development of that relationship from stage to stage reflecting the relative amount of time you spent in each stage. You can also indicate whether you backed up to a previous stage at any point.

If possible, have your relational partner fill out a similar graph and compare your perceptions of how the relationship has developed. What differences are there and why?

Intimacy

Intensification

Exploration

Initiation

Pre-Interaction Awareness

Time

You also might want to share your graph with those of classmates to compare how different relationships develop. What can you tell from the graphs about the nature of their relationships?

Relational De-Escalation

Sometimes, for a variety of reasons, you might decide that you want to leave an intimate relationship. But as you may already know, the process of ending it is not as simple as going down the same elevator you came up on; it is not a reversal of the formation stage.[5]

You can hardly make a friend in a year, but you can lose one in an hour.

—CHINESE PROVERB

When an intimate relationship is not going well, it usually enters either the *turmoil* or *stagnation* stage. Turmoil involves an increase in conflict, as one or both partners tend to find more faults in the other. The definition of the relationship seems to lose its clarity, and mutual acceptance declines. The communication climate is tense and exchanges are difficult.

Stagnation occurs when the relationship loses its vitality and the partners become complacent. Communication and physical contact between the partners decrease; they spend less time together, but do not necessarily fight. Partners in a stagnating relationship tend to go through the motions of an intimate relationship without the commitment; they simply follow their established relational routines.

As with the up elevator, individuals can stop at this point on the down elevator and decide to quit descending. The relationship can remain in turmoil or stagnate for a long time, or the individuals can repair, redefine, or revitalize the relationship and return to intimacy.

If the turmoil or stagnation continues, however, the individuals might move down to the *de-intensification stage,* decreasing their interactions; increasing their physical, emotional, and psychological distance; and decreasing their dependence upon the other for self-confirmation. They might discuss the definition of their relationship, question its future, and assess each partner's level of satisfaction or dissatisfaction. The relationship can be repaired and the individuals can move back up to intensification and intimacy, but that is more difficult to accomplish now.

On the next floor down, the *individualization stage*, the partners tend to define their lives more as individuals and less as a couple. Neither views the other as a partner or significant other anymore. Interactions are limited. The perspective changes from "we" and "us" to "you" and "me," and property is defined in terms of "mine" or "yours" rather than "ours." Both partners turn to others for confirming their self-concepts.

In the *separation stage*, individuals make an intentional decision to eliminate further interpersonal interaction. If they share custody of children, attend mutual family gatherings, or work in the same office, the nature of their interactions will change. They will divide property, resources, and friends. Early interactions in this stage are often tense and difficult, especially if the relationship has been intimate. For relationships that never went beyond exploration or intensification, however, the negotiation is often relatively painless.

For former intimates, one of the awkward things about separating is their extensive personal knowledge about one another. Their talk is limited to superficial things, although they still know a lot about each other. This tends to make the interactions fairly uncomfortable. Over time, of course, each partner knows less about who the other person has become. For example, even after spending just a few years away from your high school friends, you might have difficulty interacting with them because the knowledge you both share is out of date.

Although interaction may cease altogether, the effect of the relationship is not over. Our relational-stages high rise is like something out of the old TV

Students frequently have difficulty understanding that movement between stages does not necessarily flow in a lock-stepped sequence. The suggestion that they may want to maintain a friendship with a former intimate partner is frequently received as overly idealistic. Ask your students if this is possible. Note that the chapter stresses that maintenance and repair behaviors require a lot of effort.

MEDIA AND OUTSIDE RESOURCES
Show the film *When a Man Loves a Woman*. Discuss how trust, intimacy, and power work to help/hinder this couple's relationship.

series, *Twilight Zone*: Once you enter it, you can never leave it. The bottom floor on the down elevator, where you remain, is the *post-interaction stage*. This floor represents the lasting effects the relationship has on your self, and therefore on your other interactions and relationships. Steve Duck claims that in this final stage of terminating relationships we engage in "grave-dressing."[6] We create a public statement for people who ask why we broke up and also come to grips with losing the relationship. Sometimes our sense of self gets battered during the final stages of a relationship, and we have to work hard to regain a healthy sense of self.

Of course, we are all aware of people who hop on an express elevator to get out of a relationship, bypassing all the normal stages of decline. One study found that of the various ways to terminate a relationship, abandoned partners most dislike the quick exit without discussion.[7]

CONSIDERING OTHERS

A New Friend a Day Keeps a Cold Away

Fighting a cold? You need a friend—and not just to bring you chicken soup. The more diverse your set of relationships—friends, relatives, co-workers, neighbors—the less likely you are to catch a cold, according to a study.

People with six or more types of relationships fought off colds best after being dosed with a virus, the study of 300 healthy volunteers found. They had less than one-fourth the risk of becoming sick of those who had only one to three types of relationships.

"The notion of 'get a life' applies here," said Sheldon Coehn, professor of psychology at Carnegie Mellon University in Pittsburgh, and lead author of the federally financed study in the current *Journal of the American Medical Association*.

Part of a growing field known as psychoneuroimmunology—or the study of how such things as stress and social support affect the immune system and overall health—the study is being welcomed by specialists as an important contribution.

Other studies have found less depression and lower overall mortality among people with a broad social network or who are experiencing the least stress. But this work is "the first to show that there is a direct tie in terms of a health outcome, by actually infecting people with a cold virus and then asking, 'Did people who get colds differ in terms of social ties?'," said Janice Kiecolt-Glaser, a professor of psychiatry at Ohio State University Medical Center.

While research cannot yet explain how social support affects health, Benson said, "One possibility is that social ties decrease stress, and stress liberates hormones that lower one's resistance."

From the *Des Moines Register* June 25, 1997 p. 1

Skills for Starting Relationships

So far in this chapter, we have seen how relationships progress in stages. But the initial movement from attraction to initiation of interaction is not always an easy one. As we have discussed, there is a lot of uncertainty and apprehension involved in approaching a stranger and starting a conversation. In this section, we will suggest some specific skills for starting relationships.

Gather Information to Reduce Uncertainty

Meeting strangers and starting relationships is rarely easy. We all seem to share a fear of the unknown, which includes interacting with strangers whose behavior we cannot predict. The research team of Charles Berger, Richard Calabrese, and James Bradac[8] developed a theory to explain relational development. Their theory is based upon one basic cause-effect assumption: we like to have control and predictability in our lives; therefore, when we are faced with uncertainty, we are driven to gain information to reduce that uncertainty. Reducing uncertainty requires utilizing a number of skills we have already covered, but primarily depends on effective perception and active listening. You need to gather as much information as you can about your partner to increase predictability and reduce anxiety.

We are most comfortable in predictable situations because we can call upon familiar strategies to handle the situation. In initial interactions we often follow predictable, scripted behavior that reduces uncertainty. What if you approached a stranger and said "Hello," and the stranger responded by saying, "Bananas"? You would probably feel a little leery. You would feel even more uneasy if you then asked for the stranger's name, only to get the same reply: "Bananas." At this point you'd probably look for the nearest exit. If a person's response does not follow the normal initiation script, it might create so much anxiety that you will stop interacting.

Usually, however, we reduce uncertainty by gathering either cognitive or behavioral information about others.[9] Cognitive information relates to thoughts, attitudes, and opinions. Behavioral information relates to reactions and remarks in various situations. As we have seen, we gather some of this information during the pre-interaction stage of a relationship through observations and conversations with others who know the person. Later, we can directly observe the other's behaviors in our interactions with him or her, and

---

BUILDING YOUR SKILLS

Anxiety Level and Familiarity

Write down at least ten different social situations you can recall having been in, such as attending weddings, funerals, or ball games; going to your grandmother's for dinner; visiting your best friend's parents for the first time; or meeting your new roommate. Next to each one, indicate how nervous you felt in that situation. Use a scale from 1 to 10, with 1 being calm and cool, and 10 being highly apprehensive. After you have rated each situation, go back and rate each one on how familiar or unfamiliar the situation was. Again use a scale of 1 to 10, with 1 being very familiar and 10 being very unfamiliar.

According to uncertainty reduction theory, there should be a strong correlation between your level of anxiety and the level of familiarity. Which situations caused the most anxiety? To what degree did your unfamiliarity with the situation affect your level of anxiety? What were you most uncertain about in each situation? In which situations were you most comfortable and why? Did you feel uncomfortable under some circumstances even though the situation was familiar? Why?

DISCUSSION AND WRITING
Ask students how many of them investigated your credentials prior to enrolling in the course. Discuss the value of knowing the players prior to taking a course, going for a job interview, or attending a party.

also ask direct questions. Usually we gather behavioral information through observation and cognitive information through interactions.

We are particularly motivated to gain information early in a relationship when uncertainty is greatest, and when we are trying to evaluate the predicted outcome value.[10] We also are likely to seek out information if others behave in an unexpected way.[11] If your close friend who watches *Beavis and Butthead* every night suddenly begins reading during that time slot, you will probably ask why. Whether the friend shares with you what is going on will depend upon how comfortable he or she is in revealing information about him or herself.

Adopt an Other-Oriented Perspective

When you were frightened by an encounter with a wild animal or a neighbor's pet as a child, your parents probably told you, "It's just as afraid of you as you are of it." These words reflect an other-orientation and are useful to remember when we encounter new people as well. For all of us, meeting someone for the first time generally produces some degree of anxiety. When this happens to you, try to remember what other people did to make you comfortable in past encounters. They probably smiled a lot, actively listened, showed interest in you but didn't put you on the spot, disclosed information about themselves, and kept the conversation light. Try to use these techniques yourself to put your partner at ease.

Also, try to think about how you appear to the other person. For instance, if you are speaking to someone you just hired, he or she may feel nervous and uncomfortable because of the power and status differences between you. Do your best to minimize the differences; for example, sit in chairs that face each other without a desk between them. In general, try to apply all the information you have and that you observe about the other person to make decisions about your own behavior. Don't just re-act; take the initiative to make the first interaction pleasant and satisfying to you both.

Observe and Act on Approachability Cues

Subway riders in New York learn to avoid eye contact because it is a signal for approachability. Other ways we can signal approachability include turning toward another person, smiling, being animated (*versus* sitting very still), taking an open body posture, winking, and waving. In the absence of these cues, we generally conclude that a person wants to be left alone.

Sometimes circumstances prevent us from exchanging approachability cues. The seating arrangements in your class, for example, might discourage nonverbal exchanges. So instead, you may try to develop some sensitivity to the way other people respond to your greetings. Saying "Hello" lets people know that you are approachable, and it tests approachability. If the other person responds with a warm smile and a few words, such as, "Have you finished today's assignment yet?" then the door might be open for further interaction. But if the person gives you a silent half smile and hurries on, you can take this as a signal that the door is closed.

III INTERPERSONAL COMMUNICATION RELATIONSHIPS

DISCUSSION AND WRITING
Discuss with students whether they would enjoy a friendship with the "Star Trek: The Next Generation" character Data.

DISCUSSION AND WRITING
Try the second "Learning with Others" exercise at the end of this chapter. Have students include nonverbal cues as well.

Identify and Use Conversation Starters

We all give off a certain amount of "free" information that others can easily observe. You can use that information as a starting point for a conversation. Noting that someone is wearing a T-shirt from Glacier National Park, for example, you can ask when she or he went there and how she or he liked it. If someone is walking a dog of the same breed as your childhood pet, you can approach him or her to discuss the breed's peculiarities. If someone is carrying a book from a class you took last semester, ask him or her how the course is going. Look at Figure 10.2 to practice identifying conversation starters.

You will probably want to incorporate a greeting into your conversation starter, such as , "Hi; I see from the book you're carrying that you're taking the dreaded Dr. Bellfinger's class." You might also want to include an open question: "How do you like it?" Using an open question (for example, "What . . . ", or "How . . . ") is an effective strategy because it requests a more complete response than Yes or No. Open questions encourage the disclosure of additional information, which in turn provides opportunities for you to follow up with more questions.

Follow Initiation Norms

Many of the early interactions in a relationship are almost ritualistic, or at least scripted. In the United States, when two strangers meet for the first time they typically follow this pattern of conversation:[12]

Greetings: Say "Hello," "Hi," or "Howdy."

Introductions: Exchange names and pleasantries.

Edward Hopper, *Sunlight in a Cafe*, Yale University Art Gallery, Bequest of Stephen Carlton Clark, B.A. 1903

Figure 10.2

What conversation starters might either of the two people in this picture use to initiate a relationship?

RESEARCH AND LITERATURE

John Powell recommends that the greeting and good-bye (phatic communication) in conversation needs to be conventional and superficial. Phatic communication is used to relieve primary tension. Following successful phatic communication, factual communication becomes acceptable. Have students role-play some typical scripted conversation.

Topic 1: Discuss the present situation or weather.

Topic 2: Discuss current or past residences (where they live, hometown, etc.).

Topic 3: Determine whether they know people in common.

Topic 4: Discuss their educational backgrounds or occupations.

Topic 5: Discuss general topics such as TV, movies, music, family, sports, books, and/or travel.

Discuss Further Meeting (Optional): Say something like, "Let's get together sometime."

Exchange Pleasantries: Say, "Nice to meet you," "Hope to see you again," and so on.

Close Conversation: Indicate the intent to end the conversation with such statements as, "See you later," "Got to go to class now," or "Give me a call."

Good-Byes: Make final statements, "Bye," and move in different directions.

Following the script provides some comfort and security because both partners are able to reduce the level of uncertainty. If you deviate too much from this script, you might undermine your partner's sense of security and discourage him or her from pursuing a relationship.

As you follow the script, however, you should take advantage of opportunities to expand and develop the conversation in safe ways. Listen for details about the person's background and interests that you can inquire about, and share information about your own interests.

Provide Information About Yourself

Disclosing information about yourself allows the other person to make an informed decision about whether or not to continue the relationship. Remember, both of you need to be in a position to make such a decision. You might have found out what you want and decided that you have a lot in common with the other person, but he or she might not have reached that same point. However, you need to be careful not to violate the script or cultural expectations about what is appropriate to disclose in an initial conversation. You have probably had the experience of someone you have just met telling you his or her problems. As we mentioned earlier, such disclosures usually alienate the other, rather than advancing the relationship.

Present Yourself in a Positive Way

This may seem like a pretty obvious strategy. We tend to find people attractive who have positive self-images. And as we have mentioned, it is also against our cultural norms to disclose negative information early on in a relationship. But this doesn't mean that you should act cocky or that you should try to act ebullient if you are not that way by nature. Do not try to provide false information about yourself, but simply be selective about the information you share.

DISCUSSION AND WRITING
Four topics are commonly acknowledged as taboo in social-polite contexts: sex, religion, politics, and bodily functions. Ask students to identify these. (These are also typical topics implicit in vulgar language.)

Also keep in mind that we all have weaknesses and foibles, so the person interacting with you is probably also attempting to present a positive image. Practice the social decentering process you learned in Chapter 2 to think about the other person's thoughts and feelings as you listen to what he or she puts forward for your consideration. Being kind and responsive will win you more points than trying to act sarcastic and clever.

Ask Questions

Asking questions will accomplish two goals: first, it will help you learn about the other person, and second, it will let the other person know that you are interested in her or him. Keep your questions open and noninvasive; don't interrogate the other person. Focus on things you know you have in common and that are safe. Use the situation as a resource for questions. For example, if you are standing in line to purchase tickets for an upcoming rock concert, you could ask the person next to you how he or she got interested in the group, which of their songs he or she likes best, how many live concerts he or she has seen, and so on.

Don't Expect Too Much from the Initial Interaction

Initial interactions do not necessarily determine the future of a relationship. In movies, such as *Speed*, initial interactions between the hero and the heroine are often brusque and unfriendly, but after sharing a traumatic experience, they eventually find love. Although real life does not usually work this way, keep in mind that the scripted nature of an initial interaction limits the opportunity for you and your partner to achieve an in-depth understanding of one another. Relax and arrange another meeting if you feel the spark of attraction. It will probably take a few interactions before you can make a sound cost-benefit analysis of the relationship.

Initiating conversation is only one step in the process of developing an interpersonal relationship. Later in this chapter we will examine ways to escalate a relationship once it gets started, and in Chapter 11, we will learn strategies for strengthening relationships with family members, friends, and colleagues.

Interpersonal Communication Skills for Escalating and Maintaining Relationships

Most relationships never progress through all the stages of development to intimacy. Our lives are filled with interpersonal relationships that are maintained at one of the lower levels of development. On the other hand, having reached even the most intimate stage of development does not mean that we can take a relationship for granted. A considerable amount of effort and

INSTRUCTIONAL GOALS AND TIPS
Remind students that open-ended questions allow the respondent greater latitude and reduce defensiveness.

INSTRUCTIONAL GOALS AND TIPS
Add a bit of science to this discussion. Ask students to consider Isaac Newton's laws of motion: the object = relationship; force = communication.

1. A moving object will continue moving in a straight line at a constant speed, and a stationary object will remain at rest, unless acted on by an unbalanced force.
2. The acceleration produced on a body by a force is proportional to the magnitude of the force and inversely proportional to the mass of the object.
3. For every action, there is a reaction.

Give students some time in small groups to discuss how these laws might be used to describe relational changes.

INTERNET RESOURCE
Phatic Communication
http://www.aber.ac.uk/~dgc/trans.html
Explores the functions of phatic communication as more related to maintaining relationships than mere transmission of information. Offers a case example from Britain where phatic communication over the weather is considered.

ACTIVITY
See Activity 10.1 in the Instructor's Guide.

RESEARCH AND LITERATURE
Harriet Goldhor Lerner's book *The Dance of Intimacy* (Harper & Row, 1989, p. 79) includes some discussion of the need to appreciate differences in ways people respond to stress. She describes distancers and over-functioners and warns that "the more we get focused on the other person's behaviors rather than our own, the more stuck we become."

DISCUSSION AND WRITING
Using the skills from this chapter (and preceding ones as well), create a survey for students to self-assess their relationships. For instance:

SKILL	SELF	PARTNER
Listens	_____	_____
Expresses emotions	_____	_____

RESEARCH AND LITERATURE
Distribute these words by John Powell from his book *The Secret of Staying in Love* (Argus Communications, 1974):

> "The genius of communication is the ability to be both totally honest and totally kind at the same time. Although it is one of the stern canons of dialogue that emotions should be reported at the time they are experienced and to the person to whom these emotions are related, kindness should still have much to say about the manner of communication."

Ask students to discuss this excerpt and to role-play scenes in which emotions were revealed.

ACTIVITY
See Activity 10.2 in the Instructor's Guide.

skill is needed to maintain intimate relationships. In this section we will cover some of the skills that are needed to move a relationship toward intimacy and to maintain relationships at the stage we desire, including the most intimate.

Be Open and Self-Disclose Appropriately

In Chapter 9 we wrote about self-disclosure being a critical element for movement toward intimacy. We cannot form truly intimate relationships without mutual self-disclosure. On the other hand, restricting the amount of self-disclosure is one way to control the development of a relationship. If a relationship is moving too fast you might choose to reduce how much you are self-disclosing as a way to slow the progression of the relationship. In the interaction between Jean and Andy at the beginning of this chapter, Andy was apparently choosing to maintain the relationship as an acquaintanceship by restricting his self-disclosure. The level of self-disclosure needs to be appropriate to the level of development and both partners must be sensitive to the timing of the disclosures. Failing to disclose or disclosing the wrong thing at the wrong time can damage a relationship.

You must also be willing to accept your partner's disclosures. You expect that you can disclose your most private secrets to your intimate partners. You also expect your intimate partners to listen and provide confirming responses to you when you make such disclosures. Imagine what effect it would have on an intimate relationship if your partner turned away from you every time you tried to self-disclose highly personal information. You would become frustrated and disenchanted. The relationship would lose value.

Express Emotions

Expressing emotions is a particular form of self-disclosure and is a skill that can be improved, as discussed in Chapter 6. Many of us are embarrassed about expressing our feelings, yet sharing feelings, at the appropriate time during relational development is one way to continue its escalation. On the other hand, sharing the wrong feelings at the wrong time can have a detrimental effect.

There are two ways we share feelings with our partners. The first includes disclosing information about our past or current emotional states, such as sadness about the death of a family member, or fear about what we will do after we graduate. The second way we share emotions is the direct expression of emotions such as expressing attraction, love, or disappointment toward our partner. As relationships become more intimate, we have a greater expectation that our partner will disclose emotions openly. The amount of risk associated with such emotional disclosures varies from person to person. Most of us are comfortable sharing positive emotions such as happiness and joy, but are more reserved about sharing negative emotions such as fear or disappointment. We might think expressing negative emotions makes us appear weak or vulnerable. However, in a study of forty-six committed, romantic couples, researchers found that the number one problem was the inability to talk about negative feelings.[13] For example, partners often made the following types of observations, "When she

gets upset, she stops talking"; "He never lets me know when he's upset with something he doesn't like"; and "He just silently pouts." We generally want to know how our partners in intimate relationships are feeling, even if those feelings are negative.

On the other hand, a constant barrage of negative expressions can also alienate our partner. Research has found that marital satisfaction rises with the number of positive feelings the partners disclose, not with the number of negative ones.[14] A balance has to be found that includes expressing both positive and negative emotions at the right time in a constructive and confirming manner.

Engage in Relationship Talk

Relationship talk is talking about the nature, quality, direction, or definition of a relationship. Relationship talk is generally considered inappropriate in the early stages of a relationship. A relationship might be prematurely terminated if one partner tries to talk about the relationship too early. Willingness to talk about the relationship is one way to implicitly signal your partner about your

level of interest and commitment to the relationship. As relationships move toward greater intimacy, however, the amount of direct relationship talk increases. As the relationship escalates, we should be prepared to discuss our thoughts and feelings about it. In more intimate relationships, relationship talk helps the partners resolve differences in their perceptions of the relationship that might be contributing to conflict and dissatisfaction. Unwillingness to talk about the relationship in an intimate relationship can ultimately drive a partner away.

Monitor Your Perceptions

You need to be aware of your perceptual biases that affect your reactions to your partner. Such biases might inhibit the growth of a relationship because of an inaccurate inference. Effective perception can enhance your ability to understand and adapt to your partner as a relationship escalates. Perception checking helps you reach a more accurate understanding of your partner, and thus provides you with better information about whether to continue the relationship. Directly asking your partner for explanations about things you have perceived can potentially lead to more effective relationship management. For example, suppose you are interacting with Miguel, someone you don't know very well. During the conversation, every time you start to talk about a mutual friend of yours, Sandra, Miguel changes the subject. One interpretation of this perception is that Miguel is rude and impolite, and therefore you might decide to abandon the relationship. On the other hand, you might ask Miguel about your perception. The explanation might be that he and Sandra recently had a fight and he prefers not to talk about her. A hasty inference in this case might have precluded the development of a potentially satisfying relationship.

Listen Actively and Respond Confirmingly

Listening skills are also crucial for developing and maintaining relationships. Listening clues you into others' needs, wants, and values and it enables you to respond to them in appropriate ways. In the initial stages of a relationship, partners share a great deal of information. The amount of information tapers off in the later stages and as a relationship continues over time. This tapering off creates the illusion that you don't have to listen as much or as well

More Talk Doesn't Mean More Satisfaction

W hat we have here is a failure to communicate."

That cliche, from the movie *Cool Hand Luke*, has been quoted for years as a testament to the importance of good communication skills. If only we all knew how to talk with and listen to each other, the world would be brimming with brotherhood and amity.

Not so, say more and more researchers.

"What we really have here is a lot of talk that makes things worse," says David Stiebel, a conflict-resolution consultant in California who contends that, more often than not, we understand each other perfectly well. We just don't agree.

Nowhere has the value of communication been more oversold than in marital relationships, says Brant Burleson, a professor of communication at Purdue University.

Studies show that when one or both spouses are dissatisfied, the better the communication skills, the less satisfied they are. Why? They're using their nifty skills to stick it to each other.

Skilled communicators take the perspective of the other person, Burleson says. They know not only what will help that person but "exactly where to put the knife and twist it as well."

But what about all those "mirroring" exercises we've been drilled in? The ones in which we listen nondefensively while our partner says stuff like, "I feel embarrassed when you wear your leopard-print leggings to church."

"Mirroring can be useful if the problem is lack of clarity or people not understanding each other," Burleson says. "But not all problems in marriages are communication-related. People have affairs, spend too much money, disagree over how kids ought to be raised.

"Bad communication can exacerbate those problems, but there's no guarantee that good communication is going to solve those problems."

However, talking things out can succeed—if there's a real disagreement, and if you have a problem-solving strategy. That's the thesis of Stiebel's book, *When Talking Makes Things Worse.*

Talk It Out

Talking can help, Daniel Stiebel writes in *When Talking Makes Things Worse.* The key is to use "strategic communication," which Stiebel swears is not about manipulating your opponent. Here are the four steps:

- Decide whether you have a misunderstanding or a true disagreement.

- Create the other person's next move. Ask yourself, "What do I want this person to do?" Focus on the most he or she is willing and able to do for you right now, Stiebel suggests.

- Use other people's perceptions to persuade them to budge.

- Predict the other person's response. Learn to anticipate how the other person is likely to respond to your next move and adjust your approach accordingly.

Lorraine O'Connell

From the *Orlando Sentinel*, Sunday, May 11, 1997.

Well-adjusted couples display support and affection
for each other through
positive nonverbal cues.
(Lori Adamski Peek/Tony
Stone Images)

as you did early on. But listening is a way to demon-
strate ongoing interest in
another person. Even in
long-term relationships, you
do not know everything
your partner has to say. It is
still important to stop, look,
and listen—to put down the
newspaper or turn off the
radio when your close friend
begins talking to you.
You also need to listen
actively and provide con-
firming responses. In
Chapter 5 we discussed the
notions of confirming and
disconfirming responses.
Using confirming responses
increases your partner's
sense of self-worth and communicates the value you
place upon him or her. In
addition, if you can develop
an awareness of the biases
that prevent you from
responding with empathy, you can work deliberately to overcome them as you
ask questions and paraphrase your partner's messages.

Socially Decenter and Adapt

The skills covered in Chapter 4 for social decentering, empathizing, and
adapting to others enhances both the escalation and maintenance of relationships. Social decentering helps you better understand your partner, which provides you with a basis for choosing the most effective strategies for accomplishing your communication goals. We have been discussing the notion of "appropriateness" of your behaviors to the effective advancement and maintenance of
your relationships. Determining appropriateness depends upon your ability to
read the situation and your partner, and then to adapt or choose the best
behaviors. Essentially, you can either consider what your partner is thinking
now, or will think in response to your actions—put yourself in your partner's
shoes. For example, suppose you are on a first date and trying to decide
whether to tell your partner about a very intimate relationship you had, which
just ended. Put yourself in the other person's shoes. Would you want to hear
on a first date about someone's recent breakup? What information do you have
about your date that can help you determine your date's reaction? As relationships become more intimate, you receive more and more information that can
improve decentering and adaptation.

Managing Intimate Relationships

One technique for managing intimate relationships is to back off occasionally—periods of closeness must be balanced by periods of distance. We need time to ourselves in order to recharge and gain perspective. The following excerpt reflects the use of decentering, restraint, and effective conflict management to maintain intimate relationships.

The kinds of things we get upset about in intimacy tend to follow certain themes. Basically, we become hurt or resentful because we're getting "too much" or "too little" of something. Too many demands, too much criticism, too much domination. Or the converse, too little affectional, conversational, or sexual attention (which translates into "you don't feel I'm important" or "you don't love me"). Insufficient empathy is usually voiced as "you don't understand me," and too little responsibility translates into failure to take one's share of household and/or financial tasks. All these complaints require some attention, action, or retreat.

SHIFTING GEARS: It's not enough to identify the source of personal concern. You have to present your concerns in a way your partner can hear. If I say directly to my partner, "I'm afraid you're going to leave me," he has the opportunity to respond, "Darling, that's not true. What gave you that idea?" I get the reassurance I need. But if I toss it out in an argument, in the form of "you don't care about me," then my partner's emotional arousal keeps him from hearing me. And he is likely to back away—just when I need reassurance most.

If people were aware that intimate relationships are by nature characterized by ambivalence, they would understand the need to negotiate occasional retreats. They wouldn't feel so threatened by the times when one partner says, "I have to be by myself because I need to think about my life and where I'm going." Or "I need to be with my friends and spend time playing." If people did more backing off into constructive activities, including time to meditate or play, intimate relationships would be in much better shape today.

If couples could be direct about what they need, then the need for retreat would not be subject to the misrepresentation that now is rampant. The trouble is, we don't talk to each other that openly and honestly. What happens if one partner left behind doesn't know what the withdrawal means. But he or she draws on a personal history which provides room for all sorts of negative interpretations, the most common being "he doesn't care about me."

No matter how hard a partner tries to be all things to us, gratifying all of another's needs is a herculean task—beyond the human calling. Criticism, disappointment, and momentary rejection are intrinsic parts of intimate life; developing thicker skin can be healthy. And maintaining a life apart from the relationships is necessary. Energy invested in other people and activities provides a welcome balance.

From: Geraldine K. Piorkowski, *Psychology Today*. Reprinted with permission from *Psychology Today* magazine, copyright © 1995 (Sussex Publishers, Inc.).

Be Tolerant and Show Restraint

The most satisfying relationships are those in which both partners refrain from continually disagreeing, criticizing, and making negative comments to each other. Both individuals learn to accept the other and do not feel compelled to continually point out flaws or failures. One study found that well-adjusted couples focus their complaints on specific behaviors, whereas maladjusted couples complain about each other's personal characteristics. Well-adjusted couples are also kinder and more positive, and have more humor in their interactions. They tend to agree with each other's complaints, whereas the partners in maladjusted relationships launch countercomplaints.[15] In addition, happy couples, when compared to unhappy couples, display more affection through positive nonverbal cues, display more supportive behaviors, and make more attempts to avoid conflict.[16]

Maintaining a relationship requires tolerance. You must learn to accept your partners for who they are and put up with some things you dislike. When couples lose their tolerance, they begin focusing on and criticizing characteristics that they used to accept. Relationships begin to deteriorate.

Manage Conflict Cooperatively

Conflicts are inevitable in interpersonal relationships. As relationships develop, the individuals share more personal information and spend more time together, so the likelihood for conflict increases. The key to successful relational development and maintenance is *not* to avoid conflict altogether, but rather to manage it effectively. As we discussed in Chapter 8, a cooperative management style can actually transform conflict into an experience that strengthens a relationship. It can clarify the definition of a relationship, increase the exchange of information, and create a cooperative atmosphere for problem solving.

Seek Compliance

The final skill for developing and maintaining relationships might seem somewhat contrary to the ones we have been discussing. Strictly speaking, **compliance gaining** involves the use of persuasive strategies to accomplish your personal goals—that is, to get your own way. We are not urging you to force your will upon others. We are, however, suggesting that it is sometimes ethical and moral to persuade others to go your way. In an ideal situation, the resulting interactions will fulfill both partners' goals.

You need compliance-gaining strategies if you encounter resistance to fulfilling your goal. For example, suppose you want to go out to a movie and you need to borrow money from one of your friends to pay for it. You may simply ask, "Can I borrow five dollars so I can go to a movie?" If your friend says, "Sure," the interaction is completed. If your friend says, "No, you haven't paid me back from last time," however, you will probably use some compliance-gaining strategy.

 INTERPERSONAL COMMUNICATION RELATIONSHIPS

Compliance-gaining strategies are responsive to the ongoing, transactive nature of interpersonal relationships.[17] We plot strategies that develop over a number of interactions and modify them in accordance with others' responses. For example, before you ask to borrow money from your friend, you first might do a few favors for her during the day. Then if your friend says no, you might remind her that she owes you for all you've done for her. If she still says no, you might offer to help her over the weekend with her class project. The type of relationship you have established with the other person will affect your strategy selection. Often we face little resistance to our requests from our partners, so we have no need for any compliance-gaining strategy.

Identifying and Acting on Trouble Signs in Relationships

As the Understanding Diversity box on page 353 indicates, women usually sense trouble in a relationship earlier than do men, but what exactly do they sense? Because each stage in a relationship has unique communication qualities, specific verbal and nonverbal cues can tip us off when a relationship begins to de-escalate.[18] There is a decrease in touching and physical contact (including less sexual activity), physical proximity, eye contact, smiling, vocal variety in the voice, and ease of interaction. In addition, there is a decrease in the amount of time spent together, an increase in time between interactions, and more separation of possessions. The interactions become less personal, and so does the language.

Couples use fewer intimate terms; they use less present tense and more passive tense; they make fewer references to their future in the relationship; they use more qualified language ("maybe," "whatever," "we'll see"); make fewer evaluative statements; and spend less time discussing any given topic. They fight more, and they disclose less. If one person becomes less open about discussing attitudes, feelings, thoughts, and other personal issues, he or she is probably signaling a desire to terminate or, at least, redefine the relationship. Can you pick up the signals of the couple's difficulty reflected in the photograph on page 352?

When you pick up signals of relational problems, you have three choices: just wait and see what happens; make a decision to end the relationship; or try to repair the relationship. Repairing the relationship involves applying all the maintenance skills we talked about earlier. Some of the strategies for dealing with conflict that you learned in Chapter 8 will also help you. Underlying the success of any repair effort, however, is the degree to which both partners want to keep the relationship going. The nature of the problem, the stage of the - relationship, and the commitment and motivation of the partners all affect the success of repair efforts. There is no single quick solution to relational problems because so many factors influence each one. You need to focus on the specific concerns, needs, and issues that underlie the problem; then adapt specific strategies to resolve it. Professional counseling might be an important option.

If you do choose to end the relationship, consider your goals. Do you want to continue the relationship at a less intimate level, or terminate it altogether? Do you care enough about the other person to want to preserve his or her self-esteem? Are you aware of the costs involved in ending the relationship? There is no one correct or best way to end a relationship. Ending relationships is also not something you can practice in order to improve. But you can practice the effective relational management skills such as decentering and empathy, adaptation, and compliance gaining. These skills will also help you in ending relationships.

The final issue to consider is how to deal with someone who wants to end his or her relationship with you. Again, there is no pat answer. If a friend stops calling or visiting, should you just assume the relationship is over and leave it alone, or should you call and ask what's up? People lose contact for a myriad of reasons. Sometimes it is beneficial to ask an individual directly if he or she is breaking off the relationship, although such direct requests place your self-concept on the line. How should you react if your friend confirms a desire to end the relationship? If possible, try to have a focused discussion on what has contributed to his or her decision. You might get information you need to repair the relationship. Or you might gain information that will help you in future relationships.

When intimate relationships do end, we rely on our social networks for support and self-confirmation. Advice about how to handle the loss of a close relationship is plentiful (see the article below), but basically each person must find a way to compensate for the loss of intimacy and companionship. The loss of an important relationship hurts, but it need not put us out of commission if we make the most of our friends and family.

Loss of a Friend Can Hurt More Than a Romantic Split

You can't think of the person without a sickening lurch in your gut. You alternate between angrily wishing you'd never met the Judas and agonizing over what went wrong. It hurts when mutual friends bring up the person's name, when they tell you about the fun times you weren't invited to and wouldn't attend even if you were.

You have all the sloppy symptoms of a broken heart.

But you don't go to marriage counseling—you're not married.

You don't go to family counseling—you're not related.

You don't go to couples counseling—you're not lovers.

You don't even suggest to the person any counseling at all, lest you be thought insane.

You're "just friends," so there's no one to talk to about your shattered psyche, no words like "ex-lover" or "ex-husband" to legitimize your nemesis, no socially acceptable ritual to mourn the loss of the trusted confidant you once held dear.

Friendship—in other times and places lauded as passionately as romantic love—today takes a cultural back seat to every other important relationship.

III INTERPERSONAL COMMUNICATION RELATIONSHIPS

Yet despite society's alleged nonchalance, the loss of a friend can cut more deeply than losing a lover.

"I felt totally betrayed and completely lost," says editor Justine Kaplan, thirty-three, whose best friend, hurting from a Kaplan matchmaking attempt that went awry, told her that she no longer wanted to be friends. "I didn't understand. You're not supposed to just stop being friends with someone."

"I wanted to say, 'What the hell is this—you're breaking up with me'?"

She sighs, "With a lover, you can call them up later and say 'Let's be friends,' But when a friend rejects you, what's left to do?"

Any review of the popular media yields reams of articles on how to survive breakup of a lovematch, but almost none on losing a friend. That doesn't surprise University of South Carolina social psychologist Keith Davis, who has been researching friendship breakups for a decade.

"It's just a cultural bias," he says. "Researchers don't look at it, and people don't write about it."

He says his in-depth studies revealed two typical ways friendships end.

One is a "gradual growing apart, like when someone moves and doesn't stay in touch," he says, "The other is a betrayal, which in many ways feels quite similar to the experience with a lover."

The betrayals fall into three categories: stealing one's lover; not being there when needed; and the misuse of personal things, including property and secrets.

But whatever the betrayal, Davis says, working it through can transform the friendship into something better than it was.

"About half of my subjects said they were able to successfully repair the relationship," Davis says. "In the other half, what's learned is that the person can't be trusted, and they don't want to be around the person ever again."

Not surprisingly, Davis says anger and sadness are the most common emotions when friendships end.

"The nature of the emotion depends a lot on the specifics of the relationship," he says, "At the minimum you're angry because you've been let down. And you become very sad because you thought you had a friend you could count on."

Still, most people in the United States don't really suffer over losing friends, says Gene Gordon, a Washington, D.C., psychoanalyst and clinical professor at George Washington University.

"Friendship is just not highly valued here," he says. "Breaking up means you're close to someone, but since most people aren't close, they don't feel the breakup. It's not like in places like Central America, where friendship is taken much more seriously. Here, friendships are taken very casually."

In genuinely close friendship, Gordon says, it's natural to feel "extremely attached and very dependent." Therefore, breakups of those relationships are indeed traumatic.

"It's scary and lonely and awakens all the traumas of separation we've ever experienced in childhood," he says. "This doesn't mean one is immature. Very often, it speaks paradoxically to the maturity of the adult, that the friendship was that intimate to them."

When Laverne Left Shirley: How to Ease Breakup with Buddy

Advice for the friend-lorn:

- Remember that it's natural to feel sad, angry, or guilty when you lose an important relationship.
- Give yourself permission and time to grieve.
- Give yourself credit for having cared enough about your friend to mourn the loss.
- Talk about your feelings. If talking to other friends doesn't help, seek professional counseling.
- Know that as painful as it may feel now, time will help.
- When the pain subsides, keep yourself open and willing to make new friends and cherish the ones you already have.
- Remember that it's rarely too late to forgive or ask for forgiveness.

From: Leslie Knowlton, *Los Angeles Times.* Copyright © 1995, *Los Angeles Times.* Reprinted by permission.

De-Escalating and Ending Relationships

Relational trouble signs may signal the start of **relational de-escalation.** As Figure 10.1 shows, one half of the model for relational stages is devoted to the process of de-escalating and terminating relationships, which involves a reduction in the level of intimacy, commitment, self-disclosing, and general resources necessary to hold a relationship together. A relationship can descend through several stages before it reaches termination, or the end of interpersonal communication. As we mentioned before, no relationship ever really comes to a complete end, because each has a lasting impact. The more intimate a relationship becomes, the greater its impact. Individuals who have been married and divorced are certainly affected for a long time by that experience, even though the two partners might never see each other again.

The de-escalation and termination of a relationship is not inherently bad. Not all relationships are meant to endure. Ending a relationship can be a healthy move if the relationship is harmful, or if it no longer provides confirmation of the self or satisfies interpersonal needs; it also can open the door to new relationships. Sometimes we choose not to end a relationship, but rather to de-escalate to a less intimate stage where there is a better balance between benefits and costs.

Breaking up an intimate relationship is hard because of the degree to which we become dependent upon the other person to confirm our sense of self. When a relationship ends, we may feel as if we need to redefine who we are. The most satisfying breakups are those that confirm both partners' worth rather than degrade it. "I just can't be what you want me to be"; "I'll always love you but . . . "; or "You're a very special person, but I need other things in life" are all examples of statements that do not destroy self-esteem.

The process of ending a relationship is considerably different when only one party wants out of the relationship (unilateral) than when both are agreeable to it (bilateral).[19] In **bilateral dissolutions**, both parties are predisposed to ending the relationship; they simply need to sort out details such as timing, dividing possessions, and defining conditions for the contact after the breakup. In a **unilateral dissolution**, the person who wants to end the relationship must use compliance-gaining strategies to get his or her partner to agree to the dissolution. Sometimes, however, people simply walk out of a relationship.

How Relationships End

A declining relationship usually follows one of several paths. Sometimes a relationship loses steam and runs down like a dying battery. Instead of a single event that causes the breakup, the relationships **fades away**—the two partners just drift further and further apart. They spend less time together, let more time go by between interactions, and stop disclosing much about themselves. You've probably had a number of friendships that ended this way—perhaps long-distance relationships. Long-distance relationships require a great deal of effort to maintain, so a move can easily decrease the level of intimacy.

Some relationships end in sudden death.[20] As the name suggests, **sudden death** moves straight to separation. One partner might move away or die, or more frequently, a single precipitating event such as infidelity, breaking a confidence, a major conflict, or some other major role violation precipitates the breakup. Sudden death is like taking an express elevator from a top floor to ground level.

In between fading away and sudden death lies incrementalism. **Incrementalism** is the process by which conflicts and problems continue to accumulate in the relationship until they reach a critical mass that leads to the breakup; the relationship becomes intolerable or, from a social exchange perspective, too costly.

UNDERSTANDING DIVERSITY

Empathy and Sexual Orientation

One of your authors once volunteered as a crisis phone counselor in a large metropolitan area. We were trained to use effective counseling skills, such as empathy, in relating to the callers' crises. One night, a call came in from a very distressed and depressed man about his breakup with his homosexual partner with whom he had a long-term intimate relationship. At first I was uncomfortable dealing with the situation. Despite extensive training and roleplaying, I wondered how I, as a heterosexual male, could empathize with or relate to this caller. However, I continued to ask questions about how he felt, what he saw as his needs, and his perception of the problems. The more we talked, the more empathic I became, because I realized that his description was very familiar. I had been divorced some four years earlier, and this caller's descriptions of his feelings matched the feelings I experienced during that time. I was able to talk about some of the feelings I had experienced, and this seemed to help him understand his own situation. I realized that though the sex of our partners was different, the overriding issue was the loss of an intimate relationship. I grew a little wiser that night.

Return to science again and ask students to consider the Universal Law of Gravitation with respect to relationships. According to Newton, forces always act in pairs, and between any two objects there is an attractive force (gravity) that is proportional to the masses of the objects. Therefore, without effective communication—an elevating force—gravity will pull a relationship downward.

DISCUSSION AND WRITING
Ask students whether relationships die from too much or too little communication. Discuss this. Consider the Heisenberg Theory that you cannot measure both the velocity and the position of any particle simultaneously.

Which of the three types of relationship termination do you think is evident here: fading away—where the partners drift slowly apart, sudden death—where separation is immediate, or incremen-talism—where the conflicts gradually build until they reach the breaking point? (Donna Day/Tony Stone Images)

"I just got to a point where it wasn't worth it anymore," and "It got to the point where all we did was fight all the time" are typical statements about incremental endings. For each of the three paths, individuals can choose from a variety of strategies to end the relationship.

Strategies for Ending Relationships

When the vitality in long marriages fades away over a period of years, the individuals move slowly through the de-escalation stages before finally divorcing. Brand new relationships are far more likely to end abruptly. As you saw in Figure 10.1, the farther up the relational high rise you take the elevator, the longer the ride down.

But no matter what stage a relationship is in, partners use both direct and indirect strategies when they wish to end it. **Indirect strategies** represent attempts to break up a relationship without explicitly stating the desire to do so. **Direct strategies** involve explicit statements. The strategy that a person chooses will depend upon the level of intimacy in the relationship, the level of desire to help the partner save face, the degree of urgency for terminating the relation-ship, and the person's interpersonal skills. The Cathy cartoon illustrates the difficulties we all face in coming up with a unique and nonthreatening strategy for ending a relationship.

■ INDIRECT STRATEGIES

One researcher identifies three strategies that people use to indirectly disen-gage: withdrawal, pseudo-de-escalation, and cost escalation. *Withdrawal*

III   INTERPERSONAL COMMUNICATION RELATIONSHIPS

Gender and Ending Relationships

Men and women differ when it comes to dating and marital breakups. Women tend to be stronger monitors of the relationship, so they usually detect trouble before men do. Their sensitivity to the health of the relationship might be one factor that makes them more likely to initiate the termination of a relationship as well.[21] However, when some men want out

of a relationship, they engage in behaviors that women find totally unacceptable. This allows both partners to feel as if they were the ones who initiated the breakup and therefore to "save face."

Problems sometimes associated with behaviors that appear early in a relationship. Marriages in which the men avoid interaction by stonewalling and responding defensively to complaints are more likely to end in divorce.[22]

In one study of divorce, men tended to see the later part of the process as more difficult, whereas the women said the period before the decision to divorce was more difficult. In addition, two-thirds of the women were likely to discuss marital problems with their children as compared to only one-fourth of the men; and men were twice as likely to say that no one helped them during the worst part of the process.[23]

---

involves reducing the amount of contact and interaction without any explanation.[24] This strategy is the most dissatisfying for the other partner.[25] Withdrawal represents an attempt to avoid a confrontational scene and to save face.

In *pseudo-de-escalation* one partner claims that he or she wants to redefine the relationship at a lower level of intimacy, but in reality, he or she wants to end the relationship. Statements such as, "Let's just be friends" or "I think of you as more of a sister" might be sincere, or they might reflect an unspoken desire to disengage completely. When both parties want to end the relationship, they sometimes use mutual pseudo-de-escalation and enter into a false agreement to reduce the level of intimacy as they move to disengagement.

Cost escalation is an attempt to increase the costs associated with the relationship in order to encourage the other person to terminate it. A dissatisfied partner might ask for an inordinate amount of the other person's time, pick fights, criticize the other person, or violate relational rules. As Understanding Diversity: Gender and Ending Relationships indicates, this is a strategy that men apparently use more often than women.

■ DIRECT STRATEGIES

The same researcher also identified four direct strategies that we use to terminate relationships: negative identity management, justification, de-escalation, and positive tone.[26] *Negative identity management* is a direct statement of the desire to terminate the relationship. It does not take into account the other's feelings, and it might even include criticisms. "I want out of our relationship"; "I just can't stand to be around you anymore"; and "I'm no longer happy in

this relationship and I want to date other people" reflect negative identity management.

Justification is a clear statement of the desire to end the relationship, accompanied by an honest explanation of the reasons. Justification statements may still hurt the other person's feelings: "I've found someone else that I want to spend more time with who makes me happy" and "I feel as if I've grown a great deal and you haven't." But a person who uses justification does not fault the other person, and he or she makes some attempt to protect both parties' sense of self. One researcher found that most people on the receiving end like this strategy best.[27]

De-escalation is an honest statement of a desire to redefine the relationship at a lower level of intimacy or to move toward ending the relationship. One partner might ask for a trial separation so that both people can explore other opportunities and gain a clearer understanding of their needs:[28] "Neither of us seems to be that happy with the relationship right now, so I think we should cool it for a while and see what happens."

BUILDING YOUR SKILLS

How Your Relationships Have Ended

I dentify two relationships that you have ended and two relationships that the other person ended. For each relationship try to determine which of the indi-

rect or direct strategies were used to end the relationship. What differences were there in how the relationships ended? What effects do you think the choice of strategy had on you and your partner?

Conduct a survey of your friends by asking them these same questions. What conclusions can you draw about how people feel concerning different relationship termination strategies?

RESEARCH AND LITERATURE

For further reading about these stages, consult Diane Vaughan's *Uncoupling* (Random House, 1986).

SKILL DEVELOPMENT

Put the ending-a-relationship strategies on the board or overhead projector. Ask students to identify their preferred method for breakups in the past. Have students form groups based upon their strategies. In each group, have students consider and list all possible positive and negative effects of that particular strategy. Encourage students to consider the effects on the initiator of the breakup, the receiver of the message, and the relationship itself. After reports from each group, lead a discussion aimed at rank-ordering strategies from most to least humane.

354

Positive tone is the direct strategy that is most sensitive to the other person's sense of self. This strategy can seem almost contradictory because the initiator tries to affirm the other's personal qualities and worth at the same time that he or she calls a halt to the relationship. "I love you; I just can't live with you"; "I'm really sorry I've got to break off the relationship"; and "You really are a wonderful person, you're just not the one for me" are examples of positive tone statements.

RECAP	**Strategies for Ending Relationships**	
	Term	**Explanation**
How Relationships End	Fading Away	The relationship dissolves slowly as intimacy declines.
	Sudden Death	The relationship ends abruptly, usually in response to some precipitating event.
	Incrementalism	Relational conflicts and problems accumulate until they become intolerable, then the relationship ends.
Indirect Strategies	Withdrawal	Reducing the amount of contact, without any explanation.
	Pseudo-de-escalation	Claiming a desire for less intimacy, when you really want out.
	Cost Escalation	Increasing relational costs to encourage the other to end the relationship.
Direct Strategies	Negative Identity Management	Directly stating a desire to end the relationship, without concern for the other person's feelings.
	Justification	Directly stating a desire to end the relationship, with an explanation of the reasons.
	De-escalation	Directly stating a desire to lower the level of intimacy or move toward termination.
	Positive Tone	Directly stating a desire to end the relationship, while affirming the other person's value.

Causes of De-Escalation and Termination

The reasons for ending an interpersonal relationship are as varied as relationships themselves. In general, we end relationships when they cost us more than they reward us. This does not mean that as soon as a relationship becomes difficult we dump it. Relationships are somewhat like savings accounts. If the relationship is profitable, you deposit your excess rewards into an emotional savings account. Then at times when the costs exceed the rewards, you draw from your savings account to make up the deficit. In other words, if you have had a strong, satisfying relationship with someone for a long period of time, you will be more inclined to stay in the relationship during rough times. There might be a point, however, at which your savings account will run out, and you will decide to close your account—end the relationship. Of course, if you can foresee that you will reap more benefits in the future, you might decide to keep the account open, even when it is overdrawn. In addition, if you have had even less satisfying relationships in the past, or if your alternatives seem more dismal than your current relationships, you might decide to stick it out.[29] Of course, under those relational circumstances, when attractive alternatives do appear, relationships often suffer a sudden death.

One researcher found that most people attribute breakups to one of three main causes.[30] As Table 10.1 shows, "faults" are the number one cause. These are problems with personality traits or behaviors that one partner dislikes in the other. The number two cause, "unwillingness to compromise," represents a variety of failings on the part of one or both partners, including failure to put enough effort into the relationship, a decrease in effort, or failure to make concessions for the good of the relationship. The final cause, "feeling constrained," reflects one partner's desire to be free from the commitments and constraints of a relationship. But a variety of other elements can contribute to the breakup of both romantic and non-romantic relationships, including loss of interest in the other person, desire for independence, and conflicting attitudes about the definition of the relationship in areas such as sexual conduct, marriage, and infidelity.

Table 10.1

Reasons Given for Breakups[31]

Faults
I realized that he/she had too many personality faults.
He/she behaved in ways that embarrassed me.
His/her behaviors were more to blame for the breakup than anything else.

Unwillingness to Compromise
I realized she/he was unwilling to make enough contributions to the relationship.
I felt that he/she no longer behaved towards me as romantically as she/he once did.
I felt that he/she took me for granted.
I felt that he/she wasn't willing to compromise for the good of the relationship.

Feeling Constrained
I felt that the relationship was beginning to constrain me, and I felt a lack of freedom.
Although I still cared for him/her, I wanted to start dating other people.
Although this relationship was a good one, I started to get bored with it.
He/she made too many contributions, and I started to feel suffocated.

A Model of Ending Relationships

Steve Duck developed a model to show stages in ending a relationship.[32] As Figure 10.3 shows, first one partner reaches some threshold of dissatisfaction that prompts him or her to consider ending the relationship. In this **intra-psychic phase**, we focus on evaluating our partner's behaviors, often fixing on the reasons in Table 10.3 to justify withdrawing. We don't intentionally communicate these thoughts to our partner, however, and we often decide not to dissolve the relationship. From time to time we all become frustrated with a relationship that we consider terminating, but never proceed further than this phase. However, we might "leak" our thoughts and feelings through our communication, displaying such emotions as hostility, anxiety, stress, or guilt. We might decide to confide to a third party about our dissatisfaction. We might consider various strategies for ending the relationship.

At some point we might decide to move from our internal contemplations about the relationship to confronting our partner. This is the **dyadic phase** in the model. If our partner feels challenged and intimidated by our desire to end the relationship, we might have to justify our thoughts and feelings. Our partner might also criticize our behavior and identify our failings. He or she might raise issues that cause us to reevaluate the relationship, our partner, and the costs of dissolving the relationship. We might decide instead to work on improving and repairing the relationship.

If we agree to end the relationship, we enter the **social phase** and begin making the information public. Sometimes a person's social network will mobilize to preserve the relationship. Friends might act as mediators, encouraging reconciliation and suggesting ways to repair the relationship. Of course, friends can also reinforce a decision to separate. Rumors and stories about what happened and what is happening can fuel bad feelings and hasten the end of the relationship.

In the **grave-dressing phase**, one or both partners may attempt to place flowers on the grave of their relationship to cover up the hurt and pain associated with its death. They need a public story that they can share with others about what happened: "We still love each other; we just decided we needed more in our lives." Such a story often places blame on the other partner: "I knew he had his faults, but he thought he could change, and he just wasn't able to." During this phase, our friends encourage us to get back into social activities; they might even try to fix us up with dates. Most importantly, we go through an internal stage in which we come to accept the end of the relationship. We let go of feelings of guilt, failure, and blame.

MEDIA AND OUTSIDE RESOURCES
Show the poignant scene from the film *Joy Luck Club,* in which Rose shares with Ted her insight that "I was the one who told you that my love wasn't good enough; that your love was worth more than mine." Have the class pay particular attention to Ted's non-verbal messages of support during this disclosure and how it contributes to relational repair.

Figure 10.3

A Model of Ending
Relationships

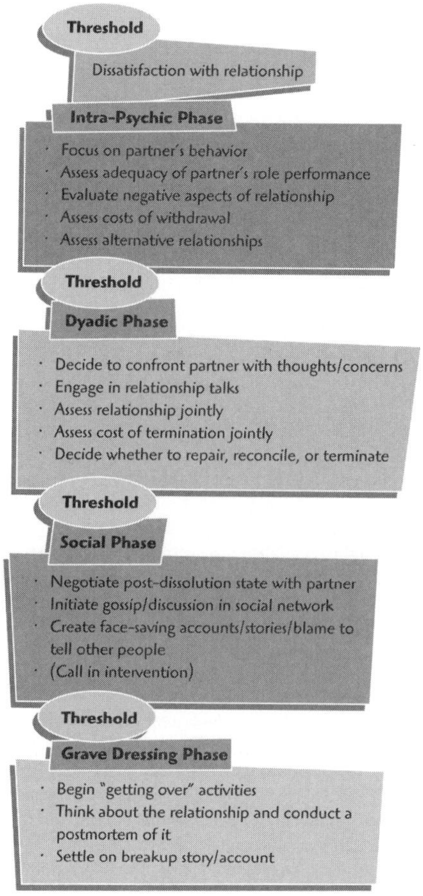

Threshold

Dissatisfaction with relationship

Intra-Psychic Phase

· Focus on partner's behavior
· Assess adequacy of partner's role performance
· Evaluate negative aspects of relationship
· Assess costs of withdrawal
· Assess alternative relationships

Threshold

Dyadic Phase

· Decide to confront partner with thoughts/concerns
· Engage in relationship talks
· Assess relationship jointly
· Assess cost of termination jointly
· Decide whether to repair, reconcile, or terminate

Threshold

Social Phase

· Negotiate post-dissolution state with partner
· Initiate gossip/discussion in social network
· Create face-saving accounts/stories/blame to
  tell other people
· (Call in intervention)

Threshold

Grave Dressing Phase

· Begin "getting over" activities
· Think about the relationship and conduct a
  postmortem of it
· Settle on breakup story/account

Summary

Relationships progress through stages, with the movement from one stage to another often signaled by turning points. As relationships escalate, they progress from pre-interaction awareness to initiation, to exploration, to intensification, and finally, to intimacy. Relationships de-escalate as we move to redefine or terminate them, moving from turmoil or stagnation, to de-intensification, to individualization, to separation, and finally, to post-interaction. Even after we end a relationship, its effects remain with us to shape our feelings and responses in other relationships. We use a variety of skills within each relational stage.

To move from initial attraction to initiation of interaction, we need to understand and utilize such skills as gathering information to reduce uncertainty, adopting an other-oriented perspective, observing and acting on approachability cues, identifying and using conversation starters, following initiation norms, providing information about ourselves, presenting ourselves in a positive way, asking questions, and not expecting too much from the initial interaction.

We disclose increasingly intimate and risky information as relationships escalate. Strategies for escalating and maintaining relationships include being open and self-disclosing appropriately; expressing emotions; engaging in relationship talk; monitoring perceptions; listening actively and responding confirmingly; social decentering, empathizing, and adapting; being tolerant and showing restraint; managing conflict cooperatively; and seeking compliance.

Certain trouble signs signal changes in relationships. A decrease in physical contact, eye contact, smiling, the amount of time spent together, intimate language, and openness in discussing thoughts and feelings are signals that a relationship is de-escalating. The partners can try to repair the relationship by applying maintenance skills, but the results will depend upon their degree of mutual commitment. When we decide to end relationships, friends and family can provide comfort and support.

On the way down, relationships can take three paths: fading away, sudden death, and incrementalism. Whether the disengagement is unilateral, with only one partner desiring it, or bilateral, with both wanting it, we can use direct or indirect strategies. Indirect strategies include withdrawal, pseudo-de-escalation, and cost escalation to end the relationship. Direct strategies are negative identity management, justification, de-escalation, and positive tone.

In general, relationships seem to end when the costs exceed the rewards over some period of time. The relationship no longer confirms an individual's sense of self enough to outweigh the demands the relationship places on the individual. The causes we give for ending a relationship fall into three categories: faults, unwillingness to compromise, and feeling constrained. We might communicate a desire to end the relationship intentionally or unintentionally through changes in our language and nonverbal communication.

1. Relationships generally escalate in systematic ways beginning with awareness, initiation, exploration, intensification, and intimacy. Likewise, relationships generally de-escalate when destructive conflict (or the lack of conflict) leads to de-intensification, individualization, separation, and grave-dressing.

2. Effective communication skills will improve relationships. These include self-monitoring, showing empathy, being flexible, adaptive, and tolerant, and using an other-orientation when trying to persuade or resolve conflict.

3. Indirect ways to end a relationship include escalating the costs for the other person by violating an expressed relationship rule or picking fights; retreating and withdrawing emotional investments; and asking to redefine the relationship. Direct ways to terminate a relationship require openly stating a desire to do so. These statements may be positive, neutral, or negative.

4. Steve Duck's phases of relational dissolution involve intrapsychic changes, dyadic changes, social changes, and finally, grave dressing.

A model for ending relationships has four phases: intra-psychic, dyadic, social, and grave-dressing. First, we internally assess the value of the relationship and consider termination; then we discuss it with our partner; we proceed by announcing the termination and interacting with friends and family; and finally, we come to grips with the consequences of separation.

For Discussion and Review

■ FOCUS ON COMPREHENSION

1. What are the five stages of relational escalation and the five stages of relational de-escalation?

2. What skills are associated with starting a relationship?

3. What interpersonal skills are associated with maintaining and escalating relationships?

4. What are direct and indirect strategies for ending a relationship?

5. What are the four phases identified in the model for ending relationships?

■ FOCUS ON CRITICAL THINKING

6. Which two skills are probably the most important for starting a relationship and which two are least important? Why?

7. How do the strategies for escalating and maintaining a relationship relate to the indirect and direct strategies used for terminating a relationship?

8. Trace two close relationships that you have had—one with a friend of the same sex, and one with a friend of the opposite sex—through the applicable stages of relational escalation and de-escalation. What differences and similarities do you find at each stage? How can you explain them?

■ FOCUS ON ETHICS

9. How ethical is it for a person who is very skilled at compliance gaining to convince another person to escalate the relationship if that person has a strong initial resistance to escalation?

10. Under what circumstances might it be ethical for a person in an intimate relationship to use sudden death withdrawal as a strategy for ending a relationship? Under what circumstances would it be unethical?

11. Lynn and Chris have had an intimate relationship and have been living together for over a year. The relationship has seemed to be comfortable for

both of them. One day Lynn comes home from work and finds that all of Chris's belongings are gone. A note from Chris says, "I couldn't bring myself to tell you I'm leaving. Sorry. Good-bye." Is Chris's behavior ethical?

For Your Journal

1. At the end of each day for three or four days, stop and assess which of the interpersonal communication skills you used the most in your interactions that day. Try to see if there is a consistent pattern in the skills you rely on. What skills do you seem to use the most? What skills do you use the least? How might using other skills affect your interactions and relationships?

2. Think about a close relationship you had that you ended. What strategy did you first use? How well did this strategy work? What was your partner's reaction to this strategy? How did you feel using this strategy? What other strategies were used, if any? What were the reactions to those? If you had it to do over again, what other strategy might you have chosen to use? How do you think your partner would have reacted to that strategy? Why? If you can't think of any relationship that you have ended, use one in which your partner has ended the relationship, and adapt the questions accordingly.

Learning with Others

1. In class, form at least five pairs of students. Each pair should choose a particular stage of relational development without telling the rest of the class. Then each pair should spend two minutes discussing plans for the upcoming weekend in a way that communicates the stage they have chosen. The rest of the class should write down what stage they think each pair is portraying. After all the pairs have finished their dialogues, score each others' responses. Which stage was easiest to portray and identify? Which stage was most difficult? How easy is it to see differences in communication behavior at various stages?

2. In small groups, brainstorm some of the turning points that each of you has experienced in important relationships. Identify the relational stages that they led to. Which stages crop up most often? Least often? What does the frequency tell you about those stages?

3. Divide into groups of four or five students. As you go around your group, have each student respond to the following request: Describe the most

successful conversation starter that has been used on you, or which you have used. What made it successful? What did you like about it? What was the outcome? Next, go around and describe the worst conversation starter that has been used on each of you, or by each of you. What made it the worst? What was the outcome?

4. Working in groups of four or five students, use your own experiences to develop an answer to the following question: Do the reasons for breaking up a relationship change as the relationship becomes more intimate? To answer this question, start with casual relationships and identify reasons that people end those relationships. Next, talk about friendships, and discuss reasons for ending them. And finally, talk about intimate relationships and the reasons they break up. What are the similarities and differences among these different types of relationships and why they break up?

■ GLOSSARY

RELATIONAL DEVELOPMENT: The process of moving from one stage to another as a relationships moves toward or away from greater intimacy.

TURNING POINT: A specific event or interaction associated with positive or negative changes in a relationship.

RELATIONAL ESCALATION: The upward movement of a relationship toward intimacy through five stages: pre-interaction awareness, initiation, exploration, intensification, and intimacy.

RELATIONAL DE-ESCALATION: The downward movement of a relationship away from intimacy through five stages: turmoil or stagnation, de-intensification, individualization, separation, and post-interaction.

NONVERBAL SENSITIVITY: The ability to pick up and accurately interpret nonverbal cues.

COMPLIANCE GAINING: The use of persuasive strategies to accomplish interpersonal goals.

BILATERAL DISSOLUTION: Ending a relationship when both parties are agreeable.

UNILATERAL DISSOLUTION: Ending a relationship when only one party is agreeable.

FADING AWAY: Ending a relationship by slowly drifting apart.

SUDDEN DEATH: Ending a relationship abruptly and without preparation.

INCREMENTALISM: Ending a relationship when conflicts and problems finally reach a critical mass.

INDIRECT RELATIONAL TERMINATION STRATEGIES: Attempts to break up a relationship without explicitly stating the desire to do so.

DIRECT RELATIONAL TERMINATION STRATEGIES: Explicit statements of a desire to break up a relationship.

INTRA-PSYCHIC PHASE: The first phase in a model of relationship termination: an individual engages in an internal evaluation of the partner.

DYADIC PHASE: The second phase in a model of relationship termination: the individual discusses termination with the partner.

SOCIAL PHASE: The third phase in a model of relationship termination: members of the social network around both parties are informed and become involved.

GRAVE-DRESSING PHASE: The final phase in a model relationship termination: the partners generate public explanations and move past the relationship.

Relating to Family, Friends, and Colleagues

After studying this chapter, you should be able to:

1. Define the term *family* and describe four types of families.

2. Describe the cohesion and adaptability model of family functioning.

3. Identify and describe the communication characteristics of a healthy family.

4. Identify characteristics of childhood, adolescent, and adult friendships as well as friendships of the elderly.

5. List and describe strategies for making and losing friends.

6. Describe principles of upward, downward, horizontal, and outward communication.

7. Identify the characteristics of an effective leader and follower in an organization.

8. Describe the role and effects of technology upon interpersonal relationships in the workplace.

- ■ RELATING TO FAMILY

- ■ RELATING TO FRIENDS AND LOVERS

- ■ RELATING TO COLLEAGUES

t has been a long, stressful day. At 11:30 P.M. Maria begins her nightly ritual of preparing for bed. Her husband is already in bed, snoring softly, with the TV flickering in the dim light of the bedroom. Her four-year-old daughter has been asleep for hours. Now it is Maria's turn for rest. Yet her mind continues to churn through a list of "to do's" for the next day. Reaching for her pad of Post-it notes she keeps by her bedside, she begins to scratch notes to jog her morning memory of the chores that must be done tomorrow. She smiles a secret smile and writes, "Buy cake for Ted. Get Chanticleer album for his birthday." On another note she pens, "Send e-mail to Hong Kong to Roseann—check on Affolter merger." On her third note she scribbles, "Pick up paper and mail for Hendersons." She lifts the covers, silently slides in beside her snoring companion, and turns out the light. Moments later she bolts upright to snap on the light and write yet another note: "Pick up Deonna from preschool. Doctor's appointment at 4:30." Somehow, writing notes before she goes to sleep frees her from worrying about tomorrow's tasks. After dashing off her fourth note, she pauses to assure herself that she's identified the important jobs and again turns off the light. She nestles herself among the covers in anticipation of sweet slumber. Tomorrow is not far off. She has much to do; so many people are counting on her.

Most of our interpersonal relationships are not single transactions with strangers. Ongoing relationships with family, friends, lovers, and colleagues occupy much of our time and energy. Although Maria writes a separate note for each of her tasks involving the people with whom she has relationships, our relationships with others cannot always be so neatly separated on individual "to do" lists. In the course of a single day you may be wife/husband, mother/father, daughter/son, friend/neighbor, boss/employee. And unlike interpersonal communication textbooks, there are no Recap Boxes or Building Your Skill reminders to fortify you for the myriad of daily tasks you must perform with those with whom you relate. Relationships in our life flow from one interpersonal exchange to another. Our relationships exist in one or more contexts, such as in our family, with friends, or at work or school.

It is in these contexts that we take a final look at communication skills and principles applied to our relationships with others. We first look at our relationships that occur in families. It is in this context that we first learned about interpersonal communication and how to relate to others. We will examine types of families, discuss the importance of communication in maintaining healthy family relationships, and offer suggestions for enriching the quality of relationships with family members. We'll then consider the nature of friendship, how our friendships change throughout our lives, and how we both make and lose friends and lovers. Finally, we will look at the role interpersonal communication plays in the workplace, offering principles for relating to bosses, subordinates, peers, and customers.

Relating to Family

Families have changed since your parents were children. In the 1950s a majority of American families were like the Cleavers from the TV sitcom *Leave It to Beaver*; almost two-thirds of them consisted of a working father, a stay-at-home mother, and at least two biological children. Today fewer than 7 percent of all American families fit that description. Divorce has dramatically increased, rising 700 percent since 1900. And many people have never been married. Although almost 95 percent of them will eventually marry, many are waiting until later in life to do so. Women's roles are changing, too. More are working outside the home, and couples now spend more time clarifying and negotiating domestic roles and responsibilities.

In the past century families have also changed from primarily agriculture-based enclaves to consuming entities. Most families do not grow and harvest their own food; they go to the mall and the market for their needs. In times past, family teamwork was vital for family survival. Today, family members function with greater autonomy. In addition, the increased mobility of families affects communication patterns with relatives. If family members find themselves living in cities distant from their families of origin, friendships develop with others who become a surrogate family.

Despite all of these changing cultural and societal conditions, however, communication still plays a pivotal role in family life. In fact, these changes should encourage us to understand how communication can reduce uncertainty as we struggle to define new roles and responsibilities for family members. But it is important to keep in mind that there is *no single best way to communicate in a family*. Each unique family comes with its own particular challenges for understanding and improving communication.

The Nature of Families

You might think that because families are basic to our existence, we do not need a formal definition of a family. Yet considerable controversy exists as to what constitutes a family unit.

Family Defined

Traditional definitions of a family focus on the roles of husbands, wives, and children who all live together under one roof. Here is one written by a sociologist in 1949:

||| INTERPERSONAL COMMUNICATION RELATIONSHIPS

TEACHING STRATEGY

Students can feel threatened by this unit. The family is so much a part of identity for most and the likelihood is that they have experienced or administered spanking as punishment. Spanking versus discussions or "timeouts" is a heated debate when it ensues. Be prepared to discuss the difference between (a) isolated behavior and statements within a family, and (b) behaviors and statements that characterize a family thematically.

INSTRUCTIONAL GOALS AND TIPS

Bring a genealogical diagram such as a family tree to illustrate this topic. Include a family crest, motto, and song. Then ask students to diagram their own families. How do the students' diagrams compare to your sample?

Today's families are often defined by interpersonal relationships and commitment rather than traditional roles. (Timothy Shonnard/Tony Stone Images)

The family is a social group characterized by common residence, economic cooperation, and reproduction. It includes adults of both sexes, at least two of whom maintain a socially approved sexual relationship, and one or more children, of one's own or adopted, of the sexually cohabitating adults.[1]

More recently, sociologists Nass and McDonald defined a family as

a social group having specified roles and statuses (e.g., husband, wife, father, mother, son, daughter) with ties of blood, marriage, or adoption who usually share a common residence and cooperate economically.[2]

Other definitions of a family deemphasize the traditional role of mother, father, and children, placing more emphasis upon interpersonal relationships and personal commitment. In 1982, the New York Supreme Court ruled that it is legal for a man to adopt his older homosexual lover as a son. The Court stated,

The best description of a family is a continuing relationship of love and care, and an assumption of responsibility for some other person. Certainly, that is present. . . ."[3]

In a survey conducted a few years later, more than 30 percent of unmarried couples believed that homosexual couples should have the same legal rights as do married couples. Art Bochner's definition of a family echoes this relational emphasis. For him, the family is

an organized, naturally occurring relational interaction system, usually occupying a common living space over an extended time period, and possessing a confluence of interpersonal images which evolve through the exchange of messages over time.[4]

11 RELATING TO FAMILY, FRIENDS, AND COLLEAGUES

DISCUSSION AND WRITING
Ask students whether children are the distinguishing feature between a family and other types of communal living. Do the characters on the situation comedy "Seinfeld" constitute a family, for instance? Ask students to count the number of families to which they belong.

For our purposes in this chapter, we synthesize these perspectives to define the **family** as a self-defined unit made up of any number of persons who live in relationship with one another over time in a common living space, and who are usually, but not always, united by marriage and kinship.

Family Types

Virginia Satir, a well-known expert in family therapy, has identified four types of families: natural, blended, single-parent, and extended.[5] The traditional family—a mother and father and their biological children—is often considered to be the **natural family**, or nuclear family. But because changes in culture, values, economics, and other factors have rendered this family type no longer typical, the traditional family is sometimes called an idealized natural family.

An increasingly common family type today is the **blended family**. This family type consists of two adults and their children. But because of divorce, separation, death, or adoption, the children may be the product of other biological parents or of just one of the adults who is raising them.

The **single-parent family** is self-explanatory. This type of family has one parent and at least one child. Divorce, unmarried parents, separation, desertion, and death make single-parent families the fastest growing type of family unit in the United States today.

The **extended family** typically refers to the relatives—aunts, uncles, cousins, or grandparents—who are part of the family unit. Some extended families also include individuals who are not related by marriage or kinship but are treated like family or share a common identity with the family. These surrogate family members may even be called Mom, Dad, Aunt, or Uncle, honoring them as part of the family circle.

In addition to Satir's categories, there is at least one other that can encompass any of her definitions. The family in which you were raised—no matter

Table 11-1

Sources of Family Difficulties

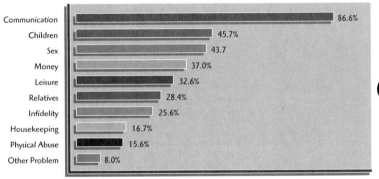

Percentage of all cases with a marital problem

Communication	86.6%
Children	45.7%
Sex	43.7
Money	37.0%
Leisure	32.6%
Relatives	28.4%
Infidelity	25.6%
Housekeeping	16.7%
Physical Abuse	15.6%
Other Problem	8.0%

what type it is—is your **family of origin**. It is in your family of origin that you learned the rules and skills of interpersonal communication and developed your basic assumptions about relationships. You may have had more than one family of origin if you come from a blended family; due to divorce, separation, or death of a parent, you may have been reared in more than one intact family of origin.

Families come in all sizes, types, and forms. A gay or lesbian couple may decide to live together and form a family and raise a child or children. At the heart of our definition of a family is the concept that it includes people who live in relationship with one another. A family is a family if it thinks it's a family.

A Model for Family Interaction

Regardless of the type of family you have, communication plays a major role in determining the quality of family life. As shown in Table 11.1, one research team found that over 86 percent of the families who reported family difficulty and stress said that communication was the key source of the problem.[6] Virginia Satir thinks good family communication is so important that she calls it "the largest single factor determining the kinds of relationships [we make] with others."[7] Howard Markman found that the more positively premarital couples rated their communication with their partner, the more satisfied they were with their marriage relationships more than five and one-half years later.[8]

More than a century ago, the Russian author Leo Tolstoy observed, "All happy families are alike. Each unhappy family is unhappy in its own way." More recently, a pair of family therapists observed, "Unhappy people came from families where there were a lot of other unhappy people."[9] As they attempted to identify causes for the problems in dysfunctional families, the therapists discovered that usually the major source of a family problem ". . . was not buried in the deep complexes and superegos and egos of the individuals, but was evident in plain daylight to the therapists. It lay in the family system: in the way the family was organized; in the way its members communicated; in the way they worked out their daily interactions."[10]

Another team of researchers have developed a model called the **circumplex model of family interaction** to explain the dynamics of both effective function and dysfunction within family systems.[11] The model's three basic dimensions, as indicated in Figure 11.1, are adaptability, cohesion, and communication. **Adaptability**, shown on the model ranging from chaotic to rigid, refers to the family's ability to modify and respond to changes in its own power structure and roles. For some families, tradition, stability, and historical perspective are important to their sense of comfort and well-being. Other families that are less tradition-bound are better able to adapt to new circumstances.

Cohesion refers to the emotional bonding and feelings of togetherness that families experience. Family cohesion ranges from excessively tight, or enmeshed, to disengaged. Because family systems are dynamic, families usually move up and down the range from disengaged to enmeshed. The originator of the circumplex model selected the three poems that follow to characterize families who are disengaged, enmeshed, and balanced, respectively.

DISCUSSION AND WRITING
Working in groups of 3–5, ask students to brainstorm as many TV families as possible for each of the family types. For instance, the natural family type would include the Huxtables ("The Bill Cosby Show") and the Ricardos ("I Love Lucy"); the single-parent family type would include the Partridges ("The Partridge Family") and the Corbetts ("The Courtship of Eddie's Father").

ACTIVITY
See Activity 11.1 in the Instructor's Guide.

MEDIA AND OUTSIDE RESOURCES
Ask students to hypothesize factors children under 12 years old are most inclined to cite as sources for marital problems. Invite a family therapist to share his or her perspectives on this topic.

MEDIA AND OUTSIDE RESOURCES
Investigate workshops and courses in your area for couples who are considering marriage. Share these resources with your class. Consider inviting a premarital counselor to describe the content and process of engaged couples workshops.

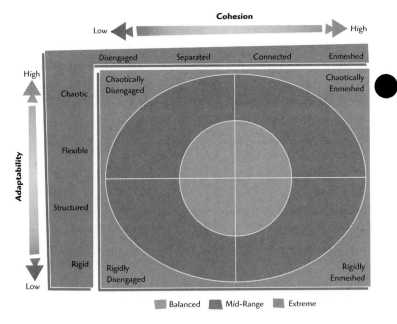

Figure 11-1

A Circumplex Model of
Family Systems
Adapted from: David Olson
and Hamilton I. McCubbin,
*Families: What Makes Them
Work* (Newbury Park: Sage
Publications, Inc., 1983).

Disengaged:

I do my thing, and you do your thing
I am not in this world to live up to your expectations
And you are not in this world to live up to mine
You are you and I am I
And if by chance we meet, it's beautiful
If not, it can't be helped.

—FRITZ PERLS

Enmeshed:

We do our thing together
I am here to meet all your needs and expectations
And you are here to meet mine
We had to meet, and it was beautiful
I can't imagine it turning out any other way.

—JERRY GILLIES

Balanced:

> Sing and dance together and be joyous,
>   but let each one of you be alone
> Even as the strings of a lute are alone
>   though they quiver with the same music
> And stand together yet not too near together;
> For the pillars of the temple stand apart,
> And the oak tree and the cypress grow
> not in each other's shadow
> But let there be spaces in your togetherness
> And let the winds of the heavens dance between you.
>
> —KAHLIL GIBRAN, *THE PROPHET*

The third key element in the model—and the most critical one—is communication. It is not labeled in the model because *everything* in the model is influenced by communication. It is through **communication** that families are able to adapt to change and maintain either enmeshed or disengaged relationships. Communication is what determines whether families are cohesive or adaptable. Communication keeps the family operating as a system.

The circumplex model helps us understand relationships among family cohesiveness, adaptability, and communication at different stages of family development. In general, families with balanced levels of cohesion and adaptability function better across the entire family life cycle than do those at the extremes of these dimensions. A balanced family has a moderate amount of cohesion and adaptability—represented by the center circle on the model. Balanced families are often better able to adapt to changing circumstances and to manage stressful periods, such as the children's adolescence. Not surprisingly, these balanced families usually have better communication skills.

As we have already emphasized, however, research suggests that *there is no single best way to be a family*. At some stages of family life, the balanced ideal of the circumplex model may not apply. Older couples, for example, seem to operate more effectively when there is more rigid structure and a lower level of cohesiveness. Families with younger children seem to function well with high levels of both cohesion and adaptability. Only one thing is constant as we go through family life: Effective communication skills play an important role in helping families change their levels of cohesiveness or adaptability. These skills include active listening, problem solving, empathy, and supportiveness. Dysfunctional families—those that are unable to adapt or alter their levels of cohesion—invariably display poor communication skills. Family members blame others for problems, criticize one another, and listen poorly.

Improving Family Communication

Wouldn't it be fantastic if you could share special secrets guaranteed to enrich your family life? But, alas, there are no surefire prescriptions for

DISCUSSION AND WRITING
Ask students to construct mobiles whose elements represent members of their immediate families. Invite students to hang these and then describe their family dynamics within small groups.

MEDIA AND OUTSIDE RESOURCES
Show the film *Ordinary People*. Ask students to discuss the effects of Buck's death upon the whole family. How does each member react and how do these responses affect the other family members?

DISCUSSION AND WRITING
Working in groups of three, ask students to define the "perfect family." Compare definitions.

ACTIVITY
See Activity 11.2 in the Instructor's Guide.

MEDIA AND OUTSIDE RESOURCES
Ask students to explore family support groups in the community. For instance, what parenting skills classes are available for new parents? What support is available for parents of teenagers? Ask students to focus on communication training and development resources.

DISCUSSION AND WRITING
Ask students to work in pairs to define and rank their top-ten family values. Ask them to compare these lists with those of other pairs in class. What are the common elements?

transforming your family system into one that a TV sitcom family would envy. Instead, we can pass on some skills and principles that researchers have either observed in healthy families or applied successfully to improve dysfunctional ones.

Virginia Satir found that in healthy families, "the members' sense of self-worth is high; communication is direct, clear, specific, and honest; rules are flexible, humane, and subject to change; and the family's links to society are open and hopeful."[12] In such families, she notes, people listen actively; they look *at* one another, not *through* one another or at the floor; they treat children as people; they touch one another affectionately regardless of age; and they openly discuss disappointments, fears, hurts, angers, and criticism, as well as joys and achievements.[13]

A study by Judy Pearson entitled *Lasting Love: What Keeps Couples Together* also sought to identify what explains marital satisfaction and stability.[14] Pearson interviewed several couples who had been together from forty to seventy years. She reports the following eight factors as hallmarks of happily married couples: (1) lowered expectations (realistic understanding of what being married means); (2) unconditional acceptance of each other; (3) seeing others in a positive way (what Pearson calls positive distortion); (4) viewing themselves as a united team (becoming one); (5) remaining separate, unique individuals (remaining two); (6) mutually satisfying sexual relations; (7) the skills to manage conflict; and (8) persistence.

These studies are descriptive rather than prescriptive. They report what satisfied married couples *do*, rather than recommend specific actions or suggestions. Perhaps you have noticed, however, that several communication-related behaviors keep cropping up in these reports. Let's explore their usefulness as skills.

Take Time to Talk about Relationships and Feelings

Healthy families talk.[15] The sheer quantity of communication depends upon family members' needs, expectations, careers, and activities. But the talking extends beyond idle chatter to focus on issues that help the family adapt to change and maintain a sense of cohesiveness.

Often, because of the crush of everyday responsibilities and tasks, family members may lapse into talking only about the task-oriented, mundane aspects of making life work: yard mowing, grocery shopping, errand running, and other uninspiring topics. Healthy families communicate about much more: their relationships; how they are feeling; how others are feeling. They make time to converse, no matter how busy they are. They have an other-orientation in these conversations, instead of focusing on themselves. In addition, they enjoy one another and don't take themselves too seriously.[16]

Navaran found that couples who are more satisfied with their marriages take time to talk.[17] In satisfied marriages, couples are more likely to:

1. Talk over pleasant things that happened during the day.

2. Feel they are understood by their spouse.

3. Discuss shared interests.

4. Avoid pouting and breaking off communication.

5. Talk with each other about personal problems.

6. Use words that have a private meaning for them.

7. Talk most important things over together.

8. Be sensitive to each other's feelings and make adjustments to take these into account when they speak.

CONSIDERING OTHERS

"Good" Apology Can Mend a Marriage

The skills of being able to make a genuine, solid apology—and being able to gracefully accept one—go a long way toward achieving a successful relationship.

"A bad apology will erode intimacy. A good apology will help restore intimacy, perhaps even deepen it," says Howard Markman, a marital researcher who is professor of psychology at the University of Denver. He is also an author of *Fighting for Your Marriage* (Jossey–Bass).

"OK, I'm sorry. Can you please just drop it now?" is a bad apology. Also, "I'm sorry I did

that, but I wouldn't have if you hadn't . . . "

"A bad apology is one that's not wanting to deal with whatever the source of the problem is," Markman says, "and it usually rests with the person trying to do the apologizing."

John Gottman, professor of psychology at the University of Washington in Seattle, has long studied what makes marriages successful. "Being able to accept influence" from one's partner is significant, Gottman says, and being able to apologize is part of this.

Men in violent marriages won't accept any suggestions from their wives that something be done differently—it's as if they're

in a batting cage, hitting back ball after ball, Gottman says. But in marriages that work, husbands accept suggestions all the time.

"In long-term happy marriages, that's a lot of what people are doing, being very respectful in the way they try to influence one another," Gottman says.

"Somebody who could really say, 'I was wrong,' or at an even higher level, 'I'm really sorry I hurt you. It hurts me that I hurt you. I don't want to hurt you,' and to really mean it—that's a very powerful interaction," says Gottman, who is author of *Why Marriages Succeed or Fail*.

Mary Jo Kochakian, *The Hartford Courant* (April 7, 1996).

Ask students to discuss some common clichés such as, "The family that prays together, stays together."

RESEARCH AND LITERATURE
On average, dual-career couples spend over an hour each day watching television and 12–21 minutes each day talking with their children. Discuss with students how much time they believe parents should spend talking with their children each day.

MEDIA AND OUTSIDE RESOURCES
Show an opening clip from the television show "The Courtship of Eddie's Father." Can a parent and a child be best friends? Invite students to debate this question.

MEDIA AND OUTSIDE RESOURCES

An excellent book for further reading is *How to Talk So Children Listen; Listen So Children Talk*, written by Adele Faber and Elaine Mazlish (Avon, 1980). The focus is on helping children deal with their feelings and working cooperatively. Another book by these authors, *Liberated Parents/ Liberated Children* (Avon, 1975), is also helpful.

ACTIVITY

See Activity 11.3 in the Instructor's Guide.

9. Discuss intimate issues without restraint or embarrassment.

10. Tell what type of day their spouse had without asking.

11. Intentionally communicate nonverbally to a greater degree; they express affection nonverbally in meaningful ways.

■ LISTEN ACTIVELY AND CLARIFY THE MEANING OF MESSAGES

Since talking about relationships is important in healthy families, it is not surprising that effective listening is also important. In the often stressful context of family life, good listening skills are essential.

Good listening requires an other-orientation. In Chapter 5, we presented fundamental skills for listening and responding to messages. Family members will communicate with greater accuracy if they learn to stop, look, and listen. Stop mental and outside distractions: Don't try to carry on a conversation over a TV blaring, a video game bleeping, or a stereo's distracting rhythmic pulse. Look: Constantly monitor the rich meaning in nonverbal messages; remember that the face and voice are prime sources for revealing emotional meaning; body posture and gestures provide clues about the intensity of an emotion. Listen: Focus on both details and major ideas. Asking appropriate follow-up questions and reflecting content and feelings are other vital skills for clarifying the mean-

---

RECAP	**Listen Actively to Family Members**
STOP:	Concentrate on your family members' messages rather than on personal evaluations. Minimize outside distractions. Seek a quiet place to talk.
LOOK:	Monitor your family member's face and voice for clues about the emotion he or she is expressing. Look at his or her posture and gestures to gauge the intensity of the emotion. Use eye contact to signal that the communication channel is open.
LISTEN:	Listen for both details and major ideas. Mentally summarize key ideas. Don't interrupt. Just listen.
ASK QUESTIONS:	Ask appropriate questions to seek more information. Ask questions to clarify what you don't understand.
REFLECT CONTENT:	Paraphrase the essential meaning of your family member's message. Use your own words with a lead-in such as, "What I hear you saying is . . ." or "You seem to be saying . . ." Don't overuse the skill of paraphrasing.
REFLECT FEELINGS:	Selectively summarize how you think your family member is feeling. Don't over-reflect feelings; reflect when you are genuinely uncertain about what someone feels or means.
CHECK PERCEPTIONS:	Ask the meaning of a specific nonverbal expression or behavior.

ing of messages. And remember the importance of checking your perceptions of the meaning of nonverbal messages.

Good listeners try to understand the feelings behind another person's words—to read between the lines. One pair of researchers suggests that you should try to interpret messages according to the sender's code system, not your own. Because you are in intimate daily contact with other family members, you have every reason and opportunity to learn their code systems. Then you can avoid becoming involved in diversionary arguments about the proper meaning of a word, phrase, or gesture.[18] Of course, after you attempt to understand your partner's meaning, you then need to relate the message to your own system of meaning.

Support and Encourage One Another

A smoothly functioning family can be a supportive, encouraging sanctuary from everyday stresses. Through communication, we can let others know that we support and value them. Satir suggests that many, if not most, sources of dysfunction in families are related to feelings of low self-worth.[19] Healthy families take time to nurture one another, express positive feelings, and take a genuine interest in each person's unique contributions to the family. It is important to learn the guidelines we discussed in Chapters 6 and 7 concerning the types of messages—verbal and nonverbal—that help establish positive, supportive relationships and an open climate for conversation.[20] It is also important to remember, however, to be selective in providing feedback and disclosing your feelings and attitudes about other family members.[21] As we saw in Chapter 9, although trust is important in developing support, total honesty and candidness, however well intended, will not necessarily strengthen your relationships. After a point, too much disclosure can lower satisfaction.[22]

Parents have a special obligation to disclose responsibly to their children. Too much negative and controlling feedback can cause permanent damage.[23] On the one hand, researchers have found that supportive messages—those that offer praise, approval, help, and affection—can lead to higher self-esteem in children, more conformity to the wishes of the parent, higher moral standards, and less aggressive and antisocial behavior.[24]

Parents frequently deliver control messages to get children to do what the parents want. Often these messages involve coercion or threats. One research team found control messages are effective in shaping a child's behavior up to a point; an overemphasis on control often results in rebellion.[25] The challenge is for parents to strike a balance between genuine support and appropriate control. Kahlil

Wise parents use support and encouragement rather than coercion as a primary strategy for shaping their children's behavior. The challenge is to find a middle ground that tempers support with appropriate control. (John Lei, Jr./ Stock Boston)

Gibran's timeless advice to parents below suggests that children need a balance of control and support as they seek their independence from parents.

Jane Howard, who traveled extensively in search of a "good family," found that "good" families have a sense of valuing and supporting each other.[26] In addition:

1. They have a chief, heroine, or founder—someone around whom others cluster.

2. They have a switchboard operator—someone who keeps track of who is doing what.

3. They maintain strong bonds within the family, but have other group associations as well.

4. They are hospitable.

5. They deal directly with stress and tragedy.

6. They cherish family rituals and traditions.

7. They express affection in a way that is meaningful to other family members.

8. They have a sense of place.

9. They find some way to connect with future generations.

10. They honor their elders.

On Parenting

Your children are not your children.
They are the sons and daughters of Life's longing for itself.
They come through you but not from you,
And though they are with you, yet they belong not to you.
You may give them your love but not your thoughts,
For they have their own thoughts.
You may house their bodies but not their souls,
For their souls dwell in the house of tomorrow,
    which you cannot visit, not even in your dreams.
You may strive to be like them, but seek not to make them like you,
For life goes not backward nor tarries with yesterday.
You are the bows from which your children as living arrows are sent forth.
The archer sees the mark upon the path of the infinite,
    and He bends you with His might that
    His arrows might go swift and far.
Let your bending in the archer's hand be for gladness;
For even as He loves the arrow that flies,
    so He loves also the bow that is stable.

—KAHLIL GIBRAN, *THE PROPHET*

All too often parents resort to violence when their children balk at their orders. The "Family Violence Almanac" below includes statistics and research conclusions about the increase in child abuse and violence in today's families. Actor Tom Cruise has self-disclosed how his father physically abused him as a child. "As a kid," says Tom, "I had a lot of hidden anger about that. I'd get hit, and I didn't understand it." When his father was dying of cancer, Cruise said, he was finally able to address the issue directly with his dad.

Learning to manage conflict with siblings is also a challenge in many families. It is with our siblings that we first learn how to manage the complexities of relationships and especially how to manage conflict. One study reported that more than half of all adolescent conflicts are between siblings.[27] The most typical method of managing sibling conflict is withdrawal. However, there is evidence that some siblings resort to violence when they run out of things to say. One survey found that 62 percent of senior high students said they had hit a brother or sister within the past year.[28] Sibling conflicts, as well as other family conflicts, often have a special intensity. Maybe that is because we drop our guard in the privacy and security of a family; we know our family members will love us no matter what, so we may express our feelings with an intensity that would be inappropriate in other social settings. Another reason conflict flares up is that we often communicate with family members when we are tired and stressed, so emotions are less controlled.

Family Violence Almanac[29]

When words are not enough to communicate anger and frustration, physical violence often takes their place in today's families. Consider the following statistics and research conclusions about family violence.

From Surveys of Research on Family Violence:

Percentage of families in which one spouse assaulted the other: 16

Percentage of children who were physically abused by a parent: 11

Percentage of children who have hit a parent: 20

Percentage of parents between the ages of 18–30 who have at least one child and use some form of physical aggression to discipline their children: 70

Percentage of husbands and wives who use physical means to resolve a conflict: 30

From a Study on the Effects of Family Violence:

Question: Do parents who use physical violence increase or decrease aggressive behavior in their children?

Answer: They increase it.

---

11 RELATING TO FAMILY, FRIENDS, AND COLLEAGUES

MEDIA AND OUTSIDE RESOURCES
Invite a family therapist or marriage counselor to come to class and speak about communication and domestic violence. Find out how professionals encourage families to manage conflict, stress, and change.

As we saw in Chapter 8, all close relationships undergo periods of conflict and stress, so families should be prepared to handle them. Satisfied couples report just as many conflicts as dissatisfied couples. The difference is that satisfied couples have learned skills and strategies for managing interpersonal differences. D. A. Infante and his colleagues found that couples who lack constructive argumentation skills are those who resort to verbal aggression (attacking their partner's self-worth to inflict psychological pain)[30] and even physical violence.[31]

John Gottman, who studied couples' relationships for over twenty years, suggests that we be on the alert for four key warning signs in our communication behavior.[32]

■ WARNING SIGNS

1. Criticism: Attacking someone's personality or character rather than specific behavior, usually with blame and personal comments.

2. Contempt: Intending to insult and psychologically abuse your partner; contempt may be verbal or nonverbal.

3. Defensiveness: Denying responsibility, making excuses, whining, repeating yourself, saying "yes, but."

4. Stonewalling: Withdrawing, not responding; becoming minimally engaged in the relationship.

Most couples experience some of these behaviors during their relationship, but the single best predictor of divorce is stonewalling. If all four warning signs are consistently present, there is a 94 percent chance the couple will eventually divorce.

Based on his extensive observations, Gottman offers the following suggestions for managing couples' conflicts. Many of them apply to parent-child and sibling conflicts as well:[33]

1. Pick your battles carefully.

2. Schedule discussions.

3. Structure your conflicts: build the agenda, persuade and argue, resolve.

4. Acknowledge your partner's viewpoint before expressing your own.

5. Moderate your emotions.

6. Trust your partner and communicate nondefensively.

7. Soothe your partner; learn how to comfort and provide positive reinforcement.

8. Take stock in your partnership.

9. Find the glory in your story as a couple and enhance romance.

10. Know when to get help or when to give up.

No list of do's and don'ts will miraculously manage all differences in a family relationship. The suggestions offered here provide only a starting point. As we have emphasized, you will need to adapt these skills and suggestions to the context of your unique family system. But research consistently shows that listening skills and empathy are strong predictors of family satisfaction.

RECAP   **How to Improve Family Relationships**

Take time to talk about relationships and feelings.

- Be other-oriented in your focus.
- Don't take yourself too seriously.

Listen and clarify the meaning of messages.

- Learn and interpret messages according to the sender's code system.

- Check your interpretation of messages.

Support and encourage one another.

- Use confirming messages.
- Be selective in disclosing your feelings.

Use productive strategies for managing conflict, stress, and change.

- Watch for communication warning signs.
- Learn to renegotiate role conflicts.

Relating to Friends and Lovers

In the scene that opens this chapter, Maria made notes not only about doing things for her family, but also about tasks she was going to do for her friends. Like Maria, many of us routinely offer help to our friends. Our friendships are one of our most valuable sources of support. In a survey of more than 100,000 men and women, single women rated friends and social life as the most important source of happiness in their lives. Single men rated friends second only to their job duties.[34] The importance of friendship is as old as the human race. More than two thousand years ago Aristotle defined the nature of friendship in his classic work, the *Nicomachean Ethics*. The motives for friendship, he wrote, are usefulness, pleasure, and a commitment to common goodness; these motives still drive us to develop friendships today.

The Nature of Friendship

A friend is someone we like and who likes us. We trust our friends. We share good and bad times with them. We want to be with them and we make time for that purpose. Or, as one armchair philosopher observed, a real friend is one who will continue to talk to you over the back fence even though he knows he's missing his favorite television program.

We expect this kind of self-sacrifice from our friends. Here are some other ideals that we hold out for friendship:

A friend will see you through after others see you are through.

A friend is one who'll tell you what you should be told even if it momentarily offends you.

A friend thinks of you when all others are thinking of themselves.

A friend is one who sticks by you even when he or she gets to know you well.

A friend is one who, when you've made a fool of yourself, doesn't feel that you've done a permanent job.

Although not every friendship we form lives up to these ideals, by nature, a friend is someone whom we choose to be with, not someone we associate with because we have to. Friendship is a relationship that exists over time between people who share a common history.[35] It is a relationship of choice, as we

A friend is someone we like and who likes us. (John Lei/Stock Boston)

defined the term in Chapter 9. Or, as one researcher suggests, "Chance makes our parents, but choice makes our friends." Friendship develops naturally into an interdependent relationship that is different from other interpersonal relationships. In friendship, we have no external constraints that keep us together, such as a job, school, or family, even though we often make friends with people in these relationships. Usually we form friendships with our equals, whereas we often form other types of relationships with people of different ages or social backgrounds.[36]

Reasons for Friendship

One of the most important functions that friends perform is to help us manage the mundane. Most friendships are not based upon unusual activities. On the contrary, most of us seek out friends just to talk, have a meal, or be entertained together. In a survey of more than 40,000 respondents, *Psychology Today* reported that the following were most often mentioned as activities to do with friends:[37]

1. Have an intimate talk

2. Have a friend ask you to do something for him or her

3. Go out to dinner in a restaurant

4. Ask your friend to do something for you

5. Have a meal together at home or at your friend's home

6. Go to a movie, play, or concert

7. Go drinking together

8. Shop together

9. Participate in sports

10. Watch a sporting event

Besides helping us enjoy a healthy life, friends help us cope with stress, take care of physical needs, and even help in the development of our personality. Friends also help shape our attitudes and beliefs. Especially during periods of change and crisis in our lives, such as adolescence and retirement, friends help us cope with uncertainty and have a profound influence on our behavior.[38]

11 RELATING TO FAMILY, FRIENDS, AND COLLEAGUES

381

ACTIVITY
See Activity 11.4 in the Instructor's Guide.

MEDIA AND OUTSIDE RESOURCES
Bring in copies of advertisements from popular magazines. Have students identify which social needs the product or service promises to fulfill. Ask students to identify how realistic these indirect promises are. Discuss the need for critical thinking when reading advertisements.

How many friends do we need? Typically, people have up to five close friends, fifteen other friends, twenty or more members in a social network (which could include family members), and many more people who are simply acquaintances.[39] In all of our social interactions, we are happiest when we are in the company of our friends. Perhaps Cicero said it best: A friend multiplies our joys and divides our sorrows.

Friends also perform other functions, such as bolstering our self-esteem. Most of us need people who provide encouragement and tell us that we are decent and likable. It is confirming to have a friend become indignant for us when we have experienced an injustice. Friends can help keep a stream of positive acceptance flowing to counteract the numerous nicks and bruises that our self-worth suffers in the course of daily living.

Friends also provide material help when we need it. When you are away on vacation, you might ask a friend to feed your cat and water your plants. If you run out of gas, you might call a friend to bring you some or pick you up.

As a relationship becomes more intimate, we expect our friends to be more aware of, and active in, meeting our personal needs. But there are still differences between our relationships with even intimate friends and those with lovers.[40] One pair of researchers suggests that love differs from friendship "in the identity of interest that the partners share. Love exists to the extent that the outcomes enjoyed or suffered by each are enjoyed or suffered by both."[41]

Another key difference between friends and lovers lies in how they talk about their relationship. Friends are less likely to talk about what attracted them to each other than are lovers. Friends are also less likely to celebrate anniversaries and mark the passage of time in formal ways, such as a card or a special dinner. Love involves an increase in a sense of "we-ness," of passionate solidarity and identification with the other.

Zick Rubin attempted to identify differences between love and friendship by developing two scales—one to measure love and the other to measure liking.[42] He found that people made distinctions between love and liking based upon these scales. Love relationships are more passionate and intimate than friendships, but interestingly, people like their lovers only slightly more than they like their friends. And women make greater distinctions between loving and liking than do men.

Two other researchers analyzed survey results of several hundred college students and identified three primary factors that determine the kind of love relationship we share with another person: intimacy, commitment, and passion.[43] Intimacy includes such attributes as trust, caring, honesty, supportiveness, understanding, and openness. As we have seen, it is a factor in all kinds of friendships. The second factor, commitment, includes loyalty, devotion, putting the other first, and needing one another. Commitment, too, characterizes all kinds of friendships. Passion, however, is unique to romantic relationships. It includes excitement, sexual passion, and butterflies in the stomach.

The closest relationship you develop with another human being will probably be a romantic one. When one research team asked a group of students, "With whom do you share your closest relationship?" 47 percent said it was with a romantic partner.[44] Thirty-six percent said they were closest to their friends, 14 percent said they were closest to a family member, and 3 percent reported "other."

Love, of course, means different things to different people. Many studies use the following six categories to classify types of love: eros, ludis, storge, mania, pragma, and agape.[45]

Eros is sexual love based upon the pursuit of beauty and pleasure. The physical need for sex brings many couples together. Erotic lovers crave sexual intimacy and passionately seek sexual activity to satisfy their need. Sexual attraction brings special needs and emotions to a relationship, sometimes obscuring other concerns. Shakespeare described this phenomenon when he wrote, "But love is blind, and lovers cannot see the folly that themselves commit."

Ludis describes love as a game, something to pursue to pass the time. Ludic lovers are not seeking long-term relationships; rather, they seek immediate gratification and to win their partner's affection. Their goal is to be in love and to enjoy their partner rather than to achieve a sexual victory.

Early dating relationships are often of the ludic type. Going on a date to a junior high dance is a casual pleasure, not a prelude to a lifelong commitment. Ludis lasts as long as the couple has fun and finds the relationship mutually satisfying.

Storge is the sort of love we find in most friendships and in relationships with siblings and other family members. Sexual consummation is not a factor in this sort of love, although sexual attraction may be present. A storgic relationship usually develops over a long period of time, and it is solid and more resistant to change than erotic love. Trust, caring, and compassion are high. Selfishness is low.

Mania describes a relationship that swings wildly between extreme highs and lows. A manic lover is one who is obsessed over the relationship with the other person. Each of the lovers may have an insatiable need for attention, often fueled by a low self-concept.

Pragma is the root word for *practical*. This kind of relationship works because the partners' personal requirements, personalities, backgrounds, likes, and dislikes are compatible. In some cultures, parents prearrange marriages because of pragmatic concerns, and if the children are lucky, passion develops later on, as the relationship takes its course.

Agape love is based upon a spiritual ideal of love. It involves giving of yourself and expecting nothing in return. The famous passage in 1 Corinthians 13 describes this love:

> Love is patient, love is kind. It does not envy, it does not boast, it is not proud. It is not rude, it is not self-seeking. It is not easily angered, it keeps no record of wrongs. Love does not delight in evil but rejoices with the truth. It always protects, always trusts, always hopes, always perseveres. Love never fails.[46]

This kind of "pure" love may characterize the relationship between a parent and a child, or the relationship between a spiritual leader and his or her followers.

11 RELATING TO FAMILY, FRIENDS, AND COLLEAGUES

DISCUSSION AND WRITING
Ask students to discuss this definition of love.

MEDIA AND OUTSIDE RESOURCES
Ask students to bring to class song lyrics which represent different types of love.

DISCUSSION AND WRITING
Working in groups of 5–7 people, ask students to brainstorm movie relationships which depict various types of love. Give a prize to the group that lists the most agapic love relationships.

Most relationships do encompass more than one kind of love. And relationships evolve. One based upon storgic love may evolve into an erotic relationship, for example. Several studies have found that men and women have different styles of loving. Men gravitate toward ludic and erotic relationships, whereas women are more likely to be manic, storgic, or pragmatic. Clyde and Susan Hendrick found that most people consider eros, agape, and storge the most important kind of love for them.[47] Manic and pragmatic were next in importance, and ludic love was the least important. The Hendricks also report that:

> Men fell in love more easily than women (eros), who were more cautious about entering relationships (pragma). Once involved in a love relationship, men were less likely than women to break it off, and it was easier for women to remain friends after the breakup (storge).[48]

Passion and love are such highly individual phenomena that we will not presume to teach you a set of skills to cultivate them. We do, however, urge you to keep in mind the skills and principles that we have emphasized throughout the book for initiating and maintaining healthy interpersonal relationships. Become other-oriented by stopping, looking, and listening to your partner. Consider his or her feelings, and try to decenter and empathize. Understand how we develop relationships through conversation. Also be mindful of the typical patterns that most meaningful relationships follow. In general, the ability to develop loving relationships with others requires sensitivity to their unique needs and personalities.

RECAP

Types of Love

EROS	Sexual, erotic love based upon the pursuit of beauty and pleasure.
LUDIS	Playful, game-playing love based upon immediate gratification and enjoyment.
STORGE	Solid love of friendship based upon trust and caring.
MANIA	Obsessive love driven by the mutual needs of both partners.
PRAGMA	Practical love based upon mutual benefits for both partners.
AGAPE	Selfless love based upon giving of oneself for others.

ACTIVITY
See Activity 11.5 in the Instructor's Guide.

Friendships at Different Stages in Life

As we saw in Chapters 9, establishing intimacy with another person takes time, so most of us have a limited number of intimate relationships. We also have different needs for intimacy at various stages of our lives. W. J. Dickens and D. Perlman examined the differences among friendships at four stages in life: childhood, adolescence, adulthood, and old age.[49]

III INTERPERSONAL COMMUNICATION RELATIONSHIPS

■ CHILDHOOD FRIENDSHIPS

At about the age of two, when we start to talk, we begin parallel play with others. As toddlers we perceive our playmates as others who can help meet our needs. Our first friendships are usually superficial and self-centered. Childhood friendships can be categorized into five sometimes overlapping stages.[50] From ages three to seven, we have *momentary playmates*—we interact with those in our presence. From ages four to nine, we have *one-way assistance*. We still view friendships from a "take" perspective, as instruments to help meet our needs, rather than from a "give" or "give-and-take" perspective.

The third stage, ages six to twelve, is the *fair-weather friend* stage. There is more give and take in friendships, but the reciprocity occurs when things are going well; the relationship is likely to end if problems and conflicts develop. The fourth stage, ages nine to fifteen, is called *mutual intimacy*. With the closeness that develops, relationships become more possessive. The last stage (twelve through adulthood) allows for more *independence* in friendships, as well as deepening interdependence with friends that permits greater levels of intimacy and sharing.

■ ADOLESCENT FRIENDSHIPS

During adolescence, beginning with the onset of puberty around age twelve, we move away from relationships with parents and other adults and toward greater intimacy with our peers. During adolescence, peer relationships are the most important social influence on our behavior. We develop cliques of friends and form friendship networks. Boys are more likely to join gangs—which might be socially acceptable groups such as a sports or debate team, or less socially desirable groups bent on violence and destruction of property. Girls are more likely to develop intimate relationships with one or two good friends. Friendship relationships usually peak in late adolescence and early adulthood, before we select a mate.[51]

During adolescence boys seem to have more friends, whereas girls appear to develop closer, more intensive and intimate relationships. The patterns of making and keeping friends we learn as children continue to affect the formation of friendships during adolescence.

Here is how one researcher described the nature of teenage friendships:

There is order in the chaos and chaos in the order, of teenage friendships. We want to hang out with the gang, but we want to be close to somebody too. We want to be close to somebody, but we don't want to shut anybody out, either. We want to trust fully, but discover that people let you down—while at the same time we are ready to drop the friendship if our needs aren't being met.[52]

■ ADULT FRIENDSHIPS

Adult friendships are among our most valued relationships. Henry Van Dyke summarized the virtues of developing a trusting, intimate relationship with a friend when he wrote the following:

But, after all, the very best thing in good talk, and the thing that helps most, is friendship. How it dissolves the barriers that divide us, and loosens all

MEDIA AND OUTSIDE RESOURCES
To illustrate the value of friendship between children, consider showing the final third of the film *My Girl*.
INSTRUCTIONAL GOALS AND TIPS
Compare this pattern to the phases of relationship development discussed in Chapter 9.

constraint, and diffuses itself like some fine old cordial through all the veins of life—this feeling that we understand and trust each other, and wish each other heartily well. Everything into which it really comes is good.[53]

Despite the value we place on friendships during adulthood, those friendships may still dissolve, for at least four reasons.[54] First, they may cool because of physical separation. One person may move to a new community, or even if the person hasn't moved, he or she may no longer travel in the same social circles. Second, new friends may replace old. Changing jobs, joining a new club or religious organization, or having new neighbors move in next door, may diminish the amount of time you can spend with former friends. A third and obvious reason for ending a friendship is that you may simply dislike something your friend did. Perhaps he or she did not help you in a time of need, betrayed a confidence, or violated another friendship rule. And, finally, if and when we begin the process of selecting a mate for life, our friendship relationships may change.

Friendships can sometimes have an adverse effect upon a couple if one partner feels that the other's friends are competing for time and intimacy. If one partner's desire to go out alone with friends becomes more important than marriage and family, then conflict flares up.

■ THE ELDERLY AND FRIENDSHIPS

Although the elderly make new friends, they value old ones most. During retirement, when individuals have more time for socializing, friendships become increasingly important; but older adults form fewer new friendships. Instead, they tend to maintain a small, highly valued network of friends.

Howard Markman and his colleagues found that self-disclosure, one of the most important components of friendship, did not seem to change in either depth or amount from young adulthood through age ninety-one.[55] They did report, however, that as friends get older, there is more negative self-disclosure; we are more willing to tell our friends less positive things about ourselves rather than limiting our disclosures to information that makes us "look good."

Yet other research suggests that changes occur in marital relationships as couples get older. Self-disclosure declines, yet retired couples tend to have fewer marital problems than younger couples. Research also suggests that, in general, older individuals express negative attitudes less frequently than younger individuals during problem-solving discussions, except during discussions in which the issue is very important. If the conflict is about an important topic, the older individuals tend to have more heated, intense disagreements with others than do younger individuals.[56]

RECAP	Friendships at Different Life Stages
Childhood Friendships	Self-focused and often superficial.
Adolescent Friendships	Peers influence social behavior. Boys often associate with others in groups, whereas girls develop deep friendships with a smaller circle of friends.
Adult Friendships	Other relationships may change if selection of a life-long mate begins.
Elderly Friendships	Old friends are valued, and friendship networks often shrink.

Making Friends

In Chapters 9 and 10 we presented some suggestions for initiating and maintaining relationships, including friendships. Some of the ideas presented in the following sections are variations on those suggestions. As you read them, however, keep Dale Carnegie's simple advice in mind: "You can make more friends in two months by becoming interested in other people than you can in two years by trying to get other people interested in you."[57]

A "friendship opportunity" is a situation in which you are likely to meet other people who may become your friends. People who develop friendships with others are good at judging where and when to meet others and with which individuals they will be compatible. We can't tell you precisely where you will meet someone who is likely to become your friend. But knowing your own interests, likes, and dislikes is a first step in choosing places to look.[58] As implied by Robert Frost in his poem "The Pasture," friendship opportunities need not always be major, preplanned events; they could involve simply inviting others to share in everyday activities.

The Pasture

I'm going out to clean the pasture spring;
I'll only stop to rake the leaves away
(And wait to watch the water clear, I may):
I sha'n't be gone long.—You come too.
I'm going out to fetch the little calf
That's standing by the mother. It's so young,
It totters when she licks it with her tongue.
I sha'n't be gone long.—You come too.

—ROBERT FROST

From: *The Poetry of Robert Frost,* edited by Connery Lathem. Copyright © 1994 by Robert Frost, Copyright © 1916 ©1969 by Henry Holt and Co., Inc. Reprinted by permission of Henry Holt and Co., Inc.

ACTIVITY
See Activity 11.6 in the Instructor's Guide.

Doing Something About Loneliness: Reaching Out to Others

The first step in overcoming loneliness is to resist the passive attitude that you can easily lapse into if you are always alone. Loneliness is a temporary condition if you are willing to take constructive actions. In order to form satisfying friendships, it is necessary to be other-oriented, to reach out and cultivate the interest of other people instead of waiting for them to come to you.

What to Do

- Accept invitations when they are offered.
- Call on someone or invite someone to visit.
- Be responsive in conversation. Let people know that you are interested in what they say by smiling and nodding.
- Ask questions to keep the conversation flowing. Others will find it rewarding to talk to you.
- Ask questions that help people to present themselves in their best light.
- Be open to the interests of other people.
- Draw attention to interests you have in common.

What Not to Do

- Do not stay away from people to hide your loneliness.
- Do not make negative remarks about yourself.
- Do not harbor critical thoughts about the people you meet.
- Do not think that you have to be exceptionally clever or attractive to be liked.

Adapted from: Peter Marsh, *Eye to Eye: How People Interact* (Topsfield, MA: Salem House, 1988).

■ ENCOURAGE OTHERS TO BE YOUR FRIEND

To develop a friendship with another person, you must show him or her something that will encourage interaction. You need skills to assess his or her interests and background, and then to communicate your interest in them.

Your encouragement may be explicit or implicit. You may explicitly ask for a date or initiate a conversation. To do this, you need effective conversation skills. How do you start a conversation? Here are several approaches:

- Volunteer your name or information about yourself followed by a question about the other person ("Hello, I'm from Missouri. Where are you from?").

- Make a comment about the other person or ask him or her a question ("That's a beautiful tie. Where did you buy it?").

- Talk about where you are, the weather, something that you are both observing ("Do you think it will ever stop raining?"). There are no surefire, prerehearsed lines for initiating conversation. Effective conversation emerges from the situation and the people involved.

Once the conversation begins, you can try out these suggestions:

- Ask questions that are open-ended and keep the conversation rolling.

- Adapt to your listener; be other-oriented.

- Remember what you talk about. Focus on what both you and your conversation partner are discussing.

- Take turns initiating and responding so that you are sharing responsibility for the conversation.

- Don't only talk about yourself.

- Don't say or do something that will cause the other person to value him- or herself less. Being rude, interrupting, and not considering the feelings of others inhibits conversation.

- Reveal information about yourself so that the other person can get to know you. If you tell nothing about yourself, your partner may perceive you as aloof. Of course, if you reveal too much too quickly, you can also violate your listener's expectations and make him or her uncomfortable.

These suggestions are consistent with the standard "script" that we follow in our culture for initial conversations, as we noted in Chapter 9. Remember that if you deviate from this script, you may make your partner feel uneasy. The *Far Side* cartoon provides some examples of disconcerting deviations.

You can also communicate your desire to make friends and to be a friend to someone through appropriate nonverbal behavior.[59] As we discussed in Chapter 7, the following nonverbal cues communicate a friendly attitude:[60]

Classic conversation stoppers

Proximity:	Move closer and lean forward if you are seated.
Orientation:	Sit directly in front of or closely beside the person.
Gaze:	Look the person in the eyes, especially when he or she looks at you.
Facial expression:	Smile.
Gestures:	Nod your head; use lively movements.
Posture:	Keep an open posture, with your arms stretched toward the other person, rather than placing your arms on your hips or folding them.
Touch:	Touch the person in a friendly, nonsexual way.
Tone of voice:	Raise your pitch; speak with a rising inflection and clear, pure tone.

DISCUSSION AND WRITING

Ask students to form small groups and to develop a list of their top-ten ways to make friends. Compare these to the tips found in this chapter.

RESEARCH AND LITERATURE

The formal term for cliché communication is *phatic communication*.

SKILL DEVELOPMENT

Ask two students to role-play the following situation: Person A: It's the first meeting of class following spring break. You sit down next to a person whom you have been attracted to for some time but haven't approached until now. Person B: You are attracted to Person A and have attempted to use cliché communication in the past. Until now, your interest hasn't been reciprocated. You're surprised and pleased to be talking with this person. Demonstrate how to use conventional conversation to promote a friendship. Following the role-play, ask students to debrief on the nonverbal messages sent between the two students.

This course in interpersonal communication may be your first formal education in how interpersonal relationships develop. You learn about relationships through your experience as well as occasional tips from parents, friends, and teachers along the way.

The information we presented in Chapters 9 and 10 explained how relationships develop, are maintained, and sometimes deteriorate. Knowing these textbook principles is no substitute for human experience, but understanding such things as the typical pace of relationship development, why we are attracted to others, the function and purpose of self-disclosure, and some of the reasons relationships deteriorate can help make you a wiser friend.

What do friends talk about? A study by Argyle and Henderson reports five major areas of conversation:[61]

1. Social talk about events, jokes, and just enjoyment of one another's company;

2. Gossip about others;

3. Common interests;

4. Sharing information and solving problems;

5. Support and encouragement in times of stress.

What do you and your friends discuss? If you are focusing on one of these areas to the exclusion of others, you may want to assess where you are in the friendship. As we discussed in Chapter 8, the depth and breadth of your self-disclosure characterizes your level of intimacy with others.

Losing Friends

We have discussed how friendships are won, but it is equally useful to know how friendships are lost. Clues about how not to make friends and influence people can be found in the pioneering work of two British researchers, Michael Argyle and Monika Henderson. They studied people who described themselves as lonely and friendless. Their research suggests that these people had developed communication patterns that discouraged close personal relationships.

Just as there are behavioral rules for making and maintaining friends, there are behaviors which, if you pursue them, will almost certainly cost you a friendship. Listed in order of offensiveness, they are as follows:[62]

1. Acting jealous or being critical of your relationship;

2. Discussing with others what your friend said in confidence;

3. Not volunteering help in time of need;

4. Not trusting or confiding in your friend;

5. Criticizing your friend in public;

6. Not showing positive regard for your friend;

7. Not standing up for your friend in his or her absence;

8. Not being tolerant of your friend's other friends;

9. Not showing emotional support;

10. Nagging your friend.

In Chapters 9 and 10 we saw how relationships intensify and sometimes become less intense in predictable stages. Relationship dissolution is not an event but a process. Love relationships usually end more abruptly and with more emotional intensity than friendships. When one researcher asked individuals to identify why their friendships with a friend of the same sex ended, first on the list was physical separation.[63] Moving away from our friends apparently takes a toll on the intensity of the relationship. Second, subjects reported that new friends replace old friends as circumstances change. Third, people often just grow to dislike a characteristic of the friend's behavior or personality. And finally, interference from dating or a couple's relationship often contributes to the decay of a friendship. It should come as no surprise that casual friendships are more likely to end than are those with close or intimate friends. Close friendships are better able to withstand change, uncertainty, and separation.

Relating to Colleagues

Perhaps, like Maria at the beginning of this chapter, you make lists of what you need to do at work. Although some of our work-related problems result from such things as a broken copy machine or an uncooperative computer, most of the problems that keep us up nights involve issues or decisions about others. One researcher estimated that 98 percent of the problems that we worry about at work are "people problems."[64] Whether this statistic is accurate or not, it is clear that "people skills" are important.

Surveys of employers have sought to answer the question: what are the most important skills people need to be successful on the job? The results of these research efforts are dramatically consistent. The number one skill you need to perform your job well, according to the experts and practitioners, is an ability to communicate effectively with others.[65] You get your job through a face-to-face interview. You keep your job based upon your ability to do the work, which usually involves a large measure of interpersonal interaction. One study specifically asked employers to identify the most important factors in helping graduating college students obtain employment. The number one skill: speaking.[66] The number two skill: listening. The entire list of important factors is presented in Table 11.2 These survey results suggest that interpersonal communication skills are more highly valued, more cherished, in fact, than your grade point average, the specific degree you hold, or the school you attended.

The higher you go in an organization, the more your job involves communicating with others. Harvey Mintzberg observed chief executive officers for five

DISCUSSION AND WRITING
Encourage students to monitor the answers they receive from family and friends to the inquiry, "How was work today?" Were the responses focused on technical work issues, people concerns, or something else? Have students report their findings after a week.

weeks. He found that managers spend most of their time communicating with others. Here are the specific activities and corresponding percentages of time they devote to each:[67]

Attending scheduled meetings	59%
Handling mail and memos	22%
Attending unscheduled meetings	10%
Talking on the phone	6%
Visiting others	3%

In all, managers spend almost 80 percent of their day communicating orally with others.

Charles Redding, a pioneer in teaching and research about communication in organizations, recommends the following bare minimum competencies for anyone who manages others:[68]

1. Be an effective speaker and listener.

2. Possess the ability to be an empathic listener and effective reader.

3. Have an understanding of how corporate decisions are made.

4. Identify the communication roles of both superiors and subordinates.

ACTIVITY
See Activity 11.7 in the Instructor's Guide.

TEACHING STRATEGY
Students often show special interest in the information on effectively interviewing for a job. Have students plan role-play interview questions—in advance— and come to class dressed for success. Videotaping their role-plays and allowing them viewing access afterwards provides very welcome feedback.

Table 11.2

Factors Most Important in Helping Graduating College Students Obtain Employment.

Rank/Order	Factors/Skills Evaluated
1	Oral (speaking) communication
2	Listening ability
3	Enthusiasm
4	Written communication skills
5	Technical competence
6	Appearance
7	Poise
8	Work experience
9	Resume
10	Specific degree held
11	Grade point average
12	Part-time summer employment
13	Accreditation of program
14	Leadership in campus/community activities
15	Participation in campus/community activities
16	Recommendations
17	School attended

5. Have an understanding of the communication policies and programs of an organization.

6. Develop a knowledge of how to communicate in an organization, using various media and methods (such as computers, public speaking, and memos).

In most organizations, working is communicating; communicating is working. Understanding the role and function of your communication with others can help you get your job done well and efficiently. Researchers who study how communication flows in the workplace perceive four directions: upward, downward, horizontal, and outward. We'll consider the function of each.

Upward Communication: Talking with Your Boss

"Please place your suggestions in the suggestion box," announces the boss. The suggestion box is the symbol for upward communication. **Upward communication** involves the flow of communication from subordinates up to superiors. The only person in an organization who does not communicate upward is the boss, president, or chief executive officer (CEO). And even those individuals usually answer to a governing board or to stockholders. Although today's organizational emphasis on quality encourages communication from lower levels to higher levels, effective upward communication is still far from the norm. Many employees fear that their candid comments will not be well received. Others may wonder, "Why bother?" If managers offer no incentive for sharing information up the line, it is unlikely that their subordinates will make the effort. If a supervisor stays holed up in an office away from his or her employees, opportunities for sharing ideas will be limited. Remember the proximity hypothesis described in Chapter 9? We are more likely to talk with those people who are physically close to us.

If there is little upward communication, the organization may be in a precarious situation. Those lower down in the organization are often the ones who make contact with the customer, make the product, or work most closely with the development and delivery of the product or service; they hear feedback about the product's virtues and problems. If supervisors remain unaware of these problems, productivity or quality may suffer. In addition, if employees have no opportunities to share problems and complaints with their boss, their frustration level may be dangerously high. Upward communication helps managers to deal quickly with problems and to hear suggestions for improving processes and procedures.

The Broadway show "How to Succeed in Business Without Really Trying" suggests that you can get ahead by manipulating your boss. Although we do not encourage you to try this approach, we do suggest that developing a positive relationship with your supervisor can help you succeed. One pair of researchers suggests that subordinates can "manage up" by being sensitive to the needs of supervisors.[69] If you know what your boss's most important goals are, along with his or her strengths, weaknesses, and preferred working style, you will be in a good position to establish a more meaningful relationship that will benefit both of you.

SKILL DEVELOPMENT
Explore with students their thoughts about the strengths and weaknesses of your college or university. As a group, draft and send a letter to either complain or compliment the president or provost. Invite this person to the class or share his or her response.

MEDIA AND OUTSIDE RESOURCES

Invite the dean of student services to your class to discuss the communication opportunities available for and to students. Use the questions in the second "Learning with Others" exercise at the end of this chapter.

RESEARCH AND LITERATURE

Investigate your institution's policy on harassment. For more information about sexual harassment on campus, consult the American Association of University Professors and the Center for Women Policy Studies.

TEACHING STRATEGY

Ask students to discuss the link between assertiveness and sexual harassment. It is a link that students often fail to see. Sexual harassment suits often are not entertained unless the person being filed against has received an assertive notification about the offensiveness of his or her behavior. That a superior who does not personally harass others, but simply fails to stop harassment, is party to sexual harassment him- or herself may seem startling. These policies make sense in light of the mutuality of responsibility suggested by the communication model and be definition of assertiveness.

If you are a manager yourself, encourage your subordinates to share both good news and bad. Be visible and cultivate their trust by developing a system that elicits feedback and comments. Use a suggestion box (paper or electronic), informal discussions, or more formal meetings and presentations. Making time for these exchanges will pay off in the long run.

Downward Communication: Talking with Your Subordinates

When the dean of your college tells your department chair that a course has to be canceled because of low enrollment, the department chair tells your instructor, and your instructor tells you, you have experienced downward communication. **Downward communication** is the flow of information from those higher up in an organization to those of lower rank. It can happen via memo, newsletter, poster, video, or, of course, face-to-face. Most downward communication consists of instruction about how to do a job, rationales for doing things, statements about organizational policies and procedures, feedback about job performance, and information that helps develop the mission or vision of the organization.[70]

What is the best way to communicate with employees—in writing or face-to-face? It depends upon the situation. Often the best method is oral, with a written follow-up. Table 11.3 suggests both effective and ineffective ways to communicate various categories of information to employees. In all of these situations, the best managers take care to develop and send ethical, other-oriented messages. Then they follow up to ensure that the receiver understood the message, and that it achieved its intended effect. Managers need to be especially other-oriented when they are sharing sensitive information or broaching personal topics.

At the opposite end of the spectrum, the worst managers indulge in an egocentric abuse of the legitimate power that accompanies their rank within an organization. Sexual harassment, which often takes place through downward communication channels, appears to be a growing problem in the workplace. U.S. Supreme Court Justice Clarence Thomas was accused of sexually harassing one of his employees prior to his Supreme Court appointment; Anita Hill's nationally broadcast Senate hearing testimony kept the nation glued to their TV sets as she described the alleged harassment. In 1994, a San Francisco jury awarded $7.1 million to a secretary who said she had been harassed by a law partner. In 1997, several scandals involving high-ranking military officers highlighted the need for greater skill and sensitivity among all individuals who have positions of power in the workplace.

There are two types of harassment. The first type is **quid pro quo**, which translates from Latin as, "you do something for me and I'll do something for you." A supervisor who says or implies, "Have sex with me or your job is in jeopardy," or "If you want the promotion you should have sex with me," is obviously using his or her power as a boss to trade sex for something the employee wants.

Table 11.3

Most Effective versus Least Effective Methods for Communicating with Employees in
Ten Different Situations

Situation	Most Effective	Least Effective
1. Communicating information requiring immediate employee action	Oral followed by written	Written only
2. Communicating information requiring future employee action	Written only	Oral only
3. Communicating information of a general nature	Written only	Oral only
4. Communicating a company directive or order	Oral followed by written	Oral only
5. Communicating information on an important company policy change	Oral followed by written	Oral only
6. Communicating with your immediate supervisor about work progress	Oral followed by written	Oral only
7. Promoting a safety campaign	Oral followed by written	Oral only
8. Commending an employee for noteworthy work	Oral followed by written	Written only
9. Reprimanding an employee for work deficiency	Oral only	Written only
10. Settling a dispute among employees about a work problem	Oral only	Written only

From: D. A. Level, Jr., "Communication Effectiveness: Method and Situation," *The Journal of Business Communication*, 10 (Fall 1972): 19–25.

The second type of harassment involves creating a **hostile environment**, in which an employee feels his or her rights are being violated because of working conditions or offensive behavior on the part of other workers. Telling lewd or obscene stories or jokes about members of the opposite sex, using degrading terms to describe women or men, or displaying risqué photographs of nude or seminude people can contribute to a hostile working environment. A supervisor who either creates, or fails to change, work situations that are threatening to a subordinate, is a party to sexual harassment. Jokes are not innocent and pictures are not "all in fun" if they make an employee feel degraded. Supervisors must adopt an other-oriented approach with respect to this issue; it is the receiver, not the sender, of the message who determines whether the behavior is hostile. Court cases have been won by defendants who were able to prove that a supervisor tolerated a hostile work environment, even if the supervisor did not directly participate in the offensive behavior. Wise supervisors do not wait for a problem to occur. They take a proactive approach, offering all workers seminars on how to avoid engaging in sexually offensive behavior and explicitly discussing what workers should do if they become the victims of sexual harassment.

DISCUSSION AND WRITING
Use your institution's policy on harassment to determine which behaviors described here are a form of harassment.

Divide the class into four groups by age and gender (< 21 males, < 21 females, > 21 males, > 21 females), and if possible separate the groups so that each has some privacy for the discussion. Explore the findings of each group with an understanding for how age and sex shape our perceptions of sexual harassment. For a variation, allow a structured debate between the groups. An independent panel of student judges will designate one group as the most "accurate" in their conclusions. If you attempt this variation, be sure that your judges are representative of your four population groups and that you have set aside a considerable amount of time for the vigorous discussion that will ensue.

BUILDING YOUR SKILLS

What Is Sexual Harassment?

Read each of the following situations and write an A in the blank if you agree that the situation depicts some form of sexual harassment, or D if you disagree. Share your answers with your classmates and discuss those situations over which you disagree. For those situations that everyone marked with an A, discuss whether the harassment is quid pro quo or whether it relates to a hostile environment.

_____ 1. Marcia is wearing a low-cut blouse and a miniskirt; a male coworker whistles at her as she is walking down the hall. The male coworker is guilty of sexual harassment.

_____ 2. Susan is the branch manager of an insurance firm. She asks one of her employees, Steve, to stay after work and discuss some work-related ideas with her. When Steve arrives, the lights are dimmed, the door is locked, Susan offers Steve a glass of wine, and she asks Steve to sit next to her on the couch. Susan is guilty of sexual harassment.

_____ 3. Jed, Lee, and Fernando usually meet for lunch in the company cafeteria. They like to tell each other sexually explicit jokes that often portray women as sex objects. Juanita overhears the jokes and complains to her supervisor. Jed, Lee, and Fernando are guilty of sexual harassment.

_____ 4. Manny is a college professor who has a *Playboy* calendar displayed in his office. He requires all of his students to visit him in his office for a private tutorial session in each of his classes. Manny is guilty of sexual harassment.

_____ 5. Cathy, Manny's department chair, has received several complaints from female students about the calendar that Manny displays on his wall. She has not asked Manny to remove the calendar. Cathy is guilty of sexual harassment.

_____ 6. At the weekly staff meeting several of the male workers secretly rate their female coworkers on a scale from 1 to 10 in terms of their physical attractiveness and then compare notes after the meeting. The supervisor knows this occurs but does not say anything about it. The supervisor is guilty of creating a hostile work environment.

_____ 7. Barbara has left Ricardo several notes asking him for a date. Ricardo keeps refusing Barbara's requests. Now Barbara sends him E-mail messages about three times each week asking Ricardo for a date. Ricardo asks Barbara to stop sending him messages, but she persists. Barbara is guilty of sexual harassment.

Horizontal Communication: Talking with Your Colleagues

You poke your head into your coworker's office and say, "Did you hear about the possible merger between Byteware and Datamass?" Or while you are tossing a crust at the Pizza Palace, one of your fellow workers asks how much pepperoni to put on a Super Duper Supreme. Both situations illustrate horizontal communication. **Horizontal communication** refers to communication among coworkers at the same level within an organization. In larger organizations you may talk with other workers in different departments or divisions who perform similar jobs at a similar level; that, too, is horizontal communication. Most often you communicate with your colleagues to coordinate job tasks, share plans and information, solve problems, make sure you understand job procedures, manage conflict, or get a bit of emotional support on the job.[71]

"I Heard It Through the Grapevine," a popular song from the 1960s, describes the way gossip travels among friends. Messages travel through the workplace the same way. Grapevine messages tend to circulate within groups and departments rather than across departmental lines. Davis and O'Connor found that information travels quickly through the organizational grapevine, and that it is also accurate from 75 to 90 percent of the time.[72] But errors do creep into these messages; details get lost and embellishments are added, much as when children play "Whisper Around the World."

Although grapevine errors can cause problems for an organization, most continue to encourage coworker communication because it enhances teamwork and allows the work group to develop a certain degree of independence. Some organizations even try to formalize it by forming *quality circles*, or groups of employees who meet together on a regular basis. These groups usually talk about such issues as how to improve the quality of services or products, reduce mistakes, lower costs, improve safety, or develop better ways of working together. This active participation in the work process encourages workers to do a better job. Moreover, the training they receive to participate in these groups—in group problem solving, decision-making skills, listening, relating, speaking, and managing conflict—applies to other areas of their work as well.

Outward Communication: Talking with Your Customers

"Attention, K-Mart shoppers: Submarine sandwiches are now a blue-light special, on sale for one dollar each for the next fifteen minutes." This is one kind of communication with customers. But in addition to just pitching to their customers, today's organizations are also asking customers what they think about the quality of the goods and services the organization produces. Increasingly, successful organizations are those that are other-oriented; they focus on the needs of those they serve through **outward communication**. They are spending time and money to find out what the *customer* perceives as quality, rather than relying solely upon the judgments of their corporate executives. And they are training their staffs to develop more empathy, better listening skills, and more awareness of nonverbal messages from customers.

Enhancing Leadership Skills

Our discussion of upward and downward communication reminds us that workplaces are hierarchies of power and influence. Some workers—those with such titles as boss or manager—have assigned leadership roles, while others follow their directives. The most successful workplaces have both effective leaders and effective followers. In most organizations today all workers are expected to exhibit some degree of leadership skill. The essence of **leadership** is the ability to influence others.

11 RELATING TO FAMILY, FRIENDS, AND COLLEAGUES

397

He Said, She Said: Gender Styles Differ at Work

So you think you're bilingual, do you? You say you speak English and Spanish—or French, or German or New Yawk or Suuuuthe'n.

Impressive, but not good enough—not in today's workplace anyway. To be truly successful in the '90s, you also must be fluent in Femalespeak and Malespeak.

Conversation is rife with ritual, according to Deborah Tannen, author of *You Just Don't Understand* and *Talking From 9 to 5*. And men and women's conversational rituals often clash, leading to misinterpretation and, in the worst cases, hindering women's progress up the male-dominated corporate ladder.

On page after page in her latest tome, Tannen reiterates her theme: Both conversational styles—men tend to be direct, blunt; women indirect and vague—are valid. Either style can

work well with others who share that style. But neither works well in every situation.

Tannen repeatedly pleads for both sexes to understand each other's style and to develop flexibility within those styles.

Men and women have very definite expectations of how members of their own sex should behave, Tannen writes.

Studies show that "individuals of both sexes who departed from the norms for their own sex were viewed negatively by subordinates of the same sex," she says.

In one study, "a male manager whose style approximated those of the women was seen as 'fairly meek' and 'weak' by men who worked for him, though he was highly praised by women subordinates," Tannen writes.

Conversely, or perversely, women managers whose style was more like those of the men in that study were criticized by female subordinates who saw them as cold and haughty.

What's a person to do?

Adapt to your audience, Tannen and others say.

For Moira Jamieson, an Orlando business consultant, the adapting has taken the form of becoming more comfy with Femalespeak, since Malespeak is her natural style.

"One of the comments I've received throughout my life is that I'm blunt, I'm direct, I'm domineering like a man," says Jamieson, 39. "For this reason, I've had great relationships with men."

But not so great with women.

"Most women find me too pushy, assertive, forceful," she says. "On several occasions, I've been called a bitch for just being blunt."

So Jamieson is modifying her style.

"It takes a great deal of conscious effort," she says. "I think about things for a couple days before I know I'll have to say them."

Around 700 B.C., Homer warned his Athenian audience to be selective in their attempts to assume control: "You will certainly not be able to take the lead in all things yourself, for to one man a god has given deeds of war, and to another the dance, to another the lyre and song, and in another widesounding Zeus puts a good mind." The first qualification for leadership, as he was trying to tell them, is skill and knowledge about the task at hand. In addition, however, you need the skills necessary to motivate, inspire, and instruct others in their work. Because not all of us are born with these skills, Stephen Covey wrote a book called *The Seven Habits of Highly Effective People* to help those of us who want to sharpen our leadership skills. To be successful as a leader, Covey suggests the following:[73]

INSTRUCTIONAL GOALS AND TIPS

Because Covey's suggestions focus on interpersonal skills, consider offering extra credit to students for writing a book report on *Seven Habits of Highly Effective People*. Ask students to concentrate upon skills for fostering interdependence.

'Til Speech Do We Part

According to Deborah Tannen, these are the conversational rituals of women and men:*

Women

- Speaking indirectly, couching criticism and commands in praise or vagueness to avoid causing offense or hurt feelings.

- Maintaining an appearance of equality.

- Playing down their authority to avoid appearing egotistical or "bossy."

- Saying "I'm sorry" not as an apology but as a way of restoring balance to a conversation.

- Feeling discomfort with boasting; downplaying their accomplishments.

- Asking questions to elicit more information.

Tips for Women

- Be cautious in offering unsolicited advice. Often, when men are given advice, they take it as criticism.

- Don't soften your opinions with qualifiers such as "I think" or "Maybe we should" or "Wouldn't it be a good idea if." Using such qualifiers weakens your message.

- Be wary of going into long explanations. Get to the point quickly—if more explanation is needed, provide it.

Men

- Speaking directly, whether giving criticism or orders.

- Using banter, teasing, and playful put-downs.

- Striving to maintain a one-up position in any interaction.

- Perceiving "I'm sorry" as putting oneself down or accepting blame.

- Boasting or "blowing their own horn" to highlight their accomplishments.

- Seeking information elsewhere rather than asking questions, for fear of appearing to lack knowledge.

According to Tannen and other researchers, here are some ways to bridge the gap between these different rituals:

Tips for Men

- Don't minimize the importance of women's feelings with statements such as, "Why are you so upset about that?" Women express their feelings more quickly and easily and need to have those feelings taken seriously.

- Don't remain silent and assume a woman will know you're absorbing what she's saying. Ask questions to show that you're interested and listening.

*Note: Remember that these generalizations do not represent *all* men or *all* women.

Excerpted and adapted from: Loraine O'Connell, *Austin American-Statesman* (January 24, 1995).

---

1. *Be proactive*: Don't wait until a situation becomes a problem to solve before starting to solve it. Don't simply react to problems, but anticipate them. Don't blame others. Accept responsibility for making decisions yourself.

2. *Begin with the end in mind*: Effective people have a vision of where they are going and what they want to accomplish.

3. *Put first things first:* In Covey's words, "Make sure the main thing is the main thing." Manage your time so that you can manage your life.

4. *Think win/win:* Don't assume someone must lose and someone must win. Approach situations attempting to maximize the benefits for all.

"That was a fine report, Barbara. But since the sexes speak different
languages, I probably didn't understand a word of it."

5. *Seek first to understand, then to be understood*. Listen effectively. Listening
skills are essential in being other-oriented.

6. *Synergize*: Synergy means that working together results in more creativity
than working alone.

7. *Sharpen the saw*: Take time out to enhance your skills rather than continuing
to work with "unsharpened" tools.

The most effective leaders combine a task orientation with a relationship
orientation to perform the following functions:[74]

Task Functions:

1. *Initiate* new ideas or approaches to achieving the task.

2. *Provide information*, such as facts, examples, statistics.

3. *Seek information* by asking for facts and other data that can help get the
work done.

4. *Seek opinions* and ask for clarification of opinions expressed by others.

5. *Offer opinions* about issues and ideas under consideration.

6. *Elaborate* and amplify the ideas of others.

7. *Evaluate* the advantages and disadvantages of issues, ideas, or proposed
solutions.

DISCUSSION AND WRITING
Ask students to work on
exercise 8 in the "Focus on
Critical Thinking" section
at the end of this chapter.

||| INTERPERSONAL COMMUNICATION RELATIONSHIPS

8. *Energize* and motivate the group to take action and be productive.

Relationship Functions:

9. *Encourage* others and offer praise and acceptance of others' ideas.

10. *Harmonize* and mediate disagreements and conflict.

11. *Compromise* and seek ways of finding common ground among group members.

12. *Be a gatekeeper* by encouraging less talkative members to participate and limiting lengthy orations from big talkers.

Enhancing Followership Skill

If you find yourself playing the role of follower in a group, remind yourself that you can still make an enormous contribution. Consider the following:

1. Seek opportunities to provide input and suggestions to leaders. Look for ways to communicate your interest in the goals of the group.

2. Listen well. This skill appears on any list for leaders or followers. Listening effectively and being able to comprehend and evaluate information is an essential followership skill.

3. Provide appropriate feedback. If you are not sure you understand directions from your superior, ask for further clarification.

4. Support your suggestions with evidence rather than with off-the-cuff opinions. Be able to document your suggestions with data, rather than relying only upon emotion-based hunches. Although you should not ignore intuitive thoughts, most supervisors will respond more positively to those ideas you can support with evidence.

5. Don't abandon your ethical principles. If you are being asked to do something that violates your sense of right and wrong, you may need to suggest tactfully that the orders you have been given by your boss are not consistent with your ethical principles. "I was only following orders," or "I was just doing what I was told," usually don't hold up in court as an excuse for violating the law.

Technology and Workplace Communication

The workplace of today is quite different from that of your parents or grandparents. Anthropologists suggest that working with tools is one of the hallmarks of any civilized society, but today's technological advances can help us transcend time and space themselves. As we noted in Chapter 1, and as you have seen in Electronic Connections features throughout the text, these days fax machines, computers, modems, pagers, and cellular telephones permit technological connections that mediate our interpersonal relationships. Marriages between computers, video, fiber optics, and electronic messaging now make it possible to interact with others when we are not in their presence. As these new technolo-

Consider Will Rogers' words: "We can't all be heroes because somebody has to sit on the curb and clap as they go by." (From *Peter's Quotations* by Laurence J. Peter, William Morrow, 1977.)

ACTIVITY
See Activity 11.8 in the Instructor's Guide.

RESEARCH AND LITERATURE
In Chapter 1 of his textbook *Organizational Communication* (William C. Brown, 1990), Gerald Goldhaber provides several examples of how advances in technological communications "are not positively related to successful interpersonal communication" (p. 6). He argues that the body, the voice, and the environment are compromised by mediated communication. Discuss this contention with students.

TEACHING STRATEGY
To address the impact of technology on interpersonal communication, ask students to address the validity of Alvin Toffler's assertion that the United States is and will grow to be more of a "throwaway" society. A throwaway society is one in which rapidity and transience are of such importance that we begin to see all aspects of life in "throwaway" terms (including our interpersonal relationships). (*Future Shock*, New York: Bantam Books, 1970) For example, Toffler suggests that we throw away friends, rather than retaining them, when we move to new geographical areas, because we can easily locate new friends. He suggests that the alarming rise in divorce rates in this country since the Industrial Revolution is evidence of this same trend. We discard mates because nothing is forever and we can always access new ones. The result, according to Toffler, is that we have more relationships of shorter duration and less depth, and we feel more and more confused and disconnected.

gies develop, they will have a potent effect upon the interactions we have with others, not just in the workplace, but also in our homes, schools, places of worship, and other arenas.

Imagine that it's time for work. But instead of hopping in your car for a forty-minute commute—the national average time for getting to work—you stroll into your media room, flip on your computer, and comb your hair so that when you talk to your boss via TV you will make a good impression. You push a button and collect your E-mail from your computer, then settle down to write your reports and talk to clients. Our homes are still our castles, but increasingly, our homes are also our workplaces, thanks to the power and ingenuity of today's technology. Even if face-to-face interaction is still required for complicated, unstructured tasks, we will undoubtedly prepare for interpersonal contacts by gathering information from a computer data base, sending and receiving faxes, or communicating with others via E-mail. The pace at which we use technology to help us do our work will quicken. As students and teachers, many of us are already using technology to increase our efficiency and to enhance learning and teaching.

Yet there is evidence that some workers are reluctant to embrace the new technology. According to a recent Gallup poll, 49 percent of the 600 white-collar workers surveyed said they were cyberphobic—afraid of computers—or resistant to new technology. Only 12 percent thought of themselves as "early adopters" who eagerly buy new hardware and software. Women (39 percent) tend to fear technology more than men (27 percent). What are some of the reasons for the anxiety? Over 56 percent said they were worried about losing their privacy, 38 percent feared information overload, and another 38 percent were worried about diminished face-to-face contact with colleagues. Thirty-five percent were afraid of having to constantly learn new skills, and 19 percent were worried about being passed over for a promotion because they lacked

Through the use of technology, the ability to communicate in our workplaces is expanding to easily allow intercontinental communication. (Matthew Borkowki/Stock Boston)

computer skills.[75] Despite these concerns, the same poll found that two thirds of those surveyed are using computers, and almost 70 percent thought the information superhighway will help their company in the future.[76]

Computers and modems have had perhaps more far-reaching effects upon workplace communication than any other technology.[77] Today, workers from the top level on down in an organization use a computer to write, track data, compute, and perform other daily functions. Using **electronic messaging**, or e-mail, you can type a message on your computer to be read by anyone who is connected to your network. The Internet, a popular and vast computer network, is one of the most widely used e-mail networks in the world. Many organizations also have developed internal computer networks that permit employees to communicate with each other. If you have a computer and modem at home, you can interact with anyone who has a similar system.

The net result of these technological advances is that your workplace is no longer confined to your own office, store, or plant, nor to people who work for your organization. Once you log on to the information superhighway, you can exchange information such as research findings, statistics, historical facts, and new ideas with others in your profession around the world. As Electronic Connections: Stay Connected After Hours suggests, your home computer can help you to plow thorough routine correspondence more efficiently, and may occasionally even permit you to avoid commuting. This, in turn, can give you more time to spend with family and friends.

Will these new technologies, and others yet to be developed, replace the need for face-to-face interpersonal relationships? Early evidence suggests that the answer is no. Communication technology is not new. Gutenberg's movable type, Morse's telegraph, and Bell's telephone all affected the speed with which we interacted with others, but they have not replaced direct interaction.

A growing collection of research studies show that we use electronic media selectively for workplace communication:[78]

1. The more positive the message, the more immediate the media we use to communicate it. We like to tell someone good news in person. We are more likely to select some other medium to communicate bad news.

2. We prefer mediated communication (e-mail) when we need to communicate data and content-rich messages, and we like face-to-face meetings for relationship messages.

3. Mediated messages work best in the workplace if the task is highly structured or involves sequential steps. Less structured tasks seem to be managed better face-to-face.

"All this E-mail . . I miss schmoozing."

The Chronicle of Higher Education

Stay Connected After Hours

One of the most frustrating experiences for a working parent is the tug of war you feel at the end of a long day. On one side, there's a stack of important documents to review and a stuffed electronic-mail message box pulling to keep you in the office. On the other side, there's dinner and kids to tuck in pulling you home. Thanks to your family PC, you can deal with those documents and answer those e-mail messages without missing a precious moment with your kids. Equipped with a host of onboard communications tools, your PC can serve as your office away from the office, allowing you to get home for dinner and tackle your day's-end chores after the kids are asleep.

With a fax modem and the e-mail (via online services) and faxing capabilities that came bundled with your computer (or that you've added on to it), you can send and receive electronic messages and files, send faxes, and tap into other computers, including the one at work. If your PC is not equipped with a fax modem, you can easily add an external modem.

E-mail management tops the list of tasks that are well suited for being done from a family computer. In fact, you can often do it better and faster after hours. Many managers habitually handle the bulk of their e-mail first thing in the morning and last thing before closing down for the day, so shifting that task to a home-based computer is a minor change in routine with big benefits on the family front.

The best strategy for setting yourself up to handle e-mail at home depends to some extent on whom you need to communicate with—whether it's with your colleagues on an internal network or with far-flung contacts outside your company—and what e-mail resources you intend to use.

Peter Scisco, Family PC.

4. Groups who use video conferences and e-mail messages are more likely to have polarized opinions than those who meet face-to-face.

5. Groups and individuals will be more productive if they have someone to help them when they experience either hardware or software problems.

6. The use of sophisticated technology does not necessarily result in improved quality. It may let us make mistakes faster.

7. In the future, people will still solve complex issues and problems face-to-face rather than through mediated messages.

Summary

We relate to others in a variety of contexts. In this chapter we have focused on interpersonal communication principles and skills applied to family, friend, and colleague relationships.

A family is a unit made up of any number of persons who live in relationship with one another over time in a common living space and are usually, but not

WEB ACTIVITY
Marriage Counseling Professional relationship and marriage counseling is widespread and varied. Have students search for many different perspectives on the process of counseling couples. Some places to begin such a search might include visiting the home pages of the following organizations: The Professional Pastoral Counseling Institute, Marriage Builders, Love Bytes, Marriage Enrichment, Inc., and Competent Couples.

always, united by marriage and kinship. One model for describing families considers family cohesion and adaptability and the role of communication in affecting family members' roles and relationships. Cohesion refers to the emotional bonding and the feeling of closeness that families experience. Family adaptability refers to the flexibility of family members in responding to changes in family roles, rules, and relationships.

There is no one best way to be a family. There are, however, several skills and strategies that can enhance the quality of family life: Take time to talk with other family members about relationship issues; listen to others; support and encourage one another; use productive strategies for managing conflict and stress.

In addition to our families, our friends are an important source of help and comfort in times of stress. They also make life more enjoyable even when all is well and we simply seek the joy of companionship. Friends are people we like and with whom we have a relationship over time, based on our own choices.

Our friendships with others evolve over time and develop in stages. Friendships also differ in importance at various stages in your life. Childhood friendships develop in intimacy and intensity through a series of stages. At around the age of twelve, family relationships often become less important, and adolescent friendships become more intense. Adult friendships often focus first on the selection of a life mate, which may supplant other relationships. Older adults appear to form fewer new friendships and to have a smaller network of friends, yet the friends that the elderly have are very important to them.

Four basic principles may help you understand how to gain and maintain friendships. First, recognize and make the most of your opportunities to make friends. Second, develop skills for encouraging others to be your friend. Conversational skills are important for both establishing and maintaining friendships. Third, try to understand how friendships evolve and grow. Finally, skills for repairing relationships can help to keep a relationship strong.

The last context we considered was the world of work and the relationships we form with our colleagues. For most people, work involves a great deal of communication with others.

In most organizations communication flows up, down, horizontally, and out to customers. Through upward communication you can share ideas and strategies for improving the work process; you can also enhance your relationships with your boss. Downward communication involves making contact with those who work for you. You should decide whether you will send messages in writing, in person, or through mediated channels. Horizontal communication concerns the communication you have with your colleagues on your level throughout the organization; most of the time, however, horizontal communication will occur with those who work in your immediate vicinity. Most organizations are encouraging better communication with customers and clients. Contacting those outside the organization who receive the organization's goods and services is an important way of ensuring that what the organization offers is of high quality.

Leadership skills are important for success in most jobs. To enhance your leadership skills you will need to cultivate such people management skills as

1. A family is a unit made up of persons who use interpersonal communication over time in a common living space and who often are united by marriage and kinship.

2. The following recommendations are for improving family relationships:

- Take time to talk about relationships and feelings;
- Listen and clarify the meanings of messages;
- Support and encourage one another;
- Use productive strategies for managing conflict, stress, and change.

3. We develop friendships to satisfy our need for inclusion, affection, and control. Friends also provide emotional support, bolster our self-esteem, help us meet material needs, and make the mundane more enjoyable.

4. *Childhood* friendships are often self-focused and superficial, whereas *adolescent* friendships are governed more by peer influence. In *adulthood,* the selection of a lifelong mate greatly influences friendships with others; networks tend to shrink for *elders,* who value their friendships highly.

5. Effective communication from any direction in the workplace requires mutual sharing of information and listening to ideas which are related to the job at hand. Colleagues should understand the role of communication in the organization and develop a knowledge of the most effective and available means of communication with superiors, subordinates, coworkers and customers.

listening, responding, organizing, and inspiring others. Leaders also need to know how to organize work, accomplish tasks, and relate well to others. An effective follower, a role most people play in organizations, makes relevant contributions, listens, follows directions, supports suggestions with evidence, and doesn't abandon ethical principles.

Technology has a growing presence in the workplace. Although mediated interaction will not replace face-to-face interpersonal contact, it clearly plays an important role in sending and receiving messages. Instead of talking to someone in person, you can send a fax, an e-mail message, or a video; or you can call on your portable phone. Although we use these technologies for much of our work, we still prefer face-to-face interaction when dealing with relationship issues and untangling complex problems.

For Discussion and Review

■ FOCUS ON COMPREHENSION

1. What is a family?

2. Identify interpersonal communication skills that can enhance the quality of family life.

3. Why do we develop friendships?

4. What are the attributes of friendships at different stages in life (e.g., during childhood, adolescence, adulthood, and old age)?

5. What are some suggestions for improving upward, downward, horizontal, and outward communication?

■ FOCUS ON CRITICAL THINKING

6. Steve and Yvette both have full-time jobs and are raising two children. A lot of the household chores simply aren't getting done, and this bothers Steve. How should Steve initiate and manage a discussion about how these chores should be handled?

7. Do you think the institution of the family is deteriorating, or is it just changing? Support your answer.

8. Bob has difficulty making friends. He is interested in outdoor activities and is a good student, but he struggles to find others who share his interests. What suggestions would you give Bob for capitalizing on "friendship opportunities"?

9. Jerry is president of Southwest Technical Computing. He has a sense that his managers are not tapping the wealth of ideas and suggestions that lower-

level employees might have for improving productivity. What specific strategies could Jerry implement to improve upward communication?

■ FOCUS ON ETHICS

10. Twelve-year-old Nathan consistently does not get along with his other brothers and sisters. He also is not doing well in school. His parents want to take him to a counselor, but Nathan does not want to go. Should Nathan's parents insist that he attend counseling?

11. Is it ethical to withhold honest thoughts and feelings from other family members? Should family members always "tell it like it is"? Should parents encourage their children to "tell everything" they know and feel?

12. Write your own definition of friendship. Select three of your good friends and discuss how their behavior illustrates your definition. What forms of support that your friends provide do you value most?

13. Is it ethical to consciously use strategies to cultivate a friendship? Shouldn't friendships develop naturally rather than by design? Explain your answer.

14. You are at a party and you overhear a group making negative comments about one of your best friends. They are not talking to you, but you hear them. Should you intervene and stick up for your friend or just ignore them?

15. Clayton has e-mail at work but not at home. His brother has e-mail at his home. Is it ethical for Clayton to use the computer at work on company time to send and receive e-mail messages from his brother three or four times a week?

For Your Journal

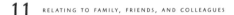

1. Select two TV situation comedies or dramas that revolve around a family. One program could be one that is still broadcast in reruns, such as *Leave It to Beaver*, *All in the Family*, or *The Brady Bunch* and the other show could be a more contemporary program. Describe the communication patterns in the TV programs that you observe. Draw upon the principles and skills presented in this chapter as you describe the family communication patterns. You may even want to discuss which of your TV families seems to do the most effective job of communicating with one another.

2. Describe what someone would learn about your family if they were to view only the nonverbal elements of the way your family interacts. For example, imagine someone viewing a videotape of your family's daily activities, with the "sound turned off." Consider not only such factors as facial expression, eye contact, touch, and use of personal space, but also the way your home is arranged and the overall appearance of your family's dwelling.

3. Write your own definition of friendship. Select three of your good friends and discuss how their behavior illustrates your definition. What forms of support that your friends provide do you value most?

4. Whether you are currently employed or are a student at a college or university, monitor each of your interactions at your institution for at least a four-hour period on a busy day. Categorize each one as upward, downward, horizontal, or outward, and record how your behavior changes when you shift categories.

5. Make a list of the workplace technology that you can now use with some skill (for example, telephone, personal computer, fax machine, and so on.) Make a second list of workplace technology with which you are familiar but do not know how to operate. Which list is longer? How has your use of technology affected your relationships with colleagues and friends?

Learning with Others

1. After you have indicated whether you agree or disagree with the following statements, break into small groups and try to agree or disagree unanimously with each statement. Try to find reasons for differences of opinion. If your group cannot reach agreement or disagreement, you may change the wording in any statement to promote unanimity.

 AGREE–DISAGREE STATEMENTS ABOUT FAMILIES

_____ 1. Most family members know how to communicate effectively; they just don't take the time to practice what they know.

_____ 2. Family conflict is a symptom rather than a cause of deteriorating family relationships.

_____ 3. Family conflict is harmful to family harmony, and all conflict should be avoided at all costs.

_____ 4. Most family conflict occurs because we don't understand the other family member; we fail to communicate effectively.

_____ 5. Families function best if there is one central leader of the family.

_____ 6. Ineffective communication is the single most important cause of family conflict, divorce, and family tension.

_____ 7. Nonverbal communication (facial expression, eye contact, tone of voice, posture, etc.) is more important than verbal communication; what you do is more important than what you say.

_____ 8. It is sometimes necessary to ignore the feelings of others in order to reach a family decision.

_____ 9. The best way to love your marriage partner is to care more for your partner than you care for yourself.

_____ 10. Generally speaking, the quality of family life is deteriorating today.

_____ 11. There is one best approach or set of rules and principles that will ensure an effectively functioning family.

2. Divide into teams of two or three people. Each team will interview a businessperson or supervisor in a nonprofit organization such as a hospital or school about the issues covered in this chapter. Ask such questions as:

- What do you do to enhance upward communication among the people you supervise?

- What is your approach to leading others? What works and what doesn't work with your subordinates?

3. This is a leadership exercise. Read the following case study and complete the instructions. Then compare your group's task list and communication strategies with those of other groups.

■ HURRICANE PREPAREDNESS CASE

Although you have idly watched local meteorologists track Hurricane Bruce's destructive course through the Caribbean for several days, you have not given any serious thought to the possibility that the number 3–rated storm might directly affect your coastal city. However, at about seven o'clock this morning, the storm suddenly veered northward, putting it on course for a direct hit. Now the National Hurricane Center in Miami has posted a Hurricane Warning for your community. Forecasters are predicting landfall in approximately nine to twelve hours. Having taken no advance precautions, you are stunned by the amount of work you now must do to secure your three-bedroom suburban home, which is about a half mile from the beach, and to protect your family—your spouse and two children, ages five and twelve.

You have enough food in the house for two days. You also have one candle and a transistor radio with one weak battery. You have no other hurricane supplies, nor have you taken any hurricane precautions. Your group's task is to identify specific strategies for (1) ensuring the survival and safety of your family and property, and (2) assigning appropriate tasks to family members to carry out these strategies. First, brainstorm a list or sequence of events or lists of tasks that you need to accomplish. Then arrange them in priority order. Finally, decide the best way to assign and explain these tasks to various family members. Make notes about your decisions.

FAMILY: Unit made up of any number of persons who live in relationship with one another over time in a common living space who are usually, but not always, united by marriage and kinship.

NATURAL FAMILY: Mother, father, and their biological children.

BLENDED FAMILY: Two adults and their children. Because of divorce, separation, death, or adoption, the children may be the product of other parents, or of just one of the adults who is raising them.

SINGLE-PARENT FAMILY: One parent raising one or more children.

EXTENDED FAMILY: Relatives such as aunts, uncles, cousins, or grandparents who are part of the family unit.

FAMILY OF ORIGIN: Family in which you were raised.

CIRCUMPLEX MODEL OF FAMILY INTERACTION: Model that shows the relationships between family adaptability, cohesion, and communication.

FAMILY ADAPTABILITY: Refers to a family member's ability to modify and respond to changes in the family's power structure and roles.

FAMILY COHESION: Refers to the emotional bonding and feelings of togetherness that families experience.

FAMILY COMMUNICATION: Way in which family members mutually influence one another.

EROS: Sexual, erotic love based upon the pursuit of physical beauty and pleasure.

LUDIS: Game-playing love based upon the enjoyment of others.

STORGE: Solid love of friendship based upon trust and caring.

MANIA: Obsessive love driven by mutual needs.

PRAGMA: Practical love based upon mutual benefits.

AGAPE: Selfless love based upon giving of yourself for others.

UPWARD COMMUNICATION: Communication in an organization that flows from subordinates to superiors.

DOWNWARD COMMUNICATION: Communication in an organization that flows from superiors to subordinates.

QUID PRO QUO: Latin phrase that can be used to describe a type of sexual harassment. The phrase means "you do something for me and I'll do something for you."

HOSTILE ENVIRONMENT: Type of sexual harassment that threatens an employee's rights through offensive working conditions or behavior on the part of other workers.

HORIZONTAL COMMUNICATION: Communication among colleagues or coworkers at the same level within an organization.

OUTWARD COMMUNICATION: Communication that flows to those outside an organization (e.g., customers).

LEADERSHIP: Behavior that influences, guides, controls, or inspires others to take action.

ELECTRONIC MESSAGING (E-MAIL): A system that allows users to generate and transmit messages via computer.